Ramanujan Revisited

Proceedings of the Centenary Conference
University of Illinois at Urbana-Champaign
June 1–5, 1987

Srinivasa Ramanujan

Ramanujan Revisited

Proceedings of the Centenary Conference
University of Illinois at Urbana-Champaign
June 1–5, 1987

Edited by

George E. Andrews

Richard A. Askey

Bruce C. Berndt

K. G. Ramanathan

Robert A. Rankin

ACADEMIC PRESS, INC.
Harcourt Brace Jovanovich, Publishers
Boston San Diego New York
Berkeley London Sydney
Tokyo Toronto

Cover design by Elizabeth E. Tustian.

Bust of Ramanujan by Paul Granlund.

Passport photo of Ramanujan reprinted courtesy of The Royal Society, London.

ACADEMIC PRESS, INC.
1250 Sixth Avenue, San Diego, CA 92101

United Kingdom Edition published by
ACADEMIC PRESS INC. (LONDON) LTD.
24-28 Oval Road, London NW1 7DX

Library of Congress Cataloging-in-Publication Data

Ramanujan revisited : proceedings of the centenary conference,
University of Illinois at Urbana-Champaign, June 1–5, 1987 / edited
by George E. Andrews . . . [et al.].
p. cm.
Bibliography: p.
ISBN 0–12–058560–X
1. Mathematics—Congresses. 2. Ramanujan Aiyangar, Srinivasa,
1887–1920—Congresses. I. Ramanujan Aiyangar, Srinivasa,
1887–1920. II. Andrews, George E., 1938–
QA1.R26 1988
510—dc 19 87–32463
CIP

88 89 90 91 9 8 7 6 5 4 3 2 1
Printed in the United States of America

January 31, 1987

As for the Centenary Conference, I wish the very best of luck and for the grand success on this auspicious occasion. I hope new talents will flow from such sources of inspiration for the advancement of mathematics.

With the very best wishes,

Yours Sincerely,

S. Janaki Ammal

(Mrs. Ramanujan)

ROW 1 (front)

Emil Grosswald, Carl Prather, James D. Louck, Alf van der Poorten, David M. Bressoud, George E. Andrews, Richard Askey, Nathan J. Fine, H. M. Srivastava, M. Ram Murty, John Friedlander, David Masson, Jon Borwein, Jet Wimp, Simka Brudno, Young Ju Choie, James Propp, J. S. Rao

ROW 2

Wolfgang Schwarz, George Gasper, Bruce Berndt, Don Redmond, Mike Hirschhorn, Frank Garvan, Cyndi Garvan, Rodney Baxter, Charles van den Eynden, Dean Hickerson, Richard Guy, C. J. Moreno, Robert Rankin, P. Swinnerton-Dyer, Peter Jau-shyong Shiue, Janice Malouf, Qi Yao, Eugene Ng, N. R. Nandakumar

ROW 3

J. L. Nicolas, T. H. Koornwinder, G. Almkvist, K. Stolarsky, H. Diamond, F. Wheeler, L. W. Kolitsch, M. Newman, James Hafner, Otto Ruehr, Reid Huntsinger, Charles Dunkl, P. Paule, A. K. Agarwal, Lou Shituo, K. Aomoto

ROW 4

Victor Moll, Lisa Jacobsen, Liang-Cheng Zhang, Elmer K. Hayashi, Vencil Skarda, Fredric T. Howard, Peter Borwein, Kevin McCurley, Freeman Dyson, John Zucker, Anthony J. F. Biagioli, Stephen C. Milne, Gérard Viennot, Robert A. Gustafson, D. Zeilberger, Kevin W. J. Kadell, S. S. Rangachari

ROW 5

Marv Wunderlich, John Hawkins, Marvin Knopp, Bill Allaway, Joseph Lehner, Paul Bateman, Sam Wagstaff, Y.-F. Pétermann, Amitabha Tripathi, Kathy O'Hara, Adolf Hildebrand, Alayne Parson, Rolf Müller, Barry Cipra, Katsuhisa Mimachi

ROW 6

Chris Caldwell, John McKay, Paul Erdös, M. Rahman, K.-H. Indlekofer, J. Brillhart, Kailash Misra, James Vaughn, Matthew Richey, Bruce Reznick, Dennis Stanton, John Greene, Michael Filaseta, Ronald J. Evans, Daniel S. Moak

Photograph of participants, Ramanujan Centenary Conference,
University of Illinois, June 1–5, 1987

SPONSORS

G. A. Miller Committee, University of Illinois

James M. Vaughn Foundation

Institute for Mathematics and Its Applications, University of Minnesota

National Science Foundation

CONTENTS

The manuscripts for the following three lectures given at the Ramanujan Centenary Conference were unavailable for publication:

KEVIN KADELL
Aomoto's Proof of Selberg's Integral and Constant Term Identities

K. G. RAMANATHAN
On Ramanujan's Continued Fractions

GÉRARD VIENNOT
Combinatorics and Continued Fractions

Participants
Ramanujan Centenary Conference
University of Illinois
Urbana, Illinois
June 1-5, 1987

William Adams
Division of Mathematical Sciences
National Science Foundation
Washington, D.C. 20550

A. K. Agarwal
Department of Mathematics
Pennsylvania State University
Mont Alto Campus
Mont Alto, PA 17237

Adebisi Agboola
Department of Mathematics
University of Illinois
1409 West Green St.
Urbana, IL 61801

William R. Allaway
Department of Mathematics
Lakehead Univ.
Thunder Bay
Ontario, P7B 5E1
Canada

Gert Almkvist
PL 500
S24300 Höör
Sweden

George Andrews
Department of Mathematics
Pennsylvania State University
University Park, PA 16802

Kazuhiko Aomoto
Department of Mathematics
Nagoya University
Chikusa-ku
Nagoya 464
Japan

Richard Askey
Department of Mathematics
Van Vleck Hall
University of Wisconsin
480 Lincoln Dr.
Madison, WI 53706

Paul T. Bateman
Department of Mathematics
University of Illinois
1409 West Green St.
Urbana, IL 61801

R. J. Baxter
Theoretical Physics IAS
Australian National University
GPO Box 4
Canberra
ACT 2601, Australia

Bruce C. Berndt
Department of Mathematics
University of Illinois
1409 West Green St.
Urbana, IL 61801

Daniel J. Bernstein
5 Brewster Lane
Bellport, NY 11713

Anthony J. F. Biagioli
Department of Mathematics
University of Missouri-Rolla
Rolla, Missouri 65401

Jonathan M. Borwein
Department of Mathematics
Dalhousie University
Halifax
Nova Scotia
Canada B3H 4H8

Peter Borwein
Department of Mathematics
Dalhousie University
Halifax
Nova Scotia
Canada B3H 4H8

David Bressoud
Department of Mathematics
Pennslyvania State University
University Park, PA 16802

John Brillhart
Department of Mathematics
University of Arizona
Tucson, AZ 85721

Chris K. Caldwell
Dept. of Mathematics & Computer Science
University of Tennessee-Martin
Martin, TN 38238

Pulak Chakravarti
1973 B Orchard
Urbana, IL 61801

S. Chandrasekhar
Laboratory for Astrophysics
& Space Research
The Enrico Fermi Institute
University of Chicago
933 East 56th St.
Chicago, IL 60637

YoungJu Choie
Department of Mathematics
Ohio State University
231 W. 18th St.
Columbus, OH 43210

S. Chowla
School of Mathematics
Institute for Advanced Study
Princeton, New Jersey 08540

David Chudnovsky
Apt. 88
423 West 120th Street
New York, NY 10027

Gregory Chudnovsky
Apt. 88
423 West 120th Street
New York, NY 10027

Barry A. Cipra
Department of Mathematics
St. Olaf College
Northfield, MN 55057

Hubert Delange
22 Alleé Troénes
F91440 Bures sur Yvette
France

Harold Diamond
Department of Mathematics
University of Illinois
1409 West Green St.
Urbana, IL 61801

Charles F. Dunkl
Department of Mathematics
Mathematics-Astronomy Bldg.
University of Virginia
Charlottesville, VA 22903

Freeman J. Dyson
School of Physics
Institute for Advanced Study
Princeton, NJ 08540

Paul Erdös
c/o R. L. Graham
Mathematical Sciences Research Center
Room 2C-382
AT&T Bell Labs
600 Mountain Ave.
Murrey Hill, NJ 07974

Ronald J. Evans
Dept. of Mathematics, C-012
University of California at San Diego
La Jolla, CA 92093

Michael Filaseta
Department of Mathematics
University of South Carolina
Columbia, SC 29208

Nathan J. Fine
Westbury F2018
Deerfield Beach, FL 33442

John Friedlander
Department of Mathematics
Scarborough College
Univ. of Toronto
Scarborough, Ontario M1C 1A4
Canada

Frank Garvan
Department of Mathematics
Van Vleck Hall
University of Wisconsin
480 Lincoln Dr.
Madison, WI 53706

George Gasper
Department of Mathematics
Northwestern Univ.
Evanston, IL 60201

Jon Gordon
Department of Mathematics
University of Illinois
1409 West Green St.
Urbana, Il 61801

R. William Gosper, Jr.
Symbolics, Inc.
845 Page Mill Rd
Palo Alto, CA 94304

Dan Grayson
Department of Mathematics
University of Illinois
1409 West Green St.
Urbana, IL 61801

John Greene
Department of Mathematics
Southern Illinois University
Carbondale, IL 62901

Emil Grosswald
11 Narwyn Lane
Narberth, PA 19072

Robert Gustafson
Department of Mathematics
Texas A&M University
College Station, TX 77840

Richard K. Guy
Department of Mathematics
The University of Calgary
Calgary, Alberta
Canada T2N 1N4

James Hafner
IBM Research K53/802
Almaden Research Center
650 Harry Road
San Jose, CA 95120

Robert Hathway
Department of Mathematics
Illinois State University
Normal, IL 61761

John Hawkins
Department of Mathematics
Bernard M. Baruch College
City University of New York
17 Lexington Ave.
New York, NY 10010

Elmer K. Hayashi
Dept. of Mathematics & Computer Science
Wake Forest University
P.O. Box 7311
Winston-Salem, NC 27109

Dean Hickerson
Department of Mathematics
University of California-Davis
Davis, CA 95616

Adolf Hildebrand
Department of Mathematics
University of Illinois
1409 West Green St.
Urbana, IL 61801

Michael Hirschhorn
Department of Mathematics
Univ. of New South Wales
P.O. Box 1
Kensington
New South Wales
Australia 2033

Fredric T. Howard
Department of Mathematics
Wake Forest University
P.O. Box 7311
Winston-Salem, NC 27109

Reid Huntsinger
Department of Mathematics
University of Illinois
1409 West Green St.
Urbana, IL 61801

Karl-Heinz Indlekofer
Füllekengrund 12
D-4799 Dörenhagen
Federal Republic of Germany

Lisa Jacobsen
Department of Mathematics
University of Trondheim
N-7055 Dragvoll
Norway

Kevin Kadell
Department of Mathematics
Arizona State University
Tempe, AZ 85287

Ambassador P. K. Kaul
Embassy of India
2107 Massachusetts Ave., N. W.
Washington, D.C. 20008

Marvin Knopp
Apt. 22
410 Lancaster Ave.
Haverford, PA 19041

Gina Kolata
Science Magazine
1333 H St., N.W.
Washington, D.C. 20005

Louis W. Kolitsch
241A Brooks Dr.
Martin, TN 38237

Tom H. Koornwinder
CWI
P.O. Box 4079
1009 AB Amsterdam
The Netherlands

Robert L. Lamphere
Dept. of Mathematics & Computer Science
Francis Marion College
Florence, SC 29501

Joseph Lehner
314-N Sharon Way
Jamesburg, NJ 08831

James D. Louck
MS B 284
Los Alamos National Laboratory
Los Alamos, NM 87545

Janice Malouf
Department of Mathematics
University of Illinois
1409 W. Green St.
Urbana, Il 61801

David R. Masson
Department of Mathematics
University of Toronto
Toronto
Ontario M5S 1A1
Canada

Kevin McCurley
Department of Mathematics
University of Southern California
Los Angeles, CA 90089

J. McKay
Department of Mathematics
University of Montreal
Montreal
Quebec H3C 3J7
Canada

Stephen C. Milne
Department of Mathematics
University of Kentucky
Lexington, KY 40506

Katsuhisa Mimachi
Department of Mathematics
Nagoya University
Chikusa-Ku
Nagoya 464
Japan

Kailash C. Misra
Department of Mathematics
North Carolina State University
Raleigh, NC 27695

Daniel S. Moak
Department of Mathematics
Michigan Tech. University
Houghton, MI 49931

Victor H. Moll
Department of Mathematics
Tulane University
New Orleans, LA 70118

Carlos Moreno
Department of Mathematics
Bernard M. Baruch College
City University of New York
17 Lexington Ave.
New York, NY 10010

Rolf Müller
Department of Mathematics
University of Illinois
1409 West Green
Urbana, IL 61801

M. Ram Murty
Department of Mathematics
McGill University
Montreal
Quebec H3A 2K6
Canada

N. R. Nandakumar
Dept. of Mathematics & Computer Science
University of Nebraska at Omaha
Omaha, Nebraska 68182

Morris Newman
Department of Mathematics
University of California-Santa Barbara
Santa Barbara, CA 93106

Eugene Ng
Department of Mathematics
University of Texas at El Paso
El Paso, TX 79968

Jean-Louis Nicolas
Department of Mathematics
University of Limoges
123 Av. A. Thomas
87060 Limoges
France

Kathleen M. O'Hara
Department of Mathematics
University of Iowa
Iowa City, IA 52290

Alayne Parson
Department of Mathematics
Ohio State University
231 W. 18th St.
Columbus, OH 43210

Peter Paule
Institut für Mathematin
Johannes Kepler Universität Linz
A-4040 Linz
Austria

Y.-F. S. Pétermann
Department of Mathematics
University of Illinois
1409 West Green St.
Urbana, IL 61801

Carl Prather
Department of Mathematics
Virginia Polytechnic Institute
& State University
Blacksburg, VA 24061

James Propp
Department of Mathematics
University of Maryland
College Park, MD 20742

Yao Qi
Department of Mathematics
University of Illinois
1409 West Green St.
Urbana, IL 61801

S. Raghavan
School of Mathematics
Tata Institute of Fundamental Research
Homi Bhabha Rd.
Bombay 400005
India

M. Rahman
Department of Mathematics
Eastern Illinois University
Charleston, IL 61920

Vijaya Ramachandran
Department of Computer Science
University of Illinois
Urbana, Il 61801

K.G. Ramanathan
School of Mathematics
Tata Institute of Fundamental Research
Homi Bhabha Road
Bombay 400005
India

S. S. Rangachari
School of Mathematics
Tata Institute of Fundamental Research
Homi Bhabha Rd.
Bombay 400005
India

Robert A. Rankin
Department of Mathematics
University of Glasgow
Glasgow G12 8QW
Scotland
U.K.

J. S. Rao
Embassy of India
2107 Massachusetts Ave., N.W.
Washington, D.C. 20008

R. Ranga Rao
Department of Mathematics
University of Illinois
1409 West Green St.
Urbana, IL 61801

Don Redmond
Department of Mathematics
Southern Illinois University
Carbondale, IL 62901

Irma Reiner
Department of Mathematics
University of Illinois
1409 West Green St.
Urbana, IL 61801

Bruce Reznick
Department of Mathematics
University of Illinois
1409 West Green St.
Urbana, IL 61801

Matthew P. Richey
Department of Mathematics
St. Olaf College
Northfield, MN 55057

Otto G. Ruehr
Department of Mathematics
Michigan Technological University
Houghton, MI 49931

Wolfgang Schwarz
Fachbereich Mathematik
der Johann Wolfgang Goethe Universität
Postfach 11 19 32
Robert-Mayer-Straße 10
D6000 Frankfurt am Main 1
Federal Republic of Germany

John Selfridge
Department of Mathematics
Northern Illinois University
DeKalb, IL 60115

Lou Shituo
Department of Mathematics
University of Illinois
1409 West Green St.
Urbana, IL 61801

Peter Jau-Shyong Shiue
Department of Mathematics
University of Nevada
Las Vegas, NV 89154

Vencil Skarda
318 TMCB
Brigham Young University
Provo, UT 84602

Claudia Sprio
Department of Mathematics
SUNY at Buffalo
Buffalo, NY 14214

Bhama Srinivasan
Department of Mathematics
University of Illinois
Chicago, IL 60680

Anupam Srivastav
Department of Mathematics
University of Illinois
1409 West Green St.
Urbana, IL 61801

H. M. Srivastava
Department of Mathematics
University of Victoria
Victoria
British Columbia V8W 2Y2
Canada

Dennis Stanton
Department of Mathematics
University of Minnesota
Minneapolis, MN 55455

Kenneth B. Stolarsky
Department of Mathematics
University of Illinois
1409 West Green St.
Urbana, IL 61801

Sir Peter Swinnerton-Dyer
14 Park Crescent
London W1N 4DH
England

S. Thangavelu
Department of Mathematics
Princeton University
Princeton, NJ 08544

Amitabha Tripathi
Department of Mathematics
SUNY at Buffalo
Buffalo, NY 14214

Stephen Ullom
Department of Mathematics
University of Illinois
1409 West Green St.
Urbana, IL 61801

Alfred van der Poorten
School of Mathematics
Macquarie University
Sydney
New South Wales
Australia 2109

Charles Vanden Eynden
Department of Mathematics
Illinois State University
Normal, IL 61761

James Vaughn, Jr.
2235 Brentwood
Houston, TX 77019

Gérard X. Viennot
Mathematiques et Informatique
Université de Bordeaux I
351, Cours de la Libération
33405 Talence Cedex
France

Samuel S. Wagstaff, Jr
Department of Computer Science
Purdue Univ.
West Lafayette, IN 47907

Ferrell Wheeler
Department of Mathematics
University of Illinois
1409 West Green St.
Urbana, IL 61801

Jet Wimp
Department of Mathematics
Drexel University
Philadelphia, PA 19104

M. C. Wunderlich
3021 Red Lion Lane
Silver Spring, MD 20904

Doron Zeilberger
Department of Mathematics
Drexel University
Philadelphia, PA 19104

Liang-Cheng Zhang
Department of Mathematics
University of Illinois
1409 West Green St.
Urbana, IL 61801

I. J. Zucker
16, Highview GDS
London N3 3EX
England

PREFACE

Shortly after the fiftieth anniversary of Ramanujan's birth, G.H. Hardy published his famous book: Ramanujan, Twelve Lectures on Subjects Suggested by His Life and Work. Hardy's book presents an overview not only of Ramanujan's contributions but also of the work of others who built on Ramanujan's ideas. At the University of Illinois in June, 1987, 125 mathematicians gathered in a conference to commemorate the one hundredth anniversary of Ramanujan's birth, and this volume contains the proceedings of that conference.

There are some natural questions that arise about this entire undertaking. Has the second fifty years provided as many interesting extensions of Ramanujan's work as the first? Is the interest in Ramanujan expanding? Is the importance of his work becoming clearer? I am certain that the answer to each of these questions is yes, and detailed positive proof is given in the following pages. At the outset we should at least mention that the amazing work of the Borwein brothers on decimal expansions of π, the beautiful solution of the hard hexagon model in statistical mechanics by Baxter and the mixture of the symbolic algebra computer language MACSYMA with Ramanujan's ideas by Gosper are three applications of Ramanujan's work which are hardly envisioned in Hardy's book. The beauty of Ramanujan's work not only attracts mathematicians but also physicists as is made clear in Dyson's article. As an interesting sidelight of the conference, a forty five year old problem posed originally by Dyson and discussed in his article was solved the day after the conference closed (see Garvan's paper for details).

Hardy's book treats broadly ten topics: primes, probabalistic number theory, asymptotics of number sequences, partitions of numbers (combinatorial), hypergeometric series, partitions of numbers (analytic), sums of squares, Ramanujan's tau function, integrals and modular functions. Besides the new topics already mentioned, each of Hardy's topics is amply addressed in the present volume.

Finally, I wish to offer a special word of thanks to Bruce Berndt. He was the person most responsible for making this conference occur and run smoothly. In addition, his tireless efforts to produce an edited complete version of Ramanujan's famous notebooks assure us that in 2037 on Ramanujan's one hundred fiftieth birthday an even bigger and more impressive conference will take place.

George E. Andrews
Pennsylvania State University

On Ramanujan[*]

S. Chandrasekhar

I cannot clearly say anything that will relate to Ramanujan as a mathematician, particularly in this company which includes, among others, Professors Richard Askey, Bruce Berndt, and George Andrews, who have devoted years to exploring and following his many trails. But I do share with Ramanujan the same cultural background in our early formative years: both of us originate in a common social background -- he from Kumbakonam and I from Tanjore, both ancient centers of Tamil culture and not very far apart. Besides, Ramanujan's parents and my own grandparents lived in very similar social and financial circumstances. On this account I can probably visualize Ramanujan's background better than even my younger Indian colleagues of later generations.

With this common background, I can perhaps throw some light on some conflicting statements that have been made about Ramanujan and 'God' by some of his Indian contemporaries. I refer here particularly to the colorful stories concerning Ramanujan's devotion to the Namakkal Goddess.

Quite generally, it may be stated that among those who were brought up in South India during the first two decades of this century, there was (and probably still is) very little correlation between observance and belief. In particular, I can vouch from my own personal experience that some of the

---

[*] Remarks made at the Banquet on June 3, 1987

ISBN 0-12-058560-X

'observances' that one followed were largely for the purposes of not offending the sensibilities of one's parents, relations, and friends.

I can say a good deal on these matters, but I shall only state that I do not accept what has commonly been said and written about Ramanujan's religious beliefs. I corresponded with Hardy on this matter while he was preparing for his Harvard Lectures; and I am personally much more inclined to accept his view as expressed in a letter to me dated February 19, 1936.

> . . . And my own view is that, at bottom and to a first approximation, R. was (intellectually) as sound an infidel as Bertrand Russell or Littlewood....
>
> One thing I am sure. R was not in the least the 'inspired idiot' that some people seem to have thought him. On the contrary, he was (except for a period when his mental equilibrium was definitely upset by illness) a very shrewd and sensible person: very individual, of course, and with a reasonable allowance of the minor eccentricities of genius, but fundamentally normal and sane.

And this view of Hardy's is corroborated by K. Ananda Rao, himself a mathematician of distinction, who had been Hardy's student and Ramanujan's contemporary in Cambridge. Ananda Rao is well known and remembered for his contributions to the theory of Tauberian theorems, function-theory and the theory of Dirichlet series. He has written:

> In his nature he was simple, entirely free from affectation, with no trace whatever of his being self-conscious of his abilities. He was quite sociable,

> very polite and considerate to others. He was a man full of humour and a good conversationalist, and it was always interesting to listen to him. On occasions when I met him, we used to talk in homely Tamil. He could talk on many things besides mathematics . . . .

This view of Ananda Rao is not surprisingly the same as Hardy's. He has written,

> . . . the picture which I want to present to you is that of a man who had his peculiarities like other distinguished men, but a man in whose society one could take pleasure, with whom one could drink tea and discuss politics or mathematics.

Let me now turn to the role of Ramanujan in the development of science in India during the early years of this century.

Perhaps the best way I can give you a feeling for what Ramanujan meant to the young men going to schools and colleges during the period 1915–1930 is to recall for you the way in which I first learned of Ramanujan's name.

It must have been a day in April 1920, when I was not quite ten years old, when my mother told me of an item in the newspaper of the day that a famous Indian mathematician, Ramanujan by name, had died the preceding day; and she told me further that Ramanujan had gone to England some years earlier, had collaborated with some famous English mathematicians, and that he had returned only very recently, and was well known internationally for what he had achieved. Though I had no idea at that time of what kind of a mathematician Ramanujan was, or indeed what scientific achievement meant, I can still recall the gladness I felt at the assurance that one brought up under circumstances similar to my own, could have achieved what I could not grasp. I am sure that others were equally gladdened. I hope that it is not hard for you to imagine what the example of Ramanujan could have provided for young men and women of those times, beginning to look at the world with increasingly different perceptions.

The fact that Ramanujan's early years were spent in a scientifically sterile atmosphere, that his life in India was not without hardships, that under circumstances that appeared to most Indians as nothing short of miraculous, he had gone to Cambridge, supported by eminent mathematicians, and had returned to India with every assurance that he would be considered, in time, as one of the most original mathematicians of the century -- these facts were enough -- more than enough -- for aspiring young Indian students to break their bonds of intellectual confinement and perhaps soar the way that Ramanujan had.

It may be argued, perhaps with some justice, that this was a sentimental attitude: Ramanujan represents so extreme a fluctuation from the norm that his being born an Indian must be considered to a large extend as accidental. But to the Indians of the time, Ramanujan was not unique in the way we think of him today. He was one of others who had, during that same period, achieved, in their judgement, comparably in science and in other areas of human activity. Gandhi, Motilal and Jawharlal Nehru, Rabindranath Tagore, J. C. Bose, C. V. Raman, M. N. Saha, S. N. Bose, and a host of others, were in the forefront of the then fermenting Indian scene. The twenties and the thirties were a period when young Indians were inspired for achievement and accomplishment by these men whom they saw among them.

I do not wish to leave the impression that Ramanujan's influence was only in this very generalized sense. I think it is fair to say that almost all the mathematicians who reached distinction during the three or four decades following Ramanujan were directly or indirectly inspired by his example.

But Ramanujan's name inspired not only ambitous young men planning scientific careers; it also stimulated to action those with public concern. Let me give one example.

When I was a student in Madras one of my classmates (who came from a very wealthy family) was one Alagappa Chettiar. We became good friends; but our lives diverged along different paths after 1930. In the years before and during the second world war, Alagappa Chettiar prospered as an entrepreneur and became a noted philanthropist. He was in fact knighted by the British government.

During the late forties after the war, Sir Alagappa Chettiar (as he was then) wrote to me inquiring if it might be useful for him to found a mathematical institute in Madras named after Ramanujan. I enthusiastically supported the idea; and when I returned to India briefly in 1951, the Ramanujan Institute had been founded a few months earlier. Its first director, T. Vijayaraghavan, was one of the most talented among Hardy's former students; he died at a comparatively early age in 1955. C. T. Rajagopal, a student of Ananda Rao, took over the directorship from him. Already at that time the financial status of the Institute seemed shaky, since Alagappa Chettiar's fortune was melting away.

In April 1957, when Alagappa Chettiar died, the fate of the Institute hung in the balance; Rajagopal wrote to me that the

Institute 'will cease to exist on the first of next month,' whereupon I wrote to the Prime Minister (Jawaharlal Nehru), explaining the origin of the Institute and the seriousness of its condition. Nehru's prompt answer was refreshing: 'Even if you had not put in your strong recommendation in favour of the Ramanujan Institute of Mathematics, I would not have liked anything to happen which put an end to it. Now that you have also written to me on this subject, I shall keep in touch with this matter and I think I can assure you that the Institute will be carried on.' And it was; but haltingly and precariously for the next twelve years. It is at this Institute in Madras that Ramanujan's Centennial will be celebrated by an International Conference in December.

There is very little more I can say. My own view, sixty-six years after my first knowing of his name, is that India and the Indian scientific community were exceptionally fortunate in having before them the example of Ramanujan. It is hopeless to try to emulate him. But he was there even as the Everest is there.

A Walk Through Ramanujan's Garden.

Lecture given at the Ramanujan Centenary Conference,

University of Illinois, June 2, 1987.

Freeman J. Dyson,

Institute for Advanced Study, Princeton, N.J.

I. ANDREWS.

I am grateful to the organizers of this conference, and to Bruce Berndt and George Andrews in particular, for bringing me here and giving me a chance to enjoy all the new flowers that have been growing in recent years in Ramanujan's garden. George Andrews is now the chief gardener and is doing a magnificent job. He is, if I may say so, doing a better job than George Watson who used to be chief gardener in the old days. Watson was chief gardener in the 1930's and worked hard to develop and elucidate Ramanujan's ideas, especially the theories of singular moduli and mock theta-functions [1]. But Watson was the sort of gardener who liked to keep human visitors as far as possible away from the flowers. He stood at the entrance to his garden like the goddess Proserpine. Proserpine stands at the entrance to her garden in the poem of Swinburne which Watson quoted at the end of his famous lecture [2] on the mock theta-functions:

"Pale, beyond porch and portal,
Crowned with calm leaves, she stands

ISBN 0-12-058560-X

Who gathers all things mortal
With cold immortal hands."

Watson was like that. My good friend Oliver Atkin had the misfortune to work on Ramanujan's discoveries during the years when Watson was in charge of the garden. Atkin discovered and proved many new congruence properties of partitions, extending and developing Watson's own work [3]. Atkin wrote letters to Watson, keeping him abreast of the progress and asking him for help and advice. When Watson died in 1965, Atkin wrote to me, "I expect you saw that Watson died. My correspondence with him is thus closed. Final score of letters: twenty-nil."

George Andrews is different. He does not stand like Proserpine, gathering all things mortal with cold immortal hands. He answers letters. He even likes to have live human beings in his garden, trampling over the flower-beds. He gives help and encouragement to anyone who comes visiting, whether it is an elderly professor like me or a raw student. As a result, the garden is now blooming and sprouting more vigorously than ever. George Andrews also enlarged the territory of the garden by finding the famous lost notebook of Ramanujan, the notebook which Watson certainly had in his possession for thirty years but apparently never examined. Andrews not only examined the notebook for the first time but also explained and displayed for all to see the treasures that it contains [4].

II. HARDY.

Mack Kac used to say, "On revient toujours à ses anciens amours," "We always come back to our old loves." So now, thanks to George Andrews, I am coming back to my old love-affair with Ramanujan's mathematics. My love-affair began 48 years ago when I was in my second year of high-school in England. I won a school mathematics prize and according to the rules I was allowed to choose any book I wanted for the prize. I chose Hardy and Wright, "An Introduction to the Theory of Numbers," the first edition which had been published that same year [5]. It was, and still is, a splendid book for a teen-ager wanting to get a taste of real mathematics on an elementary level. It is a masterpiece of clear thinking and lively exposition. A few years later I got to know Hardy in Cambridge and asked him why he spent so much time and effort writing that marvelous book when he might have been doing serious mathematics. He answered, "Young men should prove theorems, old men should write books." He was then hard at work on his last book , the Cambridge Tract on Fourier Series which he wrote with Rogosinski [6]. Now I am just about as old as he was then and I am following his good example.

The chapter in Hardy and Wright which I loved the most was Chapter 19 with the title "Partitions." This is a meaty chapter and includes a complete discussion and proof of the Rogers-Ramanujan identities. Even more exciting for me were the congruence properties of partitions discovered by Ramanujan:

$$p(5m+4) \equiv 0 (\mathrm{mod}\ 5) , \tag{1}$$

$$p(7m+5) \equiv 0 (\mathrm{mod}\ 7) , \tag{2}$$

$$p(11m+6) \equiv 0 (\mathrm{mod}\ 11) . \tag{3}$$

Hardy and Wright give elegant proofs for (1) and (2) but leave (3) aside with the remark that it is "more difficult." I tried hard to supply the missing proof of (3) but did not succeed. The first really elementary proof of (3) was found by the physicist Winquist [7] 30 years later. Winquist's proof, incidentally, was based on an identity which turned out to be one of the Macdonald Identities associated with the Lie algebra B_2. But that is another story.

While I was still in high school it occurrred to me that the congruences (1), (2) and (3) of Ramanujan raise a question which the proofs do not answer. The congruence (1), for example, says that the partitions of $(5m+4)$ must be divisible into five classes with the same number of partitions in each class. The proof tells you that it is possible to divide the partitions into five equal classes, but it does not tell you how to do it. So I began to search for a way of doing it. I wanted to find a concrete criterion, so that you could look at any particular partition of $(5m + 4)$ and use the criterion to tell which of the five equal classes it belonged to. Three years later, when I was a sophomore at Cambridge, I found it. The criterion turned out to be simple. For each partition you define a "rank." The rank of a partition is the greatest part minus the number of parts. Then for $j = 1, 2, 3, 4, 5$ you define the class $C_j(n)$, the class of partitions of n which have rank congruent to j (modulo 5). That did the trick. It turns out that, when $n = 5m + 4$, the classes C_1, C_2, C_3, C_4, C_5 are equal. I checked this the hard way, by writing down all the partitions and dividing them into the five classes according to their ranks, for $n = 4$ and $n = 9$ and $n = 14$. In the case of $n = 14$ you have 135 partitions and there are exactly 27 of them in each of the five classes. I decided that the chance that this would happen by accident was negligible. So I had found the criterion. That was a great moment. I gave thanks to Ramanujan for two things, for discovering congruence properties of partitions and for not discovering the criterion for dividing them into equal classes. That was the wonderful thing about Ramanujan. He discovered so much, and yet he left so much more in his garden for other people to discover. In the 44 years since that happy day, I have intermittently been coming back to Ramanujan's garden. Every time when I come back, I find fresh flowers blooming.

As soon as I had checked the criterion for divisibility by 5, I looked at the first cases of divisibility by 7 and 11. For 7, the same trick worked. I wrote down the partitions of 5 and 12 and divided them into 7 classes according to their ranks (modulo 7). The 77 partitions of 12 divided into 7 classes with 11 in each class. This too could not be an accident. So the rank criterion was valid for the divisibility of $p(7m + 5)$ by 7. But the trick does not work for the divisibility of $p(11m + 6)$ by 11. It fails already at the first trial. The partitions $3 + 3$ and $4 + 1 + 1$ of 6 both have rank 1, and there is no partition of 6 with rank congruent to 4 (modulo 11). I spent many happy hours searching for a criterion of divisibility for partitions (modulo 11). I never found it. It was found forty years later by Frank Garvan [8] who is here to-day to tell you about it. I will have something to say about Frank Garvan's discoveries too. But for the moment I go back to 1942.

I wanted to prove the equal division of partitions by rank (modulo 5) and (modulo 7), but I never succeeded in finding a proof. The proof was found by Oliver Atkin and Peter Swinnerton-Dyer ten years later [9]. Peter is now a baronet and a Knight of the British Empire as well as being a famous mathematician. The proof which Oliver and Peter constructed is a great work of art, in the best Ramanujan tradition. In their analysis many of Ramanujan's beloved mock theta-functions make an appearance. As Frank Garvan noticed thirty years later [8], Atkin and Swinnerton-Dyer had rediscovered for the purposes of their proof several of the striking mock-theta-function identities which were in 1953 lying buried in Ramanujan's lost notebook. The notebook was buried , not metaphorically but literally, in the deep layer of debris which covered the floor of Watson's room in Birmingham [10].

All that I managed to do in 1942 was to find a convenient generating function for partitions of a given rank. Let $p_m(n)$ be the number of partitions of n with rank m. Then the generating function is

$$P_m(x) = \sum_{n=1}^{\infty} p_m(n)x^n$$

$$= P(x) \sum_{n=1}^{\infty} (-1)^{n-1} \left(x^{\frac{1}{2}n(3n-1)} - x^{\frac{1}{2}n(3n+1)} \right) x^{|m|n} , \tag{4}$$

with

$$P(x) = \sum_{n=0}^{\infty} p(n)x^n = \left[\sum_{-\infty}^{\infty} (-1)^n x^{\frac{1}{2}n(3n-1)} \right]^{-1} . \tag{5}$$

The expression on the right of (5) is Euler's classic formula for the partition function, one of the gems to be found in Chapter 19 of Hardy and Wright [5]. The fact that the generating function (4) for partitions of a given rank is equally elegant came as an unexpected bonus. In 1942 I could prove (4) but I did not see how to give it a combinatorial meaning. I merely used (4) as a practical tool for numerical calculations.

Let $p_{q,m}(n)$ be the number of partitions of n with rank congruent to m (modulo

q). Then (4) gives us the generating function, valid for $0 \leq m < q$,

$$\begin{aligned} P_{q,m}(x) &= \sum_{n=1}^{\infty} p_{q,m}(n)x^n \\ &= P(x) \sum_{n=-\infty}^{\infty}{}'(-1)^{n-1}\ x^{\frac{1}{2}n(3n-1)+mn} \left(\frac{1-x^n}{1-x^{qn}}\right) , \end{aligned} \tag{6}$$

where the prime means that the term $n = 0$ is omitted from the sum. Using (6) it was easy, even in the days before we had electronic computers, to calculate rapidly the differences such as

$$a = p_{7,0}(n) - p_{7,3}(n),\ b = p_{7,1}(n) - p_{7,3}(n),\ c = p_{7,2}(n) - p_{7,3}(n)\ , \tag{7}$$

for values of n up to 100. The beautiful thing about such calculations is that they give you an automatic error-correction algorithm. The coefficients a, b and c are obtained by taking the quotient of two power-series according to (5) and (6). The denominator series has only sparse (+1) and (−1) coefficients, so that the process of division is easy and rapid. The resulting quotient gives coefficients a, b, c, which are always small so long as you do not make a mistake. The biggest value of a up to $n = 100$ is $a = 3$ at $n = 99$. But as soon as you make the slightest mistake in the division, the values of a rapidly blow up like $p(n)$. When you see the values blowing up, you need only glance at a table of values of $p(n)$ to see exactly where the error was. So you can happily correct each error as it arises, and you end up with a table of values of a, b and c which is guaranteed correct. This particular error-correction algorithm is of course unnecessary now that we have infallible computers and programs like SCRATCHPAD to manipulate power-series automatically. Nevertheless it may still sometimes be useful to build an error- correction algorithm of this type into a numerical computation. Even if the computer is infallible, the input data may contain errors. The essential idea of the error-correction algorithm is to make the computation numerically unstable, so that every error reveals itself in a rapid blowing-up of the output. Such an algorithm can only work in a situation where we know a priori that the correct output must be small or smooth. I found myself, thanks to Ramanujan, in a situation where the output was guaranteed to be small.

After I had calculated the differences a, b and c up to $n = 100$, I knew for certain that they would all be zero whenever $n \equiv 5 \pmod 7$. In fact I knew much more. It turned out that

$$a = 0 \text{ for } n \equiv 2, 4, 5 (\text{mod } 7), \tag{8}$$

$$b = 0 \text{ for } n \equiv 1, 3, 4, 5 (\text{mod } 7), \tag{9}$$

$$c = 0 \text{ for } n \equiv 0, 1, 5 (\text{mod } 7). \tag{10}$$

And a similar set of equalities held for the two differences

$$d = p_{5,0}(n) - p_{5,2}(n), \quad e = p_{5,1}(n) - p_{5,2}(n) \ .$$

As George Andrews and Frank Garvan have told us [32], the differences d and e are closely related to the two families of fifth-order mock theta-functions discovered by Ramanujan. Ramanujan found only three seventh-order mock theta-functions, which, as he said in his last letter to Hardy, are not related to each other. It is likely that there are in fact, waiting to be discovered, three families of seventh-order mock theta-functions related to the differences a, b, c in the same way as the fifth-order functions are related to d and e. "We are just beginning to understand Ramanujan's last brilliant creation: the mock theta-functions." Quote from Andrews [30].

The equalities (8), (9), (10) were undoubtedly true, but in 1942 I had no idea how to prove them. In the end I gave up trying to prove them and published them as conjectures in our student magazine "Eureka" [11]. Since there was half a page left over at the end of my paper, they put in a poem by my friend Alison Falconer who was a poet as well as a mathematician [12]. I was glad to have a bit of poetry mixed in with the mathematics. Since the magazine is hard to find nowadays, I take this opportunity to rescue the poem from oblivion. Here it is:

Short Vision, by A. C. Falconer.

Thought is the only way which leads to life.

All else is hollow spheres
Reflecting back
In heavy imitation
And blurred degeneration
A senseless image of our world of thought.

Man thinks he is the thought which gives him life.
He binds a sheaf and claims it as himself.
He is a ring through which pass swinging ropes
Which merely move a little as he slips.

The Ropes are Thought.
The Space is Time.
Could he but see, then he might climb.

III. BAILEY.

But I digress. My next visit to Ramanujan's garden was in 1943. By that time I had left Cambridge and was working for the Royal Air Force as a statistician. Hardy was then secretary of the London Mathematical Society, which meant that he acted as editor for the Society's Journal. Mathematics in England was at a low ebb. All the young mathematicians were involved in the war in one way or another. Most of them had disappeared into the cryptographic establishment at Bletchley, which was like a black hole. People went to Bletchley and were never seen again. I was one of the few who were not at Bletchley. I was relatively accessible, and Hardy knew that I was interested in the Rogers-Ramanujan identities. So he sent me a paper to referee. The paper was by W. N. Bailey and contained a new method of deriving identities of the Rogers-Ramanujan type. I wrote a report for Hardy, approving it for publication with some suggested improvements. Hardy saw that it was absurd for the only two people in England with a serious interest in Rogers-Ramanujan identities to be isolated from each other. So he wisely broke the rule of anonymity of the referee. He sent my report to Bailey with my name on it. Bailey immediately wrote back to me, and we continued to exchange identities back and forth while Bailey worked out his final and much more powerful "Bailey Pair" method of deriving identities [13]. Because of the wartime shortage of paper, the paper I refereed [14] did not appear in print until 1947, and the "Bailey Pair" paper [15] did not appear until 1949. But Bailey's great work was done during that winter of 1943-44, and I was lucky to be acting then as his sounding-board. I never met Bailey. During those months, he was at Manchester and I was at the Royal Air Force Bomber Command headquarters in the middle of a forest in Buckinghamshire.

It was a long, hard, grim winter. I was working a sixty-hour week at Bomber Command. The bomber losses which I was supposed to analyze were growing steadily higher. The end of the war was not in sight. In the evenings of that winter I kept myself sane by wandering in Ramanujan's garden, reading the letters I was receiving from Bailey, working through Bailey's ideas and discovering new Rogers-Ramanujan identities of my own. I found a lot of identities of the sort that Ramanujan would have enjoyed. My favorite was this one:

$$\sum_{n=0}^{\infty} x^{n^2+n} \frac{(1+x+x^2)(1+x^2+x^4)\cdots(1+x^n+x^{2n})}{(1-x)(1-x^2)\cdots(1-x^{2n+1})} = \prod_{n=1}^{\infty} \frac{(1-x^{9n})}{(1-x^n)} \,. \qquad (11)$$

In the cold dark evenings, while I was scribbling these beautiful identities amid the death and destruction of 1944, I felt close to Ramanujan. He had been scribbling even more beautiful identities amid the death and destruction of 1917.

IV. ATKIN.

When World War 2 finally ended, I decided to come to America and be a physicist. But I did not forget Ramanujan. And my interest in congruence properties of partitions was kept alive through my friendship with Oliver Atkin. Atkin kept me in touch during the long struggle which he and Swinnerton-Dyer waged against the identities (8), (9), (10), ending with the total victory recorded in their 1953 paper [9]. For fifteen years after that, Atkin together with Joe Lehner and Morris Newman was engaged in a deeper exploration of the theory of modular forms out of which the congruence properties of partitions emerge. Atkin was a pioneer in two different ways. He was one of the first people to use electronic computers creatively for purposes of mathematical discovery. He had unlimited access to the Atlas computer at Chilton and explored with it the new world of modular forms. Out of his explorations emerged occasional artifacts such as the new partition congruences [16], [17],

$$p(11^3.13n + 237) \equiv 0(\text{mod } 13) , \tag{12}$$

$$p(23^3.17n + 2623) \equiv 0(\text{mod } 17) . \tag{13}$$

Atkin shared Ramanujan's delight in the idiosyncrasies of individual integers. Littlewood once remarked that every positive integer was one of Ramanujan's personal friends. Atkin too had personal friendships with integers. You had to be a personal friend of 17 and 23 before you could hope to discover a congruence like (13). But Atkin was a pioneer in a second and more important sense. He was not content to be merely a collector of elegant identities. He had a larger vision. His vision was a grand unification of the arithmetical theory of modular forms, in which all the known and unknown congruence properties of partitions would appear as particular instances. His grand unification is not yet achieved, but he made a good beginning. The territory which he explored, bringing together ideas from group-theory, function-theory and operator-theory, now lies open for the next generation of pioneers to colonize. What Atkin has been doing is to find connections between Ramanujan's garden and the big world of modern mathematics. The garden must not be, as it was in Watson's time, a little sheltered nook with a wall around it. It is now, thanks to Atkin and others, a garden without walls, a garden with wide vistas open on all sides. Atkin's recent obituary of his student Margaret Millington-Ashworth [18] gives us a particularly clear view of the wider landscape.

While I was discussing these larger issues with Atkin in 1968, I started thinking again about a small issue, the combinatorial meaning of the generating function (4) which I had found for the partitions of a given rank 25 years earlier. It turned out that a simple combinatorial argument gives us an understanding of (4) and also a new proof of (5) into the bargain [19]. The key step is to consider partitions into non- negative parts instead of into positive parts only. A partition is allowed to have any number of zero parts. The rank of a partition is defined as before, as the largest part minus the number of parts. Let $q_m(n)$ be the number of partitions of n into non-negative parts with rank m. The table of values of $q_m(n)$ then has two separate and independent reflection symmetries, namely

$$q_m(n) + q_{1-m}(n) = p(n) \ , \tag{14}$$

and

$$q_m(n) = q_{-2-m}(n - m - 1) \ . \tag{15}$$

Both of these symmetries are easily derived from the old well-known conjugation symmetry of partitions. I take (14) first. Given any partition P into positive parts and any integer m, you construct a partition Q into non-negative parts as follows. If P has rank $r \geq m$, you add enough zeros to P to make a partition Q with rank m. If P has rank $r < m$, you take the conjugate $\bar{P}$ which has rank $(-r) \geq 1 - m$, and add enough zeros to make a partition Q with rank $(1 - m)$. The relation between P and Q is one-to-one, and this proves (14).

The proof of (15) is even simpler. Given any partition Q into non- negative parts with rank m, you add one to each part to make a partition P into positive parts, then take the conjugate $\bar{P}$ and subtract one from each part to make a partition Q' into non-negative parts. The relation between Q and Q' is one-to-one, and this proves (15). Now putting together the two symmetries (14), (15), you find

$$q_m(n) = p(n - m - 1) - q_{m+3}(n - m - 1) \ . \tag{16}$$

The product of two reflections is a translation. Notice here the translation by 3 units arising from the combination of the two reflections. When you substitute (16) repeatedly into itself, it gives

$$\begin{aligned} q_m(n) &= p(n-m-1) - p(n-2m-5) + p(n-3m-12) - \dots \\ &= \sum_{k=1}^{\infty} (-1)^{k-1}\, p\left(n - km - \frac{1}{2}k(3k-1)\right) . \end{aligned} \tag{17}$$

The series (17) comes to an end after a finite number of terms and gives the generating function

$$\begin{aligned} Q_m(x) &= \sum_{n=1}^{\infty} q_m(n) x^n \\ &= P(x) \sum_{n=1}^{\infty} (-1)^{n-1}\, x^{\frac{1}{2}n(3n-1)+mn} , \end{aligned} \tag{18}$$

valid for $m \geq 0$. Now the subtraction of a zero part from a partition into non-negative parts gives another partition with rank increased by one. Therefore

$$q_m(n) - p_m(n) = q_{m+1}(n) . \tag{19}$$

From (18) and (19), the generating-function (4) follows immediately for $m \geq 0$, and (4) holds also for negative m by symmetry. Finally, you can obtain Euler's formula (5) by adding together (18) for $m = 0$ and $m = 1$, using (14). This derivation is the only one I know that explains in a natural way why the 3 appears in Euler's formula.

V. WINQUIST.

My next stroll through Ramanujan's garden began with a letter from Winquist about his new proof [7] of Ramanujan's congruence (3). This led me into the paradise of Macdonald identities which I have spoken about on a previous occasion [20]. During the last ten years, Macdonald identities and their generalizations have become another great new domain of mathematics, extending from Ramanujan's τ-function at one end to affine Lie algebras and the Monster Group and John Conway's "Monstrous Moonshine" at the other [21, 22]. The seeds from Ramanujan's garden have been blowing on the wind and have been sprouting all over the landscape. Some of the seeds even blew over into physics. I was delighted to see a new preprint written a few weeks ago by Gregory Moore, one of the young physicists at the Institute for Advanced Study, with the title "Atkin-Lehner Symmetry" [23]. The fresh breezes of superstring theory have brought modular forms into physics in ways that Oliver Atkin and Joe Lehner never dreamed of. Here is a quote from Gregory Moore: "In some sense, a negative sign under an Atkin-Lehner transformation means that we are exchanging high-energy bosons with low-energy fermions, and vice versa." Atkin and Lehner did not have bosons and fermions in mind when they invented their operators for the classification of modular forms. But I will say no more about superstring theory. There are probably people in the audience who know more about superstrings than I do. We will have to wait a long time before we know whether the dreams of the superstring fraternity will give us a true description of physical reality. Only one conclusion is already clear. Whether or not the superstring theory is a true image of nature, it is certainly a magnificent creation of pure mathematics. As pure mathematics, it is as beautiful as any of the other flowers that grew from seeds that ripened in Ramanujan's garden.

VI. GARVAN.

After this digression into superstrings, I go back to my first love, the theory of partitions. As you will hear when Frank Garvan speaks in a few minutes' time, he has found a new way of defining partitions and their ranks [8]. With his new definitions, he can calculate the number

$$P_{q,m}{}^V(n)$$

of vector partitions of n having rank congruent to m (modulo q). I leave it to him to tell us what a vector partition is. The new definition has the consequence that

$$P_{11,m}{}^V(11k+6) = \left(\frac{1}{11}\right) p(11k+6) \ , \tag{20}$$

giving us a combinatorial interpretation of Ramanujan's third congruence (3). My old definition of rank failed to satisfy (20). I don't want to steal Garvan's thunder. I just want to say that Garvan's beautiful discovery is not an end but a beginning.

The result (20) which provided the original motivation for his work is only one of many flowers in his garden. More important for the future are the connections which he found between the $P_{q,m}{}^{V}(n)$ and mock theta-functions. The mock theta-functions give us tantalizing hints of a grand synthesis still to be discovered. Somehow it should be possible to build them into a coherent group-theoretical structure, analogous to the structure of modular forms which Hecke built around the old theta-functions of Jacobi. This remains a challenge for the future. My dream is that I will live to see the day when our young physicists, struggling to bring the predictions of superstring theory into correspondence with the facts of nature, will be led to enlarge their analytic machinery to include not only theta-functions but mock theta-functions. Perhaps we may one day see a preprint written by a physicist with the title "Mock Atkin- Lehner Symmetry." But before this can happen, the purely mathematical exploration of the mock-modular forms and their mock- symmetries must be carried a great deal farther.

VII. ANDREWS AND HICKERSON.

Just in the last few weeks, as a result of reading Frank Garvan's thesis [8] and writing letters back and forth with George Andrews, I took my most recent walk in Ramanujan's garden. This walk began with Ramanujan's function

$$R(q) = 1 + \sum_{n=1}^{\infty} \frac{q^{\frac{1}{2}n(n+1)}}{(1+q)(1+q^2)\cdots(1+q^n)} , \tag{21}$$

which George Andrews brought to our attention in two recent papers [24,25]. The function appears in Ramanujan's lost notebook, and its properties have been elucidated by Andrews and Dean Hickerson in a preprint [26]. They write

$$R(q) = \sum_{n=0}^{\infty} S(n) q^n . \tag{22}$$

The coefficients $S(n)$ have a simple combinatorial meaning,

$$S(n) = \sum_{P} (-1)^{r(P)} , \tag{23}$$

summed over partitions P of n into unequal parts, where $r(P)$ is the rank of P. Andrews computed numerically several thousand of the $S(n)$ and found that they have peculiar properties. First, all of them are small. Second, most of them are zero. He listed the first appearance of the largest values of $S(n)$ within his range, namely

$$S(22) \quad = 3 \ , \tag{24}$$

$$S(45) \quad = 4 \ , \tag{25}$$

$$S(1609) = 6 \ , \tag{26}$$

$$S(3288) = 8 \ . \tag{27}$$

I remembered that in the understanding of Ramanujan's partition congruences (1), (2), (3), things always worked better if one considered the partition-function $p(n)$ as a function of

$$N = 24n + 1 \ . \tag{28}$$

This trick succeeds because the generating-function (5) of $p(n)$ has to be multiplied by

$$x^{-(1/24)} \tag{29}$$

to become a modular form

$$x^{-1/24}P(x) = \left[\sum_{-\infty}^{\infty} (-1)^n \ x^{(6n-1)^2/24} \right]^{-1} \ . \tag{30}$$

So I tried the same trick with the values of n appearing in (24), (25), (26), (27). I found immediately

$$N = 529 \quad = 23^2 \ , \tag{31}$$

$$N = 1081 \ = 23.47 \ , \tag{32}$$

$$N = 38617 = 23^2.73 \ , \tag{33}$$

$$N = 78913 = 23.47.73 \ . \tag{34}$$

A nice piece of experimental mathematics, a genre which my colleague Armand Borel has recently extolled [27]. There was no way these factorizations into primes of the form $(24k \pm 1)$ could be accidental. Obviously these primes must play a special role in the structure of the coefficients $S(n)$. A little playing around with the first hundred values of $S(n)$ gave me an explicit formula for

$$f(N) = S(n) \ . \tag{35}$$

Every $N = 24n + 1$ has a unique factorization

$$N = \eta \left(\prod_{\alpha} p_{\alpha}{}^{s_{\alpha}} \right) \left(\prod_{\beta} q_{\beta}{}^{s_{\beta}} \right) \ , \tag{36}$$

where p_{α} is either a positive prime congruent to 1 (mod 24) or the negative of a prime congruent to (-1) (mod 24), the q_{β} are primes congruent to $\pm 5, \pm 7$ or ± 11 (mod 24), and $\eta = \pm 1$. The coefficient $f(N)$ is zero unless

$$\eta = +1 \tag{37}$$

and all the s_{β} are even,

$$s_{\beta} = 2t_{\beta} \ . \tag{38}$$

This explains why most of the $S(n)$ are zero. When (37) and (38) hold, then

$$f(N) = \left(\prod_{\alpha} (1 + s_{\alpha}) \epsilon_{\alpha}{}^{s_{\alpha}} \right) \left(\prod_{\beta} \epsilon_{\beta}{}^{t_{\beta}} \right) \ , \tag{39}$$

where the $\epsilon_{\alpha}, \epsilon_{\beta}$ are signs defined as follows. Every prime p_{α}, whether positive or negative, has a representation by the form

$$p_{\alpha} = a^2 - 72b^2 \ , \tag{40}$$

and this determines

$$\epsilon_{\alpha} = (-1)^b \ . \tag{41}$$

The representation (40) is not unique, but all representations of a given p_{α} have the same parity for b. Finally, ϵ_{β} is defined by the Legendre symbol

$$\epsilon_{\beta} = -\left(\frac{2}{q_{\beta}} \right) \ . \tag{42}$$

These results were discovered earlier, and independently, by Andrews and Hickerson [26]. What is more important, Andrews and Hickerson proved them and I didn't. Still it was a great pleasure to find such a flower growing in Ramanujan's garden.

One other little flower I found which Andrews and Hickerson missed. The function $f(N)$ defined by (39) looks as if it ought to be multiplicative, but it is not really multiplicative on the positive integers N. For example,

$$f(23.47) = 4 , \tag{43}$$

but $f(23)$ and $f(47)$ are not defined. Now the remedy is obvious. We simply extend the definition of $f(N)$ to negative $N \equiv 1 \pmod{24}$ using (39), (40) and (41). Since

$$-23 = 7^2 - 72.1^2, \ -47 = 5^2 - 72.1^2 , \tag{44}$$

the definition (39) gives

$$f(-23) = f(-47) = -2 , \tag{45}$$

and (43) is consistent with multiplicativity. Since

$$73 = 19^2 - 72.2^2 , \tag{46}$$

we have

$$f(73) = 2 , \tag{47}$$

and the values (24), (25), (26), (27) of $S(n)$ are also consistent with multiplicativity. The extended $f(N)$ is multiplicative on the set of positive and negative integers $N = 24n + 1$.

But now a new question arises. If we extend the definition of $S(n)$ to negative n, the series (22) will become a bilateral power-series

$$\sum_{n=-\infty}^{\infty} S(n)\ x^n = R(x) + L(x^{-1}) , \tag{48}$$

with the right-hand series $R(q)$ given by (21) and the left-hand series $L(q)$ given by

$$L(q) = -2q - 2q^2 - 2q^3 + 2q^7 + 2q^8 + \cdots . \tag{49}$$

What is then the meaning of the left-hand series

$$L(q) = \sum_{n=1}^{\infty} S(-n)q^n \ ? \tag{50}$$

We know that the coefficients of $R(q)$ and $L(q)$ are cross- multiplicative by virtue of the multiplicative properties of $f(N)$. But this cross-multiplicativity does not give us an explicit definition for $L(q)$. So I computed from (39) the first fifty coefficients of $L(q)$ and found the explicit formula (experimental mathematics again)

$$L(q) = 2 \sum_{n=1}^{\infty}(-1)^n \frac{q^{n^2}}{(1-q)(1-q^3)\cdots(1-q^{2n-1})} , \tag{51}$$

happily complementing Ramanujan's formula (21) for $R(q)$. Like (21), the formula (51) has a combinatorial interpretation. Instead of (23) we now have

$$S(-n) = 2 \sum_{P} (-1)^{\ell(P)} , \tag{52}$$

where P is summed over partitions of n into odd parts with maximum difference 2 between consecutive parts, and

$$\ell(P) = \frac{1}{2} \text{ (largest part} + 1) . \tag{53}$$

George Andrews and Dean Hickerson were able to supply a proof of (51), using the techniques of Bailey [10, 15]. We have then a closed set of two back-to-back functions $R(q)$ and $L(q)$, each having a series expansion of Ramanujan type, and with cross-multiplicative coefficients.

This pair of functions $R(q)$ and $L(q)$ is to-day an isolated curiosity. But I am convinced that, like so many other beautiful things in Ramanujan's garden, it will turn out to be a special case of a broader mathematical structure. There probably exist other sets of two or more functions with coefficients related by cross- multiplicativity, satisfying identities similar to those which Ramanujan discovered for his $R(q)$. I have a hunch that such sets of cross- multiplicative functions will form a structure within which the mock theta-functions will also find a place. But this hunch is not backed up by any solid evidence. I leave it to the ladies and gentlemen of the audience to find the connections if they exist.

In conclusion, I would like to urge all of you who are working in the many fields of mathematics which have been enriched by Ramanujan's ideas to go back to the source, to the collected papers and the notebooks. The collected papers [28] with an introduction by Hardy were published in 1927. The notebooks which were not "lost" [29] were published in 1957, and are now appearing in a splendidly annotated version edited by Bruce Berndt [31]. The "lost" notebook is now accessible to us through the devoted labors of George Andrews [4]. When I started my walk through Ramanujan's garden 47 years ago, only the collected papers were available. A year after I chose Hardy and Wright's "Theory of Numbers" [5] as a school prize, I won another prize. For the second prize I chose Ramanujan's collected papers. The collected papers have travelled with me from England to America and are still as fresh to-day as they were in 1940. Whenever I am angry or depressed, I pull down the collected papers from the shelf and take a quiet stroll in Ramanujan's garden. I recommend this therapy to all of you who suffer from headaches or jangled nerves. And Ramanujan's papers are not only a good therapy for headaches. They also are full of beautiful ideas which may help you to do more interesting mathematics.

REFERENCES

[1]. J. M. Whittaker, "George Neville Watson," Biographical Memoirs of Fellows of the Royal Society, 12, 521-530 (1966).

[2]. G. N. Watson, "The Final Problem: an account of the mock theta functions," J. London Math. Soc. 11, 55-80 (1936).

[3]. For example, A. O. L. Atkin, "Proof of a Conjecture of Ramanujan," Glasgow Math. Journal 8, 14-32 (1967).

[4]. G. E. Andrews, "An Introduction to Ramanujan's 'Lost' Notebook," Am. Math. Monthly 86, 89-108 (1979), and a series of papers in "Advances in Mathematics," (1981-1987).

[5]. G. H. Hardy and E. M. Wright, "An Introduction to the Theory of Numbers," (Oxford, Clarendon Press, 1938).

[6]. G. H. Hardy and W. W. Rogosinski, "Fourier Series," Cambridge Tracts in Mathematics and Mathematical Physics, No. 38 (Cambridge University Press, 1944).

[7]. L. Winquist, "An Elementary Proof of $p(11m+6) \equiv 0 (\text{mod } 11)$," J. Combinatorial Theory, 6, 56-59 (1969).

[8]. F. G. Garvan, "Generalizations of Dyson's Rank," Pennsylvania State University Ph.D. Thesis, 1986.

[9]. A. O. L. Atkin and P. Swinnerton-Dyer, "Some Properties of Partitions," Proc. London Math. Soc (3) 4, 84-106 (1953).

[10]. G. E. Andrews, "q-Series: their development and application in analysis, number theory, combinatorics, physics, and computer algebra," American Mathematical Society, Regional Conference Series in Mathematics, No.66 (1986).

[11]. F. J. Dyson, "Some Guesses in the Theory of Partitions," Eureka, 8, 10-15 (1944).

[12]. A. C. Falconer, "Short Vision," Eureka, 8, 15 (1944).

[13]. See chapter 3 of [10].

[14]. W. N. Bailey, "Some Identities in Combinatory Analysis," Proc. London Math. Soc. (2) 49, 421-435 (1947).

[15]. W. N. Bailey, "Identities of Rogers-Ramanujan Type," Proc. London Math. Soc. (2) 50, 1-10 (1949).

[16]. A. O. L. Atkin, "Multiplicative Congruence Properties and Density Problems for $p(n)$," Proc. London Math. Soc. (3) 18 , 563-576 (1968).

[17]. A. O. L. Atkin, "Congruence Hecke Operators," American Math. Soc. Proceedings of Symposia in Pure Mathematics, 12, 33-40 (1969).

[18]. A. O. L. Atkin, Obituary notice of Margaret Hillary Millington, née Ashworth, Bull. London Math. Soc. 17, 484- 486 (1985).

[19]. F. J. Dyson, "A New Symmetry of Partitions," J. Combinatorial Theory, 7, 56-61 (1969).

[20]. F. J. Dyson, "Missed Opportunities," Bull. Am. Math. Soc. 78, 635-653 (1972).

[21]. J. H. Conway and S. P. Norton, "Monstrous Moonshine," Bull. London Math. Soc. 11, 308-339 (1979).

[22]. I. B. Frenkel, J. Lepowsky and A. Meurman, "A Natural Representation of the Fischer-Griess Monster with the modular function J as character," Proc. Nat. Acad. Sci. USA, 81, 3256-3260 (1984).

[23]. G. Moore, "Atkin-Lehner Symmetry," Institute for Advanced Study Preprint HUTP-87/A013 (March 1987).

[24]. G. E. Andrews, "Ramanujan's 'Lost' Notebook V: Euler's Partition Identity," Adv. Math. 61, 156-164 (1986).

[25]. G. E. Andrews, "Questions and Conjectures in Partition Theory," Am. Math. Monthly, 93, 708-711 (1986).

[26]. G. E. Andrews and D. Hickerson, "Partitions and Indefinite Quadratic Forms," Preprint, April 1987.

[27]. A. Borel, "Mathematics: Art and Science," Math. Intelligencer, 5, No. 4, 9-17 (1983).

[28]. S. Ramanujan, Collected papers, ed. G. H. Hardy, P.V. Seshu Aiyar and B. M. Wilson, (Cambridge University Press, 1927).

[29]. "Notebooks of S. Ramanujan," 2 volumes, (Bombay, Tata Institute of Fundamental Research, 1957).

[30]. G. E. Andrews, "The Fifth and Seventh Order Mock Theta Functions," Trans. Am. Math. Soc. 293, 113-134 (1986).

[31]. B. C. Berndt, ed. Ramanujan's Notebooks, Vol. 1 (New York, Springer, 1985).

[32]. G. E. Andrews and F. G. Garvan, "Ramanujan's 'Lost' Notebook, VI: The Mock Theta Conjectures," Preprint, Pennsylvania State University (1987).

Combinatorial interpretations of Ramanujan's partition congruences

F. G. Garvan†

0. Introduction. This paper is mainly concerned with combinatorial aspects of the following congruences due to Ramanujan:

$$p(5n+4) \equiv 0 \pmod{5}, \tag{0.1}$$

$$p(7n+5) \equiv 0 \pmod{7}, \tag{0.2}$$

$$p(11n+6) \equiv 0 \pmod{11}. \tag{0.3}$$

In §1 we give a brief survey of Ramanujan's partition congruences. In §2 we state Dyson's [13] combinatorial interpretations of (0.1) and (0.2) in terms of the rank. See Dyson [14; II] for more background on the rank. Dyson conjectured the existence of what he called the *crank* which would explain (0.3) just as the rank explains (0.1) and (0.2). In §3 we give such a crank. It is in terms of a weighted count of what we call vector partitions. The results on vector partitions have been taken from [16], [17]. In §4 we show how these results are related to identities from Ramanujan's 'lost' notebook, the work of Atkin and Swinnerton-Dyer [6] and the mock theta conjectures mentioned by George Andrews in his talk.

Finally in §5 we prove some combinatorial results that are related to the crank and rank differences. The day after this conference ended the *true* crank (given in terms of ordinary partitions rather than vector partitions) was discovered by George Andrews and myself. This result is announced.

1. Ramanujan's partition congruences. The partition congruences modulo 5 and 7 namely (0.1) and (0.2) were proved by Ramanujan in [20]. In [21] he proved (0.3) by a different method. These three congruences are special cases of more general results. In 1919 Ramanujan conjectured that if $\alpha \geq 1$ and $\delta_{t,\alpha}$ is the reciprocal modulo t^α of 24 then

$$p(5^\alpha n + \delta_{5,\alpha}) \equiv 0 \pmod{5^\alpha}, \tag{1.1}$$

$$p(7^\alpha n + \delta_{7,\alpha}) \equiv 0 \pmod{7^\alpha}, \tag{1.2}$$

$$p(11^\alpha n + \delta_{11,\alpha}) \equiv 0 \pmod{11^\alpha}. \tag{1.3}$$

As noticed by Chowla [12] (1.2) fails for $\alpha = 3$ since $p(243)$ is divisible by 7^2 but not by 7^3. The correct version is

$$p(7^\alpha n + \delta_{7,\alpha}) \equiv 0 \pmod{7^{[(\alpha+2)/2]}}. \tag{1.4}$$

†Department of Mathematics, University of Wisconsin, Madison, Wisconsin, 53706.
Current Address: I.M.A., University of Minnesota, Minneapolis, Minnesota, 55455.

ISBN 0-12-058560-X

(1.1) and (1.4) were proved by Watson [27] in 1938. (1.3) was finally proved by Atkin [7] in 1967. Atkin [9] has also simplified Watson's proofs of (1.1) and (1.4). Elementary proofs of (1.1) and (1.4) have been given by Hirschhorn and Hunt [18] and Garvan [15] respectively. Congruences analogous to (0.1) – (0.3) for other primes have also been found. For example Atkin [8], [10] has found

$$p(59^4 \cdot 13n + 111247) \equiv 0 \pmod{13}, \tag{1.5}$$

$$p(23^3 \cdot 17n + 2623) \equiv 0 \pmod{17}. \tag{1.6}$$

There are further congruence results to be found in some of Ramanujan's unpublished manuscripts. As noted by Rushforth [23] and Rankin [22] Hardy extracted [21] from an unpublished manuscript entitled "*Properties of $p(n)$ and $\tau(n)$ defined by the equations*

$$\sum_{n=0}^{\infty} p(n)x^n = \frac{1}{(1-x)(1-x^2)(1-x^3)\cdots},$$

$$\sum_{n=1}^{\infty} \tau(n)x^n = x\{(1-x)(1-x^2)(1-x^3)\cdots\}^{24}."$$

Following Rankin we shall refer to this manuscript as MS. MS was sent to Hardy by Ramanujan a few months before his death. Apart from Rankin's and Rushforth's papers references to MS may be found in Birch [11] and Watson [25]. In MS Ramanujan indicates that the case $\alpha = 2$ of (1.3) can be proved in the same way as in the case $\alpha = 1$. The details are carried out by Rushforth in [23, §8]. MS also contains congruences for $p(n)$ in terms of generalizations of Ramanujan's τ-function modulo 13, 17 and 23. See Rushforth [23, §9]. The mod 13 case is closely related to work of Zuckerman [29]. Rankin [22] notes MS contains some congruences for $p(n)$ other than those mentioned in Rushforth [23]. For example, it contains the congruence

$$p\left(\frac{11 \cdot 13^\lambda + 1}{24}\right) + 2^{(5\lambda-3)/2} \equiv 0 \pmod{13}.$$

Results of this type were later discovered by Newman [19]. According to Rankin [22] there is another unpublished manuscript, referred to by Birch [11] as Fragment [VII] which is a sequel to MS. It contains amongst other things a sketch of a proof of (1.1) that is very similar to Watson's. Birch claims that Ramanujan's results are stronger than Watson's; Ramanujan states that if $\alpha \geq 1$ then there is a constant c_α such that

$$\sum_{n=0}^{\infty} p(5^\alpha n + \delta_{5,\alpha})q^n \equiv \begin{cases} c_\alpha 5^\alpha \{(1-q)(1-q^2)\cdots\}^{19} \pmod{5^{\alpha+1}}, & \text{if } \alpha \text{ odd}, \\ c_\alpha 5^\alpha \{(1-q)(1-q^2)\cdots\}^{23} \pmod{5^{\alpha+1}}, & \text{if } \alpha \text{ even}, \end{cases} \tag{1.7}$$

but this result follows almost immediately from equations (3.43) and (3.44) in Watson [27] .

2. Dyson's rank. In 1944 F.J. Dyson [13] discovered empirically some remarkable combinatorial interpretations of (0.1) and (0.2). Dyson defined the *rank* of a partition as the largest part minus the number of parts. For example, the partition $4+4+3+2+1+1+1$ has rank $4-7=-3$. Let $N(m,n)$ denote the number of partitions of n with rank m and let $N(m,t,n)$ denote the number of partitions of n with rank congruent to m modulo t. Dyson conjectured that

$$N(k,5,5n+4) = \frac{p(5n+4)}{5} \qquad 0 \le k \le 4, \tag{2.1}$$

and

$$N(k,7,7n+5) = \frac{p(7n+5)}{7} \qquad 0 \le k \le 6. \tag{2.2}$$

(2.1) and (2.2) were later proved by A.O.L. Atkin and H.P.F. Swinnerton-Dyer [6] in 1953. These are the combinatorial interpretations of (0.1) and (0.2). Atkin and Swinnerton-Dyer's proof is analytic relying heavily on the properties of modular functions. No combinatorial proof is known. All that is known combinatorially about the rank is that

$$N(m,n) = N(-m,n), \tag{2.3}$$

which follows from the fact that the operation of conjugation reverses the sign of the rank. A trivial consequence is that

$$N(m,t,n) = N(t-m,t,n). \tag{2.4}$$

More than (2.1) and (2.2) is true. Dyson also conjectured

$$N(1,5,5n+1) = N(2,5,5n+1), \tag{2.5}$$
$$N(0,5,5n+2) = N(2,5,5n+2), \tag{2.6}$$
$$N(2,7,7n) = N(3,7,7n), \tag{2.7}$$
$$N(1,7,7n+1) = N(2,7,7n+1) = N(3,7,7n+1), \tag{2.8}$$
$$N(0,7,7n+2) = N(3,7,7n+2), \tag{2.9}$$
$$N(0,7,7n+3) = N(2,7,7n+3), \quad N(1,7,7n+3) = N(3,7,7n+3), \tag{2.10}$$
$$N(0,7,7n+4) = N(1,7,7n+4) = N(3,7,7n+4), \tag{2.11}$$
$$N(0,7,7n+6) + N(1,7,7n+6) = N(2,7,7n+6) + N(3,7,7n+6). \tag{2.12}$$

These were proved by Atkin and Swinnerton-Dyer. In fact they calculated the generating functions for $N(a,t,tn+k) - N(b,t,tn+k)$ for $t=5,7$ and all possible values for a, b and k. Before giving their result for $t = 5$ we need some notation. We define

$$r_a(d) = r_a(d,t) = \sum_{n=0}^{\infty} N(a,t,tn+d)q^n \tag{2.13}$$

and

$$r_{a,b}(d) = r_{a,b}(d,t) = r_a(d) - r_b(d). \tag{2.14}$$

THEOREM 1 (ATKIN AND SWINNERTON-DYER [6]). *For* $t = 5$,

$$r_{1,2}(0) = q \prod_{n=1}^{\infty}(1-q^{5n})^{-1} \sum_{m=-\infty}^{\infty} (-1)^m \frac{q^{15m(m+1)/2}}{1-q^{5m+1}}, \tag{2.15}$$

$$r_{0,2}(0) + 2r_{1,2}(0) = \prod_{n=1}^{\infty} \frac{(1-q^{5n-3})(1-q^{5n-2})(1-q^{5n})}{(1-q^{5n-4})^2(1-q^{5n-1})^2} - 1, \tag{2.16}$$

$$r_{0,2}(1) = \prod_{n=1}^{\infty} \frac{(1-q^{5n})}{(1-q^{5n-4})(1-q^{5n-1})}, \tag{2.17}$$

$$r_{1,2}(1) = r_{0,2}(2) = 0, \tag{2.18}$$

$$r_{1,2}(2) = \prod_{n=1}^{\infty} \frac{(1-q^{5n})}{(1-q^{5n-3})(1-q^{5n-2})}, \tag{2.19}$$

$$r_{0,2}(3) = -q \prod_{n=1}^{\infty}(1-q^{5n})^{-1} \sum_{m=-\infty}^{\infty} (-1)^m \frac{q^{15m(m+1)/2}}{1-q^{5m+2}}, \tag{2.20}$$

$$r_{0,1}(3) + r_{0,2}(3) = \prod_{n=1}^{\infty} \frac{(1-q^{5n-4})(1-q^{5n-1})(1-q^{5n})}{(1-q^{5n-3})^2(1-q^{5n-2})^2}, \tag{2.21}$$

$$r_{0,2}(4) = r_{1,2}(4) = 0. \tag{2.22}$$

We shall show later that Theorem 1 is embodied in an identity from Ramanujan's 'lost' notebook. We note that (2.1), (2.5) and (2.6) follow directly from (2.18) and (2.22). Dyson also conjectured some identities for the generating functions for the rank, namely

(2.23)
$$\sum_{n=0}^{\infty} N(m,n)q^n = \sum_{n=1}^{\infty}(-1)^{n-1} q^{\frac{1}{2}n(3n-1)+|m|n}(1-q^n) \prod_{k=1}^{\infty}(1-q^k)^{-1},$$

(2.24)
$$\sum_{n=0}^{\infty} N(m,t,n)q^n = \sum_{\substack{n=-\infty \\ n\neq 0}}^{\infty} (-1)^n q^{\frac{1}{2}n(3n+1)} \frac{(q^{mn}+q^{n(t-m)})}{(1-q^{tn})} \prod_{k=1}^{\infty}(1-q^k)^{-1},$$

which were also proved by Atkin and Swinnerton-Dyer.

Finally Dyson conjectures that there exists some analog of the rank that will explain (0.3):

> I hold in fact:
>
> That there exists an arithmetical coefficient similar to, but more recondite than, the rank of a partition; I shall call this hypothetical coefficient the "crank" of the partition, and denote by $M(m,q,n)$ the number of partitions of n whose crank is congruent to m modulo q;
>
> that $M(m,q,n) = M(q-m,q,n)$;
>
> that
>
> $$\begin{aligned} M(0,11,11n+6) &= M(1,11,11n+6) = M(2,11,11n+6) \\ &= M(3,11,11n+6) = M(4,11,11n+6); \end{aligned}$$
>
> that numerous other relations exist analogous to (12)–(19), and in particular
>
> $$\begin{aligned} M(1,11,11n+1) &= M(2,11,11n+1) \\ &= M(3,11,11n+1) = M(4,11,11n+1); \end{aligned}$$
>
> that $M(m,11,n)$ has a generating function not completely different in form from (24);
>
> that the values of the differences such as $M(0,11,n) - M(4,11,n)$ are always extremely small compared with $p(n)$.
>
> Whether these guesses are warranted by the evidence, I leave to the reader to decide. Whatever the final verdict of posterity may be, I believe the "crank" is unique among arithmetical functions in having been named before it was discovered. May it be preserved from the ignominious fate of the planet Vulcan!

The equations (12)–(19) and (24) referred to in the quotation above correspond to (2.5)–(2.12) and (2.24).

3. The crank for vector partitions. In this section we give a combinatorial interpretation of (0.3) as well as new interpretations of (0.1) and (0.2). Our main result does not actually divide the partitions of $11n+6$ into 11 equal classes but rather it gives a combinatorial interpretation of $\frac{p(11n+6)}{11}$ in terms of the crank of vector partitions.

To describe our main result we need some more notation. For a partition, π, let $\sharp(\pi)$ be the number of parts of π and $\sigma(\pi)$ be the sum of the parts of π (or the number π is partitioning) with the convention $\sharp(\phi) = \sigma(\phi) = 0$ for the empty partition, ϕ, of 0. Let,

$$\begin{aligned} V = \{\, (\pi_1,\pi_2,\pi_3) \mid & \pi_1 \text{ is a partition into distinct parts} \\ & \pi_2,\pi_3 \text{ are unrestricted partitions} \}. \end{aligned}$$

We shall call the elements of V *vector partitions*. For $\vec{\pi} = (\pi_1, \pi_2, \pi_3)$ in V we define the sum of parts, s, a weight, ω, and a crank, r, by

$$s(\vec{\pi}) = \sigma(\pi_1) + \sigma(\pi_2) + \sigma(\pi_3), \tag{3.1}$$

$$\omega(\vec{\pi}) = (-1)^{\sharp(\pi_1)}, \tag{3.2}$$

$$r(\vec{\pi}) = \sharp(\pi_2) - \sharp(\pi_3). \tag{3.3}$$

We say $\vec{\pi}$ is a vector partition of n if $s(\vec{\pi}) = n$. For example, if $\vec{\pi} = (5+3+2, 2+2+1, 2+1+1)$ then $s(\vec{\pi}) = 19$, $\omega(\vec{\pi}) = -1$, $r(\vec{\pi}) = 0$ and $\vec{\pi}$ is a vector partition of 19. The number of vector partitions of n (counted according to the weight ω) with crank m is denoted by $N_V(m,n)$, so that

$$N_V(m,n) = \sum_{\substack{\vec{\pi} \in V \\ s(\vec{\pi})=n \\ r(\vec{\pi})=m}} \omega(\vec{\pi}). \tag{3.4}$$

The number of vector partitions of n (counted according to the weight ω) with crank congruent to k modulo t is denoted by $N_V(k,t,n)$, so that

$$N_V(k,t,n) = \sum_{m=-\infty}^{\infty} N_V(mt+k,n) = \sum_{\substack{\vec{\pi} \in V \\ s(\vec{\pi})=n \\ r(\vec{\pi}) \equiv k \pmod{t}}} \omega(\vec{\pi}). \tag{3.5}$$

By considering the transformation that interchanges π_2 and π_3 we have

$$N_V(m,n) = N_V(-m,n) \tag{3.6}$$

so that

$$N_V(t-m,t,n) = N_V(m,t,n). \tag{3.7}$$

We have the following generating function for $N_V(m,n)$:

$$\sum_{m=-\infty}^{\infty} \sum_{n=0}^{\infty} N_V(m,n) z^m q^n = \prod_{n=1}^{\infty} \frac{(1-q^n)}{(1-zq^n)(1-z^{-1}q^n)}. \tag{3.8}$$

By putting $z=1$ in (3.8) we find

$$\sum_{m=-\infty}^{\infty} N_V(m,n) = p(n). \tag{3.9}$$

Our main result is

THEOREM 2.

$$N_V(k,5,5n+4) = \frac{p(5n+4)}{5} \qquad 0 \le k \le 4, \tag{3.10}$$

$$N_V(k,7,7n+5) = \frac{p(7n+5)}{7} \qquad 0 \le k \le 6, \tag{3.11}$$

$$N_V(k,11,11n+6) = \frac{p(11n+6)}{11} \qquad 0 \le k \le 10. \tag{3.12}$$

We illustrate (3.10) with an example. The 41 vector partitions of 4 are given in the table below. From the this table we have

$$\begin{aligned} N_V(0,5,4) &= \omega(\vec{\pi}_6) + \omega(\vec{\pi}_9) + \omega(\vec{\pi}_{12}) + \omega(\vec{\pi}_{13}) + \omega(\vec{\pi}_{24}) \\ &\qquad + \omega(\vec{\pi}_{26}) + \omega(\vec{\pi}_{33}) + \omega(\vec{\pi}_{40}) + \omega(\vec{\pi}_{41}) \\ &= 1+1+1+1-1-1-1-1+1 \\ &= 1. \end{aligned}$$

Similarly

$$N_V(0,5,4) = N_V(1,5,4) = \cdots = N_V(4,5,4) = 1 = \frac{p(4)}{5},$$

which is (3.10) with $n = 0$.

	Weight	Crank		Weight	Crank
$\vec{\pi}_1 = (\phi,\phi,4)$	$+1$	-1	$\vec{\pi}_{22} = (1,\phi,2+1)$	-1	-2
$\vec{\pi}_2 = (\phi,\phi,3+1)$	$+1$	-2	$\vec{\pi}_{23} = (1,\phi,1+1+1)$	-1	-3
$\vec{\pi}_3 = (\phi,\phi,2+2)$	$+1$	-2	$\vec{\pi}_{24} = (1,1,2)$	-1	0
$\vec{\pi}_4 = (\phi,\phi,2+1+1)$	$+1$	-3	$\vec{\pi}_{25} = (1,1,1+1)$	-1	-1
$\vec{\pi}_5 = (\phi,\phi,1+1+1+1)$	$+1$	-4	$\vec{\pi}_{26} = (1,2,1)$	-1	0
$\vec{\pi}_6 = (\phi,1,3)$	$+1$	0	$\vec{\pi}_{27} = (1,1+1,1)$	-1	1
$\vec{\pi}_7 = (\phi,1,2+1)$	$+1$	-1	$\vec{\pi}_{28} = (1,3,\phi)$	-1	1
$\vec{\pi}_8 = (\phi,1,1+1+1)$	$+1$	-2	$\vec{\pi}_{29} = (1,2+1,\phi)$	-1	2
$\vec{\pi}_9 = (\phi,2,2)$	$+1$	0	$\vec{\pi}_{30} = (1,1+1+1,\phi)$	-1	3
$\vec{\pi}_{10} = (\phi,2,1+1)$	$+1$	-1	$\vec{\pi}_{31} = (2,\phi,2)$	-1	-1
$\vec{\pi}_{11} = (\phi,1+1,2)$	$+1$	1	$\vec{\pi}_{32} = (2,\phi,1+1)$	-1	-2
$\vec{\pi}_{12} = (\phi,1+1,1+1)$	$+1$	0	$\vec{\pi}_{33} = (2,1,1)$	-1	0
$\vec{\pi}_{13} = (\phi,3,1)$	$+1$	0	$\vec{\pi}_{34} = (2,2,\phi)$	-1	1
$\vec{\pi}_{14} = (\phi,2+1,1)$	$+1$	1	$\vec{\pi}_{35} = (2,1+1,\phi)$	-1	2
$\vec{\pi}_{15} = (\phi,1+1+1,1)$	$+1$	2	$\vec{\pi}_{36} = (3,\phi,1)$	-1	-1
$\vec{\pi}_{16} = (\phi,4,\phi)$	$+1$	1	$\vec{\pi}_{37} = (2+1,\phi,1)$	$+1$	-1
$\vec{\pi}_{17} = (\phi,3+1,\phi)$	$+1$	2	$\vec{\pi}_{38} = (3,1,\phi)$	-1	1
$\vec{\pi}_{18} = (\phi,2+2,\phi)$	$+1$	2	$\vec{\pi}_{39} = (2+1,1,\phi)$	$+1$	1
$\vec{\pi}_{19} = (\phi,2+1+1,\phi)$	$+1$	3	$\vec{\pi}_{40} = (4,\phi,\phi)$	-1	0
$\vec{\pi}_{20} = (\phi,1+1+1+1,\phi)$	$+1$	4	$\vec{\pi}_{41} = (3+1,\phi,\phi)$	$+1$	0
$\vec{\pi}_{21} = (1,\phi,3)$	-1	-1			

4. A page from Ramanujan's 'lost' notebook. For an introduction to the 'lost' notebook see Andrews [2]. We give this page below correcting typos and adding equation numbers:

$$F(q)=\frac{(1-q)(1-q^2)(1-q^3)\cdots}{(1-2q\cos\frac{2n\pi}{5}+q^2)(1-2q^2\cos\frac{2n\pi}{5}+q^4)\cdots}, \tag{4.1}$$

$$f(q)=1+\frac{q}{(1-2q\cos\frac{2n\pi}{5}+q^2)} + \frac{q^4}{(1-2q\cos\frac{2n\pi}{5}+q^2)(1-2q^2\cos\frac{2n\pi}{5}+q^4)}+\cdots,\quad n=1 \text{ or } 2, \tag{4.2}$$

$$F(q^{\frac15})=A(q)-4q^{\frac15}\cos^2\frac{2n\pi}{5}B(q)+2q^{\frac25}\cos\frac{4n\pi}{5}C(q) - 2q^{\frac35}\cos\frac{2n\pi}{5}D(q), \tag{4.3}$$

$$f(q^{\frac15})=\left\{A(q)-4\sin^2\frac{n\pi}{5}\phi(q)\right\}+q^{\frac15}B(q)+2q^{\frac25}\cos\frac{2n\pi}{5}C(q) - 2q^{\frac35}\cos\frac{2n\pi}{5}\left\{D(q)+4\sin^2\frac{2n\pi}{5}\frac{\psi(q)}{q}\right\}, \tag{4.4}$$

$$A(q)=\frac{1-q^2-q^3+q^9+\cdots}{(1-q)^2(1-q^4)^2(1-q^6)^2\cdots}, \tag{4.5}$$

$$B(q)=\frac{(1-q^5)(1-q^{10})(1-q^{15})\cdots}{(1-q)(1-q^4)(1-q^6)\cdots}, \tag{4.6}$$

$$C(q)=\frac{(1-q^5)(1-q^{10})(1-q^{15})\cdots}{(1-q^2)(1-q^3)(1-q^7)\cdots}, \tag{4.7}$$

$$D(q)=\frac{1-q-q^4+q^7+\cdots}{(1-q^2)^2(1-q^3)^2(1-q^7)^2\cdots}, \tag{4.8}$$

$$\phi(q)=-1+\left\{\frac{1}{1-q}+\frac{q^5}{(1-q)(1-q^4)(1-q^6)} + \frac{q^{20}}{(1-q)(1-q^4)(1-q^6)(1-q^9)(1-q^{11})}+\cdots\right\}, \tag{4.9}$$

$$\psi(q)=-1+\left\{\frac{1}{1-q^2}+\frac{q^5}{(1-q^2)(1-q^3)(1-q^7)} + \frac{q^{20}}{(1-q^2)(1-q^3)(1-q^7)(1-q^8)(1-q^{12})}+\cdots\right\}, \tag{4.10}$$

$$\frac{q}{1-q}+\frac{q^3}{(1-q^2)(1-q^3)}+\frac{q^5}{(1-q^3)(1-q^4)(1-q^5)}+\cdots=3\phi(q)+1-A(q), \tag{4.11}$$

(4.12)
$$\frac{q}{1-q}+\frac{q^2}{(1-q^2)(1-q^3)}+\frac{q^3}{(1-q^3)(1-q^4)(1-q^5)}+\cdots=3\psi(q)+qD(q),$$

(4.13)
$$\frac{q^2}{1-q}+\frac{q^8}{(1-q)(1-q^3)}+\frac{q^{18}}{(1-q)(1-q^3)(1-q^5)}+\cdots$$
$$=\phi(q)-q\frac{1+q^5+q^{15}+\cdots}{(1-q^4)(1-q^6)(1-q^{14})\cdots},$$

(4.14)
$$\frac{q}{1-q}+\frac{q^5}{(1-q)(1-q^3)}+\frac{q^{13}}{(1-q)(1-q^3)(1-q^5)}+\cdots$$
$$=\psi(q)+q\frac{1+q^5+q^{15}+\cdots}{(1-q^2)(1-q^8)(1-q^{12})\cdots}.$$

In (4.1)–(4.4) we may assume without loss of generality that $n=1$. If we let $\zeta=exp(\frac{2\pi i}{5})$ then we may write the definitions of $F(q)$ and $f(q)$ as

(4.15)
$$F(q)=\frac{(q)_\infty}{(\zeta q)_\infty(\zeta^{-1}q)_\infty},$$

(4.16)
$$f(q)=1+\sum_{n=1}^{\infty}\frac{q^{n^2}}{(1-\zeta q)(1-\zeta^{-1}q)\cdots(1-\zeta q^n)(1-\zeta^{-1}q^n)}$$
$$=\sum_{n=0}^{\infty}\frac{q^{n^2}}{(\zeta q)_n(\zeta^{-1}q)_n},$$

where

$$(a)_0=1,\qquad (a)_n=(1-a)(1-aq)\cdots(1-aq^{n-1})\qquad \text{for } n\ge 1$$

and
$$(a)_\infty=\lim_{n\to\infty}(a)_n=\prod_{n=1}^{\infty}(1-aq^{n-1}).$$

After replacing q by q^5 we see that (4.3) and (4.4) are identities for $F(q)$ and $f(q)$ that split each function (as a power series in q) according to the residue of the exponent modulo 5. This splitting is in terms of the functions $A(q),\ldots,D(q),\phi(q),\psi(q)$ which are defined in (4.5)–(4.10). In Theorem 3 we show that (4.3) implies (3.10) which is the combinatorial interpretation of the partition congruence mod 5 in terms of the crank. In Theorem 4 we show not only does (4.4) imply (2.1), which is Dyson's combinatorial interpretation of the partition congruence mod 5 in terms of the rank, but that (4.4) is actually equivalent to Theorem 1 (due to Atkin and Swinnerton-Dyer). (4.11)–(4.14) are mock theta function identities. In Theorem 5 we show that (4.11) and (4.12) are equivalent to Andrews and Garvan's [4] mock theta conjectures.

We note that the numerators in the definitions of $A(q)$ and $D(q)$ are theta series in q and hence may be written as infinite products using Jacobi's triple product identity:

$$\prod_{n=1}^{\infty}(1-zq^n)(1-z^{-1}q^{n-1})(1-q^n) = \sum_{n=-\infty}^{\infty}(-1)^n z^n q^{\frac{1}{2}n(n+1)}, \tag{4.17}$$

where $z \neq 0$ and $|q| < 1$. In fact we have

$$A(q) = \prod_{n=1}^{\infty}\frac{(1-q^{5n-3})(1-q^{5n-2})(1-q^{5n})}{(1-q^{5n-4})^2(1-q^{5n-1})^2}, \tag{4.18}$$

$$B(q) = \prod_{n=1}^{\infty}\frac{(1-q^{5n})}{(1-q^{5n-4})(1-q^{5n-1})}, \tag{4.19}$$

$$C(q) = \prod_{n=1}^{\infty}\frac{(1-q^{5n})}{(1-q^{5n-3})(1-q^{5n-2})}, \tag{4.20}$$

$$D(q) = \prod_{n=1}^{\infty}\frac{(1-q^{5n-4})(1-q^{5n-1})(1-q^{5n})}{(1-q^{5n-3})^2(1-q^{5n-2})^2}. \tag{4.21}$$

THEOREM 3. *(4.3) $\Longrightarrow$ (3.10).*

Proof. We first write $F(q)$ in terms of $N_V(k,5,n)$. Substituting $z=\zeta$ into both sides of (3.8) we have

$$F(q) = \frac{(q)_\infty}{(\zeta q)_\infty(\zeta^{-1}q)_\infty} = \sum_{m=-\infty}^{\infty}\sum_{n=0}^{\infty}N_V(m,n)\zeta^m q^n$$

$$= \sum_{k=0}^{4}\zeta^k\sum_{n=0}^{\infty}\Big(\sum_{\substack{m\equiv k\\ \text{mod } 5}}N_V(m,n)\Big)q^n$$

$$= \sum_{k=0}^{4}\zeta^k\sum_{n=0}^{\infty}N_V(k,5,n)q^n \qquad \text{(by (3.5))}.$$

If we assume (4.3) then we find that

$$\sum_{k=0}^{4}N_V(k,5,5n+4)\zeta^k = \text{Coeff of } q^{5n+4} \text{ in } F(q) = 0. \tag{4.22}$$

The lefthand side of (4.22) is a polynomial in ζ over $\mathbb{Z}$. It follows that

$$N_V(0,5,5n+4) = N_V(1,5,5n+4) = \cdots = N_V(4,5,5n+4).$$

From (3.9) we have

$$p(5n+4) = \sum_{k=0}^{4} N_V(k,5,5n+4) = 5N_V(0,5,5n+4)$$

and (3.10) follows. □

(4.3) is easy to prove once we observe that

$$F(q) = \frac{(q)_\infty}{(\zeta q)_\infty(\zeta^{-1}q)_\infty} = \frac{(q)^2_\infty(\zeta^2 q)_\infty(\zeta^{-2}q)_\infty}{(q^5;q^5)_\infty}$$
$$= \frac{(q)_\infty\{(\zeta^2)_\infty(\zeta^{-2}q)_\infty(q)_\infty\}}{(q^5;q^5)_\infty(1-\zeta^2)}. \tag{4.23}$$

Here $(a;q)_\infty = \prod_{n=1}^{\infty}(1-aq^{n-1})$, $|q|<1$. Now we can split $(\zeta^2)_\infty(\zeta^{-2}q)_\infty(q)_\infty$ utilizing Jacobi's triple product identity (4.17), split $(q)_\infty$ using Euler's result

$$(q)_\infty = \sum_{n=-\infty}^{\infty} (-1)^n q^{\frac{1}{2}n(3n-1)} \qquad |q|<1, \tag{4.24}$$

and (4.3) follows with not much work. (3.11) can be proved in a similar way. The proof of (3.12) is analogous but depends on Winquist's identity [28, §1]. We refer the reader to [16], [17] for details.

We now turn to (4.4) and Atkin and Swinnerton-Dyer's Theorem. We first observe that the infinite products that occur in Theorem 1 are exactly $A(q)$, $B(q)$,$C(q)$ and $D(q)$. The remaining functions turn out to be $\phi(q)$ and $\psi(q)$. Utilizing Watson's [24] q-analog of Whipple's theorem or (2.23) it can be shown that

$$-1+\sum_{n=0}^{\infty}\frac{q^{n^2}}{(z)_{n+1}(z^{-1}q)_n} = \frac{z}{(q)_\infty}\sum_{n=-\infty}^{\infty}(-1)^n\frac{q^{\frac{3}{2}n(n+1)}}{1-zq^n}, \tag{4.25}$$

where $|q|<1$, $|q|<|z|<|q|^{-1}$ and $z\neq 1$. See [17, Lemma(7.9)]. It follows that

$$\phi(q) = -1+\sum_{n=0}^{\infty}\frac{q^{5n^2}}{(q;q^5)_{n+1}(q^4;q^5)_n}$$
$$= q\prod_{n=1}^{\infty}(1-q^{5n})^{-1}\sum_{m=-\infty}^{\infty}(-1)^m\frac{q^{\frac{15}{2}m(m+1)}}{1-q^{5m+1}} \tag{4.26}$$

and

$$\frac{\psi(q)}{q} = \frac{1}{q}\left\{-1+\sum_{n=0}^{\infty}\frac{q^{5n^2}}{(q^2;q^5)_{n+1}(q^3;q^5)_n}\right\}$$
$$= q\prod_{n=1}^{\infty}(1-q^{5n})^{-1}\sum_{m=-\infty}^{\infty}(-1)^m\frac{q^{\frac{15}{2}m(m+1)}}{1-q^{5m+2}}. \tag{4.27}$$

THEOREM 4. *Theorem 1 $\Longleftrightarrow$ (4.4).*

Proof. Utilizing the concept of the Durfee square (see Andrews [3]) it can be shown that

$$\sum_{m=-\infty}^{\infty}\sum_{n=0}^{\infty} N(m,n)z^m q^n = \sum_{n=1}^{\infty}\frac{q^{n^2}}{(zq)_n(z^{-1}q)_n}. \tag{4.28}$$

Here following Atkin and Swinnerton-Dyer we agree that $N(0,0)=0$. Analogous to the proof of Theorem 3 we find that

$$\begin{aligned} f(q) &= 1+\sum_{n=1}^{\infty}\frac{q^{n^2}}{(\zeta q)_n(\zeta^{-1}q)_n}. \\ &= 1+\sum_{k=0}^{4}\zeta^k\Big(\sum_{n=0}^{\infty}N(k,5,n)q^n\Big). \end{aligned} \tag{4.29}$$

After replacing q by q^5 we can write (4.4) as

$$\begin{aligned} f(q) = \{A(q^5) &+ (\zeta+\zeta^{-1}-2)\phi(q^5)\} + qB(q^5) + (\zeta+\zeta^{-1})q^2C(q^5) \\ &- (\zeta+\zeta^{-1})q^3\left\{D(q^5) - (\zeta^2+\zeta^{-2}-2)\frac{\psi(q^5)}{q^5}\right\}. \end{aligned} \tag{4.30}$$

We now sketch how (4.4) implies Theorem 1. By picking out the coefficient of q^{5n} in both sides of (4.30) we find that

$$1+\sum_{k=0}^{4}\zeta^k N(k,5,5n) = a_n + (\zeta+\zeta^{-1}-2)\phi_n \tag{4.31}$$

where a_n, ϕ_n are the coefficients of q^n in $A(q)$, $\phi(q)$ respectively. It follows that

$$1+N(0,5,5n) - a_n + 2\phi_n = N(1,5,5n) - \phi_n = N(2,5,5n) \tag{4.32}$$

since all coefficients are rational integers. From (4.18) and (4.26) we have (2.15) and (2.16). The rest of Theorem 1 follows in the same way. □

COROLLARY.

$$r_{1,2}(0) = \phi(q), \tag{4.33}$$

$$r_{2,0}(3) = \frac{\psi(q)}{q}. \tag{4.34}$$

We now turn to the mock theta conjectures (Andrews and Garvan [4, §1]). The remainder of this section has been taken from [4]. There are ten (unproved) mock theta function identities [4, $(3.1)_R$–$(3.10)_R$]. In fact (4.11)–(4.14) are respectively $(3.1)_R$, $(3.6)_R$, $(3.2)_R$ and $(3.7)_R$. In [4] the ten identities were reduced to two combinatorial conjectures:

FIRST MOCK THETA CONJECTURE.

$$N(1,5,5n) = N(0,5,5n) + \rho_0(n), \tag{4.35}$$

where $\rho_0(n)$ is the number of partitions of n with unique smallest part and all other parts $\leq$ the double of the smallest part.

SECOND MOCK THETA CONJECTURE.

$$2N(2,5,5n+3) = N(1,5,5n+3) + N(0,5,5n+3) + \rho_1(n) + 1, \tag{4.36}$$

where $\rho_1(n)$ is the number of partitions of n with unique smallest part and all other parts $\leq$ one plus the double of the smallest part.

We need the following result of Watson [26, (A_0)]:

$$\chi_0(q) = \sum_{n=0}^{\infty} \frac{q^n}{(q^{n+1})_n} = 1 + \sum_{n=0}^{\infty} \frac{q^{2n+1}}{(q^{n+1})_{n+1}}. \tag{4.37}$$

THEOREM 5 ([4, THEOREM 2]). *(4.11) $\Longleftrightarrow$(4.35) and (4.12) $\Longleftrightarrow$ (4.36).*

Proof. Let $M_1(q) = \chi_0(q) - 2 - 3\phi(q) + A(q)$. Then (4.11) is equivalent to $M_1(q) = 0$ by (4.37). Now, by (2.17) and (4.33), we have

$$\begin{aligned} M_1(q) &= \chi_0(q) - 2 - 3\phi(q) + A(q) \\ &= \chi_0(q) - 1 + r_{0,2}(0) + 2r_{1,2}(0) - 3r_{1,2}(0) \\ &= \chi_0(q) - 1 - r_{1,0}(0). \end{aligned}$$

But by (4.37) we have

$$\chi_0(q) - 1 = \sum_{n=0}^{\infty} \rho_0(n) q^n$$

if we assume $\rho_0(0) = 0$. Hence (4.11) is equivalent to (4.35). Similarly we find (4.12) is equivalent to (4.36) by considering (2.21) and (4.34). □

5. The search for a better crank. Our crank is in terms of a weighted count of certain restricted triples of partitions. It would be nice if we could interpret $N_V(m,n)$ solely in terms of ordinary partitions. This may be possible (see **Announcement** in this section) since it turns out that all of the coefficients $N_V(m,n)$ except for one are nonnegative. All that is needed to prove this is the q-binomial theorem (Andrews [1, p.17]):

$$\sum_{n=0}^{\infty} \frac{(a)_n}{(q)_n} t^n = \frac{(at)_\infty}{(t)_\infty}, \tag{5.1}$$

where $|q| < 1$ and $|t| < 1$.

THEOREM 6. *For $m \geq 0$,*

$$\sum_{n=0}^{\infty} N_V(m,n)q^n = (1-q)\sum_{n=0}^{\infty} \frac{q^{n^2+nm+2n+m}}{(q)_{m+n}(q)_n}. \tag{5.2}$$

Proof.

$$\sum_{m=-\infty}^{\infty}\sum_{n=0}^{\infty} N_V(m,n)z^m q^n = \frac{(q)_\infty}{(zq)_\infty(z^{-1}q)_\infty} \tag{5.3}$$

$$\begin{aligned}
&= \frac{(1-z)}{(z^{-1}q)_\infty}\sum_{n=0}^{\infty}\frac{(z^{-1}q)_n z^n}{(q)_n} && \text{(by (5.1) with } a = z^{-1}q \text{ and } t = z)\\
&= (1-z)\sum_{m=0}^{\infty}\frac{z^m}{(q)_m(z^{-1}q^{m+1})_\infty}\\
&= (1-z)\sum_{m=0}^{\infty}\frac{z^m}{(q)_m}\sum_{n=0}^{\infty}\frac{(z^{-1}q^{m+1})^n}{(q)_n} && \text{(by (5.1) with } a = 0 \text{ and } t = z^{-1}q^{m+1})\\
&= (1-z)\sum_{n=0}^{\infty}\sum_{m=0}^{\infty}\frac{z^{m-n}q^{nm+n}}{(q)_m(q)_n}\\
&= (1-z)\sum_{n=0}^{\infty}\sum_{m=-n}^{\infty}\frac{z^m q^{n(m+n+1)}}{(q)_{m+n}(q)_n}\\
&= \sum_{n=0}^{\infty}\sum_{m=-n}^{\infty}\frac{z^m q^{n(m+n+1)}}{(q)_{m+n}(q)_n} - \sum_{n=0}^{\infty}\sum_{m=-n+1}^{\infty}\frac{z^m q^{n(m+n)}}{(q)_{m+n-1}(q)_n}.
\end{aligned}$$

Picking out the coefficient of z^0 in (5.3) we have

$$\begin{aligned}
\sum_{n=0}^{\infty} N_V(0,m)q^n &= \sum_{n=0}^{\infty}\frac{q^{n(n+1)}}{(q)_n^2} - \sum_{n=1}^{\infty}\frac{q^{n^2}}{(q)_{n-1}(q)_n}\\
&= \sum_{n=0}^{\infty}\frac{q^{n(n+1)}}{(q)_n^2} - \sum_{n=1}^{\infty}\frac{q^{n^2}\{q^n+(1-q^n)\}}{(q)_{n-1}(q)_n}\\
&= 1 + \sum_{n=1}^{\infty}\frac{q^{n(n+1)}(1-(1-q^n))}{(q)_n^2} - \sum_{n=1}^{\infty}\frac{q^{n^2}}{(q)_{n-1}^2}\\
&= 1 - q + \sum_{n=1}^{\infty}\frac{q^{n(n+2)}}{(q)_n^2} - \sum_{n=2}^{\infty}\frac{q^{n^2}}{(q)_{n-1}^2}\\
&= (1-q)\sum_{n=0}^{\infty}\frac{q^{n(n+2)}}{(q)_n^2},
\end{aligned}$$

which is (5.2) when $m = 0$. The general case follows in a similar fashion. □

COROLLARY.

$$N_V(m,n) \geq 0 \qquad \textit{for } (m,n) \neq (0,1). \tag{5.4}$$

Theorem 6 yields combinatorial results involving the rank that are similar to but not as deep as the mock theta conjectures.

THEOREM 7.

$$N(0,5,5n+1) = \beta_1(n) + N(2,5,5n+1), \tag{5.5}$$
$$N(1,5,5n+2) = \beta_2(n) + N(2,5,5n+2), \tag{5.6}$$

where for $i = 1, 2$ $\beta_i(n)$ denotes the number of partitions of n into i's and parts congruent to 0 or $-i$ modulo 5 with the largest part $\equiv 0 \pmod 5 \leq 5$ times the number of i's $\leq$ the smallest part $\equiv -i \pmod 5$.

Proof. From (5.3) we have

$$\frac{(q)_\infty}{(z)_\infty (z^{-1}q)_\infty} = \sum_{m=0}^{\infty} \frac{z^m}{(q)_m (z^{-1}q^{m+1})_\infty}. \tag{5.7}$$

Now the generating function for $\beta_1(n)$ is

$$\begin{aligned}\sum_{n=0}^{\infty} \beta_1(n) q^n &= \sum_{n=0}^{\infty} \frac{q^n}{(q^5;q^5)_n (q^{5n+4};q^5)_\infty} \\ &= \frac{(q^5;q^5)_\infty}{(q;q^5)_\infty (q^4;q^5)_\infty} \qquad \text{(by (5.7) with } q \text{ replaced by } q^5 \text{ and } z \text{ by } q) \\ &= r_{0,2}(1) \qquad \text{(by (2.17))}\end{aligned}$$

and (5.5) follows. Similarly we find that

$$\begin{aligned}\sum_{n=0}^{\infty} \beta_2(n) q^n &= \sum_{n=0}^{\infty} \frac{q^{2n}}{(q^5;q^5)_n (q^{5n+3};q^5)_\infty} \\ &= \frac{(q^5;q^5)_\infty}{(q^2;q^5)_\infty (q^3;q^5)_\infty} = r_{1,2}(2)\end{aligned}$$

and (5.6) follows. □

Example (1) $N(0,5,36) = 3597$, $N(2,5,36) = 3595$, $\beta_1(7) = 2$ with the relevant partitions being $5+1+1$ and $1+1+1+1+1+1+1$.

(2) $N(1,5,37) = 4328$, $N(2,5,37) = 4327$, $\beta_2(7) = 1$ with the relevant partition being $5+2$.

Announcement. The day after this conference ended the *true* crank was discovered by George Andrews and myself. This result will appear in a joint paper with George. May I introduce the crank:

DEFINITION. *For a partition π let $\lambda(\pi)$ denote the largest part of π, $\mu(\pi)$ denote the number of ones in π and let $\nu(\pi)$ denote the number of parts of π larger than $\mu(\pi)$. The crank $c(\pi)$ is given by*

$$c(\pi) = \begin{cases} \lambda(\pi), & \text{if } \mu(\pi) = 0, \\ \nu(\pi) - \mu(\pi), & \text{if } \mu(\pi) > 0. \end{cases}$$

Following Dyson we let $M(m,n)$ denote the number of partitions of n with crank m and let $M(m,t,n)$ denote the number of partitions of n with crank congruent to m modulo t. It turns out that

THEOREM 8 (ANDREWS AND GARVAN [5]). *For $n > 1$,*

$$M(m,n) = N_V(m,n). \tag{5.8}$$

Theorem 8 together with Theorem 2 yield the following new combinatorial interpretations of the congruences (0.1)–(0.3).

COROLLARY.

$$M(k,5,5n+4) = \frac{p(5n+4)}{5} \qquad 0 \le k \le 4, \tag{5.9}$$

$$M(k,7,7n+5) = \frac{p(7n+5)}{7} \qquad 0 \le k \le 6, \tag{5.10}$$

$$M(k,11,11n+6) = \frac{p(11n+6)}{11} \qquad 0 \le k \le 10. \tag{5.11}$$

The appearance of the functions $A(q)$, $B(q)$, $C(q)$ and $D(q)$ in both (4.3) and (4.4) leads to some rather *curious* relations between the rank and the crank:

THEOREM 9. *For $n > 0$,*

$$N(0,5,5n) + 2N(1,5,5n) + M(1,5,5n) = M(0,5,5n) + 3N(2,5,5n), \tag{5.12}$$

$$N(0,5,5n+1) + M(2,5,5n+1) = M(1,5,5n+1) + N(2,5,5n+1), \tag{5.13}$$

$$N(1,5,5n+2) + M(1,5,5n+2) = N(2,5,5n+2) + M(2,5,5n+2), \tag{5.14}$$

$$\begin{aligned} &2N(0,5,5n+3) + M(1,5,5n+3) \\ &\quad = M(0,5,5n+3) + N(1,5,5n+3) + N(2,5,5n+3), \end{aligned} \tag{5.15}$$

$$N(k,5,5n+4) = M(k',5,5n+4) = \frac{p(5n+4)}{5} \qquad 0 \le k, k' \le 4. \tag{5.16}$$

I offer a prize of \$25 (Australian) for a combinatorial proof of any one of the relations given above.

REFERENCES

[1] G. E. ANDREWS, *The Theory of Partitions*, Encyclopedia of Mathematics and Its Applications, Vol. 2 (G.-C. Rota ed.), Addison-Wesley, Reading, Mass., 1976. (Reissued: Cambridge Univ. Press, London and New York, 1985).

[2] ———, *An introduction to Ramanujan's "lost" notebook*, Amer. Math. Monthly, 86 (1979), pp. 89–108.

[3] ———, *Partitions: Yesterday and Today*, New Zealand Math. Soc., Wellington, 1979.

[4] G. E. ANDREWS AND F. G. GARVAN, *Ramanujan's "lost" notebook VI: the mock theta conjectures*, Advances in Math. (to appear).

[5] ———, *Dyson's crank of a partition*, submitted.

[6] A. O. L. ATKIN AND H. P. F. SWINNERTON-DYER, *Some properties of partitions*, Proc. London Math. Soc., (3) 4 (1954), pp. 84–106.

[7] A. O. L. ATKIN, *Proof of a conjecture of Ramanujan*, Glasgow Math. J., 8 (1967), pp. 14–32.

[8] A. O. L. ATKIN AND J. N. O'BRIEN, *Some properties of $p(n)$ and $c(n)$ modulo powers of* 13, Trans. Amer. Math. Soc., 126 (1967), pp. 442–459.

[9] A. O. L. ATKIN, *Ramanujan congruences for $p_{-k}(n)$*, Canad. J. Math., 20 (1968), pp. 67–78.

[10] ———, *Congruence Hecke operators*, Proc. Symp. Pure Math., 12 (1969), pp. 33–40.

[11] B. J. BIRCH, *A look back at Ramanujan's notebooks*, Proc. Cambridge Phil. Soc., 78 (1975), pp. 73–79.

[12] S. CHOWLA, *Congruence properties of partitions*, J. London Math. Soc., 9 (1934), p. 247.

[13] F. J. DYSON, *Some guesses in the theory of partitions*, Eureka (Cambridge), 8 (1944), pp. 10–15.

[14] ———, *A walk through Ramanujan's garden*, Proc. Amer. Math. Soc. (to appear).

[15] F. G. GARVAN, *A simple proof of Watson's partition congruences for powers of* 7, J. Austral. Math. Soc. Ser. A, 36 (1984), pp. 316–334.

[16] ———, *Generalizations of Dyson's rank*, Ph.D. thesis, Pennsylvania State University, 1986.

[17] ———, *New combinatorial interpretations of Ramanujan's partition congruences mod* 5, 7 *and* 11, Trans. Amer. Math. Soc. (to appear).

[18] M. D. HIRSCHHORN AND D. C. HUNT, *A simple proof of the Ramanujan conjecture for powers of* 5, J. reine angew. Math., 336 (1981), pp. 1–17.

[19] M. NEWMAN, *Congruences for the coefficients of modular forms and some new congruences for the partition function*, Canad. J. Math., 9 (1957), pp. 549–552.

[20] S. RAMANUJAN, *Some properties of $p(n)$, the number of partitions of n*, Proc. Cambridge Phil. Soc., 19 (1919), pp. 207–210.

[21] ———, *Congruence properties of partitions*, Math. Zeitschrift, 9 (1921), pp. 147–153.

[22] R. A. RANKIN, *Ramanujan's unpublished work on congruences*, Modular Functions of One Variable V, Lecture Notes in Mathematics, 601 (1977), pp. 3–15.

[23] J. M. RUSHFORTH, *Congruence properties of the partition function and associated functions*, Proc. Cambridge Phil. Soc., 4 (1952), pp. 402–413.

[24] G. N. WATSON, *A new proof of the Rogers-Ramanujan identities*, J. London Math. Soc., 4 (1929), pp. 4–9.

[25] ———, *Über Ramanujansche Kongruenzeigenschaften der Zerfällungsanzahlen I*, Math. Zeitschrift, 39 (1935), pp. 719–731.

[26] ———, *The mock theta functions (2)*, Proc. London Math. Soc., 42 (1937), pp. 274–304.

[27] ———, *Ramanujans Vermutung über Zerfällungsanzahlen*, J. reine angew. Math., 179 (1938), pp. 97–128.

[28] L. WINQUIST, *An elementary proof of $p(11m+6) \equiv 0 \pmod{11}$*, J. Combin. Theory, 6, pp. 56–59.

[29] H. S. ZUCKERMAN, *Identities analogous to Ramanujan's identities involving the partition function*, Duke Math. J., 5 (1939), pp. 88–119.

Ramanujan's Fifth Order Mock Theta Functions as Constant Terms

by

George E. Andrews[1]

1. Introduction. Twenty five years ago, F.J. Dyson [7] posed the following conjecture which arose from his studies in particle physics:

The constant term in the expanded form of

$$\prod_{1\leq i\neq j\leq k}\left(1-\frac{x_i}{x_j}\right)^{a_i} \tag{1.1}$$

is

$$\frac{(a_1+a_2+\ldots+a_k)!}{a_1!a_2!\ldots a_k!} \tag{1.2}$$

Proofs were subsequently given by K. Wilson [12], J. Gunson [9] and I.J. Good [8]. In 1975, a q-analog of Dyson's conjecture was proposed [1]:

The coefficient of $x_1^0x_2^0\ldots x_k^0$ in the expanded form of

$$\prod_{1\leq i<j\leq k}\left(\frac{x_i}{x_j}\right)_{a_i}\left(\frac{qx_j}{x_i}\right)_{a_j} \tag{1.3}$$

is

$$\frac{(q)_{a_1+a_2+\ldots+a_k}}{(q)_{a_1}(q)_{a_2}\ldots(q)_{a_k}}, \tag{1.4}$$

where

$$(A)_n = (A;q)_n = (1-A)(1-Aq)\ldots(1-Aq^{n-1}). \tag{1.5}$$

(1)Partially supported by National Science Foundation Grant DMS-8503324.

ISBN 0-12-058560-X

This conjecture was given an intricate combinatorial proof by Zeilberger and Bressoud [13] in 1985. I.G. Macdonald [11] noted that such results merely scratched the surface of infinite families of constant term identities arising from Lie algebras. An elementary survey of this topic is given in [5;Ch.4].

Indeed Macdonald's observations in [11] had their basis in his path-breaking paper [10] wherein the constant terms of certain infinite products were identified with various classical modular forms. The simplest such result is the following restatement of part of Jacobi's Triple Product Identity [2;p.21]. Let

$$\Theta(z,q) = \prod_{n=1}^{\infty} (1-zq^{n-1})(1-z^{-1}q^{n}). \tag{1.6}$$

Then the coefficient of z^0 in $\Theta(z,q)$ is

$$\prod_{n=1}^{\infty} \frac{1}{1-q^n} = \frac{q^{1/24}}{\eta(\tau)}, \quad q = e^{2\pi i\tau}, \tag{1.7}$$

where $\eta(\tau)$ is Dedekind's famous modular form [2;p.70].

Our purpose in this paper is to show that eight of Ramanujan's fifth order mock theta functions arise from constant term identities involving rational expressions of various $\Theta(z,q)$. It was our initial hope that by exhibiting the fifth order mock theta functions as constant terms we could make some progress on the Mock Theta Conjectures described in [6]. So far the Mock Theta Conjectures remain unresolved. However this new setting encompasses both mock theta functions as well as some classical modular forms like $\eta(\tau)$.

In Section 2 we prove a general constant term Lemma. It is reminiscent of the Lemma 2 in [3]; however now instead of the classical partial fraction decomposition for $1/\Theta(z,q)$ we rely on the celebrated ${}_6\psi_6$ summation formula [12;p.191].

In Section 3 we specialize to the fifth order mock theta functions. The specializations will rely heavily on the representations of the fifth order mock theta functions developed in [4].

2. The Principal Lemma.

Lemma 1. In the annulus

$$\max(|a|,|a|^{-1}) < |z| < \min(|aq^{\lambda}|^{-1},|a^{-1}q^{\lambda}|^{-1}), \tag{2.1}$$

the coefficient of z^0 in the Laurent series expansion of

$$\frac{a(q^B;q^B)_\infty(q^\lambda;q^\lambda)_\infty^2\Theta(\epsilon z^A q^C,q^B)\Theta(z,q^\lambda)\Theta(a^2,q^\lambda)}{\Theta(a/z,q^\lambda)\Theta(az,q^\lambda)\Theta(a,q^\lambda)} \tag{2.2}$$

is

$$\sum_{r=0}^{\infty}\sum_{|Aj|\leqq r}(-\epsilon)^j(-1)^{r+Aj}a^{-r}q^{B\binom{j}{2}+Cj+\binom{r+1}{2}\lambda-\binom{Aj+1}{2}\lambda}(1+a^{2r+1}), \tag{2.3}$$

where B and λ are positive real numbers and A is a nonzero integer.

Proof. We begin by observing that for $|a| < |z| < |a^{-1}q^{\lambda}|^{-1}$,

$$\sum_{r=-\infty}^{\infty}\frac{(-1)^r q^{\lambda\binom{r+1}{2}}a^r}{1-\frac{a}{z}q^{r\lambda}} \tag{2.4}$$

$$= \sum_{r=0}^{\infty}(-1)^r q^{\lambda\binom{r+1}{2}}a^r\sum_{n=0}^{\infty}z^{-n}a^n q^{r\lambda n}$$

$$+ \sum_{r=0}^{\infty}(-1)^r q^{\lambda\binom{r+1}{2}}a^{-r-1}\sum_{n=1}^{\infty}z^n a^{-n}q^{n(r+1)\lambda}$$

$$= \sum_{n=0}^{\infty}z^{-n}\sum_{r=n+1}^{\infty}(-1)^{r+n+1}(q)^{\binom{r}{2}\lambda-\binom{n+1}{2}\lambda}a^{r-1}$$

$$+ \sum_{n=1}^{\infty}z^n\sum_{r=n+1}^{\infty}(-1)^{r+n+1}q^{\binom{r}{2}\lambda-\binom{n}{2}\lambda}a^{-r}$$

$$= \sum_{n=-\infty}^{0}z^n\sum_{r\geqq|n|}(-1)^{r+n}q^{\binom{r+1}{2}\lambda-\binom{n}{2}\lambda}a^r$$

$$+ \sum_{n=1}^{\infty}z^n\sum_{r\geqq|n|}(-1)^{r+n}q^{\binom{r+1}{2}\lambda-\binom{n}{2}\lambda}a^{-r-1}.$$

Hence for $\max(|a|,|a|^{-1}) < |z| < \min(|aq^{\lambda}|^{-1},|a^{-1}q^{\lambda}|^{-1})$, we have by (2.4)

$$\sum_{r=-\infty}^{\infty} \frac{(-1)^r q^{\lambda\binom{r+1}{2}} a^r}{1-\frac{a}{z}q^{r\lambda}} + a^{-1}\sum_{r=-\infty}^{\infty} \frac{(-1)^r q^{\lambda\binom{r+1}{2}} a^{-r}}{1-\frac{a^{-1}}{z}q^{r\lambda}} \tag{2.5}$$

$$= \sum_{n=-\infty}^{\infty} z^n \sum_{r\geq|n|} (-1)^{r+n} q^{\binom{r+1}{2}\lambda-\binom{n}{2}\lambda} a^r$$

$$+ \sum_{n=-\infty}^{\infty} z^n \sum_{r\geq|n|} (-1)^{r+n} q^{\binom{r+1}{2}\lambda-\binom{n}{2}\lambda} a^{-r-1}$$

$$= \sum_{n=-\infty}^{\infty} z^n \sum_{r\geq|n|} (-1)^{r+n} a^{-r-1} q^{\binom{r+1}{2}\lambda-\binom{n}{2}\lambda}(1+a^{2r+1}).$$

Now let us examine the left-hand side of (2.5).

$$\sum_{r=-\infty}^{\infty} \frac{(-1)^r q^{\lambda\binom{r+1}{2}} a^r}{1-\frac{a}{z}q^{r\lambda}} + a^{-1}\sum_{r=-\infty}^{\infty} \frac{(-1)^r q^{\lambda\binom{r+1}{2}} a^{-r}}{1-\frac{a^{-1}}{z}q^{r\lambda}} \tag{2.6}$$

$$= \sum_{r=-\infty}^{\infty} \frac{(-1)^r q^{\lambda\binom{r+1}{2}} a^r}{1-\frac{a}{z}q^{r\lambda}} + \sum_{r=-\infty}^{\infty} \frac{(-1)^r q^{\lambda\binom{r+1}{2}} a^{r-1}}{1-\frac{1}{azq^{r\lambda}}}$$

$$= \sum_{r=-\infty}^{\infty} \frac{(-1)^r q^{\lambda\binom{r+1}{2}} a^r((1-azq^{\lambda r})-z(1-\frac{a}{z}q^{\lambda r}))}{(1-\frac{a}{z}q^{\lambda r})(1-azq^{\lambda r})}$$

$$= \sum_{r=-\infty}^{\infty} \frac{(-1)^r q^{\lambda\binom{r+1}{2}} a^r(1-z)(1+aq^{\lambda r})}{(1-\frac{a}{z}q^{\lambda r})(1-azq^{\lambda r})}$$

$$= \frac{(1-z)(1+a)}{(1-\frac{a}{z})(1-az)} \lim_{\tau\to 0} {}_4\psi_4\left[\begin{matrix} q^{\lambda}/\tau, -aq^{\lambda}, \frac{a}{z}, az; q^{\lambda}, a\tau \\ a^2\tau, -a, aq^{\lambda}/z, aq^{\lambda}z \end{matrix}\right]$$

(in the notation of [12;p.190])

$$= \frac{(1-z)(1+a)}{(1-\frac{a}{z})(1-az)} \lim_{\tau\to 0} {}_6\psi_6\left[\begin{matrix} aq^{\lambda}, -aq^{\lambda}, a, a/z, az, q^{\lambda}/\tau; q^{\lambda}, a\tau \\ a, -a, aq^{\lambda}, azq^{\lambda}, aq^{\lambda}/z, a^2\tau \end{matrix}\right]$$

$$= \frac{(q^\lambda,q^\lambda)_\infty^2 \Theta(z,q^\lambda)\Theta(a^2,q^\lambda)}{\Theta(a/z,q^\lambda)\Theta(az,q^\lambda)\Theta(a,q)^\lambda}$$

It is now a simple matter to conclude our proof. By (2.5), (2.6) and Jacobi's triple product identity, we see that under the conditions of (2.1) the coefficient of z^0 we want in (2.2) is precisely the coefficient of z^0 in

$$\left\{\sum_{j=-\infty}^{\infty} (-\epsilon)^j z^{Aj} q^{B\binom{j}{2}+Cj}\right\} \tag{2.7}$$

$$\times \left\{\sum_{n=-\infty}^{\infty} z^n \sum_{r\geq|n|} (-1)^{r+n} a^{-r-1} q^{\binom{r+1}{2}\lambda-\binom{n}{2}\lambda}(1+a^{2r+1})\right\}.$$

Thus we obtain the desired expression by taking those terms where $n = -Aj$, and that yields (2.3) immediately. □

3. The fifth order mock theta functions.

Given Lemma 1 and Theorem 9 of [4;p.125] we can easily obtain our desired representations of the fifth order mock theta functions. The only point of possible confusion is resolved when we note that

$$\sum_{j=0}^{2n} x^{\binom{j+1}{2}} = \sum_{j=-n}^{n} x^{\binom{2j+1}{2}}. \tag{3.1}$$

Consequently our proof of Theorem 2 will consist primarily of the specifications of the appropriate substitutions.

Theorem 2.

$$f_0(q) \equiv \sum_{n=0}^{\infty} \frac{q^{n^2}}{(-q;q)_n} \tag{3.2}$$

$$= \text{coefficient of } z^0 \text{ in}$$

$$\frac{(q^3;q^3)_\infty(q^5;q^5)_\infty^2 \Theta(-zq^4,q^3)\Theta(z,q^5)\Theta(q^4,q^5)}{\Theta(-q^2z^{-1},q^5)\Theta(-q^2z,q^5)\Theta(-q^2,q^5)}$$

in the annulus $|q|^{-2} < |z| < |q|^{-3}$.

$$F_0(q) \equiv \sum_{n=0}^{\infty} \frac{q^{2n^2}}{(q;q^2)_n}$$

$$= \text{coefficient of } z^0 \text{ in}$$

$$\frac{(q^6;q^6)_\infty (q^{10},q^{10})_\infty^2 \Theta(zq^7,q^6)\Theta(z,q^{10})\Theta(q^6,q^{10})}{(q^2;q^2)_\infty \Theta(q^3z^{-1},q^{10})\Theta(q^3z,q^{10})\Theta(q^3,q^{10})} \tag{3.3}$$

in the annulus $|q|^{-3} < z < |q|^{-7}$.

$$1 + \psi_0(q) \equiv 1 + \sum_{n=0}^{\infty} (-q)_n q^{\binom{n+2}{2}} \tag{3.4}$$

$$= \text{coefficient of } z^0 \text{ in}$$

$$\frac{-q^2(q)_\infty^2 (q^5;q^5)_\infty^2 \Theta(-zq^3,q^2)\Theta(z,q^5)\Theta(q^4,q^5)}{\Theta(-q^2z^{-1},q^5)\Theta(-q^2z,q^5)\Theta(-q^2,q^5)}$$

in the annulus $|q|^{-2} < |z| < |q|^{-3}$.

$$\phi_0(q) \equiv \sum_{n=0}^{\infty} (-q;q^2)_n q^{n^2} \tag{3.5}$$

$$= \text{coefficient of } z^0 \text{ in}$$

$$\frac{(q^{10};q^{10})_\infty^2 \Theta(-zq^6,q^4)\Theta(z,q^{10})\Theta(q^6,q^{10})}{\Theta(-q^3z^{-1},q^{10})\Theta(-q^3z,q^{10})\Theta(-q^3,q^{10})}$$

in the annulus $|q|^{-3} < |z| < |q|^{-7}$.

$$f_1(q) \equiv \sum_{n=0}^{\infty} \frac{q^{n^2+n}}{(-q;q)_n} \tag{3.6}$$

$$= \text{coefficient of } z^0 \text{ in}$$

$$\frac{-q(q^3;q^3)_\infty (q^5;q^5)_\infty^2 \Theta(-zq^4,q^3)\Theta(z,q^5)\Theta(q^2,q^5)}{(q)_\infty \Theta(-qz^{-1},q^5)\Theta(-zq,q^5)\Theta(-q,q^5)}$$

in the annulus $|q|^{-1} < |z| < |q|^{-4}$.

$$F_1(q) \equiv \sum_{n=0}^{\infty} \frac{q^{2n^2+2n}}{(q;q^2)_{n+1}} \tag{3.7}$$

$= \text{coefficient of } z^0 \text{ in}$

$$\frac{q(q^6;q^6)_\infty (q^{10};q^{10})_\infty^2 \Theta(zq^7,q^6)\Theta(z,q^{10})\Theta(q^2,q^{10})}{(q^2;q^2)_\infty \Theta(qz^{-1},q^{10})\Theta(qz,q^{10})\Theta(q,q^5)}$$

in the annulus $|q|^{-1} < |z| < |q|^{-9}$.

$$\psi_1(q) \equiv \sum_{n=0}^{\infty} (-q)_n q^{\binom{n+1}{2}} \tag{3.8}$$

$= \text{coefficient of } z^0 \text{ in}$

$$\frac{-q(-q)_\infty (q^5;q^5)_\infty^2 \Theta(-zq^3,q^2)\Theta(z,q^5)\Theta(q^2,q^5)}{\Theta(-qz^{-1},q^5)\Theta(-qz,q^5)\Theta(-q,q^5)}$$

in the annulus $|q|^{-1} < |z| < |q|^{-4}$.

$$\phi_1(q) \equiv \sum_{n=0}^{\infty} (-q;q^2)_n q^{(n+1)^2} \tag{3.9}$$

$= \text{coefficient of } z^0 \text{ in}$

$$\frac{-q^2(-q)_\infty (q^{10};q^{10})_\infty^2 \Theta(-zq^6,q^4)\Theta(z,q^{10})\Theta(q^2,q^{10})}{\Theta(-qz^{-1},q^{10})\Theta(-qz,q^{10})\Theta(-q,q^{10})}$$

in the annulus $|q|^{-1} < |z| < |q|^{-9}$.

Proof. The appropriate specializations of Lemma 1 are the following:

for (3.2), take $\lambda = 5$, $A = 1$, $B = 3$, $C = 4$, $\epsilon = -1$, $a = -q^2$;

for (3.3), take $q \to q^2$, then $\lambda = 5$, $A = 1$, $B = 3$, $C = \frac{7}{2}$, $\epsilon = 1$, $a = q^3$;

for (3.4), take $\lambda = 5$, $A = 1$, $B = 2$, $C = 3$, $\epsilon = -1$, $a = -q^2$;

for (3.5), take $q \to q^2$, then $\lambda = 5$, $A = 1$, $B = 2$, $C = 3$, $\epsilon = -1$, $a = -q^3$;

for (3.6), take $\lambda = 5$, $A = 1$, $B = 3$, $C = 4$, $\epsilon = -1$, $a = -q$;

for (3.7), take $q \to q^2$, then $\lambda = 5$, $A = 1$, $B = 3$, $C = \frac{7}{2}$, $\epsilon = 1$, $a = q$;

for (3.8), take $\lambda = 5$, $A = 1$, $B = 2$, $C = 3$, $\epsilon = -1$, $a = -q$;

for (3.9), take $q \to q^2$, $\lambda = 5$, $A = 1$, $B = 2$, $C = 3$, $\epsilon = -1$, $a = -q$.

After Lemma 1 is specialized as indicated, we then compare the resulting identity with the corresponding expression in Theorem 9 of [4;p.125]. We note that in (6.8) of [4;p.125] the expression $(1+q^{2n+1})$ should be $q(1-q^{2n+1})$, and we use

$$1 + \psi_0(q) = \frac{(-q)_\infty}{(q)_\infty} \sum_{\substack{n=0 \\ |j|\leqq n}}^{\infty} q^{n(5n+1)/2-j(3j+1)/2}(1-q^{4n+2})$$

instead of (6.3) of [4;p.125]. $\square$

4. Conclusion. We have restricted our attention to the fifth order mock theta functions because they provide the most elegant applications of Lemma 1. There are indeed other applications. We could treat the seventh order mock theta functions in the same manner using Theorem 13 of [4;p.132]; however now the constant term would be taken from a sum of two infinite products.

The identity [4;p.124,eq.(5.15)]

$$(q)_\infty^2(q;q^2)_\infty = \sum_{\substack{n=0 \\ |j|\leqq n}}^{\infty} (-1)^j q^{n(3n+1)/2-j^2}(1-q^{2n+1}) \tag{4.1}$$

can be proved directly using Lemma 1. Let us denote the right-hand side of (4.1) by $R(q)$. In Lemma 1 let us take $\lambda = 3$, $A = B = 1$, $C = 2$, $\epsilon = -1$, $a = -q$. Consequently $R(q)$ is the constant term in the annulus $|q|^{-1} < |z| < |q|^{-2}$ of

$$\frac{-q(q)_\infty(q^3;q^3)_\infty^2(-zq^2)_\infty(-z^{-1}q^{-1})_\infty(z;q^3)_\infty(zq^{-1}q^3;q^3)_\infty(q^2;q^3)_\infty(q;q^3)_\infty}{(-q/z;q^3)_\infty(-q^2z;q^3)_\infty(-qz;q^3)_\infty(-q^2/z,q^3)_\infty(-q;q^3)_\infty(-q^2;q^2)_\infty}$$

$$= \frac{-q(q)_\infty^2(q^3;q^3)_\infty z^{-1}q^{-1}(-zq^3;q^3)_\infty(-z^{-1};q^3)_\infty(z;q^3)_\infty(q^3/z;q^3)_\infty(-q^3;q^3)_\infty}{(-q)_\infty}$$

$$= \frac{-(q)_\infty^2}{(-q)_\infty}(q^6;q^6)_\infty z^{-2}(z^2;q^6)_\infty(z^{-2}q^6;q^6)_\infty$$

$$= \frac{-(q)_\infty^2}{(-q)_\infty} z^{-2} \sum_{n=-\infty}^{\infty} (-1)^n q^{3n^2-3n} z^{2n},$$

and the coefficient of z^0 is just

$$\frac{(q)_\infty^2}{(-q)_\infty} = (q)_\infty^2(q;q^2)_\infty$$

by [2;p.5,eq.(1.2.5)].

It remains to be seen whether arguments like the above can be applied to the fifth order mock theta functions to produce useful and interesting identities.

References

1. G.E. Andrews, Problems and prospects for basic hypergeometric functions, from Theory and Application of Special Functions, R. Askey, ed., Academic Press, New York, 1975, pp. 191-224.

2. G.E. Andrews, The Theory of Partitions, Encyclopedia of Mathematics and Its Applications, Vol. 2, G.-C. Rota ed., Addison-Wesley, Reading, 1976. (Reissued: Cambridge University Press, London and New York, 1985).

3. G.E. Andrews, Hecke modular forms and the Kac-Peterson identities, Trans. Amer. Math. Soc., 283(1984), 451-458.

4. G.E. Andrews, The fifth and seventh order mock theta functions, Trans. Amer. Math. Soc., 293(1986), 113-134.

5. G.E. Andrews, q-Series: Their Development and Application in Analysis, Number Theory, Combinatorics, Physics and Computer Algebra, CBMS Regional Conference Lecture Series, No. 66, 1986, Amer. Math. Soc., Providence.

6. G.E. Andrews and F.G. Garvan, Ramanujan's "lost" notebook, VI. the mock theta conjectures, Advances in Math., (to appear).

7. F.J. Dyson, Statistical theory of the energy levels of complex systems I, J. Math. Phys., 3(1962), 140-156.

8. I.J. Good, Short proof of a conjecture of Dyson, J. Math. Phys., 11(1970), 1884.

9. J. Gunson, Proof of a conjecture of Dyson in the statistical theory of energy levels, J. Math. Phys., 3(1962), 752-753.

10. I.G. Macdonald, Affine root systems and Dedekind's η-function, Invent. Math., 15(1972), 91-143.

11. I.G. Macdonald, Some conjectures for root systems, S.I.A.M. J. Math. Anal., 13(1982), 998-1007.

12. L.J. Slater, Generalized Hypergeometric Functions, Cambridge University Press, London and New York, 1966.

13. K. Wilson, Proof of a conjecture by Dyson, J. Math. Phys., 3(1962), 1040-1043.

14. D. Zeilberger and D.M. Bressoud, A proof of Andrews' q-Dyson conjecture, Diser. Math., 54(1985), 201-224.

The Bailey Lattice: An Introduction

D. M. Bressoud*, Pennsylvania State University,
University Park, Pa.

1. Introduction

The Bailey Chain is a systemization of the techniques first introduced by L. J. Rogers [12,13] to find q-series identities. It has had a very long genesis beginning with Rogers' own re-evaluation of his techniques in 1916 [14], continuing through the papers of F. J. Dyson [8] and W. N. Bailey [6,7] in the 1940's and finally being streamlined and clarified in 1984 by G. E. Andrews [4] who gave it its name. It constitutes a very efficient machine for discovering and proving identities of which the proto-type is the first Rogers-Ramanujan identity:

$$\sum_{r\geq 0} \frac{q^{r^2}}{(q)_r} = \prod_{m\geq 1} \frac{1}{(1-q^{5m-4})(1-q^{5m-1})} \tag{1.1}$$

$$= \frac{\sum (-1)^n q^{(5n^2-n)/2}}{\sum (-1)^n q^{(3n^2-n)/2}},$$

where

$$(a)_\infty = (a;q)_\infty = \prod_{i\geq 0} (1-aq^i),$$

$$(a)_n = (a;q)_n = \frac{(a;q)_\infty}{(aq^n;q)_\infty}.$$

*Partially supported by N.S.F. grant no. DMS-8521580

ISBN 0-12-058560-X

The second equality of equation (1.1) follows from Jacobi's Triple Product Identity [(2.2.10) in 2].

Note that if n is a positive integer, then $(a)_n$ is a product of n binomials. We shall also use negative integral n where it is useful to observe that if n is positive, then

$$\frac{1}{(q)_{-n}} = \frac{(q^{1-n};q)_\infty}{(q;q)_\infty} = 0.$$

The significance of equation (1.1) lies in the fact that the right side is a ratio of theta functions and thus is explicitly evaluable at several values of $q = e^{2\pi i\tau}$. More significantly, the knowledge of what happens under the transformation $\tau \longrightarrow -1/\tau$ gives very accurate asymptotics for the right side. On the other hand, the left side arises naturally in several contexts. It is $f(1,q)$ where

$$f(x,q) = \sum_{r\geq 0} \frac{x^r q^{r^2}}{(q)_r}, \tag{1.2}$$

is easily seen to be the solution to the difference equation

$$f(x,q) = f(xq,q) + xqf(xq^2,q), \tag{1.3}$$

$$f(0,q) = 1.$$

The problem then is to start with a function such as the left side of (1.1) and find a transformation for it. This is precisely what the Bailey Chain is set up to do for a large class of functions. We shall explain how the Bailey Chain operates on (1.1) as an example and then demonstrate how this notion can be generalized to what we call a Bailey Lattice.

2. The Bailey Chain

Let $\alpha = \{\alpha_n\}$, $\beta = \{\beta_n\}$, $n \geq 0$ be sequences of functions in q. We say that they form a Bailey pair if

$$\beta_n = \sum \frac{\alpha_r}{(q)_{n-r}(aq)_{n+r}}, \quad 0 \leq r \leq n. \tag{2.1}$$

Bailey [6,7] proved the following proposition whose proof can also be found in [4]:

Proposition 1: α, β are a Bailey pair if and only if

$$\alpha_n = \frac{(1-aq^{2n})}{(1-a)} \sum \frac{(-1)^{n-r} q^{\binom{n-r}{2}} (a)_{n+r}}{(q)_{n-r}} \beta_r, \quad 0 \leq r \leq n. \tag{2.2}$$

One implication of this lemma is that for every identity of the form of (2.1), there is a companion of the form of (2.2). To prove either is to prove both.

Given a Bailey pair: α, β, the Bailey chain constructs an infinite sequence of Bailey pairs:

Theorem 1: Let α, β be a Bailey pair and set

$$\beta'_n = \sum \frac{a^k q^{k^2}}{(q)_{n-k}} \beta_k, \tag{2.3}$$

$$\alpha'_r = a^r q^{r^2} \alpha_r. \tag{2.4}$$

Then α', β' is also a Bailey pair.

A proof of this theorem can be found in [4].

This theorem can be iterated to obtain an infinite sequence of

Bailey pairs. The chain is in fact doubly infinite for the pair α, β can be uniquely reconstructed from α', β' and so one can back up.

Given the left side of equation (1.1) we first truncate the summation by introducing a factor of $(q)_{n-r}$ in the denominator. We then define:

$$\beta''_n = \sum \frac{q^{r^2}}{(q)_{n-r}(q)_r}, \quad 0 \le r \le n. \tag{2.5}$$

The original function can be obtained by letting n approach ∞ and then multiplying by $(q)_\infty$. Comparing this with equation (2.3), we see that backing up one step yields the sequence β' with

$$\beta'_n = \frac{1}{(q)_n}. \tag{2.6}$$

We can back up once more to get the trivial sequence β:

$$\beta_n = \chi(n = 0), \tag{2.7}$$

where $\chi(A) = 1$ if A is true, 0 otherwise.

At this stage it is easy to use equation (2.2) to find the corresponding α sequence:

$$\alpha_n = (-1)^n q^{\binom{n}{2}}(1+q^n). \tag{2.8}$$

We now move two steps forward on the α side of the Bailey chain and see that α'', β'' are a Bailey pair provided:

$$\alpha''_n = (-1)^n q^{(5n^2-n)/2}(1+q^n). \tag{2.9}$$

Schematically, we have moved from β'' to the corresponding α'' in the following manner:

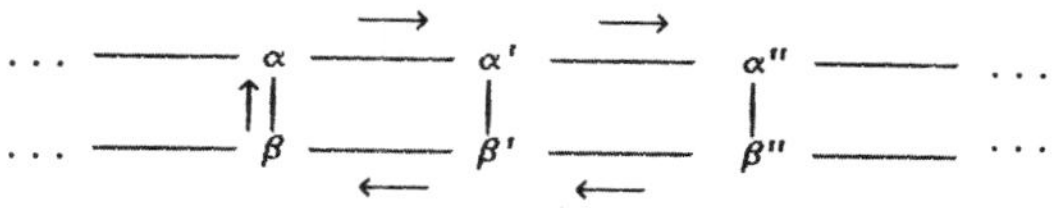

Inserting this Bailey pair into equation (2.1) yields

$$\sum_{r\geq 0} \frac{q^{r^2}}{(q)_r(q)_{n-r}} \tag{2.10}$$

$$= 1 + \sum_{r\geq 1} \frac{(-1)^r q^{(5r^2-r)/2}(1+q^r)}{(q)_{n-r}(q)_{n+r}},$$

which becomes equation (1.1) in the limit as n approaches $+\infty$.

We observe that we could have preserved the parameter a in this procedure to obtain an identity of Watson [16]:

$$\sum_{r\geq 0} \frac{a^r q^{r^2}}{(q)_r(q)_{n-r}} \tag{2.11}$$

$$= \sum_{r\geq 0} \frac{(-1)^r a^{2r} q^{(5r^2-r)/2}(aq)_{r-1}(1-aq^{2r})}{(q)_{n-r}(aq)_{n+r}(q)_r}.$$

Letting $n \rightarrow \infty$, this is the first Rogers-Ramanujan identity when $a = 1$, the second Rogers-Ramanujan identity when $a = q$, and in general gives a transformation for $f(a,q)$ as defined in equation (1.2)

If we continue along the Bailey Chain we have established, the β_n's become multiple summations while the α_n's increase by a factor of $a^n q^{n^2}$ at each step . We obtain the following general result of Andrews [3]:

$$\sum_{n_1\geq\ldots\geq n_{k-1}\geq 0} \frac{a^{n_1+\ldots+n_{k-1}} q^{n_1^2+\ldots+n_{k-1}^2}}{(q)_{n-n_1}(q)_{n_1-n_2}\cdots(q)_{n_{k-2}-n_{k-1}}(q)_{n_{k-1}}} \tag{2.12}$$

$$= \sum_{r\geq 0} \frac{(-1)^r a^{kr} q^{((2k+1)r^2-r)/2}(aq)_{r-1}(1-aq^{2r})}{(q)_{n-r}(aq)_{n+r}(q)_r}.$$

This procedure of establishing a Bailey pair by taking one of the sequences and then moving along the Bailey chain until a point is reached where it is easy or at least possible to jump to the other side of the chain is extremely powerful and has been exploited to obtain many identities similar to equation (1.1). It is the concept underlying Slater's list of 130 such identities [15]. Andrews [4,5] gives several examples of its use.

One of the drawbacks of the method as presented here, however, is that the parameter a remains invariant throughout the chain. In the next section we shall demonstrate how to pass from a Bailey pair with given parameter to a Bailey pair with arbitrary new parameter. In theory the new parameter can be chosen to be independent of the original. In practice, one chooses the new parameter to be an integral power of q times the original. This generates the Bailey Lattice in which each Bailey pair is adjacent to an infinite collection of Bailey pairs and to prove that any one pair in the lattice is a Bailey pair is to prove that they all are.

3. The Bailey Lattice

The notion of a Bailey pair can be generalized as follows. Let $M = (m_{i,j})_{i,j=0}^{\infty}$, $i > j \Rightarrow m_{i,j} = 0$, be an infinite dimensional lower diagonal matrix. If the diagonal entries are non-zero, then it has a unique inverse, say M^*. Two infinite sequences, α, β will be a Bailey pair with respect to M if and only if

$$\beta = M\alpha. \tag{3.1}$$

Equation (2.1) is simply (3.1) with

$$m_{i,j} = \frac{1}{(q)_{i-j}(aq)_{i+j}}. \tag{3.2}$$

Equation (2.2) can be trivially stated as

$$\alpha = M^*\beta. \tag{3.3}$$

Let us call the matrix defined by equation (3.2) M(a), and define M(a,b) to have entries:

$$m_{i,j}(a,b) = \frac{(b/a)_{i-j}(b)_{i+j}(1-aq^{2j})a^{i-j}}{(q)_{i-j}(aq)_{i+j}(1-a)}, \tag{3.4}$$

Up to multiplication by diagonal matrices, M(a,b) is M*(b)M(a). More precisely, we have the following lemma proved in [1]:

Lemma 1:

$$M(b,c)M(a,b) = M(a,c), \tag{3.5}$$

$$M^*(a,b) = M(b,a). \tag{3.6}$$

This makes it easy to remember M*(a,b).

Let S(b) be the diagonal matrix

$$S(b) = \left\{\frac{(\rho)_i(\sigma)_i(bq/\rho\sigma)^i}{(bq/\sigma)_i(bq/\rho)_i}\chi(i=j)\right\}_{i,j=0}^{\infty}. \tag{3.7}$$

In practice, one usually lets ρ, σ tend to ∞ so that the ith diagonal entry of S(b) becomes $b^i q^{i^2}$. We suppress the proof of the following lemma which is equivalent to the summation formula for a terminating very well poised ${}_6\varphi_5$.

<u>Lemma 2</u>: If $bcq = d\rho\sigma$, then

$$S^*(c)M(c,d)S(c) \tag{3.8}$$

$$= S^*(b)M(b,d)S(b)M(c,b).$$

Armed with these lemmas, we are now prepared to set up our Bailey lattice.

<u>Theorem 2</u>: Given that α, β are a Bailey pair with respect to $M(a,b)$, if we define α', β' by

$$\beta' = S(c)S^*(b)M(b,d)S(b)\beta,$$

$$\alpha' = S(c)M(a,c)\alpha,$$

where $bcq = d\rho\sigma$, then α', β' are a Bailey pair with respect to $M(c,d)$.

<u>Proof</u>: $\beta' = S(c)S^*(b)M(b,d)S(b)M(a,b)M(c,a)S^*(c)\alpha'$

$$= S(c)S^*(b)M(b,d)S(b)M(c,b)S^*(c)\alpha'$$

$$= S(c)S^*(c)M(c,d)S(c)S^*(c)\alpha'$$

$$= M(c,d)\alpha'.$$

Note that if $a = c$, then $\alpha' = S(a)\alpha$. The Bailey chain of Theorem 1 is the special case of this theorem where $a = c$ and $b = d = 0$. If $c = aq^{-1}$, then all entries of $M(a,c)$ are zero except those on the main diagonal or first subdiagonal. This enables us to generalize equation (2.17) to

$$\sum_{n_1 \geq \ldots \geq n_{k-1} \geq 0} \frac{a^{n_1+\ldots+n_{k-1}} q^{n_1^2+\ldots+n_{k-1}^2+n_i+\ldots n_{k-1}}}{(q)_{n-r}(q)_{n_1-n_2}\ldots(q)_{n_{k-2}-n_{k-1}}(q)_{n_{k-1}}} \tag{3.9}$$

$$= \sum_r \frac{(-1)^r a^{kr} q^{((2k+1)r^2+(2k-2i+1)r)/2}(aq)_r(1-a^i q^{2ir+i})}{(q)_{n-r}(aq)_{n+r}(q)_r} \tag{3.10}$$

by shifting from parameter aq to a after $k-i$ steps. A complete proof of equation (3.8) can be found in [1].

4. Other Bailey Pairs

The question naturally arises at this point: Are there other infinite dimensional lower triangular matrices with explicitly known inverses which satisfy a relationship analogous to equation (3.8)?

The answer to the first part of the question is "yes". Gessel and Stanton [10,11] have stated the following bi-basic generalization of $M(a)$. If we define

$$(a;q,p)_{i,j} = (a;q)_i(aq^{i-1}p;p)_j, \tag{4.1}$$

then the matrix:

$$M(a;q,p) = \left[\frac{a^{i-j}(1-ap^jq^j)}{(1-a)(q;q)_{i-j}(aq;q,p)_{i,j}}\right]_{i,j=0}^{\infty} \tag{4.2}$$

has inverse:

$$M^*(a;q,p) = \left[\frac{(a;q,p)_{j+1,i-1}}{(q;q)_{i-j}}(-1)^{i-j}q^{\binom{i-j}{2}}\right]_{i,j=0}^{\infty}. \tag{4.3}$$

While $M^*(b;q,p)M(a;q,p)$ does not collapse into a closed form, there is at least one bi-basic analog of M(a,b):

$$M(a,b;q,p) = \left\{ a^{i-j} \frac{(1-ap^j q^j)(b;q)_{i+j}(b/a;q,p)_{i+1,-1-j}}{(1-a)(q;q)_{i-j}(aq;q,p)_{i,j}} \right. \tag{4.4}$$

$$\left. * \frac{(1-ap^j/(bq^j))}{(1-a/b)} \left(\frac{q}{p}\right)^{\binom{j+1}{2}} \right\}_{i,j=0}^{\infty}$$

with inverse

$$M^*(a,b;q,p) = \left\{ \frac{(a;q,p)_{j+1,i-1}(a/b;q,p)_{1-j,i-1}}{(q;q)_{i-j}(bq;q)_{i+j}} \right. \tag{4.5}$$

$$\left. * \frac{(1-bq^{2j})}{(1-b)} b^{i-j} \right\}_{i,j=0}^{\infty} .$$

The fact that $M^*(a,b;q,p)$ is the inverse of $M(a,b;q,p)$ is equivalent to the evaluation of a certain bi-basic analog of a terminating very well poised ${}_6\varphi_5$ identity. This in turn is a special case of a bibasic result due to G. Gasper (equation (1.14) in [9]).

The inverse for $M(a;q,p)$ has been used by Gessel and Stanton [10,11] to find companion identities for many summation theorems. Unfortunately, no analog of Lemma 2 is known for the bi-basic matrices. It seems fairly clear that no useful analog of Lemma 2 exists for completely independent q and p. On the other hand, there appears to be hope that useful analogs will exist when one base is a small integral power of the other.

References

1. A.K. Agarwal, G.E. Andrews, D.M. Bressoud, The Bailey Lattice, J. Indian Math. Soc., to appear.

2. G.E. Andrews, The theory of partitions, vol. 2 in Encyclopedia of Mathematics (Addison-Wesley, Reading, Mass. 1976).

3. ____________, Problems and prospects for basic hypergeometric functions. In Theory and application of special functions, ed. R.A. Askey (Academic Press, New York, 1975).

4. ____________, Multiple series Rogers-Ramanujan type identities, Pac. J. Math., 114(1984), 267-283.

5. ____________, q-series: their development and application..., CBMS Regional Conference Series in Mathematics, 66 (AMS, Providence, 1986).

6. W.N. Bailey, Some identities in combinatory analysis, Proc. London Math. Soc. (2), 49(1947), 421-435.

7. ____________, Identities of the Rogers-Ramanujan type, Proc. London Math. Soc. (2), 50(1949), 1-10.

8. F.J. Dyson, Three identities in combinatory analysis, J. London Math. Soc., 18(1943), 35-39.

9. G. Gasper, Summation, transformation and expansion formulas for bibasic series.

10. I. Gessel and D. Stanton, Applications of q-Lagrange inversion to basic hypergeometric series, Trans. Amer. Math. Soc., 277(1983), 173-201.

11. ________________________, Another family of q-Lagrange inverstion formulas, Rocky Mtn. j. of Math., 16(1986), 373-384.

12. L.J. Rogers, Second memoir on the expansion of certain infinite products, Proc. London Math. Soc. 25(1894), 318-343.

13. ____________, Third memoir on the expansion of certain infinite products, Proc. London Math. Soc. 26(1895), 15-32.

14. ____________, On two theorems of combinatory analysis and some allied identities, Proc. London Math. Soc. (2), 16(1916), 315-336.

15. L.J. Slater, Further identities of the Rogers-Ramanujan type, Proc. London Math. Soc. (2), 54(1952), 147-167.

16. G.N. Watson, A new proof of the Rogers-Ramanujan identities, J. London Math. Soc. 4(1929), 4-9.

Ramanujan's Identities in Statistical Mechanics

R.J. Baxter

Research School of Physical Sciences
The Australian National University
GPO Box 4, Canberra A.C.T.2601
Australia

It is indicated how the Rogers-Ramanujan identities, and some of Ramanujan's "sums-of-products" identities, naturally occur in the hard hexagon model of statistical mechanics. A more general model, corresponding to Gordon's generalization of the Rogers-Ramanujan identities, is mentioned. It is remarked that typical sums-of-products identities can be put into a more transparent form by making a conjugate modulus transformation.

ISBN 0-12-058560-X

1. Introduction

A simple model in statistical mechanics is a lattice gas, in which particles are placed on the sites of a lattice, and only adjacent particles interact. Although highly idealized, such models are much studied as they give at least a qualitative understanding of more complex systems.

One is particularly interested in locating and describing any "critical points" of the system: at these points the thermodynamic properties are singular functions of the temperature, density, etc., having usually branch-point power law singularities. The exponents of these singularities are known as "critical exponents", and it seems that they are normally independent of the details of the particle interactions. (This is known as "universality".[(1)]) Thus simple models may correctly predict the critical exponents of complicated real systems.

2. Hard Hexagon Model

One such simple model is the "hard hexagon model". Here one considers a triangular lattice $\mathcal{L}$ of N sites, as in Fig.1, and places particles on $\mathcal{L}$ so that no two particles occupy the same site, or are adjacent. Thus one particle excludes any other from being next to it, or on the same site, which is a special sort of interaction.

An allowed arrangement of three particles on $\mathcal{L}$ is shown in Fig.1. One can shade the six triangular faces adjacent to each particle so as to form a hexagon, as indicated. The exclusion rule is then equivalent to saying that no two shaded hexagons can overlap: hence the name "hard hexagon model".

Let $g(n, N)$ be the number of allowed arrangements of n particles on $\mathcal{L}$. We want to calculate $g(n, N)$, or equivalently the "grand partition function"

$$\Xi_N(z) = \sum_{n \geq 0} z^n \, g(n, N) \tag{1}$$

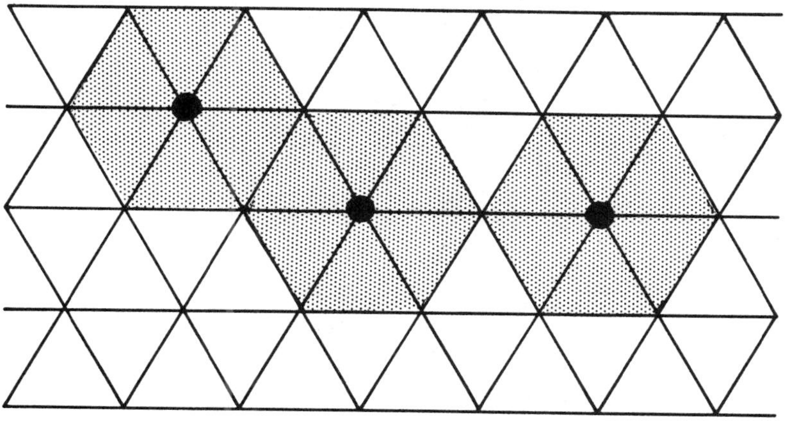

Figure 1 : An arrangement of particles (black circles) on the triangular lattice such that no two particles are together or adjacent. The six faces round each particle are shaded, forming non-overlapping ("hard") hexagons.

for positive values of z (known as the "activity"). The sum is over all possible values of n: since the closest possible packing of particles is for them to lie on one of the three sub-lattices of the triangular lattice, then apart from boundary corrections

$$0 \leq n \leq N/3 \; . \tag{2}$$

Label the sites of $\mathcal{L}$ from 1 through to N. Another way of writing (1) is to let σ_i be the number of particles on site i. Then the exclusion rule implies

$$\begin{aligned} &\sigma_i = 0 \quad \text{or} \quad 1\,, && 1 \leq i \leq N\,, \\ &\sigma_i\,\sigma_j = 0 && \text{if } i, j \text{ are adjacent.} \end{aligned} \tag{3}$$

More compactly, these rules can be written (with $\sigma_i \in \mathbb{N}$)

$$0 \leq \sigma_i + \sigma_j \leq 1 \quad \text{if } i, j \text{ are adjacent}\,. \tag{4}$$

Now (1) can be written as

$$\Xi_N(z) = \sum_{\sigma} z^{\Sigma\sigma_i} , \tag{5}$$

where the inner sum is over all sites i, the outer sum is over all values of $\sigma = \{\sigma_1,...,\sigma_N\}$ permitted by (4).

Local probabilities

In addition to $\Xi_N(z)$, we also want to calculate the probability that a particle site, say site 1, contains r particles. This is

$$p_r = \left[\Xi_N(z)\right]^{-1} \sum_{\sigma} \delta(\sigma_1, r)\, z^{\Sigma\sigma_i} , \tag{6}$$

where $\delta(a,b) = 1$ if $a = b$, else $\delta(a,b) = 0$.

These problems were solved in 1980[2,3], in the limit when $\mathfrak{L}$ becomes infinitely large in both directions (so $N \to \infty$), site 1 being infinitely deep within $\mathfrak{L}$. For z less than some critical value z_c, one defines a parameter x by

$$z = -x\left[H(x)/G(x)\right]^5 , \qquad 0 < z < z_c , \tag{7}$$

where $G(x)$, $H(x)$ are the functions:

$$\begin{aligned} G(x) &= \prod_{m=1}^{\infty} \left[\left(1 - x^{5m-4}\right)\left(1 - x^{5m-1}\right)\right]^{-1} , \\ H(x) &= \prod_{m=1}^{\infty} \left[\left(1 - x^{5m-3}\right)\left(1 - x^{5m-2}\right)\right]^{-1} . \end{aligned} \tag{8}$$

Here we must have

$$-1 < x < 0 \tag{9}$$

and z_c is given by (7) in the limit $x \to -1$, so

$$z_c = \left[\left(1+\sqrt{5}\right)/2\right]^5 = 11.09\ \ldots \tag{10}$$

By using corner transfer matrices[4], we find we can express the probabilities p_0, p_1 in terms of the functions $F_0(q), F_1(q)$, where

$$F_r(q) = \sum_{\sigma_2, \sigma_3, \sigma_4, \ldots} q^{\sigma_2 + 2\sigma_3 + 3\sigma_4 + \ldots} \quad . \tag{11}$$

Here $\sigma_1 = r$, σ_2, σ_3, σ_4, ... are the occupation numbers of a line of sites on $\mathcal{L}$, so the summation in (11) is over the values permitted by the rules (3) or (4), i.e.

$$\sigma_i = 0 \text{ or } 1 \, , \qquad \sigma_{i-1}\, \sigma_i = 0 \, , \qquad \sigma_1 = r \tag{12}$$

for $i \geq 2$. In fact it turns out p_0, p_1 are given by

$$p_r = \left[-x\, G(x)/H(x)\,\right]^r \, F_r(x^6)/c(x) \ , \tag{13}$$

where $c(x)$ is a normalization factor (independent of r) that is to be determined by the constraint

$$p_0 + p_1 = 1 \tag{14}$$

(i.e. site 1 contains either 0 or 1 particles).

Rogers-Ramanujan Identities

We can partially perform the summations in (11) by first considering the contribution when σ_2, σ_3, σ_4, ... are all zero, then the contributions when just one of them is unity, then when two are unity, and so on. This gives

$$F_0(q) = 1 + \frac{q}{1-q} + \frac{q^4}{(1-q)(1-q^2)} + \cdots + \frac{q^{n^2}}{(1-q)(1-q^2)\cdots(1-q^n)} + \cdots \quad , \tag{15a}$$

$$F_1(q) = 1 + \frac{q^2}{1-q} + \frac{q^6}{(1-q)(1-q^2)} + \cdots + \frac{q^{n(n+1)}}{(1-q)(1-q^2)\cdots(1-q^n)} + \cdots \quad . \tag{15b}$$

But these series are precisely those that occur in the famous Rogers-Ramanujan identities(5,6), so we can use these identities to obtain

$$F_0(q) = G(q) \ , \qquad F_1(q) = H(q) \ , \tag{16}$$

where $G(q), H(q)$ are the infinite products defined in (8).

We still have to determine the normalization factor $c(x)$. From (13),(14) and (16)

$$c(x)\, H(x) \ = \ H(x)\, G(x^6) - x\, G(x)\, H(x^6) \ . \tag{17}$$

The expression on the right-hand side of this equation has also been studied by Ramanujan. Define two more functions

$$Q(x) = \prod_{n=1}^{\infty} (1 - x^n) \ ,$$

$$P(x) = \prod_{n=1}^{\infty} (1 - x^{2n-1}) = Q(x) \,/ Q(x^2) \ . \tag{18}$$

Ramanujan stated (eq.8 of ref.7), and Rogers subsequently proved(8), that

$$H(x)\, G(x^6) - x\, G(x)\, H(x^6) = P(x) \,/ P(x^3) \ . \tag{19}$$

Using this identity in (17), substituting the resulting expression for $c(x)$ into (13), we obtain

$$p_0 = H(x)\, G(x^6)\, P(x^3) \,/P(x) \;,$$
$$p_1 = -x\, G(x)\, H(x^6)\, P(x^3) \,/P(x) \;. \qquad (20)$$

Critical Behaviour

This p_1 is the probability that the selected site 1 contains a particle. For $z < z_c$ all sites are equivalent, so p_1 is also the mean density ρ (the average of n/N) of the system.

We are particularly interested in examining quantities such as ρ near the critical activity $z = z_c$, i.e. near $x = -1$. All the above series and products then become poorly convergent, so are useless for examining this limit. However, thanks to the Rogers-Ramanujan identities, we have expressed our results in terms of modular functions: in particular, the RHS of (20) can be written as a ratio of products of elliptic theta functions. This means that we can use standard conjugate-modulus transformations (§§181-183 of ref.9 and §15.7 of ref.4) to re-write (20) and (7), in terms of infinite products that converge more and more rapidly as $x \to -1$. The behaviour near z_c can then be obtained from the first few terms in the new product expansions. The relevant formulae are given (for a more general model) in section 2. Here we remark only that we finally obtain

$$\rho = p_1 = \rho_c - 5^{-3/2} \left[(z_c - z)/z_c \right]^{2/3} + O(z_c - z) \;, \qquad (21)$$

where

$$\rho_c = \left(5 - \sqrt{5}\right)/10 = 0.2764 \ldots \qquad (22)$$

is the critical density.

Thus as $z \to z_c$ the derivative of ρ diverges :

$$d\rho/dz \propto (z_c - z)^{-\alpha}, \qquad (23)$$

where $\alpha = 1/3$. This α is one of the "critical exponents" mentioned above.

Experimental results

There are experimental systems that resemble hard hexagons. Bretz *et al.*[(10)] in 1973, Tejwani *et al.*[(11)] in 1980, looked at films of He_4 adsorbed onto graphite. Effectively the graphite forms a triangular lattice: the He_4 molecules lie on the sites of this lattice and tend to exclude other molecules from occupying the same or adjacent sites. Thus this sytem is an approximate realization of the hard hexagon model. At high temperatures it is a dilute fluid, but the density increases as the temperature is lowered, until at about 3°K the system passes through a critical point below which it is ordered, most of the He_4 molecules lying on just one of the three graphite sub-lattices. The experimentalists measured the exponent α : the first group found $\alpha = 0.36 \pm 0.02$, while the second found $\alpha = 0.28 \pm 0.01$. Both measurements are quite close to the exact value 1/3 of the hard-hexagon model.

Other regimes

We have only discussed the results for low-density $(z < z_c\,,\ \rho < \rho_c)$ regime of the hard hexagon model. We have not given their derivation, which involves extending the model to one on a square lattice with diagonal interactions. The high-density regime $(z > z_c\,, \rho > \rho_c)$ can also be solved, as can two other regimes that occur in the extended model. In all cases we find we need to evaluate multi-dimensional sums such as (11), and that the results can be expressed in terms of elliptic functions (simple infinite products like (8)). Further, in all cases the normalization factor $c(x)$ is the sum of two products that can be reduced to a single product by using either Ramanujan's "sums-of-products" identities[(7)], or corollaries of them. In addition to (19), one uses

$$G(x)\,G(x^9) + x^2 H(x)\,H(x^9) = Q(x^3)^2 / Q(x)\,Q(x^9) \ , \tag{24}$$

$$G(x)\,G(x^4) + x\,H(x)\,H(x^4) = P(-x)^2 \ , \tag{25}$$

$$H(x)\,G(x^{16}) - x^3\,G(x)\,H(x^{16}) = P(-x^2) \ , \tag{26}$$

$$G(x)\,G(-x^4) - x\,H(x)\,H(-x^4) = P(-x^2) \ . \tag{27}$$

The first three of these are identities (6), (2), (5) in Birch's list[7] of Ramanujan's identities. The last is a corollary of identity (23) of the list:

$$G(x)\,H(-x) + G(-x)\,H(x) = 2/P(x^2)^2 \tag{28}$$

together with two identities of Rogers[5]:

$$\begin{aligned} H(x) + H(-x) &= 2\,G(-x^4)\,Q(x^8)\big/Q(x^2) \\ G(x) - G(-x) &= 2x\,H(-x^4)\,Q(x^8)\big/Q(x^2)\ . \end{aligned} \tag{29}$$

3. <u>A more general model</u>

George Andrews suggested to the author in 1980 that there may be a generalization of the hard hexagon model that naturally involves Gordon's generalization[12,13] of the Rogers-Ramanujan identities. This was found in 1986[14-17], and has since been further extended[18]. It is a square lattice model in which particles are put on the sites subject to the rule that there be at most $k-1$ particles on each pair of adjacent sites, where k is a fixed integer greater than one. This means that there are at most $k-1$ particles on any site. There are complicated and very specific interactions between particles on each set of four sites bounding a common face of the lattice. For $k=2$ we regain the hard hexagon model.

Again there are various distinct regimes to consider: here we look at the analogue of the low density $(z < z_c\,, \rho < \rho_c)$ regime of the hard hexagon model. Then from eq.(6.11) of ref.14 (with $n, -\exp(-\lambda/2s)$ therein replaced by k, x), the probability that a selected site, deep inside the lattice, contains s particles is

$$p_s = (-x)^{s^2}\,E\left(x^{2k-2s}, x^{2k+1}\right) F_s\left(x^{4k-2}\right)\Big/d(x)\ . \tag{30}$$

Here $s = 0,1,\ldots,k-1$; x is a variable, in the interval $(-1,0)$, that is determined by the parameters of the model; $E(z, x)$ is the Jacobi triple product function (basically a theta function)

$$E(z,x) = \prod_{m=1}^{\infty} \left(1 - x^{m-1} z\right)\left(1 - x^m z^{-1}\right)\left(1 - x^m\right) \tag{31a}$$

$$= \sum_{n=-\infty}^{\infty} (-1)^n x^{n(n-1)/2} z^n \tag{31b}$$

(see Theorem 2.8 of ref.13), and $F_s(q)$ is again defined by (11), only now $\sigma_2, \sigma_3, \sigma_4, \ldots$ are non-negative integers satisfying the constraints

$$\sigma_{i-1} + \sigma_i < k \ , \qquad \sigma_1 = s \ , \tag{32}$$

for $i \geq 2$.

Gordon's generalization[12,13] of the Rogers-Ramanujan identities tells us at once that

$$F_s(q) = \prod_{\substack{j=1 \\ j \neq 0,\ \pm(k-s);\ \mathrm{mod}\ 2k+1}}^{\infty} \left(1 - q^j\right)^{-1}$$

$$= E\left(q^{k-s}, q^{2k+1}\right) / Q(q) \ , \tag{33}$$

where $Q(x)$ is defined in (18).

The normalization factor $d(x)$ in (30) is determined by the requirement that the sum of the probabilities p_s be one, i.e.

$$p_0 + p_1 + \cdots + p_{k-1} = 1 \ , \tag{34}$$

so, setting $s = k - j$,

$$Q\left(x^{4k-2}\right) d(x) = \sum_{j=1}^{k} (-x)^{(k-j)^2} E\left(x^{2j}, x^{2k+1}\right) E\left(x^{(4k-2)j}, x^{8k^2-2}\right) \ . \tag{35}$$

<u>Conjugate modulus transformation</u>

We shall show that the sum on the RHS of (35) is half the product of two E functions. An illuminating way to do this is to first make the conjugate modulus transformation mentioned in section 2. Let $\theta_1,\ldots,\theta_4$ be the standard Jacobi elliptic theta functions, defined (§162 of ref.9, §21.3 and 21.4 of ref.19) by

$$\theta_1(u,q^2) = 2q^{1/4}\sin u \prod_{n=1}^{\infty}\left(1-2q^{2n}\cos 2u+q^{4n}\right)\left(1-q^{2n}\right) , \tag{36.a}$$

$$\theta_4(u,q^2) = \prod_{n=1}^{\infty}\left(1-2q^{2n-1}\cos 2u+q^{4n-2}\right)\left(1-q^{2n}\right) , \tag{36.b}$$

$$\theta_2(u,q^2) = \theta_1\left(u+\tfrac{\pi}{2},q^2\right), \qquad \theta_3(u,q^2) = \theta_4\left(u+\tfrac{\pi}{2},q^2\right) . \tag{36.c}$$

(Our use of q^2 , rather than q , as the second argument of θ_i is non-standard. It is convenient in subsequent equations such as (37.c) and (55).)

Then the standard conjugate modulus identities (§§181-183 of ref.9 and §15.7 of ref.4) can be written as

$$\theta_1(u,e^{-\varepsilon}) = \left(\frac{2\pi}{\varepsilon}\right)^{1/2} e^{-(\pi-2u)^2/2\varepsilon}\, E\left(e^{-4\pi u/\varepsilon}, e^{-4\pi^2/\varepsilon}\right) , \tag{37.a}$$

$$\theta_4(u,e^{-\varepsilon}) = \left(\frac{2\pi}{\varepsilon}\right)^{1/2} e^{-(\pi-2u)^2/2\varepsilon}\, E\left(-e^{-4\pi u/\varepsilon}, e^{-4\pi^2/\varepsilon}\right) , \tag{37.b}$$

$$\theta_1(u,-e^{-\varepsilon}) = (-1)^{1/8}\left(\frac{\pi}{\varepsilon}\right)^{1/2} e^{-(\pi-4u)^2/8\varepsilon}\, E\left(e^{-2\pi u/\varepsilon}, -e^{-\pi^2/\varepsilon}\right) . \tag{37.c}$$

Defining ε, y, r, B by

$$x = -e^{-\pi^2/\varepsilon} , \qquad y = -e^{-\varepsilon/(4k^2-1)} , \tag{38}$$

$$r = 2k+1, \qquad B = (-1)^{-1/8}(-x)^{\frac{1}{2}-k} , \tag{39}$$

it follows that the RHS of (35) is

$$B\sum_{j=1}^{k}\theta_1\left(\frac{\pi j}{r}, y^{r-2}\right)\theta_1\left(\frac{\pi j}{r}, y^2\right) . \tag{40}$$

The summand is unchanged by replacing j by $r-j$, and vanishes when $j=r$. Hence (40) is equal to

$$\tfrac{1}{2}B\sum_{j=1}^{r}\theta_1\left(\frac{\pi j}{r},y^{r-2}\right)\theta_1\left(\frac{\pi j}{r},y^{2}\right) . \tag{41}$$

Some general "sums-of-products" identities

The summand in (41) is obviously a periodic function of j, of period r. This makes it clear that we are dealing with a Fourier-type sum, over a full period of the summand. Consider the more general quantity

$$S = \sum_{j=1}^{r}\theta_1\left(\frac{\pi j}{r},y^{a}\right)\theta_1\left(\frac{\pi j}{r},y^{b}\right) , \tag{42}$$

where a, b are positive integers,

$$a+b = r , \tag{43}$$

and r may now be either odd or even.

The function $\theta_1(u, q^2)$ can be expanded (§161 of ref.9; §21.11 of ref.19) :

$$\theta_1(u, q^2) = i\sum_{m}(-1)^{(m+1)/2}q^{m^2/4}e^{imu} , \tag{44}$$

the sum being restricted to odd integer values of m. Using this, (42) can be written

$$S = \sum_{m,n}(-1)^{(m+n)/2}y^{(am^2+bn^2)/8}\sum_{j=1}^{r}e^{i(m+n)\pi j/r} , \tag{45}$$

m and n being odd. The $j-$ summation vanishes unless $m+n=0$, modulo $2r$, when it sums to r. Thus, setting $n=2pr-m$ (p any integer) :

$$S = r\sum_{p}(-1)^{pr}\sum_{m\text{ odd}}y^{I/8} , \tag{46}$$

where, using (43),

$$I = am^2 + b(2pr - m)^2$$

$$= r\left[m^2 - 4bpm + 4brp^2\right] . \tag{47}$$

Setting $m = 2bp + s$ (s odd), we get

$$I = rs^2 + 4abrp^2 . \tag{48}$$

Hence

$$S = r \sum_p (-1)^{pr} y^{abrp^2/2} \sum_{s \text{ odd}} y^{rs^2/8} \tag{49}$$

$$= r\, \theta_\nu\left(0, y^{rab}\right) \theta_2\left(0, y^r\right) , \tag{50}$$

where $\nu = 3$ if r is even, $\nu = 4$ if r is odd.

Thus we have established the identity

$$\sum_{j=1}^{r} \theta_1\left(\frac{\pi j}{r}, y^a\right) \theta_1\left(\frac{\pi j}{r}, y^b\right) = r\, \theta_\nu\left(0, y^{rab}\right) \theta_2\left(0, y^r\right) , \tag{51}$$

true for all positive integers a, b, r satisfying (43), and all complex numbers y inside the unit circle $|y| < 1$. If we take y to be positive and use the conjugate modulus relations (37), we obtain the equivalent identity

$$\sum_{j=1}^{r} q^{(r-2j)^2/8} E\left(q^{aj}, q^{ra}\right) E\left(q^{bj}, q^{rb}\right)$$

$$= E\left(-q^{1/2}, q\right) E\left(q^{ab/2}, q^{ab}\right) \quad \text{if } r \text{ is even}$$

$$= q^{1/8} E(-1, q)\, E\left(q^{ab/2}, q^{ab}\right) \quad \text{if } r \text{ is odd} , \tag{52}$$

true for all complex numbers q with $|q| < 1$. This identity is a special case of those discussed by Rogers (section 9 of ref.8), his $p, \alpha, \beta, m, \lambda$ being replaced by $r, a, b, 1, 1$.

Expressions for the local probabilities

We now return to the original problem of evaluating the RHS of (35). Take $r = 2k+1$, $a = 2k-1$, $b = 2$ in (51): then the $j = r$ term vanishes and the j, $r-j$ terms are equal, so we can replace the sum from $j = 1$ to r by twice the sum from $j = 1$ to k. Take y to be negative, as in (38): because $\theta_4(0, p)$, from (30.b), is a two-valued function of p, this means that we should replace $\theta_4(0, y^{rab})$ in (51) by its other branch $\theta_3(0, y^{rab})$. Now perform a conjugate modulus transformation. We obtain the identity

$$\sum_{j=1}^{k} (-x)^{(k-j)^2} E\left(x^{2j}, x^{2k+1}\right) E\left(x^{(4k-2)j}, x^{8k^2-2}\right) = \tfrac{1}{2} E\left(x, x^2\right) E\left(-1, x^{2k-1}\right) . \qquad (53)$$

Thus the RHS of (35) is half the product of two E functions, as we asserted earlier. Solving for $d(x)$, substituting into (30), using (33), we obtain

$$P_{k-j} = \frac{2\,(-x)^{(k-j)^2} E\left(x^{2j}, x^{2k+1}\right) E\left(x^{(4k-2)j}, x^{8k^2-2}\right)}{E\left(x, x^2\right) E\left(-1, x^{2k-1}\right)} . \qquad (54)$$

Alternatively, the conjugate modulus expression is

$$P_{k-j} = \frac{2\,\theta_1\left(\frac{\pi j}{r}, y^{r-2}\right) \theta_1\left(\frac{\pi j}{r}, y^2\right)}{r\,\theta_4\left(0, y^{2r(r-2)}\right) \theta_2\left(0, y^r\right)} , \qquad (55)$$

where x and y are related by (38).

Special cases

The identity (52) is equivalent, for $r = 2k+1$, $a = 2k-1$, $b = 2$, to (53): both are obtained by a conjugate modulus transformation of (51), the first with y positive, the second with y negative. Taking $k = 2$, $r = 5$, they reduce respectively to :

$$G(q^2)\,G(q^3) + q\,H(q^2)\,H(q^3) = P(q^3)/P(q) ,$$

$$H(x)\,G(x^6) - x\,G(x)\,H(x^6) = P(x)/P(x^3) . \qquad (56)$$

Both these identities were obtained by Ramanujan (eqns.7 and 8 of ref.7): we see that they are equivalent.

Another interesting special case is obtained by taking $a = 1, b = 4, r = 5$ in (52): we then obtain Ramanujan's identity (25).

4. Conclusions

It is remarkable how many of Ramanujan's and Rogers' identities lurk within the hard hexagon model: not only the famous Rogers-Ramanujan identities (15) - (16), but also the "sums-of-products" identities (19), (24) - (29). These enable one to readily determine the behaviour near $q = 1$ of the series (15), and hence to obtain the critical properties of the model. In particular, one obtains the critical exponent $\alpha = 1/3$.

Toward the end of section 2 we remarked that this value of α agrees quite well with experimental measurements for a film of helium adsorbed onto a graphite surface. The Rogers-Ramanujan identities are perhaps not so remote from "ordinary human activity" as Hardy would have liked (chapter 21 of ref.20)!

In section 3 we have remarked that there exists a more general model, corresponding to Gordon's generalization of the Rogers-Ramanujan identities. In this model, (19) generalizes to (53). We have shown how this identity can be put into a more illuminating Fourier-sum type form by making a conjugate modulus transformation. It is then a special case of the quite elegant identity (51).

References

1. R.B. Griffiths, Phys. Rev. Lett. **24** : 1479-1482 (1970).

2. R.J. Baxter, J. Phys. A. **13** : L61-L70 (1980).

3. R.J. Baxter, J. Stat. Phys. **26** : 427-452 (1981).

4. R.J. Baxter, "Exactly Solved Models in Statistical Mechanics" (Academic, London, 1982).

5. L.J. Rogers, Proc. London Math. Soc. (1), **25** : 318-343 (1894).

6. S, Ramanujan, Proc. Cambridge Phil. Soc. **19** : 214-216 (1919).

7. B.J. Birch, Math. Proc. Cambridge Phil. Soc. **78** : 73-79 (1975).

8. L.J. Rogers, Proc. London Math. Soc. (2) **19** : 387-397 (1921).

9. J. Tannery and J. Molk, "Eléments de la thèorie des Fonctions Elliptiques", reprinted by Chelsea Publishing Co., New York (1972).

10. M. Bretz, J.G. Dash, D.C. Hickernell, E.O. McLean, O.E. Vilches, Phys. Rev. A**8**, 1589-1615 (1973).

11. M.J. Tejwani, O. Ferreira and O.E. Vilches, Phys. Rev. Lett. **44**, 152-155 (1980).

12. B. Gordon, Am. J. Math. **83** : 393-399 (1961).

13. G.E. Andrews, "The Theory of Partitions" (Addison-Wesley, Reading, Massachusetts, 1976).

14. R.J. Baxter and G.E. Andrews, J. Stat. Phys. **44**, 249-271 (1986).

15. G.E. Andrews and R.J. Baxter, J. Stat. Phys. **44**, 713-728 (1986).

16. G.E. Andrews and R.J. Baxter, J. Stat. Phys., to appear (1987).

17. A. Kuniba, Y. Akutsu and M. Wadati, J. Phys. Soc. Japan **55** : 1092-1101; 2166-2176; 3338-3353 (1986).

18. E. Date, M. Jimbo, A. Kuniba, T. Miwa and M. Okado, Research Institute for Math. Sciences (Kyoto) pre-prints 564 and 566 (1987).

19. E.T. Whittaker and G.N. Watson, "A Course of Modern Analysis", Cambridge University Press (1962).

20. G.H. Hardy, "A mathematician's apology", Cambridge Univ. Press (1948).

Specialized characters for affine Lie algebras and the Rogers-Ramanujan identities

Kailash C. Misra*
Department of Mathematics
North Carolina State University
Raleigh, N.C. 27695-8205.

Introduction

As it is clear from the articles in this volume, Ramanujan's work has influenced many different areas of mathematics and physics. In this paper we will discuss how the celebrated Rogers-Ramanujan identities enter the representation theory of affine Lie algebras. Affine Lie algebras form an important class of infinite-dimensional Kac-Moody Lie algebras. The study of Kac-Moody Lie algebras started with the work of Victor Kac [5] and Robert Moody [32] around 1968. Since then the theory of Kac-Moody Lie algebras has attracted the attention of many researchers in mathematics and physics because of its surprising connections with different areas of mathematics and physics. Most of the connections known to date are related to the theory of affine Lie algebras. One of the reasons for this might be that the theory of affine Lie algebras has been well understood. Recently Mathieu [22] has shown that affine Lie algebras admit a concise characterization similar to simple finite-dimensional Lie algebras. One of the important features of the theory of affine Lie algebras which makes them so special is the existence of explicit constructions of some nontrivial irreducible highest weight representations. This leads to a

1980 Mathematics subject classification (Amer. Math. Soc.): 17 B 65, 05 A 19.
*partially supported by the Physical and Mathematical Sciences Foundation of N.C. State University.

ISBN 0-12-058560-X

number of interesting connections of affine Lie algebras with combinatorial identities. For a beautiful exposition on the interaction between theory of affine Lie algebras and combinatorial identities the reader is referred to [15]. In this note we will discuss only one aspect of these connections.

In [7] Kac started the study of the 'standard' (or 'integrable highest weight') representations of Kac-Moody Lie algebras. These are natural infinite-dimensional analogues of the finite-dimensional semisimple Lie algebras. Kac also proved the generalization of Weyl character formula for these representations of Kac-Moody Lie algebras associated to symmetrizable generalized Cartan matrices. More recently Kumar [12] and Mathieu [23] independently have generalized the Weyl-Kac character formula for certain representations of arbitrary Kac-Moody Lie algebras. It was first observed by Lepowsky and Milne [16] that the 'principal specialization' of the characters of certain standard representations of the affine Lie algebra $A_1^{(1)}$ differ by a simple factor from the product sides of the famous Rogers-Ramanujan identities. Further investigations were made in [3]. Then Lepowsky [13,14] proved the 'numerator formula' which implied that the principal specialization of the characters of the standard representations of any affine Lie algebra has a product expansion. Subsequently, Wakimoto [34] extended the numerator formula to some other specializations of the same representations.

In 1978 Lepowsky and Wilson [17] gave the first explicit construction of the level one standard representations of the affine Lie algebra $A_1^{(1)}$ on a certain polynomial algebra in infinitely many variables. This construction was generalized to all affine Lie algebras of ADE type in [10]. Using the concrete realizations of level one standard representations of $A_1^{(1)}$ Lepowsky and Wilson [19] gave the first Lie theoretic proof of the Rogers-Ramanujan identities. While trying to understand these connections between the representation theory of affine Lie algebras and the identities of Rogers-Ramanujan type Lepowsky and Wilson [18,20] discovered a new family of algebras, called $\underline{Z}$-algebras associated to each highest weight representation of an affine Lie algebra. These are algebras which centralize the action of certain infinite Heisenberg subalgebra of the affine Lie algebra. Lepowsky and Wilson [21] used these $\underline{Z}$-algebras and the generalized Rogers-Ramanujan identities due to Gordon, Andrews and Bressoud (cf. [1,2]) to give explicit constructions of all standard representations of $A_1^{(1)}$. Misra [26-29] used these $\underline{Z}$-algebras to construct certain standard representations of the affine Lie algebras $A_n^{(1)}$ and $C_n^{(1)}$. In the process Misra gave two new Lie theoretic proofs of the Rogers-Ramanujan identities. In [24] Mandia used the $\underline{Z}$-algebras and the Rogers-Ramanujan identities to construct the level one representations of the affine Lie algebras $B_n^{(1)}$, $G_2^{(1)}$ and $F_4^{(1)}$. More recently Meurman and Primc [25] have given Lie theoretic proofs of the generalized Rogers-Ramanujan identities using the higher level standard representations of $A_1^{(1)}$. Thus it has been established (for example, see [16-21,24-31] time and again that representation theory of affine Lie algebras can be used to proved combinatorial identities of Rogers-Ramanujan type. On the other hand identities of Rogers-Ramanujan type may be used to study the representation theory of affine Lie algebras.

In this paper our aim is to explain how the identities of Rogers-Ramanujan type enter the representation theory of affine Lie algebras. We have tried to make this paper self-contained as far as possible. At the end we have listed the principal characters of the affine Lie algebra representations which differ by a simple factor from the product sides of the Rogers-Ramanujan identities.

§1. Affine Lie algebras:

The Kac-Moody Lie algebras associated with an affine (or Euclidean) generalized Cartan matrix (GCM) are called affine Lie algebras. A GCM $A = (A_{ij})$ is an integral square matrix satisfying:

(i) $A_{ii} = 2$, for all i ,

(ii) $A_{ij} \leq 0$, for all $i \neq j$,

(iii) $A_{ij} = 0 \iff A_{ji} = 0$, for all $i \neq j$.

Two GCMs are said to be equivalent if one can be obtained from the other by a permutation of the indices. Any GCM $A = (A_{ij})$ is said to be indecomposable if it is not equivalent to a matrix of the form $\begin{bmatrix} B & 0 \\ 0 & B' \end{bmatrix}$ with B and B' nontrivial square matrices. An indecomposable GCM $A = (A_{ij})$ is an affine GCM if there is a nonzero column vector C of nonnegative integers such that $AC = 0$. Such a vector C is called a null vector. It can easily be checked that the transpose A^T of an affine GCM is again an affine GCM. A GCM $A = (A_{ij})$ is said to be symmetrizable if there exists a nonsingular diagonal matrix D such that DA is symmetric. It is not hard to see that an affine GCM is symmetrizable. The GCM $A = (A_{ij})$ is said to be of finite type if it is a Cartan matrix of a finite-dimensional split semisimple Lie algebra. It is worth pointing out that every principal submatrix of an affine GCM is of finite type.

The (complex) Kac-Moody Lie algebra corresponding to a (symmetrizable) GCM $A = (A_{ij})_{i,j=0}^{n}$ is defined (cf. [9]) to be the Lie algebra $\underline{\ell} = \underline{\ell}(A)$ on $3(n+1)$ (canonical) generators e_i, f_i, h_i $(i = 0,1,\cdots,n)$ and the following defining relations $(i,j = 0,1,\cdots,n)$:

$$(1.1)\quad \begin{cases} [h_i,h_j] = 0\ ,\ [e_i,f_i] = h_i\ ,\ [e_i,f_j] = 0 \quad \text{if} \quad i \neq j\ , \\ [h_i,e_j] = A_{ij}e_j\ ,\ [h_i,f_j] = -A_{ij}f_j \\ (\operatorname{ad} e_i)^{1-A_{ij}}e_j = 0\ ,\ (\operatorname{ad} f_i)^{1-A_{ij}}f_j = 0 \quad \text{if} \quad i \neq j\ . \end{cases}$$

The Lie algebra $\underline{\ell} = \underline{\ell}(A)$ corresponding to an affine GCM $A = (A_{ij})$ is called an affine Lie algebra. These algebras are infinite dimensional. Observe that a finite-dimensional (complex) simple Lie algebra $\underline{g}$ is a Kac-Moody Lie algebra whose GCM is the Cartan matrix of $\underline{g}$, and whose canonical generators are the usual canonical generators of $\underline{g}$. Also note that if A and B are equivalent GCM's, then the Kac-Moody Lie algebras $\underline{\ell}(A)$ and $\underline{\ell}(B)$ are isomorphic in an obvious way. The Lie algebra $\underline{\ell}(A^T)$ is said to be dual to the Lie algebra $\underline{\ell}(A)$ and will sometimes be denoted by $\underline{\ell}^\vee = \underline{\ell}(A)^\vee$. Hence dual of an affine Lie algebra is again an affine Lie algebra. Affine Lie algebras have been completely classified (cf.[9]) and they are one of the following:

Table Aff 1

$A_1^{(1)}$

$A_n^{(1)}$ $(n \geq 2)$

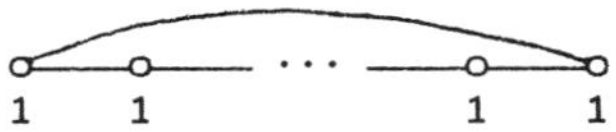

$B_n^{(1)}$ $(n \geq 3)$

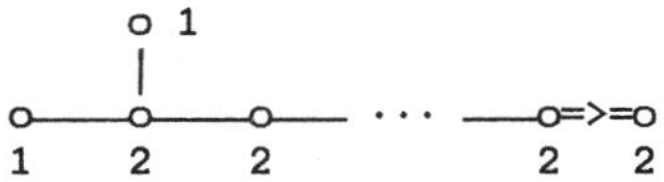

$C_n^{(1)}$ $(n \geq 2)$

$D_n^{(1)}$ $(n \geq 4)$

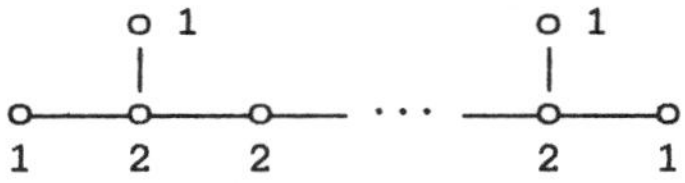

$G_2^{(1)}$

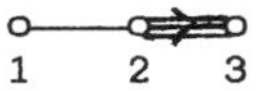

$F_4^{(1)}$

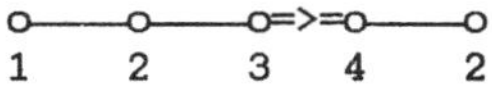

$E_6^{(1)}$

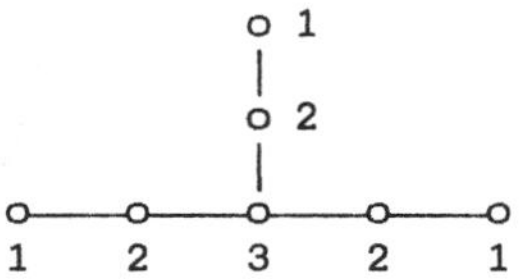

$E_7^{(1)}$

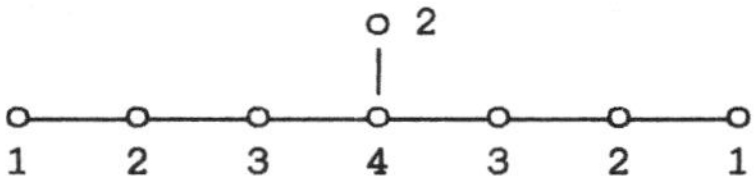

$E_8^{(1)}$

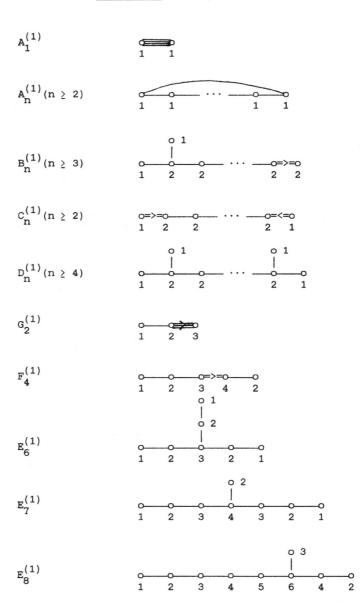

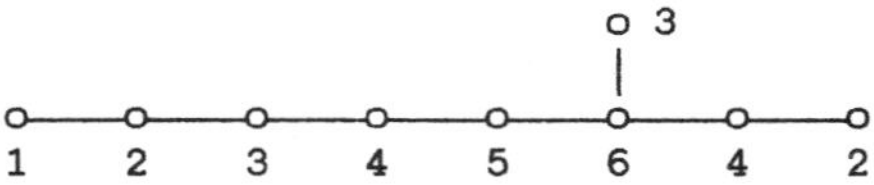

Table Aff 2

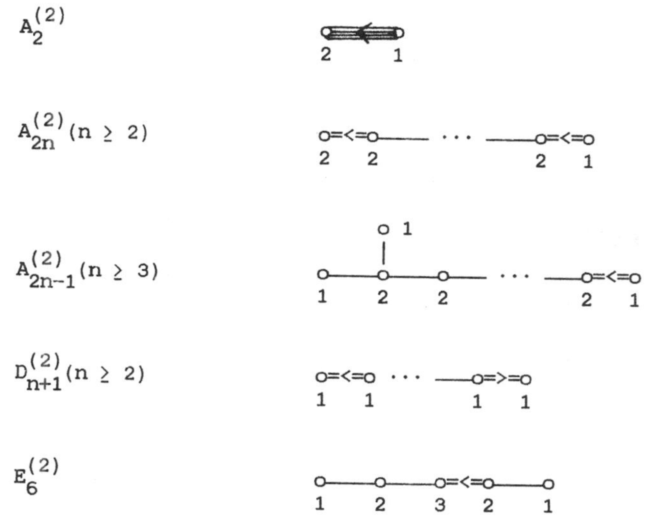

$A_2^{(2)}$

2   1

$A_{2n}^{(2)}\,(n \geq 2)$

2 2   2 1

$A_{2n-1}^{(2)}(n \geq 3)$

1 2 2   2 1

$D_{n+1}^{(2)}(n \geq 2)$

1 1   1 1

$E_6^{(2)}$

1 2 3 2 1

Table Aff 3

$D_4^{(3)}$

1 2 1

More precisely, in Table Aff 1 - 3, we have listed the Dynkin diagrams of the affine GCMs associated to the corresponding affine Lie algebras. The Dynkin diagram of the GCM $A = (A_{ij})_{i,j=0}^n$ consists of $n+1$ nodes $p_0, p_1, \cdots, p_n$. The nodes p_i and p_j are connected by $A_{ij}A_{ji}$ lines. Furthermore, if $|A_{ij}| > |A_{ji}|$ then there is an arrow pointing toward the node p_i. The numerical labels $a_0, a_1, \cdots, a_n$ in the tables are the smallest positive integral entries in the null vector of the corresponding GCM $A = (A_{ij})_{i,j=0}^n$. Note that $a_0 = 1$ except for $A_{2n}^{(2)}(n \geq 1)$, in which case $a_0 = 2$. Now observe that the Dynkin diagrams of the dual affine Lie algebras $\underline{\ell}(A)$ and $\underline{\ell}(A^T)$ can be obtained from each other by reversing the arrows. Also note that:

$$B_n^{(1)\vee} = A_{2n-1}^{(2)} , \quad C_n^{(1)\vee} = D_{n+1}^{(2)}$$

$$G_2^{(1)\vee} = D_4^{(3)} , \quad F_4^{(1)\vee} = E_6^{(1)} ,$$

and in all the other cases, the algebras are self-dual. Denote by $a_0', a_1', \cdots, a_n'$ the numerical labels in the Dynkin diagram of the dual algebra $\underline{\ell}(A^T)$ when $a_0, a_1, \cdots, a_n$ are the numerical labels in the Dynkin diagram of $\underline{\ell}(A)$. Note that in all cases $a_0' = 1$. The affine Lie algebra $\underline{\ell} = \underline{\ell}(A)$ with generators e_i, f_i, h_i $(i = 0,1,\cdots,n)$ has a 1-dimensional center spanned by $c = \sum_{i=0}^{n} a_i' h_i$. This element c is called the <u>canonical</u> <u>central</u> <u>element</u>.

§2. Root systems:

Let $\underline{\ell} = \underline{\ell}(A)$ be any affine Lie algebra with canonical generators e_i, f_i, h_i $(i = 0,1,\cdots,n)$. Then there exists unique derivations $D_0, \cdots, D_n$ of $\underline{\ell}$ such that for all $i,j = 0,1,\cdots,n$,

$$(2.1) \quad D_i e_j = \delta_{ij} = -D_i f_j .$$

Let d be the derivation

$$(2.2) \quad d = \sum_{i=0}^{n} s_i D_i$$

of $\underline{\ell}$, where $(s_0,s_1,\cdots,s_n)$ is some nonzero sequence of nonnegative integers. Consider the semidirect product Lie algebra

$$(2.3)\quad \tilde{\underline{\ell}} = \tilde{\underline{\ell}}(A) = \underline{\ell} \oplus \mathbb{C}d\ .$$

Let $\tilde{\underline{t}}$ denote the abelian subalgebra $\underline{t} \oplus \mathbb{C}d$, where $\underline{t} = \mathrm{span}\{h_0,h_1,\cdots,h_n\}$. For $0 \neq \alpha \in \tilde{\underline{t}}^*$, define

$$\underline{\ell}^{\alpha} = \{x \in \underline{\ell} \mid [h,x] = \alpha(h)x \quad \text{for all} \quad h \in \tilde{\underline{t}}\}.$$

Then

$$\Delta = \{\alpha \in \tilde{\underline{t}}^* \mid \alpha \neq 0 \quad \text{and} \quad \underline{\ell}^{\alpha} \neq (0)\}$$

is called the set of <u>roots</u>. The <u>simple</u> roots $\{\alpha_0,\alpha_1,\cdots,\alpha_n\} \subseteq \Delta$ are defined by the conditions $e_i \in \underline{\ell}^{\alpha_i}$, $i = 0,1,\cdots,n$. The simple roots are linearly independent. The set of <u>positive</u> roots Δ_+ is the set of roots which are nonnegative integral linear combinations of the simple roots. A root $\alpha \in \Delta$ is said to be <u>negative</u> if $-\alpha \in \Delta_+$. Let Δ_- be the set of negative roots. Then $\Delta = \Delta_+ \dot{\cup} \Delta_-$ and we have the triangular decompositions

$$\tilde{\underline{\ell}} = \underline{n}^- \oplus \tilde{\underline{t}} \oplus \underline{n}^+ \quad , \quad \underline{\ell} = \underline{n}^- \oplus \underline{t} \oplus \underline{n}^+$$

where $\underline{n}^{\pm} = \coprod_{\alpha\in\Delta_+} \underline{\ell}^{\pm\alpha}$.

For $i = 0,1,\cdots,n$ define the linear automorphisms r_i of $\tilde{\underline{t}}^*$ by:

(2.4) $r_i\beta = \beta - \beta(h_i)\alpha_i$

for all $\beta \in \tilde{\underline{t}}^*$. The Weyl group is the group W generated by $r_0, r_1, \cdots, r_n$. It is known that W is a Coxeter group. For $w \in W$, denote by $\ell(w)$ the length of a shortest expansion of w as a product of r_i's. Let ρ be any fixed element of $\tilde{\underline{t}}^*$ such that $\rho(h_i) = 1$ for all $i = 0, 1, \cdots, n$. Then it is known that for each $w \in W$, $\rho - w\rho$ is a sum of positive roots. Also if $w_1, w_2 \in W$, $w_1 \neq w_2$, then $\rho - w_1\rho \neq \rho - w_2\rho$.

A root $\alpha \in \Delta$ is called a real root if there exist an $w \in W$ such that $w\alpha = \alpha_i$ for some $i = 0, 1, \cdots, n$. If a root $\alpha \in \Delta$ is not real then it is called an imaginary root. A major deviation from finite dimensional semisimple theory is the existence of imaginary roots for affine Lie algebras. Let Δ^{re} denote the set of real roots and Δ^{im} denote the set of imaginary roots. Then $\Delta = \Delta^{re} \dot{\cup} \Delta^{im}$. Denote by

(2.5) $$\gamma = \sum_{i=0}^{n} a_i \alpha_i .$$

Then $\gamma \in \Delta^{im}$ and (cf. [9])

(2.6) $$\Delta^{im} = \{ j\gamma \mid 0 \neq j \in \mathbb{Z} \} .$$

For any $\alpha \in \Delta$, let $\mathrm{mult}(\alpha)$ denote the dimension of the α-root space $\underline{\ell}^{\alpha}$. Then it is known that

$$\mathrm{mult}(\alpha) = 1 , \quad \text{for all } \alpha \in \Delta^{re}$$

$$\text{and } \mathrm{mult}(\alpha) = \mathrm{rank}(A), \quad \text{for all } \alpha \in \Delta^{im},$$

where A is the affine GCM associated with the affine Lie algebra $\underline{\ell}$.

§3. Standard modules and the character formula

The standard modules (also known as 'integrable highest weight modules') are natural analogues of finite-dimensional irreducible modules. In 1974 Kac [7] started the study of these modules by proving a character formula (in the symmetrizable case) similar to Weyl character formula. More recently Kumar [12] and Mathieu [23] have proved similar character formula for arbitrary Kac-Moody Lie algebras.

Now we will define the standard module for our affine Lie algebra $\underline{\ell} = \underline{\ell}(A)$ and the extended affine Lie algebra $\tilde{\underline{\ell}} = \tilde{\underline{\ell}}(A)$. However, the corresponding definition holds for any Kac-Moody Lie algebra associated with a generalized Cartan matrix A.

Recall the abelian subalgebra $\tilde{\underline{t}}$ of $\tilde{\underline{\ell}}$ spanned by $h_0, h_1, \cdots, h_n$ and d. Let $\lambda \in \tilde{\underline{t}}^*$. A $\tilde{\underline{\ell}}$-module V generated by a vector $v_0 \neq 0$ such that $e_i \cdot v_0 = 0$ for $i = 0,1,\cdots,n$ and $h \cdot v_0 = \lambda(h)v_0$ for all $h \in \tilde{\underline{t}}$, is called a <u>highest weight module</u> with <u>highest weight</u> λ and <u>highest weight vector</u> v_0 (uniquely determined up to a scalar multiple). The scalar $\lambda(c) \in \mathbb{C}$ is said to be the <u>level</u> of V.

A highest weight $\tilde{\underline{\ell}}$-module with highest weight λ and corresponding highest weight vector v_0 is called a <u>standard $\tilde{\underline{\ell}}$-module</u> if there is an integer $r \geq 1$ such that $f_i^r \cdot v_0 = 0$ for $i = 0,1,\cdots,n$, which in turn implies that λ is <u>dominant integral</u>, that is, $\lambda(h_i) \in \mathbb{N}$ for $i = 0,1,\cdots,n$ (cf. [13]). For each dominant integral $\lambda \in \tilde{\underline{t}}^*$, there is a unique (up to isomorphism) standard $\tilde{\underline{\ell}}$-module $L(\lambda)$ and it is irreducible (cf. [9,13]).

In this paper, for convenience we will restrict our attention to the standard $\tilde{\underline{\ell}}$-modules $L(\lambda)$ with $\lambda(d) = 0$ so that $\lambda \in \mathrm{span}\{h_i^* | 0 \leq i \leq n\} \subseteq \tilde{\underline{t}}^*$

where $h_i^*(h_j) = \delta_{ij}$ and $h_i^*(d) = 0$, $0 \leq i, j \leq n$.

A standard $\underline{\ell}$-module by definition is the restriction to $\underline{\ell}$ of a standard $\tilde{\underline{\ell}}$-module.

Recall the simple roots $\alpha_0, \alpha_1, \cdots, \alpha_n \in \Delta$ of the affine Lie algebra $\underline{\ell}$ with respect to $\tilde{\underline{t}}$. Let $\underline{A} = \mathbb{Z}[[e(-\alpha_0), \cdots, e(-\alpha_n)]]$ be the ring of formal power series in analytically independent variables $e(-\alpha_0), \cdots, e(-\alpha_n)$. Here $e(\cdot)$ denotes a formal exponential with the property that $e(\alpha + \beta) = e(\alpha)e(\beta)$. Consider the standard $\tilde{\underline{\ell}}$-module $L = L(\lambda)$, with dominant integral weight $\lambda \in \tilde{\underline{t}}^*$ such that $\lambda(d) = 0$. Recall $\rho \in \tilde{\underline{t}}^*$ with $\rho(h_i) = 1$, $i = 0, 1, \cdots, n$. Then for each $w \in W$, $(\lambda + \rho) - w(\lambda + \rho)$ is a nonnegative integral linear combination of $\alpha_0, \alpha_1, \cdots, \alpha_n$. For $\mu \in \tilde{\underline{t}}^*$, define

$$(3.1) \quad L_\mu = \{x \in L \mid h \cdot x = \mu(h)x \text{ for all } h \in \tilde{\underline{t}}\} .$$

Then $L = \coprod_{\mu \in \tilde{t}^*} L_\mu$ with $\dim L_\mu < \infty$ for all $\mu \in \tilde{\underline{t}}^*$. Also $L_\mu \neq \{0\}$ implies that $\lambda - \mu$ is a nonnegative integral linear combination of $\alpha_0, \alpha_1, \cdots, \alpha_n$. Define the <u>character</u> $ch(L)$ of $L = L(\lambda)$ by the formal expression

$$(3.2) \quad ch(L) = \sum_{\mu \in \tilde{t}^*} (\dim L_\mu) e(\mu).$$

Then $e(-\lambda)ch(L) \in \underline{A}$ and we have Kac's generalization of Weyl's character formula:

<u>Theorem 3.1</u> (cf. [9,13]): In $\underline{A}$,

$$(3.3) \quad e(-\lambda)ch(L(\lambda)) = \underline{N}(\lambda)/\underline{D} ,$$

where the <u>numerator</u> is

(3.4) $$\underline{N}(\lambda) = \sum_{w\in W} (-1)^{\ell(w)} e(w(\lambda + \rho) - (\lambda + \rho))$$

and the denominator is

(3.5) $$\underline{D} = \prod_{\alpha\in\Delta_+} (1 - e(-\alpha))^{\mathrm{mult}(\alpha)}.$$ □

§4. Realizations of affine Lie algebras:

In this section we will follow the exposition in [20]. For more details see [20].

Let $\underline{g}$ be a finite-dimensional (complex) simple Lie algebra. Fix some Cartan subalgebra of $\underline{g}$. Let $<\ ,\ >$ denote the normalized Killing form of $\underline{g}$ so that the square length of a long root with respect to the fixed Cartan subalgebra is two. Let θ be an automorphism of $\underline{g}$ of order $K(= 1,2$ or $3)$ induced by an automorphism of order K of the Dynkin diagram of $\underline{g}$ with respect to the fixed Cartan subalgebra of $\underline{g}$. Let ϵ be a primitive K^{th} root of unit and for $i \in \mathbf{Z}$, let $\underline{g}_{[i]}$ denote the ϵ^i-eigenspace of θ in $\underline{g}$. Then the fixed space $\underline{g}_{[0]}$ is a simple subalgebra of $\underline{g}$. In fact, if $\underline{g}$ is of type $A_n, B_n, \cdots, G_2$, then the Dynkin diagrams of $\underline{g}_{[0]}$ can be obtained by removing the 0th node (i.e. the left most node) from the Dynkin diagram of $A_n^{(K)}, B_n^{(K)}, \cdots, G_2^{(1)}$, respectively, in Table Aff 1-3. Moreover, the $\underline{g}_{[0]}$-modules $\underline{g}_{[1]}$ and $\underline{g}_{[-1]}$ are irreducible and contragredient.

Fix a Cartan subalgebra $\underline{h}$ of $\underline{g}_{[0]}$ and let E_i, F_i, H_i $(i = 1,2,\cdots,n)$ be a corresponding set of canonical generators and $\beta_1, \beta_2, \cdots, \beta_n$ be the simple roots of $\underline{g}_{[0]}$. Choose a lowest weight vector E_0 of the $\underline{g}_{[0]}$-module $\underline{g}_{[1]}$ and a highest weight vector F_0 of the $\underline{g}_{[0]}$-module $\underline{g}_{[-1]}$ such that $[H_0, E_0] = 2E_0$, where $H_0 = [E_0, F_0]$. Let β_0 denote the lowest weight of the $\underline{g}_{[0]}$-module $\underline{g}_{[1]}$. For $i,j = 0,1,\cdots,n$, set $A_{ij} = \beta_j(H_i)$. Then the matrix $A = (A_{ij})_{i,j=0}^n$ is an affine GCM and all affine GCM's arise this way. Let $a_0, a_1, \cdots, a_n$ denote the smallest positive integral coefficients of linear dependence of the columns of the matrix A. Note that $a_0, a_1, \cdots, a_n$ are precisely the labels on the corresponding diagrams in Table Aff 1-3.

Let $(s) = (s_0, s_1, \cdots, s_n)$ be a sequence of nonnegative integers, not all zero. Take $m = K \sum_{i=0}^{n} s_i a_i$ and define the automorphism ν of $\underline{g}$ by the following conditions

$$(4.1) \quad \nu H_i = H_i \ , \ \nu E_i = \omega^{s_i} E_i \ , \ \nu F_i = \omega^{-s_i} F_i \ ,$$

$i = 0,1,\cdots,n,$ where ω is a primitive m^{th} root of unit. Call ν the (s)-automorphism of $\underline{g}$. For $p \in \mathbf{Z}_m = \mathbf{Z}/m\mathbf{Z}$ define

$$(4.2) \quad \underline{g}_{(p)} = \{x \in \underline{g} \,|\, \nu x = \omega^p x\} \ .$$

For $i \in \mathbf{Z}$, define $\underline{g}_{(i)} = \underline{g}_{(\bar{i})}$, where $\bar{i}$ denotes i reduced modulo m. This defines a $\mathbf{Z}_m$-gradation of $\underline{g}$ called the (s)-gradation in the sense that

$$\underline{g} = \coprod_{p \in \mathbf{Z}_m} \underline{g}_{(p)} \ , \ [\underline{g}_{(p)}, \underline{g}_{(r)}] \subseteq \underline{g}_{(p+r)}$$

for all $p, r \in \mathbf{Z}_m$. Consider the Lie algebra

$$(4.3) \quad \hat{\underline{g}}(1) = \underline{g} \otimes_{\mathbf{C}} \mathbf{C}[t,t^{-1}] \oplus \mathbf{C}c$$

where $\mathbf{C}[t,t^{-1}]$ denotes the commutative algebra of Laurent polynomials in the indeterminate t, c is a nonzero central element of $\hat{\underline{g}}(1)$ and

$$(4.4)\quad [x \otimes t^i, y \otimes t^j] = [x,y] \otimes t^{i+j} + m^{-1} i \delta_{i+j,0} \langle x,y\rangle c$$

for $x,y \in \underline{g}$ and $i,j \in \mathbb{Z}$. Let d be the derivation of $\hat{\underline{g}}(1)$ defined by the conditions

$$(4.5)\quad \begin{cases} d = 1 \otimes t \dfrac{d}{dt} \quad \text{on} \quad g \otimes \mathbb{C}[t,t^{-1}] \\ \text{and} \quad d(c) = 0 . \end{cases}$$

Consider the semidirect product Lie algebra

$$(4.6)\quad \tilde{\underline{g}}(1) = \hat{\underline{g}}(1) \oplus \mathbb{C}d .$$

Extend ν to a Lie algebra automorphism of $\tilde{\underline{g}}(1)$ by defining

$$(4.7)\quad \begin{cases} \nu(c) = c \ , \ \nu(d) = d \\ \nu(x \otimes t^i) = \nu x \otimes \omega^{-i} t^i \end{cases}$$

for $x \in \underline{g}$, $i \in \mathbb{Z}$. Let $\hat{\underline{g}}$ and $\tilde{\underline{g}}$ denote the ν-fixed points of $\hat{\underline{g}}(1)$ and $\tilde{\underline{g}}(1)$ respectively. Then observe that

$$(4.8)\quad \begin{cases} \hat{g} = \left[\coprod_{i\in\mathbb{Z}} g_{(i)} \otimes t^i \right] \oplus \mathbb{C}c \\ \\ \text{and} \quad \tilde{\underline{g}} = \hat{\underline{g}} \oplus \mathbb{C}d. \end{cases}$$

In $\hat{\underline{g}}$, set

$$(4.9)\quad \begin{cases} e_i = E_i \otimes t^{s_i} \\ \\ f_i = F_i \otimes t^{-s_i} \\ h_i = H_i \otimes 1 \oplus 2s_i \langle \beta_i,\beta_i\rangle^{-1} m^{-1} c \end{cases}$$

for $i = 0,1,\cdots,n$. The Lie algebra $\hat{\underline{g}} = \hat{\underline{g}}(A)$ with the system of canonical generators $\{e_i, f_i, h_i\}$ is isomorphic to the affine Lie algebra $\underline{\ell}(A)$ corresponding to the affine GCM $A = (\beta_j(H_i))_{i,j=0}^{n}$. This is called the (s)-realization of the affine Lie algebra $\underline{\ell}(A)$. The derivation d of $\hat{\underline{g}}$ defined by (4.5) is called the (s)-derivation of $\hat{\underline{g}}$. Observe that

$$(4.10)\quad d(h_i) = 0,\ d(e_i) = s_i e_i,\ d(f_i) = -s_i f_i$$

for $i = 0,1,\cdots,n$. For $j \in \mathbb{Z}$, define

$$(4.11)\quad \tilde{\underline{g}}_j = \{x \in \tilde{\underline{g}} \mid [d,x] = jx\}.$$

Then

$$(4.12)\quad \tilde{\underline{g}} = \coprod_{j\in\mathbb{Z}} \tilde{\underline{g}}_j ,$$

which gives a $\mathbb{Z}$-gradation of $\tilde{\underline{g}} = \tilde{\underline{g}}(A)$ in the sense that $[\tilde{\underline{g}}_i, \tilde{\underline{g}}_j] \subseteq \tilde{\underline{g}}_{i+j}$. This induces naturally a $\mathbb{Z}$-gradation in the universal enveloping algebra $U(\tilde{\underline{g}})$:

$$(4.13)\quad U(\tilde{\underline{g}}) = \coprod_{i\in\mathbb{Z}} U(\tilde{\underline{g}})_i .$$

Consider the abelian subalgebra

$$(4.14)\quad \tilde{\underline{h}} = \underline{h} \oplus \mathbb{C}c \oplus \mathbb{C}d$$

spanned by $h_0, h_1, \cdots, h_n$ and d. Let $\lambda \in \tilde{\underline{h}}^*$, with $\lambda(h_i) \in \mathbb{N}$, $\lambda(d) = 0$, $i = 0,1,\cdots,n$. Consider the standard $\tilde{\underline{g}}$-module $L = L(\lambda)$ with highest weight λ and highest weight vector $v_0 \neq 0$. Denote by $L_i \subseteq L(\lambda)$ the eigenspace of d with eigenvalue $i \in \mathbf{Z}$. Then

$$(4.15)\quad L(\lambda) = \coprod_{i \le 0} L_i ,$$

where $L_0 = \mathbf{C}v_0$, $L_i = U(\tilde{\underline{g}})_i \cdot v_0$ and $\dim(L_i) < \infty$. Define the <u>(s)-character</u> of $L = L(\lambda)$ by

$$(4.16)\quad \chi(L) = \sum_{i \ge 0} (\dim L_{-i}) q^i \in \mathbf{Z}[[q]],$$

where q is an indeterminate.

§5. Specialized characters and the numerator formula:

Let $(s) = (s_0, s_1, \cdots, s_n)$ be a sequence of positive integers. Then the <u>(s)-specialization</u> <u>homomorphism</u> $f_{(s)}$ is defined by

$$f_{(s)} : \underline{A} \longrightarrow \mathbf{Z}[[q]]$$

$$e(-\alpha_i) \longrightarrow q^{s_i} , \quad i = 0,1,\cdots,n .$$

The homomorphism $f_{(s)}$ is also called the <u>specialization</u> <u>of</u> <u>type (s)</u>. The specialization of type $(1) = (1,1,\cdots,1)$ is called the <u>principal specialization</u>.

Let $L = L(\lambda)$ be a standard $\tilde{\underline{g}}$-module with highest weight λ $(\lambda(d) = 0)$. Recall that $e(-\lambda)\mathrm{ch}(L) \in \underline{A}$. For the (s)-specialization $f_{(s)}(e(-\lambda)\mathrm{ch}(L))$ is called the <u>(s)-specialized</u> <u>characters</u>. The principal specialization $f_{(1)}(e(-\lambda)\mathrm{ch}(L))$ is called the <u>principally</u> <u>specialized</u> <u>character</u> (or the <u>principal</u> <u>character</u>). Observe that the (s)-character of L:

$$(5.1) \quad \chi(L) = f_{(s)}(e(-\lambda)ch(L)),$$

that is to say that the (s)-character is the same as the (s)-specialized character of the standard $\tilde{\underline{g}}$-module $L = L(\lambda)$.

Fix an affine GCM $A = (A_{ij})_{i,j=0}^{n}$. Choose a sequence of positive integers $(s) = (s_0, s_1, \cdots, s_n)$ such that $A' = (A'_{ij})_{i,j=0}^{n}$ is again an affine GCM where $A'_{ij} = s_j A_{ji} s_i^{-1}$, $i,j = 0,1,\cdots,n$. For example the sequence $(1) = (1,1,\cdots,1)$ satisfies this condition. Now consider the two extended affine Lie algebras $\tilde{\underline{g}} = \tilde{\underline{g}}(A)$ and $\tilde{\underline{g}}' = \tilde{\underline{g}}(A')$. Recall the denominator (see (3.5))

$$\underline{D} = \prod_{\alpha\in\Delta_+} (1 - e(-\alpha))^{\mathrm{mult}(\alpha)},$$

for $\tilde{\underline{g}}$. Let $\underline{D}'$ denote the corresponding denominator for $\tilde{\underline{g}}'$. For a standard $\tilde{\underline{g}}$-module $L = L(\lambda)$ with dominant integral highest weight λ recall the numerator (see (3.4)),

$$\underline{N}(\lambda) = \sum_{w\in W} (-1)^{\ell(w)} e(w(\lambda + \rho) - (\lambda + \rho)).$$

Now we are ready to state the following numerator formula:

<u>Theorem 5.1</u> [13,14,34]: For the above choice of the sequence $(s) = (s_0, s_1, \cdots, s_n)$, the (s)-specialization of the numerator $N(\lambda)$ equals to the $(s_0(\lambda(h_0) + 1), \cdots, s_n(\lambda(h_n) + 1))$-specialization of the denominator $\underline{D}'$ for the Lie algebra $\tilde{\underline{g}}'$. □

As an immediate consequence of Theorems 3.1, 5.1 and Equation 5.1, we have the following:

Corollary 5.2: For the above choice of the sequence $(s) = (s_0, s_1, \cdots, s_n)$, the (s)-specialized character of the standard $\tilde{\underline{g}}$-module $L = L(\lambda)$ with highest weight λ has an infinite product expansion. □

Theorem 5.1 was first proved by Lepowsky [13,14] for the principal specialization case, that is when $(s) = (1) = (1,1,\cdots,1)$. It was subsequently generalized by Wakimoto [34].

§6. Principal character and the Rogers-Ramanujan identities:

In this section we will discuss the case $(s) = (1)$, meaning the $(1,1,\cdots,1)$-specialization, that is the principal specialization only. The (1)-realization of the affine Lie algebra $\underline{\ell}(A)$ is called the principal realization, the (1)-character is called the principal character, the (1)-automorphism ν is called the principal automorphism and so on.

Recall the denominator $\underline{D}$ (see (3.5)) for the Lie algebra $\tilde{\underline{g}} = \tilde{\underline{g}}(A)$. Denote the denominator for the dual Lie algebra $\tilde{\underline{g}}^{\vee} = \tilde{\underline{g}}(A^T)$ by $\underline{D}^{\vee}$. Then we have the following:

Lemma 6.1 [13,14]: The principal specialization of $\underline{D}$ is equal to the principal specialization of $\underline{D}^{\vee}$. □

Consider the standard $\tilde{\underline{g}}$-module $L = L(\lambda)$ with highest weight $\lambda = \sum_{i=0}^{n} k_i h_i^* \in \tilde{\underline{h}}^*$ $(\lambda(d) = 0)$ (see Section 3). We will sometimes write the principal character $\chi(L)$ as $\chi(k_0,\cdots,k_n)$. Now it follows from Theorems 3.1, 5.1 and Lemma 6.1 that the principal character $\chi(L) = \chi(k_0,\cdots,k_n)$ of the standard $\tilde{\underline{g}}$-module has a product expansion given by the following formula:

(6.1) $\chi(k_0,\cdots,k_n)$

$$= \frac{(k_0+1,\cdots,k_n+1)\text{-specialization of } D^{\vee}}{(1,\cdots,1)\text{-specialization of } D^{\vee}} .$$

From Section 4, recall the Lie algebra $\underline{g}_{[0]}$, the θ-fixed points of the finite-dimensional simple Lie algebra $\underline{g}$. Note that E_i, F_i, H_i $(i = 1,2,\cdots,n)$ are the canonical generators of $\underline{g}_{[0]}$ with respect to the Cartan subalgebra $\underline{h}$. Define $E = \sum_{i=0}^{n} E_i$ (E_0 being the lowest weight vector of the $\underline{g}_{[0]}$-module $\underline{g}_{[1]}$) and $\underline{a} = \{x \in \underline{g} \mid [x,E] = 0\}$, the centralizer of E. Then $\underline{a}$ is a Cartan subalgebra of $\underline{g}$ [8,11] and it is stable under the principal automorphism ν. Hence $\underline{a}$ is $\mathbb{Z}_m$-graded. The <u>principal Heisenberg subalgebra</u> $\underline{s}$ of $\tilde{\underline{g}}$ is defined by

(6.2) $\underline{s} = \underline{s}^- \oplus \mathbb{C}c \oplus \underline{s}^+$

where

$$\underline{s}^+ = \coprod_{i>0} (a_{(i)} \otimes t^i)$$

and

$$\underline{s}^- = \coprod_{i<0} (a_{(i)} \otimes t^i) .$$

Denote by $\Omega(L) = \Omega(L(\lambda))$ the vacuum space of $L = L(\lambda)$, that is,

(6.3) $\Omega(L) = \{v \in L \mid \underline{s}^+ \cdot v = 0\}$.

Then we have a linear isomorphism (see [19]):

(6.4) $\Psi: U(\underline{s}^-) \otimes_{\mathbb{C}} \Omega(L) \longrightarrow L$

$$u \otimes v \longmapsto u \cdot v$$

In particular,

(6.5) $\chi(L) = F\,\chi(\Omega(L))$

where

$$F = \chi(U(\underline{s}^-)) = \prod_{i>0} (1 - q^i)^{-\dim a_{(i)}}$$

is called the <u>fundamental</u> <u>character</u>. These fundamental characters are listed in Table E of [10] for each affine Lie algebra. Let us write

(6.6) $\Omega(k_0, \cdots, k_n) = \chi(\Omega(L))$

where $L = L(\lambda)$ has highest weight $\lambda = k_0 h_0^* + \cdots + k_n h_n^*$. Note that in this case the level of L is equal to $k = \lambda(c) = \sum_{i=0}^{n} a_i^\prime k_i$. Also let us denote the two famous Rogers-Ramanujan products by

(6.7) $G(q) = \prod_{j=0}^{\infty} (1 - q^{5j+1})^{-1}(1 - q^{5j+4})^{-1}$

(6.8) $H(q) = \prod_{j=0}^{\infty} (1 - q^{5j+2})^{-1}(1 - q^{5j+3})^{-1}$.

Then using (6.1) and (6.5) one can easily check the following:

I. For the affine Lie algebra $A_1^{(1)}$:

(6.9) $\Omega(1,2) = \Omega(2,1) = G(q)$.

(6.10) $\Omega(0,3) = \Omega(3,0) = H(q)$.

II. For the affine Lie algebra $A_2^{(2)}$:

(6.11) $\Omega(2,0) = G(q^2)$.

(6.12) $\Omega(0,1) = H(q^2)$.

III. For the affine Lie algebra $A_2^{(1)}$:

(6.13) $\Omega(1,1,0) = \Omega(0,1,1) = \Omega(1,0,1) = G(q)$.

(6.14) $\Omega(2,0,0) = \Omega(0,2,0) = \Omega(0,0,2) = H(q)$.

IV. For the affine Lie algebra $C_3^{(1)}$:

(6.15) $\Omega(0,1,0,0) = \Omega(0,0,1,0) = G(q^2)$.

(6.16) $\Omega(1,0,0,0) = \Omega(0,0,0,1) = H(q^2)$.

V. For the affine Lie algebra $G_2^{(1)}$:

(6.17) $\Omega(0,0,1) = G(q^3)$.

(6.18) $\Omega(1,0,0) = H(q^3)$.

VI. For the affine Lie algebra $F_4^{(1)}$:

(6.19) $\Omega(0,0,0,1) = G(q^4)$.

(6.20) $\Omega(1,0,0,0) = H(q^4)$.

VII. For the affine Lie algebra $A_7^{(2)}$:

(6.21) $\Omega(1,1,0,0,0) = G(q)$.

(6.22) $\Omega(0,0,0,1,0) = H(q)$.

These are the only cases where the Rogers-Ramanujan products appears explicitly in the principal characters of the corresponding representations.

Similarly using (6.1) one can check that the generalized Rogers-Ramanujan products due to Gordon, Andrews and Bressoud (cf. [1,2]) appear in (i) the higher level standard $A_1^{(1)}$-modules, (ii) the level two standard $A_n^{(1)}$-modules, (iii) the level one standard $C_n^{(1)}$-modules, (iv) the higher level standard $G_2^{(1)}$-modules, (v) the higher level standard $F_4^{(1)}$-modules, etc. As we have pointed out earlier these informations have already proved to be very useful not only by establishing new connections between combinatorial identities and theory of Kac-Moody Lie algebras, but also providing new ideas leading to better understanding of the representation theory of Kac-Moody Lie algebras. We believe that once these connections are fully understood then the representation theory of affine Lie algebras can be used to generate new identities of Rogers-Ramanujan type.

References

[1] Andrews, G. E.: The theory of partitions, Encyclopedia of Mathematics and its applications, Vol. 2, ed. G.-C. Rota, Addison-Wesley, Reading, Mass., 1976.

[2] Bressoud, D.: Analytic and combinatorial generalizations of the Rogers-Ramanujan identities. Memoirs Amer. Math. Soc. 24 (1980), Number 227.

[3] Feingold, A., Lepowsky, J.: The Weyl-Kac character formula and power series identities. Advances in Math. 29 (1978), 271-309.

[4] Humphreys, J. E.: Introduction to Lie Algebras and Representation Theory. Springer-Verlag, Berlin-Heidelberg-New York, 1972.

[5] Kac, V. G.: Simple irreducible graded Lie algebras of finite growth. Izv. AAkad. Nauk USSR 32 (1968), 1323-1367. English translation: Math. USSR Izv. 2 (1968), 1271-1311.

[6] Kac, V. G.: Automorphisms of finite order of semisimple Lie algebras. Funkcional. Anal. i Prilozhen. 3 (1969), 94-96, English translation: Functional Anal. Appl. 3 (1969), 252-254.

[7] Kac, V. G.: Infinite-dimensional Lie algebras and Dedekind's η-function. Funkcional. Anal. i Prilozhen. 8 (1974), 77-78, English translation: Functional Anal. Appl. 8 (1974), 68-70.

[8] Kac, V. G.: Infinite-dimensional algebras, Dedekind's η-function, classical Mobius function and the very strange formula. Advances in Math. 30 (1978), 85-136.

[9] Kac, V. G.: Infinite-dimensional Lie Algebras, Second edition. Cambridge University Press, Cambridge (1985).

[10] Kac, V. G., Kazhdan, D. A., Lepowsky, J., Wilson, R. L.: Realization of the basic representations of the Euclidean Lie algebras. Advances in Math. 42 (1981), 83-112.

[11] Kostant, B.: The principal three-dimensional subgroup and the Betti numbers of a complex simple Lie group. Amer. J. Math. 81 (1959), 973-1032.

[12] Kumar, S.: Demazure character formula in arbitrary Kac-Moody setting. Invent. Math. 89 (1987), 395-423.

[13] Lepowsky, J.: Lectures on Kac-Moody Lie algebras. Université Paris VI, Spring, 1978.

[14] Lepowsky, J.: Application of the numerator formula to k-rowed plane partitions. Advances in Math. 35 (1980), 179-194.

[15] Lepowsky, J.: Affine Lie algebras and combinatorial identities. Proc. 1981 Rutgers Conference on Lie algebras and related topics. Springer-Verlag Lecture notes in Mathematics 933 (1982), 130-156.

[16] Lepowsky, J., Milne, S.: Lie algebraic approaches to classical partition identities. Advances in Math. 29 (1978), 15-59.

[17] Lepowsky, J., Wilson, R. L.: Construction of the affine Lie algebra $A_1^{(1)}$. Comm. Math. Phys. 62 (1978), 43-53.

[18] Lepowsky, J., Wilson, R. L.: A new family of algebras underlying the Rogers-Ramanujan identities and generalizations. Proc. Nat. Acad. Sci. U.S.A. 78 (1981), 7254-7258.

[19] Lepowsky, J., Wilson, R. L.: A Lie theoretic interpretation and proof of the Rogers-Ramanujan identities. Advances in Math. 45 (1982), 21-72.

[20] Lepowsky, J., Wilson, R. L.: The structure of standard modules, I: Universal algebras and the Rogers-Ramanujan identities. Invent. Math. 77 (1984), 199-290.

[21] Lepowsky, J., Wilson, R. L.: The structure of standard modules, II: The case $A_1^{(1)}$, principal gradation. Invent. Math. 79 (1985), 417-442.

[22] Mathieu, O.: Classification des algèbres de Lie graduées simples de croissance $\leq$ 1. Invent. Math. 86 (1986), 371-426.

[23] Mathieu, O.: The Demazure-Weyl formulas and generalizations of the Borel-Weil-Bott theorem. C.R. Acad. Sc. Paris, t. 303, Serie I, No. 9 (1986), 391-394.

[24] Mandia, M.: Structure of the level one standard modules for the affine Lie algebras $B_\ell^{(1)}$, $F_4^{(1)}$, and $G_2^{(1)}$. AMS Memoirs, 362, (1987).

[25] Meurman, A., Primc, M.: Annihilating ideals of standard modules of $\underline{sl}\ (2,C)^{\sim}$ and combinatorial identities. Advances in Math. (1987).

[26] Misra, K. C.: Structure of certain standard modules for $A_n^{(1)}$ and the Rogers-Ramanujan identities. J. Algebra 88 (1984), 196-227.

[27] Misra, K. C.: Structure of some standard modules for $C_n^{(1)}$. J. Algebra 90 (1984), 385-409.

[28] Misra, K. C.: Standard representations of some affine Lie algebras. In: Vertex Operators in Mathematics and Physics, eds. J. Lepowsky, S. Mandelstam and I. M. Singer. Publ. Math. Sci. Res. Inst. #3, Springer-Verlag, New York, (1985), 163-183.

[29] Misra, K. C.: Constructions of fundamental representations of symplectic affine Lie algebras. In: Topological and geometrical methods in field theory, ed. J. Hietarinta and J. Westerholm. World Scientific, Singapore, (1986), 147-169.

[30] Misra, K. C.: Basic representations of some affine Lie algebras and generalized Euler identities. J. Austral. Math. Soc. (Series A) 42 (1987), 296-311.

[31] Misra, K. C.: Level two standard representations of some affine Lie algebras and generalized Rogers-Ramanujan identities. manuscript in preparation.

[32] Moody, R. V.: A new class of Lie algebras. J. Algebra 10 (1968), 211-230.

[33] Moody, R. V.: Euclidean Lie algebras. Canad. J. Math. 21 (1969), 1432-1454.

[34] Wakimoto, M.: Two formulae for specialized characters of Kac-Moody Lie algebras. Hiroshima University preprint.

THE EXACT FORMULA FOR THE WEIGHT MULTIPLICITIES OF AFFINE LIE ALGEBRAS, I

by

C.J. MORENO AND A. ROCHA-CARIDI

Baruch College, CUNY

New York, NY 10010

Table of Contents

Proceedings of the Ramanujan Centenary Conference, June 1-5, 1987, University of Illinois, Urbana, IL 61801

ISBN 0-12-058560-X

"...one of the crowning achievements in the theory of partitions: the exact formula for p(n), an achievement undertaken and mostly completed by G. H. Hardy and S. Ramanujan and fully completed and perfected by H. Rademacher."

— George Andrews, The Theory of Partitions, Encyclopedia of Mathematics and its Applications, 2, Addison-Wesley, Reading, Massachusetts (1976).

1. Introduction

The analytic theory of partitions seems to have originated with Ramanujan; in fact in one of his early letters to Hardy, Ramanujan already proposes what he believed to be a good approximation for the n-th Fourier coefficient of the reciprocal of one of Jacobi's even theta functions (Hardy [8], p.8, eqn. 1.14). Later on, while in England, in joint work with Hardy, Ramanujan developed along the lines of the circle method and using the modular properties of the generating function, a finite asymptotic expression capable of producing fairly accurate numerical results (Ramanujan [24], no. 36). It was shown by Lehmer that the Hardy-Ramanujan formula when extended to infinity diverges. Subsequently it was shown by Rademacher ([21]) that the parameters needed in the circle method could be kept free until the last step when the contributions from all the rational points were taken into consideration. In this way Rademacher not only arrived at an exact formula given by an infinite series, but also showed that a finite number of terms would give good approximations to the partition function. The rest of the story of how Rademacher and his school developed these ideas into a powerful tool in the theory of modular forms of negative weight is well known.

The purpose of the present paper is to apply the Hardy-Ramanujan-Rademacher approach to the string functions associated with affine Lie algebras. These are the generating functions for the dimensions of the weightspaces, also called weight multiplicities, of the integrable irreducible highest weight representations of the affine Lie algebras. Kac and Peterson ([14,15]) have shown that the string functions behave like modular forms of negative weight. In this paper we use the modular transformation properties obtained by Kac and Peterson to adapt the circle method to the string functions. The result is an exact formula for the weight multiplicities! The formula obtained here is our starting point for further investigations on the string functions. For a brief announcement of our results we refer the reader to [19].

The plan of the paper is as follows. In §1 the basic definitions and results on the affine Lie algebras are recalled. Here, the modular transformation formula for the string functions, on which the treatment of the subject is based, is given in a form suitable to our approach. In §2 the actual proof of the Rademacher formula is given. The main difficulty that arises here is due to the fact that the string functions are not exactly modular forms for the full modular group; they transform under a finite dimensional representation of the quotient group $\Gamma/\Gamma(N^*)$ for a certain N^*. The reason for not applying the Rademacher-Zuckerman variant of the method ([26]) to the subgroup $\Gamma(N^*)$ is that for subsequent applications it is desirable to work with the group Γ. In §3 we present a series of examples of the type of formulas we obtain. Of particular interest is the case of the affine Lie algebra of type $C_\ell^{(1)}$ and level 1. We also present other examples which are quite interesting both from physical and group theoretical points of view; notably the generating function for the number of open bosonic strings is related to the string function for the affine Lie algebra $A_{24}^{(1)}$. This string function also appears to be related to the classical modular invariant j which enters in the infinite dimensional graded representation of the Fischer-Griess group F_1 constructed by Frenkel, Lepowsky and Meurman ([4]) in accordance to the Conway-Norton conjectures.

Acknowledgement: We thank J. Lepowsky for stimulating discussion on the Monster and the modular invariant j.

§1. String Functions

In this section we shall primarily review the results of [14] and [15] on string functions. Our main purpose is to state a version of the transformation law for string functions obtained in [14] and [15]. This result will be used in the next section to derive explicit formulas for the coefficients of the string functions.

We begin by recalling some basic definitions and results from the theory of affine Lie algebras. Complete details are found in [10], [17], [18], [11], [6] and [12].

Let $\underline{g}$ be a complex simple Lie algebra. Let $\underline{h}$ be a Cartan subalgebra of $\underline{g}$ and denote by Δ the root system of $(\underline{g},\underline{h})$. Then $\underline{g} = \underline{h} \oplus (\bigoplus_{\alpha\in\Delta} \underline{g}_\alpha)$, where $\underline{g}_\alpha = \{X \in g \mid [H_1 X] = \alpha(H)X$ for all $H \in \underline{h}\}$. We fix a set of positive roots Δ_+ and let $\Pi = \{\alpha_1,\ldots,\alpha_\ell\}$ be the set of simple roots. Let θ be the highest root of Δ_+. Let $(X,Y) = (2g)^{-1}B(X,Y)$ for all $X,Y \in \underline{g}$, where B is the killing form of $\underline{g}$ and $g = B(\theta,\theta)^{-1}$. W denotes the Weyl group of $(\underline{g},\underline{h})$.

We denote by $\hat{\underline{g}}$ the (untwisted) affine Lie algebra associated with $\underline{g}$. That is,

$$\hat{\underline{g}} = (\mathbb{C}[t,t^{-1}] \otimes \underline{g}) \oplus \mathbb{C}c \oplus \mathbb{C}d, \text{ where } c \text{ is central}$$

and we define

$$[P \otimes X, Q \otimes Y] = PQ \otimes [X,Y] + \operatorname{Res}\left(\frac{dp}{dt} Q\right)(X,Y)\,c,$$
$$[d, P \otimes X] = t\,\frac{dp}{dt} \otimes X \quad\text{and}\quad [d,d] = 0,$$

for all $P,Q \in \mathbb{C}[t,t^{-1}]$, $X,Y \in g$. $\hat{\underline{h}} = \underline{h} \oplus \mathbb{C}c \oplus \mathbb{C}d$ is the Cartan

<u>subalgebra</u> of $\hat{\underline{g}}$. We extend (,) to $\hat{\underline{h}} \times \hat{\underline{h}}$ by setting $(H,C) = (H,d) = 0$ for all $H \in \underline{h}$, $(c,d) = 1$, and $(c,c) = (d,d) = 0$. For each $\lambda \in \hat{\underline{h}}^*$ let H_λ be the unique element in $\hat{\underline{h}}$ such that $(H_\lambda, H) = \lambda(H)$ for all $H \in \hat{\underline{h}}$ and set $(\lambda,\mu) = (H_\lambda, H_\mu)$, $\lambda,\mu \in \hat{\underline{h}}^*$.

We view $\underline{h}^*$ as a subspace of $\hat{h}^*$ by setting $\lambda(c) = \lambda(d) = 0$ for $\lambda \in \underline{h}^*$. Let δ be the unique element of $\hat{\underline{h}}^*$ such that $\delta(\underline{h} \oplus \mathbb{C}c) = (0)$ and $\delta(d) = 1$, and put $\alpha_o = \delta - \theta$. One has $\hat{\underline{g}} = \hat{\underline{h}} \oplus (\bigoplus_{\alpha \in \hat{\Delta}} \underline{g}_\alpha)$, where $\hat{\underline{g}}_\alpha = \{X \in \hat{\underline{g}} \mid [H,X] = \alpha(H)X$ for all $H \in \hat{h}\}$ and $\hat{\Delta}$ is the <u>root system</u> of $(\hat{g},\hat{h})$, that is, $\hat{\Delta} = \{\alpha \in \hat{h}^* \mid \hat{g}_\alpha \neq (0)\}$. Then $\hat{\Pi} = \{\alpha_o, \alpha_{-1}, \cdots, \alpha_\ell\} \subset \hat{\Delta}$. $\hat{\Pi}$ is the set of <u>simple roots</u> of $\hat{\Delta}$. Let $\hat{Q} = Z\hat{\Pi}$ be the root lattice and let $\hat{Q}_+ = Z_+\hat{\Pi}$ be the subsemigroup of $\hat{Q}$ generated by $\hat{\Pi}$. $\hat{\Delta}_+ = \Delta \cap Q_+$ is the <u>set of positive roots</u> of $\hat{\Delta}$.

Let $\sigma_i : \hat{\underline{h}}^* \longrightarrow \hat{\underline{h}}^*$ be the reflection: $\sigma_i(\lambda) = \lambda - 2\dfrac{(\lambda_i,\alpha_i)}{(a_i \cdot \alpha_i)}\alpha_i$ $i = 0,1,\cdots,\ell$. The Weyl group $\hat{W}$ of $(\hat{\underline{g}},\hat{\underline{h}})$ is the subgroup of $\mathrm{Aut}(\hat{\underline{h}}^*)$ generated by $\{\sigma_i\}_{i=o}^{\ell}$.

We now describe the representations of $\hat{\underline{g}}$ that give rise to the string functions. Their construction is standard in representation theory (see [11] and [6]). Set $\hat{\underline{n}}_\pm = \bigoplus_{\alpha \in \hat{\Delta}_+} \underline{g}_\alpha$, $\hat{\underline{b}} = \hat{\underline{h}} \oplus \hat{\underline{n}}_+$. For each $\Lambda \in \hat{\underline{h}}^*$, let $\mathbb{C}(\Lambda)$ be the one-dimensional $U(\hat{b})$-module annihilated by $\hat{\underline{n}}_+$ and with $\hat{\underline{h}}$ - action given by Λ. (Here $U(\underline{a})$ is the universal enveloping algebra of $\underline{a}$.) Let $M(\Lambda) = U(\hat{g}) \otimes_{U(\hat{b})} \mathbb{C}(\Lambda)$ be the <u>Verma module</u> associated with $\hat{\underline{g}}, \hat{\underline{b}}$ and Λ. We denote by $L(\Lambda)$ its unique irreducible quotient. $L(\Lambda)$ has a <u>weightspace decomposition</u>. $L(\Lambda) = \bigoplus_{\lambda \in P(\Lambda)} L(\Lambda)_\lambda$, where $L(\Lambda)_\lambda = \{v \in L(\Lambda) \mid Hv = \lambda(H)v$, for all $H \in \hat{\underline{h}}\}$ is the λ-<u>weightspace</u> of $L(\Lambda)$ and $P(\Lambda) = \{\lambda \in \hat{\underline{h}}^* \mid L(\Lambda)_\lambda \neq (0)\}$ is the set of <u>weights</u> of $L(\Lambda)$. The <u>character</u> of $L(\Lambda)$ is defined to be the formal sum

$$(1.1) \qquad \mathrm{Ch}\, L(\Lambda) = \sum_{\lambda \in P(\Lambda)} \dim L(\Lambda)_\lambda e^\lambda,$$

where e^{λ} is the characteristic function of $\{\lambda\}$.

Let P(resp. P^+) denote the set of integral (resp. <u>dominant integral</u>) weights, i.e., P (resp. P^+) $= \{\lambda \in \underline{h}^* | 2\frac{(\lambda,\alpha_i)}{(\alpha_i,\alpha_i)} \in Z$ (resp. Z_+) for $i = 0,1,\cdots,\ell\}$. As in the classical theory, P^+ indexes an important class of representations $L(\Lambda)$ known as standard or <u>integrable modules</u>. From now on we assume that $\Lambda \in P^+$. If $\lambda \in P(\Lambda)$ one has

$$(1.2) \qquad \dim L(\Lambda)_{\lambda} = \dim L(\Lambda)_{w\lambda}$$

for all $w \in \hat{W}$. We now state the counterpart of Weyl's character formula for standard modules. Let ρ be the element of $\underline{h}^*$ such that $2\frac{(\rho,\alpha_i)}{(\alpha_i,\alpha_i)} = 1$ for all $i = 0, 1,\cdots,\ell$ and $\rho(d) = 0$. Clearly $\rho \in P^+$. Then

$$(1.3) \qquad \mathrm{Ch}\, L(\Lambda) = \frac{\sum_{w\in\hat{W}} (\det w)\, e^{w(\Lambda+\rho)}}{\sum_{w\in\hat{W}} (\det w)\, e^{w\rho}} \qquad ([11]).$$

There is a simple description of $P(\Lambda)$:

<u>Proposition 1.1</u> ([15]) $P(\Lambda) = \hat{W}\{\lambda \in P_+ | \lambda \leq \Lambda\}$.

The formal sum $\mathrm{Ch}\, L(\Lambda)$, viewed as a function of $H \in \hat{\underline{h}}$, converges absolutely on $Y = \{H \in \underline{h} | \mathrm{Re}\, \delta(H) > 0\}$ ([14], [15]). Next, following [15], we will express $\mathrm{Ch}\, L(\Lambda)$ in terms of classical theta functions and the string functions. Let M be the Z-span of $W\theta$. For $\gamma \in M$, let t_{γ} be the autmorphism of $\hat{\underline{h}}^*$ defined by $t_{\gamma}(\lambda) = \lambda + (\lambda,\delta)\gamma - (\frac{1}{2}(\lambda,\delta)|\gamma|^2 + (\gamma,\lambda))\delta$, where $|\mu|^2 = (\mu,\mu)$ for any $\mu \in \hat{\underline{h}}^*$. For each $\lambda \in \hat{\underline{h}}^*$ such that $m = \lambda(c) > 0$, put

$$(1.4) \qquad \Theta_{\lambda} = e^{-|\lambda|^2\delta/2m} \sum_{\gamma\in M} e^{t_{\gamma}(\lambda)}.$$

Using the decomposition $\hat{\underline{h}}^* = \underline{h}^* \oplus \mathbb{C}\Lambda_o \oplus \mathbb{C}\delta$, where Λ_i is defined by $\Lambda_i(d) = 0$, $\Lambda_i(h_j) = \delta_{ij}$, $i,j \in \{0,1,\cdots,\ell\}$, we have

$$(1.5) \qquad \Theta_\lambda = e^{m\Lambda_0} \sum_{\gamma \in M + m^{-1}\bar{\lambda}} e^{m\gamma - \frac{1}{2}m|\gamma|^2\delta}$$

where $\bar{\lambda}$ is the orthogonal projection of λ in $\underline{h}^*$. Θ_λ is an absolutely convergent series on Y. Also

$$(1.6) \qquad \Theta_{\lambda+m\gamma+z\delta} = \Theta_\lambda \quad \text{for all } \gamma \in M, z \in \mathbb{C}.$$

Θ_λ is the <u>classical theta function</u> (on Y) of degree m.

We set $m = \Lambda(c)$ and assume that $m > 0$, i.e., $\dim L(\Lambda) > 1$. Let

$$(1.7) \qquad s_\Lambda = \frac{|\Lambda + \rho|^2}{2(m+g)} - \frac{|\rho|^2}{2g}.$$

Taking into consideration that $\hat{W} = W \ltimes T$, where T is the subgroup of $\hat{W}$ generated by $\{t_\gamma | \gamma \in M\}$, one has from (1.3):

$$(1.8) \qquad e^{-s_\Lambda\delta} \operatorname{ch} L(\Lambda) = \frac{\sum_{w\in W} (\det w)\, \Theta_{w(\Lambda+\rho)}}{\sum_{w\in W} (\det w)\, \Theta_{w\rho}} \qquad ([14], [15]).$$

Let $\max(\Lambda) = \{\lambda \in P(\Lambda) | \lambda + \delta \notin P(\Lambda)\}$. One has

<u>Proposition 1.2</u> [12] $\max(\Lambda) = \hat{W}(\max(\Lambda) \cap P^+)$.

<u>Proposition 1.3</u> [12] $P(\Lambda) = \max(\Lambda) - Z_+\delta$.

For $\lambda \in P(\Lambda)$ set

(1.9) $$s_\Lambda(\lambda) = s_\Lambda - \frac{|\lambda|^2}{2m}$$

For $\lambda \in \max(\Lambda)$ set

(1.10) $$c_\lambda^\Lambda = e^{-s_\Lambda(\lambda)\delta} \sum_{n\geq o} \dim L(\Lambda)_{\lambda-n\delta} e^{-n\delta}.$$

Now let $\lambda \in \underline{h}^*$. If $\lambda \notin \max(\Lambda) + \mathbb{C}d$ then set $c_\lambda^\Lambda = 0$. If $\lambda \in \max(\Lambda) + \mathbb{C}\delta$ there is a unique $\mu \in \max(\Lambda)$ such that $\mu - \lambda \in \mathbb{C}d$. Then set $c_\lambda^\Lambda = c_\mu^\Lambda$. c_λ^Λ is the <u>string function</u> of λ. The number $m = \Lambda(c)$ is the level of $L(\Lambda)$ or of c_λ^Λ. It is a holomorphic function on Y. We note that $c_\lambda^\Lambda = c_\lambda^{\Lambda'}$ if $\Lambda-\Lambda' \in \mathbb{C}\delta$. Furthermore it is clear that

(1.11) $$c_{w\lambda}^\Lambda = c_\lambda^\Lambda \quad \text{for all} \quad w \in \hat{W},\ \lambda \in \hat{\underline{h}}^*$$

From (1.11) one sees immediately that

(1.12) $$c_{w\lambda+m\gamma+z\delta}^\Lambda = c_\lambda^\Lambda \quad \text{for} \quad w \in W,\ \lambda \in \underline{h}^*,\ \gamma \in M,\ z \in \mathbb{C}.$$

(1.4) and (1.10) now give

(1.13) $$e^{-s_\Lambda\delta} \operatorname{Ch} L(\Lambda) = \sum_{\substack{\lambda\in P/mM+\mathbb{C}\delta \\ \lambda(c)=m}} c_\lambda^\Lambda \Theta_\lambda.$$

The next result describes the set $\max(\Lambda) \cap P^+$. Let $\bar{P} = \{\bar{\lambda} | \lambda \in P\}$ and $\bar{Q} = \{\bar{\alpha} | \alpha \in Q\}$. Set $a_{ij} = 2\dfrac{(\alpha_i,\alpha_j)}{(\alpha_i.\alpha_i)}$ for all $i,j \in \{0,1,\cdots,\ell\}$. Let a_i^Λ (resp. $a_i^\vee$) be the relatively prime positive integers such that $\sum_{j=0}^{\ell} a_j a_{ij} = 0$ (resp. $\sum_{j=0}^{\ell} a_j^\vee a_{ji} = 0$) for all $i = 0,1,\cdots,\ell$.

Proposition 1.4 [15] Let $\Lambda \in P^{+}$ with $\Lambda(c) = m \in \mathbb{N}$, $\Lambda(d) = 0$. Let $\bar{\lambda} \in \bar{P}$ be such that $\bar{\lambda} \in \bar{\Lambda} + \bar{Q}$ and $m_i = (\bar{\lambda}, \alpha_i) \geq 0$, $i = 1, \cdots, \ell$, $\sum_{i=1}^{\ell} a_i m_i \leq m$. Then there exists $n_0 \in Z$ such that $m\Lambda_0 + \bar{\lambda} - a_o^{-1} n_o \delta \in \max(\Lambda) \cap P_+$. Every element of $\max(\Lambda) \cap P^+$ can be obtained this way.

Remark: n_0 is the smallest $n \in Z$ such that $\bar{\Lambda} - \bar{\lambda} \geq - a_o^{-1} n\delta$. Propositions 1.2 and 1.4 imply that there is only a finite number of distinct c_λ^Λ for a given Λ. In particular, the sum in (1.13) is finite.

Further reduction of the number of string functions can be obtained using the next result. If w is an automorphism of the Dynkin diagram of A (see [2] for the definition of the Dynkin diagram of a generalized Cartan matrix), we also denote by ω the unique automorphism of $\hat{\mathfrak{g}} = \hat{\mathfrak{g}}(A)$ such that $\omega(e_i) = e_{\omega(i)}, \omega(f_i) = f_{\omega(i)}, i = 0, \cdots, \ell, \omega(d) = d$. Here h_i, e_i, f_i $(i = 0, \cdots, \ell)$ are the canonical generators of $\hat{\mathfrak{g}}$. $(h_i, e_i, f_i$ $(i = 1, \cdots, \ell)$ are the canonical generators of $\mathfrak{g}$. $h_o = c - \sum_{j=0}^{\ell} a_i^\vee h_i$, $e_o = x \otimes t$, $f_o = y \otimes t^{-1}$, where x(resp. y) is a root vector corresponding to $-\theta$ (resp. θ)). ω extends uniquely to an automorphism of $U(\hat{\mathfrak{g}})$, which we again denote by w. If $\lambda \in \hat{\underline{h}}^*$, let $w^*\lambda(H) = \lambda(w^{-1}(H))$ for all $H \in \hat{\underline{h}}$.

Proposition 1.5 (a) Let $\Lambda \in \underline{h}^*$. The map $w : M(\Lambda) \longrightarrow M(\omega^*\Lambda)$ defined by $\omega(Xv_\Lambda) = \omega(X)v_{\omega^*\Lambda}$ for all $X \in U(\hat{\mathfrak{g}})$ is a linear isomorphism, where $v_\Lambda = 1 \otimes 1$ in $M(\Lambda)$.

(b) Let $\Lambda \in P^+$. Then linear isomorphism of (a) induces a linear isomorphism $\omega : L(\Lambda) \longrightarrow L(\omega^*\Lambda)$.

Proof: Let $H \in \underline{h}$. $H\omega(v_\Lambda) = \omega(\omega^{-1}(H)v_\Lambda) = \omega(\Lambda(\omega^{-1}H)\ v_\Lambda) = \Lambda\ (\omega^{-1}H)\omega(v_\Lambda) = \omega^*\Lambda(H)\ \omega v_\Lambda)$. This proves (a). Now, it is known that $L(\Lambda) =$

$M(\Lambda)/\sum_{i=0}^{\ell} f_i^{\Lambda(h_i)+1} M(\Lambda)$ for $\Lambda \in P^+$. Since $\omega^*\Lambda\ (h_{\omega(i)}) = \omega\ (\omega^{-1}(h_{\omega(i)})) =$ $\Lambda\ (h_i)$ we see that $(\sum_{i=0}^{\ell} f_i^{\Lambda(h_i)+1} M\ (\Lambda)) = \sum_{i=0}^{\ell} f_i^{\omega^*\Lambda(h_i)+1} M(\omega^*\Lambda)$, so that ω factors through to give an isomorphism $\omega : L(\Lambda) \longrightarrow L\ (\omega^*\Lambda)$. This proves (b). Q.E.D.

Corollary 1.6. $\dim L(\Lambda)_\lambda = \dim L(\omega^*\Lambda)_{\omega^*\lambda}$. In particular, Corollary 1.6 says that $c_\lambda^\Lambda = c_{\omega^*\lambda}^{\omega^*\Lambda}$. We now come to the main result of this section. We write $e^{2\pi i z}$ for $e^{-\delta}$. Then Y becomes

$$\{-2\pi i\ (H + \mu c + zd)\,|\,H \in \underline{h},\ u,\ z \in \mathbb{C},\ \mathrm{Im}(z) > 0\}.$$

We write $c_\lambda^\Lambda(z)$ for c_λ^Λ viewed as a function on $\mathcal{H} = \{\tau \in \mathbb{C}\,|\,\mathrm{Im}\ z > 0\}$.

Theorem 1.7. ([14,15])

$$(1.14)\qquad c_\lambda^\Lambda\left(-\frac{1}{z}\right) = \left(\frac{z}{i}\right)^{-\frac{\ell}{2}} \sum_{\Lambda',\lambda'} b(\Lambda,\lambda,\Lambda',\lambda')\, c_{\lambda'}^{\Lambda}(z),$$

where

$$b(\Lambda,\lambda;\ \Lambda',\lambda') = i^{|\Delta_+|}\,|\bar{P}/M|^{-1}(m(m + g))^{-\frac{\ell}{2}} \exp\left(2\pi i\,\frac{(\bar{\lambda},\bar{\lambda}')}{m}\right)$$

$$\cdot \sum_{\omega\in W} (\det w) \exp\left(-2\pi i\,\frac{(\bar{\Lambda} + \bar{P},\ w(\bar{\Lambda}' + \bar{P}))}{m + g}\right),$$

and the sum is over all $\Lambda' \in P_+/\mathbb{C}\delta$ and $\lambda' \in P/(mM + \mathbb{C}\,\delta)$ with $\Lambda'(c) = \lambda'(c) = m$.

Furthermore, if $s_\Lambda(\lambda) = [s_\Lambda(\lambda)] + \alpha$, with $0 \le \alpha < 1$, then

(1.15) $$c_\lambda^\Lambda(z+1) = e^{2\pi i\alpha} c_\lambda^\Lambda(z).$$

Let Γ be the group of linear fractional transformations σ on $\mathcal{H} : \sigma = \begin{bmatrix} a & b \\ c & d \end{bmatrix} \in SL(2,\mathbb{Z})$. Since Γ is generated by $z \longrightarrow -1/z$ and $z \longrightarrow z+1$, we deduce, from (1.14):

Corollary 1.8. Let $\sigma \in \Gamma$. Then

(1.16) $$c_\lambda^\Lambda(\sigma(z)) = \left[\frac{cz+d}{i}\right]^{-\frac{\ell}{\alpha}} \sum_{\Lambda',\lambda'} b_\sigma(\Lambda,\lambda,\Lambda',\lambda') c_{\lambda'}^{\Lambda'}(Z),$$

where the sum is as in (1.14) and $b_\sigma(\Lambda,\lambda,\Lambda',\lambda') \in \mathbb{C}$.

§2. Rademacher's Identity

2.1. Modular Forms

We retain the notation of §1. In particular, let $\mathcal{H}$ and Γ be as before. By a modular form of weight r and multiplier

$$\chi : \Gamma \longrightarrow \mathbb{C}^\times,$$

we understand, as usual, a complex valued function $F(z)$ defined on $\mathcal{H}$ with at most poles as singularities and which satisfies

(2.1.1) $$F\left[\frac{az+b}{cz+d}\right] = \chi(\sigma)\ (cz+d)^r\ F(z)$$

where $\sigma = \begin{bmatrix} a & b \\ c & d \end{bmatrix} \in \Gamma$ and $(cz+d)^r$ has its principal value:

$$(cz + d)^r = |cz + d|^r \exp (r \arg (cz + d))$$

with the determination $-\frac{\pi}{2} < \arg (cz + d) < \frac{\pi}{2}$. In the following we shall consider mainly modular forms of negative weight, e.g., $\eta(z)^{-1}$, where $\eta(z) = e^{\pi iz/12} \prod_{n=1}^{\infty} (1 - e^{2\pi i\eta z})$ is Dedekind's η-function. It is known from the classical theory that $\eta(z)$ is a cusp form (i.e., analytic modular form) of weight 1/2:

$$\eta \left(\frac{az + b}{cz + d}\right) = \varepsilon\ (cz + d)^{\frac{1}{2}}\eta(z)$$

where $\varepsilon = \varepsilon(a,b,c,d)$ is a 24th root of unity.

Another version of Theorem 1.7 ([14,15]) states that the string functions satisfy the relation (2.1.1) for σ in certain congruence subgroups. As we shall work directly with the modular group, we must replace the relation (2.1.1) by a weaker version where the right-hand side is given by a sum of similar functions F(z).

2.2 Farey Fractions and Ford Circles

Let N be a positive integer; the set of all reduced fractions r/s between 0 and 1 whose denominators satisfy $s \leq N$, arranged in increasing order, form the so called Farey sequence. For example, the Farey sequence of order N = 3 is

$$\frac{0}{1}, \frac{1}{3}, \frac{1}{2}, \frac{2}{3}, \frac{1}{1}.$$

The basic properties of these fractions are in (Rademacher [23], 265). The Farey fractions of a fixed order are used to construct a sequence of non-overlapping circles tangent to the real axis which will serve as paths of integration.

To each Farey fraction $\frac{h}{k}$ there corresponds a Ford circle $C(h,k)$

$$\left|z - \left(\frac{h}{k} + \frac{i}{2k^2}\right)\right| = \frac{1}{2k^2}$$

in the upper half plane. These circles have the following two properties:

(i) Two Ford circles $C(h,k)$ and $C(\ell,m)$ do not intersect. They are tangent to each other if and only if the corresponding fractions $\frac{h}{k}$ and $\frac{\ell}{m}$ are adjacent in some Farey sequence.

(ii) If $\frac{h_1}{k_1} < \frac{h}{k} < \frac{h_2}{k_2}$ are three adjacent fractions in a Farey sequence, then $C(h,k)$ touches $C(h_1,k_1)$ and $C(h_2,k_2)$ respectively in the points

$$\frac{h}{k} + \xi'_{hk} \quad \text{and} \quad \frac{h}{k} + \xi''_{hk}$$

where

$$\xi'_{hk} = (-k_1/k + i)/(k^2 + k_1^2), \quad \xi''_{hk} = (k_2/k + i)/(k^2 + k_2^2).$$

For the Farey fractions of order $N = 3$ the Ford circles have the following shape:

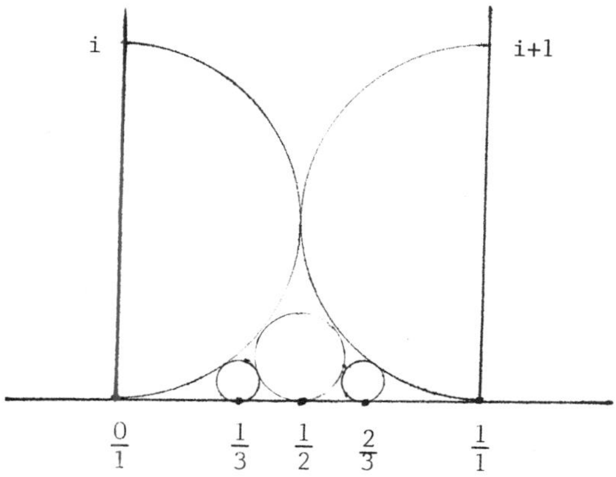

Remark 1 The set of all images of the line $\mathbb{R} + i$ in the upper half plane under all unimodular transformations in Γ corresponds in a one-to-one

manner with the set of all Ford circles at all rational points $\frac{h}{k}$, $-\infty < \frac{h}{k} < \infty$.

The Farey fractions of order N give rise to paths of integration on the corresponding Ford circles as follows: on each circle $C(h,k)$ an arc γ_{hk} is chosen joining the two points of tangency of $C(h,k)$ with the Ford circles pertaining to adjacent fractions and which does not touch the real axis. The circles $C(0,1)$ and $C(1,1)$ are congruent and as a path of integration we choose one half of each of the corresponding arcs on $C(0,1)$ and on $C(1,1)$, say from i to $\frac{0}{1} + \xi''_{01}$ and from $i + 1$ to $\frac{1}{1} + \xi'_{11}$; we let γ_{01} denote the union of these two. See the figure above for the case $N = 3$. These paths γ_{hk} will play a role in the calculation of the Fourier coefficients of a string function as an integral of a periodic function over an interval of length 1.

2.3 FOURIER COEFFICIENTS: THE MAIN FORMULA

From the definition of the number $\alpha = \alpha(\Lambda,\lambda)$ corresponding to the string functions $c_\lambda^\Lambda(z)$ we readily see that

$$f(z) = e^{-2\pi i\alpha z}c_\lambda^\Lambda(z) = \sum_{n=-\mu}^{\infty} a(n)e^{2\pi inz}$$

is a periodic function of period 1, and $\mu = -[s_\Lambda(\lambda)]$. The number $\mu = \mu(\Lambda,\lambda)$ is the order of the pole of $f(z)$ at $i\infty$. If $s_\Lambda(\lambda)$ is already an integer, then we take $\alpha = 0$ and $\mu = -s_\Lambda(\lambda)$. Set $\mathrm{mult}_\Lambda(\lambda) = \dim L(\Lambda)_\lambda$. In the notation of §1 we have

$$a(n) = \mathrm{mult}_\Lambda(\lambda - (\mu + n)\delta).$$

Since $f(z)$ is periodic of period 1 and analytic as a power series in $q = e^{2\pi iz}$ in any finite part of the upper half plane, we can write using

Cauchy's integral formula

$$a(n) = \int_{\tau_0}^{\tau_0+1} f(\tau)e^{-2\pi in\tau}d\tau,$$

where τ_0 is an arbitrary point in the upper half plane and any path from τ_0 to $\tau_0 + 1$ is permissible. In the following we use the points $\tau_0 = i$ and $\tau_0 + 1 = i + 1$ and the path of integration is taken to be the union of the arcs γ_{hk} corresponding to the Farey fractions of order N. In fact we have

$$a(n) = \int_{i}^{i+1} f(\tau)e^{-2\pi in\tau}d\tau = \sum_{h,k}{}' \int_{\gamma_{hk}} f(\tau)e^{-2\pi in\tau}d\tau,$$

where the sum $\sum_{h,k}{}'$ is over all pairs of non-negative integers h,k with $0 \leq h,k$ and $(h,k) = 1$ when $h > 0$. Here we set $\xi'_{01} = i$. Since the end points of the arc γ_{hk} are ξ'_{hk} and ξ''_{hk}, we can also write the above expression as

$$a(n) = \sum_{h,k}{}' \int_{\xi'_{hk}}^{\xi''_{hk}} f\left(\frac{h}{k} + \xi\right)e^{-2\pi in\left(\frac{h}{k} + \xi\right)}d\xi.$$

We can think of each of the above integrals as corresponding to the Ford circle $C(h,k)$, where the variable ξ runs over an arc of the circle $|\xi - \frac{i}{2k^2}| = \frac{1}{2k^2}$. If in such an integral we make the change of variable $\xi = \frac{iz}{k^2}$, we obtain

$$a(n) = \sum_{h,k}{}' \frac{i}{k^2} e^{-2\pi inh/k} \int_{z'_{hk}}^{z''_{hk}} f\left(\frac{h}{k} + \frac{zi}{k^2}\right)e^{-2\pi nz/k^2} dz \tag{2.3.1}$$

where z now runs along the arc of the circle $|z - \frac{1}{2}| = \frac{1}{2}$ between the points $z'_{hk} = k^2 \xi'_{hk}/i$ and $z''_{hk} = k^2\xi''_{hk}/i$ which does not touch the imaginary axis. Using the expressions for ξ' and ξ'' given in (2.2(ii)) we obtain

$$z_{hk} = (k^2 + ikk_1)/(k^2 + k_1^2),\ z''_{hk} = (k^2 - ikk_2)/(k^2 + k_2^2).$$

To proceed further with the above integrals we use the theorem of Kac-Peterson in the form of Corollary 1.8 of §1. Recall from the definition of $f(\tau)$ that with $\tau = \frac{h}{k} + \frac{iz}{k}$ we have

$$(2.3.2)\qquad f\left(\frac{h}{k} + \frac{iz}{k}\right) = e^{-2\pi i\alpha\left(\frac{h}{k} + \frac{zi}{k}\right)} c_\lambda^\Lambda\left(\frac{h}{k} + \frac{iz}{k}\right).$$

We now choose h' so that

$$hh' + 1 \equiv 0 \bmod k;$$

the matrix $\sigma = \sigma(h,k) \in \Gamma$ defined by

$$\sigma = \begin{pmatrix} a & b \\ c & d \end{pmatrix} = \begin{pmatrix} h & -\frac{hh' + 1}{k} \\ k & -h' \end{pmatrix}$$

satisfies

$$(2.3.3)\qquad \frac{a\left(\frac{h'}{k} + \frac{i}{kz}\right) + b}{c\left(\frac{h'}{k} + \frac{i}{kz}\right) + d} = \frac{h}{k} + \frac{iz}{k},$$

and

$$(2.3.4) \qquad \frac{c\left(\frac{h'}{k} + \frac{i}{kz}\right) + d}{i} = z^{-1};$$

combining (2.3.2), (2.3.3), (2.3.4) and the modified form of the theorem of Kac-Peterson, we obtain

$$f\left(\frac{h}{k} + \frac{iz}{k}\right) = e^{-2\pi i\alpha\left(\frac{h}{k} + \frac{zi}{k}\right)} c_\lambda^\Lambda\left(\frac{a\left(\frac{h'}{k} + \frac{i}{kz}\right) + b}{c\left(\frac{h'}{k} + \frac{i}{kz}\right) + d}\right)$$

$$= e^{-2\pi i\alpha\left(\frac{h}{k} + \frac{zi}{k}\right)} z^{\ell/2} \sum_{\Lambda',\lambda'} b_\sigma(\Lambda,\lambda;\ \Lambda',\lambda')\ c_{\lambda'}^{\Lambda'}\left(\frac{h'}{k} + \frac{i}{kz}\right).$$

Remark 2. It is important to keep track of the fact that f and α depend on Λ,λ; to make our notation precise we shall write when necessary

$$f = f_\lambda^\Lambda \quad \text{and} \quad \alpha = \alpha_\lambda^\Lambda ,$$

with a similar notation for the objects associated to $c_{\lambda'}^{\Lambda'}$.

From the relation

$$c_{\lambda'}^{\Lambda'}(\tau) = e^{2\pi i\alpha_{\lambda'}^{\Lambda'}\tau} f_{\lambda'}^{\Lambda'}(\tau)$$

we obtain

$$f_\lambda^\Lambda\left(\frac{h}{k} + \frac{iz}{k}\right) = z^{\ell/2} \sum_{\Lambda',\lambda'} b_\sigma(\Lambda,\lambda;\ \Lambda',\lambda') e^{-2\pi i\left\{\alpha_\lambda^\Lambda\left(\frac{h + iz}{k}\right) - \alpha_{\lambda'}^{\Lambda'}\left(\frac{h' + i/z}{k}\right)\right\}}$$

$$\times\ f_{\lambda'}^{\Lambda'}\left(\frac{h' + i/z}{k}\right).$$

In this last identity we make the substitution $z \longmapsto z/k$ to obtain

$$f_{\lambda}^{\Lambda}\left(\frac{h}{k}+\frac{iz}{k^2}\right) = \left(\frac{z}{k}\right)^{\ell/2} \sum_{\Lambda',\lambda'} b_{\sigma}^{*}(\Lambda,\lambda;\ \Lambda',\lambda') e^{2\pi\left\{\frac{\alpha_{\lambda}^{\Lambda} z}{k^2} - \frac{\alpha_{\lambda'}^{\Lambda'}}{z}\right\}} f_{\lambda'}^{\Lambda'}\left(\frac{h'}{k}+\frac{i}{z}\right),$$

where

$$b_{\sigma}^{*}(\Lambda,\lambda;\ \Lambda',\lambda') = b_{\sigma}(\Lambda,\lambda;\ \Lambda',\lambda') e^{2\pi i\{\alpha_{\lambda'}^{\Lambda'} h' - \alpha_{\lambda}^{\Lambda} h\}/k}.$$

To simplify the notation we put in the following

$$\psi_k(\Lambda,\lambda;\ \Lambda',\lambda';\ z) = e^{2\pi\left\{\frac{\alpha_{\lambda}^{\Lambda} z}{k^2} - \frac{\alpha_{\lambda'}^{\Lambda'}}{z}\right\}} z^{\ell/2}.$$

Substituting the above expression for f_{λ}^{Λ} into (2.3.1) we obtain

$$a(n) = \sum_{h,k}{}' \frac{i}{k^2} e^{-2\pi i n h/k} \int_{z'_{hk}}^{z''_{hk}} k^{-\ell/2}$$

$$\times \sum_{\Lambda',\lambda'} b_{\sigma}^{*}(\Lambda,\lambda\ ;\Lambda',\lambda') \psi_k(\Lambda,\lambda;\ \Lambda',\lambda';\ z) f_{\lambda'}^{\Lambda'}\left(\frac{h'}{k}+\frac{i}{z}\right) e^{\frac{2\pi n z}{k^2}}\, dz$$

$$(2.3.5) \qquad = \sum_{\Lambda',\lambda'} \sum_{h,k}{}' \frac{i e^{-2\pi i n h/k}}{k^{2+\ell/2}} b_{\sigma}^{*}(\Lambda,\lambda;\ \Lambda',\lambda') \int_{z'_{hk}}^{z''_{hk}} \psi_k(\Lambda,\lambda;\ \Lambda',\lambda';z) \times f_{\lambda'}^{\Lambda'}\left(\frac{h'}{k}+\frac{i}{z}\right) e^{\frac{2\pi n z}{k^2}}\, dz.$$

We now separate $f_{\lambda'}^{\Lambda'}$ into its integral and its polar part:

$$f^{\Lambda'}_{\lambda'}(\tau) = P^{\Lambda'}_{\lambda'}(\tau) + Q^{\Lambda'}_{\lambda'}(\tau),$$

where

$$P^{\Lambda'}_{\lambda'}(\tau) = \sum_{\upsilon=-\mu}^{-1} a_{\upsilon}(\Lambda',\lambda')e^{2\pi i v\tau}$$

and

$$Q^{\Lambda'}_{\lambda'}(\tau) = \sum_{v=0}^{\infty} a_{v}(\Lambda',\lambda')e^{2\pi i v\tau}.$$

We write (2.3.5) as a sum of two parts, of which the first yields the main contribution

(2.3.6)
$$\begin{aligned} a(n) = &\sum_{\Lambda',\lambda'} \sum_{h,k}{}' e^{-2\pi inh/k} \frac{ib^{*}_{\sigma}(\Lambda,\lambda;\ \Lambda',\lambda')}{k^{2+\ell/2}} \\ &\times \int_{z'_{hk}}^{z''_{hk}} \psi_k(\Lambda,\lambda;\Lambda',\lambda';z)P^{\Lambda'}_{\lambda'}\left[\frac{h'}{k} + \frac{i}{z}\right]e^{2\pi hz/k^2}dz \\ + &\sum_{\Lambda',\lambda'} \sum_{h,k}{}' e^{-2\pi inh/k} \frac{ib^{*}_{\sigma}(\Lambda,\lambda;\ \Lambda',\lambda')}{k^{2+\ell/2}} \\ &\times \int_{z'_{hk}}^{z''_{hk}} \psi_k(\Lambda,\lambda;\Lambda',\lambda';z)Q^{\Lambda'}_{\lambda'}\left[\frac{h'}{k} + \frac{i}{z}\right]e^{2\pi nz/k^2}dz \\ = &S_1 + S_2. \end{aligned}$$

<u>Remark 3</u>: In the sum $\sum_{\upsilon=-\mu}^{-1}$, the index $\mu = \mu(\Lambda',\lambda')$ depends on Λ',λ'. We also note the abbreviation $a(\upsilon) = a_{\upsilon}(\Lambda,\lambda)$.

The proofs of the following lemmas are obtained using the estimates of [23].

Lemma 2.1: With the above notation we have

$$|S_2| = O(N^{-\frac{\ell}{2}}).$$

Proof: We have: $|z|^2 \leq \text{Re } z$ for z in and on the circle $|z - \frac{1}{2}| = \frac{1}{2}$, $z \neq 0$. Hence, $\text{Re } \frac{1}{z} = \frac{\text{Re } z}{|z|^2} \geq 1$ in and on the circle, $z \neq 0$. In S_2 we are allowed to and do integrate along the chord from z'_{hk} to z''_{hk} in the interior of the circle $|z - \frac{1}{2}| = \frac{1}{2}$, since the integrand is regular. On the chord $|z| \leq \max\{|z'_{hk}|, |z''_{hk}|\}$ now,

$$|z'_{hk}|^2 = |(k^2 + ikk_1)/(k^2 + k_1^2)|^2 = \frac{k^4 + k^2k_1^2}{(k^2 + k_1^2)^2} = \frac{k^2}{k^2 + k_1^2}$$

$$= \frac{2k^2}{(k + k_1)^2 + (k - k_1)^2} \leq \frac{2k^2}{(k + k_1)^2} \leq \frac{2k^2}{N^2} .$$

Similarly, $|z''_{hk}|^2 < \frac{2k^2}{N^2}$. Therefore $|z| \leq \frac{k\sqrt{2}}{N}$. An analogous argument shows that $0 < \text{Re } z < \frac{2k^2}{N^2}$ on the chord. The length of the chord is $\leq |z'_{hk}| + |z''_{hk}| < \frac{2\sqrt{2}\, k}{N}$. This implies that

$$\left|\int_{z'_{hk}}^{z''_{hk}} z^{\frac{\ell}{2}} e^{2\pi\left\{\frac{\alpha_\lambda^\Lambda z}{k^2} - \frac{\alpha_{\lambda'}^{\Lambda'}}{z}\right\}} \sum_{\nu=0}^{\infty} a_\nu(\Lambda',\lambda') e^{2\pi i\nu\left[\frac{h'}{k} + \frac{i}{z}\right]} e^{2\pi nz/k^2} dz\right|$$

$$\leq \frac{2\sqrt{2}\, k}{N} \left[\frac{k\sqrt{2}}{N}\right]^{\frac{\ell}{2}} e^{\frac{4\pi}{N^2}\left[\alpha_\lambda^\Lambda + |n|\right]} \sum_{\nu=0}^{\infty} |a_\nu(\Lambda',\lambda')| e^{-2\pi\nu}$$

$$\leq C \left[\frac{k}{N}\right]^{\frac{\ell}{2} + 1} e^{\frac{4\pi}{N^2}(|n| + 1)} .$$

Therefore

$$|S_2| \le C\, e^{\frac{4\pi}{N^2}(|n|+1)} \frac{1}{N^{\ell/2+1}} \sum_{0\le h<k\le N}' \frac{1}{k} < C\, e^{\frac{4\pi}{N^2}(|n|+1)} N^{-\frac{\ell}{2}} = O(N^{-\frac{\ell}{2}})$$

for n fixed. Q.E.D.

Lemma 2.2: Let $K^{(-)}$ denote the circle $|z - \frac{1}{2}| = \frac{1}{2}$ travelled in the negative sense. We have

$$S_1 = \sum_{\Lambda',\lambda'} \sum_{h,k}' e^{-2\pi inh/k} \frac{ib^*_\sigma(\Lambda,\lambda;\ \Lambda',\lambda')}{k^{\frac{\ell}{2}+2}} \int_{K^{(-)}} \psi(\Lambda,\lambda;\ \Lambda',\lambda',z)$$

$$\times\, P^{\Lambda'}_{\lambda'}\left[\frac{h'}{k} + \frac{i}{z}\right] e^{\frac{2\pi nz}{k^2}} dz + O(N^{-\frac{\ell}{2}}),$$

where $\int_{K^{(-)}}$ is an improper integral.

Proof: To prove the lemma it suffices to show that if we replace the improper integral $\int_{K^{(-)}}$ by the improper integrals $\int_0^{z'_{hk}}$ and $\int_{z''_{hk}}^0$ then the same estimate holds. Clearly, on the circle $K^{(-)}$ the length of the arc from 0 to z'_{hk} is $\le \frac{\pi}{2}|z'_{hk}| \le \frac{\pi}{\sqrt{2}}\frac{k}{N}$. Therefore,

$$\left|\int_0^{z'_{hk}} z^{\frac{\ell}{2}} e^{2\pi\left\{\frac{\alpha^\Lambda_\lambda z}{k^2} - \frac{\alpha^{\Lambda'}_{\lambda'}}{z}\right\}} P^{\Lambda'}_{\lambda'}\left[\frac{h'}{k} + \frac{i}{z}\right] e^{\frac{2\pi n2}{k^2}} dz\right|$$

$$\le \frac{\pi}{\sqrt{2}}\frac{k}{N}\left[\frac{k\sqrt{2}}{N}\right]^{\frac{\ell}{2}} e^{\frac{4\pi}{N^2}\alpha^\Lambda_\lambda - 2\pi\,\alpha^{\Lambda'}_{\lambda'}} \sum_{\upsilon=1}^{\mu} |a_{-\upsilon}(\Lambda',\lambda')|e^{2\pi\upsilon} e^{\frac{4\pi|n|}{N^2}}$$

$$< C \left[\frac{k}{N}\right]^{1 + \frac{\ell}{2}}$$

for any fixed n. Hence,

$$\Big| \sum_{\Lambda',\lambda'} \sum_{h,k}' e^{-2\pi inh/k} \frac{ib_\sigma^*(\Lambda,\lambda;\ \Lambda',\lambda')}{k^{\frac{\ell}{2}+2}} \int_0^{z'_{hk}} \Big| \leq \frac{C}{N^{\frac{\ell}{2}+1}} \sum_{h,k}' \frac{1}{k} \leq \frac{C}{N^{\frac{\ell}{2}}} .$$

The improper integral $\int_{z''_{hk}}^{0}$ is estimated similarly. Q.E.D.

<u>Remark 4</u>: The integral $\int_{K^{(-)}}$ is to be understood as an improper integral with a path of integration not a complete circle $K^{(-)}$ but rather as an integral over a sequence of arcs $K_i^{(-)}$, open near the imaginary axis, with $K_i^{(-)} \longrightarrow K^{(-)}$ as $i \longrightarrow \infty$.

Substituting the series for $P_{\lambda'}^{\Lambda'}$ we obtain

$$a(n) = \sum_{\Lambda',\lambda'} \sum_{h,k}' \frac{ie^{-2\pi inh/k}}{k^{2+\ell/2}} b_\sigma^*(\Lambda,\lambda;\ \Lambda',\lambda') \int_{K^{(-)}} \psi_k(\Lambda,\lambda;\ \Lambda',\lambda',z)$$

$$\times \sum_{\upsilon=-\mu}^{-1} a_\upsilon(\Lambda',\lambda')e^{2\pi i\upsilon\left[\frac{h'}{k}+\frac{i}{z}\right]+\frac{2\pi hz}{k^2}} dz$$

$$+ O(N^{-\ell/2})$$

$$(2.3.7) \qquad = \sum_{\Lambda',\lambda'} \sum_{h,k}' \frac{ie^{-2\pi inh/k}}{k^{2+\ell/2}} b_\sigma^*(\Lambda,\lambda;\ \Lambda',\lambda') \sum_{\upsilon=-\mu}^{-1} a_\upsilon(\Lambda',\lambda')e^{\frac{2\pi ih'}{k}\upsilon}$$

$$\times \int_{K^{(-)}} z^{\ell/2}\, e^{2\pi\left\{\left[\alpha_\lambda^\Lambda + n\right]\frac{z}{k^2} - \left[\alpha_{\lambda'}^{\Lambda'} + \upsilon\right]\frac{1}{z}\right\}} dz$$

$$+ O(N^{-\ell/2}).$$

The substitution $w = \frac{1}{z}$ turns the last integral into the following

$$\text{(2.3.8)} \qquad i\int_K(-) = \frac{1}{i}\int_{1-i\infty}^{1+i\infty} w^{-2-\frac{\ell}{2}} e^{2\pi\left\{\left[\alpha_\lambda^\Lambda + n\right]\frac{1}{k^2 w} - \left[\alpha_{\lambda'}^{\Lambda'} + \upsilon\right]w\right\}} dw.$$

Remark 5. From the definition of $\alpha_{\lambda'}^{\Lambda'}$ and v we have $-\alpha_{\lambda'}^{\Lambda'} - v > 0$.

To simplify the shape of the final formula we use the modified Bessel function

$$L_s(y) = \frac{1}{2\pi i}\int_{1-i\infty}^{1+i\infty} w^{-s-1} e^{w + y/w} dw = \sum_{q=0}^{\infty} \frac{y^q}{\Gamma(1 + s + q)q!} .$$

If we introduce the change of variable

$$W = -(\alpha_{\lambda'}^{\Lambda'} + \upsilon)2\pi w$$

in (2.3.8), we obtain

$$i\int_K(-) = \frac{1}{i}\int_{1-i\infty}^{1+i\infty}\left[\frac{W}{-2\pi\left[\alpha_{\lambda'}^{\Lambda'} + \upsilon\right]}\right]^{-2-\ell/2} e^{2\pi\left\{\frac{(\alpha_\lambda^\Lambda + n)}{k^2}\cdot\frac{(-\alpha_{\lambda'}^{\Lambda'} - \upsilon)2\pi}{W} + \frac{W}{2\pi}\right\}}$$

$$\times \frac{dW}{-2\pi(a_{\lambda'}^{\Lambda'} + \upsilon)}$$

$$= \frac{2\pi}{(-2\pi(a_{\lambda'}^{\Lambda'} + \upsilon))^{-1-\ell/2}} \cdot \frac{1}{2\pi i}\int_{1-i\infty}^{1+i\infty} W^{-2-\ell/2}$$

$$e^{\frac{4\pi^2}{k^2}\frac{(\alpha_\lambda^\Lambda + n)(-\alpha_{\lambda'}^{\Lambda'} - \nu)}{W} + W} dW$$

$$= \frac{2\pi}{\{-2\pi(a_{\lambda'}^{\Lambda'} + \nu)\}^{-1-\ell/2}} L_{1+\ell/2}\left[\frac{4\pi^2(\alpha_\lambda^\Lambda + n)(-\alpha_{\lambda'}^{\Lambda'} - \nu)}{k^2}\right].$$

The main formula reduces to

$$a(n) = \sum_{\Lambda',\lambda'} \sum_{h,k}{}' \sum_{\nu=-\mu}^{-1} a_\nu(\Lambda',\lambda') \frac{i}{k^{2+\ell/2}} b_\sigma^*(\Lambda,\lambda;\ \Lambda',\lambda') e^{\frac{2\pi i\nu h'}{k} - \frac{2\pi i n h}{k}}$$

$$\times \int_{K(-)} z^{\ell/2} e^{2\pi\{(\alpha_\lambda^\Lambda + n)\frac{z}{k^2} - (\alpha_{\lambda'}^{\Lambda'} + \nu)\frac{1}{z}\}} dz$$

$$+ O(N^{-\ell/2}).$$

For a fixed positive integer k, we put

$$A_k(\Lambda,\lambda;\ \Lambda',\lambda';\ n,v) = \sum_{\substack{h \bmod k\\(h,k)=1}} b_\sigma^*(\Lambda,\lambda;\Lambda',\lambda') e^{2\pi i(\nu h'-nh)/k}$$

$$= \sum_{\substack{h \bmod k\\(h,k)=1}} b_\sigma(\Lambda,\lambda;\Lambda',\lambda') e^{2\pi i\{(\alpha_{\lambda'}^{\Lambda'}+\nu)h' - (\alpha_\lambda^\Lambda+n)h\}/k},$$

where

$$\sigma = \begin{bmatrix} h & \frac{hh'+1}{k} \\ k & -h \end{bmatrix}$$

and h' is chosen so that $hh' + 1 \equiv 0 \pmod k$. The formula for $a(n)$

can thus be written as

$$a(n) = \sum_{1\le k\le N} \sum_{\Lambda',\lambda'} \sum_{\nu=-\mu}^{-1} \frac{\alpha_\nu(\Lambda',\lambda')}{k^{2+\ell/2}} A_k(\Lambda,\lambda;\Lambda',\lambda';n,\nu)$$

$$\times\ i \int_{K(-)} z^{\ell/2} e^{2\pi\{(\alpha_\lambda^\Lambda+n)\frac{z}{k^2} - (\alpha_{\lambda'}^{\Lambda'}+\nu)\frac{1}{z}\}} dz$$

$$+\ O(N^{-\ell/2}).$$

Therefore we have

$$a(n) = \sum_{1\le k\le N} \sum_{\Lambda',\lambda'} \sum_{\nu=-\mu}^{-1} a_\nu(\Lambda',\lambda')A_k(\Lambda,\lambda;\ \Lambda',\lambda';\ n,\nu)k^{-2-\frac{\ell}{2}}$$

$$\times\ (2\pi)^{2+\frac{\ell}{2}}(-\alpha_{\lambda'}^{\Lambda'} - \nu)^{1+\frac{\ell}{2}} L_{1+\frac{\ell}{2}}\left[\frac{4\pi^2}{k^2}(\alpha_\lambda^\Lambda+\mu)(-\alpha_{\lambda'}^{\Lambda'}-\nu)\right] + O(N^{-\ell/2}).$$

Letting $N \longrightarrow \infty$ we finally obtain our main formula:

Theorem 2.3. With the notations above, let $a(n) = \mathrm{mult}_\Lambda(\lambda - (\mu + n)\delta)$ be the n-th coefficient of the string function $c_\lambda^\Lambda(z)$ (similarly for $a_n(\Lambda',\lambda')$ and $c_{\lambda'}^{\Lambda'}$). Then we have

$$a(n) = \sum_{k=1}^{\infty} \sum_{\Lambda',\lambda'} \sum_{\nu=-\mu}^{-1} a_\nu(\Lambda',\lambda')A_k(\Lambda,\lambda;\ \Lambda',\lambda';\ n,\nu)$$

$$\times\ k^{-2-\frac{\ell}{2}}(2\pi)^{2+\frac{\ell}{2}}(-\alpha_{\lambda'}^{\Lambda'} - \nu)^{1+\frac{\ell}{2}} L_{1+\frac{\ell}{2}}\left[\frac{4\pi^2}{k^2}(\alpha_\lambda^\Lambda+n)(-\alpha_{\lambda'}^{\Lambda'}-\nu)\right].$$

Note: The above theorem in the case of twisted affine Lie algebras can be proved exactly as above by using Theorem A.1 of [14] instead of the special case used here.

§3. Examples

3.1. Affine Lie algebras of type $C_\ell^{(1)}$, $\ell \geq 2$.

Let $\hat{\Delta}$ be the root system given by the Dynkin diagram of type $C_\ell^{(1)}$:

$$\underset{1}{0}\Rightarrow\underset{2}{0}—\cdots—\underset{2}{0}\Leftarrow\underset{1}{0}.$$

The dual root system $\hat{\Delta}^\vee$ has Dynkin diagram

$$\underset{1}{0}\Rightarrow\underset{1}{0}—\cdots—\underset{1}{0}\Leftarrow\underset{1}{0}.$$

The labels in the Dynkin diagram of $\hat{\Delta}$ (resp. $\hat{\Delta}^\vee$) are the integers a_i (resp. $a_i^\vee$), $i = 0,1,\ldots,\ell$, that were introduced in §1.

We saw in §1 that a complete listing of the non-zero level one string functions is given by the pairs (Λ,λ) where $\Lambda(c) = \lambda(c) = 1$, $\Lambda \in P^+$ mod $\mathbb{C}\delta$ and $\lambda \in \mathrm{Max}(\Lambda) \cap P^+$. We begin by listing these pairs. We set $h_i = a_i(a_i^\vee)^{-1}H_{\alpha_i}$, $i = 0,1,\ldots,\ell$. Note that $h_i = a_i H_{\alpha_i}$, $H_{\Lambda_0} = a_0^{-1}d = d$ and $H_\delta = c = \sum_{i=0}^{\ell} a_i^\vee h_i = \sum_{i=0}^{\ell} h_i$. Every $\Lambda \in \underline{\hat{h}}^*$ has the form $\Lambda = \sum_{i=0}^{\ell} b_i\Lambda_i$ mod $\mathbb{C}\delta$, $b_i \in \mathbb{C}$. Now, $\Lambda \in P^+$ if and only if $b_i = \Lambda(h_i) \in \mathbb{Z}_+$, $i = 0,1,\ldots,\ell$. Hence $\Lambda \in P^+$, $\Lambda(c) = 1$ if and only if $1 = \Lambda(c) = \sum_{i=0}^{\ell} a_i^\vee\Lambda(h_i) = \sum_{i=0}^{\ell}\Lambda(h_i) = \sum_{i=0}^{\ell}\sum_{j=0}^{\ell} b_j\Lambda_j(h_iJ) = \sum_{i=0}^{\ell} b_i$. Therefore $\{\Lambda \in P + \text{mod } \mathbb{C}\delta \,|\, \Lambda(c) = 1\} = \{\Lambda_i \,|\, i = 0,1,\ldots,\ell\}$.

Next, we use Proposition 1.4 to determine $\{\lambda \in \mathrm{Max}(\Lambda) \cap P^+ | \lambda(c) = 1\}$ for $\Lambda \in \{\Lambda_i | i = 0,1,\ldots,\ell\}$. For $\bar{\lambda} \in \underline{h}^*$ let $m_i = (\bar{\lambda},\alpha_i), i = 1,\ldots,\ell$, as in Proposition 1.4 now $\bar{\lambda}(h_i) = a_i(a_i^\vee)^{-1}m_i = a_i m_i$. Hence, $\bar{\lambda} \in \bar{P} \Leftrightarrow m_\ell \in \mathbb{Z},\ 2m_i \in \mathbb{Z},\ i = 1,\ldots,\ell - 1$. Furthermore, $m_i \geq 0,\ i = 1,\ldots,\ell$ and $\sum_{i=1}^{\ell} a_i m_i \leq 1$ if and only if $\bar{\lambda}$ is in the set $\{\bar{\Lambda}_i | i = 1,\ldots,\ell\} \cup \{0\}$, since $\bar{\lambda} = \sum_{i=1}^{\ell} m_i a_i (a_i^\vee)^{-1}\bar{\Lambda}_i = 2m_1\bar{\Lambda}_1 + 2m_2\bar{\Lambda}_2 + \cdots + 2m_{\ell-1} + m_\ell\bar{\Lambda}_\ell$.

From the Dynkin diagram we obtain the Cartan matrix $A = (a_{ij})$ $(i,j = 0,1,\ldots,\ell)$ of Δ:

$$A = \begin{bmatrix} 2 & -1 & 0 & 0 & \cdots & 0 & 0 \\ -1 & 2 & -1 & 0 & \cdots & 0 & 0 \\ 0 & -1 & 2 & -1 & \cdots & 0 & 0 \\ 0 & 0 & -1 & 2 & \cdots & 0 & 0 \\ \cdots & \cdots & \cdots & \cdots & \cdots & \cdots & \cdots \\ 0 & 0 & 0 & 0 & \cdots & 2 & -2 \\ 0 & 0 & 0 & 0 & \cdots & -1 & 2 \end{bmatrix}.$$

Let $\bar{A} = (a_{ij})$ $(i,j = 1,\ldots,\ell)$. Since $\alpha_i(h_j) = a_{ji}$, $\bar{A}$ is the transition matrix from $\{\alpha_i\}$ to $\{\bar{\Lambda}_i\}$ $(i = 1,\ldots,\ell)$. Hence, from

$$\bar{A}^{-1} = \begin{bmatrix} 1 & 1 & 1 & 1 & \cdots & 1 & 1 \\ 1 & 2 & 2 & 2 & \cdots & 2 & 2 \\ 1 & 2 & 3 & 3 & \cdots & 3 & 3 \\ 1 & 2 & 3 & 4 & \cdots & 4 & 4 \\ \cdots & \cdots & \cdots & \cdots & \cdots & \cdots & \cdots \\ 1 & 2 & 3 & 4 & \cdots & \ell-1 & \ell-1 \\ \frac{1}{2} & \frac{2}{2} & \frac{3}{2} & \frac{4}{2} & \cdots & \frac{\ell-1}{2} & \frac{\ell}{2} \end{bmatrix}$$

we obtain:

$$\bar{\Lambda}_i = \alpha_1 + 2\alpha_2 + 3\alpha_3 + 4\alpha_4 + \cdots + i\alpha_i + i\alpha_{i+1} + \cdots + i\alpha_{\ell-1} + \frac{i}{2}\alpha_\ell \quad (i = 1,\ldots,\ell).$$

Using Proposition 1.4 and the remark that follows it we obtain:

Proposition 3.1.1. Let $S = \{(\Lambda_i,\Lambda_j) \mid i \geq j\} \cup \{(\Lambda_i,\Lambda_j - \frac{j-1}{2}\delta) \mid i < j\}$ where $i,j \in \{0,1,\ldots,\ell\}$ and $i - j \in 2\mathbb{Z}$. Then a complete list of all nonzero level one string functions is:

$$c^{\Lambda}_{\lambda},\ (\Lambda,\lambda) \in S.$$

Next, we calculate the characteristics $s_\Lambda(\lambda)$ of the string functions described above. Let $c = ((\alpha_i,\alpha_j))$ $(i,j = 1,\ldots,\ell)$. Since $(\alpha_i,\alpha_j) = a_i^{-1}\overset{\vee}{a}_i a_{ij} = \overset{\vee}{a}_i a_{ij}$, $i,j = 1,\ldots,\ell$, we obtain

$$C = \begin{bmatrix} 1 & -\frac{1}{2} & 0 & 0 & \cdots & 0 & 0 \\ -\frac{1}{2} & 1 & -\frac{1}{2} & 0 & \cdots & 0 & 0 \\ 0 & -\frac{1}{2} & 1 & -\frac{1}{2} & \cdots & 0 & 0 \\ 0 & 0 & -\frac{1}{2} & 1 & \cdots & 0 & 0 \\ \cdots & \cdots & \cdots & \cdots & \cdots & \cdots & \cdots \\ 0 & 0 & 0 & 0 & \cdots & 1 & -1 \\ 0 & 0 & 0 & 0 & \cdots & -1 & 2 \end{bmatrix}.$$

Let $D = ((\bar{\Lambda}_i,\bar{\Lambda}_j))$ $(i,j = 1,\ldots,\ell)$. Since $D = (\bar{A}^{-1})^t\, C\, \bar{A}^{-1}$, we calculate D to be

$$D = \frac{1}{2}\begin{bmatrix} 1 & 1 & 1 & 1 & \cdots & 1 & 1 \\ 1 & 2 & 2 & 2 & \cdots & 2 & 2 \\ 1 & 2 & 3 & 3 & \cdots & 3 & 3 \\ 1 & 2 & 3 & 4 & \cdots & 4 & 4 \\ \cdots & \cdots & \cdots & \cdots & \cdots & \cdots & \cdots \\ 1 & 2 & 3 & 4 & \cdots & \ell-1 & \ell-1 \\ 1 & 2 & 3 & 4 & \cdots & \ell-1 & \ell \end{bmatrix}.$$

Using the matrix D and observing that $(\Lambda_0,\Lambda_0) = (\Lambda_0,\bar{\Lambda}_i) = 0$, for all i, we obtain

(3.1.1) $$(\Lambda_i,\Lambda_i) = \frac{i}{2}$$

(3.1.2) $$(\Lambda_i,\rho) = \frac{i(2\ell + 1 - i)}{4}$$

(3.1.3) $$|\rho|^2 = \frac{\ell(\ell + 1)(2\ell + 1)}{12}\,.$$

Now, $g = \sum_{i=0}^{\ell} a_i^\vee = \ell + 1$, $(\Lambda_i,\delta) = \Lambda_i(c) = \Lambda_0(c) = 1$, $i = 0,\dots,\ell$. From (1.7), (1.9) and (3.1.1)-(3.1.3) above we obtain:

Proposition 3.1.2. The characteristics of the string functions listed in Proposition 3.1.1. are:

(3.1.4) $$s_{\Lambda_i}(\Lambda_j) = \frac{i(2\ell + 2 - i) - j(\ell + 2)}{4(\ell + 2)} - \frac{\ell(2\ell + 1)}{24(\ell + 2)}$$

(3.1.5) $$s_{\Lambda_i}\left(\Lambda_j - \frac{(j - 1)}{2}\,\delta\right) = \frac{j(\ell + 2) - i(i + 2)}{4(\ell + 2)} - \frac{\ell(2\ell + 1)}{24(\ell + 2)}\,.$$

Remark 1: The sum in Theorem 2.3 can be taken over all Λ' mod $\mathbb{C}\delta$ and $w\lambda'$ mod $mM + \mathbb{C}\delta$ where $(\Lambda',\lambda') \in S$ (as in Proposition 3.1.1) and $w \in W$. Also $\alpha_{\lambda'}^{\Lambda'} = \alpha_{w\lambda'}^{\Lambda'}$ and $\mu(\Lambda',\lambda') = \mu(\Lambda',w\lambda')$ for all $w \in W$ by (1.11).

Propositions 3.1.1 and 3.1.2., and the algorithm for the b_σ's given in the Appendix provide, by the above remark, all the ingredients needed for determining the Fourier coefficients $a(n)$ in the case of $A = C_\ell^{(1)}$, $m = 1$. We note, however, that it is possible to have $c_\lambda^\Lambda = c_{\lambda'}^{\Lambda'}$ for two distinct pairs (Λ,λ), (Λ',λ') listed in Proposition 3.1.1. To further simplify the formula for $a(n)$ we use Corollary 1.6 applied to the automorphism ω of the Dynkin diagram that interchanges the vertices i and $\ell - i$, $i = 0,1,\dots,\ell$. This allows us to cut down cardinality of the labeling set S practically in half from $\frac{(\ell + 1)^2 + 1}{2}$ $\left[\text{resp. } \frac{(\ell + 1)^2}{2}\right]$

to $\frac{(\ell+1)^2+3}{4}$ $\left[\text{resp. } \frac{(\ell+1)^2}{4}\right]$ for ℓ even (resp. ℓ odd). In summary, we obtain the following refinement of Proposition 3.1.1:

<u>Proposition 3.1.1′</u>. Let $S' = \{(\Lambda_i,\Lambda_j) \mid i \geq j\} \cup \{(\Lambda_i,\Lambda_j - \frac{(j-i)}{2}\delta \mid i < j\}$ where $i - j \in 2\mathbb{Z}$, $j = 0,\ldots,\ell$, $i = 0,\ldots,\frac{\ell}{2}$ $\left[\text{resp. } i = 0,\ldots,\frac{\ell-1}{2}\right]$ for ℓ even (resp. ℓ odd). Then, a complete list of all nonzero level one string functions is: c_λ^Λ, $(\Lambda,\lambda) \in S'$.

<u>Remark 2</u>: The sum $\sum_{\Lambda',\lambda'}$ in Theorem 2.3 can be taken over all Λ' mod $\mathbb{C}\delta$ and $w\lambda'$ mod $mM + \mathbb{C}\delta$ where $(\Lambda',\lambda') \in S'$ or $(\omega^*\Lambda',\omega^*\lambda') \in S'$, $w \in W$, ω as above. Also, $\alpha_{\lambda'}^{\Lambda'} = \alpha_{w\lambda'}^{\Lambda'} = \alpha_{\omega^*\lambda'}^{\omega^*\Lambda'} = \alpha_{w\omega^*\lambda'}^{\omega^*\Lambda'}$ by (1.11) and Corollary 1.6. Similar equations hold for μ.

We now write the final formula for $\ell = 2$, $\ell = 3$ and $\ell = 4$.

In Tables 1 and 2 below we list the characteristics $s = s_\Lambda(\lambda)$, the exponent of the periodicity factor $\alpha = \alpha_\lambda^\Lambda$ and the order of the pole $\mu = \mu(\Lambda,\lambda)$ of $e^{-2\pi i\alpha z}c_\lambda^\Lambda(z)$ for $\ell = 2$ and 3, respectively (For $\ell =$ 4 see [19]).

Table 1

Λ	λ	s	α	μ
Λ_0	Λ_0	$-\frac{5}{48}$	$\frac{43}{48}$	-1
Λ_0	$\Lambda_2-\delta$	$\frac{19}{48}$	$\frac{19}{48}$	0
Λ_1	Λ_1	$-\frac{1}{24}$	$\frac{23}{24}$	-1

Table 2

Λ	λ	s	α	μ
Λ_0	Λ_0	$-\frac{7}{40}$	$\frac{33}{40}$	-1
Λ_0	$\Lambda_2-\delta$	$\frac{13}{40}$	$\frac{13}{40}$	0
Λ_1	Λ_1	$-\frac{3}{40}$	$\frac{37}{40}$	-1
Λ_2	Λ_0	$\frac{17}{40}$	$\frac{17}{40}$	0

For $C_2^{(1)}$ we have

$$\mathrm{mult}_\Lambda(\lambda - (n+1)\delta) = \sum_{k=1}^{\infty} \sum_{w\in W} \sum_{(\Lambda',\lambda')\in\mathcal{L}} A_k(\Lambda,\lambda;\ \Lambda' w\lambda';n,-1)$$

$$\times\ k^{-3}(2\pi)^3(1-\alpha_{w\lambda'}^{\Lambda'})^2 L_2\left[\frac{4\pi^2}{k^2}(\alpha_\lambda^\Lambda + n)(1-\alpha_{w\lambda'}^{\Lambda'})\right],$$

where $\mathcal{L} = \{(\Lambda_0,\Lambda_0),\ (\Lambda_1,\Lambda_1),\ (\Lambda_2,\Lambda_2)\}$, $\alpha_{\Lambda_2}^{\Lambda_2} = \alpha_{\Lambda_0}^{\Lambda_0}$ and $\mu(\Lambda_2,\Lambda_2) = \mu(\Lambda_0,\Lambda_0)$. For $C_3^{(1)}$ we have

$$\mathrm{mult}_\Lambda(\lambda - (n+1)\delta) = \sum_{k=1}^{\infty} \sum_{w\in W} \sum_{(\Lambda',\lambda')\in\mathcal{L}} A_k(\Lambda,\lambda;\ \Lambda',w\lambda',n,-1)$$

$$\times\ k^{-\frac{7}{2}}(2\pi)^{\frac{7}{2}}(1-\alpha_{w\lambda'}^{\Lambda'})^{\frac{5}{2}} L_{\frac{5}{2}}\left(\frac{4\pi^2}{k^2}(\alpha_\lambda^\Lambda + n)(1-\alpha_{w\lambda'}^{\Lambda'})\right),$$

where $\mathcal{L} = \{(\Lambda_i,\Lambda_i)\,|\,i = 0,3\}$, $\alpha_{\Lambda_2}^{\Lambda_2} = \alpha_{\Lambda_1}^{\Lambda_1}$, $\alpha_{\Lambda_3}^{\Lambda_3} = \alpha_{\Lambda_0}^{\Lambda_0}$ and similarly for μ. The formula for $C_4^{(1)}$ in [19] contain some attention errors. The correct formula for $C_4^{(1)}$ is

$$\mathrm{mult}_{\Lambda}(\lambda - (n+1)\delta) = \sum_{k=1}^{\infty} \sum_{w\in W} \sum_{(\Lambda',\lambda')\in\mathcal{L}} A_k(\Lambda,\lambda;\ \Lambda',w\lambda',n,-1)$$

$$\times\ k^{-4}(2\pi)^4(1-\alpha_{w\lambda'}^{\Lambda'})^3\ L_3\left(\frac{4\pi^2}{k^2}(\alpha_{\lambda}^{\Lambda}+n)(1-\alpha_{w\lambda'}^{\Lambda'})\right)$$

where $\mathcal{L} = \{(\Lambda_i,\Lambda_i)\,|\,i = 0,\ldots,4\}$, $\alpha_{\Lambda_3}^{\Lambda_3} = \alpha_{\Lambda_1}^{\Lambda_1}$, $\alpha_{\Lambda_4}^{\Lambda_4} = \alpha_{\Lambda_0}^{\Lambda_0}$ and similarly for μ.

Notes: (1) In the above we have used the fact that a $(\Lambda,\Lambda) = \mathrm{mult}_{\Lambda}(\Lambda) = 1$ all $\Lambda \in P^+$.

(2) The determiniation of the level one string functions for $C_{\ell}^{(1)}$ was left as an open problem in [14]. After this work was completed we received the preprint [16] where these string functions are given in terms of the discrete series characters of the Virasoro algebra which were obtained in [25].

3.2. Affine Lie Algebras of Type $A_{\ell}^{(1)}$.

Let us first recall a simple result of Kac-Peterson.

Lemma 3.2 (Kač-Peterson [13], p. 197). Let $\mathfrak{g}$ be an affine Lie algebra of type $A_{\ell}^{(1)}$, $D_{\ell}^{(1)}$, $E_6^{(1)}$, $E_7^{(1)}$, $E_8^{(1)}$ or $A_{2\ell}^{(2)}$ and let $\Lambda \in P^+$ be of level 1. Then every non-zero string function of $L(\Lambda)$ is W-equivalent to c_{Λ}^{Λ} and is equal to $\eta(z)^{-\ell}$.

Let $\ell = 24L + r$, $0 \le r < 24$. We let $\alpha = 0$ if $r = 0$ and $\alpha = 1 - \frac{r}{2q}$ if $r \ne 0$. Let $\mu = L$ if $\alpha = 0$ and $\mu = L + 1$ otherwise. We then have

$$c_{\Lambda}^{\Lambda}(z) = q^{\alpha} \sum_{n=-\mu}^{\infty} a(n)q^n,\quad q = \exp(2\pi iz).$$

A straightforward application of the Rademacher formula in its original form (Rademacher [22], p. 70) gives the following result.

Theorem 3.2. *With notations as in the main theorem we have for the n-th Fourier coefficients of the string function* $c_\Lambda^\Lambda(z)$ *the representation*

$$\mathrm{mult}_\Lambda(\Lambda - (m+1)\delta) = \sum_{\nu=-\mu}^{-1} \sum_{R=1} a_\nu(\mathcal{L}) A_k(\mathcal{L},n,\nu)$$

$$\cdot\, k^{-2-\ell/2}(2\pi)^{2+\ell/2}(-\alpha-\nu)^{1+\ell/2} L_{1+\ell/2}\left[\frac{4\pi^2}{k^2}(\alpha+n)(-\alpha-\nu)\right],$$

where $\mathcal{L} = (\Lambda,\Lambda)$ *and* $a_\nu(\mathcal{L}) = a(\nu)$.

In the case $\ell = 1$ the formula reduces to

$$\mathrm{mult}_\Lambda(\Lambda - n\delta) = 2\pi\left[\frac{\pi}{12}\right]^{3/2} \sum_{k=1}^{\infty} A_k(\mathcal{L},n-1,-1)k^{-5/2}$$

$$\cdot\, L_{3/2}\left[\left(\frac{\pi}{12k}\right)^2(24n-1)\right],$$

with

$$A_k(\mathcal{L},n-1,-1) = \sum_{\substack{h \bmod k\\(h,k)=1}}^{\infty} b_\sigma(\mathcal{L}) e^{\left[\frac{\pi i}{12}\right](h-h')} e^{-2\pi i hn/k},$$

which is precisely Rademacher's formula for $p(n)$ [22]. The case $\ell = 24$ is very interesting for many reasons. Firstly, the corresponding string function

$$C_{\Lambda}^{\Lambda}(z) = \frac{1}{\Delta(z)} = \sum_{n=-1}^{\infty} \tilde{\tau}(n)q^n,$$

is the reciprocal of the well-known Ramanujan modular form of weight 12, also known as the discriminant in the theory of elliptic modular functions. The multiplier is trivial and indeed for a modular transformation $\sigma = \begin{bmatrix} a & b \\ c & d \end{bmatrix}$ we have

$$C_{\Lambda}^{\Lambda}(\sigma(z)) = (cz + d)^{-12} C_{\Lambda}^{\Lambda}(z).$$

$C_{\Lambda}^{\Lambda}(z)$ has a simple pole at infinity with residue 1, and $\alpha = 0$. The formula in this case takes the simple form

$$\tilde{\tau}(n) = \sum_{k=1}^{\infty} \frac{A_k(n)}{k^{14}} (2\pi)^{14} L_{13} \left[\frac{4\pi^2 n}{k^2}\right],$$

where

$$A_k(n) = \sum_{\substack{h \bmod k \\ (h,k)=1}} e^{2\pi i\{-h'-nh\}/k}, \quad hh' + 1 \equiv 0 \bmod k,$$

is the Kloosterman sum.

The coefficients $\tilde{\tau}(n)$ grow very rapidly and have many interesting number theoretic properties. Secondly, in the light cone formulation of string theory, the coefficients $\tilde{\tau}(n)$ have an exact meaning as level densities (Green, Schwarz and Witten [7], p. 117):

Theorem 3.3 [7]. Let α' denote the Regge slope. Then the number of open string states with mass M such that $\alpha' M^2 = n$ is $\tilde{\tau}(n)$.

The coefficients $\tilde{\tau}(n)$ can also be given a different but somewhat equivalent formulation which is connected with the so called No-Ghost Theorem. Before we state it in this form, we need some preliminary definitions. The Virasoro algebra is defined by $\mathcal{L} = \coprod_{n\in\mathbb{Z}} \mathcal{L}_n$ where

$$\mathcal{L}_n = \mathbb{C}L_n, \; n \in \mathbb{Z} - \{0\} \quad \text{and} \quad \mathcal{L}_0 = \mathbb{C}L_0 \oplus \mathbb{C}Z$$

and for $m,n \in \mathbb{Z}$

$$[L_m,L_n] = (m - n)\, L_{m+n} + \frac{m^3 - m}{12}\, \delta_{m+n,0}\, Z, \quad [L_n,Z] = 0.$$

Let $E = \mathbb{R}^{26}$ be the Euclidean space endowed with the Lorentzian metric $(,)$ of signature $(25,1)$. Let p be a linear functional on E and denote by $V(E,p)$ the Fock space representation of the Virasoro algebra realized via the Sugawara-Segal operators. As a consequence of the study of the semi-infinite Lie algebra cohomology of the module $V(E,p)$ over the Virasoro algebra relative to the subalgebra $\mathcal{L}_0 = \mathbb{C}L_0 \oplus \mathbb{C}Z$, the following result holds.

Theorem 3.4. (Frenkel-Garland-Zukerman [5]). *Let p be a linear functional on E with $n = -(p \cdot p)/2$ a positive integer. Then the dimension of physical space*

$$\mathcal{H}(n) = H^0_\infty(\mathcal{L},\mathcal{L}_0,V(E,p))$$

is $\tilde{\tau}(n)$.

The reader interested in understanding the meaning and significance of this result should consult [5].

The following is a table of values of $\tilde{\tau}(n)$.

n	$\tilde{\tau}(n)$	n	$\tilde{\tau}(n)$
-1	1	13	156883829400
0	24	14	563116739584
1	324	15	1956790259235
2	3200	16	6599620022400
3	25650	17	21651325216200
4	176256	18	69228721526400
5	1073720	19	216108718571250
6	5930496	20	659641645039360
7	30178575	21	1971466420726656
8	143184000	22	5776331152550400
9	639249300	23	16610409114771900
10	2705114880	24	46925988716146176
11	10914317934		
12	42189811200		

Note that $\tilde{\tau}(0) = 24$ and $\tilde{\tau}(1) \equiv 196884 \bmod 13$.

3.3 The Griess-Norton Algebra.

The last example which we want to point out is that connected with the classical modular invariant; it is not exactly a string function in the sense of §2 but is closely related to the formal character of a representation of the Fischer-Griess group F_1. Let the Eisenstein series of weight k be defined by

$$E_k(z) = 1 + \frac{2k}{\zeta(1-k)} \sum_{n=1}^{\infty} \sigma_{k-1}(n)\, q^n,$$

where $\zeta(s)$ is the Riemann zeta function and $\sigma_\ell(n)$ is the sum of the ℓ-th powers of the positive divisors of n. The j-function is defined by

$$j(z) = \frac{E_4(z)^3}{\Delta(z)} = \frac{1}{q} + 744 + \sum_{n=1}^{\infty} c(n) q^n.$$

Both Rademacher [22] and Petersson [20], working in different directions with respect to the weight found the following beautiful formula for the coefficients $c(n)$:

$$c(n) = \sum_{k=1}^{\infty} \frac{A_k(n)}{k^2} (2\pi)^2 L_1 \left[\frac{4\pi^2 n}{k^2}\right],$$

where $A_k(n)$ is the same Kloosterman sum introduced above.

Associated with the Fischer-Griess simple group F_1 there is a graded module V related to the representation of the Virasoro algebra on the Fock space resulting from the Leech lattice. V is a graded vector space with grading running from $+1$ to $-\infty$:

$$V = \coprod_{n=-1}^{\infty} V_{-n}.$$

We recall the following result:

<u>Theorem 3.5</u> (Frenkel-Lepowsky-Meurman [4]). <u>For the formal</u> q-<u>character series</u>

$$f_V(q) = \sum_{n=-1}^{\infty} (\dim V_{-n}) q^n$$

<u>we have the identity</u>

$$f_V(q) = j(z) - 744.$$

We end this paper with a simple but tantalizing example which adds substance to the relation between the monster group and the physical universe. It is a well known consequence of the structure of the ring of modular forms that

$$E_4(2)^3 = E_{12}(z) + \frac{24\cdot 2730}{691}\Delta(z).$$

Hence we have the identity

$$j(z) = \frac{E_{12}(z)}{\Delta(z)} + \frac{24\cdot 2730}{691}.$$

Now we observe that the number $24\cdot 2730$ is divisible by $\ell = 2,3,5,7,13$. Hence, since for any prime p we have $E_{p-1}(z) \equiv 1 \bmod p$, we obtain that $j(z) \equiv \frac{1}{\Delta(z)} \bmod \ell$. In particular we have that modulo 13, physical space in the sense of string theory and the Norton-Griess algebra V are related by the congruence

$$\dim \mathcal{H}(n) \equiv \dim V_{-n} \bmod 13.$$

Appendix

A. <u>Algorithm for determining the</u> b_σ's.

It is well known that the unimodular group Γ is generated by the elements

$$W = \begin{bmatrix} 0 & 1 \\ -1 & 0 \end{bmatrix}, \quad T = \begin{bmatrix} 1 & 1 \\ 0 & 1 \end{bmatrix}.$$

Using an elementary result of Gauss and Dirichlet from the theory of binary quadratic forms, we give below a procedure for calculating b_σ in terms of b_W and b_T, which are already given by the theorem of Kač–Peterson.

Lemma A.1. A necessary and sufficient condition for a 2×2 integral matrix to be uniquely representable in the form

$$\begin{bmatrix} a & b \\ c & d \end{bmatrix} = \pm \begin{bmatrix} n_j & 1 \\ -1 & 0 \end{bmatrix} \begin{bmatrix} n_{j-1} & 1 \\ -1 & 0 \end{bmatrix} \cdots \begin{bmatrix} n_1 & 1 \\ -1 & 0 \end{bmatrix}$$

with the $n_1, \ldots, n_j$ a sequence of integers which alternate in sign is that

(i) $ad - bc = 1$,

(ii) $|a| \geq |b| \geq |d|$,

(iii) $|a| \geq |c| \geq |d|$.

We shall apply this lemma to the matrix

$$\sigma = \begin{bmatrix} h & -\frac{hh'+1}{k} \\ k & h' \end{bmatrix} .$$

To satisfy the conditions (i) – (iii) we use instead the matrix

$$\sigma' = \begin{bmatrix} 0 & 1 \\ -1 & 0 \end{bmatrix} \sigma = \begin{bmatrix} k & -h' \\ -h & \frac{hh'+1}{k} \end{bmatrix} .$$

Recall that $(h,k) = 1$, $1 \leq h \leq k - 1$, and $h'h + 1 \equiv 0 \bmod k$; thus h' can be chosen so that $1 \leq h' \leq k - 1$. As for the first inequality we certainly have $|k| \geq |h|$. Now the inequality $|h| \geq |\frac{hh' + 1}{k}|$ is equivalent to

$$hk \geq hh' + 1;$$

but this is clear since $h(k - h') \geq 1$. By the same reasoning, the second inequality is also satisfied. The result we obtain is then the following:

Lemma A.2. *Let* k *be a positive integer and* h *an integer satisfying* $1 \leq h \leq k$, $(h,k) = 1$. *Let* h' *be a reduced residue modulo* k *satisfying* $hh' + 1 \equiv 0 \bmod k$. *Then we have a unique representation*

$$\sigma =: \begin{bmatrix} h & -\frac{hh'+1}{k} \\ k & h' \end{bmatrix} = (-1)^{\varepsilon(\sigma)} \begin{bmatrix} 0 & 1 \\ -1 & 0 \end{bmatrix} \begin{bmatrix} -n(\ell) & 1 \\ -1 & 0 \end{bmatrix} \begin{bmatrix} -n(j-1) & 1 \\ -1 & 0 \end{bmatrix} \cdots \begin{bmatrix} -n(1) & 1 \\ -1 & 0 \end{bmatrix},$$

where $n(1), n(2), \ldots, n(\ell)$ *is a sequence of integers which alternates in sign*.

Remark 1. From the identity $\begin{bmatrix} -n & 1 \\ -1 & 0 \end{bmatrix} = \begin{bmatrix} 1 & n \\ 0 & 1 \end{bmatrix} \begin{bmatrix} 0 & 1 \\ -1 & 0 \end{bmatrix}$ we see that the above representation for σ can also be given as

$$(*) \qquad \sigma = (-1)^{\varepsilon(\sigma)}\, W \prod_{j=0}^{\ell-1} (T^{n(\ell-j)}W).$$

2. The proof of the lemma is straightforward.

The effective calculation of the integers $n(1), \ldots, n(\ell)$ can be carried out by means of the continued fraction expansion of $\frac{h}{k}$.

To complete the algorithm for calculating the b_σ's we observe that the map $\sigma \longmapsto b_\sigma$ is a homomorphism and hence the matrices b_σ also satisfy the same relation as (*). The matrices for b_T and b_W for c_λ^Λ as well as for q^{-s_Λ} ch $L(\Lambda)$ are given in [14] and [15] (see also [16]).

REFERENCES

[1] Borcherds, R., Vertex algebras, Kac-Moody algebras and the Monster, P.N.A.S. 83(1986), 3068-3071.

[2] Bourbaki, N., Groupes et algèbres de Lie, Hermann, chapitres IV-VI (1968).

[3] Feingold, A. I. and Lepowsky, J., The Weyl Character formula and power series identites, Adv. in Math. 29(1978), 271-309.

[4] Frenkel, I., Lepowsky, J. and Meurman, A., A natural representation of the Fischer-Griess Monster with the modular function J as character, P.N.A.S. 81(1984), 3256-3260.

[5] Frenkel, I., Garland, H. and Zuckerman, G., Semi-infinite cohomology and string theory, P.N.A.S. 83(1986), 8440-8446.

[6] Garland, H. and Lepowsky, J., Lie algebra homology and the Macdonald-Kac formulas, Inventiones Math. 34(1976), 37-76.

[7] Green, M., Schwarz, J. and Witten, E. Superstring Theory, vol. I, Cambridge University Press, New York (1987).

[8] Hardy, G., Ramanujan, Chelsea Publ. Co., New York (1940).

[9] Jimbo, M. and Miwa, J., in Vertex Operators in Mathematics and Physics, ed. by J. Lepowsky, S. Mandelstam and I. M. Singer, M.S.R.I. 3, Springer-Verlag, New York (1985), 207-216.

[10] Kac, V. G., Simple irreducible graded Lie algebras of finite growth, Math. USSR Izv. 2(1968), 1271-1311.

[11] __________, Infinite dimensional Lie algebras and Dedekind's η-functions, Funkt. Anal. i ergo Prilozheniya 8(1974), 77-78.

[12] __________, Infinite dimensional algebras, Dedekind's η-function, classical Möbius function and the very strange formula, Adv. in Math. 30(1978), 85-136.

[13] __________, Infinite dimensional Lie algebras, Cambridge University Press, New York (1985).

[14] Kac, V. G. and Peterson, D. H., Affine lie algebras and Hecke modular forms, Bull. Amer. Math. Soc. 3(1980), 1057-1061.

[15] __________________________, Infinite dimensional Lie algebras, theta functions and modular forms, Adv. in Math. 53(1984), 125-264.

[16] Kac, V. G. and Wakimoto, M., Modular and conformal invariance in representation theory of affine Lie algebrass, preprint.

[17] Moody, R. V., A new class of Lie algebras, J. Algebra 10(1968), 211-230.

[18] ____________, Euclidean Lie algebras, Canad. J. Math. 21(1969), 1432-1454.

[19] Moreno, C. J. and Rocha-Caridi, A., Rademacher-Type formulas for the multiplicities of irreducible highest-weight representations of affine Lie algebras, Bull. Amer. Math. Soc. 16, number 2 (1987), 292-296.

[20] Petersson, H., Über die Entwicklungskoeffizienten der ganzen Modulformen und ihre Bedeutung für die Zahlentheorie; Abh. Math. Seminar, Univ. Hamburg, 8(1931), 215-242.

[21] Rademacher, H., A convergent series for the partition function p(n), P.N.A.S. 23(1937), 78-84.

[22] ______________, Fourier expansions of modular forms and problems of partition, Bull. A.M.S. 46(1940), 59-73.

[23] ______________, Topics in analytic number theory, Springer-Verlag, New York (1973).

[24] Ramanujan, S., Collected Papers, Chelsea Publ. Co., New York (1962).

[25] Rocha-Caridi, A., Vacuum vector representations of the Virasoro algebra, in Vertex Operators in Mathematics and Physics, ed. by J. Lepowsky, S. Mandelstam and I. M. Singer, M.S.R.I. 3 Springer-Verlag, New York (1985), 451-473.

[26] Zuckerman, H. S., On the coefficients of certain modular forms belonging to subgroups of the modular group, T.A.M.S. 45(1939), 298-321.

CORRECTIONS TO REF. [19].

p. 292 line 8 ↑ should read: $(X,Y) = (2g)^{-1}B(X,Y)$.

p. 295 line 4 ↑ should read: $e^{(\pi i/12kk)(h - h')}$.

line 6 ↑ should read: $L_{3/2}\left[(\frac{\pi}{12k})^2 (24n - 1)\right]$

line 8 ↑ should read: $c\tau + d$ instead of $\tau + d$.

p. 296 lines 6,7 ↑: the formula for $\text{mult}_\Lambda(\lambda - (n + 1)\delta)$

should read as in §3.1 of the present paper.

PROBABILISTIC NUMBER THEORY

Hubert Delange

I am expected to give an expository lecture on what is commonly called "probabilistic number theory". I actually think that it would be more proper to say "probabilistic theory of arithmetic functions" for the theory deals with arithmetic functions while probability occurs in some other parts of number theory.

There exists an extremely abundant literature on this subject. A few years ago P.D.T.A. Elliott wrote on it a book in two volumes, of 700 pages altogether. It contains a very great number of references. So the account that I will give will necessarily be very far from complete. I must restrict to few basic problems.

I just said that the theory is concerned with arithmetic functions. An arithmetic function is merely a function whose domain is the set $\mathbb{N}$ of all positive integers. Of course such a function f is particularly interesting if the definition of $f(n)$ depends upon arithmetic properties of the integer n.

Some familiar examples are the following ones :

$d(n)=$ number of divisors of n.
$\sigma(n)=$ sum of the divisors of n.
$\omega(n)=$ number of prime divisors of n.
$\Omega(n)=$ total number of prime factors in the factorization of n.
$\varphi(n)=$ number of the positive integers $\leq n$ and coprime to n.
$p(n)=$ number of partitions of n, i.e. number of ways in which n can be expressed as a sum of positive integers, regardless to the order of the summands.

This function p has been extensively studied by Ramanujan.

Some arithmetic functions have a regular behavior as n tends to infinity. For instance

$$p(n) \sim \frac{1}{4n\sqrt{3}} e^{\pi\sqrt{2n/3}}$$

as was proved by Hardy and Ramanujan.

On the other hand $\omega(n)$ is equal to 1 when n is prime but, given any positive ϵ, $\omega(n)$ is $>(\log n)^{1-\epsilon}$ for infinitely many n. It is so in particular for n equal to the product n_k of the first k primes as soon as k is large enough. In fact it follows from the prime number theorem that, as k tends to infinity, $\omega(n_k) \sim \frac{\log n_k}{\log\log n_k}$.

ISBN 0-12-058560-X

In general those arithmetic functions whose value depends upon the multiplicative structure of n have a very erratic behavior.

This is usually the case of additive and of multiplicative functions.

I recall that the arithmetic function f is said to be additive if

$$f(mn)= f(m)+f(n) \quad \text{whenever} \quad (m,n)=1.$$

Note that this obviously implies that $f(1)=0$

f is said to be multiplicative if

$$f(mn)= f(m)f(n) \quad \text{when} \quad (m,n)=1 \quad \text{and} \quad f(1)=1.$$

Some authors omit the condition that $f(1)=1$.

The only difference is that in that case one has to admit as a multiplicative function the function which is equal to zero for every n. I think that it is better to exclude it.

An arithmetic function f is said to be "completely additive" if the equality $f(mn)= f(m)+f(n)$ holds for every pair (m,n) of positive integers.

It is said to be "strongly additive" if it is additive and, for every prime p, $f(p^r)$ is independent of r. Then $f(n)= \sum_{p|n} f(p)$ (it is understood that throughout this lecture the letter p will always be used to denote prime numbers).

There are similar definitions for a completely multiplicative or a strongly multiplicative function.

The functions d, σ and φ are multiplicative. Ω is completely additive, ω is strongly additive.

It is clear that an additive, or multiplicative, function is completely determined by its values on the powers of the primes.

Most results in the probabilistic number theory concern real-valued additive functions. Here I will consider only the results which concern these functions.

Because of the irregular behavior of such a function one is led to consider, instead of the value $f(n)$ for a single n, the set of the values $f(1), f(2),\ldots,$ up to $f(N)$ and to examine how these values are distributed when N is large.

The first research of this kind was done by Hardy and Ramanujan for the function ω. They proved in 1917 the following theorem :

Let g be any positive increasing function of the real variable x which tends to infinity as x tends to infinity.

Then, as x tends to infinity,

$$\#\{n\le x : |\omega(n)-\log\log x|>g(x)\sqrt{\log\log x}\} = o(x)$$

(we denote by the sign # the number of elements of the set which follows it).

Using the fact that $\log\log x-\log 2<\log\log n\le\log\log x$ for $\sqrt{x}<n\le x$, Hardy and Ramanujan remarked that <u>this is equivalent to the same statement with</u> $\log\log x$ <u>replaced by</u> $\log\log n$.

The result can be expressed roughly by saying that, when x is large, for almost all $n\le x$ $\omega(n)$ is not much different from $\log\log n$. Hardy and Ramanujan said that "the normal order of $\omega(n)$ is $\log\log n$".

Returning to the first statement we see that it can be expressed as follows :

If we choose at random an n among the positive integers $\le x$, all of these having the same probability $1/[x]$ to be chosen, then the probability that

$$|\omega(n)-\log\log x|>g(x)\sqrt{\log\log x}$$

tends to zero as x tends to infinity.

There is an obvious analogy with the weak law of large numbers.

Although Hardy and Ramanujan did not use this formulation in language of probability I think that one can say that their theorem is the very beginning of the probabilistic number theory.

Their proof was purely arithmetic. Denoting by $\varpi_\nu(x)$ the number of the $n\le x$ for which $\omega(n)=\nu$, they showed that for $x\ge3$

$$\varpi_\nu(x) \le A\,\frac{x}{\log x}\cdot\frac{(\log\log x+B)^{\nu-1}}{(\nu-1)!}$$

where A and B are constants independent of ν. The result was derived from this inequality.

In 1934 Turan gave a new proof which is very simple. He showed, very easily indeed, that

$$\sum_{n\le x}(\omega(n)-\log\log x)^2 = O(x\log\log x),$$

say $\le M\,x\log\log x$ for $x\ge3$ for instance.

This obviously implies that for $x\ge3$

$$\#\{n\le x: |\omega(n)-\log\log x|>g(x)\sqrt{\log\log x}\} \le \frac{Mx}{g(x)^2}.$$

This argument is similar to the classical proof of the weak law of large numbers by means of Tchebychef's inequality. I must say that Turan was not aware of that, for in 1934 he did not know what Tchebychef's inequality was, as he told Elliott in a letter written in 1976.

The calculation of Turan has been extended by Kubilius to an arbitrary additive function. This yields the well known "Turan-Kubilius inequality".

For the distribution of the values of the function ω, we know since 1940 a result which is much more precise than the theorem of Hardy and Ramanujan :

<u>As</u> x <u>tends to infinity, for every real</u> t

$$\frac{1}{x} \# \{n \leq x : \frac{\omega(n)-\log\log x}{\sqrt{\log\log x}} \leq t\} \quad \underline{\text{tends to}} \quad \frac{1}{\sqrt{2\pi}} \int_{-\infty}^{t} e^{-u^2/2}\, du.$$

In other words the numbers $\frac{\omega(n)-\log\log x}{\sqrt{\log\log x}}$ where n runs through the set of the positive integers $\leq x$ tend to be distributed according to the normal law of Gauss.

This follows from the famous theorem of Erdös and Kac :

<u>Let</u> f <u>be a real-valued strongly additive function</u>. <u>Suppose that</u> f(p) <u>is bounded and that</u> $\sum \frac{f(p)^2}{p} = \infty$. <u>Set</u> $A(x) = \sum_{p \leq x} \frac{f(p)}{p}$ <u>and</u> $B(x) = \left(\sum_{p \leq x} \frac{f(p)^2}{p}\right)^{1/2}$ (so B(x) tends to infinity as x tends to infinity).

<u>As</u> x <u>tends to infinity, for every real</u> t

$$\frac{1}{x} \# \{n \leq x : \frac{f(n)-A(x)}{B(x)} \leq t\} \quad \underline{\text{tends to}} \quad \frac{1}{\sqrt{2\pi}} \int_{-\infty}^{t} e^{-u^2/2}\, du.$$

It is easy to see that this still holds if A(x) and B(x) are replaced by $A^*(x)$ and $B^*(x)$ satisfying

$$B^*(x) \sim B(x) \quad \text{and} \quad A^*(x)-A(x) = o(B(x)) \quad (x \longrightarrow \infty).$$

As $\sum_{p \leq x} \frac{1}{p} = \log\log x + O(1)$ this gives the result stated above for $\omega(n)$.

The proof given by Erdös and Kac uses the theory of sums of independent random variables. This is the origin of the general theory developed by Kubilius in his book "Probabilistic methods in the theory of numbers".

Now, after this exposition of the origin of probabilistic number theory, I will give an account of the basic problems of that theory.

These problems can be expressed alternatively in language of measure or in language of probability. Of course the latter choice is better to justify the appellation of "probabilistic number theory"!

From now on it will be understood that f is a real-valued arithmetic function.

I think that it is natural to consider for each positive integer n the discrete measure μ_n on the set $\mathbb{R}$ of all real numbers defined as follows :

For each subset E of $\mathbb{R}$, $\mu_n(E)=\frac{1}{n}\#\{m\in\mathbb{N}:m\leq n$ and $f(m)\in E\}$. You certainly agree that $\mu_n(E)$ is the probability that $f(m)\in E$ if one chooses m at random among the positive integers $\leq n$, all of these having the same probability $1/n$ to be chosen.

I think that a careful probabilist would prefer to express this in the following way :

For each n we consider the probability space whose elements are the positive integers $\leq n$, the probability of each element being equal to $1/n$, and on this space the random variable X_n which is the restriction of f to its elements.

$$\mu_n(E) \text{ is the probability that } X_n\in E.$$

The distribution function σ_n of X_n is given by

$$\sigma_n(t) =: \text{Prob}(X_n\leq t)=\frac{1}{n}\#\ \{m\in\mathbb{N} : m\leq n \text{ and } f(m)\leq t\}.$$

The question which occurs most naturally is the following one :

<u>Problem 1</u> : <u>Is the sequence</u> $\{\mu_n\}$ <u>weakly convergent to a measure</u> μ <u>such that</u> $\mu(\mathbb{R})=1$? <u>Or, equivalently, does the sequence</u> $\{X_n\}$ <u>possess a limit law</u> ?

The existence of a limit law is equivalent to the existence of a distribution function σ such that $\sigma_n(t)$ converges to $\sigma(t)$ at each point of continuity of σ (I recall that a distribution function is a non--decreasing function of a real variable t which is right-continuous and which tends to zero as t tends to $-\infty$ and to 1 as t tends to $+\infty$).

If the answer is yes, then we will say that f possesses a limiting distribution.

In the contrary case we may pose the following question :

<u>Problem 2</u> : <u>Is it possible to obtain, by performing a suitable translation on each measure</u> μ_n, <u>a new sequence</u> $\{\mu'_n\}$ <u>weakly convergent to a measure</u> μ <u>such that</u> $\mu(\mathbb{R})=1$?

In other words, <u>is it possible to find a sequence</u> $\{\alpha_n\}$ <u>of real numbers such that the sequence of the random variables</u> $X_n-\alpha_n$ <u>has a limit law</u> ? (if the translation $-\alpha_n$ changes μ_n into μ'_n, then for each $E\subset\mathbb{R}$ we have

$$\mu'_n(E) = \mu_n(E+\alpha_n) = \mathrm{Prob}(X_n \in E+\alpha_n) = \mathrm{Prob}(X_n - \alpha_n \in E)).$$

If it is so, then we will say that $f(m)-\alpha_n$ has a limiting distribution.

Problem 2 is obviously a generalization of problem 1, which corresponds to $\alpha_n=0$.

One can still generalize and pose the following question :

Problem 3 : Is it possible to find two sequences of real numbers $\{\alpha_n\}$ and $\{\beta_n\}$, with $\beta_n>0$, such that the sequence of the random variables $(X_n-\alpha_n)/\beta_n$ possess a limit law ?

If it is so, then we will say that $(f(m)-\alpha_n)/\beta_m$ has a limiting distribution.

Problems 1 and 2 are completely solved for additive functions.

The solution of problem 1 is given by the theorem of Erdös and Wintner (1939) :

Define the notation $\|\ \|$ by $\|u\| = \begin{cases} u & \text{if } |u| \le 1, \\ 1 & \text{if } |u| > 1. \end{cases}$

f (supposed to be additive) has a limiting distribution if and only if the series

$$\sum \frac{\|f(p)\|}{p} \quad \text{and} \quad \sum \frac{\|f(p)\|^2}{p} \quad \text{(where } p \text{ runs through the primes)}$$

are convergent.

Erdös proved the sufficiency of these conditions in the last of three successive papers published in the Journal of the London Mathematical Society (1935-37-38). He used purely arithmetical methods with no consideration of probability. Finally Erdös and Wintner proved in 1939 that the conditions are necessary.

The theorem of Erdös and Wintner shows in particular that the additive functions $\log \frac{\varphi(n)}{n}$ and $\log \frac{\sigma(n)}{n}$ possess limiting distributions. It follows immediately that $\frac{\varphi(n)}{n}$ and $\frac{\sigma(n)}{n}$ also have limiting distributions.

The existence of a limiting distribution for $\frac{\varphi(n)}{n}$ had already been proved in 1928 by Schönberg, by use of a generalization of the theorem of H. Weyl on the uniform distribution modulo 1.

The existence of a limiting distribution for $\frac{\sigma(n)}{n}$ had been proved by Davenport in 1933 by a purely arithmetical method.

The theorem of Erdös and Wintner is proved in the books of Kubilius and Elliott by use of independent random variables.

I think that the simplest - and perhaps most natural - method to prove it is to use the following well known theorem of Paul Lévy :

A sequence of random variables possesses a limit law if and only if the sequence of their characteristic functions converges to a function which is continuous at the point zero.

I gave this proof in 1961.

The characteristic function of a random variable X is the function of a real variable t whose value is the expectation of e^{itX}.

For the random variable X_n considered above the characteristic function is equal to

$$\frac{1}{n}\sum_{m=1}^{n} F_t(n), \quad \text{where} \quad F_t(m) = e^{itf(m)}.$$

By the theorem of Paul Lévy f has a limiting distribution if and only if the function F_t has a mean-value for every real t and this mean--value is a continuous function of t at the point $t=0$.

F_t is a complex-valued multiplicative function whose absolute value is 1.

I proved in 1961 a theorem which gives a necessary and sufficient condition for a complex-valued multiplicative function F of absolute value ≤ 1 to possess a non-zero mean-value (the condition is that the series $\sum \frac{1-F(p)}{p}$ should converge and that $F(2^r) \neq -1$ for at least one r. The convergence of the series is sufficient for the existence of a mean--value equal to $\prod (1-\frac{1}{p})(1+\sum_{r=1}^{\infty}\frac{F(p^r)}{p^r}))$.

Using this theorem it is easy to obtain the conditions of Erdös and Wintner. We also see that the characteristic function of the limiting distribution is equal to

$$\prod (1-\frac{1}{p})(1+\sum_{r=1}^{\infty}\frac{e^{itf(p^r)}}{p^r}).$$

I ought to mention that Schönberg had already obtained a partial solution of the problem by use of the theorem of Paul Lévy.

Problem 2 is also easily solved for additive functions by means of the theorem of Paul Levy, using now the more complete results of G. Halász concerning the behavior of the mean $\frac{1}{n}\sum_{m=1}^{n} F(m)$ where F is a multiplicative function of absolute value ≤ 1.

By the theorem of Paul Lévy $f(m)-\alpha_n$ has a limiting distribution if and only if there exists a function Φ continuous at the point $t=0$ such that, as n tends to infinity,

$$\frac{1}{n}\sum_{m=1}^{n} e^{it(f(m)-\alpha_n)} = \Phi(t)+o(1).$$

This is equivalent to $\frac{1}{n}\sum_{m=1}^{n} F_t(m) = \Phi(t)e^{it\alpha_n}+o(1)$.

Here one can use the results of Halász.

This leads to the following theorem :

<u>In order that there exist a sequence</u> $\{\alpha_n\}$ <u>such that</u> $f(m)-\alpha_n$ <u>possess a limiting distribution the following condition is necessary and sufficient</u> :

<u>There exists a real</u> a <u>such that the function</u> $g(n)= f(n)-a\log n$ <u>satisfies</u>

$$\sum \frac{\|g(p)\|^2}{p} < \infty.$$

<u>When this condition is satisfied</u> $f(m)-\alpha_n$ <u>possesses a limiting distribution if and only if</u>

$$\alpha_n = \sum_{p\leq n} \frac{\|g(p)\|}{p} + a\log n + \text{constant} + o(1).$$

This result has been found independently by Elliott and Ryavec, Levin and Timofeev, Kubilius, and myself.

An additional problem to problems 1 and 2 is the study of the limiting distribution when it exists.

It follows from a general theorem of Jessen and Wintner on infinite convolutions that in both cases the limiting distribution is of pure type, i.e. discrete, absolutely continuous or singular.

In the case of problem 1 and also in the case of problem 2 if $a=0$, the limiting distribution is continuous if and only if

$$\sum_{f(p)\neq 0} \frac{1}{p} = \infty.$$

Erdös had proved this for problem 1 by purely arithmetical (rather complicated) arguments. In fact it follows quite easily from a theorem of Paul Lévy.

For problem 2, if $a \neq 0$, then the limiting distribution is absolutely continuous.

Now I turn to problem 3.

The theorem of Erdös and Kac gives a solution in the particular case of strongly additive functions which are bounded on the set of all primes and satisfy

$$\sum \frac{f(p)^2}{p} = \infty.$$

I think it is interesting to give here an outline of their proof for the general theory developed by Kubilius has its roots in it.

The basic idea is the following one :

To each prime p associate the function ρ_p defined by

$$\rho_p(n) = \begin{cases} f(p) & \text{if } p \mid n, \\ 0 & \text{if } p \nmid n. \end{cases}$$

We have $f(n) = \sum \rho_p(n)$, the sum containing only a finite number of non-zero terms.

The set of those n which are divisible by p has the density $\frac{1}{p}$ and the set of those n which are not divisible by p has the density $1 - \frac{1}{p}$.

This suggests to think of ρ_p as taking on the value $f(p)$ with probability $\frac{1}{p}$ and the value 0 with probability $1 - \frac{1}{p}$.

The functions ρ_p appear as "statistically independent" for, if E and E' are disjoint finite sets of primes, then the set of those n which are divisible by the p's of E and are not divisible by the p's of E' has the density

$$\left(\prod_{p \in E} \frac{1}{p}\right)\left(\prod_{p \in E'} \left(1 - \frac{1}{p}\right)\right).$$

But this approach fails because

- the subsets of $\mathbb{N}$ which possess a density do not constitute a σ-algebra,
- the density is not countably additive.

To overcome this difficulty Erdős and Kac̆ introduce the "truncated function"

$$f_y = \sum_{p\le y} \rho_p \qquad \text{(i.e. } f_y(n) = \sum_{\substack{p|n \\ p\le y}} f(p)\text{)},$$

where $y\ge 2$.

As y tends to infinity $f_y(n)$ tends to $f(n)$.

The function f_y takes on a finite number of distinct values.

If P_y is the set of the primes $\le y$, then these values are the sums $\sum_{p\in E} f(p)$ where E is a subset of P_y.

If a is one of these values, then the set of the positive integers n for which $f_y(n)=a$ possesses a density because it is the union of the disjoint sets

$$\{n\in\mathbb{N} : p|n \text{ if } p\in E \text{ and } p\nmid n \text{ if } p\in P_y\setminus E\}$$

where E runs through the set of the subsets of P_y for which $\sum_{p\in E} f(p)=a$.

Let us introduce a family $\{X_p\}$ of independent random variables, where

$$X_p = \begin{cases} f(p) & \text{with probability } \frac{1}{p}, \\ 0 & \text{with probability } 1-\frac{1}{p}. \end{cases}$$

The sum $\sum_{p\le y} X_p$ takes on the same values as the function f_y and the density of the set of the n's for which $f_y(n)=a$ is equal to $\text{Prob}(\sum_{p\le y} X_p=a)$.

Consequently, for any y such that $B(y)>0$, the set of the n's for which

$$\frac{f_y(n)-A(y)}{B(y)} \le t$$

has the density $\sigma_y(t)$, where σ_y is the distribution function of the random variable $\frac{1}{B(y)}(\sum_{p\leq y} X_p - A(y))$, i.e. as x tends to infinity

$$\frac{1}{x} \# \{n \leq x : \frac{f_y(n)-A(y)}{B(y)} \leq t\} \text{ tends to } \sigma_y(t).$$

Erdös and Kac show that, if x and y tend to infinity in such a way that $\frac{\log y}{\log x}$ tends to zero, then the difference

$$\frac{1}{x} \# \{n \leq x : \frac{f_y(n)-A(y)}{B(y)} \leq t\} - \sigma_y(t)$$

tends to zero (the proof uses Brun's sieve).

They also prove (more easily) that, if $\frac{\log x}{\log y} = o\,(B(x))$, then the difference

$$\frac{1}{x} \# \{n \leq x : \frac{f_y(n)-A(y)}{B(y)} \leq t\} - \frac{1}{x} \# \{n \leq x : \frac{f(n)-A(x)}{B(x)} \leq t\}$$

tends to zero.

They choose y as a function of x so that $\frac{\log y}{\log x}$ tends to zero and $\frac{\log x}{\log y} = o(B(x))$. So the difference

$$\frac{1}{x} \# \{n \leq x : \frac{f(n)-A(x)}{B(x)} \leq t\} - \sigma_y(t)$$

tends to zero.

They deduce from the central limit theorem for sums of independent random variables that

$$\sigma_y(t) \text{ tends to } \frac{1}{\sqrt{2\pi}} \int_{-\infty}^{t} e^{-u^2/2} du$$

(the expectation of X_p is $\frac{f(p)}{p}$ and its variance is $(1-\frac{1}{p})\frac{f(p)^2}{p}$. So $\sum_{p\leq y} \text{Expect } X_p = A(y)$ and $\sum_{p\leq y} \text{Var } X_p = B(y)^2 + 0(1))$.

The idea of introducing independent random variables is due to Kac. The proof was made rigorous by Erdös.

Kubilius has systematized this method of proof.

By it he proved in particular the general result that I will state presently, where f is still supposed to be strongly additive and $A(x)$ and $B(x)$ are defined as above.

Let us say that f belongs to the class (H) if as x tends to infinity $B(x)$ tends to infinity and $B(x^\lambda) \sim B(x)$ for every $\lambda>1$.

Suppose that f belongs to the class (H).

Then, in order that $(f(m)-A(n))/B(n)$ possess a limiting distribution of variance 1, it is necessary and sufficient that there exist a distribution function K such that, as x tends to infinity,

$$\frac{1}{B(x)^2} \sum_{\substack{p \leq x \\ f(p) \leq uB(x)}} \frac{f(p)^2}{p}$$ converges to $K(u)$ at each point of continuity of K

The characteristic function of the limiting distribution is

$$\exp\left(\int_{-\infty}^{\infty} \frac{e^{itu}-itu-1}{u^2}\, dK(u)\right).$$

Here I wish to emphasize that the condition "of variance 1" is essential. It was missing in the first paper of Kubilius and the theorem has been sometimes quoted without it - including by myself. It is so in particular in Elliott's book.

It is possible to give a condition for the existence of a limiting distribution whose variance is not necessarily one.

The condition is that the measure μ_n defined on $\mathbb{R}$ by

$$\mu_n(E) = \frac{1}{B(x)^2} \sum_{\frac{f(p)}{B(x)} \in E} \frac{f(p)^2}{p}$$

should converge weakly to some measure μ.

The variance of the limiting distribution is $\mu(\mathbb{R})$ (which is ≤ 1).

It is easy to see that Kubilius' theorem implies the theorem of Erdős and Kač.

It was suggested by Kač to try to prove the latter by use of the moments. For that one should prove that each of the moments of the distribution of the numbers $(f(n)-A(x))/B(x)$ where $n \leq x$ converges as x tends to infinity to the corresponding moment of the normal law of Gauss. This was achieved for the first time in the general case by Halberstam. His proof used rather complicated calculations. I published a simpler proof and later I found further simplifications that I did not publish.

Kubilius' theorem gives a solution of problem 3 in the particular case of strongly additive functions of class (H). Here the sequences $\{\alpha_n\}$ and

$\{\beta_n\}$ are determined a priori from the function f : $\alpha_n=A(n)$ and $\beta_n=B(n)$. It was not so in the initial statement of the problem.

It is easy to see that, if problem 3 has a solution, then β_n must tend to a finite positive limit or to $+\infty$. One sees also that in the first case there is also a solution where $\beta_n=1$, i.e. problem 2 has a solution. So to treat problem 3 one may assume that β_n tends to infinity.

It is convenient to take $\alpha_n=\alpha(n)$, $\beta_n=\beta(n)$, where α and β are functions of a real variable whose domain is some interval $[x_o,\infty[$ where $x_o\geq 0$.

The main results were obtained by Levin and Timofeev and by Elliott.

These authors consider a given function β and search conditions for the existence of a function α such that $(f(m)-\alpha(n))/\beta(n)$ have a limiting distribution. They use the theory of Dirichlet series.

Necessary and sufficient conditions are obtained in the case when, as x tends to infinity, $\beta(x^\lambda)/\beta(x)$ tends to 1 uniformly on every compact set contained in the interval $]0,\infty[$.

These conditions are too complicated to be stated here.

Any stable law may be obtained as limit law. Certain laws cannot occur.

There are also results for the case when $\beta(x^\lambda)/\beta(x)$ tends to λ^δ, $\delta>0$.

Now I will end this lecture saying that probabilistic number theory deals with many problems other than those that I have considered here. Among those I may quote the following ones :

- study of the distribution of the values of an additive function when n runs through certain special sequences, such as the sequence of the values of a polynomial with integral coefficients on the positive integers, or on the primes. A particularly interesting case is the sequence of "shifted primes".
- study of the distribution modulo 1 of an additive function.
- evaluation of the number of the n's$\leq x$ for which the function has a given value ("local laws").
- rate of convergence to the normal law in the theorem of Erdős and Kac.

On the number of prime factors of an integer

Adolf Hildebrand

1. Introduction: The paper of Hardy and Ramanujan.

During the time Ramanujan spent in England he collaborated with Hardy on six papers. One of these [HR] was entitled "The normal number of prime factors of a number n". I want to begin by describing its contents.

There are two ways of defining the number of prime factors of an integer n; first, as the number of distinct prime factors in the prime factorization of n, and secondly as the total number of prime factors, i.e., the number of distinct prime factors counted with multiplicity. The first function is denoted by $\omega(n)$, the second by $\Omega(n)$. (For example, $\omega(12) = \omega(2^2 \cdot 3) = 2$, $\Omega(12) = 3$). Both functions provide a natural measure for the degree of "compositeness" of an integer: the smaller $\omega(n)$ or $\Omega(n)$ is, the closer in a certain sense n is to being a prime.

In their paper, Hardy and Ramanujan study both of these functions. They begin by observing that, trivially,

$$\Omega(n) \leq \frac{\log n}{\log 2}$$

for all n, with equality when n is a power of 2, and, less trivially though not difficult to show,

$$\omega(n) \leq (1 + o(1)) \frac{\log n}{\log \log n},$$

for $n \to \infty$, with asymptotic equality when n is the product of the first k primes and $k \to \infty$. They express this by saying that the "maximal order"

ISBN 0-12-058560-X

of the functions $\Omega(n)$ and $\omega(n)$ are $\log n/\log 2$ and $\log n/\log\log n$, respectively. The concept of the maximal order of an arithmetic function plays an important role in another paper of Ramanujan [Ra] (cf. Nicolas' paper in these Proceedings).

After briefly mentioning the problem of the "average order" of the functions $\omega(n)$ and $\Omega(n)$, Hardy and Ramanujan go on to discuss the "normal order" of these functions. They define an arithmetic function $f(n)$ as having normal order $\phi(n)$, if, for every $\varepsilon > 0$, the inequality

$$(1 - \varepsilon)\phi(n) < f(n) < (1 + \varepsilon)\phi(n)$$

holds for "almost all" positive integers n, i.e., for all except $o(x)$ integers $1 \leq n \leq x$, as $x \to \infty$. The main result of the paper is that the functions $\omega(n)$ and $\Omega(n)$ have normal order $\log\log n$, in the following more precise form.

<u>Theorem</u> (Hardy-Ramanujan [HR]): Let $f(n)$ denote either $\omega(n)$ or $\Omega(n)$. Then, given any function $\psi(x)$ satisfying $\psi(x) \to \infty$ $(x \to \infty)$, the inequality

$$|f(n) - \log\log n| \leq \psi(n)\sqrt{\log\log n} \tag{1}$$

holds for almost all positive integers n.

Hardy and Ramanujan deduce this result from the following lemma, which gives an upper bound for the quantities

$$\pi(x,k) = \sum_{\substack{n\le x\\ \omega(n)=k}} 1, \qquad N(x,k) = \sum_{\substack{n\le x\\ \Omega(n)=k}} 1.$$

<u>Lemma</u> (Hardy-Ramanujan [HR]). There exist positive constants c_1 and c_2 such that, for every positive integer k and all $x \geq 2$,

$$\left.\begin{matrix}\pi(x,k)\\ N(x,k)\end{matrix}\right\} \leq c_1 \frac{x}{\log x} \cdot \frac{(\log\log x + c_2)^{k-1}}{(k-1)!} \tag{2}$$

The deduction of the theorem from the lemma is relatively easy; the lemma is used to obtain an upper bound for the number of integers $n \leq x$ for which (1) fails. The proof of the lemma itself is achieved by induction on k, using Chebycheff's bound for the number of primes $\leq x$ in the case $k = 1$. The argument is elementary and not very complicated, although some technical difficulties have to be overcome.

Hardy and Ramanujan's theorem and the concepts it involved ("normal order", "almost all integers") clearly have a probabilistic flavor. In fact, one can regard it as the first result of "probabilistic number theory", a new branch in number theory whose development was to a large extent influenced by Hardy and Ramanujan's paper. The importance of their result lies mainly in the fact that it is susceptible to far-reaching generalizations and refinements. Results of the same type, it turned out, hold for a large class of arithmetic functions, the so-called additive functions, i.e., functions $f(n)$ satisfying

$$f(nm) = f(n) + f(m) \quad \text{if} \quad (n,m) = 1.$$

The study of the behavior of such functions and their "value distribution" forms the core of probabilistic number theory; see, for example, Elliott's two-volume monograph [El] or Delange's survey paper in these Proceedings.

Here I want to confine myself to the original problem considered by Hardy and Ramanujan, namely the number of prime factors of an integer and more specifically the estimation of $\pi(x,k)$ and $N(x,k)$. Hardy and Ramanujan's lemma gives an upper bound for these quantities that is valid uniformly in k. This uniformity is crucial for their application.

For fixed k, Landau [La] had earlier obtained the asymptotic formula

$$(3) \qquad \pi(x,k) \sim N(x,k) \sim \frac{x}{\log x} \cdot \frac{(\log\log x)^{k-1}}{(k-1)!} \quad (x \to \infty).$$

The problem therefore arises to extend this formula to one that is valid uniformly in k, or at least in a certain range of values k. In 1948 Erdös showed that (3) also holds when k is close to $\log\log x$. An extension of (3) to the range $k \ll \log\log x$ has been given in 1954 by Sathe and Selberg. However, it was only quite recently that asymptotic formulae valid for larger values of k had been obtained. In the following sections I will survey these developments.

2. An asymptotic formula for $k \approx \log\log x$.

Of particular interest is the behavior of $\pi(x,k)$ and $N(x,k)$ when k is close to the "normal" number of prime factors of an integer $\leq x$, i.e., when k is about $\log\log x$. In 1948, Erdös obtained an asymptotic formula for this range.

Theorem (Erdös [Er]). For any fixed constant C the asymptotic formula

$$(4) \qquad \pi(x,k) \sim N(x,k) \sim \frac{x}{\log x} \cdot \frac{(\log \log x)^{k-1}}{(k-1)!} \sim \frac{x}{\sqrt{2\pi \log \log x}} \exp\left\{-\frac{1}{2} \cdot \frac{(k - \log \log x)^2}{\log \log x}\right\}$$

holds, as $x \to \infty$, uniformly in the range

$$(5) \qquad |k - \log \log x| \leq C\sqrt{\log \log x} .$$

In (4) two different expressions are given, both of which are asymptotically equal to $\pi(x,k)$ or $N(x,k)$. The first of these is the same as the one Landau had obtained for fixed k (cf. (3)). The second does not appear in Erdös' paper, but is easily seen (using Stirling's formula) to be asymptotically equal to the first in the range (5). This last expression sheds more light on the finer behavior of $\pi(x,k)$ and $N(x,k)$, for it shows that $\pi(x,k)/x$ and $N(x,k)/x$ are approximately equal to the density function of a normally distributed random variable with mean $\log \log x$ and standard deviation $\sqrt{\log \log x}$. Erdös' theorem refines the following result, proved a few years earlier by Erdös and Kac.

Theorem (Erdös-Kac [EK]): Let $f(n)$ denote either $\omega(n)$ or $\Omega(n)$. For any fixed real numbers $a < b$, the proportion of integers $n \leq x$, for which

$$a < \frac{f(n) - \log \log n}{\sqrt{\log \log n}} \leq b$$

holds, approaches

$$\frac{1}{\sqrt{2\pi}} \int_a^b e^{-t^2/2} dt,$$

as $x \to \infty$.

This is the celebrated "Erdös-Kac theorem" which is the archetype for a large class of "limit theorems for addition functions" that are studied in probabilistic number theory. It says, in essence, that the number of prime factors of an integer n obeys the normal law with mean $\log \log n$ and standard deviation $\sqrt{\log \log n}$. It thus constitutes a striking refinement of the theorem of Hardy and Ramanujan.

Erdös proves his theorem in an essentially elementary, but ingenious manner. He remarks that his method does not work when k is substantially smaller that $\log \log x$, but conjectures that a formula of the same type should be valid for all $k \ll \log \log x$.

3. The Sathe-Selberg formulae.

The gap left between the results of Landau and Erdös was closed in 1954 by Sathe and Selberg who, independently and by different methods, obtained an asymptotic formula that is valid uniformly in $k \leq C \log \log x$.

Theorem (Sathe [Sa]; Selberg [Se]). Let

$$F(z) = \frac{1}{\Gamma(z+1)} \prod_p \left(1 + \frac{z}{p-1}\right)\left(1 - \frac{1}{p}\right)^z,$$

$$G(z) = \frac{1}{\Gamma(z+1)} \prod_p \left(1 - \frac{z}{p}\right)^{-1}\left(1 - \frac{1}{p}\right)^z,$$

where the products are extended over all primes. Then the relations

$$(6)\qquad \pi(x,k) \sim F\left(\frac{k}{\log\log x}\right)\frac{x}{\log x}\cdot\frac{(\log\log x)^{k-1}}{(k-1)!}$$

and

$$(7)\qquad N(x,k) \sim G\left(\frac{k}{\log\log x}\right)\frac{x}{\log x}\cdot\frac{(\log\log x)^{k-1}}{(k-1)!}$$

hold, as $x \to \infty$, uniformly in the range

$$(8)\qquad 1 \leq k \leq C \log\log x$$

for any fixed positive constant $C < 2$. Moreover, (6) remains valid when in (8) C is an arbitrary positive constant.

The function $F(z)$ is entire, but $G(z)$ has a pole at $z = 2$. Thus (7) cannot be valid when k is close to $2 \log\log x$. However, as Selbrg in his paper indicated, one can obtain a modified form of (7) that is valid in the range (8) with an arbitrary fixed C. Note that the factors $F(\ldots)$ and $G(\ldots)$ in (6) and (7) are bounded from above and below in the considered range, and approach 1 if $k/\log\log x \to 1$ or if $k/\log\log x \to 0$. In these cases, therefore, Landau's formula (3) is valid.

Sathe's proof was essentially elementary, but very complicated. His paper, published in several parts, had a total length of about 130 pages. Selberg's proof, on the other hand, was short and elegant, and his method proved to be a widely applicable one. I will briefly describe Selberg's method, considering only the case of $\pi(x,k)$.

The basic idea is to write

$$\pi(x,k) = \sum_{\substack{n\le x\\ \omega(n)=k}} 1$$

and "resolve" the arithmetic conditions $n \le x$ and $\omega(n) = k$ using two analytic devices. The first is Cauchy's integral formula, which gives

$$\sum_{\substack{n\le x\\ \omega(n)=k}} 1 = \frac{1}{2\pi i}\oint_{|z|=r}\Big(\sum_{n\le x} z^{\omega(n)}\Big)\frac{dz}{z^{k+1}} \tag{9}$$

for any positive real number r. The second is the so-called Perron formula, well-known in Analytic Number Theory, which gives

$$\sum_{n\le x} z^{\omega(n)} = \frac{1}{2\pi i}\int_{\sigma-i\infty}^{\sigma+i\infty}\Big(\sum_{n\ge 1}\frac{z^{\omega(n)}}{n^s}\Big)\frac{x^s}{s}\,ds \tag{10}$$

for any real number $\sigma > 1$. Using (10) Selberg proved

$$\sum_{n\le x} z^{\omega(n)} = xzF(z)(\log x)^{z-1} + O(x(\log x)^{\mathrm{Re} z-2}) \tag{11}$$

uniformly for $x \ge 2$ and all complex numbers z satisfying $|z| \le C$, for any fixed constant C. Inserting (11) into (9), with an appropriate choice of r, easily yields the formula (6) for $\pi(x,k)$.

Formula (11) is in fact a particular case of a class of similar formulae that Selberg had obtained in his paper and which have since become known as "Selberg's formulae". These formulae proved to be very useful in establishing results involving the functions $\omega(n)$, $\Omega(n)$ or similar functions that go far beyond the applications Selberg gave in his paper. The full scope of these formulae has been first realized by Delange who in [De 1] gave a large number of interesting applications.

4. Asymptotic formulae for large k: the case of $N(x,k)$.

For a long period the behavior of $\pi(x,k)$ and $N(x,k)$ outside the range of validity of the Sathe-Selberg formulae remained oscure. Extending this range appeared to be difficult, if at all possible. It came therefore as a surprise when a few years ago Nicolas discovered a very simple asymptotic formula for $N(x,k)$ that is valid essentially in the complement of the Selberg-Sathe range.

Theorem (Nicolas [Ni]). With a certain positive constant C we have

$$N(x,k) \sim C \frac{x}{2^k} \log \frac{x}{2^k} \tag{12}$$

as $x \to \infty$, uniformly for all k satisfying

$$(2 + \varepsilon) \log \log x \leq k = o(\log x), \tag{13}$$

for any fixed $\varepsilon > 0$.

That $N(x,k)$ has such a simple asymptotic behavior for large k is rather surprising. The explanation lies in the fact that when k is large then most integers counted in $N(x,k)$ are of a very special type, namely a product of a high power of 2 and a number having very few prime factors. Specifically, let $N_\ell(x,k)$ denote the number of integers $n \leq x$ that are of the form $n = 2^{k-\ell}m$, where m is an odd number having ℓ prime factors (in the Ω-sense). Then

$$N(x,k) = \sum_{\ell=0}^{k} N_\ell(x,k),$$

but Nicolas' proof shows that in the range (13) the first few $N_\ell(x,k)$ already almost exhaust $N(x,k)$. Thus, estimating $N(x,k)$ essentially reduces to estimating $N_\ell(x,k)$ for fixed small values of ℓ, and this is relatively easy to carry out.

For the success of this argument it is crucial that the number of prime factors are counted with multiplicity. The argument therefore cannot be applied to $\pi(x,k)$.

5. Elementary bounds for $\pi(x,k)$.

With Nicolas' result the problem of estimating $N(x,k)$ is essentially solved. What remained was to determine the asymptotic behavior of $\pi(x,k)$ for $k \gg \log\log x$. This turned out to be a much more difficult problem and to this date an asymptotic formula for $\pi(x,k)$ comparable to that of Nicolas has not been found.

Upper and lower bounds for $\pi(x,k)$, however, have been known for some time. The simplest and most elegant of these is Hardy and Ramanujan's upper bound (2) that is valid without any restriction on k. Erdös and Nicolas [EN] obtained an equally uniform lower bound, namely

$$\pi(x,k) \geq \pi\left(\frac{x}{p_1 \cdots p_{k-1}}\right) - k + 1,$$

where $p_1 < p_2 < \ldots$ denotes the sequence of primes and $\pi(y)$ is the number of primes $\leq y$. They also showed that if $0 < c < 1$ is fixed, then

$$\sum_{k > c \log x/\log\log x} \pi(x,k) = x^{1-c+o(1)} \quad (x \to \infty).$$

More recently, Pomerance [Po] established the estimate

$$\pi(x,k) = \frac{x}{k! \log x} \exp\{k(\log L + \frac{\log L}{L} + O_\varepsilon(\frac{1}{L}))\}, \tag{14}$$

where

$$L = \log \frac{\log x}{k \log k},$$

for the range

$$(\log\log x)^{1+\varepsilon} \leq k \leq \frac{\log x}{3 \log\log x}.$$

For a large portion of this range, the upper bound in (14) supersedes that in Hardy-Ramanujan's result (3).

Pomerance [Po] also proved that for

$$\frac{\log x}{3 \log\log x} < k \leq \frac{\log x}{\log\log x}\left(1 - \frac{1}{\log\log x}\right)$$

the estimate

$$\pi(x,k) = \frac{x}{k^k}\left(1 - \frac{k \log\log x}{\log x}\right)^k \exp\{O(k)\}$$

holds. The upper bound in the last range represents a natural limit, for $\pi(x,k) = 0$ if $k \geq (1 + \varepsilon) \log x/\log\log x$ and $x \geq x_0(\varepsilon)$, as one can show using the prime number theorem.

These estimates were obtained by various elementary-conbinatorial arguments of "ad hoc" character, none of which gave any hope for obtaining an asymptotic formula.

6. Asymptotic formulae for large k: the case of $\pi(x,k)$.

A first attempt to obtain an asymptotic formula for $\pi(x,k)$ for large k was made by Kolesnik and Straus [KS] who proved that, for $k \leq (\log x)^{3/5-\varepsilon}$, $\pi(x,k)$ is asymptotically equal to a certain, rather complicated expression. However, this result proved to be of little use, since the behavior of the expression they showed to be equivalent to $\pi(x,k)$ is virtually impossible to analyze when k is large.

It was only quite recently that a significant breakthrough had been obtained by the following result of Hensley.

Theorem (Hensley [He]). The Sathe-Selberg formula (6) holds uniformly in the range

$$(15) \qquad 1 \leq k = o((\log\log x)^2/(\log\log\log x)^2).$$

Hensley in fact obtained an asymptotic formula for a range slightly larger than (15) that coincides with the Sathe-Selberg formula if and only if k satisfies (15). In particular, for the validity of the Sathe-Selberg formula the upper bound in (15) is best-possible.

Hensley's result gave some hope for obtaining an asymptotic formula in a still larger range. This turned out to be justified, as the following result shows.

<u>Theorem</u> (Hildebrand-Tenenbaum [HT]). For $k \ll (\log x)/(\log\log x)^2$, $k/\log\log x \to \infty$, we have

$$(16)\qquad \pi(x,k) \sim \frac{x^{\alpha}\rho^{-k}F(\rho,\alpha)}{2\pi\log x\sqrt{\log\frac{\log x}{k\log k}}},$$

where

$$F(z,s) = \sum_{n=1}^{\infty}\frac{z^{\omega(n)}}{n^s}$$

and $\alpha > 1$ and $\rho > 0$ are determined by

$$(17)\qquad x^{\alpha}\rho^{-k}F(\rho,\alpha) = \min_{\substack{\sigma>1\\ r>0}} x^{\sigma}r^{-k}F(r,\sigma).$$

A simple argument shows that the quantity (17), i.e., the numerator in (16), provides an upper bound for $\pi(x,k)$. Namely, we have, for any $\sigma > 1$ and $r > 0$,

$$\pi(x,k) = \sum_{\substack{n\le x\\ \omega(n)=k}} 1 \le \sum_{n=1}^{\infty}\left(\frac{x}{n}\right)^{\sigma} r^{\omega(n)-k}$$

$$= x^{\sigma}r^{-k}F(r,\sigma),$$

and by (17) this upper bound becomes minimal at $(\sigma,r) = (\alpha,\rho)$. Formula (16) then shows that dividing this upper bound by $2\pi\log x\sqrt{\log(\log x/k\log k)}$ yields an expression that is asymptotically equal to $\pi(x,k)$ over a surprisingly large range for k. By slightly modifying the right-hand side of (16), one can actually obtain an asymptotic formula valid for $1 \leq k \ll (\log x)/(\log\log x)^2$.

The formula (16) involves the implicitly defined quantities ρ and α, and therefore does not seem to be easily applicable. Nevertheless, one can use this formula to recover and slightly improve Hensley's theorem as well as the elementary estimate (14) of Pomerance. Moreover, the formula leads to a very simple relation between $\pi(x,k)$ and $\pi(x,k+1)$, namely

$$(18) \qquad \frac{\pi(x,k+1)}{\pi(x,k)} \sim \frac{\log(\log x/k \log k)}{k},$$

that is valid for $k \ll (\log x)/(\log\log x)^2$. This last result is of interest in connection with a conjecture of Erdös [Er] that $\pi(x,k)$ is a unimodal function of k for sufficiently large x, i.e., that for some k_0

$$\pi(x,1) \leq \pi(x,2) \leq \cdots \leq \pi(x,k_0) \geq \pi(x,k_0+1) \geq \cdots.$$

It follows from (18) that $\pi(x,k)$ is increasing for $1 \leq k \leq (1-\varepsilon)\log\log x$, and decreasing for $(1+\varepsilon)\log\log x \leq k \leq (\log x)/(\log\log x)^2$, provided $x \geq x_0(\varepsilon)$. Thus $\pi(x,k)$ is unimodal except possibly in the ranges $(1-\varepsilon)\log\log x \leq k \leq (1+\varepsilon)\log\log x$ and $k > (\log x)/(\log\log x)^2$. The unimodality in the first of these ranges has been proved quite recently by M. Balazard (unpublished), that in the second range remains an open problem.

The proof of (16) is based on the representation

$$(19) \qquad \pi(x,k) = \frac{-1}{4\pi^2} \oint_{|z|=r} \int_{\sigma-i\infty}^{\sigma+i\infty} F(z,s)\, \frac{x^s}{s} \cdot \frac{1}{z^{k+1}}\, ds\, dz,$$

which follows from (9) and (10), with an appropriate choice of $r > 0$ and $\sigma > 1$. The optimal choice of (r,σ), which is crucial for the success of the method, turns out to be (ρ,α), defined by (17). This choice is suggested by the saddle point method, since the function $x^s z^{-k} F(z,s)$ has a (two-dimensional) saddle point at $(z,s) = (\rho,\alpha)$. With $(r,\sigma) = (\rho,\alpha)$ the main contribution to the integral in (19) then comes from a small neighborhood of this saddle point in which the behavior of the integrand can be easily determined by Taylor's formula. In fact, in this neighborhood the integrand can be written as $x^\alpha \rho^{-k} F(\rho,\alpha)$ times a "decay factor" of relatively simple shape, and integration over this "decay factor" produces the denominator in (16).

7. Further results.

I want to mention here some related results that have been obtained in the literature. A considerable body of work has been published on the subject, and I am making no attempt for completeness. Instead, I will concentrate on a handful of typical results all of which were at least indirectly influenced by Hardy and Ramanujan's theorem.

At the end of their paper, Hardy and Ramanujan asked whether other well-known arithmetic functions posses a normal order $\phi(n)$. In order to avoid trivial cases, one has to impose some regularity condition on $\phi(n)$. Hardy and Ramanujan required the function $\phi(n)$ to be "elementary", but it is more appropriate to simply require $\phi(n)$ to be non-decreasing. With this restriction on a normal order, Birch [Bi] proved that the only multiplicative functions having a normal order are the obvious ones, namely the functions $f(n) = n^\alpha$ with fixed $\alpha \geq 0$. The problem which additive functions have a normal order turned out to be more difficult. In

Chapter 15 of his book [El], Elliott obtained a complete characterization of these functions.

As already mentioned, Selberg's formulae proved to be an important tool in a number of applications. Delange [De 1][De 2] has drawn some remarkable consequences of the formula (11). He showed, for example, that for any irrational number λ the sequence $\{\lambda\omega(n)\}$ is uniformly distributed modulo 1. Moreover, he proved that the values of $\omega(n)$ are uniformly distributed in residue classes, in the sense that, for any positive integers a and b,

$$\#\{n \le x : \omega(n) \equiv a \bmod b\} \sim \frac{x}{b} \ (x \to \infty).$$

Another observation of Delange is that formula (11) can be used to prove the Erdös-Kac theorem, quoted in Section 2, and in fact gives a quantitative form of that theorem with best-possible error term. In [De 2] Delange sharpened (11) (and related formulae) by replacing the error term $O(x(\log x)^{\mathrm{Re}z-2})$ by an expansion of the type

$$x(\log x)^z\{\sum_{j=2}^{k} a_j(\log x)^{-j} + O((\log x)^{-k-1})\}.$$

Several authors have obtained analogues of Selberg's formulae when n is restricted to an arithmetic progression ℓ mod k. Delange [De 2] proved such a result for the case of a fixed modulus k. Rieger [Ri] gave a result that is uniform in $k \le (\log x)^c$. This has been recently sharpened by Spiro [Sp]. Results of this type are useful when studying the number of prime factors of integers restricted to an arithmetic progression.

As a natural generalization of the functions $\omega(n)$ and $\Omega(n)$ one can consider the functions $\omega(n;E)$ and $\Omega(n;E)$ defined as the number prime factors of n, counted without resp. with multicity, that belong to a given set E of primes. The study of these functions has been initiated by Halász [Ha] who obtained results of remarkable generality. For example, he showed that if

$$E(x) = \sum_{\substack{p \leq x \\ p \in E}} \frac{1}{p}$$

is unbounded, then, as $x \to \infty$, the asymptotic formula

$$\#\{n \leq x : \omega(n;E)\} = k\} \sim \frac{xE(x)^k}{k!} e^{-E(x)}$$

holds whenever $k \sim E(x)$. This generalizes Erdös' result (4) which corresponds tot he case when E is the set of all primes. For further results in this direction see Norton [No] and Balazard [Ba].

Finally, I should mention that the error terms implied in the relations " $\sim$ " of the quoted asymptotic results can all be made explicit, and in most cases this has already been done in the original papers. For example, in the Sathe-Selberg formula (6) the left- and right-hand sides differ by a factor $1 + O(1/\log \log x)$ uniformly for k lying in the range (8) (see [Se]).

References

[Ba] M. Balazard, Sur la répartition des valeurs de certaines fonctions arithmétiques additives. Thèse, Limoges 1987.

[Bi] B. J. Birch, Multiplicative functions with non-decreasing normal order. J. London Math. Soc. 42(1967), 149-151.

[De 1] H. Delange, Sur les formules dues à A. Selberg. Bull. Sci. Math. 83(1959), 101-111.

[De 2] H. Delange, Sur les formules de A. Selberg. Acta Arith. 19(1971), 105-149.

[EL] P. D. T. A. Elliott, Probabilistic Number Theory I, II. Springer-Verlag 1979/1980.

[EN] P. Erdös and J.-L. Nicolas, Sur la fonction: nombre de facteurs premiers de n. L'Enseignement Math. 27(1981), 3-27.

[Er] P. Erdös, On the integers having exactly K prime factors. Ann. Math. (2) 49(1948), 53-66.

[Ha] G. Halász, On the distribution of additive and mean values of multiplicative arithmetic functions. Studia Scient. Math. Hungar. 6(1971), 211-233.

[He] D. Hensley, The distribution of round numbers. Proc. London Math. Soc. (3) 54(1987), 412-444.

[HR] G. H. Hardy and S. Ramanujan, The normal number of prime factors of a number n. Quart. J. Math. 48(1917), 76-92.

[HT] A. Hildebrand and G. Tenenbaum, On the number of prime factors of an integer. Duke J. Math., to appear.

[KS] G. Kolesnik and E. G. Straus, On the distribution of integers with a given number of prime factors. Acta Arith. 37(1980), 181-199.

[La] E. Landau, Handbuch der Lehre von der Verteilung der Primzahlen. Chelsea, New York, 1953, p. 211.

[Ni] J.-L. Nicolas, Sur la distribution des entiers ayant une quantité fixée de facteurs premiers. Acta Arith. 44(1984), 191-200.

[No] K. K. Norton, On the number of restricted prime factors of an integer I, Illinois J. Math. 20(1976), 681-705; II, Acta Math. 143(1979), 9-38; III, L'Enseignement Math. 28(1982), 31-52.

[Po] C. Pomerance, On the distribution of round numbers. In: K. Alladi (Ed.), Number Theory (Proc. Ootacamund, India 1984), 173-200. Springer Lecture Notes 1122.

[Ra] S. Ramanujan, Highly composite numbers. Proc. London Math. Soc. (2) 14(1915), 347-409.

[Ri] G. J. Rieger, Zum Teilerproblem von Atle Selberg, Math. Nachr. 30(1965), 181-192.

[Sa] L. G. Sathe, On a problem of Hardy on the distribution of integers having a given number of prime factors. J. Indian Math. Soc. 17(1953), 63-141; 18(1954), 27-81.

[Se] A. Selberg, Note on a paper by L. G. Sathe. J. Indian Math. Soc. 18(1954), 83-87.

[Sp] C. Spiro, Extensions of some formulae of A. Selberg. Internat. J. Math. & Math. Sci. 8(1985), 283-302.

Department of Mathematics
University of Illinois
1409 West Green Street
Urbana, IL 61801

RAMANUJAN EXPANSIONS OF ARITHMETICAL FUNCTIONS

Wolfgang Schwarz (Frankfurt am Main)

Contents

1. Introduction

The aim of this survey lecture[1,2] is to sketch some aspects of the development of a part of a theory of arithmetical functions beginning with the first far-sighted ideas of Srinivasa RAMANUJAN (Dec.22, 1887 - April 26, 192o) until now. This talk deals with the possibility of associating infinite

[1]Slightly enlarged version of a talk given at the Ramanujan Centenary Conference, Urbana, June 4, 1987.

[2]Closely related survey lectures were given by the author in Warszawa and Vilnius (see [77] and [78]).

ISBN 0-12-058560-X

series $f \sim \sum_{1 \leq r < \infty} a_r \cdot c_r$ to certain arithmetical functions $f\colon \mathbf{N} \to \mathbf{C}$. This vague general idea easily leads to a theory of almost-even arithmetical functions; these constitute a subspace of the (Banach-) space of almost-periodic arithmetical functions.[1] Many number-theorists have contributed to this field, as is shown by the long bibliography (which certainly is not complete), for example N.G.de BRUIJN, E.COHEN, H.DABOUSSI, H.DELANGE, P.DELSARTE, P.ELLIOTT, P.ERDÖS, A.HILDEBRAND, K.-H.INDLEKOFER, J.KNOPFMACHER, Z.KRYŽIUS, J.KUBILIUS, J.-L.MAUCLAIRE, E.V.NOVOSELOV, E.M. PAUL, J.SPILKER, A.WINTNER, and many others.

2. S.Ramanujan's and G.H.Hardy's Contributions

In his paper "On certain trigonometrical sums and their applications in the theory of numbers" RAMANUJAN [67] investigated the exponential sums

$$c_r(n) = \sum_{\substack{1 \leqq a \leqq r \\ \gcd(a,r)=1}} \exp\left(2\pi i \cdot \frac{a}{r} n\right) = \sum_{d \mid \gcd(r,n)} d \cdot \mu\left(\frac{r}{d}\right) \tag{2.1}$$

which now bear his name, the **Ramanujan sums**[2]. These real-valued functions

---

[1] We do not deal with the still larger class $\mathbf{L}^*$ of "uniformly summable" functions, introduced by K.-H.INDLEKOFER (see [39], [43]). f is u.s. iff $\lim_{K \to \infty} \sup_{x \geqq 1} x^{-1} \cdot \sum_{n \leqq x, |f(n)| \geqq K} |f(n)| = 0$.

[2] There are many papers giving generalizations of Ramanujan sums with similar properties, for example by E.COHEN (Duke Math.J. **16**, 85-9o (1949); 22, 543-55o (1955); **25**, 4o1-421 (1958); **26**, 165-182 (1959)), by M.V. SUBBA RAO and V.C.HARRIS (J.London Math.Soc.**41**, 595-6o4 (1966)), by D.SURYANARAYANA (Boll.Un.Mat.Ital. **15**, 424-43o (1978)) and others. G. J.RIEGER [69] investigates Ramanujan sums in algebraic number fields.

c_r, $r = 1,2,\ldots$, have a number of remarkable properties:

- the map $n \mapsto c_r(n)$ is periodic with period r.
- $c_r(n)$ is **even mod r**, that means $c_r(n) = c_r(\gcd(r,n))$. The notion of even-ness seems to be due to E.COHEN [6].
- the map $r \mapsto c_r(n)$ is multiplicative: If $\gcd(r,r') = 1$, then $c_{r\cdot r'}(n) = c_r(n)\cdot c_{r'}(n)$. The values $c_r(n)$ for $r = p^k$ (a prime-power) are easily calculated.
- the characteristic functions $\chi_r(n) = 1$ if $r|n$, $= 0$ if $r\nmid n$, may be expressed by the c_r, $\chi_r(n) = r^{-1}\cdot\sum_{d|r} c_d(n)$ and vice versa (reformulating (2.1)) $c_r(n) = \sum_{d|n} d\,\mu(\frac{r}{d})\,\chi_d(n)$.
- obvious from (2.1) is the estimate

$$|c_r(n)| \leq \min\ \{\varphi(r),\ n\cdot\tau(n)\}. \tag{2.2}$$

It was RAMANUJAN's aim to obtain expressions of (wellknown) arithmetical functions in the form of an infinite (convergent) series

$$f(n) = \sum_{1\leq r<\infty} a_r\cdot c_r(n) \tag{2.3}$$

by using elementary transformations; for example RAMANUJAN got the expansions

$$n^{-1}\cdot\sigma(n) = \frac{1}{6}\pi^2\cdot\sum_{r\geq 1} r^{-2}\cdot c_r(n),$$

$$n^{-1}\cdot\varphi(n) = 6\,\pi^{-2}\cdot\sum_{r\geq 1} \mu(r)\,\{\varphi_2(r)\}^{-1}\cdot c_r(n)$$

(where $\varphi_2(r) = \prod_{p|r}(p^2-1)$), and other expansions of a similar kind.

Furthermore RAMANUJAN produced some deeper examples which depend on the prime number theorem (in the form $\sum_{1\leq n<\infty} n^{-1}\cdot\mu(n) = 0$) like

$$\left.\begin{array}{l} 0 = \sum\limits_{r \geq 1} r^{-1} \cdot c_r(n) \; , \qquad \tau(n) = - \sum\limits_{r \geq 1} \dfrac{\log r}{r} \cdot c_r(n) \; , \\ r(n) = \pi \cdot \sum\limits_{r \geq 1} (-1)^{r-1} \cdot (2r-1)^{-1} \cdot c_{2r-1}(n) \; , \end{array}\right\} \tag{2.4}$$

where $\tau(n)$ is the number of divisors of n and $r(n)$ denotes the number of representations of n as a sum of two squares. Moreover RAMANUJAN proves similar formulae (partly with error terms) for the number of representations of n as a sum of $2s$ squares or $2s$ triangular numbers. According to HARDY [3o] these series have "a peculiar interest because they show explicitly the source of the irregularities in the behaviour of their sums."

In the same paper HARDY wrote "Ramanujan's proofs of his principal formulae are very interesting and ingenious, but are not, I think, the simplest or most natural." HARDY deduced RAMANUJANs formulae by a more uniform method, and he showed in addition

$$n^{-1} \cdot \varphi(n) \cdot \Lambda(n) = \sum_{r \geq 1} \frac{\mu(r)}{\varphi(r)} \cdot c_r(n) \; , \qquad 0 = \sum_{r \geq 1} \frac{c_r(n)}{\varphi(r)} \; .$$

3. Orthogonality and Ramanujan-Fourier-Coefficients

I think, R.CARMICHAEL [4] was the first to notice the important **orthogonality** property

$$M(c_r \cdot c_s) = \begin{cases} \varphi(r) \; , & \text{if } r = s \; , \\ 0 & \text{otherwise} \end{cases} \tag{3.1}$$

of Ramanujan sums, where

$$M(f) = \lim_{x \to \infty} \frac{1}{x} \cdot \sum_{n \leq x} f(n) \tag{3.2}$$

denotes the **mean-value** of $f : \mathbf{N} \to \mathbf{C}$ (if it exists). There is an **inner product**

$$< f,g > = M(f \cdot \overline{g}) \tag{3.3}$$

(on certain spaces of arithmetical functions), and this product suggests **Ramanujan expansions**

$$f \sim \sum_{r \geq 1} a_r(f) \cdot c_r \tag{3.4}$$

for arithmetical functions f in a suitable Hilbert space (see e.g. [7o], Chapter 4) with the "natural coefficients"

$$a_r(f) = \{ \varphi(r) \}^{-1} \cdot < f, c_r > . \tag{3.5}$$

In order to get a somehow satisfactory theory of Ramanujan expansions (3.4) the case of functions f satisfying $M(f) = 0$ will not be considered (and so expansions like $\sum_{r \geq 1} r^{-1} \cdot c_r(n) = 0$ are not dealt with in the sequel).

One of the early general results is due to A.WINTNER [9o] , §33, §35. If $\sum_{n \geq 1} n^{-1} \cdot |f'(n)|$ is absolutely convergent, where $f' = \mu * f$ denotes the convolution of the Moebius function μ with f, then the coefficients (3.5) exist. If moreover [1]

$$\sum_{n \geq 1} n^{-1} \cdot |f'(n)| \cdot \tau(n) < \infty \tag{3.6}$$

then the Ramanujan expansion (2.3) is pointwise convergent.[2]

---

[1] In [9o] , § 34 it is shown that the absolute convergence of $\sum_{n \geq 1} n^{-1} \cdot |f'(n)|$ is compatible with the divergence of $\sum_{r \geq 1} a_r c_r(n)$.

[2] In fact, it is absolutely convergent.

Independently two years later M.J.DELSARTE [23] also published some general results on the convergence of Ramanujan expansions.
Condition (3.6) was weakened by E.COHEN [7] and by H.DELANGE [18], and there is a recent result of DELANGE [22] on the existence of the coefficients (3.5). If $\sum_{n\leq x} |f(n)| = O(x)$ and if the limit $\lim_{x\to\infty} x^{-1}\cdot\sum_{n\leq x,\gcd(r,n)=d} f(n)$ exists for any $d|r$, then

$$\sum_{n\geq 1} (n\cdot r)^{-1}\cdot f'(nr) = \{\varphi(r)\}^{-1}\cdot\lim_{x\to\infty} x^{-1}\cdot\sum_{n\leq x} f(n)\cdot c_r(n) .$$

E.COHEN [8] began with the development of a general theory of almost-even functions defined on rather general structures, which later was continued by J.KNOPFMACHER (see [48]) .

4. Spaces of Almost-Periodic and Almost-Even Functions

Writing, as usual,

$$e_\beta(n) = \exp(2\pi i\beta n), \tag{4.1}$$

we define the vector spaces

$$\mathbf{A} = \mathrm{Lin}_{\mathbf{C}}\{e_\alpha;\alpha\in\mathbf{R/Z}\},\quad \mathcal{D} = \mathrm{Lin}_{\mathbf{C}}\{e_\alpha;\ \alpha\in\mathbf{Q/Z}\}, \tag{4.2}$$
$$\mathcal{B} = \mathrm{Lin}_{\mathbf{C}}\{c_r;\ r = 1,2,\dots\} = \{f:\mathbf{N}\to\mathbf{C};\ \exists\, k \text{ s.t. } f(n) = f(\gcd(n,k))\}.$$

The functions in $\mathcal{D}$ resp. $\mathcal{B}$ are the periodic resp. even functions. The supremum norm ("uniform" norm)

$$\|f\|_u = \sup_{n\in\mathbf{N}} |f(n)| \tag{4.3}$$

enables us to obtain the spaces

$$\mathbf{A}_u = \|\cdot\|_u\text{- closure of } \mathbf{A},\ \mathbf{B}_u,\ \mathbf{D}_u \tag{4.4}$$

of **uniformly-almost-periodic**, **uniformly-almost-even**, resp. **uniformly-limit-periodic** functions. However, these spaces are rather small, as old results of de BRUIJN [3] and others show.

Assume f to be multiplicative. Then $f \in \mathbf{B}_u$ if and only if
(i) $\lim_{k\to\infty} f(p^k)$ exists for any prime p,
(ii) $\sum_p \sup_k |f(p^k)-1| < \infty$.
Therefore even the nice function $n \to \varphi(n)/n$ is **not** in $\mathbf{B}_u$.

The multiplicative function f is in $\mathbf{A}_u$ iff there exists a character χ mod N such that
(i) $\lim_{k\to\infty} f(p^k) = 0$, if $p|N$,
(ii) $\lim_{k\to\infty} \chi(p^k)\cdot f(p^k) \neq 0$ exists for any $p \nmid N$,
(iii) $\sum_p \sup_k |\overline{\chi}(p^k) f(p^k) - 1| < \infty$ (de BRUIJN).

Assume f to be additive. Then $f \in \mathbf{B}_u$ iff $f \in \mathbf{A}_u$ iff
(i) $\lim_{k\to\infty} f(p^k)$ exists for any prime p,
(ii) $\sum_p \sup_k |f(p^k)| < \infty$.
[Van KAMPEN [45], J.KNOPFMACHER [48], SCHWARZ & SPILKER [81].]

By the way, GELFANDs theory[1] of commutative Banach algebras shows that

$$\mathbf{B}_u \cong C(\mathbf{N}^*) \tag{4.5}$$

[similarly $\mathbf{D}_u \cong C(\mathbf{N}^{**})$ and $\mathbf{A}_u \cong C(\mathbf{N}^{***})$] with the maximal ideal space $\mathbf{N}^*$, a compactification of the set $\mathbf{N}$ of positive integers. This compactification[2], as shown in SPILKER & SCHWARZ [80], may be given explicitly by $\mathbf{N}^* = \prod_p \mathbf{N}_p$, where $\mathbf{N}_p = \{1, p, p^2, \ldots, p^\infty\}$ is the ALEXANDROFF one-point-compactification of the discrete topological space $\{1, p, p^2, \ldots\}$.[3]

---

[1] See, for example, RUDIN [70], § 18, or [71], Chapter 11.
[2] See also KNOPFMACHER [48], Chapter 7.
[3] KRYŽIUS [50] explicitly describes further compactifications.

Denoting the image of $f \in \mathcal{B}_u$ under the isomorphism (4.5) by f^*, then the mean-value operator $M^*: \mathcal{C}(\mathbf{N}^*) \to \mathbf{C}$, defined by $M^*(f^*) = M(f)$, induces a measure μ on some σ-algebra on $\mathbf{N}^*$ (via the Riesz representation theorem). This measure is a product measure (see [81])

$$\mu = \prod_p \mu_p \text{ , where } \mu_p(p^m) = p^{-m} \cdot (1 - p^{-1}) \text{ .} \tag{4.6}$$

Unfortunately, **N** is a set of measure zero in **N***.

There are more useful (semi-) norms

$$\| f \|_q = \left\{ \limsup_{x \to \infty} x^{-1} \cdot \sum_{n \le x} |f(n)|^q \right\}^{1/q} , \quad q \ge 1, \tag{4.7}$$

which permit the definition of the larger spaces

$$\mathbf{A}^q = \|.\|_q \text{ - closure of } \mathbf{A} \text{ , } \quad \mathcal{D}^q \text{ and } \quad \mathcal{B}^q \tag{4.8}$$

of q-**almost-periodic**, q-**limit-periodic**, resp. q-**almost-even** functions. Diagram 1 shows relations of inclusion between these spaces. For arithmetical applications it is important to notice that $f \in \mathbf{A}^1$ implies the existence of $M(f)$. J. KNOPFMACHER [49] showed that $\mathcal{B}^q \cong L^q(\mathbf{N}^*, \mu)$ with the measure μ defined by (4.6).

Diagram 1

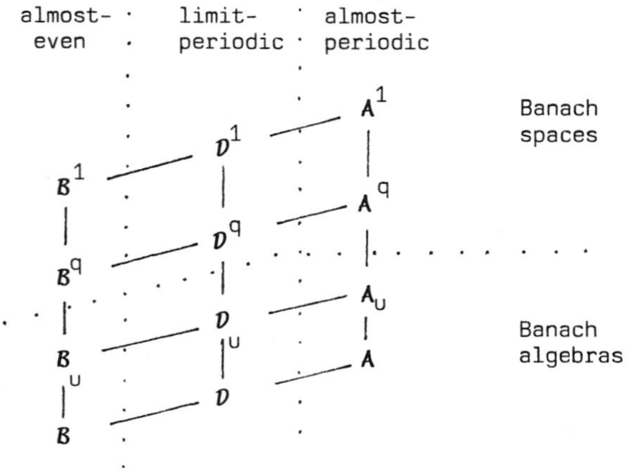

A deep and thorough study of the use of integration on extensions of **N** (resp. **Z**) for number theory was performed by E.V.NOVOSELOV [64], [65], later this theory was used again by Z.KRYŽIUS [5o], [51]. Important contributions to "integration and number theory" are due to J.-L.MAUCLAIRE (see his book [62] and his papers quoted there).[1]

First results giving criteria for the membership of multiplicative functions in $\mathcal{B}^1$ or $\mathcal{B}^2$ are due to KAC, van KAMPEN & WINTNER [44] and A.WINTNER [9o]. The necessary and sufficient conditions for multiplicative functions to belong to $\mathcal{B}^q$ due to DABOUSSI, DELANGE, ELLIOTT will be dealt with in §7.

A class of functions in $\mathcal{D}^1$ is given by MAUCLAIRE [59], VIII (with a different proof by H.DELANGE [21]). <u>If the characteristic function</u> 1_A <u>of a subset</u> A <u>of</u> $\mathbf{N}$ <u>is in</u> $\mathcal{D}^1$ <u>with mean-value</u> $M(1_A) > 0$, <u>then the function</u> δ <u>is in</u> $\mathcal{D}^1$ <u>too</u>, <u>where</u> $\delta(n) = 0$, <u>if</u> $n \notin A$, <u>and</u> $= \min_{m\in A, m>n} (m-n)$ <u>otherwise.</u>

A totally different kind of investigation is to be found in CODECÀ [5]. He gives sufficient conditions ensuring that the convolution $\sum_{n\leq x} n^{-1}\alpha(n)\times$ $\times f(x/n)$ is a B^λ-almost-periodic function on $\mathbf{R}$.

5. Properties of the Spaces Defined in Section 4

Simple approximation arguments (including the use of the Weierstraß approximation theorem) give most of the results quoted on the lefthand side of

---

[1] By the way, K.-H.INDLEKOFER's lecture at this conference also dealt with connections between integration theory and the theory of numbers.

the following diagram 2; the number-theoretical consequences often only depend on the simple fact that $f \in \mathbf{A}^1$ implies the existence of the mean-value $M(f)$.[1] [2]

Diagram 2

Properties of the spaces $\mathbf{A}^q,\ldots$	Arithmetical consequences
(a) $\mathbf{A}_u \cdot \mathbf{A}^q \subset \mathbf{A}^q$ $\mathcal{B}_u \cdot \mathcal{B}^q \subset \mathcal{B}^q$	$f \in \mathbf{A}^q \Longrightarrow \chi \cdot f \in \mathbf{A}^q$, χ character, $f \in \mathcal{B}^q \Longrightarrow f \cdot c_r \in \mathcal{B}^q$. Fourier-coefficients $f\hat{}(\alpha) = M(f \cdot \overline{e}_\alpha)$ and Ramanujan-Fourier coefficients $a_r(f)$ exist for $f \in \mathbf{A}^q$ resp. $f \in \mathcal{B}^q$.
(b) $\mathbf{A}^q \cdot \mathbf{A}^{q'} \subset \mathbf{A}^1$, if $\frac{1}{q} + \frac{1}{q'} = 1$. If $f \in \mathbf{A}^1$ then the shifted function $n \to f(n+a)$ is in $\mathbf{A}^1$	If $f_1,\ldots,f_k \in \mathbf{A}^k$, then $F \in \mathbf{A}^1$ and $M(F)$ exists[3], where $F(n) = \prod_{1 \le \varkappa \le k} f_\varkappa(a_\varkappa n + b_\varkappa)$.
(c) $f \in \mathbf{A}^q \Longrightarrow |f|, \overline{f}$, Re f, Im $f, \ldots \in \mathbf{A}^q$.	
(d) $g \in \mathbf{A}^1$ bounded, $f \in \mathbf{A}^q$ $\Longrightarrow g \cdot f \in \mathbf{A}^q$ (DABOUSSI [1o])	$f \in \mathbf{A}^1 \Longrightarrow M(\mu^2 \cdot f)$ exists.
(e) $f \in \mathcal{B}^1$, $[\![f]\!]_q < \infty \Longrightarrow f \in \mathcal{B}^r$ for any $r<q$ (**not** true for $r=q$)	
(f) $\{\varphi(r)\}^{-1/2} \cdot c_r$ is a complete orthonormal system in $\mathcal{B}^2$.	Parseval's equation[4] : If $f,g \in \mathcal{B}^2$ then $\sum_{r \ge 1} a_r(f) \cdot \overline{a}_r(g) \cdot \varphi(r) = M(f \cdot \overline{g})$.

1 See, for example, DABOUSSI [1o] , see also [77] .

2 If the existence of M(f) is known, then the actual calculation of the mean-value is - at least for multiplicative functions - a minor problem by using the Abel continuity theorem for Dirichlet series.

3 The existence of M(F) under more restrictive assumptions was proved by L.LUCHT [55], [56] .

4 For strongly multiplicative functions see KAC et al.[44] . For multiplicative functions see TUTTAS [86], WARLIMONT [88]. See also [37] .

(g) If $g \geq 0$, $\alpha \geq 1$, $\beta \geq 1$, then $g^{\alpha} \in \mathcal{A}^{\beta} \iff g \in \mathcal{A}^{\alpha\beta}$ (DABOUSSI [1o]).

(h) If $\psi: U \to \mathbf{C}$ is Lipschitz continuous, $f \in \mathcal{B}^1$, $f(\mathbf{N}) \subset U$, then $\psi \circ f$ is in $\mathcal{B}^1$.

Important example: $\psi(x) = e^{itx}$, t real.

$f \in \mathcal{B}^1 \implies M(1/f)$, $M(\log f)$, $M(\exp f)$, ... exist under suitable precautions.[1]

If $g \in \mathcal{B}^1$ is real-valued, then there is a limit-distribution for g, that means the limit

$$\lim_{N\to\infty} N^{-1} \cdot \# \{n \leq N;\ g(n) \leq x\} = \psi_g(x)$$

exists for any point of continuity of ψ_g.[2] [3]

An interesting result, related to (e) and proved by functional analytic tools, is due to Peter KUNTH [53]: Assume $q \geq 1$. Then $f \in \mathcal{B}^q$ is equivalent with

(i) $f \in \mathcal{B}^1$

(ii) $\|f\|_q < \infty$

(iii) $\lim_{1 \leq r < q,\, r \to q} \|f\|_r = \|f\|_q$.

The number-theoretical applications mentioned in Diagram 2 and others[4]

---

[1] For multiplicative functions see SCHWARZ [74].

[2] See KNOPFMACHER [49]. A thorough study of limit-distributions of multiplicative functions is contained in INDLEKOFER [42].

[3] The proof depends on the continuity theorem for characteristic functions, see LUKACS [57].

[4] DELANGE ([21], see also MAUCLAIRE [59], III) announces that for a function f in $\mathcal{A}^1$ (resp. $\mathcal{D}^1$ or $\mathcal{B}^1$) the composed function $I_y \circ f$ is again in $\mathcal{A}^1$ (resp. $\mathcal{D}^1$ or $\mathcal{B}^1$). Here $I_y(x) = 1$, if $x < y$, and $I_y(x) = 0$, if $x \geq y$.

make it an important question to look for conditions on f guaranteeing that $f \in \mathcal{A}^q$ (resp. $f \in \mathcal{D}^q$ resp. $f \in \mathcal{B}^q$). We shall return to this question in §7.

In the next section we are going to discuss a question which is nearer to RAMANUJAN's paper [67] - the question of pointwise convergence of the Ramanujan expansion

$$f(n) = \sum_{r=1}^{\infty} a_r(f) \cdot c_r(n) . \tag{5.1}$$

6. Pointwise Convergence of Ramanujan Expansions

The question of obtaining "good" convergence results for Ramanujan expansions does not seem to be uninteresting. R.BELLMAN [2] suggested deducing results on sums like

$$\sum_{n \leq x} f\left(P(n)\right) , \tag{6.1}$$

where $P \in \mathbf{Z}[X]$ is a polynomial with integer coefficients, by inserting for f its Ramanujan expansion (5.1) and using (2.2) to get estimates of the remainder term. However, the convergence properties of Ramanujan expansions are too bad in general to obtain good results - for example the method does not work for $f = \mu^2$ (if deg(P) > 1).

J.SPILKER [85] showed: For any bounded arithmetical function f there is a pointwise (absolutely) convergent Ramanujan expansion $f(n) = \sum_r b_r c_r(n)$. A.HILDEBRAND (in [36]) gave a simpler proof, without assuming boundedness. However, the coefficients b_r are not the natural ones {see (3.5)} , and therefore this result does not seem to be applicable.

WINTNER's criterion (3.6) for pointwise convergence of the Ramanujan expansion with the "normal" coefficients (3.5) has been mentioned already; the same remark applies to the fact that there are functions satisfying $\sum |f'(n)|\cdot n^{-1} < \infty$ with divergent Ramanujan expansion.[1]

In his long and interesting paper [36] A.HILDEBRAND proved by skilful calculations that for any function in $\mathcal{B}_u$ the Ramanujan expansion is pointwise convergent. This seems to be the most general result concerning pointwise convergence.

Next, in the same paper HILDEBRAND also showed, that there are functions in $\mathcal{B}_u$, for which the Ramanujan expansion $\sum a_r \cdot c_r(n)$ is **not** absolutely convergent (for any n).

For more specialized arithmetical functions, namely additive and multiplicative ones, there are reasonable results, for example. If $f \in \mathcal{B}^2$ is multiplicative, and $M(f) \neq 0$, then the Ramanujan expansion (5.1) is pointwise convergent.[2] This result is true for (multiplicative) functions in $\mathcal{B}^q$, with $M(f) \neq 0$, too.[3] If $f \in \mathcal{B}^q$, $q \geq 1$, is additive, then its Ramanujan expansion is pointwise convergent.[4]

D.KLUSCH [47] obtained results on the **absolute** convergence of Ramanujan expansions for functions in a certain class K_α ($\mathrm{Re}\,\alpha \geq 0$), which is

---

[1] Pointwise convergence of Ramanujan expansions in a more general setting is investigated in KNOPFMACHERs book [48] , Chapter VII.

[2] SCHWARZ [73], if $|f| \leq 1$ and $M(f) \neq 0$ exists. TUTTAS [86] , if $\|f\|_2 < \infty$ and $M(f) \neq 0$ exists.

[3] See H.DELANGE [17] and R.WARLIMONT [88].

[4] HILDEBRAND & SPILKER [38].

defined as follows: $f_\alpha \in K_\alpha$ iff $f_\alpha(n) = \sum_{d|n} d^{1-\alpha}\cdot w(d)$, where $w(x)$ is real-valued, piecewise continuously differentiable, and such that the integral $F(s) = \int_0^\infty x^{s-1}\cdot w(x)\,dx$ is absolutely convergent in the strip $\delta_1 < \operatorname{Re} s < \delta_2$ and moreover $\int_{-\infty}^{\infty} |F(\sigma+it)|\,dt < \infty$ in $\delta_1 < \operatorname{Re} s < \delta_2$.

Examples of functions in K_0 are $\sum_{d|n} (d+1)^{-1}$, $\sum_{d|n} d^2\cdot e^{-2ad}$ (if $\operatorname{Re} a > 0$).

7. Characterization of Multiplicative and Additive Functions in $\mathcal{B}^q$

This characterization (resp. the characterization of functions with mean-value $M(f) \neq 0$ and some growth condition in the multiplicative case, where the same conditions are obtained) was done by H.DABOUSSI [1o], [11], H.DELANGE [16], P.D.T.A.Elliott ([24] - [27]), A.HILDEBRAND & J.SPILKER [38], K.-H.Indlekofer [39], and variants of proofs, using simple ideas from functional analysis, were given by J.SPILKER and the author [82][1] - [84]. Generalizations and the use of ideas from harmonic analysis are due to J.-L.MAUCLAIRE [58] - [62], and there is a recent interesting paper "Functional analysis and additive integer functions" by ELLIOTT [28], dealing - amongst other things- with the distribution of the values of additive functions.

I think, this topic of "characterization" began with the famous theorem of DELANGE [16] for multiplicative functions of absolute value at most one, giving necessary and sufficient conditions for such functions to

[1] Proposition 4 in [82] is not correct as it stands (there are counter-examples), however, it is correct for multiplicative functions. Corrections of the proof were sketched in the survey article [77] and in [76].

have a non-zero mean-value.[1] The extension to multiplicative functions with finite (semi-) norm $\|f\|_q$ was done by ELLIOTT ([24] for $q = 2$, [26] for $q > 1$; see also [25]), and independently by H.DABOUSSI [9] (for $q \geq 1$). K.-H.INDLEKOFER [39] extended these results to the class of "uniformly summable functions", which properly contains $\mathbf{A}^1$.

Let us quote the theorem of ELLIOTT and DABOUSSI. For $q \geq 1$ define the set E_q by the following conditions.

$f \in E_q$ if and only if the four series

$$\left.\begin{aligned} S_1(f) &= \sum_p p^{-1}\cdot\{f(p) - 1\} , \\ S_2(f) &= \sum_{p,\,|f(p)|\leq 2} p^{-1}\cdot|f(p) - 1|^2 , \\ S_{3,q}(f) &= \sum_{p,\,|f(p)|>2} p^{-1}\cdot|f(p)|^q , \quad \text{and} \\ S_{4,q}(f) &= \sum_p \sum_{k\geq 2} p^{-k}\cdot|f(p^k)|^q \end{aligned}\right\} \tag{7.1}$$

are convergent.[2]

Next denote the factors of the Euler product of the generating Dirichlet series $\sum f(n)\cdot n^{-s}$ (for a multiplicative function f) by

$$\varphi_f(p,s) = 1 + f(p)\cdot p^{-s} + f(p^2)\cdot p^{-2s} + \ldots . \tag{7.2}$$

Theorem of ELLIOTT. Assume that the arithmetical function $f\colon \mathbf{N} \to \mathbf{C}$ is multiplicative, and let $q > 1$. Then the following conditions are equivalent.

---

[1] About the same time E.WIRSING (Math.Ann.**143**, 75-1o2 (1961)) proved a theorem extremely useful for applications, giving sufficient conditions for multiplicative functions f, which guarantee asymptotic formulae for $\sum_{n<x} f(n)$.

[2] These convergence conditions mean that the values f(p) are "in general near 1"; large values f(p) are rare, and the values $f(p^k)$ are not too big. The philosophy behind this is that multiplicative functions f are determined by their values at the primes, and that due to the rareness of higher powers the values of f at prime powers cannot spoil too much.

(1) $M(f)$ exists, $M(f) \neq 0$ and $\|f\|_q < \infty$.

(2) $f \in \mathcal{E}_q$ and $\varphi_f(p,1) \neq 0$ for every prime p .

In fact, DELANGE's and ELLIOTT's theorems give necessary and sufficient conditions for a multiplicative functions to belong to $\mathcal{B}^q$. This was explicitly stated and proved by DABOUSSI [10] and extended to the characterization of multiplicative functions in $\mathcal{A}^q$ - see his Theorem B below.

In [82] (+ [76]) and [83], using RENYIs method [68] , the DABOUSSI-DELANGE result [13] and some simple approximation arguments, the following result was proved.

Theorem A. Assume $f: \mathbf{N} \to \mathbf{C}$ is multiplicative and $q \geq 1$.

(1) If $f \in \mathcal{E}_q$, then $f \in \mathcal{B}^q$.

(2) If $f \in \mathcal{A}^q$ and $M(f) \neq 0$, then $f \in \mathcal{E}_q$ and $\varphi_f(p,1) \neq 0$ for every prime p.

DABOUSSI [1o] showed

Theorem B. Assume $f: \mathbf{N} \to \mathbf{C}$ is multiplicative and $q \geq 1$.

(1) If $f \in \mathcal{A}^q$ and $\mathrm{spec}(f) \neq \emptyset$, then condition D_χ holds.

(2) Condition D_χ implies $f \in \mathcal{D}^q$.

Here "**condition D_χ**" means

There exists a Dirichlet character χ such that the four series $S_1(\chi f)$, $S_2(\chi f)$, $S_{3,q}(f)$ and $S_{4,q}(f)$ are convergent.

With the usual notation $f\hat{}(\alpha) = M(f \cdot \mathbf{e}_\alpha)$ for the Fourier-coefficients of f ($\mathbf{e}_\alpha(n) = \exp(2\pi i \alpha n)$) the **spectrum** of the function f is defined by

$$\operatorname{spec}(f) = \{ \alpha \in \mathbf{R} \bmod \mathbf{Z} , \quad \hat{f}(\alpha) \neq 0 \} .$$

It seems plausible that these two theorems are related, and after having presented the necessary tools in section 8, a direct proof that Theorem A implies Theorem B will be sketched in §9.

For the sake of completeness the corresponding characterization of additive functions will be quoted from HILDEBRAND & SPILKER [38].[1]

<u>Assume</u> g <u>to be additive and</u> $q \geq 1$. <u>Then the following three conditions are equivalent.</u>

(i) $g \in \mathcal{B}^q$.

(ii) $M(g)$ <u>exists and</u> $\|g\|_q < \infty$.

(iii) <u>The following three series are convergent:</u>

$$\sum_{|g(p)|\leq 1} p^{-1}\cdot g(p) \ , \quad \sum_{|g(p)|\leq 1} p^{-1}|g(p)|^2, \quad \sum_{p}\ \sum_{\substack{k\geq 1 \\ |g(p^k)|>1}} p^{-k}|g(p^k)|^q .$$

8. The Relationship Theorem and Daboussi's Theorem

A useful tool is the "relationship theorem" of E.HEPPNER and the author [35], which depends on the vague idea that multiplicative functions differing not

[1] See also ELLIOTT [27], Theorem 4, where real-valued additive functions g with $\|g\|_q < \infty$ are characterized by the boundedness of the partial sums $\sum_{p\leq x, |g(p)|\leq 1} p^{-1}\cdot g(p)$ and the convergence of the two last series in (iii).

too much at the primes behave similarly; therefore this theorem may be used to reduce proofs to the simplest possible cases.

Relationship Theorem. Let f, g : $\mathbf{N} \to \mathbf{C}$ be multiplicative and assume that f and g are related ($f \sim g$), i.e.

$$\sum_p p^{-1} \cdot |f(p) - g(p)| < \infty . \tag{8.1}$$

Define the subsets G and G^* of the set of multiplicative functions by

$$G = \{ f \text{ multiplicative}; \; S_{4,1}(f) = \sum_p \sum_{k\geq 2} \frac{|f(p^k)|}{p^k} < \infty, \; \sum_p \frac{|f(p)|^2}{p^2} < \infty \},$$

and (recall that $\varphi_f(p,s)$ is defined by (7.2))

$$G^* = \{ f \in G \,, \varphi_f(p,s) \neq 0 \text{ in } \operatorname{Re} s \geq 1 \text{ for every prime } p \} .$$

Suppose that $g \in G$ and $f \in G^*$. Then the convolution h of g and the convolution inverse f^{-1} of f , $h = g * f^{-1}$, satisfies

$$\sum_{n=1}^{\infty} n^{-1} \cdot |h(n)| < \infty . \tag{8.2}$$

COROLLARY. Under the assumptions from above the following assertions hold.

(1) If $M(f)$ exists, then $M(g)$ exists.

(2) If $f \in \mathcal{A}^1$ then $g \in \mathcal{A}^1$.

(3) If $f \in \mathcal{B}^1$ then $g \in \mathcal{B}^1$.

(4) If $f \in \mathcal{A}^1$ and $\operatorname{spec}(f) = \emptyset$, then $\operatorname{spec}(g) = \emptyset$.

Sometimes it is difficult to satisfy the condition $f \in G^*$. Then the following remark may be useful.

REMARK. If the condition $\varphi_f(p,s) \neq 0$ in $\mathrm{Re}\, s \geq 1$ is violated for some "bad" primes (at most finite in number) then the theorem remains true if in addition

$$f(p^k) = g(p^k) \quad \text{for } k = 1,2,\ldots \text{ and all these bad primes } p. \tag{8.3}$$

Of course, the idea of "related multiplicative functions" is wellknown. For earlier variants of this theorem see for example L.LUCHT [54]. For functions of several variables, see E.HEPPNER [32] .

Next a theorem of H.DABOUSSI (and H.DELANGE, see [12]; for the formulation given here, see DABOUSSI & DELANGE [14]) will be needed.
<u>If</u> f <u>is multiplicative with finite semi-norm</u> $\|f\|_2 < \infty$, <u>and if the values</u> $|f(p)| \leq A$ <u>are bounded for any</u> p , <u>then the Fourier-coefficients</u> $f\hat{}(\beta)$ <u>vanish for any irrational</u> β .

A quantitative sharpening of this result is due to H.MONTGOMERY and R.C. VAUGHAN (see [63] and [87]). DABOUSSIs theorem can be extended by the relationship theorem (for other proofs see DABOUSSI & DELANGE [14],[15]).

THEOREM D. <u>If</u> $f \in \mathbf{A}^1$ <u>is multiplicative</u>, <u>then</u> $f\hat{}(\beta) = 0$ <u>for any irrational</u> β.

Idea of proof (see [84]). $|f| \in \mathbf{A}^1$, and so Theorem A implies the convergence of the series $S_i(|f|)$ (if $M(|f|) = 0$ then $f\hat{}(\beta) = 0$ for any β). Change f to a multiplicative function f^* with bounded values $f(p)$ and relate the Fourier coefficients of f to those of f^*.

9. Some Indications of Proofs [1]

In order to deduce Theorem B from Theorem A at first the case of a completely multiplicative function f is dealt with.

THEOREM 9.1. If $f \in \mathbf{A}^q$ is completely multiplictive, $q \geq 1$, and spec(f) $\cap\, \mathbf{Q} \neq \emptyset$, then there exists a Dirichlet character χ for which $M(\chi f) \neq 0$ [and so by Theorem A the series $S_i(\chi \cdot f)$ are convergent].

The idea of proof is to reduce the Fourier coefficients $M(f \cdot \overline{\mathbf{e}}_\alpha)$, $\alpha \in \mathbf{Q}$, to sums over arithmetic progressions, $\sum_{n \leq x,\ n \equiv c \bmod r} f(n)$. By complete multiplicativity gcd(c,r)=1 may be assumed without loss of generality. Then the sum above is expressed by sums $\sum_{n \leq x} \chi(n) \cdot f(n)$.

THEOREM 9.2. If $f \in \mathbf{A}^q$ is multiplicative and spec(f) $\neq \emptyset$, $q \geq 1$, then Daboussi's Theorem B (1) holds.

It is known from Theorem D that spec(f) $\subset \mathbf{Q}$. Since $|f| \in \mathbf{A}^q$ the series $S_i(|f|)$ converge by Theorem A. The relationship theorem allows one to replace f by an "almost-completely" multiplicative function f*. A cutting-off-argument changes f* to a completely multiplicative function, and Theorem 9.1 gives the assertion.

The reverse direction (f multiplicative, $q \geq 1$, $S_1(\chi f)$, $S_2(\chi f)$, $S_{3,q}(f)$, $S_{4,q}(f)$ converge for some character $\Longrightarrow f \in \mathbf{A}^q$) is more straightforward.

---

[1] See [84].

10. Concluding Remarks

S.RAMANUJAN investigated expansions of arithmetical functions into infinite series - which now bear his name - only in one single paper, and so this topic was certainly outside the main stream of RAMANUJAN's interest. However, as I think, it shows RAMANUJAN's deep understanding, feeling that Ramanujan expansions (not Fourier expansions) are well adapted to multiplicative (and additive) arithmetical functions.

There are reasonable convergence properties, the map $r \to a_r(f)/a_1$ is multiplicative (if $f \in \mathcal{B}^1$ is multiplicative and $M(f) \neq 0$), there are adequate formulae for the coefficients in the additive case too, the intersections of the set of additive functions (resp. the set of multiplicative functions with mean-value $M(f) \neq 0$) with $\mathcal{A}^1$ and with $\mathcal{B}^1$ coincide.

The topic, the surface of which was scratched by RAMANUJAN, developed into a lively theory, and the bibliography shows continued interest, with many of the papers bringing together number theory, functional analysis, harmonic analysis and probability theory.

So RAMANUJAN far-sightedly opened the trail where many mathematicians are hunting now.

11. Bibliography

[1] *Babu,G.J.* Probabilistic methods in the theory of arithmetic functions. New Delhi **1978** vii+118 pp.

[2] *Bellman, R.* Ramanujan sums and the average value of arithmetical functions. Duke Math.J.**17**,159-168 (195o)

[3] *Bruijn, N.G.de*,Bijna periodieke multiplicative functies. Nieuw Archief voor Wiskunde **32**, 81-95 (1943)

[4] *Carmichael, R.* Expansions of arithmetical functions in infinite series. Proc.London Math.Soc.(2) **34**, 1-26 (1932)

[5] *Codecà, P.* Sul comportamento quasi periodico del resto di una certa classe di funzioni fortemente moltiplicative. Ann.Univ.Ferrara - Sez.VII Sc.Mat. **27**, 229-244 (1981)

[6] *Cohen, E.* A class of arithmetical functions. Proc.Nat.Acad.Sci.USA **41**, 939-944 (1955)

[7] *Cohen, E.* Fourier expansions of arithmetical functions. Bull.Amer. Math.Soc. **67**, 145-147 (1961)

[8] *Cohen, E.* Almost even functions of finite abelian groups. Acta Arithm. **7**, 311-323 (1961/62)

[9] *Daboussi, H.* Fonctions multiplicatives presque périodiques B. D'après un travail commune avec Hubert Delange. J.Arithm.Bordeaux (Conf.1974), Astérisque **24/25**, 321-324 (1975)

[1o] *Daboussi, H.* Caractérisation des fonctions multiplicatives p. p.B^{λ} à spectre non vide. Ann.Inst.Fourier Grenoble **3o**, 141-166 (198o)

[11] *Daboussi, H.* Sur les fonctions multiplicatives ayant une valeur moyenne non nulle. Bull.Soc.Math.France **1o9**, 183-2o5 (1981)

[12] *Daboussi, H. & Delange,H.* Quelques propriétés des fonctions multiplicatives du module au plus égal à 1. C.R.Acad.Sci.Paris Sér.A **278**, 657-66o (1974)

[13] *Daboussi,H. & Delange, H.* On a theorem of P.D.T.A.Elliott on multiplicative functions. J.London Math.Soc.(2) **14**, 345-356 (1976)

[14] *Daboussi, H. & Delange, H.* On multiplicative arithmetical functions whose modulus does not exceed one. J.London Math.Soc.(2) **26**, 245-264 (1982)

[15] *Daboussi, H. & Delange, H.* On a class of multiplicative functions. Acta Scient.Math.Szeged **49**, 143-149 (1985)

[16] *Delange, H.* Sur les fonctions arithmétiques multiplicatives. Ann.Sci. de l'École Norm.Sup. **78**, 273-3o4 (1961)

[17] *Delange, H.* Quelques résultats sur les fonctions multiplicatives. C. R.Acad.Sci.Paris Sér.A **281**, A 997 - A 1ooo (1975)

[18] *Delange, H.*On Ramanujan expansions of certain arithmetical functions. Acta Arithm. **31**, 259-27o (1976)

[19] *Delange, H.* Generalization of Daboussi's theorem. Topics in classical number theory, Vol.I,II. Coll.Math.Soc.János Bolyai **34**, Budapest 1981, 3o5-318 (1984)

[2o] *Delange, H.* Sur certaines sous-ensembles de **N*** de fonction caractéristique presque-périodique-B. Journées de Théorie Analytique et Elémentaire des Nombres. 4 pp. Reims 1981

[21] *Delange, H.* On a theorem of J.-L.Mauclaire on limit-periodic sequences. Bull.London Math.Soc. **17**, 518-526 (1985)

[22] *Delange, H.* On a formula for almost-even arithmetical functions. Ill. J.Math. **31**, 24-35 (1987)

[23] *Delsarte, J.M.* Essai sur l'application de la théorie des fonctions presque-périodiques à l'arithmétique. Ann.Sci.de l'École Norm. Sup. **62**, 185-2o4 (1945)

[24] *Elliott, P.D.T.A.* A mean-value theorem for multiplicative functions. Proc.London Math.Soc. (3) **31**, 418-438 (1975)

[25] *Elliott, P.D.T.A.* Probabilistic Number Theory, Vol.I/II. New York - Heidelberg - Berlin 1979/198o

[26] *Elliott, P.D.T.A.* Mean-value theorems for functions bounded in mean α - power,$\alpha > 1$. J.Austral.Math.Soc. **29**, 177-2o5 (198o)

[27] *Elliott, P.D.T.A.* High-power analogues of the Turán-Kubilius inequality, and an application to number theory. Canad.Math.J. **32**, 893-9o7 (198o)

[28] *Elliott, P.D.T.A.* Functional analysis and additive arithmetic functions. Bull.Amer.Math.Soc. **16**, 179-223 (1987)

[29] *Erdös, P. & Wintner, A.* Additive functions and almost periodicity (B^2). Amer.J.Math. **62**, 635-645 (194o)

[3o] *Hardy, G.H.* Note on Ramanujan's trigonometrical function $c_q(n)$ and certain series of arithmetical functions. Proc.Cambridge Phil. Soc. **2o**, 263-271 (1921)

[31] *Hartmann, P. & Wintner, A.* On the almost - periodicity of additive number-theoretical functions. Amer.J.Math. **62**, 753-758 (194o)

[32] *Heppner, E.* Über benachbarte multiplikative zahlentheoretische Funktionen mehrerer Variabler. Archiv Math. **35**, 454-46o (198o)

[33] *Heppner, E.* Über Mittelwerte multiplikativer zahlentheoretischer Funktionen mehrerer Variabler. Monatsh.Math. **91**, 1-9 (1981)

[34] *Heppner, E.* On the existence of mean-values of multiplicative functions. Topics in Classical Number Theory. Vol.I/II. Coll.Math. Soc.Jânos Bolyai 34, Budapest 1981, 717-729 (1984)

[35] *Heppner, E. & Schwarz, W.* Benachbarte multiplikative Funktionen. Studies in Pure Mathematics (To the Memory of Paul Turân). Budapest 1983, 323-336

[36] *Hildebrand, A.* Über die punktweise Konvergenz von Ramanujan-Entwicklungen zahlentheoretischer Funktionen. Acta Arithm. **44**, 1o9-14o (1984)

[37] *Hildebrand, A., Schwarz, W. & Spilker, J.* Still another proof of Parseval's formula. Preprint 1987

[38] *Hildebrand, A. & Spilker, J.* Charakterisierung der additiven, fastgeraden Funktionen. Manuscripta Math. **32**, 213-23o (198o)

[39] *Indlekofer, K.-H.* A mean-value theorem for multiplicative functions. Math.Z. **172**, 255-271 (198o)

[4o] *Indlekofer, K.-H.* Remark on a theorem of G. Halász. Archiv Math. **36**, 145-151 (1981)

[41] *Indlekofer, K.-H.* Some remarks on almost-even and almost-periodic functions. Archiv Math. **37**, 353-358 (1981)

[42] *Indlekofer, K.-H.* Limiting distributions and mean-values of arithcal functions. J.Reine Ang.Math. **328**, 116-127 (1981)

[43] *Indlekofer, K.-H.* On multiplicative arithmetical functions. Topics in Classical Number Theory. Vol.I/II. Coll.Math.Soc.János Bolyai 34, Budapest 1981, 731-748 (1984)

[44] *Kac, M., Kampen, E.R.van & Wintner, A.* Ramanujan sums and almost periodic behaviour. Amer.J.Math. **62**, 1o7-114 (194o)

[45] *Kampen, E.R. van* On uniformly almost periodic multiplicative and additive functions. Amer.J.Math. **62**, 627-634 (194o)

[46] *Kampen, E.V. van & Wintner, A.* On the almost-periodic behaviour of multiplicative number-theoretical functions. Amer.J.Math. **62**, 613-626 (194o)

[47] *Klusch, D.* Mellin Transforms and Fourier-Ramanujan Expansions. Math. Z. **193**, 515-526 (1986)

[48] *Knopfmacher, J.* Abstract Analytic Number Theory. Amsterdam/Oxford 1975

[49] *Knopfmacher, J.* Fourier analysis of arithmetical functions. Annali Mat. Pura Appl. (IV) **1o9**, 177-2o1 (1976)

[5o] *Kryžius, Z.* Almost even arithmetic functions on semigroups (Russ.). Litovsk.Mat.Sbornik **25**, No.2, 9o-1o1 (1985)

[51] *Kryžius, Z.* Limit periodic arithmetical functions. Litovsk.Mat.Sb. **25** , No.3, 93-1o3 (1985)

[52] *Kubilius, J.* Probabilistic methods in the theory of numbers. (Engl.Transl.) Providence R.I. 1964. 182pp

[53] *Kunth, P.* Multiplikative Funktionen in B^q. - Preprint Frankfurt 1987

[54] *Lucht, L.* Über benachbarte multiplikative Funktionen. Archiv Math. **3o**, 4o-48 (1978)

[55] *Lucht, L.* Mittelwerte zahlentheoretischer Funktionen und lineare Kongruenzsysteme. J.Reine Ang.Math. **3o6**, 212-22o (1979)

[56] *Lucht, L.* Mittelwerte multiplikativer Funktionen auf Linearformen. Archiv Math. **32**, 349-355 (1979)

[57] *Lukacs, E.* Characteristic Functions. Sec.Ed. 35o pp, London 197o

[58] *Mauclaire, J.-L.* Fonctions arithmétiques et analyse harmonique. Analytic Number Theory , Proc.Symp.Tokyo 198o, 83-94 (1981)

[59] *Mauclaire, J.-L.* Suites limite-périodiques et théorie des nombres. II, III, VII, VIII, IX. Proc.Japan Acad.Ser.A Math.Sci. 56, 223-224 (198o); **56**, 294-295 (198o); **59**, 26-28 (1983); **59**, 164-166 (1983); **6o**, 13o-133 (1984)

[6o] *Mauclaire, J.-L.* On multiplicative arithmetical functions. Number Theory and Combinatorics. Japan 1984 (Tokyo, Okayama and Kyoto 1984), 297-3o3. Singapore 1985

[61] *Mauclaire, J.-L.* Sur la notion de fonction multiplicative et quelques problèmes qui lui sont associés. Proc.J.Acad.Sci.Ser.A Math. Sci. **61**, 228-231 (1985)

[62] *Mauclaire, J.-L.* Intégration et Théorie des Nombres. Paris 1986

[63] *Montgomery, H. & Vaughan, R.C.* Exponential sums with multiplicative coefficients. Invent.Math. **43**, 69-82 (1977)

[64] *Novoselov, E.V.* A new method in probabilistic number theory (Russ.). Nauk SSSR Ser.Mat. **28**, 3o7-364 (1964)

[65] *Novoselov, E.V.* Introduction to polyadic analysis (Russ.). Petrozavodsk.Gos.Univ. 1982 (112pp)

[66] *Paul, E.M.* Density in the light of probability theory. I, II, III. Sankhya, The Indian J. of Statistics Ser.A **24**, 1o3-114, 2o9-212, (1962), **25**, 273-28o (1963)

[67] *Ramanujan, S.* On certain trigonometrical sums and their applications in the theory of numbers. Trans.Cambr.Phil.Soc. **22**, 259-276 (1918) - Collected papers 179-199

[68] *Rényi, A.* A new proof of a theorem of Delange. Publ.Math.Debrecen **12**, 323-329 (1965)

[69] *Rieger, G.J.* Ramanujan'sche Summen in algebraischen Zahlkörpern. Math.Nachrichten **22**, 371-377 (196o)

[7o] *Rudin, W.* Real and complex analysis. New York, St.Louis et al.1966

[71] *Rudin, W.* Functional Analysis. New York, St.Louis et al.1973

[72] *Schwarz, W.* Ramanujan-Entwicklungen stark multiplikativer Funktionen. J.Reine Ang.Math. **262/263**, 66-73 (1973)

[73] *Schwarz, W.* Ramanujan-Entwicklungen multiplikativer Funktionen. Acta Arithm. **27**, 269-279 (1975)

[74] *Schwarz, W.* Some applications of Elliott's mean-value theorem. J. Reine Angew.Math. **3o7/3o8**, 418-423 (1979)

[75] *Schwarz, W.* Fourier-Ramanujan-Entwicklungen zahlentheoretischer Funktionen mit Anwendungen. Festschrift Wiss.Ges.Univ.Frankfurt, 399-415, Wiesbaden 1981

[76] *Schwarz, W.* A correction to "Remarks on Elliott's Theorem on Mean-Values of Multiplicative Functions" (Durham 1979/81) and some remarks on almost-even number-theoretical functions. Actes Coll.C.I.R.M (1983), Théorie analytique et élémentaire des nomres. Publ.Math. d'Orsay, 139-158

[77] *Schwarz, W.* Remarks on the theorem of Elliott and Daboussi, and Applications. Proc. 2oth sem. Warszawa 1982, 463-498. Banach Center Publications 17, Warszawa 1985

[78] *Schwarz, W.* Almost-even number-theoretical functions. Prob.Theory and Math.Stat. Vol. 2, 581-587, 1986 VNU Science Press

[79] *Schwarz, W.* Einführung in die Zahlentheorie, 2.Aufl.Darmstadt 1987

[8o] *Schwarz, W. & Spilker, J.* Eine Anwendung des Approximationssatzes von Weierstraß-Stone auf Ramanujan-Summen. Nieuw Archief Wisk.(3) **19**, 198-2o9 (1971)

[81] *Schwarz, W. & Spilker, J.* Mean values and Ramanujan expansions of almost even arithmetical functions. Coll.Math.Soc.J.Bolyai **13**. Topics in Number Theory, 315-357, Debrecen 1974

[82] *Schwarz, W. & Spilker, J.* Remarks on Elliott's theorem on mean-values of multiplicative functions. Recent Progress in Analytic Number Theory, Durham 1979, 325-339; London 1981

[83] *Schwarz, W. & Spilker, J.* Eine Bemerkung zur Charakterisierung der fastperiodischen multiplikativen zahlentheoretischen Funktionen mit von Null verschiedenem Mittelwert. Analysis **3**, 2o5-216 (1983)

[84] *Schwarz, W. & Spilker, J.* A variant of proof of Daboussi's theorem on the characterization of multiplicative functions with non-void Fourier-Bohr spectrum. Analysis **6**, 237-249 (1986)

[85] *Spilker, J.* Ramanujan expansions of bounded arithmetical functions. Archiv Math. **35**, 451-453 (198o)

[86] *Tuttas, F.* Über die Entwicklung multiplikativer Funktionen nach Ramanujan-Summen. Acta Arithm. **36**,257-27o (198o)

[87] *Vaughan, R.C.* On the estimation of trigonometrical sums over primes and related questions. Report 9 (1977), Institut Mittag Leffler

[88] *Warlimont, R.* Ramanujan expansions of multiplicative functions. Acta Arithm. **42**, 111-12o (1983)

[89] *Wintner, A.* On a statistics of the Ramanujan sums. Amer.J.Math. **64**, 1o6-114 (1942)

[9o] *Wintner, A.* Eratosthenian Averages. Baltimore 1943

Author's address.

Schwarz, Wolfgang (Karl)
Department of Mathematics
Johann Wolfgang Goethe-University
Robert-Mayer-Straße 1o
D 6ooo F r a n k f u r t am Main

On highly composite numbers

by Jean-Louis Nicolas

University of Limoges, France

ABSTRACT

Let $d(n)$ be the number of divisors of n. S. Ramanujan has defined n to be highly composite, if, for any $m < n$, we have $d(m) < d(n)$. We shall try to describe the results obtained by Ramanujan about these numbers, and improvements and generalizations of his work. The main problem, which is not completely solved, is to estimate the number of highly composite numbers (or of similar numbers defined with some others arithmetical functions) up to x.

I. **Introduction and notations.**

In 1915, S. Ramanujan published in the Proceedings of the London Mathematical Society a memoir of sixty-three pages entitled "highly composite numbers" and consisting of 52 paragraphs (cf. [54] and [55], no. 15). The purpose of this memoir was to study how large the number of divisors of an integer n can be when n tends to infinity. We shall try to describe the results obtained by Ramanujan, and the improvements and generalizations of his work.

We shall use the following classical notations:

$p_1 = 2$, $p_2 = 3, \ldots, p_k = k^{th}$ prime;

p, P, q will denote prime numbers;

ISBN 0-12-058560-X

$$d(n) = \sum_{d|n} 1 = \text{number of divisors of } n;$$

$$\sigma_s(n) = \sum_{d|n} d^s = \text{sum of } s^{th} \text{ power of divisors of } n$$

(observe that $\sigma_{-s}(n) = \sigma_s(n)/n^s$);

$$\sigma(n) = \sigma_1(n) = \sum_{d|n} d;$$

$$\omega(n) = \sum_{p|n} 1 \ ; \quad \varphi(n) = \text{Euler's totient function};$$

$$d_2(n) = d(n) \ ; \quad d_k(n) = \sum_{d|n} d_{k-1}(d) \quad \text{for } k \geq 3;$$

$$\pi(x) = \sum_{p \leq x} 1 \ ; \quad \theta(x) = \sum_{p \leq x} \log p \quad \text{is the Chebyshev function};$$

$$\text{Li } x = \lim_{\varepsilon \to 0} \left[\int_0^{1-\varepsilon} + \int_{1+\varepsilon}^{x} \frac{dt}{\log t} \right] \quad \text{is the integral logarithm.}$$

The notation $f \ll g$ (or $g \gg f$) will mean $f = O(g)$.

If f is an arithmetical function, we shall define n as an f-champion number if $m < n \Rightarrow f(m) < f(n)$.

For real x, $[x]$ will denote the integral part of x.

The memoir of Ramanujan encompasses 5 parts: Elementary results on the maximal order of $d(n)$, the definition and the structure (that is to say the form of the standard factorization in primes) of the highly composite numbers, the superior highly composite numbers, the maximal order of $d(n)$

with or without the assumption of the Riemann hypothesis, and special forms of N.

In the last part (§46-51), the value of $d(N)$ is studied for various N's: N a perfect power, $N = \text{l.c.m.}(1,2,\dots,n)$, $N = n!$. The smallest integer N with exactly 2^n divisors is also determined, and this is a good contest question.

In the very last paragraph (§52) a few words are said about the iterated d-function: $d^{(1)} = d$, and $d^{(k)}(n) = d(d^{k-1}(n))$. A deeper study of $d^{(k)}$ has been undertaken by Erdös and Kátai (cf. [8]).

II. Elementary results concerning the maximal order of $d(n)$.

It was proved by C. Runge in 1885 (cf. [68]) that for fixed $\varepsilon > 0$,

$$(1)\qquad \lim d(n)/n^{\varepsilon} = 0.$$

S. Wigert proved in 1907 (cf. [74]) that the maximal order of $\log d(n)$ is $\dfrac{\log n \log 2}{\log\log n}$, that is to say that

$$(2)\qquad \overline{\lim}\, \frac{(\log d(n))(\log\log n)}{(\log n)(\log 2)} = 1.$$

For this result, S. Wigert uses the prime number theorem: $\pi(x) \sim x/\log x$.

S. Ramanujan proved (2) without assuming the prime number theorem, as is mentioned in the notes in Hardy and Wright's book (cf. [19], Chapter 18).

The upper bound of (2) is based on the inequality, valid for all N with $\omega(N) = k$,

$$(3) \qquad d(N) < \frac{((\theta(p_k) + \log N)/k)^k}{(\log p_1)(\log p_2) \cdots (\log p_k)}$$

and on the relation

$$(4) \qquad \pi(x)\log x - \theta(x) = \int_2^x \frac{\pi(t)}{t}\,dt.$$

It is easy to deduce from the prime number theorem that, as $k \longrightarrow \infty$,

$$\theta(p_k) \sim p_k \sim k \log k,$$

but, using (4), it is possible to prove $\theta(p_k) \sim k \log k$ without the prime number theorem (cf. [62]), and this was mainly Ramanumjan's idea.

Let us define the multiplicative function $r(n)$ as follows:

if $p \equiv 1 \bmod 4$, $r(p^k) = d(p^k) = k + 1$;

if $p \equiv 3 \bmod 4$, $r(p^k) = 0$ for k odd, and $r(p^k) = 1$ for k even;

if $p \equiv 2$, $r(2^k) = 1$ for all k.

It is known that the number of ways in which n can be written as a sum of two squares is equal to $4r(n)$ (cf. [19], Chapter 16).

An application of (2) with Ramanujan's proof gives the maximal order of $r(n)$ (cf. [37]):

$$(5) \qquad \overline{\lim} \frac{(\log r(n))(\log\log n)}{(\log 2)(\log n)} = 1.$$

Actually $r(n)$ counts (crudely) the divisors of n made up of primes $\equiv 1 \bmod 4$; these primes are about half of all the primes, but the maximal orders of $\log r(n)$ and $\log d(n)$ are the same. This is somewhat surprising and sometimes misleading. For instance, Theorem 338 in [19] gives erroneously 1/2 instead of 1 on the right hand side of (5).

III. **Highly composite numbers.**

S. Ramanujan defined an integer n to be highly composite (we shall write h.c.) if for all $m < n$, we have $d(m) < d(n)$. So, with our definition, h.c. numbers are d-champion numbers.

For every integer $n \geq 1$, let us draw a point with coordinates $(n, d(n))$ and look at the increasing envelope of these points, that is the smallest nondecreasing function lying above all these points. This envelope is a step function, and the vertices of the steps correspond to h.c. numbers.

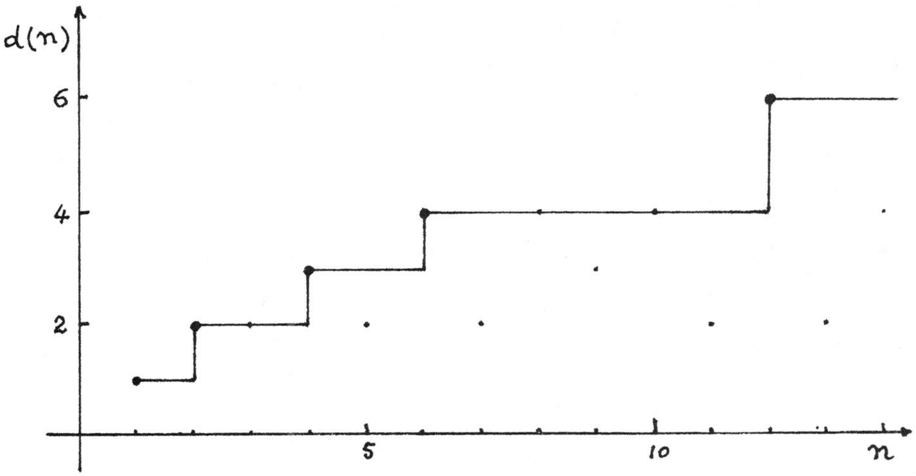

Now, let us write the standard factorization of an integer n in the form

$$n = \prod_{i=1}^{\infty} p_i^{\alpha_i} \quad \text{with} \quad \alpha_i = \alpha_i(n),$$

where only finitely many α_i are non-zero. Then we have

$$d(n) = \prod_{i=1}^{\infty} (\alpha_i + 1).$$

An integer n is said to be w.n.i.e. (with nonincreasing exponent) if the sequence $(\alpha_i)_i$ is nonincreasing. Clearly, a h.c. number is w.n.i.e..

For a w.n.i.e. integer, we define $q_1 = \max_{p|n} p$ (so that all the primes $\leq q_1$ divide n), and

$$q_j = \max_{p^j|n} p.$$

The nonincreasing sequence $(q_j)_{j\geq 1}$ characterizes n.

IV. **Superior highly composite numbers.**

Let $\varepsilon > 0$ be fixed. It follows from (1) that $d(n)/n^{\varepsilon}$ is bounded and reaches its maximum in one or several points. Ramanujan has defined an integer N to be superior h.c. (s.h.c.) if there exists $\varepsilon > 0$ such that for all n we have

$$\frac{d(n)}{n^{\varepsilon}} \leq \frac{d(N)}{N^{\varepsilon}} .$$

For $n < N$ we have $d(n) \leq \left[\frac{n}{N}\right]^{\varepsilon} d(N) < d(N)$, which shows that a s.h.c. number is h.c..

The stucture of these numbers has been completely determined by Ramanujan. Let us define

$$E = \left\{\frac{\log(1 + 1/k)}{\log p} \; ; \; k \geq 1, \; p \text{ prime}\right\}.$$

If $\varepsilon \notin E$, then the maximum of $d(n)/n^{\varepsilon}$ is attained at only one integer N_{ε}, and we have

$$(6) \qquad N_{\varepsilon} = \prod_{i=1}^{\infty} p_i^{\alpha_i} \quad \text{with} \quad \alpha_i = [1/(p_i^{\varepsilon} - 1)].$$

It was known by Siegel (cf. [1], p. 455) that for real λ and three different primes p,q,r, the numbers $p^{\lambda}, q^{\lambda}, r^{\lambda}$ cannot be all rational, except when λ is an integer (cf. [27] and [28], Chapter 2). This implies that three elements of E cannot be equal. It seems very likely that two elements of E are always distinct, but this is still unproved. If it is true, then, for $\varepsilon \in E$, the maximum of $d(n)/n^{\varepsilon}$ is attained at two integers. If it is false, this maximum is attained at four integers for some ε (cf. [9], p. 71). This question was probably overlooked by Ramanujan; for instance, the result of §44 is false in the latter case.

In both cases, the integer N_{ε} defined by (6) is a s.h.c. number, maximizing $d(n)/n^{\varepsilon}$. If we set

(7) $x = 2^{1/\varepsilon}, \; x_k = x^{\log(1+1/k)/\log 2}$ for $k \geq 1$,

then we have $x_1 = x$ and $x_2 = x^{\theta}$ with

(8) $$\theta = \frac{\log (3/2)}{\log 2} = 0.585 \ldots,$$

and from (6) we see that

$$p \,|\, N_{\varepsilon} \Leftrightarrow p \leq x,$$

$$\alpha_i = k \Leftrightarrow x_{k+1} < p_i \leq x_k,$$

$$\alpha_1 \leq \frac{1}{2^{\varepsilon} - 1} \leq \frac{1}{\varepsilon \log 2} = \frac{\log x}{(\log 2)^2},$$

(9) $$\log N_{\varepsilon} = \sum_{1 \leq k \leq \alpha_1} \theta(x_k).$$

(10) $$\log d(N_{\varepsilon}) = \sum_{1 \leq k \leq \alpha_1} \pi(x_k) \log(1 + 1/k).$$

It follows from (9) that $\log N_{\varepsilon} \sim x$.

V. **The number of highly composite numbers up to x.**

Let us define $Q(X)$ as the number of h.c. numbers $\leq X$. It is easy to see that between X and $2X$ there is always a h.c. number (because $d(2n) > d(n)$), and this implies that $Q(X) \gg \log X$.

It was proved by Ramanujan that $\lim Q(X)/\log X = +\infty$ (cf. [54], §28). Given a h.c. number n, the idea is to construct n' as close as possible to n, and with $d(n') > d(n)$. Then there exists a h.c. number n'' with $n < n'' \le n'$. Ramanujan chose n' with the same exponents as n for the large primes, modifying only the exponents of the small primes.

The problem of estimating $Q(X)$ was of some interest to Ramanujan. In a joint paper with Hardy (cf. [18] and [55], no. 34), the number of w.n.i.e. (cf. §III) integers up to X is estimated. The introduction mentions: "That class of numbers includes as a subclass the h.c. numbers recently studied by Mr. Ramanujan. The problem of determing the number $Q(X)$ of h.c. numbers not exceeding X appears to be one of extreme difficulty. It is still uncertain whether or not the order of $Q(X)$ is greater than that of any power of $\log X$".

P. Erdös proved in 1944 that for a positive c_1 we have $Q(X) \gg (\log X)^{1+c_1}$. A new tool was Hoheisel's theorem (cf. [21]): for some $0 < \tau < 1$,

$$(11) \qquad \pi(x + x^\tau) - \pi(x) \gg x^\tau/\log x$$

(the best τ is now $\frac{11}{20} - \frac{1}{384} = 0.547396\ldots$, cf. [32]).

Erdös used it to construct n' by multiplying and dividing n by large primes, and using the diophantine approximations of θ (defined by (8)) given by Dirichlet's theorem (cf. [7]).

In 1971, I proved (cf. [36]) that $Q(X) \ll (\log X)^{c_2}$. I used for this the result of Feldmann (cf. [15]) that there exists κ such that for all integers $u, v \geq 1$ we have:

$$(12) \qquad |v\theta - u| \gg v^{-\kappa}.$$

I also used the structure of the h.c. numbers between two consecutive s. h. c. numbers that we shall describe in the next paragraph.

Let us define $c(X)$ by

$$Q(X) = (\log X)^{c(X)},$$

and let us assume two very strong conjectures: first, (11) holds for all $\tau > 0$, and secondly, for all $\eta > 0$, there exists a positive constant $B = B(\eta)$ such that for all u, v, w in $\mathbb{Z}$ we have:

$$|u \log 5 + v \log 3 + w \log 2| \geq B((|u| + 1)(|v| + 1))^{-1-\eta}.$$

Then the method of [36] shows that (cf. [73])

$$\lim c(X) = (\log 30)/(\log 16) = 1.227\ldots .$$

More recently (cf. [48]) I used the value $\kappa = 2^{49}\log 3$ given by M. Waldschmidt to show that $\overline{\lim}\, c(X) \leq 3.48$, and a new result of G. Rhin (cf. [57]), namely $\kappa = 7.616$, implies $\overline{\lim}\, c(X) \leq 1.71$. I also show that $\underline{\lim}\, c(X) \leq 1.44$. It was proved in [36] that

$$\underline{\lim}\, c(X) \geq \frac{1}{3}\, \frac{\log(15/8)}{\log 2}\, (1 - \tau) = 1.13682\ldots$$

with Mozzochi's value $\tau = 11/20 - 1/384$.

All these results are based on diophantine approximations of $\theta = \frac{\log(3/2)}{\log 2}$, and similar numbers arising from the values of the function d. Actually the 3 is $d(p^2)$ and both 2's occuring in the definition of θ are $d(p)$. Now, suppose we consider a multiplicative function δ, such that $\delta(p^\alpha)$ depends only on α and $\hat{\theta} = \frac{\log(\delta(p^2)/\delta(p))}{\log(\delta(p))}$ is, say, a Liouville number. Then the method of [36] no longer works (cf. [73]). For such a function δ, let $Q_\delta(X)$ be the number of champion numbers up to X. It is an open question whether there exists $c(\delta)$ such that

$$Q_\delta(X) \ll (\log x)^{c(\delta)}.$$

Another open question is the following: Let n_i be the ith h.c. number. Erdös proved in [7] that there exists $c > 0$ such that, for i large enough,

$$n_{i+1}/n_i \leq 1 + (\log n_i)^{-c},$$

and deduced from this that $Q(X) \geq (\log X)^{1+c+o(1)}$. But does there exist c' such that $n_{i+1}/n_i - 1 \gg (\log n_i)^{-c}$? In [48] it is only proved that

$$n_{i+1}/n_i - 1 \gg \exp(-(\log n_i)^{1/4}).$$

VI. The structure of highly composite numbers.

Let n be a h.c. number, and q_1 its largest prime divisor. We write

$$n = \prod_{p \le q_1} p^{a_p}.$$

Ramanujan has proved that $a_{q_1} = 1$ unless $n = 4$ or $n = 36$. Then he divides the primes from 2 to q_1 in five ranges and for each range gives an asymptotic estimate of a_p in terms of q_1. For instance, he has proved that

$$(13) \qquad a_p \log p = \frac{\log q_1}{\log 2} + O(\sqrt{\log q_1 \operatorname{loglog} q_1})$$

holds for $\log p = O(\operatorname{loglog} q_1)$.

The study of the structure of h.c. numbers takes up about half of the whole paper. In the introduction to the "Collected Papers" (cf. [55], p. xxxiv) Hardy has written that this study is "most remarkable, and shows very clearly Ramanujan's extraodinary mastery over algebra of inequalities."

To estimate a_p, the idea of Ramanujan is to write $d(m) < d(n)$ for an appropriate choice of $m < n$. In [1], Alaoglu and Erdös have improved Ramanujan's estimations for a_p, mainly using Hoheisel's result in the construction of a better m.

In [36] and [48] estimates of a_p are obtained with the so-called "benefit" method. Let n be h.c. and N the s.h.c. number just preceding n. Let ε be any parameter such that $N = N_\varepsilon$, and $x = 2^{1/\varepsilon}$. We write (cf. (6))

$$N = \prod_{p \le x} p^{b_p} \quad \text{with} \quad b_p = [1/(p^\varepsilon - 1)].$$

The benefit of n (relative to N and ε) is

$$(14) \qquad \begin{aligned} \text{ben } n &= \log \frac{d(N)}{N^\varepsilon} - \log \frac{d(n)}{n^\varepsilon} \\ &= \sum_{p \le \max(q_1, x)} \left[\log\left(\frac{b_p + 1}{a_p + 1}\right) - \varepsilon(b_p - a_p)\log p\right]. \end{aligned}$$

From the definition of the s.h.c. numbers, each term in the above sum in nonnegative. In [36] I proved that there exists C, such that, when n is h.c.,

$$\text{ben } n \le C\, x^{-\gamma}$$

for $\gamma = \theta(1 - \tau)(\kappa + 1) = 0.0307\ldots$ with the Mozzochi and Rhin values of τ and κ. Using this I showed:

$$(15) \quad \begin{cases} \text{if } \varepsilon \log p - \log\left[1 + \dfrac{1}{b_p + 1}\right] \le Cx^{-\gamma}, & \text{then } a_p = b_p \text{ or } a_p = b_p + 1; \\ \text{if } \log\left[1 + \dfrac{1}{b_p + 1}\right] - \varepsilon \log p \le Cx^{-\gamma}, & \text{then } a_p = b_p \text{ or } a_p = b_p - 1; \\ \text{in other cases, } a_p = b_p. \end{cases}$$

Formulas (15) show that $|a_p - b_p|$ is at most 1. If q_k is the largest prime dividing n with exponent $\ge k$, and x_k is defined by (7), then we have for $k \le k'$, $k' = [1/(e^{\gamma \log 2} - 1)] = 46$, (cf. [48])

$$(16) \qquad |\pi(x_k) - \pi(q_k)| \ll \sqrt{x_k x^{-\gamma}},$$

and for $k' < k \le a_2$

$$|\pi(x_k) - \pi(q_k)| \le 1.$$

With $k = 1$, we get, by Hoheisel's theorem

$$q_1 = x + O(x^\tau) \sim \log N \sim \log n. \tag{17}$$

From this we can see that in (13) the error term is in fact $O(1)$. Moreover, from (15) and (17), when q_1 is given, we can calculate a_p with an error of at most 1, for all p's between 2 and q_1.

VII. **Effective upper bounds.**

For each integer $n \ge 1$, let us draw a point with coordinates $\log n$ and $\log d(n)$, and then consider the convex envelope of all these points.

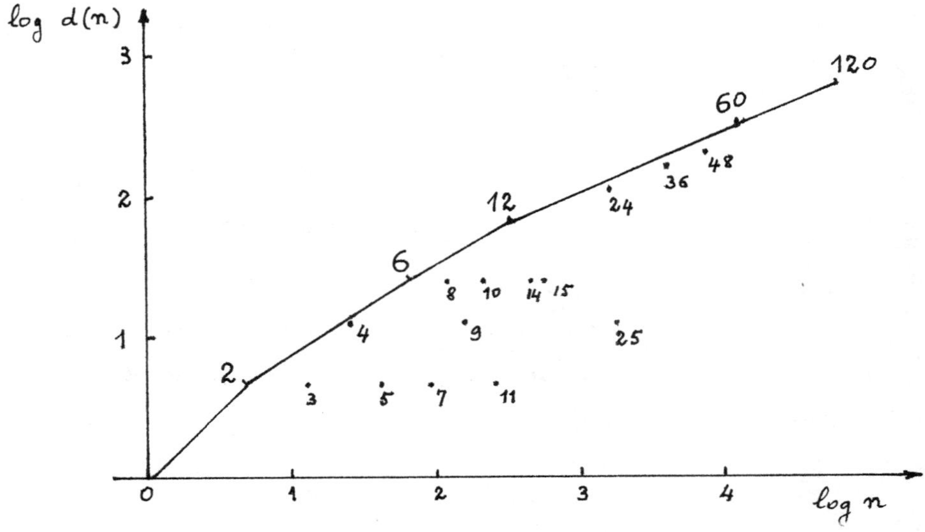

The first s.h.c. numbers are 2,6,12,60. Observe that h.c. numbers which are not superior such that 4,24,36,48 are close to the convex envelope, The vertical distance from them to the convex envelope measures the "benefit".

Now consider all the straight lines with fixed slope ε and going through the points $(\log n, \log d(n))$. These lines cut the y-axis in a point whose ordinate is $\log d(n) - \varepsilon \log n$, and so, from the definition of s.h.c. numbers, the highest possible such line, is going through $(\log N, \log d(N))$ where $N = N_\varepsilon$. Thus s.h.c. numbers are characterized by the vertices of the preceding convex envelope.

It follows from (2) that there exists an absolute constant A such that

$$\frac{\log d(n)}{\log 2} \leq A \frac{\log n}{\log\log n} \quad \text{for all} \quad n \geq 3 \tag{18}$$

($n = 2$ is not possible because $\log\log 2$ is negative).

We now observe that the function $x \longmapsto \frac{Ax}{\log x}$ is concave for $x \geq e^2$ and that 2520 is the smallest s.h.c. number bigger than $\exp(e^2)$. So to prove (18) for a certain A, it is sufficient to prove it for all $n \leq 2520$, and then for all s.h.c. number bigger than 2520, because, if the curve $y = Ax/\log x$ is above all the vertices of the convex envelope, it will be above all the points $(\log n, \log d(n))$.

Calculations can be carried out easily for two reasons: first, s.h.c. numbers are rare, and secondly, their factorization into primes is known by (6) or (9), and effective estimates of Rosser and Schoenfeld can be used (cf. [66], [67], [70]). The result is that

$$\frac{\log d(n)}{\log 2} \leq 1.5379 \ldots \frac{\log n}{\log\log n}, \qquad n \geq 3$$

with equality for $n = 6983776800$ cf ([43]). By the same method more accurate estimates can be given (cf. [61]):

$$\frac{\log d(n)}{\log 2} \leq \frac{\log n}{\log\log n}\left[1 + \frac{1.9349\ \ldots}{\log\log n}\right], \quad n \geq 3;$$

$$\frac{\log d(n)}{\log 2} \leq \frac{\log n}{\log\log n}\left[1 + \frac{1}{\log\log n} + \frac{4.7624\ \ldots}{(\log\log n)^2}\right], \quad n \geq 3;$$

$$\frac{\log d(n)}{\log 2} \leq \frac{\log n}{\log\log n - 1.39177\ \ldots}, \quad n \geq 56.$$

Under the assumption of the Riemann hypothesis, it follows from the upper bound obtained by Ramanujan (cf. [54], §43, and (19) below), that there exists c such that

$$\frac{\log d(n)}{\log 2} \leq \mathrm{Li}(\log n) + c(\log n)^{\theta}$$

with θ defined by (8). The above method enables one to find the best possible c, but the calculations have not yet been done.

VIII. The maximal order of d(n).

Using the definition of s.h.c. numbers, Ramanujan has defined the maximal order of $d(n)$ as a certain function D (cf. [54], §38). Consider the piecewise linear function $u \longmapsto \Delta(u)$ such that for all s.h.c. numbers N, $\Delta(\log N) = \log d(N)$, that is the convex envelope of the set of points $(\log n, \log d(n))$ considered in the preceding paragraph. Then Ramanujan's D-function is equal to

$$D(t) = \exp\left(\Delta(\log t)\right)$$

and satisfies $d(n) \leq D(n)$ for all n, with equality when n is s.h.c.

The reasons why Ramanujan chose D as the maximal order of $d(n)$ are not clear to me. $F(t) = \max_{n \le t} d(n)$ might be a better choice. Anyway D and F are very close (cf. [41], p. 13–15, where more about this notion of maximal order can be found).

However, it was a great idea of Ramanujan to use s.h.c. numbers to get a good estimate of the maximal order, that is to find an analytic function as close as possible to the maximal order. His estimation for D, under the assumption of the Riemann hypothesis,

$$(19) \qquad \frac{\log D(n)}{\log 2} = \mathrm{Li}(\log n) + \theta\, \mathrm{Li}((\log n)^{\theta}) - \frac{(\log n)^{\theta}}{\log\log n} - R(\log n) + O\left[\frac{\sqrt{\log n}}{(\log\log n)^{3}}\right]$$

with

$$R(x) = \left[2\sqrt{x} + \sum_{\rho} \frac{x^{\rho}}{\rho^{2}}\right] / (\log x)^{2}$$

where the sum is over all the nonreal zeroes of the Rieman ζ-function, is certainly very nice.

Let $\lambda > 1$, and let

$$f_{\lambda}(n) = \frac{\log d(n)}{\log 2} - \lambda \frac{\log n}{\log\log n}.$$

It follows from (2) that $\lim_{n\to\infty} f_{\lambda}(n) = -\infty$, and therefore $f_{\lambda}(n)$ has an absolute maximum attained for at least one integer $\tilde{N}_{\lambda}$ (cf. [64]). Little is known about these integers $\tilde{N}_{\lambda}$, but they are still closer to the maximal order of $d(n)$ than the s.h.c. numbers themselves.

IX. **Tables.**

In his memoir, Ramanujan has included a table of the first one hundred h.c. numbers, and of the first fifty s.h.c. numbers. It is worth while mentioning that the table on pp. 2 and 3 in the notebooks (cf. [56], Vol. 2) is a table of the h.c. numbers.

In [60], Robin has calculated the first 5000 h.c. numbers, and independently the same calculation was carried out by te Riele. They used a method of dynamical programming. Let us define S_k as the set of integers made up of primes $p_1, \dots p_k$. We say that n is k - h.c. if $n \in S_k$ and if

$$m \in S_k \text{ and } m < n \Rightarrow d(m) < d(n).$$

These k - h.c. numbers are easily determined by induction, and small k - h.c. numbers are actually h.c.

A theoretical study of 2 - h.c. numbers (of the form $2^{\alpha}3^{\beta}$) has been undertaken in [2], using the continued fraction expansion of $\log 3/\log 2$.

A more powerful algorithm is also given in [60]. It allows one to calculate h.c. numbers between two consecutive s.h.c. numbers. This algorithm uses the "benefit" method mentioned in §VI. First you guess a positive real number B which should be the maximal value of the benefit of a h.c. number. Then you calculate all integers n in the considered range, the benefit of which is smaller than B. From these n's you calculate an exact upper bound B' for the maximal benefit of a h.c. number. If $B' \leq B$, h. c. numbers are included in the calculated n's. If $B' > B$, you start again with B' instead of B.

Robin has used this algorithm to determine the smallest number which has more than 10^{1000} divisors. It is an integer of 13198 decimal digits, the largest prime factor of which is 30113.

Aloaglu and Erdös conjectured in [1] that if n is h.c., then there exist two primes p and q such that Np and N/q are h. c.. G. Robin has found a counterexample to this conjecture (cf. [60]).

X. **Optimization problems in integers.**

Calculation of the largest h.c. numbers $\leq A$ is equivalent to solving

$$
(20) \qquad \begin{cases} \max \displaystyle\sum_{k=1}^{\infty} \log(x_k + 1), \\ \\ \displaystyle\sum_{k=1}^{\infty} x_k \log p_k \leq a = \log A, \ x_k \in \mathbb{N}. \end{cases}
$$

As $p_k \leq A$, the number of variables is finite, and solving (20) with x_k real is easy using Lagrange multipliers.

In fact, it is also possible to use Lagrange multipliers to solve (20) when the x_k's are integers. Suppose that f and g are two real-valued functions defined on a subset Ω of $\mathbb{R}^n$, and that g is nonnegative. We want to solve

$$
(21) \qquad \begin{cases} \max\limits_{x \in \Omega} f(x) \\ \\ g(x) \leq C \end{cases}
$$

for different values of C. Suppose that for $\lambda \geq 0$ there exists x_0 such that $f - \lambda g$ is maximal at x_0, that is to say

$$
\forall x \in \Omega, \ f(x) - \lambda g(x) \leq f(x_0) - \lambda g(x_0).
$$

Then x_0 is a solution of (21) for $C = g(x_0)$. Indeed, we have for $x \in \Omega$, with $g(x) \leq C = g(x_0)$:

$$f(x) \leq f(x_0) + \lambda(g(x) - g(x_0)) \leq f(x_0).$$

Such C's which can be written in the form $g(x_0)$ are called Lagrange bounds for the problem (21). Lagrange bounds of (20) are logarithms of s.h.c. numbers.

In general, not all possible values of C in (21) are Lagrange bounds, and to solve (20) when C is not a Lagrange bound, we can use Everett's method (cf. [14]) which is about the same as the benefit method I used in §VI.

A few bridges have been built between h.c. numbers and optimization problems in integers. (cf. [38], [39], [40], [58], [60]). Probably it is worthwhile working in that area. In my opinion, optimization theory sheds an interesting light on h.c. numbers, and from this point of view it can no longer be said that h.c. numbers are in a backwater of mathematics.

XI. **Other champion numbers.**

Ramanujan's work on h.c. numbers has been first extended to the sum of the divisors of n by Alaoglu and Erdös (cf. [1], [51] and [69]). They define a highly abundant (h.a.) number as a champion number for the function $n \longmapsto \sigma(n)$, and a superabundant (s.a.) number as a champion number for the function $n \longmapsto \sigma(n)/n$. Furthermore they say that n is colossally abundant (c.a.) if there exists $\varepsilon > 0$ such that for all m,

$$\frac{\sigma(m)}{m^{1+\varepsilon}} \leq \frac{\sigma(n)}{n^{1+\varepsilon}} .$$

It is easy to see that c.a. $\Rightarrow$ s.a. $\Rightarrow$ h.a.

Let n be h.a. and P its largest prime divisor. It is not knwon whether $P \sim \log n$, or if P^2 divides n for infinitely many n's. Let $Q_h(X)$ and $Q_s(X)$ be the number of h.a. and s.a. numbers up to X. It has been proved in [9] that $Q_s(X) \gg (\log X)^{1+\delta}$. We don't know whether $Q_h(X)$, or even $Q_s(X)$, is smaller than $(\log X)^c$.

More recently, Masser and Shiu (cf. [31] and [4]) have studied sparsely totient numbers, that is to say integers n such that $m > n \Rightarrow \varphi(m) > \varphi(n)$. In this case the superior numbers are easy: they are the product of the first k primes (cf. [49], Chapter 1), but that does not make the study of sparsely totient numbers really easier.

Landau has defined $g(n)$ as the maximal order of an element in the symmetric group of n elements. Let ℓ be the additive function defined by $\ell(p^\alpha) = p^\alpha$. One can prove that

$$g(n) = \max_{\ell(M) \le n} M$$

and

$$N \in g(\mathbb{N}) \Leftrightarrow M > N \Rightarrow \ell(M) > \ell(N).$$

So the values of $g(n)$ appear as a generalization of h.c. numbers (cf. [34], [35], [29], [30]).

Let us define n to be largely composite (l.c.) if

$$m \le n \Rightarrow d(m) \le d(n).$$

These numbers are not necessarily w.n.i.e. (cf. §III), and they are much more numerous than h.c. numbers (cf. [42]). An open question is whether between two consecutive h.c. numbers that are large enough there is always a l.c. number.

Champion numbers are considered in [52] for $d_k(n)$ (cf. §1), in [3] for the function $f(n)$, defined as the number of unordered factorizations of n into factors > 1, in [48] for the function $n \longmapsto d(n) + d(n+1)$, in [10] for the function

$$F(n) = \max_t \Big[\sum_{\substack{d|n \\ t/2 \le d < t}} 1 \Big],$$

in [13] for the function $f(n) = \sum_{i=1}^{k-1} q_i/q_{i+1}$ where $n = q_1^{\alpha_1}, \ldots, q_k^{\alpha_k}$ with $q_1 < q_2 < \ldots < q_k$, and for the function $\omega - f$, and in [11] for the function f, where $f(n)$ is the largest integer k for which there exists m such that n divides the product $\prod_{1 \le i \le k} (m+i)$, but does not divide this product if any of its factors is omitted.

Champion numbers for ω are the products of the first primes. Integers n such that

$$m \le n \Rightarrow \omega(m) \le \omega(n)$$

have been studied in [12].

XII. **Maximal order of various functions.**

It has been proved by Landau (cf. [26]) that

$$\overline{\lim} \frac{n}{\varphi(n) \operatorname{loglog} n} = e^{\gamma},$$

where γ is Euler's constant. In [45] and [46] it is proved that for infinitely many n's,

$$n > e^{\gamma}\varphi(n) \operatorname{loglog} n$$

holds.

The maximal order of $\sigma(n)$ was first obtained by Gronwall (cf. [16]) who showed

$$\overline{\lim} \frac{\sigma(n)}{n \operatorname{loglog} n} = e^{\gamma}$$

Robin has proved in [63] that the property

$$\forall n \geq 5041, \ \sigma(n) < e^{\gamma} n \operatorname{loglog} n$$

is equivalent to the Riemann hypothesis (cf. also [59] and [65]).

Let $a(n)$ be the number of abelian groups of order n. This is a multiplicative function, and $a(p^{\alpha})$ is equal to the number of partitions of α. The maximal order of $a(n)$ is a little more difficult to study than that of $d(n)$. The reason is that the "superior" numbers are more complicated. Schwarz and Wirsing have proved in [71] that the maximal order of $a(n)$ is

$$(\log 5)\mathrm{Li}\left[\frac{\log n}{4}\right] + O(\log n \exp(-c\sqrt{\log\log n})),$$

improving the results of [22] and [25]. In [41] the maximal order of a(n) under the assumption of the Riemann hypothesis is given.

When dealing with an arithmetical function, it is now a classical problem to study its maximal order. This has been done for the coefficients of some modular forms and especially Ramanujan's function τ (cf. [5] and [33]), and some other functions (cf. [17], [23] and [24]).

A more general study has been undertaken for those multiplicative functions f(n) for which $f(p^{\alpha})$ does depend on α, but not on p. (cf. [6], [53], [20], [72], and [44]).

Explicit upper bounds for $d_3(n)$ and r(n) defined in §II can be found in [61].

XIII. **The unpublished manuscript.**

In the notes on the memoir "Highly composite numbers" at the end of the "Collected Papers" of S. Ramanujan (cf. [55], p. 339), it is stated: "The paper, as long as it is, is not complete. The London Math. Soc. was in some financial difficulty at the time, and Ramanujan suppressed part of what he had written, in order to save expense."

During the Ramanujan centenary conference at Urbana, many documents were displayed, and among them, I have found about 20 pages, handwritten by Ramanujan, that belong to this suppressed part. This unpublished part deals with the maximal order of some arithmetical functions under the assumption of the Riemann hypothesis, and generalizes the results of §§ 39-43. One type of these arithmetical functions is the number of representations of n by a sum of 2, 4,, 6, 8 squares, or by some other simple quadratic forms. Large values of $d_k(n)$ are also studied.

The more interesting part of this manuscript pertains to the maximal order of

$$\sigma_{-s}(n) = \sum_{d|n} d^{-s}$$

where $s > 0$. We have

$$\sigma_s(n) = n^s \sigma_{-s}(n)$$

and Ramanujan studied in detail those functions $\sigma_s(n)$ which occur in Eisenstein series. To study the maximal order of $\sigma_{-s}(n)$, generalized superior h.c. numbers are introdcued. In the case $s = 1$, these numbers were rediscovered by Alaoglu and Erdös who call them colossally abundant numbers.

Three cases are to be considered: $0 < s < 1/2$, $s = 1/2$ and $s > 1/2$. When $s = 1$, Ramanujan gives the formula

$$\overline{\lim}\, (\sigma_{-1}(n) - e^{\gamma}\log\log n)(\sqrt{\log n}) \leq e^{\gamma}(4 - 2\sqrt{2} + \gamma - \log 4\pi)$$

$$= 1.39\ldots ,$$

which was rediscovered by Robin (cf. [63], p. 194). In fact, Ramanujan has estimations for every s.

I shall try to get this manuscript of Ramanujan published elsewhere.

REFERENCES

[1] L. Alaoglu and P. Erdös. "On highly composite and similar numbers", Trans. Amer. Math. Soc. 56,1944, pp. 448-469.

[2] G. Bessi and J. L. Nicolas. "Nombres 2-hautement composés", J. Math. pures et appliquées 56, 1977, pp. 307-326.

[3] E. R. Canfield, P. Erdös and C. Pomerance. "On a problem of Oppenheim concerning Factorisation Numerorum", J. Number Theory 17, 1983, pp. 1-28.

[4] J. Chidambaraswamy and P. V. Krishnaiah. "On integers n with $J_t(n) < J_t(m)$ for $n < m$", Abstracts A.M.S., no. 45, 1986, pp. 279.

[5] P. Deligne and J. P. Serre. "Formes modulaires de poids 1", Annales Scientifiques de l'E.N.S., 4ème série, 7, 1974, pp. 507-530.

[6] A. A. Drozdova and G. A. Freiman. "The estimation of certains arithmetical functions", Elabuz. Gas. Pad. Inst. Ucen. Zap. 3, 1958, p. 160-165, MR 40#7213.

[7] P. Erdös, "On highly composite numbers", J. London Math. Soc. 19, 1944, pp. 130-133.

[8] P. Erdös and I. Kátai. "On the growth of $d_k(n)$", Fibonacci Quart. 7, 1969, pp. 267-274.

[9] P. Erdös and J. L. Nicolas. "Répartition des nombres superabondants", Bull. Soc. Math. France 103, 1975, pp. 65-90.

[10] P. Erdös and J. L. Nicolas. "Méthodes probabilistes et combinatoires en théorie des nombres", Bull. Sc. Math. 2e serie, 100, 1976, pp. 301-320.

[11] P. Erdös and J. L. Nicolas. "Grandes valeurs d'une fonction liée au produit d'entiers consécutifs", Annales Fac. Sci. Toulouse 3, 1981, pp. 173-199.

[12] P. Erdös and J. L. Nicolas. "Sur la fonction: nombre de diviseurs premiers de n", l'Enseignement Mathématique 27, 1981, pp. 3-27.

[13] P. Erdös and J. L. Nicolas. "Grandes valeurs de fonctions liées aux diviseurs premiers consécutifs d'un entier", preprint.

[14] H. Everett. "Generalized Lagrange Multiplier method for solving problems of optimum allocations of resources", Operations Research 11, 1963, pp. 399-417.

[15] N. Feldmann. "Improved estimate for a linear form of the logarithms of algebraic numbers", Mat. Sb. 77(119), 1968, pp. 423-436 (in Russian). Math. USSR-Sb. 6, 1968, pp. 393-406.

[16] T. H. Gronwall. "Some asymptotic expressions in the theory of numbers", Trans. Amer. Math. Soc. 14, 1913, pp. 113-122.

[17] G. E. Hardy and M. V. Subbarao. "Highly powerful numbers", Congressus Numerantium 37, 1983, pp. 277-307.

[18] G. H. Hardy and S. Ramanujan. "Asymptotic formulae for the distribution of integers of various types", Proc. London Math. Soc. (2) 16, 1917, pp. 112-132.

[19] G. H. Hardy and E. M. Wright. "An introduction to the theory of numbers, Oxford at the Clarendon Press, 5th edition (1979).

[20] E. Heppner. "Die Maximale Ordnung primzahl-unabhängiger multiplikativer Funktionen", Arch. Math. 24, 1973, pp. 63-66.

[21] G. Hoheisel. "Primzahlproblem in der Analysis", Berlin Math. Ges. Sitzungsber., 1930, pp. 550-558.

[22] D. G. Kendall and R. A. Rankin. "On the number of abelian groups of a given order", Quart. J. Math. Oxford 18, 1947, pp. 197-208.

[23] J. Knopfmacher. "Arithmetical properties of finite rings and algebras, and analytic number theory", I - VI, J. Reine Angew. Math. 252, 1972, pp. 16-43; 254, 1972, pp. 74-99; 259, 1973, pp. 157-170; 270, 1974, pp. 97-114; 271, 1974, pp. 95-121; 277, 1975, pp. 45-62.

[24] J. Knopfmacher. "A prime divisor function", Proc. Amer. Math. Soc. 40, 1973, pp. 373-377.

[25] E. Krätzel. "Die maximale Ordnung der Anzahl der wesentlich verschiedenen Abelschen Gruppen n-ter Ordnung", Quart. J. Math. Oxford (2) 21, 1970, pp. 273-275.

[26] E. Landau. "Handbuch der Lehre von der Verteilung der Primzahlen", Leipzig und Berlin, B. G. Teubner, 1909.

[27] S. Lang. "Nombres transcendants", Séminaire Bourbaki, 18éme année, 1965-66, no. 305, 8 p.

[28] S. Lang. "Introduction to transcendental numbers", Addison Wesley Series in Math., 1966.

[29] J. P. Massias. "Majoration explicite de l'ordre maximum d'un élément du groupe symétrique", Annales Fac. Sci. Toulouse 6, 1984, pp. 269-281.

[30] J. P. Massias, J. L. Nicolas, and G. Robin. "Evaluation asymptotique de l'ordre maximum d'un élément du groupe symétrique", to be published in Acta Arithmetica 50, no. 3.

[31] D. W. Masser and P. Shiu. "On sparsely totient numbers", Pacific J. Math. 121, 1986, pp. 407-426.

[32] C. J.Mozzochi. "On the difference between consecutive primes", J. Number Theory 24, 1986, pp. 181-187.

[33] R. Murty. "Oscillations of Fourier coefficients of modular forms", Math. Annalen 262, 1983, pp. 431-446.

[34] J. L. Nicolas. "Sur l'ordre maximum d'un élément dans le groupe S_n des permutations", Acta Arithmetica 14, 1968, pp. 315-332.

[35] J. L. Nicolas. "Ordre maximal d'un élément du groupe des permutations et highly composite numbers". These, Bull. Soc. Math. France 97, 1969, pp. 129-191.

[36] J. L. Nicolas. "Répartition des nombres hautement composés de Ramanujan", Can. J. Math. 23, 1971, pp. 116-130.

[37] J. L. Nicolas. "Grandes valeurs des fonctions arithmétiques", Séminaire D.P.P., Paris, 16éme année, 1974/75, no. G 20, 5 p.

[38] J. L. Nicolas. "Problèmes d'optimisation en nombres entiers", Astérisque 24-25, 1975, pp. 325-333.

[39] J. L. Nicolas. "Sur un problème d'optimisation en nombres entiers de T. L. Saaty", R.A.I.R.O. 9, 1975, V2, pp.67-82.

[40] J. L. Nicolas. "Algorithmes d'optimisation en nombres entiers", Astérisque 38-39, 1976, pp. 169-182.

[41] J. L. Nicolas. "Sur les entiers n pour lesquels il y a beaucoup de groupes abéliens d'ordre n", Annales de l'Institut Fourier 28, 1978, pp.1-16.

[42] J. L. Nicolas. "Répartition des nombres largement composés", Acta Arithmetica 34, 1980, pp. 379-390.

[43] J. L. Nicolas and G. Robin. "Majorations explicites pour le nombre de diviseurs de n", Bull. Can. Math. 26, 1983, pp.485-492.

[44] J. L. Nicolas. "Grandes valeurs d'une certaine classe de fonctions arithmétiques", Studia Scientiarum Math. Hung. 15, 1980, pp. 71-77.

[45] J. L. Nicolas. "Petites valeurs de la fonction d'Euler", J. of Number Theory 17, 1983, pp. 375-388.

[46] J. L. Nicolas. Petites valeurs de la fonction d'Euler et hypothèse de Riemann", Sém. Th. des Nombres DPP, Paris 1981-82, Birkhäuser, Progress in Mathematics, no. 38, pp. 207-218.

[47] J. L. Nicolas. "Responses to the queries no. 341", Notices A.M.S., 1986, p. 629.

[48] J. L. Nicolas. "Nombres hautement composés", to be published in Acta Arithmetica, 49, no. 4, dedicated to P. Erdös' 75th birthday .

[49] D. P. Parent. "Exercices de théorie des nombres", Gauthiers-Villars, Paris, 1978, collection MU. English translation, Springer-Verlag, 1984, Problem books in Mathematics.

[50] S. Pillai. "On $\sigma_{-1}(n)$ and $\varphi(n)$", Proc. Indian Math. Soc. 17, 1943, pp. 67-70.

[51] S. Pillai. "Highly abundant numbers", Bull. Calcutta Math. Soc. 35, 1943, pp. 141-156.

[52] S. Pillai. "Highly composite numbers", J. Indian Math. Soc. 8, 1944, pp. 61-74

[53] A. G. Postnikov. "Introduction to analytic theory of numbers", Izdat. "Nauka", Moscow, 1971, (in Russian). MR 55#7895.

[54] S. Ramanujan. "Highly composite numbers", Proc. London Math. Soc., (2) 14, 1915, pp. 347-409.

[55] S. Ramanujan. "Collected papers", Chelsea, 1927.

[56] S. Ramanujan. "Note books of Srinivasa Ramanujan", Tata Inst. of Fundamental Research, Bombay, 1957, vol. 1 and 2.

[57] G. Rhin. Approximants de Padé et mesure d'irrationalité, Sém. Th. des nombres D.P.P., Paris, 1985-1986, to be published in Birkhäuser, Progress in Math.

[58] G. Robin. "Sur un problem d'optimisation en nombres entiers", Math. Oper. Stat. Ser. Opt. 11, 1980, pp. 403-420.

[59] G. Robin. "Sur l'ordre maximum de la fonction somme des diviseurs", Sém. Th. des Nombres DPP, Paris, 1981-82, Birkhäuser. Progress in Mathematics, no. 38, pp. 233-244.

[60] G. Robin. "Méthodes d'optimisation pour un problème de théorie des nombres", R.A.I.R.O. Informatique théorique 17, no. 3, 1983, pp. 239-247.

[61] G. Robin. Thèse d'état, Université de Limoges, France, 1983.

[62] G. Robin. "Estimation de la fonction de Tchebychef θ sur le k-ième nombre premier et grandes valeurs de la fonction $\omega(n)$ nombre de diviseurs premiers de n", Acta Arith. 42, 1983, pp. 367-389.

[63] G. Robin. "Grandes valeurs de la fonction somme des diviseurs et hypothèse de Riemann", J. Math. pures et appl. 63, 1984, pp. 187-213.

[64] G. Robin. "Sur une famille de nombres hautement composés supérieurs", to be published in Studia Sci. Math. Hung.

[65] G. Robin. "Grandes valeurs de la fonction somme des diviseurs dans les progressions arithmétiques", to be published in J. Math. pures et appl.

[66] J. B. Rosser and L. Schoenfeld. "Approximate formulas for some functions of prime numbers", Illinois J. Math. 6, 1962, pp. 64-94.

[67] J. B. Rosser and L. Schoenfeld. "Sharper bounds for the Chebyshev functions $\theta(x)$ and $\psi(x)$", Math. Comp. 29, 1975, pp. 243-269.

[68] C. Runge. "Über die auflösbaren Gleichungen von der Form $x^5 + ux + v = 0$", Acta Mathematica 7, 1885, pp. 173-186.

[69] H. Salié. "Über abundante Zahlen", Math. Nachr. 9, 1953, pp. 217-220.

[70] L. Schoenfeld. "Sharper bounds for the Chebyshev functions $\theta(x)$ and $\psi(x)$", II, Math. Comp. 30, 1976, pp. 337-360.

[71] W. Schwarz and E. Wirsing. "The maximal number of non-isomorphic abelian groups of order n", Arch. Math., t.24, 1973, pp. 59-62.

[72] P. Shiu. "The maximum order of multiplicative functions", Quart. J. Math., Oxford, (2) 31, 1980, pp. 247-252.

[73] T. H. Tran. "Nombres hautement composés de Ramanujan généralisés", C.R. Acad. Sci. Paris, Sér A-B, 282, 1976, no. 17, pp. A939-A942.

[74] S. Wigert. "Sur l'ordre de grandeur du nombre de diviseurs d'un entier", Arkiv för Mathematik, vol. 3, no. 18, 1906-1907, pp. 1-9.

J. L. Nicolas
Département de Mathématiques
Université de Limoges
123 Ave Albert Thomas
87060 Limoges, France

Ramanujan's tau-function and its generalizations

By R.A. Rankin

1. Introduction. The tau-function provides a good illustration of Ramanujan's insight and ingenious ability to find new and interesting facts in areas negected by other mathematicians. In several cases many years have elapsed before subjects that he founded have been studied by others and have revealed their richness and importance.

The tau-function is defined as the nth Fourier coefficient of the discriminant function

$$\Delta(z) = e^{2\pi iz} \prod_{m=1}^{\infty} (1 - e^{2\pi imz})^{24} = \sum_{n=1}^{\infty} \tau(n)e^{2\pi inz}, \tag{1.1}$$

where Im $z > 0$. Δ is so named, since it is essentially the discriminant of the cubic polynomial appearing on the right-hand side of the differential equation satisfied by the Weierstrass $\wp$ -function

$$y^2 = 4x^3 - g_2x - g_3 \qquad (x = \wp(u),\ y = \wp'(u))$$

and therefore, except in degenerate cases, is never zero, as is shown by the infinite product. In the theory of modular forms the fact that $\Delta(z)$ does not vanish in the finite upper half-plane is of supreme importance, since it allows one to take fractional powers of Δ , which remain holomorphic and remain modular forms.

So far as I know, Ramanujan was the first person to take any interest in the coefficients $\tau(n)$. The properties which he found and investigated were of three main types:

ISBN 0-12-058560-X

(i) Multiplicative properties, namely

$$\tau(mn) = \tau(m)\tau(n) \quad \text{for} \quad (m,n) = 1, \tag{1.2}$$

$$\tau(p^{r+1}) = \tau(p)\tau(p^r) - p^{11}\tau(p^{r-1}) \quad (p \ \text{prime}, \ r \geq 1). \tag{1.3}$$

(ii) Order of magnitude of $\tau(n)$, and, in particular, the conjecture

$$|\tau(p)| < 2\, p^{11/2} \quad (p \ \text{prime}). \tag{1.4}$$

Both these topics are discussed in the famous 1916 paper 'On certain arithmetical functions' [27].

(iii) Congruence properties. These are of two types, typified by

(a) $\tau(n) \equiv \sigma_{11}(n) \pmod{691}$, where

$$\sigma_r(n) = \sum_{d|n} d^r. \tag{1.5}$$

(b) $\tau(n)$ is almost always divisible by 691. See §4.

Ramanujan was interested in similar properties for a number of other arithmetical functions which, like $\tau(n)$, are Fourier coefficients of cusp forms.

I shall discuss (i) and (ii) fairly fully. On (iii)(a) I shall say very little, while on (iii)(b) my main concern will be his unpublished work [29] and not later developments.

2. Multiplicative properties. Ramanujan was not the first person to work in this area. He was preceded by the English mathematician J.W.L. Glaisher (1848-1928). They must have met, since both were at Trinity College, Cambridge, but probably had few contacts. However, Ramanujan was certainly familiar with Glaisher's papers. In these, by methods that must have been, even in 1900, somewhat old-fashioned,

Glaisher obtained formulae for the number $r_s(n)$ of representations of a number n as the sum of s squares for the cases s = 2, 4, 6, ...,18 [6],[7],[8]. These formulae were obtained by juggling with the expansions of the functions

$$k^q \, k'^r \, \rho^{s/2},$$

where k an k' are the so-called modulus and complementary modulus of elliptic function theory and where ρ is now called ϑ_3^2 or θ_3^2 , the square of the simplest theta-function.

In more modern notation the problem boils down to expressing ϑ_3^s as $E_s + C_s$, where E_s is a combination of Eisenstein series, having divisor functions as coefficients, and C_s is a cusp form. For $s \leq 8$, $C_s = 0$, while for s = 10, 12, 14 and 16 the vector space of cusp forms has dimension 1 and Glaisher, who, like Ramanujan, was an indefatigable calculator, noticed that, when C_s was divided by a suitable constant, its coefficients were multiplicative. For example, when s = 12, the cusp form is 16 $\Delta^{\frac{1}{2}}(z)$, and, with the help of Mordell [20], he was able to give an elementary proof of the multiplicative properties.

For s = 18, however, the space has dimension 2 and he tried, with only partial success, to find two spanning cusp forms with multiplicative coefficients. The work had become very complicated and he stopped there.

Ramanujan continued Glaisher's work for the case s = 24, where he found that $\tau(n)$ and $\tau(n/2)$ occurred in the formula for $r_{24}(n)$. This result appears in the 1916 paper [27] already mentioned. From a table of 30 values of $\tau(n)$ he conjectured the properties given in (i) above and at once noted the application to Dirichlet series, a type of formula that does not occur in any of Glaisher's papers, namely the identity

$$\sum_{n=1}^{\infty} \frac{\tau(n)}{n^s} = \prod_p \{1 - \tau(p)p^{-s} + p^{11-2s}\}^{-1}. \qquad (2.1)$$

It was presumably by considering the quadratic

$$1 - \tau(p)T + p^{11}T^2$$

that he observed that the roots were not real for the values of p in his table and so conjectured that (1.4) holds for all p. For a later purpose, we express the conjecture by setting

$$1 - \tau(p)T + p^{11}T^2 = \{1 - \alpha(p)T\}\{1 - \beta(p)T\}, \qquad (2.2)$$

where $$|\alpha(p)| = |\beta(p)| = p^{11/2}. \qquad (2.3)$$

This conjecture was later extended by Petersson [23] to certain other cusp form coefficients and is known as the Ramanujan-Petersson conjecture.

In 1917 Mordell [21] proved the multiplicative properties of $\tau(n)$ and the analogous results for certain other such functions. His method was essentially that later developed by Hecke, although made simpler in detail by the fact that $\Delta(z)$ vanishes only at ∞ and at rational points on the real axis. Whether because his results came out in war-time, or because his paper was difficult to read, they were virtually ignored outside the United Kingdom and Mordell never returned to the subject.

In fact, when Hecke first published his work on Euler products in 1935, he was unaware of Mordell's work and [11] claimed the results on $\tau(n)$ as new. By the time, however, that he had written his full exposition of the subject [12], published in the following year, he was aware of Mordell's earlier work.

I now describe the work of Hecke [12], Petersson [24], Atkin-Lehner [1], Li [19] and others and begin with some definitions.

We take two positive integers k and N, called the weight and level, respectively. For technical reasons we exclude $N = 2$. Further, χ is an arbitrary Dirichlet character modulo N satisfying $\chi(-1) = (-1)^k$, so that k is even when $N = 1$. Write

$$\Gamma(1) = SL(2,Z) \tag{2.4}$$

and put

$$T = \begin{bmatrix} a & b \\ c & d \end{bmatrix}, \qquad Tz = \frac{az + b}{cz + d}, \tag{2.5}$$

$$\Gamma_0(N) = \{T \in \Gamma(1) : c \equiv 0 (\mathrm{mod}\ N)\}. \tag{2.6}$$

The group $\Gamma_0(N)$ has finite index in $\Gamma(1)$. Note that we have $\Gamma_0(1) = \Gamma(1)$. We also define

$$\chi(T) = \chi(d) \quad (T \in \Gamma_0(N)), \tag{2.7}$$

and put

$$H = \{z \in C : \mathrm{Im}\ z > 0\}. \tag{2.8}$$

We now define $C(k,N,\chi)$ to be the vector space of functions, called cusp forms, satisfying

(i) f is holomorphic on H.

(ii) For all $T \in \Gamma_0(N)$ and $z \in H$,

$$f(Tz) = \chi(T)(cz + d)^k f(z). \tag{2.9}$$

(iii) For $z \in H$ the function f has an absolutely convergent Fourier expansion

$$f(z) = \sum_{r=1}^{\infty} a(r)\, e^{2\pi i r z}. \tag{2.10}$$

This can be expressed by saying that f vanishes at the cusp ∞. We demand further that f vanishes at every cusp L_∞, for $L \in \Gamma(1)$, but do not spell this out in detail. Also, if $a(1)=1$, we say that f is primitive.

For each triple (k, N, χ), $C(k, N, \chi)$ is a finite-dimensional vector space. Hecke [12] introduced a family of operators $T_n (n \in N)$ acting on $C(k, N, \chi)$ as follows:

$$f(z)|T_n = \frac{1}{n} \sum_{d|n} \sum_{\nu=1}^{n/d} \chi(d)\, d^k\, f\{(dz + \nu)d/n\}. \tag{2.11}$$

It is easy to show that $f|T_n \in C(k, N, \chi)$ for all $n \in N$, and that

$$f(z)|T_n = \sum_{r=1}^{\infty} a_n(r) e^{2\pi i r z}, \tag{2.12}$$

where

$$a_n(r) = \sum_{d|(n,r)} \chi(d)\, d^{k-1}\, a(nr/d^2). \tag{2.13}$$

We call n good when $(n,N)=1$ and bad when n is composed entirely of primes dividing N. In this latter case we have $a_n(r) = a(nr)$.

It can be shown that the T_n commute with each other and that

$$T_m\, T_n = \sum_{d|(m,n)} \chi(d)\, d^{k-1}\, T_{mn/d^2} \quad (m, n \in N). \tag{2.14}$$

If for some scalar $\lambda_f(n)$

$$f|T_n = \lambda_f(n)\, f. \tag{2.15}$$

We call f an eigenform for T_n, with eigenvalue $\lambda_f(n)$. If this holds for all good n, we say that f is a good

<u>eigenform</u> ; further, if it holds for all positive integers n, and if in addition f is primitive, we call f a <u>super eigenform</u>. Needless to say, this terminology is not standard.

If f is a primitive good eigenform, it is easy to deduce from (2.10), (2,13) and (2.15) that $\lambda_f(n) = a(n)$ for good n and that

$$\lambda_f(m)\lambda_f(n) = \sum_{d|(m,n)} \chi(d)\, d^{k-1}\, \lambda_f(mn/d^2), \tag{2.16}$$

when both m and n are good. Moreover, if f is a super eigenform, this result holds for all m and n. Formula (2.16) combines in a single equation the multiplicative properties (1.2) and (1.3) stated for $\tau(n)$, where $\chi(d) = 1$, of course.

If f is a super eigenform, we write

$$F(s) = \sum_{n=1}^{\infty} a(n)n^{-s} (\sigma = \text{Re } s > (k + 1)/2). \tag{2.17}$$

Then (2.16) implies that F(s) possesses the Euler product

$$F(s) = \prod_p \{1 - a(p)p^{-s} + \chi(p)p^{k-1-2s}\}^{-1}. \tag{2.18}$$

It seems that Hecke would have liked to show that the space $C(k, N, \chi)$ has a basis of super eigenforms. However, the most that he was able to prove was that any subspace C of $C(k, N, \chi)$, invariant under all his operators, contains at least one super eigenform. This, of course, solves the problem when dim $C(k, N, \chi) = 1$, and this is how he proved the multiplicative properties of $\tau(n)$.

Hecke was followed by Petersson, whose great contribution was to show [24] that $C(k, N, \chi)$ is a finite-dimensional Hilbert space and that the good Hecke operators are normal, i.e. that they commute with their adjoint operators. In fact, he showed that

$$(f|T_n, g) = \chi(n)\,(f, g|T_n) \quad \text{for} \quad (n,N) = 1, \tag{2.19}$$

but this does not necessarily hold for other values of n. Since the operators commute, Petersson was able to deduce that $C(k, N, \chi)$ has an orthogonal basis of good eigenforms, but from this he could only conclude that, instead of (2.18), each Dirichlet series associated with a basis form can be written as

$$F(s) = H_N(s) \prod_{p \nmid N} \{1 - a(p)p^{-s} + \chi(p)p^{k-1-2s}\}^{-1}, \tag{2.20}$$

where $H_N(s)$ is a Dirichlet series of the form

$$\sum_{n \text{ bad}} a(n)\, n^{-s}.$$

These difficulties were finally solved by Atkin and Lehner [1] in 1970. Their work covered the case when χ is the principal character modulo N, but was extended to all characters in 1975 by Winnie Li [19]. It is perhaps fairly obvious that one cannot expect that $H_N(s)$ can be expressed as an Euler product in every case. For since, for example, a form of level N is also of level N/d for every $d|N$, what is a bad number for N may be good for N/d. This no doubt motivated Atkin and Lehner to write

$$C(k, N, \chi) = C^- \oplus C^+, \tag{2.21}$$

where in C^- we take all forms of lower level (this is a somewhat vague statement, which it would take too much time to make absolutely precise), and C^+ is the orthogonal complement.

Since everything is straightforward for N = 1, in which case C^- is the zero space, we can, by induction, regard the situation in C^- as known and concentrate on C^+, which can be shown to be invariant under all the operators T_n. C^+ is spanned by good eigenforms. If f is such a good eigenform and is non-zero, we write [f] for the set of forms f^* in C^+ having the same eigenvalues $\lambda_f(n)$ for good n. The crucial result is that dim [f] = 1 and that, by multiplication by a suitable scalar, f may be taken to be primitive. It follows that f is a super eigenform and we call it a newform, the eigenforms in C^- being labelled as oldforms. For newforms additional information is sometimes available regarding the eigenvalues $\lambda_f(p)$ for bad primes p. For example, when χ is a primitive character it can be shown that

$$|\lambda_f(p)| = p^{(k-1)/2}. \tag{2.22}$$

In the work I have described the weight k is an integer and the group is a congruence group. Hecke operators have been defined for non-integral weight and non-congruence groups [47], but there are substantial difficulties, except in the case of half-integral weight, where a satisfactory theory has been developed by Shimura [41], generalizing earlier work by Hecke and others. Here the operators T_n

work smoothly when n is a square, but there are complications in other cases. See also the more recent work by Waldspurger [44].

Before passing to my next topic I return to Ramanujan. Vector space theory as we know it today was unknown to him. Nevertheless he listed, in an unpublished fragment published by B.J. Birch [2], several examples of newforms spanning vector spaces of dimension greater than 1 ; these have been investigated, and proofs given, by Rangachari [30] and Raghavan [25].

3. Orders of magnitude. Although Ramanujan may not have been the first to consider the multiplicative properties of cusp form coefficients, I believe he was the first to estimate their orders of magnitude. He made various conjectures, not only for $\tau(n)$, but also for other cusp form coefficients, including those arising from representations of an integer as a sum of squares.

For $\tau(n)$ he proved that

$$\tau(n) = 0(n^7) \tag{3.1}$$

and this was improved by Hardy to

$$\tau(n) = 0(n^6), \tag{3.2}$$

who also showed that, for certain positive constants A and B, we have

$$A\, n^{12} \le \sum_{m \le n} |\tau(m)|^2 \le B\, n^{12}. \tag{3.3}$$

Hardy's proof was not immediately applicable to other cusp form coefficients, since it depended strongly on the product formula for $\Delta(z)$. It was published in 1927, although the work had been done ten years earlier. However, in 1927 Kloosterman [14] considered the problem from a more general point of view and, by use of the Hardy-Littlewood circle method, he, and later Salié [36] and Davenport [3], were able to obtain better estimates, such as ,for any $\varepsilon > 0$,

$$\tau(n) = O(n^{6-\frac{1}{6}+\varepsilon}), \tag{3.4}$$

due to the last two mentioned.

At about the same time Petersson [23] had published his important work, that showed that the spaces of cusp forms were spanned by Poincaré series, whose Fourier coefficients could be expressed explicitly as infinite series involving Kloosterman sums and Bessel functions. It followed that the use of the Hardy-Littlewood method could be avoided. It followed, for example, that

$$\tau(n) = A\, n^{11/2} \sum_{q=1}^{\infty} \frac{S(1,n,q)}{q} J_{11}\left(\frac{4\pi\sqrt{n}}{q}\right) \tag{3.5}$$

for a certain constant A. Here

$$S(m,n,q) = \sum_{\substack{h=1 \\ (h,q)=1}}^{q} \exp\{(mh + nh')/q\}, \tag{3.6}$$

where $hh' \equiv 1 \pmod q$. These improvements in the order of $\tau(n)$ were obtained by successive improved estimates of the magnitude of Kloosterman sums. It seems likely that in the infinite series the oscillations of the Kloosterman sums and the Bessel functions cancel out considerably, but at present there appears to be no method of estimating the extent of this cancellation, so that absolute values of each term have to be taken.

In order to continue this method to its logical conclusion, I leap-frog over an intermediate method of a different kind in order to mention the work of André Weil on Kloosterman sums. He [45] was able to prove that

$$|S(m,n,p)| < 2\, p^{1/2} \quad (p \ \text{prime},\ p \nmid (m,n)) \tag{3.7}$$

as a corollary of his deep work on the Riemann hypothesis for curves over finite fields. This yielded the estimate

$$\tau(n) = O(n^{6-\frac{1}{4}+\varepsilon}). \tag{3.8}$$

It should be mentioned that Stepanov [42] has obtained the same estimates for the Kloosterman sum by elementary (but complicated) methods.

I now back-track to a different analytic method [31], [37] developed, not primarily to estimate the magnitude of an individual coefficient, but to study the sum-function

$$\sum_{n \leq x} |a(n)|^2.$$

For simplicity I confine my attention to the case when we have $a(n) = \tau(n)$. For whereas, in the study of multiplicative properties, the main difficulties arise from congruence groups of level $N > 1$ and the bad prime factors of N, in order of magnitude investigations the extra complications arising from a level $N > 1$ are purely technical.

Write

$$D(s) = \sum_{n=1}^{\infty} |\tau(n)|^2 n^{-s} \quad (\sigma > 12). \tag{3.9}$$

Then, by term-by-term integration we have

$$(4\pi)^{-s}\Gamma(s)D(s) = \iint_S y^{s-1}|\Delta(z)|^2\, dxdy \quad (\sigma > 12),$$

where S is the strip $y > 0$, $|x| < 1/2$. We partition S into fundamental regions for $\Gamma(1)$ and, by a change of variable, find that

$$(4\pi)^{-s}\Gamma(s)D(s) = \iint_{\mathcal{D}} y^{s-1}\, |\Delta(z)|^2\, E(s,z)\, dxdy, \tag{3.10}$$

where $\mathcal{D}$ denotes the standard fundamental region

$$\mathcal{D} = \{z \in C : |x| \leq \tfrac{1}{2},\ |z| > 1,\ y > 0\} \tag{3.11}$$

and

$$E(s,z) = \sum |cz + d|^{-2s+22}, \tag{3.12}$$

the summation being over all c, d such that

$$(c,d) = 1, \quad c \geq 0, \quad \text{but} \quad d > 0 \quad \text{if} \quad c = 0.$$

We then have

$$\xi(s) = 2\,\zeta(2s - 22)E(z,s) = \sum_{m=-\infty}^{\infty} \sum_{n=-\infty}^{\infty}{}' |mz + n|^{-2s+22}, \tag{3.13}$$

where the dash denotes the omission of the term with $m=n=0$. It can be shown that $\xi(s)$ can be continued as a holomorphic function over the whole s-plane, apart from a simple pole, and that it satisfies the functional equation

$$(y/\pi)^{s-11}\Gamma(s - 11)\xi(s) = (y/\pi)^{12-s}\Gamma(12 - s)\xi(23 - s). \tag{3.14}$$

It follows that $D(s)$ may be continued as a meromorphic function over the whole plane, that it has a simple pole at $s=12$ with residue

$$\alpha = \frac{(4\pi)^{11}}{11!} \iint_{\mathcal{D}} y^{10}\, |\Delta(z)|^2\, dxdy, \tag{3.15}$$

and that it satisfies the functional equation

$$\phi(s) = \phi(23 - s), \tag{3.16}$$

where

$$\phi(s) = (2\pi)^{-2s}\Gamma(s)\Gamma(s - 11)\zeta(2s - 22)D(s). \tag{3.17}$$

The only singularities of $\phi(s)$ are simple poles at s=11 and 12.

The application of a famous theorem of Landau [16] now gives

$$\sum_{n \leq x} |\tau(n)|^2 = x^{12} + 0(x^{12-2/5}), \tag{3.18}$$

a generalization of Hardy's inequalities (3.3). From this we deduce as a corollary that

$$\tau(n) = 0(n^{6-1/5}), \tag{3.19}$$

an estimate inferior to that obtained from Weil [45], but better than the earlier estimate (3.4).

I have given this argument in some detail, since the ideas involved were, together with other ingredients, used by Deligne [4] in his proof of the Riemann hypothesis for varieties over finite fields, from which he deduced the truth of the Ramanujan-Petersson conjecture . His work applies more generally to the coefficients of any newform of level N and integral weight $k \geq 2$.

An important ingredient in the proof just sketched is the fact that the function D(s), defined by (3.9), is a meromorphic function over the whole plane with a simple pole at s=12. Because of the multiplicative properties of $\tau(n)$, D(s) has an Euler product, namely

$$D(s) = \frac{\zeta^2(s - 11)}{\zeta(2s - 22)} \prod_p [(1 - \alpha^2(p)p^{-s})(1 - \beta^2(p)p^{-s})]^{-1}, \tag{3.20}$$

where, as previoualy,

$$\alpha(p) + \beta(p) = \tau(p), \quad \alpha(p)\beta(p) = p^{11}.$$

In 1974 R.P. Langlands [17] had remarked that the ideas of [31] could be used to prove the Ramanujan conjecture if one had information concerning the analytic behaviour of the more general family of functions

$$L_n(s) = \prod_p \prod_{\nu=0}^{n} \{1 - \alpha^\nu(p)\beta^{n-\nu}(p)p^{-s}\}^{-\binom{n}{\nu}}, \tag{3.21}$$

where n runs through all the even positive integers. Note that

$$\begin{aligned} L_2(s) &= \zeta^2(s - 11) \prod_p \{(1 - \alpha^2(p)p^{-s})(1 - \beta^2(p)p^{-s})\}^{-1} \\ &= D(s)\zeta(2s - 22). \end{aligned} \tag{3.22}$$

The functions $L_n(s)$ are typical of various families of Dirichlet L-series studied in recent years. Deligne realized that Grothendieck's cohomological theory [9] of such L-series provided a clue. However, another ingredient was necessary, and this goes back to Lefschetz's great work [18] on the topology of algebraic varieties, published as long ago as 1924, and to a more recent result on the monodromy of Lefschetz pencils proved by D.A. Kazdan and G.A. Margoulis ; see N. Katz [13], p.285. By combining these two main strands, and others that I have not mentioned, Deligne was able to prove the Riemann hypothesis for varieties over finite fields, and with it the Ramanujan-Petersson conjecture as a corollary.

Deligne's proof applied for any weight $k \geq 2$. A proof

of an entirely different character was given later by Deligne and Serre for k=1 [5]. For this purpose they required the estimate [32]

$$\sum_{p\le x} |\lambda(p)|^2 p^{1-k} \log p \sim x. \tag{3.23}$$

Deligne's result gives upper and lower bounds for $\tau(p)$, but states nothing about possible oscillations between these bounds. Similarly, from (1.4) we deduce that, for arbitrary n,

$$|\tau(n)| \le n^{11/2}\sigma_0(n),$$

but this gives no information about how much $\tau(n)$ can vary. This has been a subject of study ever since Ramanujan's day. He showed that $|\tau(n)| \ge n^{11/2}$ for infinitely many n. The methods that have been used to tackle this problem make strong use of the multiplicative properties of eigenvalues and of certain Dirichlet series of a type similar to the functions $L_n(s)$ defined in (3.21). I confine myself to three examples, stated for $\tau(n)$, for simplicity :

$$\tau(n) = \Omega_{\pm}\left\{n^{11/2}\exp\left(\frac{c \log n}{\log \log n}\right)\right\} \qquad [26], \quad (3.24)$$

$$\sum_{n\le x} |\tau(n)|^4 \sim A\, x^{23} \log x \qquad [22], \quad (3.25)$$

and

$$x^{13/2}(\log x)^{-\alpha} \ll \sum_{n\le x} |\tau(n)| \ll x^{13/2}(\log x)^{-\beta} \qquad [34] \quad (3.26)$$

where

$$\alpha = 1 - 1/\sqrt{2} = 0.2929, \; \beta = (8 - 3\sqrt{6})/10 = 0.0652. \tag{3.27}$$

Here, for example, (3.25) comes from the fact that $L_4(s)$ has a double pole at s=12, but is otherwise holomorphic and nonzero for $\sigma \geq 12$. An unproved conjecture of Sato and Tate states that, if we put

$$\tau(p) = 2\, p^{11/2} \cos \theta_p \quad (0 \leq \theta_p \leq \pi), \tag{3.28}$$

then the angles θ_p are uniformly distributed with respect to the measure $(2/\pi) \sin^2\theta\, d\theta$. If we had more information about the analytic behaviour of an infinite family of L-series, similar to the $L_n(s)$, we might be able to prove this. If it does hold, then the correct order of magnitude of the sum in (3.26) would be

$$x^{13/2}(\log x)^{-\gamma}, \tag{3.29}$$

where $\gamma = 1 - 8/(3\pi) = 0.1512.$

See [35] for other results.

4. Congruence properties. So far as I am aware, Ramanujan was the first person to take an interest in the congruence properties of the coefficients of modular forms. In two of his papers that were accepted for publication before his death, he gave a number of congruences satisfied by the partition function $p(n)$, and at the end of the second paper ([28], p.230) he mentions briefly congruences satisfied by $\tau(n)$ to the moduli 5, 7 and 23. A third long paper [29] on congruence properties, entitled "Properties of $p(n)$ and $\tau(n)$ " exists in manuscript form in the library of Trinity College, Cambridge. Those parts of the paper dealing with $p(n)$ were prepared for publication by G.H. Hardy, and appeared in the Mathematische Zeitschrift in 1921; see [28], p.232. The unpublished part contains a great variety of coefficients. Between the years 1920 and 1950 several of these congruences were rediscovered and proved by various authors, and numerous other congruences of similar type were found. This fascinating, but uncoordinated rag-bag of formulae was finally explained and given a structure by Serre [38], [39] and Swinnerton-Dyer [43] approximately twenty years ago.

I am not concerned here with this more recent work, but should like to say something about the results stated by Ramanujan in his manuscript. By way of illustration I confine my attention in the main to the special prime 691.

The congruence

$$\tau(n) \equiv \sigma_{11}(n) \pmod{691} \tag{4.1}$$

was first stated explicitly in a paper [46] by J.R. Wilton in 1929. It occurs in [29], but it is implicit in one of the formulae in [27].

However, in this lecture I am more interested in Ramanujan's result that $\tau(n)$ is almost always divisible by 691 and similar statements for other moduli. Here 691 is one of a set of 5 exceptional primes ℓ (as defined by Swinnerton-Dyer) considered by Ramanujan, namely

$$\ell = 3, \quad 5, \quad 7, \quad 23, \quad 691.$$

Put α_ℓ = $1/2$, $1/4$, $1/2$, $1/2$, $1/690$.

Then $\tau(n)$ is almost always divisible by ℓ in the sense that

$$A_1(x) := \sum_{n \leq x,\, \ell \nmid \tau(n)} \ell = o(x). \tag{4.2}$$

In fact, more is known and Ramanujan asserted that

$$A_\ell(x) \sim \frac{A_2 x}{(\log x)^{\alpha_\ell}}, \tag{4.3}$$

where A_ℓ is a certain positive constant. In the manuscript he gives the indices α_ℓ as defined above, and explicit values of A_ℓ for $\ell = 3$, 7 and 23. He also gives numerous results to composite moduli, such as that, for almost all values of n

$$\tau(n) \equiv 0 \pmod{2^5 \cdot 3^3 \cdot 5^2 \cdot 7^2 \cdot 23 \cdot 691} \tag{4.4}$$

and notes, by way of contrast, that 1381 is the smallest value of n for which $691 | \tau(n)$.

What is interesting about these 'almost all' results is that it is generally believed that Ramanujan knew no complex function theory, and he certainly does not appear to have used the theory of residues to evaluate the numerous definite integrals he studied. However, the proof of results like (4.3) use complex function theory applied to Dirichlet series having algebraic singularities on their abscissa of convergence. The first application of methods of this kind that I know of is Landau's 1908 paper [15] on the density of integers expressible as the sum of two squares, a problem mentioned by Ramanujan in his first letter to Hardy in 1913 ; see p.xxiv of [28]. It seems clear that Hardy must have drawn Ramanujan's attention to this work of Landau and that Ramanujan must have attained sufficient understanding of Landau's method to use it to deduce results of the type (4.3). In the manuscript he gives no proofs, but states that results like (4.2) can be obtained by elementary methods, while those of type (4.3) are obtained by 'transcendental methods'.

From the work of Serre [40] it is now known that $\tau(n)$ is almost always divisible by ℓ, for any positive integer ℓ, and more precise estimates of the form (4.3) can be given. Ramanujan realized that his method would not work for values of ℓ other than those considered earlier ; for there are only finitely many such values for which $\tau(n)$ is congruent to a combination of divisor functions $\sigma_r(n)$. Nevertheless, with his remarkable insight, he guessed that there were 'unexceptional' primes, such as 11, for which such results continued to hold, although he was unable to provide a complete proof.

In this lecture I have confined my attention to the three topics mentioned in my opening remarks. Even within this narrow area I need hardly state that there are numerous results that I have not had time to discuss — for example, estimates of sum-functions of other types — but I hope that I have said enough to give some flavour of the methods that have been employed.

REFERENCES

[1] A.O.L. ATKIN and J. LEHNER. Hecke operators on $\Gamma_0(m)$. Math. Ann. 185 (1969), 134-160.

[2] B.J. BIRCH. A look back at Ramanujan's notebooks. Math. Proc. Cambridge Philos. Soc. 78 (1975), 73-79.

[3] H. DAVENPORT. On certain exponential sums. J. Reine Angew. Math. 169 (1932), 158-176.

[4] P. DELIGNE. La conjecture de Weil. I. Inst. Hautes Etudes Sci. Publ. Math. 53 (1974), 273-307.

[5] P. DELIGNE and J.-P. SERRE. Formes modulaires de poids 1. Ann. Sci. Ec. Norm. Sup. (4) 7 (1974), 507-530.

[6] J.W.L. GLAISHER. On the representations of a number as the sum of two, four, six, eight, ten and twelve squares. Quart. J. Math. 38 (1907), 1-62.

[7] J.W.L. GLAISHER. On the number of representation of a number as the sum of fourteen and sixteen squares. Quart. J. Math. 38 (1907), 178-236.

[8] J.W.L. GLAISHER. On the representations of a number as the sum of eighteen squares. Quart. J.Math. 38 (1907), 38 (1907), 289-351.

[9] A. GROTHENDIECK. Formule de Lefschetz et rationalité des fonctions L. Séminaire Bourbaki 1965/66, Exposé 279. W.A. Benjamin, New York, 1966.

[10] G.H. HARDY. Note on Ramanujan's arithmetical function $\tau(n)$. Proc. Cambridge Philos. Soc. 23 (1927), 675-680.

[11] E. HECKE. Die Primzahlen in der Theorie der elliptischen Modulfunktionen. Kgl. Danske Videnskabernes Selskab. Math.-fys. Meddelser XIII. 10 (1935), 1-16; [22], pp. 577-590.

[12] E. HECKE. Ueber Modulfunktionen und die Dirichletschen Reihen mit Eulerscher Produktentwicklung. I. Math. Ann. 114 (1937), 1-28; II. ibid., 316-351.

[13] N.M. KATZ. An overview of Deligne's proof of the Riemann hypothesis for varieties over finite fields. Proceedings of Symposia in Pure Mathematics 28 (1976), 275-305.

[14] H.D. KLOOSTERMAN. Asymptotische Formeln für die Fourierkoeffizienten ganzer Modulformen. Abh. Math. Sem. Univ. Hamburg 5 (1927), 337-352.

[15] E. LANDAU. Ueber die Einteilung der positiven ganzen Zahlen in vier Klassen nach der Mindestzahl der zu ihrer additiven Zusammensetzung erforderlichen Quad-

rate. Ann. Math. Phys. (3) 13 (1908), 305-312.

[16] E. LANDAU. Ueber die Anzahl der Gitterpunkte in gewissen Bereichen. II. Nachr. Ges. Wiss. Göttingen (1915), 209-243.

[17] R. LANGLANDS. Problems in the theory of automorphic forms. Lectures in modern analysis and applications. III.Lecture Notes in Mathematics 170 (1970), 18-61.

[18] S. LEFSCHETZ. L'analysis situs et la géométrie algébrique. Gauthier-Villars, Paris, 1924.

[19] W.-C. LI. Newforms and functional equations. Math. Ann. 212 (1975), 285-315.

[20] L.J. MORDELL. On the solutions of $x^2 + y^2 + z^2 + t^2 = 4m_1m_2$. Messenger Math. 47 (1918), 142-144.

[21] L.J. MORDELL. On Mr Ramanujan's empirical expansions of modular functions. Proc. Cambridge Philos. Soc. 19 (1917), 117-124.

[22] C.J. MORENO and F. SHAHIDI. The fourth moment of Ramanujan's τ-function. Math. Ann. 266 (1983), 233-239.

[23] H. PETERSSON. Theorie der automorphen Formen beliebiger reeler Dimension und ihre Darstellung durch eine neue Art Poincaréscher Reihen. Math. Ann. 103 (1930), 369-436.

[24] H. PETERSSON. Konstruktion der sämtlichen Lösungen einer Riemannschen Funktionalgleichung durch Dirichlet-Reihen mit Eulerscher Produktentwicklung. I. Math. Ann. 116 (1939), 401-412; II. Math. Ann 117 (1939), 39-64; III. Math. Ann. 117 (1940), 277-300.

[25] S. RAGHAVAN. On Ramanujan and Dirichlet series with Euler products. Glasgow Math. J. 25 (1984), 203-206.

[26] M. RAM MURTY. Oscillations of Fourier coefficients of modular forms. Math. Ann. 262 (1983), 431-446.

[27] S. RAMANUJAN. On certain arithmetical functions. Trans. Cambridge Philos. Soc. 22 (1916), 159-184.

[28] S. RAMANUJAN. Collected Papers. Cambridge University Press, 1927.

[29] S. RAMANUJAN. Properties of p(n) and τ(n) .... Unpublished manuscript.

[30] S.S. RANGACHARI. Ramanujan and Dirichlet series with Euler products. Proc. Indian Acad. Sci. (Math. Ser.) 91 (1982), 1-15.

[31] R.A. RANKIN. Contributions to the theory of Ramanujan's function $\tau(n)$ and similar functions. II. The order of the Fourier coefficients of integral modular forms.

Proc. Cambridge Philos. Soc. 35 (1939), 357-373.

[32] R.A. RANKIN. An Ω-result for the coefficients of cusp forms. Math. Ann. 203 (1973), 239-250.

[33] R.A. RANKIN. Modular forms and functions. Cambridge University Press, 1977.

[34] R.A. RANKIN. Sums of cusp form coefficients. II. Math. Ann. 272 (1985), 593-600.

[35] R.A. RANKIN. Fourier coefficients of cusp forms. Math. Proc. Cambridge Philos. Soc. 100 (1986), 5-29.

[36] H. SALIE. Zur Abschätzung der Fourierkoeffizienten ganzer Modulformen. Math. Z. 36 (1933), 263-278.

[37] A. SELBERG. Bemerkungen über eine Dirichletsche Reihe, die mit der Theorie der Modulfunktionen nahe verbinden ist. Arch. Math. Naturvid. 43 (1940), 47-50.

[38] J.-P. SERRE. Une interprétation des congruences relatives à la fonction τ de Ramanujan. Séminaire Delange-Pisot-Poitou 1967/68, Exposé 14.

[39] J.-P. SERRE. Congruences et formes modulaires. Séminaire Bourbaki 416 (1972).

[40] J.-P. SERRE. Divisibilité des coefficients des formes modulaires de poids entier. C.R. Acad. Sci. Paris. Sér. A 279 (1974), 679-682.

[41] G. SHIMURA. On modular forms of half integral weight. Ann. of Math. 97 (1973), 440-481.

[42] S.A. STEPANOV. Estimation of Kloosterman sums. Izv. Akad. Nauk. SSSR. Ser. Mat. 35 (1971), 308-323.

[43] H.P.F. SWINNERTON-DYER. On ℓ-adic representations and congruences for coefficients of modular forms. Modular functions of one variable. III. Lecture Notes in Mathematics 350 (1973), 1-55.

[44] J.-L. WALDSPURGER. Sur les coefficients de Fourier des formes modulaires de poids demi-entier. J. Math. Pures Appl. 60 (1981), 375-484.

[45] A. WEIL. On some exponential sums. Proc. Acad. Sci. U.S.A. 34 (1948), 204-207.

[46] J.R. WILTON. Congruence properties of Ramanujan's function $\tau(n)$. Proc. London Math. Soc. 31 (1930), 1-10.

[47] K. WOHLFAHRT. Ueber Operatoren Heckesche Art bei Modulformen reeler Dimension. Math. Nachr. 16 (1957), 233-256.

UNIVERSITY OF GLASGOW,
GLASGOW G12 8QQ,
SCOTLAND.

THE RAMANUJAN τ FUNCTION

M. Ram Murty

§1. Ramanujan

In a classic paper written in 1916, Ramanujan [26] introduced the τ function. It is defined by the power series expansion of an infinite product:

$$\sum_{n=1}^{\infty} \tau(n) q^n = q \prod_{n=1}^{\infty} (1 - q^n)^{24}.$$

Let $q = e^{2\pi i z}$ and set

$$\Delta(z) = \sum_{n=1}^{\infty} \tau(n) e^{2\pi i n z}.$$

Then, $\Delta(z)$ is a modular form of weight 12 for the full modular group $SL_2(\mathbf{Z})$. In particular,

$$\Delta\left(\frac{az+b}{cz+d}\right) = (cz+d)^{12}\Delta(z) \quad \forall \begin{pmatrix} a & b \\ c & d \end{pmatrix} \in SL_2(\mathbf{Z}).$$

The purpose of this paper is to discuss various conjectures about the τ function enunciated by Ramanujan and others, and relate what is known and unknown about these conjectures at the present time.

Ramanujan was the first to foresee the arithmetical significance of $\tau(n)$, for he was the first to investigate the divisibility properties of these coefficients. From the work of Shimura, Serre, and Deligne, it is now known that the decomposition laws of primes in certain non-solvable extensions of $\mathbf{Q}$ are given by divisibility criteria for the τ function. The first indications of a general reciprocity law and non-abelian class field theory lie hidden in the divisibility properties of Fourier coefficients of cusp forms.

In [26], Ramanujan proposed three conjectures:

(i) $\tau(n)$ is multiplicative: $\tau(nn') = \tau(n)\tau(n')$ whenever $(n, n') = 1$.

(ii) if p is prime, $\tau(p^{n+1}) = \tau(p)\tau(p^n) - p^{11}\tau(p^{n-1})$, for $n > 1$, and

(iii) $|\tau(p)| \le 2p^{11/2}$.

Mordell [16] proved (i) and (ii) in 1917. Hecke [9] generalised his proof and unravelled the underlying theory. But (iii) defied many attempts. A succession of

ISBN 0-12-058560-X

analytic methods failed to hit the mark. The best result by analytic methods was obtained by Rankin [27] who showed that

$$\tau(n) = O(n^{\frac{11}{2}+\frac{3}{10}}).$$

Inspired by E. Artin, Weil [39] introduced in 1949 the zeta function of an algebraic variety over a finite field. He conjectured that this zeta function is a rational function which satisfies an appropriate functional equation and an analogue of the Riemann hypothesis. These formed the famous Weil conjectures. Shortly thereafter, experts in the theory of modular forms began to suspect a relationship between the Ramanujan conjecture (iii) and the Weil conjectures. Eichler [5], Ihara [10], Kuga and Shimura [12] began to search for a smooth projective variety X over $\mathbf{F}_p$ such that the polynomial

$$1 - \tau(p)T + p^{11}T^2$$

appears as a factor in the zeta function of X. They constructed an X which almost worked (the 10 fold product of a generic elliptic curve) but was not compact. Deligne [4] showed how to compactify their X and so the Ramanujan conjecture (iii) turned out to be a consequence of his proof of the Weil conjectures [3].

§2. Linnik - Selberg

Partly motivated by the Ramanujan conjecture (iii), Selberg [29] and Linnik [15] independently proposed the following conjecture. Let

$$S(m,n;c) = \sum_{\substack{a\bar{a}\equiv 1 \pmod{c} \\ (a,c)=1}} e^{\frac{2\pi i}{c}(ma+n\bar{a})}$$

be the Kloosterman sum. Then:

Linnik - Selberg conjecture:

$$\sum_{c\leq x} \frac{S(1,n;c)}{c} \ll x^{\epsilon}.$$

where the implied constant depends only on ϵ.

Theorem 1. The Linnik-Selberg conjecture implies

$$\tau(p) = O_{\epsilon}(p^{\frac{11}{2}+\epsilon})$$

for every $\epsilon > 0$.

This fact was certainly known to Selberg [29, p. 9]. A proof appears in [18].

The set S_k of all cusp forms of weight k for $SL_2(\mathbf{Z})$ forms a finite dimensional vector space over $\mathbf{C}$. Let $k \geq 4$. An explicit basis for S_k can be constructed as follows. Define the m-th Poincaré series as

$$P_m(z) = \frac{1}{2} \sum_{(c,d)=1} \frac{e^{2\pi i m(\frac{az+b}{cz+d})}}{(cz+d)^k},$$

where the summation is over all pairs of integers c, d satisfying $(c, d) = 1$ and a, b are integers chosen so that $ad - bc = 1$. (The sum is independent of the choice, as can be easily checked.) $P_m(z)$ is a modular form of weight k Rfor $SL_2(\mathbf{Z})$. If r is the dimension of S_k, then it was proved by Petersson [25] that $P_1, ..., P_r$ form a basis of S_k. In particular, since S_{12} is one dimensional and generated by Δ, it follows that

$$P_1(z) = c\Delta(z),$$

for some non-zero constant c. The advantage in considering P_m is that one can derive an explicit formula for the n-th Fourier coefficient. An explicit calculation of the Fourier coefficient of P_1 reveals that

$$\tau(n) = 2\pi n^{11/2} \sum_{c=1}^{\infty} \frac{S(1,n;c)}{c} J_{11}(\frac{4\pi\sqrt{n}}{c})$$

where J_{11} denotes the Bessel function of order 11. If J_{11} is replaced by J_{k-1}, then the resulting expression gives a formula for the n-th Fourier coefficient of a Poincaré series of weight k. Thus, if in the above sum J_{11} is replaced by J_9, the resulting expression is identically zero as $S_{10} = \{0\}$.

Proof of Theorem 1. On the basis of the Selberg-Linnik conjecture it follows that

$$\sum_{c>\sqrt{n}} \frac{S(1,n;c)}{c} J_{11}(\frac{4\pi\sqrt{n}}{c}) \ll n^{\epsilon}$$

by partial summation and standard estimates for the Bessel function. As there are no cusp forms of weight 10, it also follows by a similar estimation that

$$\sum_{c<\sqrt{n}} \frac{S(1,n;c)}{c} J_9(\frac{4\pi\sqrt{n}}{c}) \ll n^{\epsilon}.$$

It remains to estimate

$$\sum_{c<\sqrt{n}} \frac{S(1,n;c)}{c} J_{11}(\frac{4\pi\sqrt{n}}{c}).$$

By utilising the key identity,

$$J_9(x) + J_{11}(x) = \frac{20J_{10}(x)}{x}$$

we are reduced to estimating

$$\frac{1}{\sqrt{n}} \sum_{c<\sqrt{n}} S(1,n;c) J_{10}(\frac{4\pi\sqrt{n}}{c}).$$

Familiar estimates for the Bessel function and a straightforward partial summation yields the desired result. This completes the proof.

The Ramanujan conjecture implies that

$$|\tau(n)| \leq n^{11/2} d(n)$$

where $d(n)$ denotes the number of divisors of n. From estimates on the divisor function, it follows that

$$\tau(n) = O(n^{11/2} \exp(\frac{c \log n}{\log\log n})),$$

for any positive constant $c > \log 2$. It was long conjectured that this was sharp in the following sense.

Theorem 2.

$$\tau(n) = \Omega_{\pm}(n^{11/2} \exp(\frac{c \log n}{\log\log n}))$$

for some constant $c > 0$.

Remarks.

1. We write $f(n) = \Omega_{\pm}(g(n))$ to mean that

$$f(n) > g(n)$$

for an infinity of n and

$$f(n) < -g(n)$$

for an infinity of n.

2. The constant c in this result is not optimal. On the Sato-Tate conjecture (discussed in §3) any $c > \log 2$ is valid.
3. This was proved in Ram Murty [19]. It has a long history. As a consequence of his conjectures (i), (ii), and (iii), Ramanujan [26] showed that

$$|\tau(n)| \geq n^{11/2}$$

for infinitely many values of n. Hardy [8] gave an unconditional proof of this. Then Rankin [28] proved that

$$\limsup_{n\to\infty} \frac{|\tau(n)|}{n^{11/2}} = +\infty.$$

Joris [11] improved upon this and showed that

$$\tau(n) = \Omega\left(n^{11/2} \exp\left(\frac{c(\log n)^{1/22}}{(\log\log n)^{23/22}}\right)\right).$$

Then, R. Balasubramanian and M. Ram Murty [2] proved that

$$\tau(n) = \Omega\left(n^{11/2} \exp((\log n)^{2/3-\epsilon})\right).$$

The final result, which is best possible, was obtained in [19].

Theorem 2 can be used to prove:

Theorem 3.

$$\sum_{c\leq x} \frac{S(1,n;c)}{c} = \Omega(\exp(\frac{\log x}{\log\log x})).$$

This says that we cannot expect too much cancellation to occur in the sum of Kloosterman sums that appears in the Linnik-Selberg conjecture. The idea of the proof is that if the sum in Theorem 3 is too small, then the explicit formula for $\tau(n)$ would imply that $\tau(n)$ itself is too small. This would then contradict Theorem 2. The details can be found in [19].

§3. Sato - Tate

If for each prime p, we write

$$\tau(p) = 2p^{11/2}\cos\theta_p$$

then it is conjectured that the θ_p's are uniformly distributed in $[0, \pi]$ with respect to the measure

$$\frac{2}{\pi}\sin^2\theta d\theta.$$

This was first proposed by Serre [32, p. I - 21] and is called the Sato - Tate conjecture because of the close analogy it bears to a conjecture of Sato and Tate on elliptic curves. Serre [32] suggested a general procedure for such questions. If for each prime p we associate a conjugacy class X_p in a compact group G, then given an irreducible representation ρ of G, define the L-series

$$L(s,\rho) = \prod_p det(1 - \rho(X_p)p^{-s})^{-1}.$$

Serre [32] proved that if for every non-trivial irreducible representation ρ of G,

(a) $L(s,\rho)$ has an analytic continuation to $Re(s) \geq 1$ and

(b) $L(1+it,\rho) \neq 0$ for $t \in \mathbf{R}$,

then the X_p's are uniformly distributed in G with respect to the Haar measure of G.

In our case, let $G = SU_2(\mathbf{C})$. The conjugacy classes of G are parametrized by $0 \leq \theta \leq \pi$ and each class has a representative of the form

$$\begin{pmatrix} e^{i\theta} & \\ & e^{-i\theta} \end{pmatrix}.$$

The irreducible representations are given by the sequence $\rho_0, \rho_1, \ldots$ where ρ_n has character χ_n given by

$$\chi_n \begin{pmatrix} e^{i\theta} & \\ & e^{-i\theta} \end{pmatrix} = \frac{\sin(n+1)\theta}{\sin\theta}.$$

Therefore, Serre's theorem states that if for $n \geq 1$,

(a) $L(s,\rho_n)$ has an analytic continuation to $Re(s) \geq 1$ and

(b) $L(1+it,\rho_n) \neq 0$, for $t \in \mathbf{R}$,

then the Sato-Tate conjecture is true. Kumar Murty [23] subsequently showed that (a) alone suffices to imply the Sato-Tate conjecture. That is, the non-vanishing turns out to be a consequence of the analytic continuation to the line $Re(s) = 1$.

Not much is known about $L(s, \rho_n)$. For instance, if $n = 0$, then $L(s, \rho_0) = \zeta(s)$, the Riemann zeta function. If $n = 1$, then

$$L(s, \rho_1) = \sum_{n=1}^{\infty} \frac{\tau(n)}{n^{s+\frac{11}{2}}}$$

is the series introduced by Ramanujan [26] and further studied by Hecke [9]. For $n = 2$, Rankin [27] and Selberg [30] independently showed that $\zeta(s)L(s, \rho_2)$ has an analytic continuation and a functional equation, except for a simple pole at $s = 1$. Shimura [36] finally showed that $L(s, \rho_2)$ is in fact entire. Recently, Shahidi [35] proved that $L(s, \rho_3), L(s, \rho_4), L(s, \rho_5)$ each has an analytic continuation for $Re(s) \geq 1$.

Let $\pi(x)$ denote the number of primes up to x. The Sato - Tate conjecture is equivalent to the assertion that for each k,

$$(A_k) \qquad \sum_{p \leq x} (2\cos\theta_p)^{2k} \sim \frac{1}{k+1}\binom{2k}{k}\pi(x)$$

as $x \to \infty$. One can prove [19] :

Theorem 4. If for $n \leq N$, $L(s, \rho_n)$ has analytic continuation for $Re(s) \geq 1$, then A_k is true for $k \leq [N/2]$.

In particular, Theorem 4 is true for $N = 4$ and hence,

$$\sum_{p \leq x} (2\cos\theta_p)^4 \sim 2\pi(x)$$

as $x \to \infty$.

Proof of Theorem 2. It follows from (A_2) that for some $\delta > 0$, there are at least $\delta x/\log x$ primes satisfying

$$|2\cos\theta_p| > 2^{1/4}, \quad \frac{x}{2} < p < x.$$

Let n be defined by

$$\log n = \sum_{\substack{\frac{x}{2} < p < x \\ |2\cos\theta_p| > 2^{1/4}}} \log p.$$

Then,

$$|\tau(n)| \geq n^{11/2} \exp(\frac{c\delta x}{\log x})$$

where $c = \frac{\log 2}{4}$. Since, $\delta x \leq \log n \leq 2x$, it follows that

$$|\tau(n)| \geq n^{11/2} \exp(\frac{c_1 \log n}{\log \log n})$$

for some $c_1 > 0$. This completes the proof.

§4. Lehmer

Based on empirical evidence, Lehmer [14] conjectured that $\tau(p) \neq 0$, for every prime p. This is equivalent to the non-vanishing of the Poincaré series P_n of weight 12, for every natural number n. This is unknown at present.

In 1967, Serre [33] conjectured the existence of an ℓ-adic representation

$$\rho_\ell : \text{Gal}(\overline{\mathbf{Q}}/\mathbf{Q}) \to GL_2(\mathbf{Z}_\ell)$$

such that if σ_p is the Frobenius automorphism of p, then

$$tr\ \rho_\ell(\sigma_p) = \tau(p), \quad det\ \rho_\ell(\sigma_p) = p^{11}.$$

This conjecture was proved by Deligne [4]. Serre [34] noticed that this fact can now be utilised, in conjunction with the Chebotarev density theorem, to show that $\tau(p) = 0$ very rarely. If we consider reduction (mod ℓ),

$$GL_2(\mathbf{Z}_\ell) \to GL_2(\mathbf{F}_\ell)$$

then an extension $K_\ell/\mathbf{Q}$ is determined by the kernel of the composition of this map with ρ_ℓ. This extension has the property that if σ_p represents the Frobenius automorphism of $\text{Gal}(K_\ell/\mathbf{Q})$ then

$$tr\ \rho_\ell(\sigma_p) \equiv \tau(p) \pmod{\ell}$$
$$det\ \rho_\ell(\sigma_p) \equiv p^{11} \pmod{\ell}.$$

Serre and Swinnerton-Dyer [38] showed that for sufficiently large ℓ,

$$\text{Gal}(K_\ell/\mathbf{Q}) = \{g \in GL_2(\mathbf{F}_\ell) : det\ g \in (\mathbf{F}_\ell^*)^{11}\}.$$

The number of primes $p \leq x$ such that $\tau(p) = 0$ is contained in the set of primes such that $\tau(p) \equiv 0 \pmod{\ell}$. A quick calculation of the number of elements of trace zero in $\mathrm{Gal}(K_\ell/\mathbf{Q})$ and an application of the effective Chebotarev density theorem shows that

$$\#\{p \le x : \tau(p) = 0\} \ll \frac{x}{(\log x)^{1+\gamma}}$$

for some $\gamma > 0$. This was proved by Serre [34]. Serre [34] further showed that if the generalised Riemann hypothesis for Artin L-series is assumed then

$$\#\{p \le x : \tau(p) = 0\} = O(x^{3/4}).$$

§5. Lang-Trotter

As part of more general conjectures on Fourier coefficients of cusp forms, Lang and Trotter [13] have conjectured that if for each integer a, we set

$$\pi_a(x) = \#\{p \le x : \tau(p) = a\}$$

then $\pi_a(x) = O_a(1)$. That is, for each a, the equation $\tau(p) = a$ has only finitely many solutions. A variant of this conjecture was proved recently by M. Ram Murty, V. Kumar Murty and T. N. Shorey [17] *for odd values of a*. More precisely:

Theorem 5. If a is odd, and $\tau(n) = a$ then $n \le \exp((2|a|)^c)$ for some effectively computable constant $c > 0$.

Corollary. If $\tau(n)$ is odd, then $|\tau(n)| \ge (\log n)^c$ for some effectively computable absolute constant $c > 0$.

The starting point is the observation that $\tau(p)$ is even for every prime p. To see this note that

$$\begin{aligned}\sum_{n=1}^{\infty} \tau(n) q^n &= q \prod_{n=1}^{\infty} (1-q^n)^{24} \\ &\equiv q \prod_{n=1}^{\infty} (1+q^{8n})^3 \pmod 2 \\ &\equiv q \sum_{n=0}^{\infty} q^{4n^2+4n} \pmod 2\end{aligned}$$

by an identity of Jacobi. Thus, $\tau(n)$ is odd if and only if $n = (2m+1)^2$.

A natural number n is called *squarefull* if for every prime $p|n$, we have $p^2|n$. Thus, if $\tau(n)$ is odd, then n is squarefull. By using techniques from transcendence, it is possible to prove that there is an effectively computable positive constant c such that

$$|\tau(n)| \geq (\log n)^c$$

whenever n is squarefull. Following Ramanujan [26] we can write

$$\tau(p^m) = \frac{\alpha_p^{m+1} - \overline{\alpha}_p^{m+1}}{\alpha_p - \overline{\alpha}_p}$$

utilising the truth of (ii) and (iii). If $\tau(p) \neq 0$, it follows that

$$\begin{aligned} |\tau(p^m)/\tau(p)| &= \left| \frac{\alpha_p^{m+1} - \overline{\alpha}_p^{m+1}}{\alpha_p^2 - \overline{\alpha}_p^2} \right| \\ &\geq \frac{1}{2} p^{\frac{11}{2}(m-1)} \left| \left(\frac{\alpha_p}{\overline{\alpha}_p} \right)^{m+1} - 1 \right|. \end{aligned}$$

There is a theorem of Baker [1] which states that if α is an algebraic number, then there is an effectively computable positive constant c such that $\alpha^n = 1$ or

$$|\alpha^n - 1| > \exp(-cH(\alpha) \log n)$$

where $H(\alpha)$ denotes the logarithm of the absolute values of the coefficients of the minimal polynomial of α over $\mathbf{Q}$. If we apply this here, we obtain

$$|\tau(p^m)| \geq |\tau(p)| p^{\frac{11}{2}(m - c_1 \log m)}$$

for some $c_1 > 0$. This gives us a good lower bound provided m is sufficiently large, say for $m \geq C_2$.

For small values of m, a subtler approach is needed. The key observation is that

$$\tau(p^m) = \gamma_m(p) \prod_{r=1}^{[m/2]} (\tau(p)^2 - 4p^{11} \cos^2 \frac{\pi r}{m+1})$$

where

$$\gamma_m(p) = \begin{cases} 1 & \text{if } m \text{ is even,} \\ \tau(p) & \text{if } m \text{ is odd.} \end{cases}$$

That is, $\tau(p^m)$ is a binary form in $\tau(p)^2$ and p^{11}. Moreover, this binary form has degree ≥ 3 when $m \geq 6$. There is a result of Feldman [6] which states that if f is an irreducible binary form of degree ≥ 3 with rational integer coefficients and $m \neq 0$, then the equation $f(x,y) = m$ forces

$$\max\{|x|,|y|\} \leq m^C$$

for some effectively computable constant C depending only on f. Applying this to the case of the $\tau(p^m)/\gamma_m(p)$ function, we obtain for $m \geq 6$ that

$$|\tau(p^m)| \geq p^C$$

where C depends only on m. Thus, for $6 \leq m \leq C_2$, there is an absolute constant $c_3 > 0$ such that

$$|\tau(p^m)| \geq p^{mc_3}.$$

Combining this with our previous lower bound enables us to deduce that

$$|\tau(p^m)| \geq p^{mc}$$

for some effectively computable positive constant c. To treat $2 \leq m \leq 5$, the approach is similar, but the results are not as sharp. For instance,

$$\tau(p)^2 = p^{11} + \tau(p^2)$$

so that the point $(p, \tau(p))$ lies on the hyperelliptic curve

$$y^2 = x^{11} + a,$$

with $a = \tau(p^2)$. A theorem of Sprindzuk [37] on the solutions of hyperelliptic equations tells us that if (x,y) lies on the above curve, then,

$$\log\max\{|x|,|y|\} \ll |a|^C$$

for some effectively computable positive constant C. This implies that

$$|\tau(p^2)| \geq (\log p)^c$$

for some positive constnat c. Putting all these facts together, yields the result that if n is squarefull then, either $\tau(n) = 0$ or

$$|\tau(n)| \geq (\log n)^C$$

for some positive constant C.

Serre [34] showed that if we assume the generalised Riemann hypothesis, then

$$\pi_a(x) = O(x^{7/8}).$$

This was improved in [22] to:

Theorem 6. Assuming *GRH*, for $a \neq 0$,

$$\pi_a(x) = O(x^{4/5}).$$

The proof of Theorem 6 is based on ℓ-adic representations and an improved version of the Chebotarev density theorem. This improvement is based on a simple group theoretic idea. Let G be a finite group and let

$$\pi : \hat{G} \to \mathbf{C}$$

be a function defined on the irreducible characters of G. For each conjugacy class C of G, let g_C be a representative of C and define

$$\pi_C = \frac{|C|}{|G|} \sum_{\chi} \overline{\chi(g_C)} \pi(\chi)$$

where the summation is over irreducible chracters of G. The orthogonality relations imply that

$$(\dagger) \qquad \sum_C \frac{1}{|C|} |\pi_C - \frac{|C|}{|G|} \pi(1)|^2 = \frac{1}{|G|} \sum_{\chi \neq 1} |\pi(\chi)|^2$$

where the first sum is over conjugacy classes C of G.

Now let $K/\mathbf{Q}$ be a normal extension with Galois group G. For each prime p, let σ_p denote the Frobenius automorphism and set

$$\pi(x, \chi) = \sum_{p \leq x} \chi(\sigma_p).$$

Assuming Artin's conjecture on the holomorphy of $L(s, \chi)$ and the analogue of the Riemann hypothesis, it is essentially deduced that for $\chi \neq 1$,

$$\pi(x, \chi) = O(\chi(1) x^{1/2} \log x),$$

apart from a few minor logarithmic factors. Now,

$$\pi_C(x) = \frac{|C|}{|G|} \sum_{\chi} \overline{\chi(g_c)} \pi(x, \chi)$$

enumerates the number of primes $p \leq x$ such that $\sigma_p \in C$. Therefore, the above identity implies that

$$\frac{1}{|C|} |\pi_C(x) - \frac{|C|}{|G|} \pi(x)|^2 = O(x \log^2 x)$$

in view of the group theoretic identity

$$\sum_{\chi} \chi(1)^2 = |G|.$$

Thus, ignoring a few logarithmic factors,

$$(\ddagger) \qquad |\pi_C(x) - \frac{|C|}{|G|} \pi(x)| \ll |C|^{1/2} x^{1/2} \log x.$$

By using the Cauchy-Schwarz inequality and the identity (†), it follows that the same estimate is true for any set C stable under conjugation.

The number of primes $p \leq x$ such that$\tau(p) = a$ is certainly bounded by the number of primes $p \leq x$ satisfying

$$(*) \qquad \tau(p) \equiv a \pmod{\ell}.$$

By the result of Serre and Swinnerton-Dyer [38] on the shape of the Galois group, cited earlier, the primes p satisfying the above congruence have Frobenius automorphism $\sigma_p \in GL_2(\mathbf{F}_\ell)$ of trace a. This comprises a set C_ℓ which is stable under conjugation. Moreover, the size of this set is roughly ℓ^3, so that the number primes satisfying $(*)$ is

$$\ll \frac{1}{\ell} \pi(x) + O(\ell^{3/2} x^{1/2}).$$

Choosing $\ell = x^{1/5}$ yield the result

$$\pi_a(x) = O(x^{4/5})$$

which is Theorem 6. It would appear that we have assumed the truth of Artin's conjecture. This hypothesis can be removed by very nice arguments of a group-theoretic nature. The details can be found in [22].

If $a = 0$, Serre [34] proved that $\pi_0(x) = O(x^{3/4})$. Kumar Murty [24], proceeding differently, proved the following:

Theorem 7. If $L(s, \rho_n)$ have an analytic continuation to the entire complex plane, satisfy appropriate functional equations for $n \geq 1$ and the analogue of the Riemann hypothesis, then

$$\pi_a(x) = O(x^{3/4})$$

for all integers a.

It should be noted that the ℓ-adic approach does not yield as good a result for all a.

§6. Atkin-Serre

There is an even more ambitious conjecture about the growth of $\tau(p)$.

Namely, Atkin-Serre [31, eqn. 4.11k] have conjectured that

$$|\tau(p)| \gg_\epsilon p^{9/2-\epsilon}.$$

Using methods of analytic number theory, we can obtain information for almost all primes p.

For instance, let $\nu(n)$ denote the number of prime factors of n. It is a classical result of Hardy and Ramanujan [7] that

$$\sum_{n \leq x} (\nu(n) - \log\log n)^2 = O(x \log\log x).$$

Such a result implies that

$$(\star) \qquad |\nu(n) - \log\log n| < (\log\log n)^{\frac{1}{2}+\epsilon}$$

for all $n \leq x$ apart from

$$O(\frac{x}{(\log\log x)^\epsilon})$$

exceptional values of n. That is, a natural number "usually" has $\log\log n$ prime factors. If n satisfies $(\star)$, it is called a normal number. If we treat $\tau(p)$ as a normal number, we would expect that it too should have "usually" $\log\log p$ prime factors. This is indeed the case. One can establish the following "modular analogue" :

Theorem 8. On the generalised Riemann hypothesis for Dedekind zeta functions (*GRH*)

$$\sum_{\substack{p\le x\\ \tau(p)\neq 0}} (\nu(\tau(p)) - \log\log p)^2 = O(\frac{x\log\log x}{\log x}).$$

This implies that for $p \le x$,

$$|\nu(\tau(p)) - \log\log p| < (\log\log p)^{\frac{1}{2}+\epsilon}$$

apart from

$$O(\frac{x}{(\log x)(\log\log x)^{\epsilon}})$$

exceptional primes. If we now consider $\tau(n)$, then it seems plausible to expect

$$\sum_{p|n} \log\log p$$

prime divisors in view of the fact that $\tau(n)$ is multiplicative. The above sum behaves like

$$\frac{1}{2}(\log\log n)^2$$

on the average. This heuristic reasoning is also correct and in a similar way, one can prove [20]: on GRH,

$$\sum_{\substack{n\le x\\ \tau(n)\neq 0}} (\nu(\tau(n)) - \frac{1}{2}(\log\log n)^2)^2 = O(x(\log\log x)^{3+\epsilon})$$

More generally:

$$Pr\{\frac{\nu(\tau(n)) - \frac{1}{2}(\log\log n)^2}{(\log\log n)^{3/2}} \le \frac{\alpha}{\sqrt{3}}\} = \frac{1}{\sqrt{2\pi}}\int_{-\infty}^{\alpha} e^{-t^2/2}dt.$$

This is the "modular analogue" of the celebrated Erdös - Kac theorem.

The implications of these results is that if $\tau(p)$ has usually $\log\log p$ distinct prime factors, then it cannot be too small. The full strength of the GRH is not necessary. Let

$$\pi(x,\ell) = \#\{p \le x : \tau(p) \equiv 0 \pmod{\ell}\}.$$

Then the Chebotarev density theorem implies that

$$\pi(x,\ell) \sim \delta(\ell) li\ x$$

where

$$li\ x = \int_2^x \frac{dt}{\log t}.$$

We make the hypothesis:

$$(H) \qquad \sum_{\ell \le X} |\pi(x,\ell) - \delta(\ell) li\ x| \ll \frac{x}{(\log x)^3}$$

for $X = \exp(\log x / \log\log x)$. (H) is a consequence of GRH but is considerably weaker. It can be viewed as a non-abelian analogue of the Bombieri - Vinogradov theorem on primes in arithmetic progressions.

The proof of Theorem 8 requires asymptotic formulas for

$$\sum_{\substack{p \le x \\ \tau(p) \ne 0}} \nu(\tau(p)), \qquad \sum_{\substack{p \le x \\ \tau(p) \ne 0}} \nu^2(\tau(p)).$$

In order to see how this is done, let us consider the first sum:

$$\begin{aligned} \sum_{\substack{p \le x \\ \tau(p) \ne 0}} \nu(\tau(p)) &= \sum_{\substack{p \le x \\ \tau(p) \ne 0}} \left(\sum_{\substack{\ell \mid \tau(p) \\ \ell < X}} 1 \quad + \sum_{\substack{\ell \mid \tau(p) \\ \ell > X}} 1 \right) \\ &= \sum_{\ell < X} \pi(x,\ell) \quad + \quad O(\frac{x \log\log x}{\log x}). \end{aligned}$$

The desired asymptotic formula follows from (H) on noting that

$$\delta(\ell) \sim 1/\ell.$$

The second sum is handled similarly.

Results of this nature allow us to obtain lower bounds for $\tau(p)$ for almost all p.

Theorem 9. For all but $O(\pi(x)(\log\log x)^{-\epsilon})$ primes $p \le x$,

(i) $|\tau(p)| \ge (\log p)^{1-\epsilon}$, unconditionally,

(ii)

$$|\tau(p)| \ge \exp((\log p)^{1-\epsilon}),$$

assuming (H).

The improved effective Chebotarev density theorem [22] leads to the following:

Theorem 10. On GRH,

$$|\tau(p)| > p^{\frac{1}{4}-\epsilon}$$

with at most $O(x^{1-\epsilon})$ exceptional primes $p \leq x$.

The proof of Theorem 10 is curious. In view of Theorem 6, it is only immediate that

$$|\tau(p)| \geq p^{\frac{1}{5}-\epsilon}$$

for all but $O(x^{1-\epsilon})$ primes $p \leq x$. The improvement is obtained by considering the union of all conjugacy classes of trace $< X^{\frac{1}{4}-\epsilon}$ and then invoking the estimate (‡).

These results reveal to some extent the arithmetic significance of the τ function and Fourier coefficients of cusp forms in general. The story is not yet over. The future awaits for some deeper connections between non-abelian class field theory and Fourier coefficients of cusp forms.

REFERENCES

[1] A. Baker, A sharpening of the bounds for linear forms in logarithms, I, *Acta. Arith.*, **21** (1972) 117-129.

[2] R. Balasubramanian and M. Ram Murty, An Ω theorem for Ramanujan's τ-function, *Inventiones Math.* **68** (1982) 241-252.

[3] P. Deligne, La conjecture de Weil, I, *Publ. Math. I.H.E.S.*, **43** (1974)273-307.

[4] P. Deligne, Formes modulaires et representations ℓ-adiques, *Lecture Notes in Mathematics,* **179** (1971) 139-172, Springer-Verlag.

[5] M. Eichler, Eine verallgemeinerung der Abelschen integrale, *Math. Zeit.*, **67** (1967) 267-298.

[6] N. Feldman, An effective refinement of the exponent in Liouville's theorem (Russian), *Izv. Akad. Nauk.*, **35** (1971) 973-990, (*AMS Translations* **5** (1971) 985-1002).

[7] G.H. Hardy and S. Ramanujan, The normal number of prime factors of a number n, *Quarterly Journal of Mathematics,* **48** (1920) 76-92.

[8] G.H. Hardy, A note on Ramanujan's arithmetical function $\tau(n)$, *Proc. Cambridge Phil. Soc.*, **23** (1927) 675-680.

[9] E. Hecke, Über Modulfunktionen und die Dirichletschen Reihen mit Eulerscher Produktentwicklung, I, *Math. Ann.*, **114** (1937) 1-28; II, *Math. Ann.*, **114** (1937) 316-351.

[10] Y. Ihara, Hecke polynomials as congruence zeta functions in elliptic modular case, *Annals of Math.*, **Ser. 2, 85** (1967) 267-295.

[11] H. Joris, An Ω result for coefficients of cusp forms, *Mathematika*, **22** (1975) 12-19.

[12] M. Kuga and G. Shimura, On the zeta function of a fibre variety whose fibres are abelian varieties, *Annals of Math.*, **Ser. 2, 82** (1965) 478-539.

[13] S. Lang and H. Trotter, Frobenius distributions in GL_2 extensions, *Springer Lecture Notes in Mathematics*, **504** (1976) Springer-Verlag.

[14] D. H. Lehmer, Ramanujan's function $\tau(n)$, *Duke Math. J.*, **10** (1943) 483-492.

[15] U. V. Linnik, Additive problems and eigenvalues of the modular operators, *Proc. International Cong. Math. Stockholm*, (1962) 270-284.

[16] L. J. Mordell, On Ramanujan's empirical expansions of modular functions, *Proc. Camb. Phil. Soc.*, **19** (1920) 117-124.

[17] M. Ram Murty, V. Kumar Murty and T.N. Shorey, Odd values of the Ramanujan τ function, *Bull. Soc. Math. France*, **115** (1987)

[18] M. Ram Murty, On the estimation of eigenvalues of Hecke operators, *Rocky Mountain J.*, **15** (1985) 521-533.

[19] M. Ram Murty, Oscillations of Fourier coefficients of modular forms, *Math. Annalen*, **262** (1983) 431-446.

[20] M. Ram Murty and V. Kumar Murty, Prime divisors of Fourier coefficients of modular forms, *Duke Math. J.*, **51** (1984) 57-76.

[21] M. Ram Murty and V. Kumar Murty, An analogue of the Erdös-Kac theorem for Fourier coefficients of modular forms, *Indian Journal of Pure and Applied Mathematics*, **15**(10) (1984) 1090-1101.

[22] M. Ram Murty, V. Kumar Murty and N. Saradha, Modular forms and the Chebotarev density theorem, *Amer. Journal of Math., to appear.*

[23] V. Kumar Murty, On the Sato-Tate conjecture, in *Number Theory related to Fermat's Last Theorem*, ed. N. Koblitz, (1982) 195-205, Birkhauser-Verlag, Boston.

[24] V. Kumar Murty, Explicit formulae and the Lang-Trotter conjecture, *Rocky Mountain J.*, **15** (1985) 535-551.

[25] H. Petersson, Theorie der automorphen Formen beliebiger reeller Dimension und ihre Darstellung durch eine neue Art Poincaréscher Reihen, *Math. Ann.*, **103** (1930) 369-436.

[26] S. Ramanujan, On certain arithmetical functions,*Trans. Camb. Phil. Soc.*, **22** (1916) 159-184.

[27] R. A. Rankin, Contributions to the theory of Ramanujan's function $\tau(n)$ and similar arithmetical functions, II, The order of the Fourier coefficients of integral modular forms, *Proc. Camb. Phil. Soc.*, **35** (1939) 357-372; III, A note on the sum of the Fourier coefficients of integral modular forms, *Proc. Camb. Phil. Soc.*, **36** (1940) 150-151.

[28] R. A. Rankin, An Ω result for the coefficients of cusp forms, *Math. Ann.*, **203** (1973) 239-250.

[29] A. Selberg, On the estimation of Fourier coefficients of modular forms, *Proc. Symposia in Pure Math.*, **VIII** (1965) 1-15, AMS, Providence.

[30] A. Selberg, Bemerkungen über eine Dirichletsche Reihe die mit der Theorie der Modulformen nahe verbinden ist, *Arch. Math. Naturvid.*, **43** (1940)47-50.

[31] J.-P. Serre, Divisibilité de certaines fonctions arithmétiques, *L'Ens. Math.*, **22** (1976) 227-260.

[32] J.-P. Serre, Abelian ℓ-adic representations and elliptic curves, Benjamin.

[33] J.-P. Serre, Facteurs locaux des fonctions zeta des variétés algébriques (definitions et conjectures), *Sém. Délange-Pisot-Poitou, exposé 19* (1969/70).

[34] J.-P. Serre, Quelques applications du théoréme de densité de Chebotarev, *Publ. Math. IHES*, **54** (1982) 123-201.

[35] F. Shahidi, On certain L-functions, *Amer. J. Math.*, **103** (1981) 297-355.

[36] G. Shimura, On the holomorphy of certain Dirichlet series, *Proc. London Math. Soc.*, **31** (1975) 79-98.

[37] V. Sprindzuk, Hyperelliptic diophantine equations and class numbers of ideals (Russian) *Acta Arith.*, **30** (1976) 95-108.

[38] H.P.F. Swinnerton-Dyer, On ℓ-adic representations and congruences for coefficients of modular forms, *Lecture Notes in Mathematics,* **350** (1973) Springer.

[39] A. Weil, Number of solutions of equations in finite fields, *Bulletin of A.M.S.*, **55** (1949) 497-508.

M. Ram Murty
Department of Mathematics
McGill University
Montréal, Canada

Congruence Properties of $\tau(n)$

H. P. F. Swinnerton-Dyer

Ramanujan had a particular interest in the coefficients of the power series

$$\{(1 - q)(1 - q^2)(1 - q^3) \dots\}^\alpha$$

for various values of α, notably $\alpha = -1$ and α dividing 24. The case $\alpha = -1$ gives the partitio function, for which he discovered congruences modulo powers of 5,7 and 11. Some of the proofs which he gave depended heavily on classical modular form theory; for example

$$p(5n + 4) \equiv 0 \bmod 5$$

follows immediately from the beautiful identity

$$p(4) + p(9)q + p(14)q^2 + \dots = 5 \frac{\{(1 - q^5)(1 - q^{10})\dots\}^5}{\{(1 - q)(1 - q^2)\dots\}^6} .$$

Of the positive values of α the most interesting is $\alpha = 24$, which gives

$$\Delta = q\{(1 - q)(1 - q^2) \dots\}^{24} = \sum \tau(n)q^n,$$

the unique cusp form of weight 12 for the full modular group. Ramanujan conjectured, and Mordell proved, that the $\tau(n)$ are multiplicative--a fact most conveniently expressed in the form

$$\sum \tau(n)n^{-s} = \Pi (1 - \tau(p)p^{-s} + p^{k-1-2s})^{-1} \tag{1}$$

ISBN 0-12-058560-X

where $k = 12$ is the weight of the modular form Δ. To prove (1), Mordell invented Hecke operators a decade before Hecke did; but since he was using them on a one-dimensional subspace he overlooked the key fact that Hecke operators always commute.

The coefficents $\tau(n)$ have a richer and more diverse set of congruence properties than the $p(n)$, and Ramanujan stated a number of these. Write

$$\sigma_r(n) = \sum d^r \text{ taken over all } d|n;$$

in particular σ_r is multiplicative and

$$\sigma_r(p) = 1 + p^r$$

when p is prime. The following congruences can be found in Ramanujan's writings; we can be confident that he had proofs of all of them, though the proofs do not all appear to have survived.

$$\begin{aligned} \tau(n) &\equiv \sigma_{11}(n) \bmod 2^8 \quad \text{for } n \text{ odd}, \\ \tau(n) &\equiv n^2\sigma_7(n) \bmod 3^3, \\ \tau(n) &\equiv n\,\sigma_9(n) \bmod 5^2, \\ \tau(n) &\equiv n\,\sigma_3(n) \bmod 7, \\ \tau(n) &\equiv 0 \bmod 23 \text{ if } \left(\frac{n}{23}\right) = -1, \end{aligned} \tag{2}$$

$$\tau(n) \equiv \sigma_{11}(n) \bmod 691. \tag{3}$$

Of these, the easiest to prove are the last two. Ramanujan's proof of (2) was as follows,

$$\sum \tau(n)q^n = q\{(1 - q)(1 - q^2)\ldots\}^{23}\{(1 - q)(1 - q^2)\ldots\}$$

$$\equiv q\ f(q^{23}) \sum (-1)^m q^{m(3m+1)/2} \tag{4}$$

by Euler's identity, where

$$f(q^{23}) = (1 - q^{23})(1 - q^{46}) \dots .$$

The only exponents that can appear in (4) are congruent mod 23 to

$$m(3m + 1)/2 + 1 \equiv (6m + 1)^2$$

and so no n with $\left[\frac{n}{23}\right] = -1$ can occur.

Ramanujan would seem to have missed a trick here; for if we also apply Euler's identity to $f(q^{23})$ then (4) becomes

$$q \sum \sum (-1)^{m+r} q^{m(3m+1)/2+23r(3r+1)/2}$$

and from this one can easily deduce Wilton's congruences (13). But he may have thought that this was outside the rules of the game, because the expression to which $\tau(n)$ is proved to be congruent is not a straightforward enough function of n.

The surviving proofs of the congruences other than (2) all depend on using the functions

$$\left.\begin{aligned} P &= 1 - 24 \sum \sigma_1(n)q^n, \\ Q &= 1 + 240 \sum \sigma_3(n)q^n, \\ R &= 1 - 504 \sum \sigma_5(n)q^n, \end{aligned}\right\} \tag{5}$$

and the operator

$$\theta = q\frac{d}{dq} . \tag{6}$$

Q and R are multiples of the Eisenstein series of weights 4 and 6 respectively. P is defined by analogy. It is not a modular form, though it is related to modular forms. Also θ does not take modular forms into modular forms; but it is needed if one is to form series $\sum n^r\sigma_s(n)q^n$ with $r > 0$. The reason why P and θ can play a part in proofs based on modular forms will appear below.

We can now give a simple proof of (3). It is well known that

$$1728\Delta = Q^3 - R^2. \tag{7}$$

Moreover Q^3 and R^2 form a base for the modular forms of weight 12, so that in particular the Eisenstein series

$$G_{12} = \frac{691}{65520} + \sum \sigma_{11}(n)q^n$$

is equal to a linear combination of them; comparing coefficients now gives

$$65520\ G_{12} = 441\ Q^3 + 250\ R^2. \tag{8}$$

Combining (7) and (8) we obtain

$$65520\ G_{12} + 432000\ \Delta = 691\ Q^3;$$

comparing coefficients of q^n and noting that 65520 + 432000 is divisible by 691, we obtain (3).

This is presumably the form in which Ramanujan would have written the proof, but nearly all the numbers are in fact superfluous; the result only depends on the presence of 691 in the numerator of the constant term in G_{12}. For use a Tilde to denote that coefficients are to be taken mod 691. Then $\tilde{G}_{12}$ and $\tilde{\Delta}$ must be linear combinations of $\tilde{Q}^3$ and $\tilde{R}^2$; and since they have zero constant terms they must both be multiples of $\tilde{Q}^3 - \tilde{R}^2$, and hence multiples of each other. Comparing coefficients of q, we find $\tilde{G}_{12} = \tilde{\Delta}$, which is just (3).

Most of Ramanujan's congruences can be strengthened, though only with a good deal of effort. So far as I know, the strongest results obtained by traditional methods are those given below, all of which are stated under the condition that n(or p) is prime to the modulus of the congruence. Because $\tau(n)$ is multiplicative, this is not a serious reduction of generality; and it does make it possible to state the congruences in a form more appropriate to what follows.

$$\tau(n) \equiv \begin{cases} \sigma_{11}(n) \bmod 2^{11} & \text{if} \quad n \equiv 1 \bmod 8, \\ 1217\, \sigma_{11}(n) \bmod 2^{13} & \text{if} \quad n \equiv 3 \bmod 8, \\ 1537\, \sigma_{11}(n) \bmod 2^{12} & \text{if} \quad n \equiv 5 \bmod 8, \\ 705\, \sigma_{11}(n) \bmod 2^{14} & \text{if} \quad n \equiv 7 \bmod 8, \end{cases} \tag{9}$$

$$\tau(n) \equiv n^{-610}\, \sigma_{1231}(n) \begin{cases} \bmod 3^6 & \text{if} \quad n \equiv 1 \bmod 3, \\ \bmod 3^7 & \text{if} \quad n \equiv 2 \bmod 3, \end{cases} \tag{10}$$

$$\tau(n) \equiv n^{-30} \sigma_{71}(n) \bmod 5^3 \quad \text{if} \quad (n,5) = 1, \tag{11}$$

$$\tau(n) \equiv n\, \sigma_9(n) \begin{cases} \bmod 7 & \text{if} \quad n \equiv 0,1,2, \text{ or } 4 \bmod 7, \\ \bmod 7^2 & \text{if} \quad n \equiv 3,\ 5 \quad \text{or } 6 \bmod 7, \end{cases} \tag{12}$$

$$\tau(p) \equiv \begin{cases} 0 \bmod 23 & \text{if} \quad \left(\frac{p}{23}\right) = -1, \\ 2 \bmod 23 & \text{if} \quad p = u^2 + 23v^2 \quad \text{with} \quad u \neq 0, \\ -1 \bmod 23 & \text{for other} \quad p \neq 23 \end{cases} \tag{13}$$

$$\tau(n) \equiv \sigma_{11}(n) \bmod 691. \tag{14}$$

Another way of expressing the distinction between the second and third lines of (13), which will turn out to be significant later, is that among the primes p which split in $\mathbb{Q}(\sqrt{-23})$ the second line describes those which are products of two principal ideals and the third line those which are products of two non-principal ideals.

One reason for improving Ramanujan's congruences was the hope of proving by congruence considerations Lehmer's conjecture that $\tau(n)$ never vanishes. In particular, the last congruence (9) and earlier weaker results gave rise to the

Conjecture: if $2^N \| (p + 1)$ then $2^N \| \tau(p)$.

It follows from (9) that this holds for each $N \leq 13$. Unfortunately the developments reported below show that it is false for all larger N. Indeed, given any 2-adic numbers α, β such that

$$\alpha \equiv 7 \bmod 8, \ \beta \equiv 705(1 + \alpha^{11}) \bmod 2^{14}$$

we can find a prime p which is as near as we like to α and for which $\tau(p)$ is as near as we like to β. This means that the last equation (9) is best possible in a very strong sense.

If one considers these results, three questions natually arise: can these congruences be further improved, are there congruences modulo powers of other primes, and can the results be fitted into a systematic pattern? The necessary tools for answering these questions only became available in the early seventies; they are the Serre-Deligne representation theorem and the theory of modular forms mod ℓ. It is natural to look not just at Δ but at the six modular forms

$$\Delta, \ Q\Delta, \ R\Delta, \ Q^2\Delta, \ QR\Delta \ \text{and} \ Q^2R\Delta, \tag{15}$$

all of which have coefficients which are multiplicative in the sense of (1) for appropriate k and which are rational integers. In what follows, we denote the power series expansion of any one of them by $\sum \tau_k(n)q^n$, and we normally omit the subscript k.

Let ℓ be prime, and let K_ℓ be the maximal algebraic extension of $\mathbb{Q}$ unramified except at ℓ. The Serre–Deligne representation theorem, applied to any of the six functions (15), says that there is a continuous homomorphism

$$\rho_\ell : \mathrm{Gal}(K_\ell/\mathbb{Q}) \longrightarrow \mathrm{GL}_2(\mathbb{Z}_\ell)$$

such that for any $p \neq \ell$ the matrix $\rho_\ell(\mathrm{Frob}(p))$ has characteristic polynomial

$$X^2 - \tau(p)X + p^{k-1}. \tag{16}$$

Note that (16) is essentially the same as the factors on the right hand side of (1).

By class-field theory, any continuous homomorphism from $\mathrm{Gal}(K_\ell/\mathbb{Q})$ to a commutative group must factor through a power of

$$\chi_\ell : \mathrm{Gal}(K_\ell/\mathbb{Q}) \longrightarrow \mathrm{Gal}(K_\ell^{ab}/\mathbb{Q}) \simeq \mathbb{Z}_\ell^*, \tag{17}$$

and this has the property that $\chi_\ell(\mathrm{Frob}\ (p)) = p$. Hence in particular

$$\det \circ \rho_\ell = \chi_\ell^{k-1}.$$

Suppose now that the image of ρ_ℓ is small enough; then approximate ℓ-adic knowledge of the determinant of an element of the image of ρ_ℓ will carry with it some approximate ℓ-adic information about its trace. In other words, if we know enough about p we know something about $\tau(p)$. Conversely, the existence of a congruence for $\tau(p)$ means that the image of ρ_ℓ must be unexpectedly small--using the fact that Frobenius elements are dense in the Galois group. But the image is contained in the group of those elements of $GL_2(\mathbb{Z}_\ell)$ whose determinant is in $(\mathbb{Z}_\ell^*)^{k-1}$, and is equal to this group if and only if the image contains $SL_2(\mathbb{Z}_\ell)$.

Consider the composite map

$$\tilde{\rho}_\ell : \mathrm{Gal}(K_\ell/\mathbb{Q}) \longrightarrow GL_2(\mathbb{Z}_2) \longrightarrow GL_2(\mathbb{F}_\ell),$$

where the right hand map is reduction $\bmod \ell$. A tedious but elementary argument shows that for $\ell > 3$ the image of ρ_ℓ contains $SL_2(\mathbb{Z}_\ell)$ if and only if the image of $\tilde{\rho}_\ell$ contains $SL_2(\mathbb{F}_\ell)$; and for $\ell = 2$ or 3 enough is known about K_ℓ to show that neither of these can happen. We therefore define ℓ to be an <u>exceptional prime</u> if the image of ρ_ℓ does not contain $SL_2(\mathbb{Z}_\ell)$, or equivalently if the image of $\tilde{\rho}_\ell$ does not contain $SL_2(\mathbb{F}_\ell)$. Finding the exceptional primes will be the first step towards finding all congruences for $\tau(p)$, but we have to attack this in a roundabout way.

Suppose that ℓ is an exceptional prime; what are the possibilities for the image of $\tilde{\rho}_\ell$ and what properties of $\tau(p)$ correspond to each of them? The classification of the subgroups of $GL_2(\mathbb{F}_\ell)$ has been known for a century, though the language in which it is expressed changes from time to time. However, some of these subgroups cannot be the image of $\mathrm{Gal}(K_\ell/\mathbb{Q})$, for fairly straightforward number-theoretic reasons, and one obtains the following result.

<u>Lemma 1</u>. <u>Let</u> ρ_ℓ <u>be any continuous homomorphism</u> $\mathrm{Gal}(K_\ell/\mathbb{Q}) \longrightarrow GL_2(\mathbb{Z}_\ell)$ <u>such that</u> $\det \circ \rho_\ell = \chi_\ell^{k-1}$ <u>for some even integer</u> k. <u>Let</u> G <u>be the image of</u> $\tilde{\rho}_\ell$ <u>in</u> $GL_1(\mathbb{F}_\ell)$ <u>and suppose that</u> G <u>does not contain</u> $SL_2(\mathbb{F}_\ell)$. <u>Then</u>

(i) G _is contained in a Borel subgroup of_ $GL_2(\mathbb{F}_\ell)$; _or_

(ii) G _is contained in the normalizer of a Cartan subgroup, but not in the Cartan subgroup itself; or_

(iii) _the image of_ G _in_ $PGL_2(\mathbb{F}_\ell)$ _is isomorphic to_ S_4.

In case (ii) $\ell > 2$; _in case_ (iii) $\ell > 3$.

A Borel subgroup is any subgroup conjugate to the upper triangular matrices. Taking it actually to be the group of upper triangular matrices, we see that each of the two diagonal elements gives a homomorphism $\mathrm{Gal}(K_\ell/\mathbb{Q}) \longrightarrow \mathbb{F}_\ell^*$. This must be a power of $\tilde{\chi}_\ell$, and therefore the two diagonal elements must be $\tilde{\chi}_\ell^m$ and $\tilde{\chi}_\ell^{k-1-m}$ for some m.

A Cartan subgroup consists of all matrices which have the same pair of eigenvectors, and the remaining elements of its normalizer are those matrices which interchange these two vectors. The latter elements therefore all have trace 0. In case (ii) the map

$$\mathrm{Gal}(K_\ell/\mathbb{Q}) \longrightarrow G \longrightarrow \text{Normalizer/Cartan}$$

is onto, and clearly the image of Frob(p) is the identity (that is, $\tilde{\rho}_\ell(\mathrm{Frob}(p))$ is in the Cartan subgroup) if and only if $\left[\frac{p}{\ell}\right] = 1$.

Finally in case (iii) G and the traces of its elements are known. Thus we obtain

Corollary. Under the conditions of the Lemma, let $\tau(p)$ _be the trace of_ $\rho_\ell(\mathrm{Frob}(p))$. _Corresponding to the three cases listed in the Lemma, we have_

(i) _there is an integer_ m _such that_ $\tau(p) \equiv p^m + p^{k-1-m} \bmod \ell$;

(ii) $\tau(p) \equiv 0 \bmod \ell$ _whenever_ $\left[\frac{p}{\ell}\right] = -1$;

(iii) $p^{1-k}\,\tau^2(p) \equiv 0, 1, 2,$ _or_ $4 \bmod \ell$.

Strictly speaking, (iii) is not a congruence for $\tau(p)$; but it is undoubtedly a constraint on the values of $\tau(p)$. By contrast, if ℓ is not an exceptional prime the knowledge of $p \bmod \ell$ carries no information about $\tau(p) \bmod \ell$.

To find the exceptional primes, we have to discover for which ℓ one of the congruences in the Corollary holds. Consider first (iii). Taking say $p = 2$, we obtain a finite list of possible ℓ; and a small amount of further arithmetic reduces us to the one candidate $k = 16$, $\ell = 59$. The numerical evidence that this is a genuine example of case (iii) is overwhelming, and a recipe for constructing a proof can be found in [1], pp. 34-36; but so far as I am aware, this is still an unresolved problem.

Congruences of types (i) and (ii) are classical, and we know how to prove them for given values of ℓ and m. But the problem we have to attack is more complicated: it is to find those values of ℓ and m for which a proof of the corresponding congruence exists. The key to this is to develop a systematic theory of modular forms mod ℓ, of which there are hints but no more in Ramanujan's work.

In what follows, we shall systematically use a Tilde to denote reduction mod ℓ; in the case of a modular form this will mean reduction mod ℓ of the coefficients of the q-series expansion, and the result will be a formal power series with coefficients in $\mathbb{F}_\ell$. Let $\tilde{f}$ be any formal power series with coefficients in $\mathbb{F}_\ell$; we say that it is a modular form mod ℓ if it is the reduction mod ℓ of a power series with coefficients in $\mathbb{Z}_\ell \cap \mathbb{Q}$ (that is, rational and without ℓ in the denominator) which is the q-series expansion of a modular form for the full modular group. There are of course similar definitions for subgroups of the modular group.

Let E_k denote the Eisenstein form of weight k, normalized to have constant term 1; thus $Q = E_4$ and $R = E_6$ in the notation of (5). The cases $\ell = 2$ and $\ell = 3$ are untypical and will be described separately; for $\ell > 3$ there is a polynomial $A(Q,R)$ such that

$$E_{\ell-1} = A(Q,R)$$

and the coefficients of A are in $\mathbb{Z}_\ell \cap \mathbb{Q}$. In what follows, it is important to distinguish between $\tilde{A}(Q,R)$, which is a polynomial, and $\tilde{E}_{\ell-1} = \tilde{A}(\tilde{Q},\tilde{R})$ which is a formal power series.

Lemma 2. Suppose that $\ell > 3$. The algebra of modular forms mod ℓ is naturally isomorphic to $\mathbb{F}_\ell[Q,R]/(\tilde{A}(Q,R) - 1)$ and has a natural grading with values in $\mathbb{Z}/(\ell - 1)$; and θ given by (6) is an operator of weight 2. Moreover

$$\tilde{E}_{\ell-1} = 1 \quad \text{and} \quad \tilde{E}_{\ell+1} = \tilde{P}. \tag{18}$$

The grading is of course derived from the weight of the underlying modular form; that it has to be taken mod $(\ell - 1)$ ties in with the first equation (18). The important roles which P and θ play in Ramanujan's proofs become more natural in the light of their appearance in the Lemma.

The cases $\ell = 2$ and $\ell = 3$ are less interesting. In both cases $\tilde{P} = \tilde{Q} = \tilde{R} = 1$; the ring of modular forms mod ℓ is $\mathbb{F}_\ell[\tilde{A}]$ and is annihilated by θ, and there is no grading.

The congruences in (i) and (ii) of the Corollary to Lemma 1 can be written respectively in the forms

$$\theta\tilde{f} = \theta^{m+1}\,\tilde{G}_{k-2m} \tag{19}$$

and

$$\theta\tilde{f} = \theta^{(\ell+1)/2}\,\tilde{f} \tag{20}$$

where f, of weight k, is the relevent one of the forms (15) and

$$G_k = -b_k/2k + \sum \sigma_{k-1}(n)q^n$$

is the Eisenstein series of weight k. For any particular values of k,ℓ,m these can be tested and proved (when true) by means of Lemma 2. But to ensure that we have only a finite list of ℓ to consider, we need a further idea.

Let $\widetilde{M}$ be the algebra of modular forms mod ℓ, and let $\widetilde{M}_k$ be the vector space of forms mod ℓ which are reductions of forms of weight k. Let $\widetilde{f}$ be a graded element of $\widetilde{M}$, that is to say a sum of elements of various $\widetilde{M}_k$ for which all the relevent k are congruent $\bmod(\ell - 1)$. By multiplying the summands by suitable powers of $\widetilde{E}_{\ell-1} = 1$, we can make them all belong to the same $\widetilde{M}_k$, so that $\widetilde{f}$ itself belongs to an $\widetilde{M}_k$. Define $\omega(\widetilde{f})$, the <u>filtration</u> of $\widetilde{f}$, to be the least k such that $\widetilde{f}$ belongs to $\widetilde{M}_k$. The key result now is

<u>Lemma 3</u>. <u>Let</u> $\widetilde{f}$ <u>be a graded element of</u> $\widetilde{M}$. <u>Then</u>

$$\omega(\theta\widetilde{f}) \leq \omega(\widetilde{f}) + \ell + 1 \tag{21}$$

<u>with equality if and only if</u> $\omega(\widetilde{f})$ <u>is not a multiple of</u> ℓ.

Applying this to (19) and (20) we find without much difficulty that for (19) <u>either</u> $2m < \ell < k$ <u>or</u> $m = 0$ and ℓ divides the numerator of b_k, and for (20) $\ell < 2k$. The underlying idea is as follows. Suppose first that we have (19) with $m = 0$; then $(\widetilde{f} - \widetilde{G}_k)$ has fitration at most k and is annihilated by θ. Hence by Lemma 3 its filtration is divisible by ℓ, and either $\ell \leq k$ or $\widetilde{f} = \widetilde{G}_k$. In the latter case, consideration of the constant terms gives the desired result. Suppose instead that we have (19) with $m > 0$ or (20). Then the filtration of the left hand side is at most $k + \ell + 1$. On the other hand, θ is applied at least twice on the right hand side, and if $\ell > k$ this means that we must have inequality in (21) for at least one of the applications of θ. The inequalities claimed now follow easily from Lemma 3.

We can now complete the discussion of case (ii). It turns out there are just two instances--one being $k = 12$, $\ell = 23$ which was already known to Ramanujan and the other being $k = 16$, $\ell = 31$; and in most respects they are very similar. But (20) only proves (2) and (13) shows that this is not the full story. There are two natural ways to prove the rest of (13). One is to prove the identity

$$2\tilde{\Lambda} = \sum\sum q^{m^2+mn+6n^2} - \sum\sum q^{2m^2+mn+3n^2}$$

where the coefficients of the right hand side are in $\mathbb{F}_{23}$. This follows easily from Euler's identity, as has already been remarked. But the corresponding identity

$$2\tilde{Q}\tilde{\Lambda} = \sum\sum q^{m^2+mn+8n^2} - \sum\sum q^{2m^2+mn+4n^2},$$

where now the coefficients on the right are in $\mathbb{F}_{31}$, seems to need a much more sophisticated approach, for which see [1], p. 34.

The alternative is as follows. Let G, as in Lemma 1, be the image of $\tilde{\rho}_\ell$ in $GL_2(\mathbb{F}_\ell)$; then there is a field $L \subset K_\ell$ such that $\tilde{\rho}_\ell$ factors as

$$\mathrm{Gal}(K_\ell/\mathbb{Q}) \longrightarrow \mathrm{Gal}(L/\mathbb{Q}) \simeq G \hookrightarrow GL_2(\mathbb{F}_\ell).$$

We know that G has an abelian subgroup of index 2, but is not itself abelian; so L must be abelian over $\mathbb{Q}(\sqrt{-\ell})$ but not over $\mathbb{Q}$. Since L is also unramified outside ℓ, there are very few choices for L and the embedding of G into $GL_2(\mathbb{F}_\ell)$. Each of these choices would give a congruence rule for $\tau(p) \bmod \ell$, and examination of small values of p shows all but one of the congruence rules to be false. This constitutes a rigorous proof (though of a rather unusual kind) that the remaining rule is true.

In both cases it turns out that L is the absolute class field of $\mathbb{Q}(\sqrt{-\ell})$ and G is isomorphic to S_3; hence we obtain (13) and the corresponding result for τ_{16} with $\ell = 31$. But this is not the end of the story, for we can improve the middle equation (13) almost effortlessly to

$$\tau(p) \equiv 1 + p^{11} \bmod 23^2 \quad \text{if} \quad p = u^2 + 23v^2,\ u \neq 0. \tag{22}$$

The point is that for such a prime we have just seen that $\tilde{\rho}_{23}(\text{Frob } p)$ is the identity and hence $\rho_{23}(\text{Frob } p)$ has

$$\text{trace} \equiv 1 + \det \bmod 23^2.$$

The same argument applies equally to τ_{16} with $\ell = 31$.

For the remainder of this paper, we shall be concerned with case (i). So far as congruences mod ℓ are concerned, all the machinery is now set up, and it is just a matter of checking which of the finite number of possible congruences actually occur. For $m = 0$ in (19) we have the following table:

k	12	16	18	20	22	26
Form	Δ	$Q\Delta$	$R\Delta$	$Q^2\Delta$	$QR\Delta$	$Q^2R\Delta$
ℓ	691	3617	43867	283, 617	131, 593	657931

The primes here are all the ones that divide the numerator of the relevent Bernoulli number, and the proofs can be reduced to handwaving along the lines sketched above for the case of Δ. There remain the primes $\ell < k$, and in each such case the following table gives the value of m if ℓ is exceptional, or the word 'No' if it is not:

Form	k	$\ell = 2$	3	5	7	11	13	17	19	23
Δ	12	0	0	1	1	No				
$Q\Delta$	16	0	0	1	1	1	No			
$R\Delta$	18	0	0	2	1	1	1	No		
$Q^2\Delta$	20	0	0	1	2	1	1	No	No	
$QR\Delta$	22	0	0	2	1	No	1	1	No	
$Q^2R\Delta$	26	0	0	2	2	1	No	1	1	No

In each case the possible value of m, if any, can be found by considering $\tau(2)$ and $\tau(3)$, and the rest is just a matter of checking the truth or falsehood of (19) by means of Lemma 2.

What we have done so far in case (i) is far less than the full truth, as (9) to (12) show: and it is a poor return for this sophisticated machinery to show that there are no values of ℓ which classical machinery overlooked (in the case of Δ) or would have been likely to overlook (in the case of the other five forms). We now turn, therefore, to congruences modulo higher powers of ℓ, and from now on we assume that $\ell > 2$. The case $\ell = 2$ is much more complicated, as the Appendix to [1] already shows, but it is unlikely to require fundamentally new ideas; it can be recommended only to a doctoral student desperate for a soluble but not-yet-solved problem.

The first step is to list the possible images of ρ_ℓ, at least up to conjugacy; and for this purpose some normalization is helpful. Choose once for all a prime p_0 which generates $\mathbb{Z}_\ell^*$ as a topological group--that is, the powers of p_0 are dense in $\mathbb{Z}_\ell^*$. The quadratic equation

$$\tau(p_0) = x + x^{-1}p_0^{k-1}$$

has both its roots in $\mathbb{Z}_\ell$ by Hensel's Lemma, because the corresponding congruence mod ℓ has the distinct roots p_0^m and p_0^{k-1-m}. Let x_0 be the root which is congruent to p_0^m mod ℓ and choose μ so that $x_0 = p_0^\mu$; we shall eventually be able to replace μ, which lies in $\varprojlim \mathbb{Z}/(\ell^n(\ell - 1))$, by an integer congruent to it mod $\ell^N(\ell - 1)$, but we cannot yet tell how big N will need to be. It follows from the Serre-Deligne representation theorem, described above, that the characteristic roots of $\rho_\ell(\text{Frob } p_0)$ are p_0^μ and $p_0^{k-1-\mu}$, and therefore (having chosen a conjugate representation if necessary) we can assume that

$$\rho_\ell(\text{Frob } p_0) = \begin{bmatrix} p_0^\mu & 0 \\ 0 & p_0^{k-1-\mu} \end{bmatrix}. \tag{23}$$

The advantage of this is that the image of ρ_ℓ now contains $\text{Diag}(c^\mu, c^{k-1-\mu})$ for every c in $\mathbb{Z}_\ell^*$. Hence we know explicitly an element of the image with any allowable determinant, so that instead of studying the whole image we can concentrate on the elements of determinant 1. In fact we go further and write

$$\Gamma = \{\rho_\ell(\sigma) \mid \chi_\ell(\sigma) = 1\}$$

where χ_ℓ is given by (17). We shall also write

$$\rho_\ell(\sigma) = \begin{bmatrix} a(\sigma) & b(\sigma) \\ c(\sigma) & d(\sigma) \end{bmatrix}.$$

It is easily shown that neither $b(\sigma)$ nor $c(\sigma)$ can vanish identically.

We still need a further normalization. Let ℓ^n be the largest power of ℓ which divides every $b(\sigma)$. Conjugating our representation ρ_ℓ by $\text{Diag}(\ell^n, 1)$ multiplies every $c(\sigma)$ and divides every $b(\sigma)$ by ℓ^n; so it enables us to make the additional assumption that not all $b(\sigma)$ are divisible by ℓ.

Now let $N_1 > 0$ and $N_2 > 0$ be the largest integers such that

$$a(\sigma) \equiv d(\sigma) \equiv 1 \bmod \ell^{N_1} \quad \text{and} \quad c(\sigma) \equiv 0 \bmod \ell^{N_2}$$

for all σ in Γ. Elementary arguments show that

$$N_1 = N_2 = N, \text{ say;}$$

and it is easy to see that N depends only on ℓ and the cusp form we are discussing. Essentially, ℓ^N measures how near the representation ρ_ℓ is to one composed from powers of the one-dimensional representation χ_ℓ. To examine the nature of the departure, we denote by $\alpha, \beta, \gamma, \delta$ the reductions mod ℓ of

$$\ell^{-N}(a - 1),\ b,\ \ell^{-N}c,\ \ell^{-N}(d - 1)$$

respectively, for any element of Γ. Since elements of Γ have determinant 1,

$$\alpha + \delta = \beta\gamma;$$

and the potential tetrads $\{\alpha, \beta, \gamma, \delta\}$ form a group $\tilde{G}$ of order ℓ^3, with a group law inherited from matrix multiplication in Γ. The homomorphism $\Gamma \longrightarrow \tilde{G}$ has non-trivial image, by the definition of N, and elementary calculation shows that the non-trivial subgroups of $\tilde{G}$ are of three kinds:

(a) the whole group $\tilde{G}$;

(b) the elements with $\beta = \lambda\gamma$, for some fixed λ in $\mathbb{F}_\ell^*$;

(c) the cyclic group generated by some $\{\alpha_0, \beta_0, \gamma_0, \delta_0\}$.

In case (c), the previous normalizations show that $\beta_0\gamma_0 \neq 0$.

For reasons of classfield theory, not all these subgroups can occur. In fact the image of Γ in $\tilde{G}$ must be of type (c) if

$$2(k - 1 - 2m) \equiv 0 \bmod(\ell - 1) \tag{24}$$

and of type (a) otherwise; it can never be of type (b). The relevence of condition (24) is that conjugation by (23) induces an automorphism of the subgroup which has the form

$$\{\alpha,\beta,\gamma,\delta\} \longrightarrow \{\alpha,\beta\upsilon,\gamma\upsilon^{-1},\delta\}$$

where υ is the image of p_0^{k-1-2m} in $\mathbb{F}_\ell^*$. If (24) is false then $\upsilon \neq \pm 1$ and this automorphism does not preserve any subgroup of type (b) or (c); so the image of Γ must be the whole of $\tilde{G}$. The case when (24) holds is more complicated. It turns out that (a) or (b) would then imply the existence of an abelian extension of $\mathbb{Q}(\sqrt{-\ell})$, unramified outside ℓ, with Galois group C_ℓ^3. This means that the class number of $\mathbb{Q}(\sqrt{-\ell})$ would have to be divisible by ℓ, and crude estimates show that this is impossible. So if (24) holds, the image of Γ must be of type (c). But we can go further than that, for now $\upsilon = -1$ and the cyclic group generated by $\{\alpha_0,\beta_0,\gamma_0,\delta_0\}$ must contain $\{\alpha_0,-\beta_0,-\gamma_0,\delta_0\}$. But

$$\{\alpha,\beta,\gamma,\delta\}^n = \{n\alpha + \frac{1}{2}n(n-1)\beta\gamma, n\beta, n\gamma, n\delta + \frac{1}{2}n(n-1)\beta\gamma\}$$

and it follows easily that $\alpha_0 = \delta_0 = \frac{1}{2}\beta_0\gamma_0$.

In both cases (a) and (c), it follows from the definition of N that for $p \neq \ell$,

$$\tau(p) \equiv p^\mu + p^{k-1-\mu} \bmod \ell^N. \tag{25}$$

Since Frobenius elements are dense in the Galois group, it is easy to show that in case (a) we cannot say anything more about $\tau(p) \bmod \ell^{N+1}$, however good an ℓ-adic approximation we have to p. In case (c), the same is true provided $\left[\frac{p}{\ell}\right] = 1$; but if $\left[\frac{p}{\ell}\right] = -1$ it follows from what we have just proved that

$$\tau(p) \equiv p^{\mu} + p^{k-1-\mu} \bmod \ell^{N+1} \quad \text{whenever} \quad \left[\frac{p}{\ell}\right] = -1. \tag{26}$$

The derivation of this will be given in more detail below. These two patterns correspond to the known results (10), (11), (12) and (14) for τ_{12}.

But (25) and (26) are not much use until one knows the value of N. To prove that $N = 1$, when that is true, is easy; it is enough to find some p with

$$\tau(p) \not\equiv p^{\mu} + p^{k-1-\mu} \bmod \ell^{2}.$$

Trial and error is in practice good enough; but there are more systematic methods available, analogous to but not identical with those described below for $N > 1$. By this means we show that $N = 1$ whenever $\ell > 7$ in case (a), or $\ell > 3$ in case (c); this leaves for more detailed enquiry in case (a) the six instances with $\ell = 5$ and the two instances $k = 16, 22$ with $\ell = 7$, and in case (c) the six instances with $\ell = 3$. In these instances, the way we determine the value of N and prove that it is correct is as follows. We exhibit a prime p_1, depending only on ℓ, for which we can assert that

$$\tau(p_1) \not\equiv p_1^{\mu} + p_1^{k-1-\mu} \bmod \ell^{N+1} \tag{27}$$

without having prior knowledge of the value of N. This and (25) now enable N to be determined from $\tau(p_1)$.

We show how to find p_1 in case (c); the ideas in case (a) are similar but the details are more complicated. We have already seen that the image of Γ in $\tilde{G}$ consists of the $\{\lambda n^2, \lambda n, 2n, \lambda n^2\}$ where λ is fixed and non-zero and n runs through the elements of $\mathbb{F}_\ell$. It follows that, for fixed λ and some n,

$$\rho(\sigma) \equiv \begin{bmatrix} (1 + \lambda n^2 \ell^N)\chi^\mu & \chi^\mu \lambda n \\ 2\chi^{k-1-\mu} n \ell^N & (1 + \lambda n^2 \ell^N)\chi^{k-1-\mu} \end{bmatrix}$$

where the congruences for a,c,d are to be taken mod ℓ^{N+1} and that for b is to be taken mod ℓ. In particular

$$\tau(p) \equiv (p^\mu + p^{k-1-\mu})(1 + \lambda n^2 \ell^N) \bmod \ell^{N+1}, \tag{28}$$

and (26) follows from this and (24).

Because of (24), $\mathrm{Gal}(K_\ell/\mathbb{Q}(\sqrt{-\ell}))$ consists of those σ in $\mathrm{Gal}(K_\ell/\mathbb{Q})$ for which

$$\chi^{k-1-2\mu}(\sigma) \equiv 1 \bmod \ell.$$

The map which takes σ onto

$$(\lambda n(\sigma) \bmod \ell) \times (\chi^{\ell-1}(\sigma) \bmod \ell^2)$$

is therefore a homomorphism

$$\mathrm{Gal}(K_\ell/\mathbb{Q}(\sqrt{-\ell})) \longrightarrow C_\ell \times C_\ell \tag{29}$$

and it is easily seen to be onto. If $\left(\frac{p}{\ell}\right) = 1$ then (28) fixes $n(\mathrm{Frob}\ p) \bmod \ell$ up to sign; and it follows from this and the density of Frobenius elements that the non-trivial automorphism of $\mathbb{Q}(\sqrt{-\ell})$ over $\mathbb{Q}$

must either preserve $n(\sigma) \bmod \ell$ or change its sign. The former is impossible, because $n(\sigma) \bmod \ell$ would be a function of $\chi(\sigma)$ and (29) would not be onto; so the latter must be true. But these properties are enough to determine $n(\sigma) \bmod \ell$ up to multiplication by a constant.

In particular, when $\ell = 3$ and $p \equiv 1 \bmod 3$ we can write

$$4p = u^2 + 27v^2 = 4\pi\bar{\pi}$$

in essentially only one way, where $2\pi = u + 3v\sqrt{-3}$. Here $v/u \bmod 3$ has the properties which we established for $n(\text{Frob } p) \bmod 3$ in the previous paragraph, and hence we have

$$n(\text{Frob } p) \equiv \pm\, v/u \bmod 3.$$

In view of this and (28), the primes p_1 for which (27) holds when $\ell = 3$ are just those with $v \not\equiv 0 \bmod 3$; and the simplest example is $p_1 = 7$. Indeed (28) gives us

$$\tau(p) \equiv (p^{\mu} + p^{k-1-\mu})(1 \pm 3^N v^2) \bmod 3^{N+1} \tag{30}$$

where the sign depends only on k. This gives the following table for $\ell = 3$.

k	12	16	18	20	22	26
N	6	5	5	5	6	5
$\mu \bmod 2.3^N$	848	174	386	298	18	340
sign	+	+	−	−	−	−

But in fact even (30) is not the end of the story, for in case (c) refinements of the above argument give us congruences $\bmod\ \ell^{N+2}$ for $\tau(p)$

when $\left(\frac{p}{\ell}\right) = 1$, in terms of p and its expression by an appropriate quadratic form. Confining ourselves to the classical case of Δ, we find that we can improve the first equation (10) to

$$\tau_{12}(p) \equiv p^{119} + p^{-108} - 3^6 v^2 \bmod 3^8 \quad \text{if} \quad 4p = u^2 + 27v^2$$

and the first equation (12) to

$$\tau_{12}(p) \equiv (1 + p^9)(p - 35v^2) + 196p^{-1} v^4 \bmod 7^3 \quad \text{if} \quad 4p = u^2 + 7v^2$$

which in particular implies the Atkin conjecture

$$\tau_{12}(p) \equiv p + p^{10} - 21v^2 \bmod 7^2.$$

In case (a) the question whether or not p_1 satisfies (27) involves looking at its factors in the cyclotomic field of ℓth roots of unity. It turns out that we can take $p_1 = 11$ for $\ell = 5$ and $p_1 = 29$ for $\ell = 7$. This gives the following eight instances of case (a) with $N > 1$, where μ is to be taken mod $\ell^{N-1}(\ell - 1)$.

ℓ	5	5	5	5	5	5	7	7
k	12	16	18	20	22	26	16	22
N	3	2	3	2	2	2	3	2
μ	41	17	22	13	14	6	85	37

Thus for example, we can say that (modulo a certain amount of general theory) the congruence (11) has been proved for all p once it has been verified for $p = 2$ and $p = 11$. This is the kind of proof that Ramanujan would have enjoyed!

Full details of all this can be found in [1] and [2], and in the references given in [1].

REFERENCES

[1] H. P. F. SWINNERTON-DYER, On ℓ-adic representations and congruences for coefficients of modular forms, in Modular Functions of One Variable III (Springer Lecture Notes, vol 350), 1-55.

[2] H. P. F. SWINNERTON-DYER, On ℓ-adic representations and congruences for coefficients of modular forms (II), in Modular Functions of One Variable V (Springer Lecture Notes, vol 601), 64-90.

Ramanujan's Modular Equations

by

Bruce C. Berndt*

Recall that the complete elliptic integral $K = K(k)$ of the first kind is defined by

$$K(k) = \int_0^{\pi/2} (1 - k^2\sin^2\varphi)^{-1/2} d\varphi = \frac{\pi}{2} \sum_{n=0}^{\infty} \frac{(1/2)_n^2}{(n!)^2} k^{2n},$$

where $0 < k < 1$ and $(\alpha)_n = \alpha(\alpha + 1) \cdots (\alpha + n - 1)$. For later use, let $K' = K(k')$, where $k' = (1 - k^2)^{1/2}$. The numbers k and k' are called the modulus and complementary modulus, respectively. In a sense, the theory of modular equations begins with a theorem about K that arises from two papers written by John Landen [28], [29] in 1771 and 1775. Let

(1) $$k = \frac{2\sqrt{\ell}}{1 + \ell},$$

which trivially implies that

(2) $$k^2(1 + \ell)^2 = 4\ell.$$

Then Landen showed that

(3) $$K(k) = (1 + \ell)K(\ell).$$

*Research partially supported by a grant from the Vaughn Foundation.

ISBN 0-12-058560-X

In other words, the algebraic relation (1) between k and ℓ implies that the transcendental function K satisfies the remarkable algebraic relation (3). The equation (2) is an example of a quadratic modular equation. In practice, as we shall see in the sequel, the process is reversed, i.e., modular equations are consequences of equalities relating elliptic integrals. Thus, for example, given the relation (3), what can one say about the relationship of k and ℓ?

It is interesting to note that, in two isolated sections of Chapter 15 of his second notebook [35, Sections 15, 16], Ramanujan begins his study of modular equations in a similar manner. With

$$F(x) := (1 - x)^{-1/2} = \sum_{n=0}^{\infty} \frac{(1/2)_n}{n!} x^n, \qquad |x| < 1,$$

Ramanujan begins Section 15(i) with the trivial identity

$$F\left[\frac{2t}{1 + t}\right] = (1 + t)F(t^2),$$

which is reminiscent of (3). After setting $\alpha = 2t/(1 + t)$ and $\beta = t^2$, Ramanujan offers the "modular equation of degree 2,"

$$\beta^2(2 - \alpha)^2 = \alpha^2,$$

which, of course, is an analogue of (2). By iteration, Ramanujan then proceeds to derive "modular equations of degree 2^n." However, not all of this work is correct, because Ramanujan evidently thought that he saw a developing pattern, which unfortunately was erroneous. For a complete description of this preliminary work of Ramanujan on modular equations, see the author's book [2].

Before proceeding further, we remark that many versions of Landen's transformation (3) exist. In fact, (3) is the special case $\alpha = \pi$, $\beta = \pi/2$ of the following more general formula. If $x \sin \alpha = \sin(2\beta - \alpha)$, then

$$(4) \qquad (1 + x) \int_0^{\alpha} (1 - x^2 \sin^2 \varphi)^{-1/2} d\varphi = 2 \int_0^{\beta} \left(1 - \frac{4x}{(1 + x)^2} \sin^2 \varphi\right)^{-1/2} d\varphi,$$

which is known as Landen's transformation for incomplete elliptic integrals of the first kind. Landen's transformation (4) was rediscovered by Ramanujan and can be found in his second notebook [35, Chapter 17, Entry 7(xiii)].

There are several definitions for a modular equation. Very simply, a modular equation is an algebraic relation connecting one or more elliptic functions or modular forms at different values of the argument. Usually, different powers of the argument are involved. Although not immediately obvious, (2) satisfies this admittedly vague definition, as we shall see in the sequel. Alternatively, and still imprecisely, a modular equation is an algebraic relation among moduli of elliptic integrals.

Klein's absolute modular invariant $J(\tau)$, where $\mathrm{Im}(\tau) > 0$, is perhaps the function that has captured the most attention in the theory of modular equations. Thus, for example, Schoeneberg [39, p. 142] defines a modular equation exclusively in terms of $J(\tau)$. See also Rankin's book [38, pp. 209-212].

It also should be mentioned that various forms of modular equations exist in the literature. See the classical treatises of H. Weber [47], [48] and F.Klein [25] as well as the recent book of J. and P. Borwein [8]. A paper of M. Hanna [17] in 1928 summarizes a century's work on modular equations and presents modular equations in various forms. For an excellent history of the theory of modular equations before 1890, see Enneper's treatise [14, pp. 477-483].

In this paper, we employ a somewhat less general definition of modular equation than was indicated above. However, this is the definition that Ramanujan used; see [34], [36, p. 31]. This is also the definition given by Hardy [18, p. 214] in his brief description of a very small portion of Ramanujan's work on modular equations. Let K, K', L, and L' denote the complete elliptic integrals of the first kind associated with the moduli k, k', ℓ, and ℓ', respectively. Suppose that the equality

$$n\frac{K'}{K} = \frac{L'}{L} \tag{5}$$

holds for some positive integer n. Then a modular equation of degree n is a relation between the moduli k and ℓ which is induced by (5). Ramanujan writes his modular equations in terms of α and β, where $\alpha = k^2$ and $\beta = \ell^2$.

Furthermore, let

$$\varphi(q) = \sum_{r=-\infty}^{\infty} q^{r^2}, \tag{6}$$

where $q = e^{-\pi K'/K}$. The multiplier m for a modular equation of degree n is defined by

$$m = \frac{z_1}{z_n}, \tag{7}$$

where

$$z_j = \varphi^2(q^j). \tag{8}$$

One of the most important results in the theory of elliptic functions is the formula [49, p. 500]

(9) $$K(k) = \frac{\pi}{2} z_1.$$

For $n = 2$, observe that, by (3) and (9), $m = 1 + \ell$.

With this definition of a modular equation, the theory commenced with Legendre's [30] modular equation of degree 3 in 1825 and Jacobi's modular equations of degrees 3 and 5 found in his epic Fundamenta Nova [23], [24] published in 1829. Subsequently, in the century that followed, contributions were made by several mathematicians, including C. Guetzlaff, L. A. Sohncke, H. Schröter, L. Schläfli, F. Klein, A. Hurwitz, E. Fiedler, A. Cayley, R. Fricke, R. Russell, and H. Weber.

Now, in fact, in Chapter 20 of his second notebook [35], Ramanujan actually considers another type of modular equation, a "mixed" modular equation or a modular equation of composite degree. To define a "mixed" modular equation, let K, K', L_1, L_1', L_2, L_2', L_3, and L_3' denote complete elliptic integrals of the first kind associated, in pairs, with the moduli $\sqrt{\alpha}$, $\sqrt{\beta}$, $\sqrt{\gamma}$, and $\sqrt{\delta}$, and their complementary moduli, respectively. Let n_1, n_2, and n_3 be positive integers such that $n_3 = n_1 n_2$. Suppose that the equalities

(10) $$n_1 \frac{K'}{K} = \frac{L_1'}{L_1}, \quad n_2 \frac{K'}{K} = \frac{L_2'}{L_2}, \quad \text{and} \quad n_3 \frac{K'}{K} = \frac{L_3'}{L_3}$$

hold. Then a "mixed" modular equation is a relation between the moduli $\sqrt{\alpha}$, $\sqrt{\beta}$, $\sqrt{\gamma}$, and $\sqrt{\delta}$ that is induced by the relations (10). In such an instance, we shall say that β, γ, and δ are of degrees n_1, n_2, and n_3, respectively. To indicate the vast extent of Ramanujan's findings on "mixed" modular equations, we remark that in Chapter 20 of his second notebook, Ramanujan states "mixed" modular equations for a total of 20 distinct triples of positive integers n_1, n_2, and n_3. He also offers "mixed" modular equations for one set of three distinct moduli. Other than Ramanujan's findings, we know of no other work in the literature on "mixed" modular equations.

Before describing Ramanujan's contributions and relating methods for deriving modular equations, we delineate a few reasons for studying and calculating modular equations.

First, the modular equation for Klein's absolute invariant $J(\tau)$ was employed by D. H. Lehmer [31] to help derive congruential properties of the Fourier coefficients of $J(\tau)$.

Secondly, Hermite [19], [20] showed how to solve the general quintic and septic polynomials via modular equations of degrees 5 and 7, respectively. An outline of Hermite's method for degree 5 may be found in the Borweins' book [8, pp. 135, 136]. An account of Hermite's theorem on the quintic is also given in the book of Dutta and Debnath [13, pp. 276-279].

Thirdly, we recall that Ramanujan made some very famous conjectures on congruences involving the partition function $p(n)$. We state two of them, the second being a corrected reformulation given by G. N. Watson.

$$\text{If } 24m \equiv 1 \pmod{5^n}, \quad \text{then } p(m) \equiv 0 \pmod{5^n}.$$

$$\text{If } 24m \equiv 1 \pmod{7^n}, \quad \text{then } p(m) \equiv 0 \pmod{7^{[(n+2)/2]}}.$$

Here m and n are positive integers. These conjectures were first proved by G. N. Watson [46]. Later, A. O. L. Atkin simplified Watson's work; for an account of Atkin's proofs, see Knopp's book [26, Chapters 7, 8]. The proofs of both Watson and Atkin crucially utilize modular equations of degrees 5 and 7.

Fourthly, in recent times, modular equations have been employed to rapidly compute π. See a paper of J. Borwein [7], the Borweins' book [8, Chapter 5], and, in particular, their paper published in these proceedings [9].

In [27], Kondo and Tasaka define theta-functions for sublattices of the Leech lattice. They show how to express these theta-functions in terms of the classical Jacobian theta-functions. An important feature of their calculations is the employment of modular equations.

More recent work on the calculation of modular equations has been accomplished by Hiramatsu and Mimura [21] and Yui [50].

In the past two decades, interest has shifted from the explicit determination of modular equations to parametrization problems involving elliptic curves and modular equations. Thus, for example, see the papers of Igusa [22], Deligne and Rapoport [12], and Mazur [32].

Various algebraic and analytic methods have been devised to find modular equations, but generally it can be said that the difficulty of finding modular equations increases very rapidly with n, no matter what methods are used. This paper features certain analytic methods; the reader desiring to learn about some algebraic methods should consult Cayley's book [11] and paper [10] or the Borweins' treatise [8]. Most of the older methods, when successful, yield modular equations of formidable complexity. One feature of Ramanujan's modular equations is that they are generally quite elegant, and so some older methods do not appear to be applicable. In fact, Watson [18, p. 220] has declared that "when dealing with Ramanujan's modular equations generally, it has always seemed to me that knowledge of other people's work is a positive disadvantage in that it tends to put one off the shortest track."

In attempting to establish Ramanujan's modular equations in Chapters 19 and 20 of his second notebook [35], we have utilized three approaches. The first relies heavily on the theory of theta-functions and frequently employs Schröter's formulas, first established in his dissertation [40] in 1854. Schröter's formulas may also be found in the treatises of Tannery and Molk [44, pp. 163-167] and J. and P. Borwein [8, p. 111]. A simple proof of these formulas is given in a paper of Kondo and Tasaka [27].

Proofs of the formulations that we employ may be found in [1, pp. 65-69]. Schröter [40], [41], [42], [43] used his formulas to find several modular equations, although, except for his thesis [40], he never published complete proofs of his results. Ramanujan, to our knowledge, has not explicitly stated Schröter's formulas in any of his published papers, notebooks, or unpublished manuscripts. But, it seems clear, from the theory of theta-functions that he did develop, that Ramanujan must have been aware of these formulas or at least of the principles that yield the many special cases that Ramanujan doubtless used. However, the majority of Ramanujan's modular equations do not appear to be direct results of Schröter's formulas. We conjecture that Ramanujan knew other general formulas involving theta-functions, which are still unknown to us, and which he used to derive further modular equations. In particular, we think that Ramanujan derived an unknown general formula involving quotients of theta- functions. In fact, Watson [45, p. 150] asserts that "A prolonged study of his modular equations has convinced me that he was in possession of a general formula by means of which modular equations can be constructed in almost terrifying numbers." Watson then intimates that Ramanujan's "general formula" is, in fact, Schröter's most general formula. However, it is highly probable that Ramanujan possessed other formulas or analytic techniques which have escaped us.

The second method utilizes previously derived modular equations and a heavy dosage of tedious elementary algebra. The primary idea is to find expressions for α and β in terms of another parameter. These parametric representations are then employed to verify a given modular equation by elementary algebra. Possibly, Ramanujan used such methods for very small values of n. However, the algebraic difficulties increase very rapidly with n. It seems doubtful that Ramanujan used such tedious techniques, for his mathematics is normally characterized by beauty and elegance. Moreover, this method seems to depend upon knowing the modular equation in advance. Thus, the proofs are more in the nature of verifications.

Our third method employs the theory of modular forms. In some ways, this represents the best approach. First, the theory of modular forms provides the structure which explains why certain identities among theta-functions exist. Secondly, this approach does not usually become too much more complicated with increasing n, and so proofs remain comparatively short. The primary disadvantage to the method is that the modular equation must generally be known in advance, and so, as in the second method, the proofs are really verifications. The principal idea is to show that the multiplier systems for certain modular forms agree and that the coefficients in the expansion of a certain modular form are equal to zero up to a certain prescribed point and then conclude that the modular form must identically be equal to zero. It could be argued that Ramanujan knew that modular forms generate finite dimensional vector spaces and so searched for the right combination of expressions involving theta-functions in order to make the coefficients vanish. However, there is no evidence whatsoever that Ramanujan possessed such ideas. Moreover, it is extremely difficult and tedious to find the proper linear combination from a myriad of possible quotients and products of theta-functions at various arguments.

Except for Hardy's [18, pp. 214-223] brief description and some results stated by Ramanujan without proof in [34], [36, pp. 23-39], none of Ramanujan's work on modular equations has ever been published until recently. Proofs of some of Ramanujan's modular equations may be found in three papers by A. J. Biagioli, J. M. Purtilo, and the author [4], [5], [6], written for special issues in observance of the centenary of Ramanujan's birth. The extent of Ramanujan's findings in the theory of modular equations is incredible. For some values of n, Ramanujan offers perhaps 10-15 different modular equations. In fact, it is no exaggeration to claim that Ramanujan likely found more modular equations than what were discovered by the combined efforts of his predecessors in the previous century. In view of the complexity of the work, it is also remarkable that only a couple of Ramanujan's modular equations contain errors. Complete proofs of Ramanujan's modular equations in Chapters 19-21 of his second notebook will be given in the author's book [3]. But even if proofs of all of Ramanujan's modular equations are found, more study is necessary in order to find more "natural" approaches and to better understand Ramanujan's work.

We now introduce the theta-functions which arise in Ramanujan's theory. Let

$$f(a,b) = \sum_{r=-\infty}^{\infty} a^{r(r+1)/2} b^{r(r-1)/2},$$

where $|ab| < 1$. Note that $f(a,b) = f(b,a)$ and $f(q,q) = \varphi(q) = \theta_3(0,q)$, where φ is defined by (6) and where we have used a standard notation [49, p. 464] in the theory of theta-functions. If $\psi(q) = f(q,q^3)$, then $2q^{1/8}\psi(q) = \theta_2(0,\sqrt{q})$, which is Schläfli's modular function. Also,

$$f(-q,-q^2) = \sum_{r=-\infty}^{\infty} (-1)^r q^{r(3r-1)/2} = \prod_{n=1}^{\infty}(1 - q^n) = e^{-\pi i\tau/12}\eta(\tau^2),$$

by Euler's pentagonal number theorem, where $q = e^{\pi i\tau}$ and η denotes Dedekind's eta-function.

To transcribe Modular equations into identities relating theta-functions, we shall need the following formulas:

(11) $\varphi(\sqrt{q}) = \sqrt{z}\,(1 + \sqrt{\alpha})^{1/2},$

(12) $$\varphi(\sqrt{-q}) = \sqrt{z}\,(1-\alpha)^{1/4},$$

(13) $$\varphi(-q^2) = \sqrt{z}\,(1-\alpha)^{1/8},$$

(14) $$\varphi(q^4) = \frac{1}{2}\sqrt{z}\,\{1+(1-\alpha)^{1/4}\},$$

(15) $$\psi(q) = \sqrt{\frac{1}{2}z}\,(\alpha/q)^{1/8},$$

(16) $$\psi(-q) = \sqrt{\frac{1}{2}z}\,\{\alpha(1-\alpha)/q\}^{1/8},$$

(17) $$\psi(q^2) = \frac{1}{2}\sqrt{z}\,(\alpha/q)^{1/4},$$

and

(18) $$\psi(q^8) = \frac{1}{4}\sqrt{z}\,\{1-(1-\alpha)^{1/4}\}/q,$$

where $z = z_1$ is defined by (8). If q is replaced by q^n, then α is to be replaced by β and z by z_n. These evaluations are found in Chapter 17 of Ramanujan's second notebook [35] and follow very easily from basic properties of theta-functions.

Before proceeding further, we prove Landen's modular equation (2) of degree 2, which, in Ramanujan's notation is expressible in the form

$$\alpha(1+\sqrt{\beta}) = 4\sqrt{\beta}\ .$$

Translating this proposed equation by means of (8), (11), and (15), we find that

$$\frac{16q\,\psi^8(q)}{\varphi^8(q)}\,\frac{\varphi^4(q)}{\varphi^4(q^2)} = 4\,\frac{4q\psi^4(q^2)}{\varphi^4(q)}\ ,$$

or

$$\psi^2(q) = \varphi(q)\psi(q^2).$$

But this last equality is elementary. (In fact, it is Entry 25 (iv) of Chapter 16 [35].) Thus, Landen's modular equation (2) has been established.

We now prove the simplest of the eleven modular equations of degree 7 given in Entry 19 of Chapter 19 in Ramanujan's second notebook [35].

<u>Theorem 1</u>. If β is of degree 7 over α, then

$$(\alpha\beta)^{1/8} + \{(1-\alpha)(1-\beta)\}^{1/8} = 1.$$

In fact, Theorem 1 is due to Guetzlaff [16] in 1834. Schröter [40], [41], [43] and Fiedler [15] also established Theorem 1.

<u>Proof</u>. Let μ and ν denote integers with $0 \leq \nu < \mu$ and μ even. Then Schröter [40] (see also [1, equa. (36.8)]) proved that

$$(19) \qquad \psi(q^{\mu+\nu})\psi(q^{\mu-\nu}) = \varphi(q^{\mu(\mu^2-\nu^2)})\psi(q^{2\mu})$$

$$+ \sum_{m=1}^{\frac{1}{2}\mu-1} q^{\mu m^2-\nu m} f(q^{(\mu+2m)(\mu^2-\nu^2)}, q^{(\mu-2m)(\mu^2-\nu^2)}) f(q^{2\nu m}, q^{2\mu-2\nu m})$$

$$+ q^{\frac{1}{4}\mu^3 - \frac{1}{2}\mu\nu} \psi(q^{2\mu(\mu^2-\nu^2)}) f(q^{\mu\nu}, q^{2\mu-\mu\nu}).$$

Setting $\mu = 4$ and $\nu = 3$, we deduce that

$$(20)\qquad \psi(q)\psi(q^7) = \varphi(q^{28})\psi(q^8) + q\psi(q^{14})\psi(q^2) + q^{10}\psi(q^{56})f(q^{12},q^{-4})$$

$$= \varphi(q^{28})\psi(q^8) + q\psi(q^{14})\psi(q^2) + q^6\psi(q^{56})\varphi(q^4).$$

Here we have used the equality

$$q^4 f(q^{12},q^{-4}) = f(q^4,q^4) = \varphi(q^4),$$

which is a special instance of the basic identity

$$f(a,b) = a^{n(n+1)/2}b^{n(n-1)/2}f(a(ab)^n,b(ab)^{-n}),$$

where n is any integer [35, Entry 18 (iv)], [1]. If we now apply (14), (15), (17), and (18), we find that (20) is transformed into the equality

$$\frac{1}{2}(\alpha\beta)^{1/8} = \frac{1}{8}\{1 - (1-\alpha)^{1/4}\}\{1 + (1-\beta)^{1/4}\} + \frac{1}{4}(\alpha\beta)^{1/4}$$

$$+ \frac{1}{8}\{1 + (1-\alpha)^{1/4}\}\{1 - (1-\beta)^{1/4}\}.$$

Simplifying, transposing, and then taking the square root of each side, we complete the proof of Theorem 1.

As an illustration of one of Ramanujan's formulas for the multiplier m, when $n = 7$, we record that

$$(21)\qquad m^2 = \left[\frac{\beta}{\alpha}\right]^{1/2} + \left[\frac{1-\beta}{1-\alpha}\right]^{1/2} - \left[\frac{\beta(1-\beta)}{\alpha(1-\alpha)}\right]^{1/2} - 8\left[\frac{\beta(1-\beta)}{\alpha(1-\alpha)}\right]^{1/3}.$$

To put such a result in the context of this paper's introduction, observe that, by (7) and (9), (21) implies a "7th degree transformation" relating the elliptic integrals $K(\sqrt{\alpha})$ and $K(\sqrt{\beta})$.

Secondly, we prove one of Ramanujan's "mixed" modular equations. (See Section 11 of Chapter 20 in Ramanujan's second notebook [35], [3].)

<u>Theorem 2</u>. Let β, γ, and δ be of degrees 3, 5, and 15, respectively. Let $m = z_1/z_3$ and $m' = z_5/z_{15}$. Then

$$(\beta\gamma)^{1/8} - \{\beta\gamma(1-\beta)(1-\gamma)\}^{1/8} = (\alpha\delta)^{1/4}\left[\frac{m}{m'}\right]^{1/2}.$$

<u>Proof</u>. Let $\mu = 4$ and $\nu = 1$ in (19) to find that

$$\psi(q^3)\psi(q^5) = \psi(q^8)\varphi(q^{60}) + q^{14}\varphi(q^4)\psi(q^{120}) + q^3\psi(q^2)\psi(q^{30}).$$

Now replace q by $-q$ and subtract the result from the equality above to deduce that

$$\psi(q^3)\psi(q^5) - \psi(-q^3)\psi(-q^5) = 2q^3\psi(q^2)\psi(q^{30}).$$

Translating this equality via (15) - (17), we deduce Theorem 2 at once.

We relate one additional "mixed" modular equation. Let α, β, γ, and δ be as above. If

$$P = \{256\alpha\beta\gamma\delta(1-\alpha)(1-\beta)(1-\gamma)(1-\delta)\}^{1/48}$$

and

$$Q = \left[\frac{\alpha\delta(1-\alpha)(1-\delta)}{\beta\gamma(1-\beta)(1-\gamma)}\right]^{1/16},$$

then

$$Q + \frac{1}{Q} = \sqrt{2}\left[P + \frac{1}{P}\right].$$

This complicated, but elegant, modular equation is Entry 11 (xv) of Chapter 20 in the second notebook [35].

We have proved only two of Ramanujan's simpler modular equations. Both proofs utilized just one, (19), of Schröter's formulas. Several additional formulas akin to (19) and essentially due to Schröter have also been employed to prove many of Ramanujan's modular equations. Further techniques and theorems are needed to establish Ramanujan's remaining modular equations. Most of the basic properties of theta-functions that Ramanujan probably employed are found in Sections 24-31 of Chapter 16 in his second notebook [35], [1]. In addition, the Jacobi triple product identity is used repeatedly. The quintuple product identity is also quite useful. (Although not found in the notebooks [35], Ramanathan [33] has pointed out that the quintuple product identity is found, in somewhat disguised form, in Ramanujan's "lost" notebook [37].) Various Lambert series expansions for products of theta-functions, the Fourier series for the Jacobian elliptic functions, and Ramanujan's celebrated $_1\psi_1$ summation formula are also some of the tools that have proven to be helpful in establishing Ramanujan's modular equations. Consult the author's book [3] to learn how these results are employed in deriving modular equations.

Unfortunately, however, these classical ideas have not always been successful. We thus have had to invoke the theory of modular forms in order to verify several of Ramanujan's modular equations. In this work, we are gratefully indebted to our collaborator A. J. Biagioli.

We shall briefly outline the theory that we need and apply it to establish a modular equation of degree 17. Complete details may be found in [3] and [4].

First, the modular equation to be proved is translated into a proposed identity involving theta-functions. Then this identity is written in terms of modular forms. For the proof of Theorem 3 below, we define the functions $g_j(\tau)$ and $h_j(\tau)$, $0 \le j \le 2$, by

$$g_0(\tau) = \varphi(-q) = \frac{\eta^2(\tau/2)}{\eta(\tau)},$$

$$g_1(\tau) = \varphi(q) = \frac{\eta^2((\tau+1)/2)}{\eta(\tau+1)},$$

$$g_2(\tau) = q^{1/4}\psi(q^2) = \frac{\eta^2(2\tau)}{\eta(\tau)},$$

(22)

$$h_0(\tau) = q^{1/8}\psi(q) = \frac{\eta^2(\tau)}{\eta(\tau/2)},$$

$$h_1(\tau) = q^{1/8}\psi(-q) = e^{-\pi i/8}\frac{\eta^2(\tau+1)}{\eta((\tau+1)/2)},$$

and

$$h_2(\tau) = \varphi(-q^2) = \frac{\eta^2(\tau)}{\eta(2\tau)},$$

where $q = e^{\pi i\tau}$. It can be shown that $g_j(\tau)$ and $h_j(\tau)$, $0 \le j \le 2$, are modular forms of weight 1/2 on $\Gamma(2)$. Furthermore, if n is an odd positive integer and $F(\tau)$ is any of the six functions defined above, then both $F(\tau)$ and $F(n\tau)$ are modular forms on $\Gamma(2) \cap \Gamma_0(n)$. The multiplier systems of $F(\tau)$ and $F(n\tau)$ may be derived from the multiplier system of the eta-function $\eta(\tau)$.

Let Γ be any subgroup of finite index in the full modular group $\Gamma(1)$. Suppose that $\mathcal{F}$ is a fundamental set for Γ. The order of a modular form F at z with respect to Γ is denoted by $\mathrm{Ord}_\Gamma(F;z)$. We are now in a position to state the valence formmula. If $F(\not\equiv 0)$ is a modular form of weight r on Γ, then

(23) $$\sum_{z\in\mathcal{F}} \mathrm{Ord}_\Gamma(F;z) = r\rho_\Gamma,$$

where

$$\rho_\Gamma = \frac{1}{12}(\Gamma(1) : \Gamma).$$

In particular, let $\Gamma = \Gamma(2) \cap \Gamma_0(n)$, where n is odd and square-free. If $F = g_j$ or h_j, $0 \le j \le 2$, then $\mathrm{Ord}_\Gamma(F;z) \ge 0$, for $z \in \mathcal{H} \cup Q \cup \{\infty\}$, where, as usual, $\mathcal{H} = \{\tau : \mathrm{Im}\,\tau > 0\}$ and Q denotes the set of rational numbers. Furthermore,

(24) $$\rho_\Gamma = \frac{1}{2}\prod_{p|n}(p + 1),$$

where the product is over all primes p dividing n.

Lastly, we take the proposed identity involving modular forms, clear denominators (if necessary), and collect terms on one side to obtain an equation of the form

(25) $$F := F_1 + \cdots + F_m = 0,$$

where F is a modular form of weight r on $\Gamma = \Gamma(2) \cap \Gamma_0(n)$. If the coefficients of $q^0, q^1, \ldots, q^\mu$ in F are equal to zero, it follows that $\mathrm{Ord}_\Gamma(F;\infty) \ge \mu + 1$. Suppose further that $\mu + 1 > r\rho_\Gamma$. Then

(26) $$\sum_{z\in\mathcal{F}} \mathrm{Ord}_\Gamma(F;z) \ge \mathrm{Ord}_\Gamma(F;\infty) \ge \mu + 1 > r\rho_\Gamma.$$

We conclude that $F \equiv 0$, for otherwise we have a contradiction to the valence formula (23).

We now apply the theory outlined above to sketch a proof of the following theorem from Section 12 of Chapter 20 [35].

Theorem 3. If β is of degree 17, then

$$m = \left(\frac{\beta}{\alpha}\right)^{1/4} + \left(\frac{1-\beta}{1-\alpha}\right)^{1/4} + \left(\frac{\beta(1-\beta)}{\alpha(1-\alpha)}\right)^{1/4}$$

$$- 2\left(\frac{\beta(1-\beta)}{\alpha(1-\alpha)}\right)^{1/8}\left\{1 + \left(\frac{\beta}{\alpha}\right)^{1/8} + \left(\frac{1-\beta}{1-\alpha}\right)^{1/8}\right\}.$$

Sketch of proof. Using (8), (12), (13), (15) - (17), and the definitions (22), we find that it suffices to prove that

$$(27) \qquad 1 = \frac{g_2(17\tau)g_1(17\tau)}{g_2(\tau)g_1(\tau)} + \frac{g_0(17\tau)g_1(17\tau)}{g_0(\tau)g_1(\tau)} + \frac{g_2(17\tau)g_0(17\tau)}{g_2(\tau)g_0(\tau)}$$

$$- 2\,\frac{h_1(17\tau)g_1(17\tau)}{h_1(\tau)g_1(\tau)} - 2\,\frac{h_2(17\tau)g_2(17\tau)}{h_2(\tau)g_2(\tau)} - 2\,\frac{h_0(17\tau)g_0(17\tau)}{h_0(\tau)g_0(\tau)}.$$

The multiplier system for each of the six quotients above is identically equal to 1. Transforming (27) into the form (25), we find that F is a modular form of weight 3 on the subgroup $\Gamma = \Gamma(2) \cap \Gamma_0(17)$. By (24), $\rho_\Gamma = 9$. Thus, by (26), if we can show that the coefficients of $q^0, q^1, \ldots, q^{27}$ in the expansion of F are equal to 0, then $F \equiv 0$ and the proof of (27) is complete. Indeed, using the computer algebra system MACSYMA, we have shown this.

Our work on modular equations has been greatly aided by notes compiled by G. N. Watson. We are grateful to the Master and Fellows of Trinity College, Cambridge for a copy of these notes.

References

1. C. Adiga, B. C. Berndt, S. Bhargava, and G. N. Watson, Chapter 16 of Ramanujan's second notebook: Theta-functions and q-series, Memoir No. 315, American Mathematical Society, Providence, 1985.

2. B. C. Berndt, Ramanujan's notebooks, Part II, Springer-Verlag, New York, to appear.

3. B. C. Berndt, Ramanujan's notebooks, Part III, Springer-Verlag, New York, to appear.

4. B. C. Berndt, A. J. Biagioli, and J. M. Purtilo, Ramanujan's modular equations of "large" prime degree, J. Indian Math. Soc., to appear.

5. B. C. Berndt, A. J. Biagioli, and J. M. Purtilo, Ramanujan's modular equations of degrees 7 and 11, Indian J. Math., to appear.

6. B. C. Berndt, A. J. Biagioli, and J. M. Purtilo, Ramanujan's "mixed" modular equations, J. Ramanujan Math. Soc., to appear.

7. J. Borwein, Some modular identities of Ramanujan useful in approximating π, Proc. Amer. Math. Soc. 95(1985), 365-371.

8. J. M. and P. B. Borwein, Pi and the AGM, John Wiley, New York, 1987.

9. J. M. and P. B. Borwein, More Ramanujan-type series for $1/\pi$, these Proceedings.

10. A. Cayley, A memoir on the transformation of elliptic functions, Philos. Trans. Royal Soc. London 164(1874), 397-456.

11. A. Cayley, An elementary treatise on elliptic functions, Deighton, Bell, and Co., Cambridge, 1876.

12. P. Deligne and M. Rapoport, Les schémas de modules des courbes elliptiques, Lecture Notes in Math., No. 349, Springer-Verlag, New York, 1973, pp. 143-316.

13. M. Dutta and L. Debnath, Elements of the theory of elliptic and associated functions with applications, World Press, Calcutta, 1965.

14. A. Enneper, Elliptische Functionen, Louis Nebert, Halle, 1890.

15. E. Fiedler, Ueber eine besondere Classe irrationaler Modulargleichungen der elliptischen Functionen, Vierteljahrsschrift Naturforschenden Gesell., Zurich 30(1885), 129-229.

16. C. Guetzlaff, Aequatio modularis pro transformatione functionum ellipticarum septimi ordinis, J. Reine Angew. Math. 12(1834), 173-177.

17. M. Hanna, The modular equations, Proc. London Math. Soc. (2) 28(1928), 46-52.

18. G. H. Hardy, Ramanujan, third ed., Chelsea, New York, 1978.

19. C. Hermite, Sur la théorie des équations modulaires, C. R. Acad. Sci. (Paris) 48(1859), 940-947, 1079-1084, 1095-1102; 49(1859), 16-24, 110-118, 141-144..

20. C. Hermite, Oeuvres, Tome II, Gauthier-Villars, Paris, 1908, pp. 5-12, 38-82.

21. T. Hiramatsu and Y. Mimura, The modular equation and modular forms of weight 1, Nagoya Math. J. 100(1985), 145-162.

22. J. Igusa, Fibre systems of Jacobian varieties. III. Fibre systems of elliptic curves, Amer. J. Math. 81(1959), 453-476.

23. C. G. J. Jacobi, Fundamenta nova theoriae functionum ellipticarum, Sumptibus fratrum Bornträger, Regiomonti, 1829.

24. C. G. J. Jacobi, Gesammelte Werke, Erster Band, G. Reimer, Berlin, 1881.

25. F. Klein, Vorlesungen über die Theorie der elliptischen Modulfunctionen, zweiter Band, B. G. Teubner, Leipzig, 1892.

26. M. Knopp, Modular functions in analytic number theory, Markham, Chicago, 1970.

27. T. Kondo and T. Tasaka, The theta functions of sublattices of the Leech lattice, Nagoya Math. J. 101(1986), 151-179.

28. J. Landen, A disquisition concerning certain fluents, which are assignable by the arcs of the conic sections; wherein are investigated some new and useful theorems for computing such fluents, Philos. Trans. Royal Soc. London 61(1771), 298-309.

29. J. Landen, An investigation of a general theorem for finding the length of any arc of any conic hyperbola, by means of two elliptic arcs, with some other new and useful theorems deduced therefrom, Philos. Trans. Royal Soc. London 65(1775), 283-289.

30. A. M. Legendre, Traité des fonctions elliptiques, t. 1, Huzard-Courcier, Paris, 1825.

31. D. H. Lehmer, Properties of the coefficients of the modular invariant $J(\tau)$, Amer. J. Math. 64(1942), 488-502.

32. B. Mazur, Modular curves and the Eisenstein ideal, Publ. I. H. E. S. No. 47(1978), 33-186.

33. K. G. Ramanathan, Generalizations of some theorems of Ramanujan, to appear.

34. S. Ramanujan, Modular equations and approximations to π, Quart. J. Math. (Oxford) 45(1914), 350-372.

35. S. Ramanujan, Notebooks (2 volumes), Tata Institute of Fundamental Research, Bombay, 1957.

36. S. Ramanujan, Collected papers, Chelsea, New York, 1962.

37. S. Ramanujan, "Lost notebook", manuscript at Trinity College, Cambridge.

38. R. A. Rankin, Modular forms and functions, Cambridge Univ. Press, Cambridge, 1977.

39. B. Schoeneberg, Elliptic modular functions, Springer-Verlag, New York, 1974.

40. H. Schröter, De aequationibus modularibus, Dissertatio Inauguralis, Albertina Litterarum Universitate, Regiomonti, 1854.

41. H. Schröter, Extrait d'une lettre adressee A. M. Liouville, J. Math. (2) 3(1858), 258-264.

42. H. Schröter, Ueber Modulargleichungen der elliptischen Functionen, Auszug aus einem Schreiben an Herrn L. Kronecker, J. Reine Angew. Math. 58(1861), 378-379.

43. H. Schröter, Beiträge zur Theorie der elliptischen Funktionen, Acta Math. 5(1884), 205-208.

44. J. Tannery and J. Molk, Éléments de la théorie des fonctions elliptiques, Tome 2, Chelsea, New York, 1972.

45. G. N. Watson, Ramanujan's notebooks, J. London Math. Soc. 6(1931), 137-153.

46. G. N. Watson, Ramanujans Vermutung über Zerfällungsanzahlen, J. Reine Angew. Math. 179(1938), 97-128.

47. H. Weber, Elliptische Functionen und algebraische Zahlen, Friedrich Vieweg und Sohn, Braunschweig, 1891.

48. H. Weber, Lehrbuch der Algebra, dritter Band, Friedrich Vieweg und Sohn, Braunschweig, 1908.

49. E. T. Whittaker and G. N. Watson, A course of modern analysis, fourth ed., Cambridge Univ. Press, Cambridge, 1966.

50. N. Yui, Explicit form of the modular equation, J. Reine Angew. Math. 299/300 (1978), 185-200.

Department of Mathematics
University of Illinois
1409 West Green St.
Urbana, IL 61801
U. S. A.

Euler products, modular identities and elliptic integrals in Ramanujan's manuscripts I

By

S. Raghavan

In the Notebooks of Srinivasa Ramanujan, as well as in his so-called "Lost Notebook", one finds beautiful 'modular identities' i.e. identities between modular forms of a given type written down quite systematically to make significant and interesting applications later. These applications are surprisingly enough diverse in nature and indeed encompass congruences for partition functions, formidable elliptic integrals occurring together with a solitary hyperelliptic integral and non-linear differential equations for Eisenstein series of low stufe. The 'modular identities' involve modular forms naturally of low weight and small stufe, however, they appear to be key identities constituting perhaps a striking prototype (and possibly a veritable fountainhead) of such identities concerning monomials in transforms of Dedekind's η-function (or of Eisenstein series). They can be found to be strewn over the Notebooks and look somewhat tailor-made for subsequent applications and by no means, just isolated. The elliptic integrals considered by Ramanujan are associated with modular curves of small conductor, the genus of the congruence subgroup $\Gamma_0(N)$ being small only for small values of the level N; the genus is 0, in particular, for $N = 5,7$ so that the corresponding function field is rational while for $N = 14,15$, it is 1. Ramanujan seems to have been the first to have discussed concrete elliptic integrals of this kind, although elliptic integrals have been studied in depth by Jacobi, Cayley and others. Further, much ahead of Hecke, Ramanujan appears to have been conscious of the dichotomy of elliptic integrals into those

ISBN 0-12-058560-X

of elementary type (i.e. involving only logarithms of modular functions) and otherwise. It is certainly desirable to make a systematic study of the elliptic integrals featuring in the Notebooks and the cryptic formulae associated therewith.

Before we describe a few of Ramanujan's modular identities, let us recall one of his well-known partition congruences: $p(5n+4)\equiv 0 \pmod 5$, $n=0,1,2,\ldots$ for the partition function $p(m)$:= the coefficient of x^m in $\prod_{r=1}^{\infty}(1-x)^{-1}$. This congruence was derived by Ramanujan from his "remarkable identity"

$$x\,\frac{\prod_{n=1}^{\infty}(1-x^{5n})^5}{\prod_{n=1}^{\infty}(1-x^n)} = \sum_{n=0}^{\infty}\sum_{a=1}^{4}\left(\frac{a}{5}\right)\frac{x^{5n+a}}{(1-x^{5n+a})^2} \tag{1}$$

(with $(-)$ denoting the Legendre symbol) by applying to both sides of (1), an averaging operator U_5 (occurring in Hecke theory as well) which takes $\phi(x)$ to $(U_5\phi)(x) := \frac{1}{5}\sum_{r=0}^{4}\phi(x^{1/5}e^{2\pi i r/5})$ and obtaining, as a result, the "beautiful formula":

$$\sum_{n=0}^{\infty} p(5n+4)x^n = 5.\ \frac{\prod_{n=1}^{\infty}(1-x^{5n})^5}{\prod_{n=1}^{\infty}(1-x^n)^6}\ .$$

On setting $x = e^{2\pi i z}$ with $\operatorname{Im} z>0$ and considering Dedekind's function $\eta(z) := e^{\pi i z/12}\prod_{n=1}^{\infty}(1-e^{2\pi i n z})$, the left hand side of (1) turns out to be precisely $\eta^5(5z)/\eta(z)$ which is a modular form of real Nebentypus $(-2,5,\chi_5)$ in the sense of Hecke. We recall that a holomorphic function $f(z) = \sum_{n=0}^{\infty} a_n e^{2\pi i n z}$ for z in the upper half-plane $\mathfrak{h}$ which satisfies the condition $f((\alpha z+\beta)(\gamma z+\delta)^{-1}) = (\gamma z+\delta)^k \chi_\ell(\delta) f(z)$ (respectively $(\gamma z+\delta)^k f(z)$) for every $\begin{pmatrix}\alpha & \beta\\ \gamma & \delta\end{pmatrix}$ in $\Gamma_0(\ell) := \{\begin{pmatrix}a & b\\ c & d\end{pmatrix} \in SL_2(\mathbb{Z}) \mid c \equiv 0 \pmod{\ell}\}$ with $\chi_\ell(\delta) := (\frac{\delta}{\ell})$ is said to be a modular form of real Nebentypus $(-k,\ell,\chi_\ell)$ (respectively of Haupttypus $(-k,\ell,1)$) The right hand side of (1) is just the Eisenstein series $E_2^0(z : \chi_5)$ of Nebentypus $(-2,5,\chi_5)$ not vanishing at the cusp 0 but vanishing at the other cusp ∞ for $\Gamma_0(5)$. Now the space of modular forms of Nebentypus $(-2,5,\chi_5)$ contains no cusp forms (i.e. modular forms vanishing at both the cusps $0, \infty$) and is, in fact, generated over $\mathbb{C}$ by $E_2^0(z;\chi_5)$ above and another Eisenstein series $E_2(z;\chi_5) := -\frac{1}{5} + \sum_{t=1}^{\infty} e^{2\pi i t z} \sum_{1\le d|t} (\frac{d}{5})d$. From this fact, not only is the identity (1) immediate but also Ramanujan's identity 'allied' to the identity (1 namely

$$\frac{\prod_{n=1}^{\infty}(1-x^n)^5}{\prod_{n=1}^{\infty}(1-x^{5n})} = 1-5\sum_{n=0}^{\infty}\sum_{r=1}^{4}(\frac{r}{5})\frac{(5n+r)x^{5n+r}}{(1-x^{5n+r})} \qquad (2)$$

The modular form $\eta^5(z)/\eta(5z)$ of Nebentypus $(-2,5,\chi_5)$ is of the form $\lambda E_2^0(z;\chi_5) + \mu E_2^\infty(z;\chi_5)$ with constants λ,μ and indeed it is equal to $-5E_2^\infty(z)$ on comparing the constant Fourier coefficient on both sides, as asserted by the identity (2).

Similarly, Ramanujan derives the partition congruence $p(7n + 5)\equiv 0 \pmod$ from an identity analogous to (1) which we rewrite in terms of the η-function

$$8\ \eta^7(7z)/\eta(z) + \eta^3(z)\eta^3(7z) = E_3^0(z;\chi_7) (:= \sum_{n=1}^{\infty}(\frac{n}{7})\frac{e^{2\pi i n z}(1+e^{2\pi i n z})}{(1-e^{2\pi i n z})^3}) \qquad (3)$$

The space of modular forms of Nebentypus $(-3,7,\chi_7)$ is spanned by the two Eisenstein series $E_3^0(z,\chi_7)$, $E_3^\infty(z:\chi_7) = -\frac{8}{7} + \sum_{t=1}^{\infty} e^{2\pi itz} \sum_{1\leq d|t} (\frac{d}{7})d^2$ and the cusp form $\eta^3(z)\eta^3(7z)$. Identity (3) follows on expressing $\eta^7(7z)/\eta(z)$ in terms of these generators. A companion identity to (3) involving $\eta^7(z)/\eta(7z)$ is proved in the same fashion.

Remarks. There exist in the literature several proofs of (2), e.g. one due to H.B.C. Darling using theta functions heavily, followed by Mordell's proof using the 'Hauptmodul' for the congruence subgroup of level 5 and two proofs given by W.N. Bailey of which one depends on a formula for well-posed bilateral hypergeometric series and the other on Weierstrass' $\wp$-function. For (3), however, a formal proof has been given only recently. A uniform approach to the identities above via modular forms on the other hand, makes it entirely plausible that Ramanujan's own perception of the same was motivated by his anticipation, by several years, of (Hecke theory and) Hecke's results on Eisenstein series (i.e. decomposition of the space of modular forms). With his powerful intuition, Ramanujan was perhaps influenced by the fact that a modular form cannot afford to have zeros of a very large order without vanishing identically or equivalently that in order to check the equality of two modular forms of the same genre, it suffices to compare the first few coefficients (e.g. for modular forms of Nebentypus $(-k,\ell,\chi_\ell)$ for prime ℓ, the first $1+\frac{k}{12}(\ell+1)$ coefficients, as we know from Hecke [4]).

Let $E_2(z) := 1-24 \sum_{n=1}^{\infty} (\sum_{1\leq d|n} d)e^{2\pi inz}$ which is the same as P in Ramanujan's notation, $E_4(z) := 1+240 \sum_{n=1}^{\infty} (\sum_{1\leq d|n} d^3)e^{2\pi inz}$ and $E_6(z)=1-504 \sum_{n=1}^{\infty} (\sum_{1\leq d|n} d^5)e^{2\pi inz}$;

the latter are Eisenstein series of weights 4 and 6 respectively for the modular group and generate the algebra of elliptic modular forms. For prime ℓ, $E_2(z;1;\Gamma_0(\ell)):=E_2(z)-\ell E_2(\ell z)$ is the unique Eisenstein series of Haupttypus $(-2,\ell,1)$. In the case of forms of Nebentypus $(-k,\ell,\chi_\ell)$ with $k\geq 2$ and $\chi_\ell(-1) = (-1)^k$, however, there exist two Eisenstein series $E_k^0(z;\chi_\ell), E_k^\infty(z;\chi_\ell)$ corresponding to the two cusps $0,\infty$ for $\Gamma_0(\ell)$. For $k = 2$ and $\ell = 5$, let us denote $E_2^\infty(z;\chi_5)$ merely by $E_2(z;\chi_5)$. We know that $E_2(z;\chi_5) = -\frac{1}{5}\eta^5(z)/\eta(5z)$ from above and also that $E_2^0(z;\chi_5) = \eta^5(5z)/\eta(z)$. For any $N\geq 1$, let us define the function η_N by $\eta_N(z) := \eta(Nz)$ for $z \in \mathfrak{H}$. The following two key identities involving monomials in η_N, besides being noteworthy for intrinsic interest and sheer elegance, come in quite handy for the simplification carried out by Ramanujan on some of his elliptic integrals and also for verifying other modular identities stated by him, e.g. $\psi^2(x)-x\psi^2(x^5) = f(x,x^4)f(x^2,x^3)$ where $\psi(x) := x^{-1/8}\eta_2^2(z)/\eta(z)$, $f(x,x') := \prod_{n=0}^{\infty}(1+x(xx')^n)(1+x'(xx')^n)(1-(xx')^{n+1})$.

The identity above involving ψ and f was proved by Watson [10].

<u>Proposition</u>. (i) $\eta_2^4\eta_5^2 - 5\,\eta^2\eta_{10}^4 = \eta^5\,\eta_5\,\eta_{10}/\eta_2$

(ii) $\eta_2^4\eta_5^2 - \eta^2\,\eta_{10}^4 = \eta\eta_2\,\eta_5^5\,/\eta_{10}$

<u>Proof</u>. Using the Hauptmodul $\tau := 10\,\eta_2\,\eta_{10}^3/\eta^3\eta_5$ for the group $\Gamma_0(10)$ of genus 0 and the Eisenstein series $E_2^0(z;\chi_5) = \eta_5^5/\eta$, $E_2(z;\chi_5) = -\frac{1}{5}\eta^5/\eta_5$ above, the identities may be rewritten as

$$\text{(i)}'\quad E_2(z;\chi_5) - E_2(2z;\chi_5) = -\frac{\tau}{2}E_2(z;\chi_5)$$

$$\text{(ii)}'\quad E_2^0(z;\chi_5) + E_2^0(2z;\chi_5) = \frac{\eta_2^4\,\eta_5^2}{\eta^2\,\eta_{10}^4}E_2^0(2z;\chi_5)$$

Now τ has a simple zero at $i\infty$ and a simple pole at 0 while $E_2(z:\chi_5)$ is regular at $i\infty$ and vanishes at 0, since $E_2(-\frac{1}{z};\chi_5) = (z^2/\sqrt{5})E_2^0(z;\chi_5)$. Thus $(\tau/2+1)\ E_2(z;\chi_5)$ is an entire modular form of weight 2 and Nebentypus for $\Gamma_0(10)$. The proof of (i) reduces to showing that $(\tau/2+1)E_2(z;\chi_5)=E_2(2z;\chi_5)$. By Hecke, it suffices to check the equality of the first $1+(2(\Gamma(1):\Gamma_0(10))/12 =)3$ Fourier coefficients on both sides. This verification is immediate from the Fourier expansions

$$E_2(z;\chi_5) = -\frac{1}{5} + e^{2\pi iz} - e^{4\pi iz} - 2e^{6\pi iz} + \ldots.$$

$$(\tau/2+1) = 1 + 5\,e^{2\pi iz} + 15\,e^{4\pi iz} + 40\,e^{6\pi iz} + \ldots.$$

$$(\tau/2+1)\ E_2(z:\chi_5) = -\frac{1}{5} + 0\cdot e^{2\pi iz} + e^{4\pi iz} + 0\cdot e^{6\pi iz} + \ldots.$$

Using (i), we may rewrite $\eta_2^4\,\eta_5^2\,/(\eta^2\eta_{10}^4)$ as $5+10/\tau$ and then (ii)' will follow, once we establish that $(\tau/(4\tau+10))E_2^0(z,\chi_5) = E_2^0(2z,\chi_5)$. Now $\tau/(4\tau+10)$ is regular at all the cusps of $\Gamma_0(10)$ except those equivalent to $\pm 1/5$ where it has a simple pole. Further $E_2^0(z,\chi_5)$ which is of Nebentypus $(-2,5,\chi_5)$ has a zero at ∞ and hence at $\pm 1/5$ equivalent to ∞ under $\Gamma_0(5)$. This means that $(\tau/(4\tau+10))E_2^0(z,\chi_5)$ is an entire modular form of weight 2 and Nebentypus for $\Gamma_0(10)$. The proposition is now immediate on comparing the first three Fourier coefficients of

$$(\tau/(4\tau+10))\ E_2^0(z;\chi_5) = (e^{2\pi iz} - e^{4\pi iz} + 0\cdot e^{6\pi iz} + \ldots)(e^{2\pi iz} + e^{4\pi iz} + 2\cdot e^{6\pi iz} + \ldots)$$

with those of $E_2^0\ (2z,\ \chi_5)$.

There is another η-identity of striking elegance lurking in Ramanujan's "Lost Notebook":

$$\eta_3^5\eta_5^5/(\eta\eta_{15})-\eta^4\eta_5^4-5(\eta\eta_3\eta_5\eta_{15})^2-9(\eta_3\eta_{15})^4-\eta^5\eta_{15}^5/\eta_3\eta_5 = 0$$

involving modular forms of weight 4 for $\Gamma_0(15)$. Its proof boils down, in view of Hecke's theorem, just to checking that the coefficient of $e^{2\pi inz}$ for $0\le n\le 8 = 4(\Gamma_0(1):\Gamma_0(15))/12$ vanish. This occurs in Ramanujan's reduction of the following elliptic integral arising from $\Gamma_0(15)$ to (4);

$$\int_0^x \eta(z)\eta(3z)\eta(5z)\eta(15z)\,\frac{dx}{x} = \frac{1}{5}\int_{2\tan^{-1}\left(\frac{1}{\sqrt{5}}\sqrt{\frac{1-11v-v^2}{1+v-v^2}}\right)}^{2\tan^{-1}(1/\sqrt{5})} \frac{d\phi}{\sqrt{1-\frac{9}{25}\sin^2\phi}}$$

$$= \frac{1}{5}\int_{2\tan^{-1}\left(\frac{1-3v_1}{\sqrt{5}(1+3v_1)}\right)}^{2\tan^{-1}(1/\sqrt{5})} \frac{d\phi}{\sqrt{1-\frac{9}{25}\sin^2\phi}} \tag{4}$$

where $x = e^{2\pi iz}$, $v := \eta^3\eta_{15}^3/(\eta_3^3\eta_5^3)$, $v_1 = \eta_3^2\eta_{15}^2/(\eta^2\eta_5^2)$.

In precisely the same spirit as above, one can uphold the following identities noted down by Ramanujan connecting E_4, E_6 and their transforms under $z \longrightarrow \ell z$ ($\ell = 5,7$) with monomials in η, η_5, η_7:

$$E_4^3 = (\eta^{10}/\eta_5^2 + 250\,\eta^4\eta_5^4 + 3125\,\eta_5^{10}/\eta^2)^3$$

$$E_4^3(5z) = (\eta^{10}(z)/\eta^2(5z)+10\eta^4(z)\eta^4(5z)+5\eta^{10}(5z)/\eta^2(z))^3$$

$$E_6^2 = \eta^{24}(\eta^3/\eta_5^3 - 500\eta_5^3/\eta^3-5^6\eta_5^9/\eta^9)^2(1+22\eta_5^6/\eta^6+125\eta_5^{12}/\eta^{12})$$

$$E_6^2(5z) = \eta^{24}(5z)(\eta^{15}(z)/\eta^{15}(5z)-\eta^3(z)/\eta^3(5z)+4\eta^9(z)/\eta^9(5z))^2(1+22\eta^6(5z)/\eta^6(z) + 125\eta^{12}(5z)/\eta^{12}(z))$$

$$E_4^3 = (\eta^7/\eta_7+5.7^2\eta^3\eta_7^3+7^4\eta_7^7/\eta)^3(\eta^7/\eta_7+13\eta^3\eta_7^3 + 49\eta_7^7/\eta) \tag{5}$$

and three more such identities corresponding to the prime 7 in lieu of 5. These eight identities however follow at once from Klein's formulae [5] involving the modular invariant $j := E_4^3/(E_4^3-E_6^2)$ and $\tau_5:=-\eta^6/\eta_5^6$, $\tau_7:=\eta^4/\eta_7^4$ (see Greenhill's book on "The applications of elliptic functions"). Ramanujan must have had his own approach to them. Any way, it is remarkable that he quietly notes down in the "Lost Notebook" that 'the cube root' of the factor $\eta^7/\eta_7 + 13\eta^3\eta_7^3 + 49\eta_7^7/\eta$ in (5) is just the Eisenstein series $E_1(z,\chi_7) := 1+2\sum_{m,n\geq 1}\chi_7(n)e^{2\pi imnz}$ whose square turns out to be $-\frac{1}{6}E_2(z,1;\Gamma_0(7))$; Ramanujan simply revels in exhibiting such an "algebra of identities" in his manuscripts! Striking and more complicated identities such as

$$(E_4^2(z)+94E_4(z)E_4(5z)+625E_4^2(5z))^{\frac{1}{2}}=12\sqrt{5}\left(\frac{\eta^{10}(z)}{\eta^2(5z)}+26\eta^4(z)\eta^4(5z)+125\frac{\eta^{10}(5z)}{\eta^2(z)}\right)$$

involving E_4 and η (and likewise E_6,η) which may be established with the help of the identities above are also to be found in the "Lost Notebook". Ramanujan's motivation for these is not clear to us though.

Using the basis $\{\eta^{10}/\eta_5^2,\ \eta^4\eta_5^4, \eta_5^{10}/\eta^2\}$ for modular forms of Haupttypus (-4,5,1), one shows that $E_2(z)-5E_2(5z) = -4\ g_5\sqrt{h_5(\lambda_5)}$ where $g_5\ := \eta^5/\eta_5, \lambda_5 := \eta_5^6/\eta^6$, $\lambda_5(X) := 1+22X+125X^2$, simply by squaring both sides and checking the first four Fourier coefficients in view of Hecke's theorem; recall that the same method gave us the identity $E_4 = (\eta^{10}/\eta_5^2 + 250\eta^4\eta_5^4+3125\eta_5^{10}/\eta$ leading the eight identities above. The two identities just mentioned imply the consistency of the two defining relations

$$E_2(z)=g_5(\sqrt{h_5(\lambda_5)}-30F(\lambda_5)), E_2(5z)=g_5(\sqrt{h_5(\lambda_5)}-6F(\lambda_5)) \tag{6}$$

for the function $F(\lambda_5)$ of the 'Hauptmodul' λ_5 for $\Gamma_0(5)$. Ramanujan has stated an interesting non-linear differential equation for $F(\lambda_5)$:

$$\sqrt{h_5(\lambda_5)}\,\frac{dF}{d\lambda_5} = 1 + \frac{25}{2}\lambda_5 + \frac{5}{2\lambda_5}F^2 \tag{7}$$

which can be proved by using the above identity for E_4, the first relation in (6) and the Ramanujan differential equation $E_4 - E_2^2 = -(12/2\pi i)\frac{dE_2}{dz}$ (This differential equation along with two others for E_4, E_6 is of basic importance for the theory of p-adic modular forms due to Serre; "Formes modulaires et fonctions zêta p-adiques", Springer Lecture Notes No.350,1973,191-268. Introducing $\mathcal{E}_5(z) := \frac{1}{24}(E_2(z) - E_2(5z)) = -g_5 F(\lambda_5)$ in view of (6), we may rewrite the differential equation (7) as

$$\frac{1}{2\pi i}\frac{d\mathcal{E}_5}{dz} - \frac{5}{2}\mathcal{E}_5^2 = -\eta^4\eta_5^4 - \frac{25}{2}\frac{\eta_5^{10}}{\eta^2} \tag{8}$$

This seems to play for the Eisenstein series (of weight 2) for $\Gamma_0(5)$ the same rôle as the Ramanujan differential equation for E_2 above in the case of the modular group. For $\mathcal{E}_7(z) := \frac{1}{24}(E_2(z) - E_2(7z))$, the analogue of (8) may be realized as

$$\frac{1}{2\pi i}\frac{d\mathcal{E}_7}{dz} - \frac{7}{3}\mathcal{E}_7^2 = -\eta^3\eta_7^3\, E_1(z,\chi_7) - \frac{28}{3}\frac{\eta_7^7}{\eta}\, E_1(z,\chi_7). \tag{9}$$

We know from Hecke that Eisenstein series of weight 2 for congruence subgroups of level N are linearly expressible in terms of N-divisor values of Weierstrass' $\wp$ - function. Recent work of Eichler and Zagier (Math. Ann.258(1982),399-407) provides non-linear differential equations of degree 2 for these N-divisor values, with coefficients independent of N. On the other hand, the coefficients of the non-linear differential equations (8), (9) evidently depend on the stufe.

Ramanujan's "Lost Notebook" contains a number of elliptic integrals arising from modular curves of low conductor and reductions carried out with successive transformations such as Landen's transformation or Gauss' transformation (which incidentally figure already in the Notebooks, with innumerable applications). We have indeed given above such an elliptic integral arising from $\Gamma_0(15)$.

Ramanujan also seems to have anticipated to an extent Hecke's observation that 'special integrals of the third kind of stufe N' (i.e. with the integrand having logarithmic singularities at most, at the cusps of the congruence subgroup $\Gamma(N)$) are of elementary type (i.e. expressible in terms of logarithms of functions invariant under $\Gamma(N)$). As two typical examples, one may quote

$$\int_{e^{-2\pi}}^{x} \sqrt{E_4}\,\frac{dx}{x} = \log \frac{E_4^{3/2}-E_6}{E_4^{3/2}+E_6}, \quad \frac{8}{5}\int_{0}^{x} \frac{\psi^5(x)}{\psi(x)}\,\frac{dx}{x} = \log u^2 u_2^3 + \sqrt{5}\log \frac{1+\varepsilon^{-3} u u_2^2}{1-\varepsilon^3 u u_2^2} \tag{10}$$

where $x = e^{2\pi iz}$, $u = \frac{x^{1/5}}{1+}\,\frac{x}{1+}\,\frac{x^2}{1+}\ldots$, $u_2(x) = u(x^2)$, $\psi(x) = x^{-1/8}\eta_2^2(z)/\eta(z)$ and $\varepsilon = (1+\sqrt{5})/2$. The evaluation of the latter invokes the modular identities in the Proposition above and an identity of Ramanujan for ψ proved by Berndt [2]. Other elliptic integrals discussed by Ramanujan involve monomials in η and its transforms (i.e. cusp forms of weight 2 and not Eisenstein series) and thus turn out to be 'non-elementary' and more complicated than (10).

References

[1] W.N. Bailey: A note on two of Ramanujan's formulae, Quart. J. Math.

Oxford Series 3 (1952), 29-31.

[2] B.C. Berndt: Chapter 19 of Ramanujan's second notebook (Preprint).

[3] H.B.C. Darling: Proofs of certain identities and congruences enunciated by S. Ramanujan, Proc. London Math. Soc. (2), 19 (1921), 350-373.

[4] E.Hecke: Gesammelte Abhandlungen,van den Hoeck u.Ruprecht, Gottingen, 195 pp.811, 953.

[5] F. Klein: Gesammelte Abhandlungen, Bd.III,p.46.

[6] L.J. Mordell: Note on certain modular relations considered by Messrs. Ramanujan, Darling and Rogers, Proc. London Math. Soc. (2), 20 (1922), 408-416.

[7] S. Raghavan: On certain identities due to Ramanujan, Quart. J. Math. Oxford (2), 37 (1986), 221-229.

[8] S. Ramanujan: Congruence properties of p(n), Unpublished manuscript, 1920, Trinity College.

[9] S. Ramanujan: Notebooks of Srinivasa Ramanujan, Tata Institute of Fundamental Research, 1957.

[10] G.N. Watson: Proof of certain identities in combinatory analysis, Jour. Ind. Math. Soc. 20 (1933), 57-69.

Euler Products, Modular Identities and elliptic integrals in Ramanujan's manuscripts II

By
S.S. Rangachari

1. Euler Products

The term "Euler Product" comes from the infinite product representation of Riemann ζ - function ,the product taken over all primes. In other words, $\zeta(s) = \sum_{n=1}^{\infty} n^{-s} = \prod_{p} (1-p^{-s})^{-1}$, Res > 1. This is a consequence of the fundamental theorem of arithmetic. We also have similar representations for Dirichlet L-series namely if χ is a Dirichlet character $\chi(n) = (\frac{d}{n})$, then $L(s, \chi) = \prod_{p} (1-\chi(p)p^{-s})^{-1}$. One observes that in these cases, the p-component is a linear polynomial in p^{-s}. It is quite natural to ask whether we can have Euler products of Dirichlet series in which the p-component is a polynomial in p^{-s} of degree greater than 1. One obvious way is to take products of zeta functions and L-series (with translations of variable s). In fact, such Euler products do occur as Mellin transforms of Eisenstein series. Perhaps Ramanujan was the first one to consider Euler products where the p-component is an irreducible polynomial in p^{-s} of degree 2. The most prominent example of this is of course the Dirichlet series $\sum \tau(n) n^{-s} = \prod_{p} (1-\tau(p)p^{-s} + p^{11-2s})^{-1}$ associated with $\Delta(z) = \eta^{24}(z)$ where η is the Dedekind η - function defined by the infinite product $e^{\pi i z/12} \prod_{n=1}^{\infty} (1-e^{2\pi i n z})$. This was introduced by him in his paper on "Arithmetical Functions" [5]. In the same paper, he also considers

ISBN 0-12-058560-X

Euler products for Dirichlet series associated with $\eta^k(\frac{24z}{k})(k|24)$. Besides these published results of Ramanujan, we also find some more Dirichlet series with Euler products scattered in his unpublished manuscripts. [A complete list was made by Professor Ramanathan some years ago.] Of course Ramanujan never gave any indications of proofs for these Euler products.

The Euler products occurring in Ramanujan manuscripts are of two types (a) those published by Birch in his paper [1] and (b) those that have been now termed 'Lost Note Book' by Professor Andrews[6]. We shall give a brief account of these in this lecture. The types of Dirichlet series occurring in the manuscripts published by Birch are associated to cusp forms belonging to subgroups of the type $\Gamma(n)$ $(n|24)$ and some multiplier. More precisely they are all of the form $\eta^k E_{2\ell}$ (k even and $E_{2\ell}$: Eisenstein series of weight 2ℓ belonging to the full modular group). His examples vary from $k=2$, $\ell=0$ to $k=22$, $\ell=2$. For a detailed list, see Table at the end.

We shall quote here just a sample, changing his notations slightly. In the following Q and R stand for E_4, E_6.

$$\sum_{n=1}^{\infty} a_0(n)q^n = \eta^4(6z), \quad \sum_{n=1}^{\infty} a_2(n)q^n = \eta^4 Q(6z)$$

$$\sum_{n=1}^{\infty} a_3(n)q^n = \eta^4 R(6z), \quad \sum_{n=1}^{\infty} a_4(n)q^n = \eta^4 Q^2(6z) + 288\sqrt{70}\,\eta^{20}(6z)$$

$$\sum_{n=1}^{\infty} a_5(n)q^n = \eta^4 QR(6z), \quad \sum_{n=1}^{\infty} a_7(n)q^n = \eta^4 Q^2 R(6z) + 100\,88\sqrt{280}\;\eta^{20} R$$

In all these cases $\sum_{n=1}^{\infty} a_k(n)n^{-s} = \prod_{p>3} (1 - a_k(p)p^{-s} + p^{2k+1-2s})^{-1}$.

If $k = 0, 2, 3, 5$, then $a_k(p) = 0$ for $p \equiv 5 \pmod 6$ and

$$a_k(p) = (A + \sqrt{-3}\,B)^{2k+1} + (A - \sqrt{-3}\,B)^{2k+1} \quad \text{for} \quad p \equiv 1 \pmod 6$$

where $A^2 + 3B^2 = p$ (A, B integers with $A \equiv 1 \pmod 3$).

$a_4(p)$ and $a_7(p)$ do not seem to have such simple laws.

It can be easily seen that the modular forms occurring above are cusp forms belonging to $\Gamma_0(6)$ and some multiplier. Using Rankin's results [8] on the dimension of these spaces, we see that when $k = 0, 2, 3, 5$ the dimension is 1 and hence the Dirichlet series is an Euler product whereas in the cases of $k = 4, 7$, the dimension is 2. Hence the Euler product corresponds to a suitable linear combination of the basis forms $\eta^4 Q^2$, η^{20} ($k=4$) and $\eta^4 Q^2 R$ and $\eta^{20} R$ ($k=7$). The actual coefficients can be determined by studying the effect of the Hecke operator T_2 on these forms.

The explicit descriptions of $a_k(p)$ shows that these Dirichlet series are nothing but Hecke L-series associated to $\mathbb{Q}(\sqrt{-3})$. In other words the cusp forms η^4, $\eta^4 Q$, $\eta^4 QR$ are all theta series with Hecke characters of $\mathbb{Q}(\sqrt{-3})$ or in present day parlance, "forms of CM type".

It has been observed by Serre that forms of CM type are lacunary and vice versa. The remark of Ramanujan on a_4 (p) and a_7 (p) seem to indicate that the corresponding forms are <u>not</u> of CM type.

Ramanujan gives similar results for $\eta^k E_{2\ell}$ (k=6, 8 and ℓ=2, 3, 4, 5, i.e. Euler products and representations as Hecke L- series. In the case of $\eta^2 E_{2\ell}$ (ℓ = 2, 3, 4, 5, 7) he gives only Hecke eigen functions. The actual Euler products and their representation as Hecke L-series are not available. But it is quite possible the manuscripts are lost since all the other details are correct. One interesting point to be noted is that Ramanujan does not consider $\eta^k E_{12}$ in any of his manuscripts. These forms are also of interest as can be seen from the recent work of Serre on the lacunarity of η^{26}. Now, observe that all the forms of CM type that occur in Ramanujan's papers are for the imaginary quadratic fields $\mathbb{Q}(\sqrt{-1})$, $\mathbb{Q}(\sqrt{-3})$. In fact Serre has proved that if η^{2r} is lacunary (or of CM type) then it necessarily comes from $\mathbb{Q}(\sqrt{-1})$ or $\mathbb{Q}(\sqrt{-3})$. Ramanujan's results on $\eta^k Q$, $\eta^k R$, $\eta^k QR$ indicate a possible generalisation of Serre's results to forms of the type $\eta^k E_{2\ell}$.

The other types of Euler products which occur in Ramanujan's work are Dirichlet series associated with $\eta(z)\eta(7z)$, $\eta(z)\eta(11z)$, $\eta(z)\eta(2$ (all of weight 1) ($\eta(z)\eta(11z))^2$ and $(\eta(z)\eta(7z))^3$. The case $\eta(z)\eta(23z)$ has been studied by Rankin and Serre. Other forms can be handled in a similar fashion.

2. <u>Modular Identities</u>: The type of modular identities we would be considering is somewhat different from the ones stated by Raghavan in his lecture. These are usually known as the "40 identities of Ramanujan" and occur in the same paper of Birch where he discusses the Euler products of $\eta^k E_{2\ell}$. Some of these identities have been proved by Ramanujan, Watson, Rogers. Finally due to the work of Bressoud as well as of Biagioli are the proofs for all of them are at hand. Our object in this lecture is to look at some of these identities as a relation between "modular units", i.e. units in modular function fields.

Following Bressoud's notation, we define, for $x=e^{2\pi i w}$. Im$w > o$

$$G(x)=\prod_{n=0}^{\infty}((1-x^{5n+1})(1-x^{5n+4}))^{-1}, \quad H(x)=\prod_{n=0}^{\infty}((1-x^{5n+2})(1-x^{5n+3}))^{-1}.$$

$g_\alpha = g_\alpha(x) = x^{-\alpha/60} G(x^\alpha)$, $h_\alpha = h_\alpha(x) = x^{11\alpha/60} H(x^\alpha)$, for any natural number α. Then Ramanujan's identities are of the following type.

If $\alpha \equiv \beta \pmod 5$, $g_\alpha h_\beta - g_\beta h_\alpha$ is a rational function of η_γ-s for some γ and if $\alpha \equiv -\beta \pmod 5$ $g_\alpha g_\beta + h_\alpha h_\beta$ is a rational function of η_δ -s for some δ. Sometimes his identities involve.

$(g_\alpha h_\beta - g_\beta h_\alpha)(g_{\alpha'} g_{\beta'} + h_{\alpha'} h_{\beta'})$ or $(g_\alpha h_\beta - g_\beta h_\alpha)/g_{\alpha'} g_{\beta'} + h_{\alpha'} h_{\beta'})$.

Our object in this lecture is to give an alternative proof of the simpler identities involving $g_\alpha h_\beta - g_\beta h_\alpha$ for some values of α and β.

Firstly we observe that these functions belong to $\Gamma_o(\alpha\beta)$ with some multiplier. For the same, we introduce the Klein representation of the homogeneous icosahedral group in 2 variables. If $w = \frac{w_1}{w_2}$ with Im $w > o$, define for $\nu = 1, 2$

$$z_\nu (w_1, w_2) = (-1)^\nu \left(\frac{w_2}{\pi}\right)^7 q^{\nu^2/5} \frac{\theta_1(\nu w \pi, q^5)}{\theta_1'(o, q)^5}$$

where $g = e^{\pi i w}$ $(x = g^2)$. We now have a 2-dimensional representation of the homogeneous icosahedral group by means of $(z_1(w_1, w_2), z_2(w_1, w_2))$. Using the infinite product representations of θ_1 and θ_1', we have the following relations

$$z_1(w_1, w_2) = -\frac{i}{2^5} \cdot h_1(w_1, w_2)(\eta(w_1, w_2))^{-14} \quad \text{and}$$

$$z_2(w_1, w_2) = \frac{i}{2^5} \; g_1(w_1, w_2)(\eta(w_1, w_2))^{-14}$$

where $g_1(w_1, w_2) = g(x)$, $h_1(w_1, w_2) = h(x)$ and

$$\eta(w_1, w_2) = \left(\frac{w_2}{\pi}\right)^{-\frac{1}{2}} q^{1/12} \prod_{n=1}^{\infty} (1 - x^n).$$

Now $g_\alpha(x) = g(\alpha w_1, w_2)$, $h_\alpha(x) = h(\alpha w_1, w_2)$ and it can be checked that the 2-dimensional icosahedral representation gives a 2-dimensional representation of $\Gamma_o(\alpha\beta)$ by means of $(g_\alpha \eta_\alpha^{-14}, h_\alpha \eta_\alpha^{-14})$ and similarly $(g_\beta \eta_\beta^{-14}, h_\beta \eta_\beta^{-14})$. This gives a 1-dimensional representation of $\Gamma_o(\alpha\beta)$ by means of $(g_\alpha h_\beta - g_\beta h_\alpha)(\eta_\alpha \eta_\beta)^{-14}$. From the transformation formula for $(\eta_\alpha \eta_\beta)^{-14}$, we deduce that $g_\alpha h_\beta - g_\beta h_\alpha$ is a modular function for $\Gamma_o(\alpha\beta)$ with some multiplier. We shall examine the cases in which this is a unit. In other words $g_\alpha h_\beta - g_\beta h_\alpha$ has zeros and poles concentrated at the cusps of $\Gamma_o(\alpha\beta)$. This can happen if and only if $\frac{g_\alpha}{h_\alpha} - \frac{g_\beta}{h_\beta}$ has no zero in the upper half plane (since $h_\alpha h_\beta$ has no zero in the upper half plane). In other words, $\frac{g_\alpha}{h_\alpha} \neq \frac{g_\beta}{h_\beta}$. Since $\frac{g}{h}$ is generating function (Hauptmodul) for the function field of $\Gamma(5)$ this is equivalent to saying that αz is not equivalent to βz under $\Gamma(5)$ for z in the upper half plane. If $\begin{pmatrix} a & b \\ c & d \end{pmatrix} \in \Gamma(5)$, this amounts to saying that $(d\beta + a\alpha)^2 - 4\alpha\beta \geq o$. We can find a set of sufficient conditions on α, β for this property to be satisfied. Since $\alpha \equiv \beta \pmod 5$, we can prove that when $\alpha = 1$, $\beta = 6, 11, 16, 36$ this is satisfied. Similarly for $\alpha = 2$, $\beta = 7$, $\alpha = 3$, $\beta = 8$, $\alpha = 4$, $\beta = 9$ this is satisfied.

To get an explicit expression for the unit $g_\alpha h_\beta - g_\beta h_\alpha$ in these cases, we use a result of Biagioli in his thesis. He gives a method of constructing η - quotients which have a simple zero at one cusp and no zeros at all other cusps. Using this, one can obtain the following results of Ramanujan.

1) $g_{11} h_1 - g_1 h_{11} = 1$

2) $g_{16} h_1 - h_{16} g_1 = \dfrac{\eta_4^2}{\eta_2 \eta_8}$

3) $g_6 h_1 - g_1 h_6 = \dfrac{\eta_1 \eta_6}{\eta_2 \eta_3}$

4) $g_7 h_2 - g_2 h_7 = \dfrac{\eta_1 \eta_{14}}{\eta_2 \eta_7}$

5) $g_8 h_3 - g_3 h_8 = \dfrac{\eta_1 \eta_4 \eta_6 \eta_{24}}{\eta_2 \eta_3 \eta_8 \eta_{12}}$

6) $g_9 h_4 - g_4 h_9 = \dfrac{\eta_1 \eta_6^2 \eta_{36}}{\eta_2 \eta_3 \eta_{12} \eta_{18}}$

7) $g_{36} h_1 - g_1 h_{36} = \dfrac{\eta_4 \eta_6^2 \eta_{36}}{\eta_2 \eta_3 \eta_{12} \eta_{18}}$

The above technique does not seem to work for identities involving $g_\alpha g_\beta + h_\alpha h_\beta$. It would be interesting to extend it to other identities as well, which are more complicated.

References:

1) Birch B. J.: A look back at Ramanujan's Note books, Math. Proc. Camb. Phil. Soc. 78, Part I (1975) 73-79.

2) Biagioli A. J.: Product of transforms of the Dedekind eta function Thesis (University of Wisconsin- Madison 1982).

3) Bressoud D.: Proof and generalisation of certain identities conjectured by Ramanujan (Temple University thesis, 1977).

4) Raghavan S.: On Ramanujan and Dirichlet series with Euler products, Glasgow Math. Journal 25 (1984) 203-206.

5) Ramanujan S: Collected papers. Cambridge University Press 1927

6) Ramanujan S: Unpublished manuscripts, Trinity College Library, Cambridge.

7) Rangachari S. S.: Ramanujan and Dirichlet series with Euler products Proc. Ind. Acad. Sci 91, No. 1 (1982). 1-15.

8) Rankin R. A.: Hecke operators on congruence subgroups of the modular group. Math. Ann. 168 (1967) 40-58.

9) Serre J. P.: Sur la lacunarité des puissances de η, Glasgow Mathematical Journal 27 (1985) 203 - 221.

Notation: [9] If c is a Hecke character of K of exponent k-1 and conductor f_c, then c is a homomorphism of the group $I(f_c)$ of fractionary ideals of K prime to f_c, into $\mathbb{C}^*$ with the property $c(\alpha \mathcal{O}_K) = \alpha^{k-1}$ if $\alpha \in K^*$ and $\alpha \equiv 1 \bmod {}^{x} f_c$ ($\mathcal{O}_K$: ring of integers in K and x denotes "multiplicative" sense). Then $\varphi_{K,c}(z) = \sum c(\mathfrak{a}) q^{N\mathfrak{a}}$ where $\mathfrak{a}$ runs over all integral ideals of K prime to f_c and $N\mathfrak{a}$, norm of $\mathfrak{a}$.

Table 1 (Serre 1985)

Cusp form	Form of CM type	Imaginary Quad. field K
1) $\eta^2(12z)$	$\phi_{K,c}(z)$, c of order 4 associated to $E = \mathbb{Q}(\sqrt{-1}, \sqrt[4]{12})$	$\mathbb{Q}(\sqrt{-1})$
2) $\eta^4(6z)$	$\phi_{K,c}(z)$, c of exponent 1 and conductor $f_c = (2\sqrt{-3})$	$\mathbb{Q}(\sqrt{-3})$
3) $\eta^6(4z)$	$\phi_{K,c}(z)$, c of exponent 2 and conductor $f_c = (2)$.	$\mathbb{Q}(\sqrt{-1})$
4) $\eta^8(3z)$	$\phi_{K,c}(z)$, c of exponent 3 and conductor $f_c = (\sqrt{-3})$	$\mathbb{Q}(\sqrt{-3})$

5) $\eta^{10}(12z)$ $\frac{1}{96}(\phi_{K,c_+}(z) - \phi_{K,c_-}(z))$ c_+ and c_- are of exponent 4 and conductor $f=(6)$. $\mathbb{Q}(\sqrt{-1})$

6) $\eta^{14}(12z)$ $\frac{1}{720\sqrt{-3}}(\phi_{K,c_+}(z) - \phi_{K,c_-}(z))$ c_+ and c_- are of exponent 6 and conductor $f=(4\sqrt{-3})$ $\mathbb{Q}(\sqrt{-3})$

7) $\eta^{26}(12z)$ $\frac{1}{32617728}(\phi_{K',c'_+} + \phi_{K',c'_-} - \phi_{K'',c''_+} - \phi_{K'',c''_-}$ $K' = \mathbb{Q}(\sqrt{-3})$ $K'' = \mathbb{Q}(\sqrt{-1})$

c'_+, c'_- (resp c''_+, c''_-) are Hecke char. of exponent 12 in K'(resp K'') and conductor $f' = (4\sqrt{-3})$ (resp $f'' = (6)$).

Ramanujan has (2), (3), (4). Although he gets the Hecke eigenfunctions in the case of (5) and (6), he has no explicit description of these as theta series as in the cases (2) - (4). He does not consider (7) at all. In addition to the abo[ve] he has the following results.

Cusp form	Form of CM type	Imaginary quad. field K
1) $\eta^4 Q(6z)$	$\phi_{K,c}(z)$, c of exponent 5 and conductor $f_c = (2\sqrt{-3})$	$\mathbb{Q}(\sqrt{-3})$
2) $\eta^4 R(6z)$	$\phi_{K,c}(z)$, c of exponent 7 and conductor $f_c = (2\sqrt{-3})$	$\mathbb{Q}(\sqrt{-3})$
3) $\eta^4 QR(6z)$	$\phi_{K,c}(z)$, c of exponent 11 and conductor $f_c = (2\sqrt{-3})$	$\mathbb{Q}(\sqrt{-3})$

4)	$\eta^6 Q(4z)$	$\phi_{K,c}(z)$, c of exponent 6 and conductor $f_c = (2)$	$\mathbb{Q}(\sqrt{-1})$
5)	$\eta^6 Q^2(4z)$	$\phi_{K,c}(z)$, c of exponent 10 and conductor $f_c = (2)$	$\mathbb{Q}(\sqrt{-1})$
6)	$\eta^8 R(3z)$	$\phi_{K,c}(z)$, c of exponent 9 and conductor $f_c = (\sqrt{-3})$	$\mathbb{Q}(\sqrt{-3})$.

More Ramanujan-type Series for $1/\pi$

J.M. Borwein and P.B. Borwein
Department of Mathematics,
Statistics and Computing Science
Dalhousie University
Halifax, B3H 3J5, Nova Scotia

Abstract: We present various classes of rapidly convergent power series for $1/\pi$. This allows us to give all of Ramanujan's mysterious series for $1/\pi$ and to produce some interesting additional examples. Many of these additional examples add more than 10 or 20 digits accuracy per term.

1. Introduction: In [7, §13] Ramanujan sketches the derivation of 3 remarkable series for $1/\pi$. In §14, with essentially no explanation, he gives 14 more remarkable series. Hardy [3], quoting Mordell, observes that "it is unfortunate that Ramanujan has not developed in detail the corresponding theories." In [1] we constructed seven general classes of hypergeometric-like power series for $1/\pi$. In each case the power is an invariant from elliptic function theory and the coefficients involve similar quantities. In particular, we recovered all of Ramanujan's series. In this note we concentrate on the three forms which prove the most flexible.

ISBN 0-12-058560-X

We begin by listing some additional examples. First,

$$\frac{1}{\pi} = 12 \sum_{n=0}^{\infty} (-1)^n \frac{(6n)!}{(n!)^3 (3n)!} \frac{13591409 + n545140134}{(640320^3)^{n+1/2}},$$

which arises with $N := 163$ in TYPE 3a of the tables of our final section. (This series seems to have been first observed by the Chudnovskys.) Second, with $N := 427$ in TYPE 3c of the tables we have

$$\frac{1}{\pi} = 12 \sum_{n=0}^{\infty} \frac{(-1)^n (6n)!}{(n!)^3 (3n)!} \frac{(A + nB)}{C^{n+1/2}}$$

where

$$A := 212175710912\sqrt{61} + 1657145277365$$

$$B := 13773980892672\sqrt{61} + 107578229802750$$

$$C := [5280\,(236674 + 30303\sqrt{61})]^3 .$$

This series adds roughly twenty-five digits per term, $\sqrt{C}/(12A)$ already agrees with pi to twenty-five places. Surprisingly, one also has

$$\frac{1}{\pi} = 7 \cdot 12 \sum_{n=0}^{\infty} \frac{(-1)^n (6n)!}{(n!)^3 (3n)!} \frac{\overline{A} + n\overline{B}}{\overline{C}^{\,n+1/2}}$$

where $\overline{A}$, $\overline{B}$, and $\overline{C}$ are the conjugate quadratic numbers

$$\overline{A} := 212175710912\sqrt{61} - 1657145277365$$

$$\overline{B} := 13773980892672\sqrt{61} - 107578229802750$$

$$\overline{C} := [5280\,(236674 - 30303\sqrt{61})]^3 .$$

In this case convergence is much slower - less than one digit per term.

The most recent record setting calculations of digits of pi all rely on methods that trace their genesis to related material. Details of the theory and of the calculations of Gosper, Bailey, Tamura and Kanada, and Kanada may be found in [1].

2. **Preliminary Results**: The complete elliptic integrals of the first and second kind may be defined in terms of hypergeometric functions by

$$K(k) := \frac{\pi}{2} \cdot {}_2F_1\left(\frac{1}{2}, \frac{1}{2}; 1; k^2\right), \tag{2.1}$$

and

$$E(k) := \frac{\pi}{2} \cdot {}_2F_1\left(\frac{1}{2}, \frac{-1}{2}; 1; k^2\right), \tag{2.2}$$

for $0 \leqslant k < 1$. The complementary modulus is the quantity

$k' := \sqrt{1-k^2}$ and we write $K'(k) := K(k')$, $E'(k) := E(k)$.

These are related by the differential equation

$$E = k'^2 K + kk'^2 \frac{dK}{dk} \tag{2.3}$$

They are also linked by the beautiful Legendre relation ([1], [11])

$$E'K + K'E - K'K = \pi/2 \tag{2.4}$$

We will use the following invariants employed by Ramanujan [7],

$$G := (2kk')^{-1/12}, \quad g := (2k/k')^{-1/12}$$

and (2.5)

$$2^{1/4} gG = (k^2/2k')^{-1/12}.$$

In Weber's terms [10] $2^{1/4}G = f$, $2^{1/4}g = f_1$. We also need Klein's absolute invariant J which is expressible as

$$J := \frac{(4G^{24}-1)^3}{27G^{24}} = \frac{(4g^{24}+1)^3}{27g^{24}} \tag{2.6}$$

With these invariants one can obtain the following hypergeometric equations

$$\left[\frac{2K}{\pi}(k)\right]^2 = (1+k^2)^{-1}\,{}_3F_2\left(\frac{1}{4},\frac{3}{4},\frac{1}{2};1,1;\left[\frac{g^{12}+g^{-12}}{2}\right]^{-2}\right),$$

$$= (k'^2-k^2)^{-1}\,{}_3F_2\left(\frac{1}{4},\frac{3}{4},\frac{1}{2};1,1;-\left[\frac{G^{12}-G^{-12}}{2}\right]^{-2}\right)$$

and (2.7)

$$\left[\frac{2K}{\pi}(k)\right]^2 = (1-(kk')^2)^{-1/2}\,{}_3F_2\left(\frac{1}{6},\frac{5}{6},\frac{1}{2};1,1;J^{-1}\right).$$

Finally, we will need the <u>rising factorial</u> $(a)_n = a(a+1)(a+2)\cdots(a+n-1)$.

3. Series Identities of Ramanujan-type:

The <u>singular value function</u> may be defined as the solution of

$$\frac{K'}{K}(k(N)) = \sqrt{N} \tag{3.1}$$

for positive real N. This uniquely defines k on $[0,\infty]$ as a decreasing function with $k(0) = \infty$, $k(1) = 1/\sqrt{2}$, $k(\infty) = 0$. Importantly, $k(N)$ is algebraic when N is rational [1]. Some values are given below (§4). Moreover, for some $k = k(N)$ one or more of our invariants becomes very simple. In terms of theta functions, $k(N) = (\theta_2(q)/\theta_3(q))^2$ with $q = e^{-\pi\sqrt{N}}$.

In [1] we introduced the function α (a <u>singular value</u> of <u>the second kind</u>). It connects elliptic integrals of the first and second kinds and is intimately related to Ramanujan's algebraic approximations to pi. It is defined by

$$\alpha(N) = \frac{E'}{K} - \frac{\pi}{4K^2} \qquad (k := k(N)) \tag{3.2}$$

and also is algebraic at rational values with $\alpha(1) = \frac{1}{2}$, $\alpha(\infty) = \frac{1}{\pi}$.

Additionally, α satisfies recursions which allow one to compute it at many values both numerically and explicitly. The simplest recursion is,

$$\alpha(4N) = \frac{4\alpha(N) - 2\sqrt{N}\,k^2(N)}{[1 + k'(N)]^2}, \tag{3.3}$$

and

$$k(4N) = \frac{1 - k'(N)}{1 + k'(N)}. \tag{3.4}$$

This is equivalent to the <u>Gauss-Salamin-Brent iteration</u> for pi. The recursion and its extensions lead to explicit high-order iterations for $1/\pi$ and to the recent record breaking computations of pi, [1]. Values of α are also given below (§4). The construction of α shows that

$$\frac{1}{\pi} = \sqrt{N}\ kk'^2 \frac{4K\dot{K}}{\pi^2} + (\alpha(N) - \sqrt{N}\,k^2)\frac{4K^2}{\pi^2} \qquad (k := k(N)). \tag{3.5}$$

(Here and below the dot signifies differentiation.) This follows from using Legendre's identity (2.4) to write a <u>one-sided Legendre identity</u>

$$\alpha(N) = \pi/(4K^2) - \sqrt{N}(E/K - 1)$$

and then using (2.3) to replace E by the derivative $\dot{K}$. Similarly,

$$\frac{1}{K} = \sqrt{N}\ kk'^2 \frac{4\dot{K}}{\pi} + (\alpha(N) - \sqrt{N}\ k^2)\frac{4K}{\pi} \qquad (k := k(N)). \tag{3.6}$$

Given $\alpha(N)$ and $k(N)$ we can combine (3.5) with (2.7) to produce power series for $1/\pi$ as follows. In each case we have $(\frac{2K}{\pi})^2(k) = m(k)F(\phi(k))$ for algebraic m and ϕ where $F(\phi)$ has a hypergeometric power-series expansion $\sum_{n=0}^{\infty} a_n \phi^n$.

Now

$$\frac{4K\dot{K}}{\pi^2} = \frac{1}{2}\dot{m}F + \frac{1}{2} m\dot{\phi}\,\dot{F}(\phi)$$

and substitution in (3.5) leads to

$$\frac{1}{\pi} = \sum_{n=0}^{\infty} a_n \left[\frac{\sqrt{N}}{2} kk'^2 \dot{m} + (\alpha(N) - \sqrt{N}k^2)m + n\frac{\sqrt{N}}{2} m \frac{\dot{\phi}}{\phi} kk'^2 a\right]\phi^n . \qquad (3.7)$$

Note that, for each rational N, the bracketed term is of the form $A + nB$ with A and B algebraic. We now make explicit these considerations for the three invariants which give the most remarkable and elegant special cases.

1. Series in $x_N := \left[\frac{g_N^{12} + g_N^{-12}}{2}\right]^{-1} = \frac{4k(N)k'^2(N)}{[1+k^2(N)]^2}$: For $N > 2$

$$\frac{1}{\pi} = \sum_{n=0}^{\infty} \frac{\left(\frac{1}{4}\right)_n \left(\frac{2}{4}\right)_n \left(\frac{3}{4}\right)_n}{(n!)^3} d_n(N) x_N^{2n+1} \qquad (3.8)$$

where

$$d_n(N) := \left[\frac{\alpha(N)x_N^{-1}}{1+k^2(N)} - \frac{\sqrt{N}}{4} g_N^{-12}\right] + n\sqrt{N}\left[\frac{g_N^{12} - g_N^{-12}}{2}\right] .$$

2. Series in $y_N := \left[\frac{G_N^{12}-G_N^{-12}}{2}\right]^{-1} = \frac{4k(N)k'(N)}{1-[2k(N)k'(N)]^2}$: For $N \geqslant 4$

$$\frac{1}{\pi} = \sum_{n=0}^{\infty} (-1)^n \frac{\left(\frac{1}{4}\right)_n \left(\frac{2}{4}\right)_n \left(\frac{3}{4}\right)_n}{(n!)^3} \; e_n(N) y_N^{2n+1} \tag{3.9}$$

where

$$e_n(N) := \left[\frac{\alpha(N) y_N^{-1}}{k'^2(N)-k^2(N)} + \frac{\sqrt{N}}{2} k^2(N) G_N^{12}\right] + n\sqrt{N}\left[\frac{G_N^{12}+G_N^{-12}}{2}\right].$$

3. Series in $J_N^{-1} := \frac{27G_N^{24}}{(4G_N^{24}-1)^3} = \frac{27g_N^{24}}{(4g_N^{24}+1)^3}$: For $N > 1$

$$\frac{1}{\pi} = \sum_{n=0}^{\infty} \frac{\left(\frac{1}{6}\right)_n \left(\frac{3}{6}\right)_n \left(\frac{5}{6}\right)_n}{(n!)^3} \; f_n(N) \left(J_N^{-1/2}\right)^{2n+1} \tag{3.10}$$

where

$$f_n(N) := \frac{1}{3\sqrt{3}}\left[\sqrt{N}\sqrt{1-G_N^{-24}} + 2(\alpha(N) - \sqrt{N}\, k^2(N))(4G_N^{24}-1)\right]$$

$$+ n\sqrt{N}\, \frac{2}{3\sqrt{3}}\left[(8G_N^{24}+1)\sqrt{1-G_N^{-24}}\right].$$

There are many equivalent rearrangements of the formulae for $d_n(N)$, $e_n(N)$, $f_n(N)$. (See [1] especially page 186.)

4. Specific Examples: We begin by listing values of $\alpha(N)$ and of $k(N)$ (or equivalently G_N^{-12} or g_N^{-12} whichever is simpler).

N	$2k(N)k'(N) = G_N^{-12}$	$\alpha(N)$
1	1	$1/2$
9	$(2-\sqrt{3})^2$	$(3-3^{3/4}\sqrt{2}(\sqrt{3}-1))/2$
13	$5\sqrt{13}-18$	$(\sqrt{13}-\sqrt{74\sqrt{13}-258})/2$
27	$(2^{1/3}-1)^4/2$	$3(\sqrt{3}+1-2^{4/3})/2$
37	$(\sqrt{37}-6)^3$	$(\sqrt{37}-(171-25\sqrt{37})(\sqrt{37}-6)^{1/2})/2$

N	$2k(N)/k'(N)^2 = g_N^{-12}$	$\alpha(N)$
2	1	$(\sqrt{2}-1)$
10	$(\sqrt{5}-2)^2$	$(7+2\sqrt{5})(\sqrt{10}-3)(\sqrt{2}-1)^2$
18	$(\sqrt{3}-\sqrt{2})^4$	$3(\sqrt{3}+\sqrt{2})^4(\sqrt{6}-1)^2(7\sqrt{2}-5-2\sqrt{6})$
22	$(\sqrt{2}-1)^6$	$(\sqrt{2}+1)^6(33-17\sqrt{2})(3\sqrt{22}-7-5\sqrt{2})$
58	$(\frac{\sqrt{29}-5}{2})^6$	$(\frac{\sqrt{29}+5}{2})^6(99\sqrt{29}-444)(99\sqrt{2}-70-13\sqrt{29})$

Many other values of G_N, g_N may be found in [7], [10] or [1]. Certain values of $k(N)$ are given in [12]. The computation of $k(N)$ is discussed in [1], [8] and [13]. Many values of $\alpha(N)$ are derived in [1]. For $N := 2,3,4,5,7$ they are given in [12]. From information like that in these tables and the formulae given for $1/\pi$, we may explicitly compute all but two of Ramanujan's series. These two which rely on another ${}_3F_2$ are treated in [1].

Ramanujan gives series of form (3.8) for $N := 6, 10, 18, 22, 58$ and of form (3.9) for $N := 5, 9, 13, 25, 37$. He gives series of form (3.10) for $N := 3, 7$. In each case manipulation of the formulae yields the desired result. In fact $\alpha(37)$ and $\alpha(58)$ were calculated by obtaining $d_0(58)$ and $e_0(37)$ to high precision numerically and then solving for α. Given the algebraic nature of α this ultimately suffices to verify the values. In these cases, we have

$$\frac{1}{\pi} = \sum_{n=0}^{\infty} (-1)^n \frac{\left(\frac{1}{4}\right)_n \left(\frac{2}{4}\right)_n \left(\frac{3}{4}\right)_n}{(n!)^3} \left[\frac{1123 + n21460}{4}\right] \left(\frac{1}{882}\right)^{2n+1} \tag{4.1}$$

using (3.9) for $N := 37$; and using (3.8) for $N := 58$

$$\frac{1}{\pi} = \sum_{n=0}^{\infty} \frac{\left(\frac{1}{4}\right)_n \left(\frac{2}{4}\right)_n \left(\frac{3}{4}\right)_n}{(n!)^3} \left[2\sqrt{2}\,(1103 + n26390)\right] \left(\frac{1}{99^2}\right)^{2n+1} \tag{4.2}$$

Series (4.2) is the most rapid and most celebrated of the series given by Ramanujan. It is the series with which Gosper performed his record breaking computation of more than 17,000,000 terms of the continued fraction for π in 1985.

Since $k^2(N)$ behaves like $16e^{-\pi\sqrt{N}}$ [1] it is very easy to estimate the number of digits added in each series. For N at all large, the convergence while linear is most impressive. Not surprisingly, Ramanujan has given most of the special cases of (3.8) and (3.9) for which the power is rational. We add some quadratic examples which come in conjugate pairs from invariants G_N (respectively g_N) corresponding to discriminants with one form per genus for which N is of the form PQ or P/Q (respectively 2PQ and 2P/Q) with P and Q prime. (See [1, page 293].) In these cases the invariant is a product of two algebraic units and so x_N or y_N is a real quadratic irrational. These examples are listed as TYPE 1 and TYPE 2 in the next section.

In a similar fashion we may apply (3.10) for rational or quadratic values of J_N. Ramanujan gives two of the four series for which J_N is rational and positive (N := 3 , 7) and in [1] we produced the two others (N := 2, 4). There are also eight negative rational values of J. In our terms they come from $(\sqrt{N} - i)/2$ for N := 3, 7, 11, 19, 27 ,43, 67, 163. These correspond (27 excepted) to the seven imaginary quadratic fields $Q(\sqrt{-N})$ of class number 1, with N congruent to 3 mod 4. These 7 give rise to the series listed as TYPE 3a. While we stated (3.10) for positive numbers, it continues to hold more generally by analytic continuation - as long as $J < -1$. The real part of the identity gives a series for $1/\pi$; the imaginary part an obscure formula for zero. Note that now the underlying q variable becomes $ie^{-\sqrt{N}\pi/2}$ rather than $e^{-\sqrt{N}\pi}$.

There are also many quadratic values of J both positive and negative. They again give rise to conjugate pairs of series. These are listed as TYPE 3b and TYPE 3c. It should be noted that each case the J value is a perfect cube, while the X and Y values are perfect squares. Granted the knowledge that the quantities A and B corresponding to the conjugate invariants are conjugate, the easiest way to determine their precise values is to compute the underlying q-series expansions from the information in Chapter 5 of [1] and to match off the rational coefficients. This is how the quadratic series were determined. In similar fashion, one can determine the corresponding series for many other values of the invariants: both quadratic and higher order.

Finally we should mention the interesting Log series for pi derived in [5] and [8], and the more abstract approach to Ramanujan's approximations described by the Chudnovskys in their contribution to this volume.

TYPE 1

$$\frac{1}{\pi} = \Delta \sum_{n=0}^{\infty} \frac{\left(\frac{1}{4}\right)_n \left(\frac{2}{4}\right)_n \left(\frac{3}{4}\right)_n}{(n!)^3} \frac{(A + nB)}{X^{2n+1}}$$

Here $\Delta := 1$ if the signs are "+" and $\Delta :=$ (smallest odd prime factor of N) if the signs are "-".

	(Approximate) digits correct per term (+ signs)	(- signs)
$N := 42 = 14 \cdot 3$ $A := 186\sqrt{2} \pm 151\sqrt{3}$ $B := 3780\sqrt{2} \pm 3080\sqrt{3}$ $X := 825 \pm 336\sqrt{6}$	6	<1

$N := 78 := 26\cdot 3$ $A := \sqrt{3}(4302\sqrt{2} \pm 12161/2)$ $B := \sqrt{3}(119340\sqrt{2} \pm 168740)$ $X := 33099 \pm 23400\sqrt{2}$	9	2
$N := 70 = 14\cdot 5$ $A := \sqrt{7}(1356\sqrt{2} \pm 1715/2\sqrt{5})$ $B := \sqrt{7}(35640\sqrt{2} \pm 22540\sqrt{5})$ $X := 15939 \pm 5040\sqrt{10}$	8	$\leqslant 1$
$N := 130 := 26\cdot 5$ $A := \sqrt{2}(117046\sqrt{13} \pm 188730\sqrt{5})$ $B := \sqrt{2}(4192540\sqrt{13} \pm 6760260\sqrt{5})$ $X := 1874961 \pm 232560\sqrt{65}$	12	1
$N := 190 = 38\cdot 5$ $A := \sqrt{19}(11552301/2 \pm 4084354\sqrt{2})$ $B := \sqrt{19}(250129620 \pm 176868340\sqrt{2})$ $X := 79097931 \pm 55930680\sqrt{2}$	15	1

TYPE 2

$$\frac{1}{\pi} = \Delta \sum_{n=0}^{\infty} (-1)^n \frac{\left(\frac{1}{4}\right)_n \left(\frac{2}{4}\right)_n \left(\frac{3}{4}\right)_n}{(n!)^3} \frac{(A + nB)}{Y^{2n+1}}$$

Here $\Delta := 1$ if the signs are "+" and $\Delta :=$ (smallest odd prime factor of N) if the signs are "−".

	(Approximate) digits correct per term	
	(+ signs)	(− signs)
$N := 177 = 59\cdot 3$ $A := 1781017/2\sqrt{177} \pm 47389527/4$ $B := 37219780\sqrt{177} \pm 495176085$ $Y := 21488850\sqrt{3} \pm 4845594\sqrt{59}$	15	4

$N := 253 = 23 \cdot 11$ $A := 212750712\sqrt{11} \pm 2822457127/4$ $B := 10631172240\sqrt{11} \pm 35259609385$ $Y := 2216752650 + 668376072\sqrt{11}$	19	(DIVERGES)

TYPE 3a (J<0, RATIONAL)

$$\frac{1}{\pi} = \frac{1}{\sqrt{-1728\,J}} \sum_{n=0}^{\infty} \frac{\left(\frac{1}{6}\right)_n \left(\frac{3}{6}\right)_n \left(\frac{5}{6}\right)_n}{(n!)^3} \frac{(A + nB)}{J^n}$$

	(Approximate) digits correct per term
$N := 7$ $A := 24$ $B := 189$ $J := -125/64$	$\leqslant 1$
$N := 11$ $A := 60$ $B := 616$ $J := -512/27$	1
$N := 19$ $A := 300$ $B := 4104$ $J := -512$	3
$N := 27$ $A := 1116$ $B := 18216$ $J := -64000/9$	4

N := 43 A := 9468 B := 195048 J := −512000	6
N := 67 A := 122124 B := 3140424 J := −85184000	8
N := 163 A := 163096908 B := 6541681608 J := −151931373056000	15

TYPE 3b (J>0, QUADRATIC)

$$\frac{1}{\pi} = \frac{\Delta}{\sqrt{3J}} \sum_{n=0}^{\infty} \frac{\left(\frac{1}{6}\right)_n \left(\frac{3}{6}\right)_n \left(\frac{5}{6}\right)_n}{(n!)^3} \frac{(A + nB)}{J^n}$$

Here $\Delta := 1$ if the signs are "+" and $\Delta := 2$ if the signs are "−".

	(Approximate) digits correct per term (+ signs)	(− signs)
N := 6 = 3·2 A := $15 \pm 10\sqrt{2}$ B := $228 \pm 156\sqrt{2}$ J := $1399 \pm 988\sqrt{2}$	3	$\leqslant 1$
N := 10 = 5·2 A := $62\sqrt{5} \pm 135$ B := $1224\sqrt{5} \pm 2700$ J := $123175 \pm 55080\sqrt{5}$	5	1

$N := 22 = 11 \cdot 2$	9	3
$A := 16659 \pm 11750\sqrt{2}$		
$B := 490644 \pm 346500\sqrt{2}$		
$J := 1821424375 \pm 1287940500\sqrt{2}$		
$N := 58 = 29 \cdot 2$	17	7
$A := 30282810\sqrt{29} \pm 163073763$		
$B := 1449063000\sqrt{29} \pm 7803343548$		
$J := 17497973317415837 5 \pm 32492920723263000\sqrt{29}$		

TYPE 3c (J<0, QUADRATIC)

$$\frac{1}{\pi} = \frac{\Delta}{2\sqrt{-3J}} \sum_{n=0}^{\infty} \frac{\left[\frac{1}{6}\right]_n \left[\frac{3}{6}\right]_n \left[\frac{5}{6}\right]_n}{(n!)^3} \frac{(A + nB)}{J^n}$$

Here $\Delta := 1$ if the signs are "+" and $\Delta :=$ (smallest prime factor of N) if the signs are "–".

	(Approximate) digits correct per term	
	(+ signs)	(– signs)
$N := 235 = 47 \cdot 5$	17	1
$A := 380527125 \pm 170176896\sqrt{5}$		
$B := 18326073150 \pm 8195668992\sqrt{5}$		
$J := -(238187910720320000 \pm 106520871957857280\sqrt{5})$		
$N := 267 := 89 \cdot 3$	19	4
$A := 197238000\sqrt{89} \pm 1860739157$		
$B := 10125024000\sqrt{89} \pm 95519278302$		
$J := -(569533907814800000 0 \pm 603704734875424000\sqrt{89})$		
$N := 427 = 61 \cdot 7$	25	1
$A := 212175710912\sqrt{61} \pm 1657145277365$		
$B := 13773980892672\sqrt{61} \pm 107578229802750$		
$J := -(45172035626515578471 68000 \pm 5783686501836674471 04000\sqrt{61})$		

References

[1] J.M. Borwein and P.B. Borwein, 'Pi and the AGM: A Study in Analytic Number Theory and Computational Complexity', Wiley, 1987.

[2] A. Erdelyi et al., 'Higher Transcendental Functions', McGraw-Hill, 1953.

[3] G.H. Hardy, 'Ramanujan's Collected Papers', Chelsea Publishing, 1962.

[4] W. Magnus, 'Formulas and Theorems for the Special Functions of Mathematical Physics', Springer-Verlag, 1966.

[5] M. Newman and D. Shanks, 'On a sequence arising in series for π', Math. of Computation 42 (1984), 199-217.

[6] E.D. Rainville, 'Special functions', McMillan New York, 1960.

[7] S. Ramanujan, 'Modular equations and approximations to π', Quart J. Math. Oxford, 45 (1914), 350-372.

[8] D. Shanks, 'Dihedral quartic approximations and series for π', J. Number Theory, 14 (1982), 397-423.

[9] L.J. Slater, 'Generalized hypergeometric functions', Cambridge University Press, 1966.

[10] H. Weber, 'Lehrbuch der Algebra', vol. III, Brauschweig, 1908.

[11] E.T. Whittaker and G.N. Watson, 'Modern Analysis', 4th ed., Cambridge University Press, 1927.

[12] I.J. Zucker, 'The summation of series of hyperbolic functions', SIAM J. Math. Anal., 10 (1979), 192-206.

[13] I.J. Zucker, 'The evaluation in terms of Γ-functions of the periods of elliptic curves admitting complex multiplication', Proc. Camb. Phil. Soc., 82 (1977), 111-118.

Approximations and complex multiplication according to Ramanujan

by

D.V. Chudnovsky*), G.V. Chudnovsky*)

Department of Mathematics
Columbia University
New York, NY 10027

*)This work was supported in part by the N.S.F., U.S. Air Force and O.C.R.E.A.E. program.

ISBN 0-12-058560-X

Introduction

This talk revolves around two focuses: complex multiplications (for elliptic curves and Abelian varieties) in connection with algebraic period relations, and (diophantine) approximations to numbers related to these periods. Our starting point is Ramanujan's works [1], [2] on approximations to π via the theory of modular and hypergeometric functions. We describe in chapter 1 Ramanujan's original quadratic period--quasiperiod relations for elliptic curves with complex multiplication and their applications to representations of fractions of π and other logarithms in terms of rapidly convergent nearly integral (hypergeometric) series. These representations serve as a basis of our investigation of diophantine approximations to π and other related numbers. In Chapter 2 we look at period relations for arbitrary CM-varieties following Shimura and Deligne. Our main interest lies with modular (Shimura) curves arising from arithmetic Fuchsian groups acting on H. From these we choose arithmetic triangular groups, where period relations can be expressed in the form of hypergeometric function identities. Particular attention is devoted to two (commensurable) triangle groups, (0,3;2,6,6) and (0,3;2,4,6), arising from the quaternion algebra over $\mathbb{Q}$ with the discriminant $D = 2\cdot 3$. We also touch upon the algebraic independence problem for periods and quasiperiods of general CM-varieties and particularly CM-curves associated with the triangle groups (hypergeometric curves as we call them). The diophantine approximation problem for numbers connected with periods, particularly for multiples of π, is analyzed using Padé approximations to power series representing these numbers. We give a brief review of Padé approximations, their effective construction, and problems of analytic and arithmetic (p-adic) convergence of Padé approximants. Padé approximations to nearly integral power series (G-functions) are used in connection with Ramanujan-like representations of $1/\pi$ and other similar period constants. We discuss measures of irrationality for algebraic multiples of π and related numbers that follow from Padé approximation methods.

The problem of uniformization by nonarithmetic subgroups is discussed in connection with the Whittaker conjecture [11] on an explicit expression for accessory parameters in the (Schottkey-type) uniformization of hyperelliptic Riemann surfaces of genus $g \geq 2$ by Fuchsian groups. On the basis of numerical computations of monodromy groups of linear differential equations, we concluded that the conjecture [11] is generically incorrect. Moreover, it appears that accessory parameters in the uniformization problem of Riemann surfaces defined over $\bar{\mathbb{Q}}$ are nonalgebraic with the exception of uniformization by arithmetic subgroups and of cases when the differential equations are reduced to hypergeometric ones (the monodromy group is connected to one of the triangle groups). We briefly describe numerical and theoretical results on the transcendence of elements of the monodromy groups of linear differential equations over $\bar{\mathbb{Q}}(x)$.

We conclude the paper with a discussion of numerical approximations to solutions of algebraic and differential equations. We present generalizations of our previous results [12] on the complexity of approximations to solutions of linear differential equations. We describe a new, "bit-burst" method of evaluation of solutions of linear differential equations everywhere on their Riemann surface. In the worst case, an evaluation with n bits of precision at an n-bit point requires $O(M_{bit}(n)\log^3 n)$ boolean (bit) operations, where $M_{bit}(n)$ is the boolean complexity of an n-bit multiplication. For functions satisfying additional arithmetic conditions (e.g. E-functions and G-functions) the factor $\log^3 n$ could be further decreased to $\log^2 n$ or, even, $\log n$. We also describe the natural parallelizations of the presented algorithms that are well suited for practical implementation.

We want to thank the organizers of the Ramanujan conference and, particularly, B. Berndt and R. Askey. We want to thank the IBM Computer Algebra Group for their help and access to the SCRATCHPAD System. We thank SYMBOLICS Corporation for the use of their workstation 3645.

1. Complex multiplications and Ramanujan's period relations

Most of the material in this talk evolves around mathematics closely associated with one of the earliest Ramanujan papers "Modular equations and approximations to π" [1] published in 1914, which according to Hardy [2] "is mainly Indian work, done before he came to England." In that or another way the same kind of mathematics appears in later Ramanujan research, including his notebooks. Hardy interpreted many of Ramanujan's results and identities as connected mainly with "complex multiplication", and Ramanujan's interest in resolving modular equations in explicit radicals was later picked up in Watson's outstanding series [3] of "Singular Moduli" papers. Singular moduli themselves, and general modular equations relating automorphic functions with respect to congruence subgroup of a full modular group are traditional subjects of late $\overline{\text{XIX}}$ century mathematics, whose importance is clearly realized in modern number theory and algebraic geometry, particularly in diophantine geometry in connection with arithmetic theory of elliptic curves and rational points on them. Also modular equations turned up as a convenient tool of fast operational complexity algorithms of computation of π and of values of elementary functions (see corresponding chapters in Borweins' book [5]).

Instead of complex multiplication as merely a subject of "singular moduli" of elliptic functions we will touch upon the complex multiplication in a slightly more general context: from the point of view of nontrivial endomorphisms of certain classes of Jacobians of particular algebraic curves. (We are not going to discuss a variety of complex "complex multiplication" subjects on L-functions and Abelian varieties, though we'll have to borrow particular consequences of vast theories developed in general by Shimura, Deligne and others.)

The choice of curves is clearly determined by Ramanujan's interest: these are curves with 4 critical points, whose Abelian periods are expressed via hypergeometric integrals (for simplicity one can call those curves hypergeometric ones), see [10].

Transforming one of the 4 critical points into infinity and normalizing, one recovers the Gauss hypergeometric function integrals representative of these periods. We display these well-known expressions:

$$F(a,b;c;z) = \frac{\Gamma(c)}{\Gamma(b)\Gamma(c-b)} \cdot \int_0^1 x^{b-1}(1-x)^{c-b-1}(1-xz)^{-a}dx,$$

$(c > b > 0)$, with the expansion near $z = 0$:

$$F(a,b;c;z) = 1 + \frac{a\cdot b}{c\cdot 1} \cdot z + \frac{a(a+1)\cdot b(b+1)}{c\cdot(c+1)\cdot 1\cdot 2} \cdot z^2 + \ldots .$$

Our primary interest in complex multiplication is not arithmetical but transcendental; rather than to study the number-theoretical functions associated with complex multiplication invariants, we want to know the basic facts about the values of these invariants: are these numbers transcendental (over $\mathbb{Z}$)? If algebraic relations do exist, over what fields of definition do they exist? These basic questions of transcendence, algebraic independence and linear independence are the subject of diophantine approximations. With these questions come their qualitative counterparts: when numbers are irrational (transcendental), how well are they approximated by rationals? Can these best approximations be determined effectively and/or explicitly? (Usually one asks in this context: can one determine the continued fraction expansion of the number?)

The class of numbers we are interested in is generated over $\bar{\mathbb{Q}}$ by periods and quasiperiods of Abelian varieties, i.e. by integrals

$$\int_\gamma \omega \quad \text{and} \quad \int_\gamma \eta$$

for differentials ω and η of the first and the second kind, respectively, from $H^1_{DR}(A)$, and $\gamma \in H_1(A,\mathbb{Z})$, for an Abelian variety A defined over $\bar{\mathbb{Q}}$.

In particular, when A is a Jacobian $J(\Gamma)$ of a non-singular curve Γ over $\bar{\mathbb{Q}}$, we are looking at periods and quasiperiods forming the full Riemann matrix of Γ-total of $2g \times 2g$ elements, where g denotes the genus of Γ.

In this context, complex multiplications, understood as

nontrivial endomorphisms of A, are usually expressed as non-trivial algebraic relations among the elements of Riemann's original $2g \times g$ pure period matrix π of A. These "purely period relations" are well known, and are mainly algebraic in nature, and in one-dimensional case ($g = 1$), give pairs of periods whose ratio is a "singular module". An interesting thing discovered by Ramanujan in this classical (even in his time) field was the existence of new quasiperiods relations. In the Weierstrass-like notation, commonly accepted nowdays, period and quasiperiod relations in the elliptic curve case can be described as follows.

One starts with an elliptic curve over $\bar{\mathbb{Q}}$ with a Weierstrass equation $y^2 = 4x^3 - g_2x - g_3$ ($g_2, g_3 \in \bar{\mathbb{Q}}$), having the fundamental periods ω_1, ω_2 (with $\mathrm{Im}\frac{\omega_2}{\omega_1} > 0$) and the corresponding quasi-periods η_1, η_2. The only relation between ω_i and η_j that always holds is the Legendre identity:

$$\eta_1\omega_2 - \eta_2\omega_1 = 2\pi i.$$

Thus π belongs to the field generated by periods and quasiperiods over $\bar{\mathbb{Q}}$. In the complex multiplication case $\tau = \frac{\omega_2}{\omega_1}$ is an imaginary quadratic number.

Whenever $\tau \in \mathbb{Q}(\sqrt{-d})$ for $d > 0$, invariants g_2 and g_3 can be chosen from the Hilbert class field of $\mathbb{Q}(\sqrt{-d})$, and this field is the minimal extension with this property.

A priori complex multiplication means only a single relation between ω_i.

It seems that until Ramanujan's paper nobody explicitly stated the existence of the second relation between periods and quasiperiods. This relation is the following one:

Whenever τ is a quadratic number: $A\tau^2 + B\tau + C = 0$, the four numbers: $\omega_1, \omega_2, \eta_1, \eta_2$ are linearly dependent over $\bar{\mathbb{Q}}$ only on two of them.

Explicitly:

$$\begin{aligned} &\omega_2 = \tau\omega_1, \\ &A\tau\eta_2 - C\eta_1 + \alpha\omega_1 = 0 \end{aligned} \tag{1.1}$$

for $\alpha \in \bar{\mathbb{Q}}$ $(\alpha \in \mathbb{Q}(\tau, g_2, g_3))$.

The relations (1.1) are not entirely original; Legendre's investigation of the lemmiscate case provides with (1.1) in two cases, where τ is equivalent to i or to ρ under $SL_2(\mathbb{Z})$; moreover, these cases were clearly known to Euler, who evaluated the appropriate complete elliptic integrals. However, those two particular cases are "wrong ones": in these cases the importance of the relation (1.1) is lost because $\alpha = 0$, and it is hard to understand the need for its appearance. In a few other special singular moduli cases, (1.1) appears in the classical literature, see [4].

Of course, Ramanujan did not use the Weierstrass equations and preferred the Legendre ones, where one can see the hypergeometric functions instantly.

In order to pass to Legendre notations [5], one puts $4x^3 - g_2x - g_3 = 4(x-e_1)(x-e_2)(x-e_3)$, and looks at the modular function

$$k^2 = \frac{e_2 - e_3}{e_1 - e_3}$$

(an automorphic function $k^2 = k^2(\tau)$ with respect to the principal congruence subgroup $\Gamma(2)$ of $\Gamma(1) = SL_2(\mathbb{Z})$ in the variable τ in $H = \{\tilde{z}: \operatorname{Im} \tilde{z} > 0\}$). Then the periods and quasiperiods are expressed through the complete elliptic integrals of the first and second kind:

$$K(k) = \frac{\pi}{2}\cdot F(\frac{1}{2},\frac{1}{2};1;k^2),$$

$$E(k) = \frac{\pi}{2}\cdot F(-\frac{1}{2},\frac{1}{2};1;k^2).$$

We also look at $K(k')$, $E(k')$ for $k'^2 = 1 - k^2$; then ω_1, η_1 are expressed in terms of $K = K(k)$, $E = E(k\ )$, while ω_2, η_2 are expressed in terms of iK' and iE':

$$\omega_1 = \frac{K}{\sqrt{e_1 - e_3}}, \quad \omega_2 = \frac{iK'}{\sqrt{e_1 - e_3}};$$

$$\eta_1 = \sqrt{e_1 - e_3}\cdot E - e_1\omega_1, \quad \eta_2 = -\sqrt{e_1 - e_3}\ iE' - e_3\omega_2.$$

Invariant α in (1.1)--a nontrivial part of the Ramanujan quasiperiod relation--is easily recognized as one of the simplest values of "nonholomorphic Eisenstein series". Weil's treatise [6] creates a clear impression that this quantity and its algebraicity had been known to Kronecker (or even Eisenstein). It seems to us that though similar and more general functions were carefully examined, this particular connection had been reconstructed by Weil, and cannot be easily separated from his own work on period relations. The "nonholomorphic" Eisenstein series are too important to be ignored.

The usual Eisenstein series associated with the lattice $\mathcal{L}$ of periods: $\mathcal{L} = \mathbf{Z}\omega_1 \oplus \mathbf{Z}\omega_2$ are

$$G_k(\omega_1,\omega_2) = \sum_{\substack{\omega\in\mathcal{L}\\ \omega\neq 0}} \omega^{-k} \quad \text{for } k = 4,6,\ldots .$$

The corresponding normalized inhomogeneous series $E_k(\tau)$ are defined as

$$G_k(\omega_1,\omega_2) = \left(\frac{2\pi i}{\omega_2}\right)^k \cdot \frac{-B_k}{k!} \cdot E_k(\tau),$$

or

$$E_k(\tau) = 1 - \frac{2k}{B_k} \cdot \sum_{n=1}^{\infty} \sigma_{k-1}(n) \cdot q^n$$

for $\sigma_{k-1}(n) = \Sigma_{d|n} d^{k-1}$, and $q = e^{2\pi i\tau}$.

These q-series were subject of a variety of Ramanujan's studies [1-2] with his preferred notations a P,Q,R for $E_k(\tau)$ with $k = 2,4,6$, respectively.

For $k = 2$ the proper definition of $G_k(\omega_1,\omega_2)$ is a non-holomorphic one arising from

$$H(s,z) = \sum_{\omega\in\mathcal{L}} (\bar{z}+\bar{\omega})\,|z+\omega|^{-2s}$$

as:

$$G_2(\omega_1,\omega_2) = \lim_{s\to\infty^+} \sum_{\omega\in\mathcal{L}}{}^{*} \omega^{-2} \cdot |\omega|^{-2s}.$$

In the $E_k(\tau)$ notations, the quasiperiod relation is expressed by means of the function

$$s_2(\tau) \stackrel{\text{def}}{=} \frac{E_4(\tau)}{E_6(\tau)} \cdot \left(E_2(\tau) - \frac{3}{\pi \operatorname{Im}(\tau)}\right), \tag{1.2}$$

which is invariant under the action of $\Gamma(1)$ but nonholomorphic. It is this object that was studied by Ramanujan in connection with α in (1.1). Ramanujan actually proved in [1] that this function admits algebraic values whenever τ is imaginary quadratic. Moreover, Ramanujan [1] presented a variety of algebraic expressions for this function, differentiating modular equations.

His work, or Weil's, shows that the function in (1.2) has values from the Hilbert class field $\mathbb{Q}(\tau, j(\tau))$ of $\mathbb{Q}(\tau)$ for quadratic τ. The relation of (1.2) to α is simple: for $\beta = s_2(\tau)$ from (1.2), $\alpha = (B + 2A\tau)\beta \cdot g_3/g_2$.

Amazingly, Mordell in his notes [1] on Ramanujan paper missed the true importance of (1.1) or (1.2), stating merely "... Ramanujan's method of obtaining purely algebraical approximations appears to be new." These relations were rediscovered in the 70's (among the rediscovers was Siegel [7]), see particularly [9], and stimulated search for multidimensional generalizations of the period relations promoted by Weil [8]. We'll talk about generalizations of elliptic period relations later, but meanwhile let us look on relations (1.1) once more. One can combine (1.1) with the Legendre relation to arrive to a phenomenally looking "quadratic relation" derived by Ramanujan, that expresses π in terms of squares of ω_1 and η_1 only (no ω_2 and η_2!) All this is interesting, as an algebraic identity, but Ramanujan transforms these quadratic relations into rapidly convergent generalized hypergeometric representation of simple algebraic multiples of $1/\pi$. To do this he needed not only modular functions but also hypergeometric function identities.

We reproduce first Ramanujan's own favorite [1], which was used by Gosper in 1985 in his $17.5 \cdot 10^6$ decimal digit computation of π:

$$\frac{9801}{2\sqrt{2}\pi} = \sum_{n=0}^{\infty} \{1103 + 26390n\} \frac{(4n)!}{n!^4 \cdot (4 \cdot 99)^{4n}} \qquad (44).$$

(Numeration here is temporarily borrowed from [1].)

The reason for this pretty representation of $1/\pi$ lies in the representation of $(K(k)/\pi)^2$ as a ${}_3F_2$-hypergeometric function. Apparently there are four classes of such representations all of which were determined by Ramanujan: these are <u>four</u> distinct classes of ${}_3F_2$-representation of $1/\pi$, all based on special cases of Clausen identity (and all presented by Ramanujan [1]):

$$F(a,b;a+b+\tfrac{1}{2};z)^2 = {}_3F_2\left(\begin{matrix}2a,a+b,2b \\ a+b+\frac{1}{2},2a+2b\end{matrix}\Big| z\right). \qquad (1.3)$$

Unfortunately, the Clausen identity is a unique one--no other nontrivial relation between parameters makes a product of hypergeometric functions a generalized hypergeometric function.

We display the basis for the Ramanujan's series representation for $1/\pi$. We'll discuss them later in connection with arithmetic triangle groups. Meanwhile, what is good in these identities for diophantine approximations? First of all, Ramanujan approximations to π are indeed remarkably fast numerical schemes of evaluation of π. Unlike some other numerical schemes these are series schemes, that can be accelerated into Padé approximation schemes. These Padé approximations schemes are better numerically, but more important, they are nontrivial arithmetically good rational approximations to algebraic multiples of π, that provide nontrivial measures of diophantine approximations.

(Deviating momentarily, we want to compare Padé approximations vs. power series approximations in numerical evaluation of functions and constants. Remarkably, asymptotically there is no significant difference between Boolean complexities of evaluation of Padé approximations to solutions of linear differential equations and of power series approximations within a given precision. Unfortunately, asymptotically there is no gain in the degree of approximations either; moreover there is a significant difference in storage requirements. Padé approximations require more storage. Even in cases when explicit Padé approximations are known, gains of using them can be visible only in about hundreds of digits of precision; not below or above. That is why unless special circumstances call for (like uniform approximations with a minimal storage in ordinary precision range), Padé approximations and continued fraction expansion techniques should not be used for numerical evaluation.

However, in diophantine approximations we have no choice. Only Padé approximations and a vast army of their generalizations are capable of approximating functions and constants and tell something of their arithmetic nature, of their irrationalities and transcendences, measures of approximation, etc.).

All Ramanujan's quadratic period relations (four types) can be deduced from one series by modular transformations, and we choose the series as the one associated with the modular invariant $J = J(\tau)$. In the place of Ramanujan's nonholomorphic function we take, as above in (1.2):

$$s_2(\tau) = \frac{E_4(\tau)}{E_6(\tau)}\left(E_2(\tau) - \frac{3}{\pi \mathrm{Im}(\tau)}\right).$$

Then the Clausen identity gives the following ${}_3F_2$-representation for an algebraic multiple of $1/\pi$:

$$\sum_{n=0}^{\infty} \{\frac{1}{6}(1-s_2(\tau))+n\}\cdot\frac{(6n)!}{(3n)!n!^3}\cdot\frac{1}{J(\tau)^n} = \frac{(-J(\tau))^{1/2}}{\pi}\cdot\frac{1}{(d(1728-J(\tau)))^{1/2}}. \tag{1.4}$$

Here if $\tau = (1+\sqrt{-d})/2$. If $h(-d) = 1$ the second factor in the right hand side is a rational number. The largest one class discriminat $-d = -163$ gives the most rapidly convergent series (though coefficients are slightly strange):

$$\sum_{n=0}^{\infty} \{c_1+n\}\cdot\frac{(6n)!}{(3n)!n!^3}\,\frac{(-1)^n}{(640{,}320)^n} = \frac{(640{,}320)^{3/2}}{163\cdot 8\cdot 27\cdot 7\cdot 11\cdot 19\cdot 127}\cdot\frac{1}{\pi}. \tag{1.5}$$

Here

$$c_1 = \frac{13,591,409}{163\cdot 2\cdot 9\cdot 7\cdot 11\cdot 19\cdot 127}$$

(and, of course, $J(\frac{1+\sqrt{-163}}{2}) = -(640,320)^3$).

Ramanujan [1] provides instead of this a variety of other formulas connected mainly with the three other triangle groups commensurable with $\Gamma(1)$.

Four classes of ${}_3F_2$ representations of algebraic multiples of $1/\pi$ correspond to four ${}_3F_2$ hypergeometric functions (that are squares of ${}_2F_1$ representations of complete elliptic integrals via the Clausen identity). These are

$$ {}_3F_2\left(\begin{matrix}1/2, & 1/6, & 5/6\\ 1, & 1\end{matrix}\Big| x\right) = \sum_{n=0}^{\infty} \frac{(6n)!}{(3n)!n!^3}\left(\frac{x}{12^3}\right)^n \quad (1.6)$$

$$ {}_3F_2\left(\begin{matrix}1/4, & 3/4, & 1/2\\ 1, & 1\end{matrix}\Big| x\right) = \sum_{n=0}^{\infty} \frac{(4n)!}{n!^4}\left(\frac{x}{4^4}\right)^n \quad (1.7)$$

$$ {}_3F_2\left(\begin{matrix}1/2, & 1/2, & 1/2\\ 1, & 1\end{matrix}\Big| x\right) = \sum_{n=0}^{\infty} \frac{(2n)!^3}{n!^6}\left(\frac{x}{2^6}\right)^n \quad (1.8)$$

$$ {}_3F_2\left(\begin{matrix}1/3, & 2/3, & 1/2\\ 1, & 1\end{matrix}\Big| x\right) = \sum_{n=0}^{\infty} \frac{(3n)!}{n!^3}\cdot\frac{(2n)!}{n!^2}\left(\frac{x}{3^3\cdot 2^2}\right)^n. \quad (1.9)$$

The first function is the one arising in (1.4) with $x = 12^3/J(\tau)$. Other three functions correspond to modular transformations of $J(\tau)$. This means that appropriate $x = x(\tau)$ is a modular function of higher level (e.g. in (1.8), $x = 4k^2(1-k^2)$ for $k^2 = k^2(\tau)$), and series (1.7)-(1.9) for the same τ have slower convergence rates than the series in (1.6).

Representations similar to (1.5) can be derived for any of the series (1.6)-(1.9) for any singular moduli $\tau \in \mathbb{Q}(\sqrt{-d})$

and for any class number h(-d), thus extending Ramanujan list [1] ad infinum. There is a simple recipe to generate these new identities, instead of elaborate procedure proposed in [1] (see also [5]) based on differentiating of modular equations. To derive these identities one needs the explicit expressions of $x_j = x(\tau_j)$ with the representatives τ_j in H of algebraically conjugate values of automorphic function $x = x(\tau)$ for $\tau \in \mathbb{Q}(\sqrt{-d})$ (say $\tau = \sqrt{-d}$ or $\tau = \frac{1+\sqrt{-d}}{2}$). E.g. for $x(\tau) = 12^3/J(\tau)$, τ_j: $j = 1,\ldots,h(-d)$ corresponds to the class number of $\mathbb{Q}(\sqrt{-d})$. The necessary values of $s_2(\tau_j)$ are easy to compute from q-series representation of $E_k(\tau)$, if to use the formula (1.2). These computations can be carried out in bounded precision, because, as we know, $s_2(\tau_j)$ lies in the Hilbert class field of $\mathbb{Q}(\sqrt{-d})$ and because, whenever $J(\tau_j)$ is algebraically conjugate to $J(\tau_i)$, numbers $s_2(\tau_j)$ and $s_2(\tau_i)$ are also algebraically conjugate. This allows us to express $s_2(\tau)$ in terms of $J(\tau)$ and $\sqrt{-d}$ explicitly using only finite precision approximations to all $s_2(\tau_j)$. This way one obtains rapidly convergent ${}_3F_2$ representations of algebraic multiples of π by nearly integral power series. When $h(-d) > 1$, these series contain nonrational numbers, making the series (1.5) the fastest convergent series representing a multiple of $1/\pi$, and having rational number entries only.

Even before Ramanujan's remarkable approximations to π, singular moduli evaluations were used to approximate multiples of π by logarithms of algebraic numbers (usually the values of modular invariants). One of the first series of such approximations belongs to Hermite [13]. Of course, by now it is reproduced in hundreds of papers and we have to give a customary example. One is looking here at the expansion of the modular invariant near infinity:

$$J(\tau) = q^{-1} + 744 + 196884q + 21493760q^2 + \ldots$$

for $q = e^{2\pi i\tau}$. The elementary theory of complex multiplication shows that for $\tau = (1+\sqrt{-d})/2$, $q^{-1} = e^{-\pi\sqrt{d}}$ is very close to an algebraic integer $J(\tau)$ of degree $h(-d)$. Usual examples (see description in [14]) involve the largest one class discriminant -163, $d = 163$, when:

$$e^{\pi\sqrt{163}} = -262537412640768743.9999999999992\ldots .$$

There is a variety of these and similar approximations of π by logarithms of other classical automorphic functions. One of the most popular, studied by Shanks et. al. [15], has a simple q-expansion:

For $f = f_1(\sqrt{-d})^{-24} = (k/4k'^2)^2$ at $\tau = \sqrt{-d}$,

$$\log f + \sqrt{d}\cdot\pi = 24 \sum_{k=1}^{\infty} \frac{(-1)^{k+1}}{k} q^k(1-q^k)^{-1}.$$

It is also known that the right side can be expanded in powers of f:

$$\log f + \sqrt{d}\cdot\pi = \sum_{n=1}^{\infty} (-1)^{n-1} \frac{a_n}{n}\cdot f^n.$$

Here a_n are integers. Shanks [15] looks at specialization of this formula for -d with class groups of special structure for relatively large d. These approximations are not technically approximations to π, but rather to a linear form in π and in another logarithm. All of them are natural consequences of Schwarz theory and the representation of the function inverse to the automorphic one (say $J(\tau)$) as a ratio of two solutions of a hypergeometric equation. One such formula is

$$\pi i\cdot\tau = \ell n(k^2) - \ell n(16) + \frac{G(\frac{1}{2},\frac{1}{2};1;k^2)}{F(\frac{1}{2},\frac{1}{2};1;k^2)}, \tag{1.10}$$

and another (our favorite) is Fricke's [16]

$$2\pi i\cdot\tau = \ell n\ J + \frac{G(\frac{1}{12},\frac{5}{12};1;\frac{12^3}{J})}{F(\frac{1}{12},\frac{5}{12};1;\frac{12^3}{J})}. \tag{1.11}$$

Here $G(a,b;c;x) = \Sigma_{n=0}^{\infty} \frac{(a)_n(b)_n}{(c)_n n!}\cdot\{\Sigma_{j=0}^{n-1}(\frac{1}{a+j} + \frac{1}{b+j} - \frac{2}{c+j})\}$ is the hypergeometric function (of the second kind) in the exceptional case, when there are logarithmic terms.

Perhaps the most popular approximations to linear forms in π and in another logarithm are associated with Stark-Baker solution to one-class and two-class problems (cf. [17]). Stark's approach [18] is based on Kronecker's limit formula, and in a way, similar to approximations given above, one represents

$$L(1,\chi)\cdot L(1,\chi\chi') - \frac{\pi^2}{6}\prod_{p|k}(1-\frac{1}{p^2})\Sigma_f \frac{\chi(a)}{a}$$

for $\chi(\cdot) = (\frac{k}{\cdot})$, $\chi'(\cdot) = (\frac{-d}{\cdot})$, $k > 0$ as a rapidly convergent

$q^{1/k}$-series (here $f = ax^2 + bxy + cy^2$ runs through a complete set of unequivalent quadratic forms with the discriminant $-d$). Using Dirichlet's class number formula one obtains an exceptional approximation (as above) to the linear form in two logarithms:

$$|h(-kd)\cdot\log \varepsilon_{\sqrt{k}} - q\pi\sqrt{d}| < e^{-\pi O(\sqrt{d}/k)}$$

for an arbitrary fundamental unit $\varepsilon_{\sqrt{k}}$ of $\mathbb{Q}(\sqrt{k})$ and for one-class discriminant $-d$. These remarkable linear forms were generalized by Stark to three-term linear forms in the class number two case.

(While these unusually good approximations can be used in the class number problem--approximations are so good that they are impossible for large d--these linear forms cannot be used for the analysis of arithmetic properties of the individual logarithms, like π, entering the linear form. Moreover, as the class number grows, the number of the terms in the linear form grows.)

Important developments initiated by Ramanujan in his truly algebraic approximations to $1/\pi$ can be extended to the analysis of linear forms in logarithms presented above. In fact, each term in these linear forms can be separately represented by a rapidly convergent series in $1/J$ with nearly integral coefficients.

For this one takes an automorphic function $\varphi(\tau)$ with respect to one of the congruence subgroups of $\Gamma(1)$ and expand functions like $F(\frac{1}{12},\frac{5}{12};1;12^3/J)$, $G(\frac{1}{12},\frac{5}{12};1,;12^3/J)$ in powers of $\varphi(\tau)$ instead of $J(\tau)$. Whenever $\varphi(\tau)$ is automorphic with respect to a classical triangle group, we arrive to the corresponding usual hypergeometric functions.

Other logarithms, like π, can be represented as values of convergent series satisfying Fuchsian linear differential equations. This is particularly clear for log $\epsilon_{\sqrt{k}}$ of a fundamental unit $\epsilon_{\sqrt{k}}$ of a real quadratic field $\mathbb{Q}(\sqrt{k})$. To represent this number as a convergent series (in, say, $1/J(\tau)$) one uses Kronecker's limit formula expressing this logarithm log $\epsilon_{\sqrt{k}}$ in terms of products of values of Dedekind's Δ-function ("Jugandtraum", see [6]). Such an expression of log $\epsilon_{\sqrt{k}}$ in terms of power series in $1/J(\tau)$ for $\tau = (1+\sqrt{-d})/2$ for any $d \equiv 3(8)$, depends, unfortunately, on k, because k is related to the level of the appropriate modular form $\varphi = \varphi_k(\tau)$.

For $k = 5$ Siegel [19] made an explicit computation that expresses $J(\tau)$ in terms of the resolvent $\varphi_5(\tau)$ of 5-th degree modular equation known from the classical theory of 5-th degree equations. His relations [19] were:

$$(\varphi-\varepsilon^3)((\varphi-\varepsilon)(\varphi^2+\varepsilon^{-1}\varphi+\varepsilon^{-2}))^3 + (\varphi/\sqrt{5})^5 J = 0$$

and

$$\varphi(\tau)(= \varphi_5(\tau)) = \varepsilon^{h(-5p)/2}$$

for $\tau = (1+\sqrt{-p})/2$ and $\varepsilon = \varepsilon_{\sqrt{5}}$. Here one has $p \equiv 3(5)$; if $p \equiv 2(5)$ and replaces ε by ε^{-1} in the expression of $J = J(\tau)$.

This, in combination with Ramanujan's approximation to π, allows one to express log ϵ (its multiple) as a convergent series in $1/J$ (or in $1/\omega$).

2. Period relations for Abelian varieties with complex multiplication.

The most general approach to period relations emerged in works of Shimura [20-21], Deligne [22-23] and others after extensive work in the 60's and 70's by Shimura, mainly on algebraic values of automorphic forms of $\mathbb{Q}$-rational reductive algebraic groups G (see references in [24]). In this work, with many important special examples treated by Siegel and Weil (see [8]), period relations are constructed for CM-points in bounded symmetric domains, and then values of automorphic forms at CM-points are expressed in terms of these periods. Among values of such automorphic forms are values of L-functions corresponding to Grossencharacters at integral points and values of various Eisenstein series. To describe period relations in invariant form we use the language of CM-types of Shimura-Taniyama [25].

A totally imaginary quadratic extension K of a totally real algebraic number field is called a CM-field. We look at $\mathbb{Z}$-module generated by formal sums of σ_i for embeddings σ_i of K into $\mathbb{C}$. An Abelian variety A defined over $\bar{\mathbb{Q}}$ is said to have a CM-type (K,Φ) if

$$\dim(A) = g, \quad [K:\mathbb{Q}] = 2g, \text{ there exist an injection } i: K \to \mathrm{End}(A) \otimes \mathbb{Q} \tag{2.1}$$

(i.e. A is a CM-variety), and

$$\Phi = \sum_{i=1}^{n} \sigma_i, \tag{2.2}$$

where σ_i runs through a set of representatives of pairs of complex conjugate embeddings of K into $\mathbb{C}$, and for j = 1,.. j = 1,...,n there exists a $\bar{\mathbb{Q}}$-rational holomorphic 1-form $\omega_j \neq 0$ on A such that

$$\omega_j \circ i(a) = a^{\sigma_j} \omega_j \text{ for all } a \in K$$

(with $i(a) \in \mathrm{End}(A)$).

Shimura introduces then "CM-periods" $p(\sigma_j,\Phi)$ depending on K,Φ, σ_j such that

$$\frac{\int_\gamma \omega_j}{\pi \cdot p(\sigma_j,\Phi)} \in \bar{\mathbb{Q}}$$

for all 1-cycles γ on A ($\gamma \in H_1(A,\mathbb{Z})$).

Shimura and Deligne [20-23] have shown how all periods and quasiperiods of a CM-variety A can be expressed algebraically through $p(\sigma,\Phi)$. For example, if σ is an embedding of K into $\mathbb{C}$, and $\Phi_1,\ldots,\Phi_m$ are CM-types of K, then $\prod_{i=1}^{m} p(\sigma,\Phi_i)^{c_i}$ for $c_i \in \mathbb{Z}$ depends, up to an algebraic (i.e. $\bar{\mathbb{Q}}$) factor, only on $\sum_{i=1}^{m} c_i\Phi_i$ and σ.

One of the results that determines the number of algebraically independent generators of period and quasiperiod matrix of A (the dimension of the Hodge group of A) is the following one [21,23]:

Let I_K^0 be the module of all formal linear combinations $\Sigma_\sigma c_\sigma \cdot \sigma$ for $c_\tau \in \mathbb{Q}$ such that $c_\sigma + c_{\sigma\rho}$ does not depend on σ (ρ is the complex conjugation). The rank, $r(K,\phi)$ of a CM-type (K,ϕ) is the dimension of the subspace of I_K^0 generated over $\mathbb{Q}$ by all ϕ_γ for $\gamma \in \text{Gal}(\bar{\mathbb{Q}}/\mathbb{Q})$.

Then for a CM-variety A with the CM-type (K,ϕ), the number of algebraically independent elements among periods $\int_\gamma \omega$ and quasiperiods $\int_\gamma \eta$ is bounded by the rank $r(K,\phi)$.

Here ω and η are, respectively, the differentials of the first and second kind on A, and γ is a 1-cycle.

We conjectured [26] that, in fact, the number of algebraically independent numbers among periods and quasiperiods is exactly the rank $r(K,\phi)$. This conjecture is correct at least for $g = 1$. In the case $g = 1$ the rank is always 2, there are, in fact, two algebraically independent numbers among CM periods and quasiperiods; the fact that the rank is 2 can be considered to be a consequence of Ramanujan's quasiperiod relation.

The rank is bounded as follows:

$$2 + \log_2 g \leq r(K,\phi) \leq g + 1$$

(with both inequalities achievable).

These period relations and the framework within which they are achieved: values of Eisenstein series and the theory of motives, are the most far reaching generalizations of "quadradic period relations" discovered by Ramanujan in the elliptic curve case. Additional information, also often sought by Ramanujan in the elliptic curve case, include the determination of period relations up to $\mathbb{Q}$-factors (i.e. resolution of algebraic equations in radicals), and the determination of periods in terms of products of Γ-functions in Abelian cases [22]. The Γ-product representations for periods are known in the case of elliptic curves with complex multiplication as Selberg-Chowla formulas [6]. Ramanujan [1] observed particular cases of these formulas. Important additions to Selberg-Chowla formulas include computation of algebraic factors in terms of values of p-adic Γ-functions, due to Gross and Deligne, see [27].

Most of this recently developed fascinating theory of period relations is of primary interest to algebraic geometry and escapes an easy translation into magic identities of Ramanujan type. It is therefore reasonable to restrict ourselves to the cases which Ramanujan might have himself stumbled upon by looking only on hypergeometric equations.

Instead of arithmetic quotients of general bounded symmetric domains we will look only at discrete arithmetic subgroups acting on the upper half-plane. These arithmetic subgroups were well studied by the late $\overline{\underline{\text{XIX}}}$ century, particularly by Fricke and Klein. If to restrict ourselves to automorphic forms expressed in terms of hypergeometric integrals, we arrive to the celebrated class of Schwarz triangle groups denoted according to canonical notations as

$$(0.3;\ell_1,\ell_2,\ell_3) \tag{2.3}$$

where $2 \leq \ell_i \leq \infty$.

For the triangle group with the signature (2.3) to be Fuchsian, the condition of non- Euclideanity has to be satisfied:

$$\frac{1}{\ell_1} + \frac{1}{\ell_2} + \frac{1}{\ell_3} < 1. \tag{2.4}$$

(If (2.4) is not satisfied we arrive at the famous Schwarz's cases of finite polyhedral groups, if the inequality in (2.4) is reversed, or to an elliptic case uniformizing the curves of genus 0 and 1, if the equality is substituted in (2.4).)

The triangle groups with the signature (2.3) are explicitly expressed in terms of hypergeometric functions as follows. For $\lambda = 1/\ell_1$, $\mu = 1/\ell_2$, $\nu = 1/\ell_3$ we put $a = \frac{1}{2}(1-\lambda-\mu+\nu)$, $b = \frac{1}{2}(1-\lambda-\mu-\nu)$, $c = 1-\lambda$. Then the function

$$\tau = S(\lambda,\mu,\nu;z),$$

inverse to the function $\varphi(\tau) = z$, automorphic in H with respect to the triangle group $(0,3;\ell_1,\ell_2,\ell_3)$, is expressed as the ratio of two linearly independent solutions of the hypergeometric equation with the parameters a,b,c defined above. E.g. for $\lambda(= 1/\ell_1) \neq 0$, one can put

$$\tau = C\cdot z^{1/\ell_1}\cdot\frac{F(a+1-c,b+1-c;2-c;z)}{F(a,b;c;z)}.$$

Not all triangle groups are arithmetic; one easily recognizes those arithmetic triangle groups that correspond to (are commensurable with) a full modular group $\Gamma(1)$ or its principal congruence subgroup $\Gamma(2)$. However, the list of arithmetic triangle groups is rather large. The first sequence of arithmetic triangle subgroups had been described by Fricke and Klein in [28] in connection with ternary quadratic forms. Later in the turn of the $\overline{\underline{XX}}$ century an extensive investigation of triangle groups had been conducted by Hutchinson, Young and Morris, following earlier work of Hurwitz and Burkhardt. In these works detailed investigations of special classes of arithmetic triangle groups were carried out, see references R. Morris, [29]. This American contribution was much more than just automorphic function study, because period relations on Riemann surfaces of high genera with four critical points were described in detail; unfortunately this investigation seems to be largely ignored.

Recently a complete classification of all arithmetic triangle groups was presented by Takenchi [30]. For a precise definition of an arithmetic subgroup see Swinnerton-Dyer [31]. (Roughly speaking an arithmetic triangle group is one which is commensurable with the Fuchsian group arising from the order of a quaternion algebra over a totally real field.)

Computations of Takenchi [30] confirmed the findings of Fricke-Klein [28] (essentially, up to commensurability, the arithmetic triangle subgroups were already known.)

If one looks at the commensurability classes of arithmetic triangle subgroups, one of the classes corresponds to the full modular group with its most important representative being

$$
\begin{aligned}
&(0,3;2,3,\infty),\\
&(0,3;2,4,\infty),\\
&(0,3;2,6,\infty),\\
&(0,3;2,\infty,\infty).
\end{aligned}
\tag{2.5}
$$

These are exactly four cases of hypergeometric functions studied by Ramanujan [1] in connection with period relations. Here one always has $\ell_1 = 2$ to have the Clausen identity. The squares of hypergeometric function corresponding to four classes in (2.5) are listed explicitly in (1.6)-(1.9) as ${}_3F_2$-hypergeometric functions. The four triangle subgroups listed in (2.5), two of which correspond simply to $\Gamma(1)$ and $\Gamma(2)$ and two others to Hecke groups G_q with $q = 4,6$ are well studied in classical and modern literature. The commensurability relations between groups can be easily translated into algebraic transformations of the corresponding hypergeometric functions, i.e. into modular relations of low degrees. Nothing more than the usual elliptic theory of modular functions occurs here, and one can always deduce all the identities from a single group, corresponding, say, to $(0,3;2,3,\infty)$--the case of the modular invariant $J(\tau)$--our favorite.

Other arithmetic triangle subgroups are less redundant. Among those of special interest to us are 17 classes [30] of commensurability of triangle subgroups corresponding to 12 totally real fields with class number 1 and quaternion algebras over them. In each of these cases there is a rich theory of arithmetic values of functions automorphic with respect to arithmetic triangle groups Γ acting on H with a compact H/Γ.

One of these arithmetic subgroups is a particularly distinguished Hurwitz group

$$(0,3;2,3,7).$$

This is a group with the minimal volume of H/Γ (among all Fuchsian groups of the first kind). Factors of this Hurwitz group are known to attain the maximal order 84 (g-1) of automorphism group of a Riemann surface of genus $g > 1$.

The picture of the action of this triangle subgroup often illustrates papers, books and conference posters (see Figure 1).

Remarkably, very little is known about the arithmetic properties of values of automorphic functions corresponding to Hurwitz's and other arithmetic triangle compact groups, though Shimura in his papers (see review in [24]) built a complete theory of complex multiplication in most of these cases. He determined the Hilbert class fields and the action of Frobenius there (including the case of Hurwitz group).

A single commensurability class of triangle subgroups corresponds to quaternion algebras over $\mathbb{Q}$ with discriminant $D = 2\cdot 3$. This class contains

Figure 1

(0,3;2,4,6) and (0,3;2,6,6).

These cases are quite complex from the point of view of the underlying hypergeometric integrals and were partially studied by Hutchinson and Dalaker, see [32]. (These two cases are two cases of the general curve with four critical points (hypergeometric curves) for which the moduli of all integrals of the first kind, i.e. all periods of the differential of the first kind on this curve, are expressed linearly in terms of a single parameter. The problem of determination of all hypergeometric curves possessing this property had been studied by Morris [29], who proved that in addition to 4 cases commensurable with the full modular group there are only two additional cases: (0,3;2,4,6) and (0,3;2,6,6). These two cases lead to curves of genera 23 and 6, respectively (see below). This seems slightly surprising because the monodromy groups of the corresponding differential equations are rather small as subgroups of $SL_2(\mathcal{O})$ for a ring $\mathcal{O}$ of integers in $\mathbb{Q}(\sqrt{2},\sqrt{3})$. We are dealing here, however, with Riemann surfaces depending on a single parameter that admit a large group of automorphisms some of which are nontrivial. In a sense these particular Riemann surfaces represent a one-parameter generalization of the famous Klein curves

$$x^3y + y^3z + z^3x = 0$$

--a famous genus 3 curve with 168 automorphism group, and its less famous quintic counterpart

$$x^4y + y^4z + z^4x = 0$$

studied by Snyder and Scorza.

To see why it is unusual for a hypergeometric curve to have its period matrix to depend linearly only on a single parameter, let us look at the general expression of a curve with 4 critical points:

$$y^q = (x-a_0)^{\alpha_0}(x-a_1)^{\alpha_1}(x-a_2)^{\alpha_2}(x-a_3)^{\alpha_3},$$

(when $a_0 = \infty$, one puts $\alpha_0 = 0$). Elements of Riemann's period matrix of this curve have the form of hypergeometric integrals

$$\int (x-a_1)^{\beta_1}(x-a_2)^{\beta_2}(x-a_3)^{\beta_3}dx,$$

for a variety of exponents $(\beta_1,\beta_2,\beta_3)$. Not all of these integrals can be linearly dependent; and these linear dependences are usually nontrivial automorphisms).

We look now at Jacobians of hypergeometric curves (curves with four critical points), i.e. at all periods of differentials of the first kind, and not only obvious ones, expressed by hypergeometric functions themselves.

Only the simplest case of $(0;3;\infty,\infty,\infty)$--i.e. of $K(k) = \frac{\pi}{2}F(\frac{1}{2},\frac{1}{2};1;k^2)$--clearly leads to elliptic function field. Already other triangle subgroups, commensurable with this one, give rise to nontrivial Riemann surfaces of hypergeometric type. E.g. the two Hecke triangle groups in (2.5) lead to Riemann surfaces of genra 2. These are, respectively,

$$y^3 = (x-a_0)(x-a_1)(x-a_2)^2(x-a_3)^2$$

for $(0,3;2,6,\infty)$, and

$$y^4 = (x-a_0)(x-a_1)^2(x-a_2)^2(x-a_3)^3$$

for $(0,3;2,4,\infty)$.

In both cases $g = 2$, and the Jacobian of each of the curves is isogenous to the product of two elliptic curves, which are isogenous to each other. Explicit modular equations express integrals of the first kind on these curves (and not only their periods) through classical elliptic integrals.

For two other triangle subgroups associated with quaternion algebra over $\mathbb{Q}$ with the discriminant $D = 2\cdot 3$, arising hypergeometric curves are even more complicated. For the triangle group $(0,3;2,6,6)$ we get a genus $g = 3$ equation

$$y^6 = (x-a_0)^2(x-a_1)^2(x-a_2)^3(x-a_3)^5, \tag{2.6}$$

and for $(0,3,2,4,6)$ we arrive at $g = 23$ curve

$$y^{24} = (x-a_0)(x-a_1)^{11}(x-a_2)^{17}(x-a_3)^{19}. \tag{2.7}$$

The first curve (2.6) has its Jacobian isogeneous to the product of an elliptic curve and a Jacobian of a hyperelliptic curve. The second curve is harder to describe. Its Jacobian possesses many nontrivial Jacobian factors (of genera 2 there are at least eight, and there is a factor of genera 5).

(All other (arithmetic) triangle subgroups lead to hypergeometric curves of high genera ($g > 2$), which have period matrices that cannot be expressed linearly in terms of a single parameter [29], [32]. This means that monodromy groups of more than a single hypergeometric equation are involved in the description of the monodromy group of a single hypergeometric curve. This means that the totality of numbers in the period and quasiperiod matrix of the corresponding hypergeometric Riemann surfaces involves more than values of a single automorphic function. This makes the corresponding theory of complex multiplication very complicated.)

The cases of (0,3;2,4,6) and (0,3;2,6,6) (and other arithmetic triangle groups) immediately lend themselves to the generalization of the Ramanujan period relations. For each of these cases we can look at the function $z = \varphi(\tau)$ automorphic in H with respect to the corresponding arithmetic triangle group see [24]. We normalize this function like the classical modular invariant by its values in the vertices of the fundamental triangle. (Say we put, following [24]:

$$\varphi(e_2) = 1, \ \varphi(e_m) = 0, \ \varphi(e_n) = \infty$$

for vertices e_i ($m = n = 6$ or $m = 4$, $n = 6$) that are fixed points of elliptic elements γ_i of orders i in the triangle group: $\prod \gamma_i = -I_2$.)

The theory of complex multiplication in the quaternion case (Eichler-Shimura [24]) shows that for τ in H which is imaginary quadratic, the field $\mathbb{Q}(\tau, \varphi(\tau))$ is an explicit Abelian extension of $\mathbb{Q}(\tau)$.

For example, whenever $\mathbb{Q}(\tau)$ has the class number 1, the values of $\varphi(\tau)$ have the structure similar to that of $J(\tau)$. For the numbers $z = \varphi(\tau)$ we obtain Ramanujan's period relations like in the elliptic case. Namely, we get $\underline{\underline{2}}$ new algebraic relations between values of

$$F(\frac{1}{24},\frac{5}{24};\frac{3}{4};z) \quad \text{and} \quad F'(\frac{1}{24},\frac{5}{24};\frac{3}{4};z)$$

for (0,3;2,4,6) case, and between values of

$$F(\frac{1}{12},\frac{1}{4};\frac{5}{6};z) \quad \text{and} \quad F'(\frac{1}{12},\frac{1}{4};\frac{5}{6};z)$$

for (0,3;2,6,6), where $z = \varphi(\tau)$.

When $\tau \in \mathbb{Q}(\sqrt{-d})$ and $-d$ is one of the 9 one class discriminants, we arrive at new Ramanujan-like period identities. There are 3 classes of hypergeometric functions for these two triangle subgroups, where the Clausen identity is satisfied and product of the periods can be expressed as a value of a single ${}_3F_2$ function.

Unfortunately, the convergence of series in these identities is not as fast as in the original Ramanujan case. The reason is obvious: for large values of $J(\tau)$,

$$2\pi i\tau \sim \log J;$$

because at the corresponding vertex of the triangle $\ell = \infty$. In compact case, $\varphi(\tau)$ does not grow that fast.

We now describe briefly an outline of a general theory of Ramanujan-like relations for arbitrary arithmetic groups Γ. In addition to the theory of complex multiplication for these groups (see [20]-[24], [31]) one needs an analog of Ramanujan's nonholomorphic function $s_2(\tau)$. Instead of looking at the Eisenstein series corresponding to Γ, we prefer to look directly at linear differential equation corresponding, according to a Schwarz theory, to Γ. We follow the approach presented in [33] for derivation of differential equations satisfied by Eisenstein series. In this approach we look at the derivatives of the automorphic function $\varphi(\tau)$ for the arithmetic group Γ normalized by its values at vertices. The function itself satisfies the third order (nonlinear) differential equation over $\bar{\mathbb{Q}}$ (see [30] and [31]) that follows from the determination of the Schwarzian $\{\varphi,\tau\}$ in terms of φ. An analog of $s_2(\tau)$ in (1.2) that is a nonholomorphic automorphic form for Γ is

$$-\frac{1}{\varphi'(\tau)}\cdot\{\frac{\varphi''(\tau)}{\varphi'(\tau)}-\frac{i}{\mathrm{Im}(\tau)}\} \tag{2.8}$$

For $\varphi(\tau) = J(\tau)$ one gets $s_2(\tau)$ in (2.8).

For example, let us look now at a quaternion triangle case (0,3;2,6,6). In this case, instead of an elliptic Schwarz formulas (1.10)-(1.11) one has the following representation of the (normalized) automorphic function $\varphi = \varphi(\tau)$ in H in terms of hypergeometric functions:

$$\frac{\tau+i(\sqrt{2}+\sqrt{3})}{\tau-i(\sqrt{2}+\sqrt{3})} = -\frac{3^{1/2}}{2^2\cdot 2^{1/6}}\cdot\{\frac{\Gamma(1/3)}{\sqrt{\pi}}\}^6\cdot\frac{F(\frac{1}{12},\frac{1}{4};\frac{5}{6};\varphi)}{\varphi^{1/6}\cdot F(\frac{1}{4},\frac{5}{12};\frac{7}{6};\varphi)} .$$

Thus the role of π in Ramanujan's period relations is occupied in (0,3;2,6,6)-case by the transcendence

$$\{\frac{\Gamma(1/3)}{\pi}\}^6.$$

In the case (0,3;2,4,6)-group the corresponding representation for $\varphi = \varphi(\tau)$ was actually derived in [28]:

$$\frac{(\sqrt{3}-1)\tau-i\sqrt{2}}{(\sqrt{3}-1)\tau+i\sqrt{2}} = -2(\sqrt{3}-\sqrt{2})\frac{\Gamma(-\frac{1}{24})\Gamma(-\frac{5}{24})}{\Gamma(-\frac{13}{24})\Gamma(-\frac{17}{24})}\cdot\varphi^{1/2}\cdot\frac{F(\frac{13}{24},\frac{17}{24};\frac{3}{2};\varphi)}{F(\frac{1}{24},\frac{5}{24};\frac{1}{2};\varphi)}.$$

Thus, in this case, we have a new Γ-factor:

$$\frac{\Gamma(\frac{1}{24})^4}{\{\Gamma(\frac{1}{3})\Gamma(\frac{1}{4})\}^2}.$$

Appearance of such constants can be explained from the point of view of Shimura-Deligne theory of periods of CM-varieties and values of the corresponding L-functions.

We will present the new Ramanujan-like identities for this and other arithmetic triangle subgroups corresponding to quaternion algebras elsewhere, together with applications to diophantine approximations in a fashion similar to that of Chapters 4,5 and [34].

We want to point out that, though there is no algebraic relation between automorphic functions corresponding to congruence subgroups of the elliptic modular and of quaternion groups, there are arithmetic and algebraic relations between the modular curves and the modular equations for these two classes of groups. These relations between L-functions of modular forms and modular curves are predicted by general Jaquet-Langlands theory and were investigated by Shimura in special cases (particularly in Hurwitz case) and were studied by Swinnerton-Dyer [31] and by D. Heihal [59].

The generalizations of Ramanujan identities allow us to express a variety of constants, such as π and other Γ-factors, as values of rapidly convergent series with nearly integral coefficients in an infinitude of ways (rather than a single expression) with convergence improving as the discriminant of the corresponding singular moduli increases. One can ask: what kind of constants allow these representations? Values of which hypergeometric functions can be represented by such quadratic identities?

We don't even know what kind of numbers can be expressed as values of hypergeometric functions at algebraic points. (Other than to say that they are "periods".)

New Ramanujan-like period identities let us study arithmetic nature of complicated transcendences using values of (more complicated) automorphic functions. This process gives us a hope that the best diophantine approximations to such constants as π (and also periods of elliptic curves) can be interpreted through values of modular and automorphic functions, much like the best approximations to cubic irrationalties can be interpreted through values of parabolic forms of high level (via-Weil-Taniyama conjecture).

In arithmetic applications there is one more side to Ramanujan identities--their p-adic interpretation that reveals the action of Frobenius on algebraic factors in period identities. These p-adic identities involve values of p-adic hypergeometric functions and p-adic (Morita) Γ-functions, cf. with [27].

3. Diophantine approximations to numbers and methods of Padé approximations.

The main tool in the diophantine approximations is the method of Padé-type approximations. These are auxiliary polynomial or rational approximations to functions, satisfying algebraic differential or functional equations, whose specializations at, say, algebraic points provide with unusually good approximations to numbers in question. These approximations are rational in nature and should not be confused with numerical approximations often provided by iteration of sequences of algebraic maps. The crucial property of Padé-type approximations lies in the matching of degree of approximation with the degree (as an algebraic function) of an approximant--thus Padé approximations are better than simple polynomial approximations and often better than Newton ones, with obvious known exceptions such as Newton approximations to $1/(1-x)$ and $\sqrt{1-x}$.

In order to be specific, we define one of the schemes of Padé approximations (the so-called Padê approximations of the second kind [35], [36]):

Definition 3.1: Let $f_1(x),\dots,f_n(x)$ be analytic at $x = 0$. For a given (weight) $D \geq 0$, there exist polynomials $q(x), p_1(x),\dots,p_n(x)$ of degree at most D such that

$$\text{ord}_{x=0}\{q(x)\cdot f_i(x) - p_i(x)\} \geq D + 1 + [\tfrac{D}{n}]$$

for all $i = 1,\ldots,n$.

This means that all functions $f_i(x)$ are simultaneously approximated by $\frac{p_i(x)}{q(x)}$-rational functions with the common denominator. In arithmetic applications $f_i(x)$ usually satisfy linear differential equations with additional arithmetic conditions. In our current study of periods, these equations satisfy the global nilpotence conditions [35], [37]. According to one of our results from [38] this condition is equivalent to the statement that $f_i(x)$ have convergent expansions at $x = 0$ with algebraic and nearly integral coefficients, i.e. $f_i(x)$ are Siegel's G-functions (see below [35]). Padé approximations of Definition 3.1, or Padé approximations of the second kind are used to study arithmetic properties of $f_i(x)$ at algebraic (rational) $x = z$ close to 0, by specilizing approximations x to z. Though these approximations always exist, their arithmetic properties are virtually unknown with an exception of those cases when the close form expressions are found for Padé approximations. It is not merely a closed expression that is needed, but the control on the growth of the coefficients (local, i.e. nonarchimedian conditions) versus the order of convergence of approximations (an archimedian condition).

In the simplest case this local/global condition on Padé approximations can be stated as follows:

If $f_i(x) \in \mathbb{Q}[[x]]$ $(i = 1,\ldots,n)$, can one find Padé approximants $q(x)$, $p_1(x),\ldots,p_n(x)$ of weight (degree) D from $\mathbb{Z}[x]$ such that heights of all polynomials are bounded by

$$C^D$$

for a constant $C > 1$ (independent of D)?

Unfortunately, this arithmetic condition is often not satisfied even for the simplest $f_i(x)$. This is the case when $n = 1$ and $f_1(x)$ is an algebraic function with more than 3 critical points, e.g. $f_1(x) = \sqrt{(x-a_1)\ldots(x-a_{2k})}$. In this and other generic cases the heights of Padé approximants from $\mathbb{Z}[x]$ grow as fast as

$$C^{D^2}$$

for $D \to \infty$, which make them unsuited for applications in diophantine approximations.

The typical compromise then, is to consider Padé-type approximations that reduce significantly the number of conditions on the order of approximations. This allows us to control the growth of coefficients, but results here are merely the existence ones, based on counting argument, and as a consequence, the rate of such approximations is very poor and usually involves fantastically large constants, cf. [34],[39].

There is something good in hypergeometric and generalized hypergeometric functions that allow for closed form expressions of Padé approximations to them and some of their combinations, and makes local/global conditions to be satisfied. (One can mention two reasons for this: a) an explicit expression for the monodromy group and contiguous relations; b) integral representations. In all cases, when explicit construction is possible, a) and b) play important roles, see [40-41].)

We are not going to present explicitly the corresponding systems of Padé approximations but we describe the most important cases when we have a closed form expression for simultaneous Pade approximations and the arithmetic condition on local-global behavior stated above.

These cases are (see also in [34], [40-41])

1) $f_i(x) = {}_2F_1(1,b_i;c_i;x)$ or

$f_i(x) = {}_2F_1(1,b;c;\omega_i x)$

(e.g. $f_i(x) = (1-x)^{\nu_i}$ or $f_i(x) = (1-\omega_i x)^{\nu}$): $i = 1,\ldots,n$). They are essentially classical Hermite-Padé approximations, [40].

2) Whenever

$$f(x) = {}_{p+1}F_p\left(\begin{matrix}a_1,\ldots,a_{p+1}\\ b_1,\ldots,b_p\end{matrix}\middle| x\right)$$

and we look at simultaneous Padé approximation to p functions $f_1(x),\ldots,f_p(x)$ defined as

$$(1:f_1:\ldots:f_p) = (f:\delta_x f:\ldots:\delta_x^p f_p)$$

for $\delta_x = x\frac{d}{dx}$, [34], [42]. This is a generalization of Euler-Gauss continued fraction expansions of $\frac{d}{dx}\log{}_2F_1(a,b;c;x)$.

An important counterpart to 2) is given by Padé approximations to

$${}_{p+1}F_p\left({a_1+i,a_2,\ldots,a_{p+1} \atop b_1,\ldots,b_p}\Big|\omega_j x\right):\ i = 0,\ldots,p$$

the last system of Padé approximations for $p = 2$ was used by us in applications of Ramanujan identities, see [34], [42].

In cases 1) and 2) we had determined explicitly the asymptotic expansions of Padé approximants and of the corresponding remainder functions. Explicit expressions for the asymptotics of the denominators of coefficients of Padé approximants (i.e. of heights in the integral case) turned out to be very complicated arithmetic functions of rational parameters a_i, b_i, c_i. See examples in [43].

3) Padé approximations can be also explicitly determined for Picard generalizations of hypergeometric functions (Pochhammer integrals):

$$F(\mu_0,\ldots,\mu_{d+1}) = \int_1^\infty t^{-\mu_0}(t-1)^{\mu_1} \prod_{i=2}^{d+1} (t-x_i)^{-\mu_i}\, dt.$$

Here μ_i are rational numbers and singularities x_i are linear functions of a single variable x. (These functions are general section of Picard function, where all x_i are treated as variables; in this case also one can construct multidimensional Padé approximations.)

In Picard cases there is a large class of arithmetic monodromy groups. In these cases an analog of complex multiplication theory, and theory of Ramanujan period relations can be constructed. This theory has interesting applications to diophantine approximations of numbers that arise from periods of curves and algebraic varieties; most interesting ones are not yet fully explored. The generating functions of Padé approximants to Picard integrals are themselves expressed as periods of algebraic varieties.

4) Finally, there are explicit Padé approximations to multidimensional generalization of generalized hypergeometric functions, which are expressed as integrals over powers of polynomials in complex variables taken over polytops. We present only one example of a nice multidimensional integral arising as a natural generalization of Hermite-Lindemann proof [17] of transcendence of e and π. This formula can be considered as a multidimensional analog of operational calculus formula for Laplace transforms.

In this formula:

$$I_\Delta = \int \cdots \int_\Delta e^{-\Sigma_{i=1}^n x_i y_i} \cdot P(y_1,\ldots,y_n) \prod_{i=1}^n dy_i,$$

where Δ is a polytope in n-dimensional space, P is a polynomial vanishing up to high orders at vertices of Δ. The integral I_Δ can be evaluated through values of P and its derivatives at vertices of Δ only. This is a generalization of the so called Hermite identity (see [17], [44]):

$$I_\Delta = \sum_{\bar{e}\in V(\Delta)} e^{-(\bar{x},\bar{e})} \cdot \prod_{i=1}^n (\ell_i(\frac{\partial}{\partial y_1},\ldots,\frac{\partial}{\partial y_n}) - \ell(x_1,\ldots,x_n))^{-1} \cdot P|_{\bar{y}=\bar{e}}$$

where $\ell_i(y_1,\ldots,y_n) = 0$ are hyperplane equations of sides of Δ intersecting at the vertex $\bar{e} \in V(\Delta)$.

The choice of the polytope and the polynomials vanishing

up to high order in all its vertices determines a variety of Padé approximations to linear combinations of exponents. Hermite's simultaneous Padé approximation correspond to $n = 1$ and give Padé approximations to $e^{\omega_i x}$. Whenever Δ is an n-polytop (tetrahedron in $\mathbb{R}^n$), one obtains Padé approximations used by Hermite, Mahler and Siegel to estimate diophantine approximations to e^{α} and π, see [44]. An interesting intermediate case corresponds to the so called graded Padé approximations [40], [45] that provide sharp measures of diophantine approximations to such numbers as sin 1, $J_0(1)$, etc., though for the corresponding functions (sin x, $J_0(x)$ et. al.) no regular pattern continued fraction exists and arithmetic (local/global) conditions for rational approximations (as above) are not satisfied.

We can use explicit Padé approximations, particularly those to generalized hypergeometric functions to establish sharp irrationality measures for numbers that occur as values of these functions close to the point of nearly integral power series expansions.

We used Ramanujan's amazing generalized hypergeometric identities representing quadratic period relations and their generalizations, as described in Chapter 2, to derive new bounds on measures of diophantine approximations for a variety of numbers mainly connected with π. We are able to obtain these strong bounds because Ramanujan representations give expressions for classical constants as rapidly convergent series with nearly integral (or integral) coefficients. Though from the point of view of numerical approximations these new series are not dramatically better than some of the classical ones, performing Padé approximations on them we arrive at incredibly good arithmetic rational approximations, often very close to the best rational approximations that only continued fraction expansion provides. (One cannot expect to get the continued fraction expansion this way, because no regular pattern emerges, at least experimentally, in the expansion of these numbers.)

What Ramanujan's and similar identities provide is a new identification of classical constants such as π or $\pi\cdot\sqrt{2}$ (or $\log \epsilon_{\sqrt{k}}$) as values of nearly integral power series expansions of solutions of linear differential equations (primarily of hypergeometric and generalized hypergeometric type) <u>very close</u> to the point of expansion.

The closer we are to the origin, the better is the exponent of irrationality! To give a precise statement, we quote one of our results on G-functions [35].

We recall that a function $f(x) = \Sigma_{n=0}^{\infty} a_n x^n$ with $a_n \in \mathbb{Q}$ is called Siegel's G-function [35], [38], if a_n are nearly integral, i.e. $f(x)$ converges around $x = 0$ and the common denominator of $a_0,\ldots,a_n$ grows not faster than a geometric progression in n. All generalized hypergeometric functions with rational parameters are G-functions, as well as solutions of Picard-Fuchs equations.

One of our results relating diophantine approximations of G-functions with the global nilpotence of the corresponding differential equations states:

Theorem 3.2 [35]: Let $f_1(x),\dots,f_n(x)$ be G-functions satisfying linear differential equations over $\mathbb{Q}(x)$. Let $r = a/b$, with integers a and b, be very close to the origin. Then we get the following lower bound for linear forms in $f_1(z),\dots,f_n(z)$.

For arbitrary non-zero rational integers $H_1,\dots,H_n$ and $H = \max\{|H_1|,\dots,|H_n|\}$, if $H_1f_1(r) +\dots+ H_nf_n(r) \neq 0$,

$$|H_1f_1(r) +\dots+ H_nf_n(r)| > |H_1 \cdots H_n|^{-1}\cdot H^{1-\epsilon}$$

provided that r is very close to 0:

$$|b| \geq c_1\cdot |a|^{n(n-1+\epsilon)}$$

and $H \geq c_2$ with effective constants $c_i = c_i(f_1,\dots,f_n,\tau,\epsilon)$. If r is not as close to 0, we get only

$$|H_1f_1(r) +\dots+ H_nf_n(r)| > H^{\lambda-\epsilon}$$

for $\lambda = -(n-1)\log|b|/\log|b/a^n|$ (< 0).

This theorem shows what a qualitative difference in the exponent of diophantine approximation, the rate of convergence of a series representing a constant makes.

Looking at the rate of convergence of Ramanujan-like series and combining them with the G-function theorems, one obtains extremely strong results, which might have shown that all numbers connected with π have (Roth's) exponent of irrationality $2 + \epsilon$ for any $\epsilon > 0$.

<u>Mock Proposition.</u> If there exist infinitely many negative quadratic discriminants $-d$ with a <u>fixed</u> class number, then <u>all</u> elements of the field $\mathbb{Q}(\pi^2)$, irrational over $\mathbb{Q}$, have measures of irrationality with the exponent $2 + \epsilon$ for all $\epsilon > 0$.

The same result holds also for fields generated by $\log^2 \epsilon_{\sqrt{k}}$ for real quadratic units $\epsilon_{\sqrt{k}}$.

Unfortunately, degrees of numbers $J(\tau)$ for $\tau = \frac{1+\sqrt{-d}}{2}$ grow to infinity as $d \to \infty$, thus we are confined (for a given degree) only to the finitude of cases of rapidly convergent series. This means that exponent stays away from 2. Also for all these cases, instead of general results we have to use explicit Padé approximations to generalized hypergeometric functions and Pochhammer integrals [34], [42].

We review briefly the best results on measures of diophantine approximations to number connected with π obtained using effective Padé approximations to generalized hypergeometric functions.

$$|\pi\sqrt{2} - \frac{p}{q}| > |q|^{-16.67\ldots}$$

for rational integers p, q: $|q| \geq q_0$. This is based on Ramanujan's series for $1/\sqrt{2}\pi$;

$$|\pi\sqrt{640,320} - \frac{p}{q}| > |q|^{-11.109\ldots}$$

for $|q| \geq q_1$ (see (1.5)).

For $\pi\sqrt{3}$ we use slightly different systems of Padé-type approximations [34], [46]:

$$|\pi\sqrt{3} - \frac{p}{q}| > |q|^{-5.791\ldots}$$

for $|q| \geq q_2$.

Finally, we can give one unconditional result for π:

Proposition 3.3: For arbitrary rational integers p,q with $|q| \geq 2$ we have:

$$|q\cdot\pi - p| > |q|^{-14.0}.$$

In the finite range $|q| \leq 10^{10^5}$ we had to look at the explicit continued fraction expansion of π.

In fact we know slightly better (conditional) measures of irrationality:

$$|\pi - \frac{p}{q}| > |w|^{-15.62\ldots}$$

for $|q| \geq q_3$, and the following one for π^2:

$$|\pi^2 - \frac{p}{q}| > |q|^{-7.81\ldots}$$

for $|q| \geq q_4$.

Let us look on the transcendence and algebraic independence results for periods and quasiperiods of hypergeometric curves, and the corresponding statements the transcendence of values of hypergeometric functions at algebraic points. (As it was already explained, with the exception of two classes of arithmetic triangle groups, in general, periods of a single hypergeometric curve involve values of more than a single hypergeometric function.)

First of all, trivial cases have to be excluded: we remove from consideration all hypergeometric functions reducible to algebraic ones (exclude all equations on the Schwarz's list of finite groups when ratio of two solutions is an algebraic function). Next, only rational values of parameters are to be considered. (This corresponds to the G-functions or to a finite genus case; little to nothing is known about values of hypergeometric functions with algebraic irrational parameters.) Other hypergeometric functions reducible to elementary or genus 1 cases have to be excluded too; they are analyzed by other means.

Let us start with the simplest case of Legendre functions $F(\frac{1}{2},\frac{1}{2};1;z)$. In this case (or in any other case algebraically reducible to this one including triangle cases commensurable with the modular group) it is a consequence of our 1977 [26], [39] result that:

<u>Theorem 3.4</u>: For an arbitrary algebraic $z \neq 0,1$ two numbers $F(\frac{1}{2},\frac{1}{2};1;z)$ and $F(-\frac{1}{2},\frac{1}{2};1;z)$ are algebraically independent (over $\mathbb{Q}$).

Moreover, one can get the measure of algebraic independence of these two numbers: $\alpha = F(\frac{1}{2},\frac{1}{2};1;z)$, $\beta = F(-\frac{1}{2},\frac{1}{2};1;z)$. This measure is very close to the best possible: if $P(x,y) \in \mathbb{Z}[x,y]$, $P \not\equiv 0$, P has the (total) degree d and height (the maximum of absolute values of coefficients) $H > 1$, then [39]:

$$|P(\alpha,\beta)| > H^{-c_0 d^2 \log^2(d+1)}$$

with $c_0 = c_0(\alpha,\beta,z) > 0$--an effective constant.

Theorem 3.4 can be supplemented with a stronger statement [26] that, whenever, $z \neq 0,1,\infty$ two of three numbers:

$$z, F(\tfrac{1}{2},\tfrac{1}{2},1;z) \quad \text{and} \quad F(-\tfrac{1}{2},\tfrac{1}{2};1;z)$$

are algebraically independent (over $\mathbb{Q}$).

It is natural to conjecture that for all other nontrivial (i.e. with an exception of the cases stated above) cases analog of Theorem 3.4 hold for hypergeometric functions corresponding to the hypergeometric curves of genus $g > 1$. We do not yet have such a strong result, though the analogue of Theorem 3.4 holds, if all hypergeometric functions giving periods of hypergeometric curves are considered. In particular, for all hypergeometric functions algebraically reducible to the triangle case (0,3;2,4,6) (or (0,3;2,6,6)), the values $F(z)$ and $F'(z)$ are algebraically independent over $\mathbb{Q}$, whenever z is algebraic $\neq 0,1$ and F is the corresponding hypergeometric functions. (Note that if one considers in Theorem 3.4 and its generalization <u>all</u> branches of a given hypergeometric function and its derivatives, there are still only two algebraically independent numbers, whenever z is a singular moduli. This is due to the Ramanujan period relations.)

Let us look now at the general algebraic independence results for hypergeometric function when all branches of the function are involved. In this case we use the knowledge of the monodromy group of the hypergeometric equation and the uniformization of hypergeometric functions by functions meromorphic in H. We use methods of [46] based on the uniformization $x = k^2(\tau)$ of general hypergeometric functions $F(x)$.

Theorem 3.5: Let $F_1(x)$ $(= F(a,b;c;x))$ and $F_2(x)$ $(= x^{1-c}\cdot F(a-c+1,b-c+1;2-c;x))$ be two algebraically independent (over $\mathbb{Q}(x)$) solutions of hypergeometric equation with rational a,b,c.

If F_1, F_2 do not correspond to genus $= 0,1$ cases, then for every algebraic $x \neq 0,1$ at least two of the numbers

$$F_1(x),\ F_1'(x),\ F_2(x),\ F_2'(x)$$

are algebraically independent.

There are at most 3 algebraically independent numbers among these and in singular moduli case there are exactly 2 algebraically independent ones.

4. The uniformization theory and accessory parameters for hyperelliptic curves.

In the nonarithmetic case, one is still interested in the arithmetic nature of groups (Fuchsian groups acting on H) uniformizing Riemann surfaces corresponding to algebraic curves of genus $g \geq 2$ defined over $\bar{\mathbb{Q}}$. In the uniformization problem we are using classical language of Schwarzians, Fuchsian linear differential equations, monodromy groups (representing groups of fractional transformations), and accessory parameters in the differential equations on which these groups depend. This language was used early in the development of the uniformization theory by Klein and Poincaré [47] when the continuity method was the main tool. The continuity method is no longer necessary to prove results in this theory. Nevertheless, the basis of classical theory--the one-to-one relationship between the uniformization of Riemann surfaces of genus $g \geq 2$ and certain linear differential equations of the second order depending on $3g-3$ complex accessory parameters can be used for the explicit numerical (or analytic, if possible) solution to the uniformization problem. In this approach one has to find a Fuchsian group, its fundamental domain and the uniformizing functions of a Riemann surface given by an explicit algebraic equation. There are several existing numerical approaches to this problem (Myrberg method based on Koebe theorem, methods based on integral equations for an appropriate Riemann problem), but the best method requires the determination of accessory parameters. If the uniformization problem is solved via the accessory parameters, then one has to determine $6g - 6$ real variables in the second order Fuchsian equation, for which the monodromy group of this equation is represented by real 2×2 matrices (so that this group is Fuchsian). If one has an efficient algorithm that computes the monodromy group of a second order equation, this algorithm becomes a key subroutine in the program that searches for the choice of accessory parameters for which traces of products of all monodromy matrices have zero (or very close to zero within a given precision) imaginary parts. This iterative program can be viewed, e.g. as a descent method to find the global minima of squares of these imaginary parts. The minima (equal to zero) is unique and is achieved at Fuchsian accessory parameters.

We apply our methods of fast computation of solutions of linear differential equations (see Chapter 5 and [12]) to fast computations of monodromy groups. This allows us to apply the descent method to find the Fuchsian accessory parameters, when their number is not too large. In practice, one has to be content with $g \leq 6$, when the Riemann surface and the differentials on it are known. In this lecture we report on our computations for hyperelliptic curves of genus $g \geq 2$

which had been studied in detail because of the special role of hyperelliptic curves, and also because the number of accessory parameters is smaller (only $2g-1$ accessory parameters) and the Fuchsian equation depending on them has polynomial coefficients. Some time ago we have conducted similar computations for the Riemann surfaces of genera 0 and 1 with several prescribed branch points, see [12].

In our study of hyperelliptic curves we were particularly interested in possible closed form expressions of accessory parameters in terms of known functions. The Whittaker conjecture [11] expressed the accessory parameters as algebraic functions of the branch points. This elegant conjecture turned out to be incorrect, and only special cases of algebraic expressions for accessory parameters were found.

Let us describe briefly the role of accessory parameters.

Let us consider an algebraic curve given by an equation $P(x,y) = 0$ for an irreducible polynomial $P(x,y)$. One can interpret this curve as a ramified covering of a Riemann sphere $\mathbb{CP}^1$ by looking at y as a multivalued function of x. Let us assume that this algebraic curve has a genus $g \geq 2$, and let us denote the corresponding compact Riemann surface by Γ. If $\hat{\Gamma}$ denotes the universal covering surface of Γ, then the existence theorem of the uniformization theory implies the conformal equivalence of $\hat{\Gamma}$ to the upper-half plane H. This conformal equivalence with H manifests itself as the uniformization of Γ:

$$\varphi: H \to \Gamma.$$

The group of cover transformations of Γ is $G = \{T: \varphi(T\circ z) = \varphi(z) \text{ for all } z \in H\}$. Here G is a discrete group of Mobius transformations over $\mathbb{R}$, i.e. a Fuchsian group.

It is easier to look at the inverse map $z = \varphi^{-1}$ than on φ. The function z is multivalued on Γ and its monodromy is related to the action of G: $z \to \sigma(z)$ for $\sigma \in G$. Since G is a group of Mobius transformations and the Schwarzian derivatives $\{\cdot,x\}$ ($\{f,x\} = (\frac{f''}{f'})' - \frac{1}{2}(\frac{f''}{f'})^2$) are invariant under the fractional transformations, the function $\{z,x\}$ is a single-valued function on Γ.

This means that

$$\{z,x\} = 2R(x,y) \text{ on } \Gamma \tag{4.1}$$

for some rational function $R(x,y)$. The classical relationship between the Schwarzian and the second order differential equations states that a change of variables

$$y_1 = (\frac{dz}{dx})^{-1/2}, y_2 = z(\frac{dz}{dx})^{-1/2}, \quad z = y_2/y_1$$

reduces (4.1) to a second order linear differential equation on y_1 and y_2:

$$(\frac{d^2}{dx^2} + R(x,y))y = 0. \tag{4.2}$$

Whenever z is locally one-to-one, $R(x,y)$ can be determined as [48]

$$R(x,y) = R_0(x,y) + Q(x,y),$$

where $Q(x,y)dx^2$ is a regular quadratic differential and $R_0(x,y)$ is a second derivative of an Abelian integral of the third kind (an explicit function that can be determined whenever Γ is known algebraically). If one knows the basis $\{Q_j(x,y): j = 1,\ldots,3g-3\}$ of regular quadratic differentials on Γ, then an equation (4.2) can be represented as [48]:

$$\left(\frac{d^2}{dx^2} + R_0(x,y) + \sum_{i=1}^{3g-3} c_j \cdot Q_j(x,y)\right)y = 0 \qquad (4.3)$$

for 3g-3 complex parameters c_j ($j = 1,\ldots,3g-3$)--the accessory parameters. For an analytic continuation of a (chosen) basis (y_1,y_2) of (4.3) around the loop γ of $\pi_1(\Gamma;\mathcal{O})$ we have a monodromy matrix M_γ:

$$(y_1,y_2)^t \underset{\gamma}{\rightarrow} M_\gamma (y_1,y_2)^t.$$

When the accessory parameters c_j ($j = 1,\ldots,3g-3$)in (4.3) are Fuchsian, i.e. (4.3) indeed arises, as above, from the uniformization of Γ by G: $y_2/y_1 = z = \varphi^{-1}$ of $\varphi: H \rightarrow \Gamma$-- then the monodromy group of (4.3) generated by $\{M_\gamma\}$ is G, up to conjugation in $SL_2(\mathbb{C})$.

Consequently for a given Γ (and properly chosen R_0 and Q_j in (4.3)), there existsa unique group of c_j: $j = 1,\ldots,3g-3$ (6g-6 real parameters) for which the corresponding monodromy group of (4.3) is Fuchsian (i.e. is a subgroup of $SL_2(\mathbb{R})$).

This description is slightly different for a hyperelliptic curve. In this case simple transformations allow us to reduce (4.2) to an equation with coefficients polynomial in x. Following [49] one considers a general hyperelliptic equation of genus g:

$$y^2 = (x-e_1)\dots(x-e_{2g+2}) \tag{4.4}$$

Arguments of Schottky in the general case and Whittaker [49] for hyperelliptic curves, show that the Fuchsian group G of an equation (4.4) is a subgroup of index 2 of a group G^* (of self-inverse transformations, i.e. elliptic transformations of period 2). The group G can be easily found once G^* is known. The group G^* has genus 0 and thus its automorphic function can be expressed as a rational function of a single automorphic function. This means that in equation (4.2) corresponding to the hyperelliptic curve (4.4), the right hand side is a rational function of x with singularities only at e_i's. Analyzing the behavior of the uniformizing variable at ∞ one gets a clear description of (4.2) (Whittaker, [11]): The uniformizing variable z of (4.4) is represented as a ratio of two linearly independent solutions of the following second order linear differential equation

$$\left(\frac{d^2}{dx^2} + R(x)\right)y = 0, \quad \text{where}$$

$$R(x) = \frac{3}{16}\cdot\left\{\sum_{i=1}^{2g+2}\frac{1}{(x-e_i)^2} - \frac{2(g+1)x^{2g} - 2g\sum_{i=1}^{2g+2} e_i\cdot x^{2g-1} + \sum_{i=0}^{2g-2} C_i\cdot x^{2g-2-i}}{(x-e_1)\dots(x-e_{2g+2})}\right\} \tag{4.5}$$

Here 2g-1 parameters $C_0,\dots,C_{2g-2}$ are accessory parameters. The Fuchsian accessory parameters C_i are determined uniquely by the condition that the monodromy group of (4.5) is Fuchsian, i.e. is represented by real 2×2 matrices.

Whittaker in [11], studying the birational transformations of curves (4.4) and the corresponding transformations of accessory parameters C_i in (4.5) found explicit expressions for uniformization of a special case of (4.4):

$$y^2 = x^5 + 1 \tag{4.6}$$

(here $g = 2$ and $e_6 = \infty$). The group G^* is conjugate to the group generated by the 5 transformations

$$\sigma_j^*: x \mapsto \frac{\alpha x - \epsilon_j}{\epsilon_j^* x - \alpha}: \; j = 0,\dots,4$$

for $\epsilon_j = \exp((4j+1)\pi i/10)$: $j = 0,\dots,4$ and $\alpha = \sqrt{\frac{\sqrt{5}+1}{2}}$. The group G itself is generated by $\sigma_0\sigma_1,\dots,\sigma_0\sigma_4$, and the corresponding linear differential equation in this case is reduced to a particular Gauss hypergeometric equation.

Whittaker called automorphic functions in the case (4.6) hyperlemmiscate functions, and on the basis of (4.6) and other similar examples had been led to a conjecture describing $R(x)$ in (4.5) explicitly:

Conjecture 4.1: Let $P(x) = (x-e_1)\dots(x-e_{2g+2})$. Then the Fuchsian accessory parameters $C_0,\dots,C_{2g-2}$ in (4.5) are polynomial in e_i, and we have the following explicit expression for R(x) in (4.5):

$$R(x) = \frac{3}{16}\cdot\{(\frac{P'(x)}{P(x)})^2 - \frac{2g+2}{2g+1}\cdot\frac{P''(x)}{P(x)}\}. \tag{4.7}$$

Whittaker's students and collaborators studied this conjecture. Recent results on the Whittaker conjecture belong to Rankin [50], who showed the truth of the Whittaker conjecture for a large number of equations associated with one of the finite groups on the Schwarz's list, when (4.5) is related to the hypergeometric equation.

We ran numerical checks for random curves (4.4) of genus g, $2 \le g \le 10$ (particularly with integral e_i); the Conjecture 4.1 is incorrect.

Our numerical experiments with Fuchsian accessory parameters C_i in (4.5) suggest that the form of C_i predicted by (4.7) in Conjecture 4.1 holds only in cases when the differential equation (4.5) is reducible by an algebraic transformation to Gauss hypergeometric equations. Consequently, if our evidence holds, for a given g there would be only finitely many hyperelliptic equations (4.4) for which the accessory parameters C_i in (4.5) are expressed as polynomials of e_j as in (4.7). Still there are quite a few such equations. Rankin [50] presented some interesting examples, e.g. $y^2 = x(x^{10}+11x^5-1)$ (cf. with Apéry's equation for recurrences approximating $\zeta(2)$, see last paragraph of [46] and [12], and $3y^2 - 2y^3 = 4x^3 - 3x^4$; $y^m = x^p(x^q-1)^r$; $y^m = (\frac{x^8+14x^5+1)^3}{x^4(x^4-1)^4}$ etc.

Even if accessory parameters are not globaly algebraic (as functions of branch points in case of (4.4)), one is still very much interested in their arithmetic properties. Our particular attention is focused on the following problem [12]:

Problem: Let us consider a linear differential equation (4.5) for the hyperelliptic equation (4.4) that gives a Fuchsian uniformization (or the corresponding equation (4.2) for the general algebraic curve). Let us assume that this algebraic curve is defined over $\bar{\mathbb{Q}}$ (or even $\mathbb{Q}$). Are the accessory parameters algebraic? If they are not algebraic, are they algebraically independent?

The algebraicity of accessory parameters is known only in cases when the answer to the Whittaker conjecture is positive and, in general, when the equation (4.5) is reducible to a Gauss hypergeometric equation.

We conducted multiprecision computations of accessory parameters for a generic curve (4.4) with integral e_i. Our computations seem to indicate the transcendence of accessory parameters. Namely, we determined the absence of algebraic relations of moderate degrees (100 at most) with moderate size integral coefficients (up to 10^{100}). We do not know of any examples of algebraicity of accessory parameters other than in cases arising from Schwarz triangle functions or other arithmetic subgroups.

This class of problem is a part of a more general problem

on the transcendence of elements of the monodromy matrices of Fuchsian linear differential equations. Next to nothing is known about this problem. E.g. among the second order Fuchsian linear differential equations the transcendence of elements of the monodromy matrices had been studied only in case when a monodromy group of this equation is commutative.

We are able to prove some transcendental results for monodromy groups of Fuchsian differential equations. Our methods stem from the uniformization of these Fuchsian equations by special subgroups of $SL_2(\mathbb{C})$ using the uniformization of algebraic curves by special functions in H having only 3 branch points [46]. The only condition we impose is the existence of a G-function solution for this differential equation.

Theorem 4.2: Let a Fuchsian differential equation $L[\frac{d}{dx},x]y = 0$ of order n be satisfied by a transcendental G-function $f(x)$ that does not satisfy any equation over $\bar{\mathbb{Q}}(x)$ of order less than n. If $L[\frac{d}{dx},x] \in \bar{\mathbb{Q}}(x)[\frac{d}{dx}]$, and $\mathfrak{M}$ is a monodromy group of L, corresponding to a choice of a fundamental system of solutions $y_1,\ldots,y_n$ of $Ly = 0$ with algebraic initial conditions $y_j^{(i)}(x_1)$ for an algebraic x_1, then at least one element of one matrix from $\mathfrak{M}$ is transcendental, provided that the base point x_1 of $L[\cdot]y = 0$ is nonsingular.

5. Bignum and high precision computations of solutions of linear differential equations.

Many computations associated with number theory require manipulations with integers or real numbers of large sizes. These numbers are called bignums and bigfloats as opposite to the fixed precision numbers that are primitives in computer operations and most high-level languages. Obviously, the speed of manipulation with bignums and bigfloats starts to depend on their sizes. In order to highlight this dependence we will differentiate between operational and boolean (bit) complexity. By operational complexity of computations we understand the number of operations (additions, multiplications, comparisons and copyings) independently of the sizes of numbers involved. On the other hand, by the boolean (or bit) complexity of computations we understand the total number of operations required to complete a given program. Here the primitive operations are understood to be: additions, multiplications, comparisons, storage and retrieval of short numbers (say, single digit or single bit numbers). (This definition is most closely associated with modern serial machine, where each of the primitive operations takes about the same time.)

The operational complexity does serve as a good measurement of computational time only if all intermediate operands have bounded length. This is the case of: a) floating point computations with a fixed precision M; or b) computations in modular arithmetic, where all results are considered mod a fixed number. (Still the computational time will differ from the operational complexity by a factor equal to the complexity of multiplication of primitive numbers in cases a) or b).)

To understand the differences between operations on short and long numbers one should consider the multiplication of bignums.

Let us denote by $M_{bit}(n)$ the bit complexity of multiplication of two n-bit integers. The best known upper bound on $M_{bit}(n)$ belongs to Schonhage-Strassen [51]:

$$M_{bit}(n) = O(n \log n \log\log n).$$

It is widely assumed that $M_{bit}(n) = O(n \log n)$ (and this was, in fact, proved for a large set of n). It is also conjectured, though without too much of supporting evidence, that the last bound is tight: $M_{bit}(n) = \Omega(n \log n)$. For related complexity investigation see [52], [53].

The $M_{bit}(n)$ quantity is indeed crucial. In comparison, a bit complexity of addition is relatively simple: $M_{add}(n) = O(n)$ (in the scalar case; in parallel case, or on VLSI, it is not that simple). The multiplication of bigfloats is, obviously, as bit complex as that of bignums.

A (normalized) bigfloat of precision n is denoted by $.b_0 \ldots b_n \times SIGN \times B^{EXP}$ $(= SIGN \cdot \{b_0 \cdot B^{EXP-1} + b_1 \cdot B^{EXP-2} + \ldots\})$, where B is the base: B = 2, or, say, B = 10, SIGN is the sign: 0, $\pm$ 1 and EXP is the exponent. The normalization condition is $b_0=1$ for SIGN$\neq$0 and the overflow conditions is EXP = O(nlogn).

All algebraic operations on bigfloats have bit complexity of the same order of magnitude as a multiplication. For example, let B(n) denote one of the following bit complexities: division of n-bit bigfloat numbers, square root extraction, or raising to the fixed (rational) power. Then $B(n) = O(M_{bit}(n))$, and $M_{bit}(n) = O(B(n))$. (The determination of the best constant factors in these equations is an interesting problem. E.g. if D(n) is a bit complexity of inverting an n-bit bigfloat, then the Newton iterations to $1/x-y = 0$ give a bound $D(n) \leq 4 \cdot M_{bit}(n) + O(n)$. What is the best constant instead of 4? cf. [53].)

To determine the complexity of transcendental operations on bigfloats is not that easy. A general problem of bigfloat computations can be formulated as follows:

Problem: Let F(x) be a function defined by algebraic, differential (functional or integral) equations or their combinations, with initial or boundary conditions at rational points or arbitrary bigfloats of full n-bit precision. Let this function F(x) be defined uniquely in the neighborhood of a bigfloat x_0 as an analytic function. Compute $F(x_0)$ with the full n-bit precision with the minimal bit complexity.

Though this question is a practical one, and high precision computations are often needed in mathematical physics, particularly in computation of instabilities and attractors, most often high precision computations are carried out for particular constants of number-theoretic interest. Computations of γ (the Euler constant) and, particularly, π became a major undertaking in computational mathematics, often expensive. Low operational complexity algorithms, for computation of the logarithmic function based on Landen's transformation for elliptic functions (the Gauss arithmetic-geometric mean iteration) were proposed by Salamin and improved by Brent [54] and Borwein-Borwein [5]. These low operational complexity algorithms are translated into low bit complexity algorithms for computation of values of the logarithmic function. Namely, to compute the value of log x (and to be nonambiguous, we can assume that $|x-1| < 1/2$), with the full n-bit precision, starting from the n-bit x, one needs bit-complexity of at most $O(M_{bit}(n) \cdot \log n)$. In particular, n digits of π can be computed in that many short (bit) operations. These particular methods are used in recent computation of π.

For special functions there is no low operational complexity methods of computation that are known to give low bit complexity. That is why we propose low bit complexity methods of computations of values of special functions, not related to any rapidly convergent analytic transformations. Our methods differ in bit complexity by $\log^2 n$ or $\log^3 n$ from the bit complexity of algebraic computations.

(It is an interesting problem [5], whether the computation of n digits of a classical transcendence, like π, can be done in $O(M_{bit}(n))$ only. Probably not, but a proof will be more difficult than the transcendence proof.)

Our new low bit (boolean) complexity algorithms of evaluation solutions of (linear) differential equations are based on the reduction to fast evaluation of solutions of linear difference equations with polynomial coefficients. We start first with the reduction from linear differential equations to the difference ones, and then describe low operational and bit complexity methods of solution of linear difference equations.

Let us look at an arbitrary linear differential equation with rational (polynomial) coefficients, either in the scalar form

$$a_m y^{(m)} + a_{m-1} y^{(m-1)} + \ldots + a_1 y' + a_0 y = 0, \tag{5.1}$$

or, in the general matrix form,

$$\frac{d}{dx} Y(x) = A(x) \cdot Y(x),$$

where $a_i \in \mathbb{C}(x)$, and $A(x) \in M_n(\mathbb{C}(x))$. We are interested in the evaluation of solutions of (5.1) or (5.2) with an arbitrary precision using the method of (formal) power series expansions [56]. A solution of (5.1) or (5.2) is determined by its initial conditions at $x = x_0$. If $x = x_0$ is not a singular point of (5.1) or (5.2), then the solution $y = y(x)$ of (5.1) or $y(x)$ of (5.2) is uniquely determined by its initial conditions $y(x_0),\ldots,y^{(m-1)}(x_0)$ in the case of (5.1), or $n \times n$, matrix $Y(x_0)$, in the case of (5.2), respectively. If $x = x_0$ is a regular singular point of (5.1) or (5.2), then the initial conditions take the form of a few leading terms in the expansion of $y(x)$ or $Y(x)$ in powers of $(x-x_0)^\alpha$ for various local exponents α. Finally, if $x = x_0$ is an irregular singularity of (5.1) or (5.2), one can interpret as initial conditions at $x = x_0$ few first terms in the asymptotic expansions that are linear combinations of formal powers series from $\mathbb{C}[[x-x_0]]$ times functions like $\exp(Q((x-x_0)^{-\alpha}))$ for $Q(x) \in \mathbb{C}[x]$. In all these cases, having specified initial conditions for $y(x)$ or $Y(x)$ at $x = x_0$, we want to evaluate within a given precision ℓ $y(x)$ or $Y(x)$ at another point $x = x_1$. For all practical purposes we assume that values of x_0 and x_1 are given correctly with the precision of ℓ bits (or decimal digits), or as rational or algebraic numbers of sizes less than ℓ. To determine values at $x = x_1$ from those at $x = x_0$ one has to specify a path from x_0 to x_1 on the Riemann surface (or its universal covering) of $y(x)$ or $Y(x)$. This problem of analytic continuation had been studied by us in [12], and we will return to it shortly. Now we look at the most important case when $x = x_1$ lies within the disc of convergence of power series expansions defining $y(x)$ or $Y(x)$. [In the case of a regular point $x = x_0$ this is simply the disc of convergence of $y(x)$ or $Y(x)$. If $x = x_0$ is a regular or irregular singularity, and the expansion at $x = x_0$ looks like $y(x) = \varphi_0(x)\cdot y_0(x)$, where $y_0(x) \in \mathbb{C}[[x-x_0]]$, and $\varphi_0(x) = (x-x_0)^{\alpha}$ or $\varphi_0(x) = \exp(Q((x-x_0)^{-\alpha}))$, then $x = x_1$ should lie within the disc of convergence of $y_0(x)$.]

In the cases of (5.1) and (5.2), when the coefficients are rational functions and the set S of singularities of (5.1) or (5.2) is a discrete (finite) set, the radius of convergence of $y(x)$ or $Y(x)$, if nonzero, is bounded from below by the distance from the point $x = x_0$ to the nearest point in S. We consider now only the case of nonzero radius of convergence (though, the general case can be treated in the same framework using the generalized Borel transform). For this reason we now consider the case when $x = x_0$ is a regular or a regular singular point only. For (5.1), the basis of solutions at $x = x_0$ can be expressed in terms of regular expansions

$$y(x,\alpha) = (x-x_0)^{\alpha} \sum_{n=0}^{\infty} y_n(\alpha)\cdot(x-x_0)^n \tag{5.3}$$

The coefficients $y_n(\alpha)$ are determined for $n \geq 0$ from the initial conditions at $x = x_0$ and the linear recurrence

$$\sum_{j=0}^{\min(n,d)} y_{n-j}(\alpha)\cdot f_j(\alpha+n-j) = 0, \tag{5.4}$$

$n = 1,2,3,\ldots$, with the explicit expression of coefficients $f_j(\beta)$ in terms of a_i in (5.1) as follows: if $a_j = Q_j(x)\cdot(x-x_0)^j$ $(j = 0,\ldots,m)$, then for

$f(x,\alpha) \overset{\text{def}}{\equiv} \alpha(\alpha-1)\ldots(\alpha-m+1)\cdot Q_m(x) +\ldots+ \alpha Q_1(x) + Q_0(x)$, we put $f(x,\alpha) = f_0(\alpha) + (x-x_0)f_1(\alpha) +\ldots+ (x-x_0)^d f_d(\alpha)$, where d is the bound of degrees for all polynomials $Q_j(x)$. The exponent α in (5.3) satisfies the indicial equation $f_0(\alpha) = 0$ [56].

Similarly, we look at regular solutions $Y(x)$ of (5.2) having a regular expansion of the form

$$Y(x) = \{\sum_{N=0}^{\infty} C_N(x-x_0)^N\}\cdot(x-x_0)^W, \tag{5.5}$$

where C_0 ($\in M_{n\times n}(\mathbb{C})$) is the initial condition for $Y(x)$ at $x = x_0$, and the (matrix) coefficients C_N of (5.5) are determined from the matrix linear recurrence of length d (the maximal degree of the rational function in $A(x)$ in (5.2)). To derive this recurrence, let us consider a case of a regular point $x = x_0$ when $W = 0$. For $A(x)$ from (5.2) let us put $A(x) = A_0(x)/d(x)$, where $A_0(x) \in M_{n\times n}(\mathbb{C}[x])$, $d(x) \in \mathbb{C}[x]$. We put $d(x) = \Sigma_{j=0}^{d} d_j(x-x_0)^j$, where $d_0 \neq 0$, and $A_0(x) = \Sigma_{j=0}^{d-1} A_j(x-x_0)^j$. Then we have the following recurrence on C_N:

$$C_{N+1}\cdot(N+1)\cdot d_0 = \sum_{i=0}^{\min\{N,d-1\}} A_i\cdot C_{N-i} - \sum_{i=0}^{\min\{N,d-1\}} d_{i+1}(N-i)\cdot C_{N-i}. \tag{5.6}$$

Here $d_j = d^{(j)}(x_0)/j!$, $A_i = A^{(i)}(x_0)/i!$. In applications, in order to evaluate the power series expansion (5.3) or (5.5), we should look at recurrences satisfied by $C_N(x-x_0)^N$ instead of C_N. E.g., the recurrence for $C_N(x-x_0)^N$ has the form

$$C_{N+1}(x-x_0)^{N+1} = \{\sum_{i=0}^{\min\{N,d-1\}} \alpha_{i;N}\, C_{N-i}(x-x_0)^{N-i}\}/\delta_0, \qquad (5.7)$$

where $\delta_0 = (N+1)\cdot d_0$, $\alpha_{i;N} = (x-x_0)\cdot[A_i(x-x_0)^i - d_{i+1}(N-i)(x-x_0)^i]$: $i = 0,\ldots,\min\{N,d-1\}$. This recurrence (like (5.4) or (5.6)) can be written in the matrix form. We write this matrix recurrence that computes simultaneously d consecutive coefficients $C_{N-i}(x-x_0)^{N-i}$: $i = 0,\ldots,d-1$ ($i \le \min\{N,d-1\}$), and simultaneously, the N-th partial sum $Y_N(x) = \Sigma_{i=0}^{N-1} C_i(x-x_0)^i$ of $Y(x)$. This new recurrence follows from (5.7), if to add one more formula:

$$Y_{N+1}(x) = Y_N(x) + C_N(x-x_0)^N. \qquad (5.8)$$

To represent the matrix recurrence, we introduce a $n(d+1) \times n$ matrix $\mathcal{Y}_N = (Y_n, C_N\cdot(x-x_0)^N,\ldots,C_{N-(d-1)}\cdot(x-x_0)^{N-d+1,t}$ From (5.7)-(5.8) we deduce a matrix recurrence:

$$\mathcal{Y}_{N+1} = \mathcal{G}(N)\cdot\mathcal{Y}_N,$$

where $\mathcal{G}(N)$ is a $n(d+1) \times n(d+1)$ matrix consisting of blocks of $n \times n$ matrices: $\mathcal{G}(N) = (B_{ij}(N))_{i,j=1}^{d+1}$. Here $B_{1,1}(N) = 1$, $B_{1,2}(N) = 1$, $B_{i,j}(N) = 0$ for $j = 3,\ldots,d+1$; $B_{k,\ell}(N) = \delta_{k-1,\ell}$ for $k \ge 3$, $B_{2,1}(N) = 0$, and

$$B_{2,j}(N) = \alpha_{j-2;N}/\delta_0: \ j = 2,\ldots,d+1, \qquad (5.10)$$

in the notations of (5.7). Similarly, in the case of equation (5.1), we get a matrix recurrence

$$\mathcal{Y}_{N+1} = \mathcal{G}(N)\cdot\mathcal{Y}_N,$$

for $(d+1)\times(d+1)$ matrix $\mathcal{G}(N)$ and $\mathcal{Y}_N = (y_N(x), y_N(\alpha)\cdot(x-x_0)^N, \ldots$ $\ldots, y_{N-d+1}(\alpha)(x-x_0)^{N-d+1})$, for $\mathcal{Y}_N(x) = (x-x_0)^{\alpha}\cdot\Sigma_{i=0}^{N-1} y_i(\alpha)\cdot(x-x_0)^i$.

Let us determine now the computational cost of deriving the matrix recurrence (5.9) from the original linear differential equations (5.1) and (5.2), and the dependence of $\mathcal{G}(N)$ in (5.9) on N, x_0 and x. To derive (5.9) we need to know the original coefficients of (5.1) or (5.2) and to know α or W. In all important cases α is a fixed rational number (and W is a diagonal matrix with rational number entries). To compute coefficients in (5.4) or (5.6) one needs to determine the coefficients of the translated polynomials in (5.1) or (5.2) after the translation $x \to x + x_0$. Thus the total number of operations to compute the coefficients matrix $\mathcal{G}(N)$ in (5.9) is $O(n^2 d\log d)$ in the case of (5.2), and is $O(n\, d\log d)$ in the case of (5.1) (with $d \geq n$ in the case of (5.1)). The matrix $\mathcal{G}(N)$ in (5.9) can be represented as $\mathcal{G}(N) = \mathcal{G}_0(N)/d_0(N)$, where $\mathcal{G}_0(N)$ and $d_0(N)$ are polynomial in N, x_0 and X. In the case of (5.2) (with $W = 0$), $\mathcal{G}(N)$ is an $n(d+1) \times n(d+1)$ matrix, with $\mathcal{G}_0(N)$, $d_0(N)$ linear in N, polynomial in x_0 and $x - x_0$ of degrees at most d in x_0, and with $\mathcal{G}_0(N)$ of degree d in $(x-x_0)$ ($d_0(N)$ is independent of x). More precisely, $\mathcal{G}_0(N)$, as a polynomial in $x - x_0$ and x_0 has a total degree of at most d. In the case of the equation (5.1), $\mathcal{G}_0(N)$ and $d_0(N)$ are polynomial of degree n in N; they are polynomials in $x - x_0$ and x_0. $d_0(N)$ is polynomial in x_0 of degree at most d, and $\mathcal{G}_0(N)$ is polynomial in $x - x_0$ and x_0 of total degree at most d.

The growth of coefficients in the power series expansions $y(x)$ or $Y(x)$ can be estimated e.g. from the recurrences (5.2) or (5.4) (or (5.9)) according to the Poincare-Perron theorem (see Perron [57]), which states that the asymptotics of solutions of recurrences are determined by roots of the limit characteristic equation of a linear recurrence with constant coefficients that one deduces from (5.2) or (5.4) as $N \to \infty$. An explicit form of (5.2) or (5.4) shows that these roots of the limit characteristic equation are $1/(s-x_0)$ for $s \in S$ (the set of singularities of (5.1) or (5.2)), when x_0 is a regular point. More precisely, an asymptotic analysis of recurrences (5.2) or (5.4) (or (5.9)) gives the following leading term of the asymptotics of coefficients $y_N(\alpha)$ or C_N:

$$|y_N(\alpha)| \leq \gamma_1 \cdot N^{\nu} \cdot \text{dist}^*(x_0,S)^{-N}, \tag{5.10}$$

$$\|C_N\| \leq \gamma_2 \cdot N^{\mu} \cdot \text{dist}^*(x_0,S)^{-N}. \tag{5.11}$$

Here $\text{dist}^*(x_0,S) = \min\{|s-x_0|: s \in S, x_0 \neq S\}$, and $\|.\|$ is a c_0-norm of $n \times n$ matrices. Asymptotic bounds (5.10) or (5.11) hold for arbitrary equations (5.1) or (5.2) with any initial conditions at regular (singularity) $x = x_0$. In general (i.e. for generic equations (5.1) or (5.2) or for generic initial conditions), one can complement (5.10) and (5.11) with a similar lower bound for $N \geq N_0$, but with different constants γ_1 and γ_2. Bounds (5.10) and (5.11) show that whenever $\delta > 0$, and $|x_1-x_0|/\text{dist}^*(x_0,S) < 1-\delta$, one obtains the value of $y(x_1)$ or $Y(x_1)$ from the matrix $\mathcal{Y}_N$ at $x = x_1$ because $y_N(x_1)$ or $Y_N(x_1)$

converges to $y(x_1)$ or $Y(x_1)$, respectively, as a geometric progression in N. To evaluate $y(x_1)$ or $Y(x_1)$ with the precision ℓ one needs the value of $\mathcal{Y}_N$ with the precision $\ell + O(\log \ell)$ for $N = O(-\ell \log(\frac{|x_1-x_0|}{\text{dist*}(x_0,S)}))$, if $|x_1-x_0|/\text{dist*}(x_0,S) < 1-\delta$ (for fixed $\delta > 0$).

Now we can touch upon the problem of analytic continuation studied in detail in [12]. The key is the standard superposition formula that expresses the solution $Y(x;x_0)$ of (5.2) normalized at $x = x_0$: $Y(x;x_0)|_{x=x_0} = I_n$ has the form of chain rule:

$$Y(x;x_0) = Y(x;x_1)\cdot Y(x_1;x_0) \tag{5.12}$$

for any three points x_0,x_1,x in $\mathbb{CP}^1$. This superposition formula leads to the chain rule of evaluation of an arbitrary solution $Y(x)$ with the initial conditions $Y(x)|_{x=x_0} = A$ at $x = x_0$ at a point x_{fin}, which is the end-point of a path $\overline{x_0x_1\ldots x_mx_{m+1}}$ in $\mathbb{CP}^1$ with m+2 vertices $x_0,x_1,\ldots,x_m,x_{m+1} = x_{fin}$:

$$Y(x)|_{x=x_{fin}} = Y(x_{m+1};x_m)\ldots Y(x_2;x_1)Y(x_1;x_0)\cdot A. \tag{5.13}$$

A rule (5.13) is unambiguous, whenever x_{i+1} lies within the disc of convergence of $Y(x;x_i)$, e.g. whenever for a fixed $\delta > 0$, $|x_{i+1}-x_i|/\text{dist*}(x_i,S) < 1-\delta$.

Let us estimate now the bit complexity of computing of $Y(x_1;x_0)$ using the matrix recurrence (5.9). As above, we assume that for a fixed $\delta > 0$, $|x_1-x_0|/\text{dist*}(x_0,S) < 1-\delta$. As it was shown above, to compute the $n \times n$ matrix with precision

$\ell + O(\log \ell)$ one can compute $\mathcal{Y}_N$ for $N = -O(\ell/\log(|x_1-x_0|/\mathrm{dist}^*(x_0,S)))$ from (5.9) with initial conditions $Y(x)|_{x=x_0} = I_n$. (I.e. $C_0 = I_n$.)

To estimate the bit complexity of computations of $\mathfrak{a}_N$ one needs to know the amount of bit information in the representation of x_0 and x_1. We can represent x_0 and x_1 as rational numbers p/q of logarithmic size(p,q) = log(max{1,|p|,|q|}), or as b-bit binary (floating point) numbers $\underbrace{.b_1b_2b_3 \ldots b_b}_{b} \times 2^{EXP}$ (for EXP = O(b)). The matrix of coefficients $\mathfrak{a}(N)$ in (5.9) depends polynomially on x_0 and $x_1 - x_0$. Convenient parameters can be x_0 and $x_1 - x_0$ or $\frac{x_1-x_0}{x_0}$ (if $x_0 \neq 0$). Let us look at x_0, $x_1 - x_0$ written with a common denominator: $x_0 = \frac{X_0}{D}$, $x_1-x_0 = \frac{X_{10}}{D}$ (e.g. $D = 2^b$ in the binary representation). We define then $b = \log_2\max\{1,|D|,|X_0|,|X_{10}|\}$ as the (logarithmic) size of x_0, x_1-x_0. Then $\mathfrak{a}(N) = \mathfrak{a}_0(N)/d_0(N)$ where $\mathfrak{a}_0(N), d_0(N)$ are linear in N with coefficients that are $O(d\cdot b)$-bit integers. Let $e = -\log_2(|x_1-x_0)/\mathrm{dist}^*(x_0,S)) > 0$ be the measure of closeness of x_1 to x_0. Then we need to compute $\mathcal{Y}_N$ for $N = O(\ell/e)$ with the precision $\ell + O(\log \ell)$.

To compute $\mathcal{Y}_N$ from the matrix recurrence (5.9) we use the fast binary-splitting technique of Theorem 6.1. This way we arrive at the following <u>local</u> evaluation of the solution Y(x) of (5.2), where we specify all the dependencies on the sizes of coefficients involved.

<u>Theorem 5.1</u>: Let (5.2) be a fixed matrix linear differential equation, where all elements of A(x) are rational functions of

the total degree at most d, and coefficients of these functions are rational numbers of sizes at most k (or arbitrary complex numbers represented by their binary approximations as k-bit binary floats). Let $x = x_0$ be a regular or regular singular point of (5.2) represented by a rational number of (logarithmic) size of at most b, or by a b-bit binary floating point number. Let $Y(x)$ be a solution of (5.2) with fixed initial conditions at $x = x_0$, and let x_1 be another binary b-bit number, lying within the disc of convergence of $Y(x)$. Then to compute $Y(x)$ at $x = x_1$ with precision of ℓ leading digits one needs at most

$$c_1 \cdot M_{atrix}(n) \cdot \frac{db+k}{e} \cdot M_{bit}(\ell) \cdot \log^2 \ell + O(\ell)$$

bit-operations. Here $e = -\log_2(|x_1 - x_0|/\mathrm{dist}^*(x_0,S)) > 0$, $M_{atrix}(n)$ is the number of operations needed for $n \times n$ matrix multiplications, $M_{bit}(\ell)$ ($= \ell \cdot \log(\ell) \cdot \log\log(\ell)$) is the number of operations for ℓ-bit multiplication, and c_1 is an absolute constant. The constant in $O(\ell)$ depends on initial conditions of $Y(x)$.

Theorem 5.1 is the basis of bit-burst method of fast evaluation of any solution of a linear differential equation at any point on its Riemann surface. According to this method the evaluation of any branch of any solution with the precision of ℓ leading bits (digits) requires at worst only $O(M_{bit}(\ell) \cdot \log^3 \ell \cdot (1+o(\ell))$ total bit operations.

Starting from Theorem 5.1 and using the chain rule (5.13)

of analytic continuation along any fixed path, we can evaluate $Y(x)$ (the solution of (5.2) with given initial conditions) everywhere on its Riemann surface. First, the recipes for the optimal choice of polygon $\overline{x_0 x_1 \ldots x_m x_{m+1}}$ homotopic to a given path γ in $\mathbb{CP}^1 \setminus S$ are presented in [12], so as to minimize the total number of operations of evaluations of $Y(x)$ at intermediate points x_i. Second, we are using Theorem 5.1 in a clever way to evaluate $Y(x)$ from $x = x_0$ to $x = x_1$ making several steps between x_0 and x_1 (again using the chain rule (5.13)), releasing consecutive blocks of x_1 in bursts. We call this method "bit-burst" method. In this approach one, in order to evaluate $Y(x)$ at a bigfloat $x = \Sigma_{N=0}^{\infty} b_N \cdot B^{-N}$, evaluates $Y(x)$ consecutively at $x_i = x_i + \Sigma_{N=2^i}^{2^{i+1}} b_N \cdot B^{-N}$ by analytic continuation of $Y(x)$ (rule (5.13)): "adding more bits of a number, but computing with the same accuracy". In this approach we are matching the distance from the evaluation point to the point of expansion with the size of the point of evaluation. In particular, we move initial conditions from $x = x_0$ to a nearby point $x = x_0'$ of bounded size, and then evaluate $Y(x)$ at $x = x_1$ starting from $x = x_0'$ in bit-bursts. This way we arrive at the following general theorem that gives an upper bound on the bit complexity:

Theorem 5.2: Let (5.2) be a given linear differential equation with rational function coefficients, and $Y(x)$ be its arbitrary (regular) solution with initial conditions at

$x = x_{in}$, where x_{in} is an K-bit number. Given a path γ from x_{in} to an K-bit number x_{fin} (on the Riemann surface of $Y(x)$) of length L, one can evaluate $Y(x)|_{x=x_{fin}}$ at $x = x_{fin}$ with the full K-bit precision one needs at most

$$O(M_{bit}(K)(\log^3 K + \log L))$$

bit operations.

The bit-burst method in the general form of Theorem 5.2 should be improved: one would like to see $\log^3 K$ replaced by $\log K$ always. We don't know how to do it in general, but sometimes the complexity can be lowered:

I. If x_{in} and x_{fin} are fixed rational numbers (or are given as big floats with $o(K)$ bits), then the computation of $Y(x)$ with the full K bits of precision has bit complexity at most $O(M_{bit}(K)\cdot(\log^2 K + \log L))$. (This is the case of computation of classical constants.)

II. If the differential equation (5.1) or (5.2) possesses special arithmetic properties, bit-complexity can be lowered. E.g. if the equation (5.1) is globally nilpotent or (5.1)-(5.2) possesses a solution which is either an E-function or a G-function, then the general bit bound of Theorem 5.2 can be lowered to

$$O(M_{bit}(K)\cdot(\log^2 K + \log L)).$$

If, further, like in I, x_{in} and x_{fin} are given only by a few bits (i.e. are fixed rational numbers), and $Y(x)$ is built from

E-or G-functions, then K significant digits of $Y(x_0)$ can be computed in

$$O(M_{bit}(K)\cdot(\log K + \log L))$$

bit operations.

This bound is unsurpassed by any other algorithm even for elementary functions, like the exponent, where low operational complexity algorithms are well known [5], [54-55].

Remark: The bit-burst method should not be confused with the popular bit-serial (or bit-by-bit) method, where each new bit of the evaluated function is added for a new input bit of the value. Instead, we output the full precision of evaluated function for a bit burst of an input value, and the number of input bits increases geometrically. Note a significant difference with the Newton method of computations, where input bits are also introduced in bursts, but at each step only an appropriate precision of evaluation is needed, thus making the algorithm self-correcting. Of course, the Newton method is efficient only for computation of algebraic functions. The bit burst method is particularly fast when the result is needed with full precision, but the amount of input bits is limited. This is the case, e.g. of computations of solutions of linear differential equations at fixed rational points, or of computations of invariants of differential equations such as monodromy group.

6. Fast solution of matrix difference equations and parallel algorithms.

As we saw in the proof of Theorem 5.1 the main component in the fast evaluation of solutions of differential equations using the power series method is the solution of a difference equation with rational function coefficients. Instead of the recurrence (5.9) we look at the matrix difference equation written as follows

$$A_{N+1} = C(N)\cdot A_N \tag{6.1}$$

where $C(N)$ is $n \times n$ matrix rationally dependent on N. The solution A_N of (6.1) with initial conditions $A_N|_{N=0} = A_0$ has a symbolic representation

$$A_N = \overleftarrow{\prod_{i=0}^{N-1}} C(i)\cdot A_0, \text{ or}$$
$$A_N = C(N-1)\cdot C(N-2)\cdot\ldots\cdot C(1)\cdot C(0)\cdot A_0, \tag{6.2}$$

i.e. the order of the terms in the product is reversed. The fast method of computation of A_N in (6.2) is known as the binary-splitting method (or divide and conquer method). This is a known technique to accelerate the solution of linear recurrences, and also a well known instrument in applications of the Chinese remainder theorem and interpolation. In this method a binary tree (when $N = 2^k$; otherwise more complicated trees associated with addition chain methods are used) of operations is constructed so that multiplication of terms in (6.2) proceeds in the way that operands have slow growing sizes. (This method is opposite to the obvious method of computation of (6.2) with consecutive multiplications by $C(i)$).

With notations of (6.2) we introduce the following auxiliary variables

$$\mathfrak{A}_{L;K} = \overleftarrow{\prod_{j=K}^{L-1}} C(j) \tag{6.3}$$

for $L > K$. We put $\mathfrak{A}_{K;K} = I_n$. In these notations A_N is

$$A_N = \mathfrak{A}_{N;0} \cdot A_0. \tag{6.4}$$

There is a simple chain rule of computations of $\mathfrak{A}_{L;K}$ which is the basis of any splitting method including the binary splitting method:

$$\mathfrak{A}_{L;K} = \mathfrak{A}_{L;M} \cdot \mathfrak{A}_{M;K} \quad \text{for} \quad L \geq M \geq K. \tag{6.5}$$

The chain rule (6.5) provides us with an immediate algorithm of computations of $\mathfrak{A}_{L;K}$ from the binary expansion of L and K. This method is at its best when N is a power of 2, $N = 2^k$.

The algorithm consists of the outer loop over all ℓ from 0 to k and the inner loop over all $(k-\ell)$-bit (binary) integers. We start at $\ell = 0$ with the initialization:

$$\mathfrak{A}_{K+1;K} = C(K) \text{ for all } K \text{ in } K = 0,\ldots,2^k-1 \tag{6.6}$$

At the ℓ-th step we have determined all $\mathcal{G}_{2^\ell(K+1);2^\ell\cdot K}$ for all $(k-\ell)$-bit integers K: $0 \leq K \leq 2^{\ell-k} - 1$. At the step $\ell + 1$ we use the rule (6.5), and obtain:

$$\mathcal{G}_{2^{\ell+1}(K+1);2^{\ell+1}K} = \mathcal{G}_{2^\ell(2K+2);2^\ell(2K+1)} \cdot \mathcal{G}_{2^\ell(2K+1);2^{\ell+1}\cdot K} \tag{6.7}$$

for $0 \leq K \leq 2^{k-\ell-1} - 1$, i.e. $\mathcal{G}_{2^{\ell+1}(K+1);2^{\ell+1}\cdot K}$ are determined for all $(k-\ell-1)$-bit integers.

Finally, at step k at $\ell = k$, according to (6.4), A_N is determined as: $A_N = \mathcal{G}_{2^k\cdot(K+1);2^k\cdot K} = \mathcal{G}_{2^k;0}$ at $K = 0$.

For $\ell = 1,\ldots,k$, at ℓ-th step of this algorithm we perform in (6.7) $2^{k-\ell}$ matrix multiplications. Binary-splitting method is efficient if the computations are conducted with increased precision, i.e. all bits of information in computations of A_N via (6.1)-(6.2) are preserved. In the typical case, when $C(N)$ is rational in N, the total (memory) space needed to hold all bits of A_N (as a rational number, i.e. numerator and denominator) is $O(n^2\cdot N\cdot \log_2 N)$. [Only in special cases, when the recurrence (6.1) represents a recurrence associated with a globally nilpotent Fuchsian linear differential equation the memory requirements are $O(N)$.] It is important to notice that the binary-splitting method of computation of A_N in (6.6)-(6.7) requires about the same amount of memory. Indeed, to compute the ℓ-th step of the algorithm only the previous step is needed with a total amount of memory space of $O(N \log_2 N)$.

The total amount of operations depends on the cost of the multiplication of ℓ-bit numbers $M_{bit}(\ell)$. Under the assumptions above, that $C(N)$ is a rational function of N, let

$$C(N) = \frac{C_0(N)}{d(N)} \tag{6.8}$$

where $C_0(N) \in M_{n\times n}(\mathbb{Z}[N]), d(N) \in \mathbb{Z}[N]$. Let in (6.8) d be the maximal degree of polynomials in $C_0(N)$ and $d(N)$. With (6.8) substituted in (6.2) the solution A_N of (6.1) can be represented as

$$A_N = \frac{\overleftarrow{\prod_{i=0}^{N-1}} C_0(i)}{\prod_{i=0}^{N-1} d(i)} A_0. \tag{6.9}$$

We compute $\overleftarrow{\prod}_{i=0}^{N-1} C_0(i)$ using the binary-splitting algorithm of (6.6)-(6.7) for $C_0(N)$ instead of $C(N)$. Let h be the maximum of sizes of coefficients of polynomials in $C_0(N)$ and $d(N)$. Then, as it follows from the iterative scheme (6.7), all $\mathcal{C}_{2^\ell\cdot(K+1);2^\ell\cdot K}$ for $0 \le K \le 2^{k-\ell} - 1$ are integers of sizes bounded by $O((d+h)\cdot 2^\ell \cdot \log_2 N)$ (for $\ell \le k$). [The constant under $O(.)$ depends only on n and logarithmically so; by choosing instead of h the maximum of sizes of polynomials in $C_0(N)$ and different norm of the matrix, the dependence on n can be removed.] Consequently, at every step from $\ell = 1$ to k the total number of bit operations is bounded by $2^{\ell-k} \times M_{bit}(2^\ell \log_2 N)\cdot(d+h)$. The total number of bit-operations (with $\log_2 N = k$) is $O(M_{atrix}(n)\cdot(d+h)\cdot M_{bit}(N)\cdot \log^2 N)$. This gives the numerator in (6.9). The denominator is computed the same way with the total number of operations again bounded by $O((d+h)\cdot M_{bit}(N)\cdot \log^2 N)$. [If necessary, the denominator can be computed faster using the distribution of prime ideals in the Galois group of polynomial $d(N)$. The bit complexity becomes $O(M_{bit}(N).\log N)$.]

When $N = 2^k$ we use binary-splitting method as presented above; if N is arbitrary the corresponding addition chain tree (used for fast computation of N in $O(\log N)$ additions only) is applied.

Theorem 6.1: Let in the recurrence (6.1), $C(\cdot)$ be $n \times n$ matrix whose rational function entries have sizes and degrees bounded by s. Then the bit complexity of computations of A_N in (6.2) is bounded by

$$O(M_{bit}(N)\cdot M_{atrix}(n)\cdot s\cdot \log^2 N),$$

where $M_{atrix}(n)$ is the operational complexity of $n \times n$ matrix multiplication.

(Only the term $\log^2 N$ is not the best possible. Apparently, under additional arithmetic assumptions it can be improved. This is the case when all A_N are "nearly integral," i.e. the generating function $Y(x) = \Sigma_{N=0}^{\infty} A_N x^N$ is a G-function. In this case, and also in the case when $Y(x)$ is a E-function, the $\log^2 N$ term in (6.2) can be replaced by

$$\log N\cdot (\log \log N)^{1+\epsilon}.)$$

Our best results on the upper bounds of the operational complexities of computations of solutions of the recurrence (6.1) are not as good as in Theorem 6.1.

Since in operational complexity count the sizes of operands are irrelevant, binary-splitting methods or a trivial method of computation of (6.2) give the same bound: $O(N\cdot(n^2\cdot d + n^{\mu}))$, where $\mu < 2.5$ is the exponent in the matrix multiplication problem.

The "binary splitting" method:

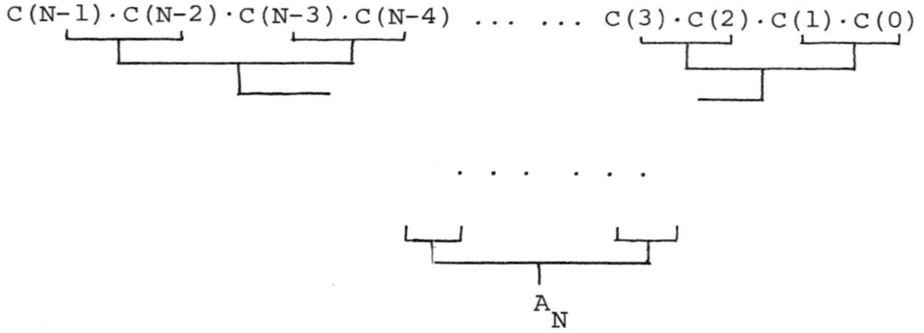

Fig. 2

The linear dependence on N is unsatisfactory. To speed up the computation of (6.2) we use a linear acceleration instead of geometric one. We start with introduction of some auxiliary cost functions. The operational complexity (cost) of multiplication of polynomials of degree d is $M_{poly}(d) = O(d\log d)$; the cost of evaluation of a polynomial $p(x)$ of degree d at $d(+1)$ consecutive points: $0,1,\ldots,d-1(d)$--is $M_{eval}(d) = O(d\log^2 d)$, with $O(d\log d)$ essential multiplications. (There is, though, a simple algorithm that requires $O(d^2)$ additions.) Similarly $M_{shift}(d)$ is the cost of a shift of a polynomial $p(x)$ to $p(x+h)$ for $p(x)$ of degree d.

Let us look at new recurrences following from (6.1)

$$A_{N+k} = C_k(N)\cdot A_N, \tag{6.10}$$

where for any $k \geq 1$

$$C_k(N) = C(N) \cdots C(N+k-1). \tag{6.11}$$

Let us consider, as above, $N = 2^a$ (again similar arguments apply to an arbitrary N):

$$\begin{aligned} A_{N+2^c} &= C_{2^c}(N)\cdot A_N, \\ C_{2^c}(N) &= C_{2^{c-1}}(N+2^{c-1})\cdot C_{2^{c-1}}(N). \end{aligned} \tag{6.12}$$

To compute $C_{2k}(N) = C_k(N+k)\cdot C_k(N)$ from $C_k(N)$, as a matrix with entrees rational in N, one needs: a) to compute the coefficients of polynomial/rational expansion of $C_k(N+k)$ in (powers of) N--it takes $O(n\ M_{shift}(d_k))$ operations: b) to multiply the rational/polynomial entries of $C_k(N+k)$ and $C_k(N)$--this takes $O(M_{atrix}(n)\cdot M_{pol}(d_k))$. Here d_k is the maximum of the degrees of elements of $C_k(N)$.

Now we remark that the scheme (6.10) for a given k is nothing but a version of a general scheme (6.1), but: (i) with a different matrix C--the size of it is the same, but the degrees of its polynomial/rational function entries are different; (ii) the length of the recurrence is k times shorter. The maximum, d_k, of degrees of rational/polynomial entries of

$C_k(N)$ is $\leq kd$; say, for simplicity, $d_k = kd$.

Let us estimate now the total cost of the trivial algorithm of computation of (6.2) in the case of recurrence (6.10) (or a binary-splitting version of this algorithm). To evaluate $A_N = A_{t\cdot k}$ in t steps, starting from A_0 following the rule (6.10) one needs: α) consecutive evaluation of $C_k(0),\ldots,C_k((t-1)\cdot k)$ at $t = N/k$ points. Once the rational function $C_k(\cdot)$ is known, the total operational complexity of α) is $O(n^2\cdot M_{eval}(d_k)\cdot[\frac{N}{kd_k}+1])$. Secondly, one needs β) t consecutive matrix multiplications $C_k(j\cdot k)\cdot A_{j\cdot k}$ for $j = 0,\ldots,t-1$ with the total cost of $O(M_{atrix}(n)\cdot t)$.

The cost of determination of $C_k(\cdot)$ for $k = 2^c$, as follows from the discussion above, is $\Sigma_{b=0}^{c-1}\{O(M_{atrix}(n).M_{pol}(2^b.d)) + O(n^2\cdot M_{shift}(2^b.d))\}$, i.e. the cost of determination of $C_k(\cdot)$ is $O(M_{atrix}(n)\cdot M_{pol}(kd) + n^2 M_{shift}(kd))$. This result is true not only for $k = 2^c$, but for any k.

Thus, whenever $N \geq k^2 d$ (so that $[N/kd_k] \geq 1$), the total cost of computation of A_N using from the scheme (6.10) is:

$$O(M_{atrix}(n)\cdot\{M_{pol}(kd)+\frac{N}{k}\} + n^2\{M_{shift}(kd)+M_{eval}(kd)\cdot\frac{N}{k^2 d}\}).$$

Substituting $M_{pol}(x) = O(x \log x)$, $M_{shift}(x) = O(x \log x)$, $M_{eval}(x) = O(x \log^2 x)$ we can derive the following upper bound on the total cost of computations of A_N using (6.10) with, say, $k = [\sqrt{N/d}] + o(\sqrt{N})$:

$$O(M_{atrix}(n)\sqrt{Nd}\ \log N + n^2\sqrt{Nd}\ \log^2 N)$$

for $N/d \gg 1$. This bound can be slightly improved, also the cost of a single multiplication has to be multiplied by the corresponding weight (if long numbers are involved). We arrive at the following result:

Theorem 6.2: Let in the recurrence

$$A_{N+1} = C(N)\cdot A_N,$$

$C(\cdot)$ be $n \times n$ matrix with rational coefficients with degrees bounded by d. Then the operational complexity (total number of operations) is bounded by

$$O(M_{atrix}(n)\cdot\sqrt{Nd}\ \log N + n^2\sqrt{Nd}\ \log^2 N),$$

with at most $O(M_{atrix}(n)\cdot\sqrt{Nd}\ \log N)$ multiplications.

A far cry from Theorem 6.1 is $O(\sqrt{N}\ \ldots)$ number of operations. Can it be reduced in general? Consider an example:

Example: Let us look on operations in modular arithmetic mod M for a fixed M. Then the cost of an operation is bounded by $O(M_{bit}(\log M)) = O(\log M\cdot \log\log M\cdot \log\log\log M)$.

To factor M one has only to compute in modular arithmetic $N!\ (\mathrm{mod}\ M)$ for $N = [\sqrt{M}]$, i.e. a solution of a simple recurrence:

$$A_{N+1} = N\cdot A_N \mod M,$$

and then check for g.c.d. of $N! \pmod{M}$ and M.

Theorem 6.2 implies that we got a simple method of factorizing M in $O(\sqrt[4]{M}.\log^2 M)$ <u>bit</u> operations. This is asymptotically equivalent to two popular factorization methods: Pollard's ρ-method and Shank's quadratic form composition method. Our method, though, is completely deterministic.

Unlike computations in modular arithmetic, where we have difficulties bounding complexity (as $N \to \infty$) of computation of solutions of (6.1), in the case of fixed precision computations the situation is different. In this case we can use asymptotic expansions of solutions of (6.1) in powers of N near ∞. Using these Borel (Birkhoff's) expansions we get the following bound:

<u>Proposition 6.3:</u> The matrix solution A_N of (6.1) can be computed within the precision M of leading digits in

$$O(\log^3(MN) \cdot M_{bit}(M))$$

bit (boolean) operations.

To prove Proposition 6.3 we use $1/N$ expansions of solutions of difference equations, and asymptotic (inverse factorial) series representation of A_N for large N. In modular arithmetic mod p we do not have similar expansions and the problem of low complexity computations of (6.2) is an open one, cf.[12].

Proposition 6.3 is interesting because many constants

that arise as values of functions not satisfying linear differential equations are well approximated by constants that are values of functions satisfying difference and differential equations. (Among such constants we can name values of Γ-function, Barnes Γ-functions, values of ζ- and L-functions associated with algebraic number fields and modular forms.)

How about nonlinear differential equations? One would like to hope that in this case, as for linear differential equations, the bit-complexity of multiprecision computations is close to the optimal one, perhaps differing by a power of log n only. Unfortunately we cannot in general prove such tight bounds because the Galois group (a rather sophisticated object in the nonlinear case) is more difficult to compute.

(For nonlinear equations with some structure, like generalized Ricatti equations, Painleve-type equations,... etc. low complexity algorithms can be constructed.)

The best bound that we have so far for n-bit precision computations of solutions of nonlinear differential equations is

$$O(\sqrt{n}\,\log^2 n \cdot M_{bit}(n)).$$

As far as massive parallelism is concerned, the full n-bit precision computations of values of nonlinear differential equations (whose right hand side is built from "known" function, that can be themselves solutions of differential equations) can be completed in only O(log n) steps with the total circuitry of $n^{O(1)}$ processors.

How efficient are these methods practically for moderate values of n compared with the standard finite-difference (Runge-Kutta,... etc.) methods of solution?

One of the advantages of the proposed methods is the low storage requirements even in the case when solutions have to be tabulated and not evaluated at a single point. Indeed, our methods determine not only a value of a function, but provide with good approximating polynomials and rational functions that can be used in large domains. Tabulation of these objects requires much less computational effort, when precision n is fixed.

Let us look now at parallel versions of these algorithms. For computations in the parallel environment one has to balance the following parameters: a) the number of parallel steps (the depth of the circuit); b) the total number of bit (boolean) operations; and c) the number of (micro) processors. For the moment we put aside important consideration of: d) communication network; 3) local-global storage and retrieval requirements; and, in the case of VLSI designs, that of f) area-time complexity.

For a problem with I or O of $O(n)$ bits, e.g. in the evaluation with the full n-bit precision of the value of an algebraic or transcendental function, one can hope for the depth of $O(\log n)$. With this depth one would like also to have parallel algorithms of total circuitry (number of processors) to be optimal as well: on the order of

$O(M_{bit}(n) \cdot \log n)$.

There are serious obstacles in generation of such fast parallel algorithms from the serial algorithms with the same bit complexity. Iterative algorithms, that are used to construct low bit (and operational) complexity serial algorithms, do not provide depth $O(\log n)$. These iterative algorithms, particularly the arithmetic-geometric mean, and also the Newton iteration method, can get the depth at best $O(\log^2 n)$.

The problem actually starts with computation of elementary functions (most notably that of division). Popular iterative methods (Sieveking-Kung,...) give depth $O(\log^2 n)$, though with only $O(M_{bit}(n))$ of total circuitry for elementary function computations. Only recently new algorithms of Reif, Bini, Schonhage and Pan, see review [58] for references, made it possible to compute elementary functions in $O(\log n)$ (or $O(\log n \cdot \log\log n)$ in Reif and Beame-Cook-Hoover algorithms) depth circuits. Unfortunately, the total circuitry significantly increases: the typical number of processor becomes $n^{O(1)}$, see [58].

The methods that we propose, bit-burst algorithms for computations of arbitrary linear differential equations, have always depth $O(\log n)$, even though, in general, the total bit operation count is $O(M_{bit}(n) \cdot \log^3 n)$. In fact, for E- and G-functions the total bit operation count with the same depth is only $O(M_{bit}(n) \cdot \log^2 n)$.

References

[1] S. Ramanujan, Collected Papers, Cambridge, 1927, 23-39.

[2] G.H. Hardy, Ramanujan, Cambridge, 1940.

[3] G.N. Watson, Some singular moduli (I);(II);(III);(IV); Quart. J. Math. Oxford, 3 (1932), 81-98; 189-212; Proc. London Math. Soc. 40 (1936), 83-142; Acta Arithmetica, 1 (1936), 284-323.

[4] J.M. Borwein, P.B. Borwein, Pi and the AGM, Wiley, 1987.

[5] E.T. Whittaker, G.N. Watson, A Course of Modern Analysis, 4 ed., Cambridge, 1927.

[6] A. Weil, Elliptic Functions According to Eisenstein and Kronecker, Springer, 1976.

[7] C.L. Siegel, Bestimmung der elliptischen Modulfunktionen durch eine Transformations gleichung, Abh. Math. Sem. Univ. Hamburg, 27 (1964), 32-38.

[8] A. Weil, Sur les Périodes des Intégrales Abéliennes, Comm. Pure Appl. Math., 29 (1976), 813-819.

[9] D. Masser, Elliptic Functions and Transcendence, Lecture Notes Math., v. 437, Springer, 1975.

[10] S. Lefschetz, On certain numerical invariants of algebraic varieties with application to Abelian varieties, Trans. Amer. Math. Soc., 22 (1921), 327-482.

[11] E.T. Whittaker, On hyperlemniscate functions, a family of automorphic functions, J. London Math. Soc., 4 (1929), 274-278.

[12] D.V. Chudnovsky, G.V. Chudnovsky, Computer assisted number theory, Lecture Notes Math., Springer, 1240, 1987, 1-68.

[13] Ch. Hermite, Sur la Théorie des Équations Modulaires, C.R. Acad. Sci. Paris., 48 (1859), 940-1079-1097; 49 (1859), 16-110-141.

[14] H.M. Stark, Class-numbers of complex quadratic fields, Lecture Notes Math., Springer, v. 320, 1973, 153-174.

[15] D. Shanks, Dihedral quartic approximation and series for π, J. Number Theory, 14 (1982), 397-423.

[16] R. Fricke, Die Elliptischen Funktionen und ihre Anwendungen, v. 1, Teubner, 1916.

[17] A. Baker, Transcendental Number Theory, Cambridge, 1979.

[18] H.M. Stark, A transcendence theorem for class number problems, I; II; Ann. Math. 94 (1971), 153-173; 96(1972), 174-209.

[19] C.L. Siegel, Zum Beweise des Starkschen Satzes, Invent. Math., 5 (1968), 180-191.

[20] G. Shimura, Automorphic forms and the periods of Abelian varieties, J. Math. Soc. Japan, 31 (1979), 561-59.

[21] G. Shimura, The arithmetic of certain zeta functions and automorphic forms on orthogonal groups, Ann. of Math., 111 (1980), 313-375.

[22] P. Deligne, Valeurs de fonctions L et périodes d'integrales, Proc. Symp. Pure Math., v. 33, Part 2, Amer. Math. Soc., Providence, R.I., 313-346.

[23] P. Deligne, Cycles de Hodge absolus et périodes des intégrales des variétés abéliennes, Soc. Math. de France, Memoire, N° 2, 1980, 23-33.

[24] G. Shimura, Introduction to the Arithmetic Theory of Automorphic Forms, Princeton, University Press, 1971.

[25] G. Shimura, Y. Taniyama, Complex Multiplication of Abelian Varieties and Its Applications to Number Theory, Publications of the Mathematical Society of Japan, N°6, 1961.

[26] G.V. Chudnovsky, Algebraic independence of values of exponential and elliptic functions. Proceedings of the International Congress of Mathematicians, Helsinki, 1979, Acad. Sci. Tennice, Helsinki, 1980, v. 1, 339-350.

[27] B.H. Gross, N. Koblitz, Gauss sums and the p-adic Γ-function, Ann. of Math., 109 (1979), 569-581.

[28] R. Fricke, F. Klein, Vorlesungen über die Theorie der Automorphen Functionen, bd. 2, Tenbner, 1926.

[29] R. Morris, On the automorphic functions of the group $(0,3;\ell_1,\ell_2,\ell_3)$, Trans. Amer. Math. Soc., 7 (1906), 425-448.

[30] K. Takeuchi, Arithmetic triangle groups, J. Math. Soc. Japan, 29 (1977), 91-106.

[31] H.P.F. Swinnerton-Dyer, Arithmetic groups in Discrete Groups and Automorphic Functions, Academic Press, 1977, 377-401.

[32] J.I. Hutchinson, On the automorphic functions of the group (0,3;2,6,6), Trans. Amer. Math. Soc., 5 (1904), 447-460.

[33] D.V. Chudnovsky, G.V. Chudnovsky, Note on Eisenstein's system of differential equations, in Classical and Quantum Models and Arithmetic Problems, M. Dekker, 1984, 99-116.

[34] D.V. Chudnovsky, G.V. Chudnovsky, The use of computer algebra for diophantine and differential equations, in Computer Algebra as a Tool for Research in Mathematics and Physics, Proceeding of the International Conference, 1984, New York University, M. Dekker, 1987.

[35] D.V. Chudnovsky, G.V. Chudnovsky, Applications of Padé approximations to diophantine inequalities in values of G-functions, Lecture Notes Math., v. 1135, Springer, 1985, 9-50.

[36] K. Mahler, Perfect systems, Compositio Math., 19 (1968), 95-166.

[37] D.V. Chudnovsky, G.V. Chudnovsky, Applications of Padé approximations to the Grothendieck conjecture on linear differential equations, Lecture Notes Math., v. 1135, Springer, 1985, 51-100.

[38] C.L. Siegel, Über einige Anwendungen diophantischer Approximationen, Abh. Preuss. Akad. Wiss. Phys. Math. Kl. 1, 1929.

[39] G.V. Chudnovsky, Contributions to the Theory of Transcendental Numbers, Mathematical Surveys and Monographs, v. 19, Amer. Math. Soc., Providence, R.I., 1984.

[40] G.V. Chudnovsky, Padé approximation and the Riemann monodromy problem, in Bifurcation Phenomena in Mathematical Physics and Related Topics, D. Reidel, Boston, 1980, 448-510.

[41] G.V. Chudnovsky, Rational and Padé approximation to solutions of linear differential equations and the monodromy theory. Lecture Notes Physics, v. 126, Springer, 1980, 136-169.

[42] G.V. Chudnovsky, Padé approximations to the generalized hypergeometric functions. I., J. Math. Pures et Appliques, Paris, 58 (1979), 445-476.

[43] G.V. Chudnovsky, On the method of Thue-Siegel, Ann. of Math., 117 (1983), 325-382.

[44] C.L. Siegel, Transcendental Numbers, Princeton University Press, 1949.

[45] G.V. Chudnovsky, Rational approximations to linear forms of exponentials and binomials, Proc. Nat'l Acad. Sci. U.S.A., 80 (1983), 3138-3141.

[46] D.V. Chudnovsky, G.V. Chudnovsky, A random walk in higher arithmetic, Adv. Appl. Math., 7 (1986), 101-122.

[47] H. Poincare, Sur les groupes des équations lineaires, Acta. Math., 4 (1884) 201-312.

[48] D.A. Hejhel, Monodromy groups and Poincaré series, Bull. Amer. Math. Soc., 84 (1978), 339-376.

[49] E.T. Whittaker, On the connexion of algebraic functions with automorphic functions, Phil. Trans., 122 A(1898), 1-32.

[50] R.A. Rankin, The differential equations associated with the uniformization of certain algebraic curves, Proc. Roy. Soc. Edinburgh, 65 (1958) 35-62.

[51] A. Schonhage, V. Strassen, Schnelle Multiplikation grosser Zahlen, Computing, 7 (1971), 281-292.

[52] D.V. Chudnovsky, G.V. Chudnovsky, Algebraic complexities and algebraic curves over finite fields, Proc. Natl. Acad. Sci. USA, 84 (1987), 1739-1743.

[53] A. Schonhage, Equation solving in terms of computational complexity, Proc. International Congress of Mathematicians, Berkeley, 1986.

[54] R.P. Brent, Multiple-precision zero-finding methods and the complexity of elementary function evaluation, in Analytic Computational Complexity, J.F. Traub, Ed., Academic Press, 1975, 151-176.

[55] R.P. Brent, The complexity of multiple-precision arithmetic, in Complexity of Computational Problem Solving, R.S. Anderson and R.P. Brent, Eds. Univ. of Queensland Press, Brisbane, Australia, 1975, 126-165.

[56] D.V. Chudnovsky, G.V. Chudnovsky, On expansions of algebraic functions in power and Puiseux series, I; II; J. of Complexity, 2 (1986), 271-294; 3 (1987), 1-25.

[57] O. Perron, Die Lehre von den Kettenbrüchen, Teubner, 1929.

[58] D. Bini, V. Pan, Polynomial division and its computational complexity, J. of Complexity, 2 (1986), 179-203.

[59] D. A. Hejhal, A classical approach to a well-known spectral correspondence on quaternion groups, Lecture Notes Math., v. 1135, Springer, 1985, 127-196.

Multiple q-Series and $U(n)$ generalizations of Ramanujan's ${}_1\Psi_1$ sum

by

S.C. Milne*

Department of Mathematics
University of Kentucky
Lexington, Kentucky 40506 - 0027

*Partially supported by NSF Grant DMS-8604232

ISBN 0-12-058560-X

Introduction.

Classical basic hypergeometric functions of one-variable (q-series) have many significant applications in several areas of pure and applied mathematics. More familiar applications include classical analysis, combinatorics and additive number theory. Recently, q-series have enriched new developments in physics, Lie algebras, transcendental number theory, and statistics. Extensive references to and accounts of the general theory and applications of basic hypergeometric functions can be found in books by G.E. Andrews [2,3,4], W.N. Bailey [33], R.J. Baxter [36], L.J. Slater [79], and in the papers of C. Adiga, B.C. Berndt, S. Bhargava, and G.N. Watson [1], G.E. Andrews [5-24], G.E. Andrews and R. Askey [25] , G.E. Andrews, R.J. Baxter, and P.J. Forrester [27], R. Askey and M. Ismail [31], R. Askey and J.A. Wilson [32] , R.J. Baxter [34,35], W. Hahn [45-48], M.E.H. Ismail [52], V.G. Kac and D.H. Peterson [57], J. Lepowsky [59], I.G. Macdonald [63-65], and D. Zeilberger and D.M. Bressoud [84].

The symmetries, transformation properties, and summation theorems for basic hypergeometric series are responsible for many of the above applications. Several higher-dimensional generalizations of some of these results for one-variable q-series are contained in the theory of (basic) Appell and Lauricella functions of several variables which have been studied in [2,4,8,9,28,33,66,79]. Generally, none of these multiple series has the depth, richness, or contact with other major areas of mathematics and physics as does classical (one-variable) basic hypergeometric series. Formally, there is simply too much freedom in the number of ways one can move from a single sum to multi-dimensional analogs.

Recently, modern mathematical physics has provided a new natural multivariable generalization of ordinary classical hypergeometric series that has subsequently led to multiple basic hypergeometric series which appear to have the required depth and rich interaction with other parts of mathematics and physics.

The three mathematical physicists L.C. Biedenharn, W.J. Holman III, and J.D. Louck showed in [50,51] how the classical work on ordinary hypergeometric series is intimately related to the irreducible representations of the compact group $SU(2)$. Similarly, they also initiated the study of the generalized multiple hypergeometric series $W_m^{(n)}$ and $F^{(n)}$ which arise in the theory of Wigner coefficients for $SU(n)$. This work was done in the context of the quantum theory of angular momentum [37,38] and the special unitary groups $SU(n)$.

By utilizing explicit expressions for the matrix elements of multiplicity-free Wigner and Racah coefficients in $U(n)$ both L.C. Biedenharn, W.J. Holman III, J.D. Louck [51] and W.J. Holman III [50] established generalizations of known one-variable hypergeometric summation theorems for $W_m^{(n)}$ and $F^{(n)}$, respectively. Essentially, the same matrix element is computed in two different ways. The methods rely upon the representation theory of $U(n)$. Recently, R.A. Gustafson [41] significantly extended this program by proving a generalized Biedenharn-Elliott identity for multiplicity-free $U(n)$ Racah coefficients. As a consequence of an explicit evaluation of a special case of this identity he then derived an elegant generalization of Whipple's [81,82] classical transformation of a very-well poised ${}_7F_6(1)$ into a balanced ${}_4F_3(1)$, to the multiple hypergeometric series $W_m^{(n)}$ and $F^{(n-1)}$, respectively. Suitable special cases and limits of this $U(n)$ generalization of Whipples transformation yield multivariable generalizations of most classical summation theorems, including W.J. Holman III's [50] $U(n)$ generalization of the summation theorems of Gauss and Pfaff-Saalschutz.

In several recent papers [68-76] we have introduced and studied natural q-analogs $[W]_m^{(n)}$ and $[F]^{(n)}$ of $W_m^{(n)}$ and $F^{(n)}$, respectively. The series $[W]_m^{(n)}$ satisfy a general q-difference equation [69] which generalizes our corresponding difference equation for $W_m^{(n)}$ from [67]. In addition [73], we have discovered basic hypergeometric series $[H]^{(n)}$ very well poised in $U(n)$ which provides an elegant, explicit, multivariable generalization of the one-variable classical, very well poised basic hypergeometric series responsible for the Rogers-Ramanujan-Schur identities [2,4].

Recently [74,75], we found direct, elementary proofs of a q-analog of W.J. Holman III's [50] $U(n)$ generalization of the summation theorems of Gauss and Pfaff-Saalschutz. The $U(n)$ Gauss summation theorem [74] for $[F]^{(n)}$ series was obtained by iterating a suitable multivariable generalization of the Gauss reduction formula for a ${}_2F_1(1)$. The $U(n)$ Pfaff-Saalschutz summation theorem [75] for $[F]^{(n)}$ series is a consequence of $q-U(n)$ Gauss and a new general q-difference equation for "balanced" basic hypergeometric series $[F]^{(n)}$ in $U(n)$. By utilizing $q-U(n)$ Pfaff-Saalschutz and our q-difference equations for $[W]_m^{(n)}$ and $[F]^{(n)}$, we found in [76] a direct, elementary proof of a q-analog of R.A. Gustafson's $U(n)$ Whipple's tranformation. Our q-difference equation approach to the theory of the mutiple q-series $[W]_m^{(n)}$, $[F]^{(n)}$, and $[H]^{(n)}$ is complimentary to the Biedenharn-Gustafson-Holman III-Louck representation - theoretic treatment of the ordinary multiple series $W_m^{(n)}$ and $F^{(n)}$. The paper [44] strongly suggests that $[W]_m^{(n)}$, $[F]^{(n)}$, and $[H]^{(n)}$ can also be studied from the viewpoint of representation theory.

In [71] basic properties of $[F]^{(n)}$ led to a $U(n)$ multiple series refinement of the q-binomial theorem [2,33,79], and a direct, elementar derivation of the Macdonald identities [40,58,60,63,83] for $A_l^{(1)}$. Subsequently, M.E.H. Ismail's proof from [52] was extended in [72] to give a $U(n)$ multiple series generalization of Ramanujan's ${}_1\Psi_1$ summation [6,7,26,29,47,55], directly from the $U(n)$ q-binomial theorem. As a consequence, we obtained a new generalization of the Macdonald identities for $A_l^{(1)}$, with extra free parameters. Very recently, R.A. Gustafson [42] put together an induction argument based upon the nonterminating $U(n)\,{}_6\Phi_5$ summation theorem [73] and certain multiple contour integrals to prove a $U(n)$ generalization of the ${}_6\Psi_6$ summation theorem [9].

In this paper we describe how the results from [41-43,67-76] provide an elegant common $U(n)$ generalization of: Ramanujan's ${}_1\Psi_1$ summation, the ${}_6\Psi_6$ summation theorem, and the Macdonald identities for $A_l^{(1)}$. We then survey the summation theorems and transformation properties for the multiple q-series $[W]_m^{(n)}$, $[F]^{(n)}$, and $[H]^{(n)}$.

The contents of this paper are organized as follows.

In section 2 we review the definitions of classical one-variable basic hypergeometric series and bilateral basic series. We state W.N. Bailey's ${}_6\Psi_6$ summation theorem and recall how both Jacobi's triple product identity [2,4] and

Ramanujan's ${}_1\Psi_1$ summation [6,7,26,29,47,52,55] are consequences of the q-binomial theorem. These applications of the q-binomial theorem motivated much of our work in [71,72].

The multiple q-series $[W]_m^{(n)}$ and $[F]^{(n)}$ are introduced in section 3. We describe here how the Macdonald identities for $A_l^{(1)}$ and our $U(n)$ multiple series generalization of Ramanujan's ${}_1\Psi_1$ summation are both consequences of the $U(n)$ q-binomial theorem [71].

Section 4 gives R.A. Gustafson's [42] $U(n)$ generalization of the ${}_6\Psi_6$ summation theorem and his extension of the $U(n)\,{}_1\Psi_1$ summation theorem in [72]. We include the hypergeometric series $[H]^{(n)}$ very well poised in $U(n)$ as part of this section.

Our q-analogs of W.J. Holman III's [50] $U(n)$ generalizations of the summation theorems of Gauss and Pfaff-Saalschutz are presented in section 5.

Section 6 contains a discussion of our q-analogs of R.A. Gustafson's $U(n)$ Whipple's transformation and $U(n)$ generalization of J. Dougall's summation theorem.

2. Background Information.

We begin with the classical q-binomial theorem [2,33,79] given by

Theorem 2.1. (q-binomial theorem). If $|q|<1$, $|t|<1$, then

$$\sum_{n=0}^{\infty}\frac{(a)_n}{(q)_n}\cdot t^n=\frac{(at)_\infty}{(t)_\infty}, \tag{2.2}$$

where $(A)_n$ and $(A)_\infty$ are defined by

$$(A)_n = (1-A)(1-Aq)\cdots(1-Aq^{n-1}), \tag{2.3a}$$

and

$$(A)_\infty = \lim_{n\to\infty} (A)_n = \prod_{r=0}^{\infty}(1-Aq^r). \tag{2.3b}$$

Note that we may define $(A)_n$ for all real numbers n by

$$(A)_n = (A)_\infty/(Aq^n)_\infty. \tag{2.4}$$

In particular,

$$(A)_0 = 1, \tag{2.5a}$$

and

$$\begin{aligned}(A)_{-n} &= (1-A/q^n)^{-1}\cdots(1-A/q)^{-1}\\ &= (-A)^{-n}\, q^{n(n+1)/2}\cdot(q/A)_n^{-1}\end{aligned} \tag{2.5b}$$

Theorem 2.1 is originally due to Cauchy [39, p.40] in 1843. To prove Theorem 2.1, just note that both sides of (2.2) satisfy the q-difference equation and initial condition

$$(1-t)F(t) = (1-at)F(tq) \tag{2.6a}$$

$$F(0) = 1 \tag{2.6b}$$

Now, Cauchy and Gauss independently utilized Theorem 2.1 to give a simple, elegant proof of the fundamental Jacobi triple product identity [56] given by

Theorem 2.7. (Jacobi). If $x \neq 0$, $|q| < 1$, then

$$\begin{aligned}\sum_{n=-\infty}^{+\infty} x^n q^{(n^2+n)/2} &= \prod_{n=0}^{\infty}(1+xq^{n+1})(1+x^{-1}q^n)(1-q^{n+1})\\ &= (-xq)_\infty(-x^{-1})_\infty(q)_\infty\end{aligned} \tag{2.8}$$

They first set

$$a = q^{-2N} \text{ and } t = -xq^{1+N} \tag{2.9}$$

in (2.2) and rewrite the resulting identity in the form

$$\sum_{n=-N}^{N} x^n q^{(n^2+n)/2} \cdot \{(q)_{2N}/((q)_{N-n}(q)_{N+n})\} \tag{2.10a}$$

$$= \prod_{n=1}^{N} (1+xq^n)(1+x^{-1}q^{n-1}). \tag{2.10b}$$

Letting $N \to \infty$ in (2.10) immediately yields (2.8).

Important applications of Theorem 2.7 to the theories of elliptic functions and partitions are described in the books of Andrews [2] and Hardy and Wright [49].

Observing that

$$\frac{1}{(q)_n} = \frac{(q^{n+1})_\infty}{(q)_\infty} \tag{2.11}$$

vanishes when $n = -1, -2, \cdots$, it is immediate that Theorem 2.1 is the $b = q$ case of

Theorem 2.12. (Ramanujan's ${}_1\Psi_1$ summation).

Let

$$0 < |q| < 1 \tag{2.13a}$$

and

$$|b/a| < |t| < 1. \tag{2.13b}$$

Then,

$$\sum_{n=-\infty}^{+\infty} \frac{(a)_n}{(b)_n} \cdot t^n = \left\{\frac{(at)_\infty(q/(at))_\infty}{(t)_\infty(b/(at))_\infty}\right\} \cdot \left\{\frac{(b/a)_\infty(q)_\infty}{(q/a)_\infty(b)_\infty}\right\}. \tag{2.14}$$

It is not difficult to see that replacing a,q,b, and t by $(-1/c),q,0$, and $(q\,x\,c)$, respectively, in Theorem 2.12, and letting $c \to 0$ yields Theorem 2.7. Thus, Ramaujan's ${}_1\Psi_1$ summation contains both the q-binomial theorem and the Jacobi triple product identity as special cases. In [29] Theorem 2.12 is viewed as an extension of the beta function given as an integral on $[0,\infty)$. Applications to orthogonal polynomials defined by basic hypergeometric series are discussed in [26,29].

In [6,7,26,29,47,55] clever rearrangements of series or q-difference equations are utilized to prove Theorem 2.12. The most elegant proof appears in [52]. First, observe that both sides of (2.14) are analytic in $z=b$ for $|z|$ sufficiently small. The q-binomial theorem immediately implies that both sides of (2.14) agree when $z=q^m$, for $m=0,1,2,\cdots$. Both sides of (2.14) are now equal for general b (subject to (2.13)) since 0 is an interior point of the domain of analyticity. We generalized this proof to higher dimensions in [72].

Motivated by Theorems 2.1, 2.7, and 2.12 we now recall the definitions of classical basic and bilateral basic hypergeometric series. We first have

Definition 2.15. (classical basic hypergeometric series). We let

$$ {}_m\Phi_n \left[\begin{matrix} a, & (\alpha) \\ & (\beta) \end{matrix} \middle| q;x \right] $$

denote the basic hypergeometric series

$$ {}_m\Phi_n \left[\begin{matrix} a, & (\alpha) \\ & (\beta) \end{matrix} \middle| q;x \right] \equiv {}_m\Phi_n \left[\begin{matrix} a, \alpha_1, \alpha_2, , \ldots, \alpha_{m-1} \\ \beta_1, \beta_2, , \ldots, \beta_n \end{matrix} \middle| q;x \right] $$

$$ = \sum_{l=0}^{\infty} \frac{(a)_l(\alpha_1)_l(\alpha_2)_l \cdots (\alpha_{m-1})_l}{(\beta_1)_l(\beta_2)_l \cdots (\beta_n)_l} \cdot \frac{x^l}{(q)_l}, \tag{2.16a} $$

where

$$(A)_l \equiv (A;q)_l = (1-A)(1-Aq)\cdots(1-Aq^{l-1}), \tag{2.16b}$$

$$|x| < 1,\ |q| < 1,\ \beta_i \neq q^{-N}, \tag{2.16c}$$

for any nonnegative integer N. The basic hypergeometric series in (2.16a) is well-poised provided that

$$m = n+1 \text{ and } aq = \alpha_1\beta_1 = \cdots = \alpha_n\beta_n, \tag{2.16d}$$

and very-well poised, if in addition,

$$\alpha_1 = q\sqrt{a},\ \alpha_2 = -q\sqrt{a},\ \beta_1 = \sqrt{a},\ \beta_2 = -\sqrt{a}. \tag{2.16e}$$

Finally, the series (2.16a) is balanced if

$$(\beta_1\beta_2\cdots\beta_n) = (a\,\alpha_1\alpha_2\cdots\alpha_{m-1})q. \tag{2.16f}$$

The a and α_i are numerator parameters and the β_i are denominator parameters.

Note that if (2.16a) is very-well poised we have

$$\frac{(q\sqrt{a})_l(-q\sqrt{a})_l}{(\sqrt{a})_l(-\sqrt{a})_l} = \frac{(1-aq^{2l})}{(1-a)}. \tag{2.17}$$

Bilateral basic series are determined by

Definition 2.18. (classical bilateral basic series). Let $n \leq m$, $|q| < 1$, and $b_i \neq q^{-N}$, $a_i \neq q^{(N+1)}$, for all nonnegative integers N. Then,

$$ {}_m\Psi_n\begin{bmatrix} a_1, & \cdots & ,a_m;\ q;z \\ b_1, & \cdots & ,b_n \end{bmatrix}$$

$$= \sum_{l=-\infty}^{\infty} \frac{(a_1)_l(a_2)_l\cdots(a_m)_l}{(b_1)_l(b_2)_l\cdots(b_n)_l}\cdot z^l, \tag{2.19}$$

where

$$|z| < 1,\ \text{ if } n < m, \tag{2.20a}$$

and

$$|(b_1 \cdots b_n)/(a_1 \cdots a_m)| < |z| < 1, \text{ if } n = m. \tag{2.20b}$$

We will sometimes use the product notation

$$\prod\left[(a);(b)\right] \equiv \prod\left[\begin{matrix} a_1, & \cdots & ,a_m; \\ b_1, & \cdots & ,b_n; \end{matrix}\ q\right] = \frac{(a_1)_\infty (a_2)_\infty \cdots (a_m)_\infty}{(b_1)_\infty (b_2)_\infty \cdots (b_n)_\infty}. \tag{2.21}$$

One of the most fundamental results in the theory of basic hypergeometric series is Watson's [80] q-analog of Whipple's [81,82] classical transformation of a very-well poised ${}_7F_6(1)$ into a balanced ${}_4F_3(1)$. This result leads to q-analogs of all the main summation theorems for classical ordinary hypergeometric series. Watson's transformation is given by

Theorem 2.22. (Watson).

$${}_8\Phi_7\left[\begin{matrix} a, q\sqrt{a}, -q\sqrt{a}, b, c, d, e, q^{-n} \\ \sqrt{a}, -\sqrt{a}, \frac{aq}{b}, \frac{aq}{c}, \frac{aq}{d}, \frac{aq}{e}, aq^{n+1} \end{matrix}\ \middle|\ \frac{a^2q^{n+2}}{bcde}\right] \tag{2.23a}$$

$$= \left\{(aq)_n\, ((aq)/(de))_n\, (aq/d)_n^{-1} (aq/e)_n^{-1}\right\} \tag{2.23b}$$

$${}_4\Phi_3\left[\begin{matrix} ((aq)/(bc)), d, e, q^{-n} \\ ((de)/(aq^n)), (aq/b), (aq/c) \end{matrix}\ \middle|\ q\right] \tag{2.23c}$$

We conclude this section with Bailey's ${}_6\Psi_6$ summation theorem in

Theorem 2.24. (Bailey)

$${}_6\Psi_6\left[\begin{matrix} q\sqrt{a}, -q\sqrt{a}, b, c, d, e & ; q; \\ \sqrt{a}, -\sqrt{a}, \frac{aq}{b}, \frac{aq}{c}, \frac{aq}{d}, \frac{aq}{e} & ; \end{matrix}\ \frac{a^2q}{bcde}\right] \tag{2.25a}$$

$$= \prod\left[\begin{matrix} aq, \frac{aq}{bc}, \frac{aq}{bd}, \frac{aq}{be}, \frac{aq}{cd}, \frac{aq}{ce}, \frac{aq}{de}, q, \frac{q}{a}; \\ \frac{q}{b}, \frac{q}{c}, \frac{q}{d}, \frac{q}{e}, \frac{aq}{b}, \frac{aq}{c}, \frac{aq}{d}, \frac{aq}{e}, \frac{a^2q}{bcde}; \end{matrix}\ q\right] \tag{2.25b}$$

The identity (2.25) is probably the most general summation identity known for bilateral basic hypergeometric series. Andrews [8, sec. 3] deduces many important diverse results in number theory from (2.25). Other q-series identities that follow from the ${}_6\Psi_6$ summation are given by Andrews [24,27] and Slater [78].

3. $U(n)$ Generalization of Ramanujan's ${}_1\Psi_1$ Summation.

Just as Theorems 2.7 and 2.12 are consequences of Theorem 2.1, their higher-dimensional generalizations in this section follow from

Theorem 3.1. ($U(n)$ refinement of the q-binomial theorem). If $0 < |q| < 1$, $|t| < 1$, then

$$\sum_{y_1,\ldots,y_n \geq 0} \left(\prod_{1 \leq i < r \leq n} (1-(z_i/z_r) \cdot q^{y_i - y_r})/(1-(z_i/z_r)) \right) \tag{3.2a}$$

$$\cdot \left(\prod_{1 \leq i,r \leq n} (a_i(z_r/z_i))_{y_r} \right) \cdot \left(\prod_{1 \leq i,r \leq n} (q(z_r/z_i))_{y_r} \right)^{-1} \tag{3.2b}$$

$$\cdot\, q^{(y_2+2y_3+\ldots+(n-1)y_n)} \cdot t^{(y_1+\ldots+y_n)} \tag{3.2c}$$

$$= (a_1 a_2 \cdots a_n t)_\infty / (t)_\infty, \tag{3.2d}$$

where

$$(z_i/z_r) \neq q^p, \text{ if } 1 \leq i < r \leq n \text{ and } p \in \mathbf{Z}; \tag{3.3a}$$

and

$$(qz_r/z_i) \neq q^{-p}, \text{ if } 1 \leq r \neq i \leq n,\ p \in \mathbf{Z}, \text{ and } p \geq -1. \tag{3.3b}$$

Clearly, the $n=1$ case of Theorem 3.1 is Theorem 2.1. Theorem 3.1 was derived in [71] by making use of the basic hypergeometric series $[F]^{(n)}$ in $U(n)$, introduced in [69]. We will discuss the proof of Theorem 3.1 at the end of this section.

Our higher-dimensional generalization of Theorem 2.12 is given by

Theorem 3.4. ($U(n)$ generalization of Ramanujan's ${}_1\Psi_1$ summation). Let

$$0 < |q| < 1 \tag{3.5a}$$

and

$$|(b^n q^{(1-n)})/(a_1 a_2 \cdots a_n)| < |t| < 1. \tag{3.5b}$$

Then

$$\sum_{y_1=-\infty}^{+\infty} \cdots \sum_{y_n=-\infty}^{+\infty} \left\{ \prod_{1 \leq i < r \leq n} (1-(z_i/z_r) \cdot q^{y_i - y_r})/(1-(z_i/z_r)) \right\} \tag{3.6a}$$

$$\cdot \left\{ \prod_{1 \leq i,r \leq n} (a_i(z_r/z_i))_{y_r} \right\} \cdot \left\{ \prod_{1 \leq i,r \leq n} (b(z_r/z_i))_{y_r} \right\}^{-1} \tag{3.6b}$$

$$\cdot\, q^{(y_2+2y_3+\ldots+(n-1)y_n)} \cdot t^{(y_1+\ldots+y_n)} \tag{3.6c}$$

$$= \left\{ \frac{(a_1 a_2 \cdots a_n t)_\infty (q(a_1 a_2 \cdots a_n t)^{-1})_\infty}{(t)_\infty (q^{(1-n)} b^n (a_1 a_2 \cdots a_n t)^{-1})_\infty} \right\} \tag{3.6d}$$

$$\cdot \left\{ \prod_{1 \leq i,r \leq n} \left[\frac{((b/a_i)(z_i/z_r))_\infty (q(z_r/z_i))_\infty}{((q/a_i)(z_i/z_r))_\infty (b(z_r/z_i))_\infty} \right] \right\}, \tag{3.6e}$$

where

$$(z_i/z_r) \neq q^p, \text{ if } 1 \leq i < r \leq n \text{ and } p \in \mathbf{Z}; \tag{3.7a}$$

$$(qz_r/z_i) \neq q^{-p}, \text{ if } 1 \leq r \neq i \leq n,\ p \in \mathbf{Z}, \text{ and} p \geq -1; \tag{3.7b}$$

$$(z_i/z_r) \neq a_i q^{-p}, \text{ if } 1 \leq i,r \leq n,\ p \in \mathbf{Z}, \text{and } p \geq 1; \tag{3.7c}$$

$$t \neq q^{-p}, \text{ if } p \in \mathbf{Z} \text{ and } p \geq 0; \tag{3.7d}$$

$$(a_1 a_2 \cdots a_n t) \neq q^p,\ p \in \mathbf{Z}; \tag{3.7e}$$

and

$$b \neq q^{-p} \cdot (z_i/z_r),\ q^{-p}(a_i z_r) z_i, \tag{3.8a}$$

or

$$(a_1 a_2 \cdots a_n t)^{1/n} \cdot q^{(1-1/n)} \cdot q^{-(p/n)}, \tag{3.8b}$$

with

$$1 \leq i, r \leq n,\ p \in \mathbf{Z}, \text{ and } p \geq 0. \tag{3.8c}$$

It is immediate that the $n=1$ case of Theorem 3.4 is Theorem 2.12, and that the $b=q$ case of Theorem 3.4 is Theorem 3.1.

Theorem 3.4 was first proven in [72]. Both sides of (3.6) are analytic in $z=b$ for $|z|$ sufficiently small. Theorem 3.1 implies that both sides of (3.6) agree when $z=q^m$, for $m=0,1,2,\cdots$. Thus, both sides of (3.6) are now equal for general b, subject ot (3.8).

From Theorem 2.12 it is not hard to see that the products in (3.6d-e) can be written as

$$\left\{ \sum_{M=-\infty}^{+\infty} \frac{(a_1 a_2 \cdots a_n)_M}{(q^{(1-n)} \cdot b^n)_M} \cdot t^M \right\} \tag{3.9a}$$

$$\cdot \left\{ \frac{(q/(a_1 a_2 \cdots a_n))_\infty (q^{(1-n)} \cdot b^n)_\infty}{(q^{(1-n)} \cdot b^n/(a_1 a_2 \cdots a_n))_\infty (q)_\infty} \right\} \tag{3.9b}$$

$$\cdot \left\{ \prod_{1 \leq i, r \leq n} \left[\frac{((b/a_i)(z_i/z_r))_\infty (q(z_r/z_i))_\infty}{((q/a_i)(z_i/z_r))_\infty (b(z_r/z_i))_\infty} \right] \right\}. \tag{3.9c}$$

It is now immediate that equating coefficients of t^M in the Laurent series (3.6a-c) and (3.9a-c) yields

Theorem 3.10. Let $M \in \mathbf{Z}$, $|q| < 1$, and assume that (3.5b), (3.7), and (3.8) hold. We then have

$$
\sum_{\substack{y_1 + \ldots + y_n = M \\ y_i \in \mathbf{Z}}} \left(\prod_{1 \le i < r \le n} (1 - (z_i/z_r) \cdot q^{y_i - y_r}) \right) \cdot \left(\prod_{1 \le i, r \le n} (a_i(z_r/z_i))_{y_r} \right) \tag{3.11a}
$$

$$
\cdot \left(\prod_{1 \le i, r \le n} (b(z_r/z_i))_{y_r} \right)^{-1} \cdot q^{(y_2 + 2y_3 + \ldots + (n-1)y_n)} \tag{3.11b}
$$

$$
= \left\{ \left[\frac{(a_1 a_2 \cdots a_n)_M}{(q^{(1-n)} \cdot b^n)_M} \right] \cdot \left(\prod_{1 \le i < r \le n} (1 - (z_i/z_r)) \right) \right\} \tag{3.12a}
$$

$$
\cdot \left\{ \frac{(q/(a_1 a_2 \cdots a_n))_\infty (q^{(1-n)} \cdot b^n)_\infty}{(q^{(1-n)} \cdot b^n/(a_1 a_2 \cdots a_n))_\infty (q)_\infty} \right\} \tag{3.12b}
$$

$$
\cdot \left\{ \prod_{1 \le i, r \le n} \left[\frac{((b/a_i)(z_i/z_r))_\infty (q(z_r/z_i))_\infty}{((q/a_i)(z_i/z_r))_\infty (b(z_r/z_i))_\infty} \right] \right\}. \tag{3.12c}
$$

The product formula for a Vandermonde determinant and an interchange of summation transforms the $M=0$ case of Theorem 3.10 into

Theorem 3.13. ($_1\Psi_i$ generalization of the Macdonald identities for $A_l^{(1)}$). Let $|q| < 1$. Assume that (3.5b), (3.7), and (3.8) hold. We then have

$$
\sum_{\sigma \in S_n} \epsilon(\sigma) \prod_{r=1}^{n} z_{\sigma(r)}^{(r - \sigma(r))} \sum_{\substack{y_1 + \ldots + y_n = 0 \\ y_i \in \mathbf{Z}}} q^{[(y_{\sigma(2)} + 2y_{\sigma(3)} + \ldots + (n-1)y_{\sigma(n)})]} \tag{3.14a}
$$

$$
\cdot \left(\prod_{1 \le i, r \le n} (a_i(z_r/z_i))_{y_r} \right) \cdot \left(\prod_{1 \le i, r \le n} (b(z_r/z_i))_{y_r} \right)^{-1} \tag{3.14b}
$$

$$
= \left\{ \frac{(q/(a_1 a_2 \cdots a_n))_\infty (q^{(1-n)} \cdot b^n)_\infty}{(q^{(1-n)} \cdot b^n/(a_1 a_2 \cdots a_n))_\infty (q)_\infty} \right\} \tag{3.15a}
$$

$$\cdot\left\{\left(\prod_{1\le i<r\le n}(1-(z_i/z_r))\right)\cdot\left(\prod_{1\le i,r\le n}\left[\frac{((b/a_i)(z_i/z_r))_\infty(q(z_r/z_i))_\infty}{((q/a_i)(z_i/z_r))_\infty(b(z_r/z_i))_\infty}\right]\right)\right\}, \quad (3.15b)$$

where $\epsilon(\sigma)$ is the sign of the permutation σ, and $\mathbf{Z}$ is the set of all integers.

Replacing b and a_i by 0 and $(-1/c)$, respectively in Theorem 3.13, simplifying, and then letting $c \longrightarrow 0$ yields Eq. (4.3) of [71] given by

$$\left\{(q)_\infty^{n-1}\cdot\left(\prod_{1\le i<r\le n}(z_i/z_r)_\infty(qz_r/z_i)_\infty\right)\right\} \quad (3.16a)$$

$$=\sum_{\sigma\in S_n}\epsilon(\sigma)\prod_{r=1}^{n}z_{\sigma(r)}^{(r-\sigma(r))}\sum_{\substack{y_1+\ldots+y_n=0\\ y_i\in\mathbf{Z}}}\left(\prod_{r=1}^{n}z_{\sigma(r)}^{(ny_{\sigma(r)})}\right) \quad (3.16b)$$

$$\cdot\left\{q^{[n/2(y_{\sigma(1)}^2+\ldots+y_{\sigma(n)}^2)+(y_{\sigma(2)}+2y_{\sigma(3)}+\ldots+(n-1)y_{\sigma(n)})]}\right\}. \quad (3.16c)$$

In [71] it is proven that (3.16) is equivalent to the Macdonald identities for $A_l^{(1)}$. Thus, Theorem 3.13 may be viewed as a generalization of the Macdonald identities for $A_l^{(1)}$ with the extra parameters $a_1, \cdots, a_n$, and b.

Recall that Theorem 2.7 is a limiting case of Theorem 2.12. A similar situation holds in higher dimensions. Consider the specialization

$$q \longrightarrow q \quad (3.17a)$$

$$b \longrightarrow 0 \quad (3.17b)$$

$$a_i \longrightarrow (-1/c),\ 1\le i\le n, \quad (3.17c)$$

$$t \longrightarrow (-1)^{(n-1)}qxc^n. \quad (3.17d)$$

In [72] we showed that substituting (3.17) into both sides of (3.6), simplifying, and then letting $c \longrightarrow 0$ gives

Theorem 3.18. ($U(n)$ generalization of the Jacobi triple product identity). If $x \neq 0$, $|q| < 1$, and $\{z_1, \cdots, z_n\}$ are indeterminants such that

$$z_i/z_r \neq q^p, \text{ if } 1 \leq i < r \leq n \text{ and } p \text{ is any integer}, \tag{3.19}$$

then we have

$$\sum_{y_1=-\infty}^{+\infty} \cdots \sum_{y_n=-\infty}^{+\infty} \left(\prod_{1 \leq i < r \leq n} (1 - (z_i/z_r) \cdot q^{y_i - y_r}) \right) \tag{3.20a}$$

$$\cdot \left(\prod_{i=1}^{n} z_i^{(ny_i - (y_1 + \cdots + y_n))} \right) \cdot (-1)^{(n-1)(y_1 + \cdots + y_n)} \tag{3.20b}$$

$$\cdot q^{[n(\binom{y_1}{2} + \cdots + \binom{y_n}{2}) + (y_1 + 2y_2 + \cdots + ny_n)]} \cdot x^{(y_1 + \cdots + y_n)} \tag{3.20c}$$

$$= [(-xq)_\infty (-x^{-1})_\infty (q)_\infty] \cdot \left[(q)_\infty^{n-1} \left(\prod_{1 \leq i < r \leq n} (z_i/z_r)_\infty (qz_r/z_i)_\infty \right) \right]. \tag{3.20d}$$

Theorem 3.18 was first derived in [71] from Theorem 3.1 in the same way that Theorem 2.7 follows from Theorem 2.1. The substitution of

$$a_i \rightarrow q^{-2N}, \text{ if } 1 \leq i \leq n, \tag{3.21a}$$

$$t \rightarrow -xq^{(1+nN)}, \tag{3.21b}$$

into both sides of (3.2) leads to a multiple series generalization of (2.10) which yields (3.20) in the limit as $N \rightarrow \infty$.

Now, (3.20) also contains the Macdonald identities for $A_l^{(1)}$. We use the same type of argument which led from (3.6) to (3.16). It is immediate from Theorem 2.7 that (3.20d) can be written as

$$\left[(q)_\infty^{(n-1)} \left(\prod_{1 \leq i < r \leq n} (z_i/z_r)_\infty (qz_r/z_i)_\infty \right) \right] \cdot \sum_{M=-\infty}^{+\infty} x^M q^{\binom{1+M}{2}}. \tag{3.22}$$

Equating coefficients of x^M in the Laurent series (3.20a-c) and (3.22), considering the case $M = 0$, and utilizing the product formula for a Vandermonde determinant and an interchange of summation gives the identity in (3.16). But,

(3.16) is equivalent to the Macdonald identities for $A_l^{(1)}$.

We close this section by describing our proof of Theorem 3.1. To this end, we recall the definitions of the multiple q-series $[W]_m^{(n)}$ and $[F]^{(n)}$ from [69].

Definition 3.23. (basic hypergeometric series well-poised in $SU(n)$). We define

$$[W]_m^{(n)}\left(\begin{array}{c|c|c|c} (A_{rs}) & (a_{rs}) & (b_{rs}) & (x_i) \\ 1\leq r<s\leq n & 1\leq r\leq n & 1\leq r\leq n & 1\leq i\leq n \\ & 1\leq s\leq k & 1\leq s\leq j & \end{array}\right) \tag{3.24a}$$

$$\equiv (1-q)^{(j-k-1)m}\,(q)_m \sum_{\substack{y_1+\cdots+y_n=m \\ y_i\geq 0}} \left(\prod_{1\leq i<r\leq n}(1-A_{ir}\cdot q^{y_i-y_r})/(1-A_{ir})\right)$$

$$\cdot\left(\prod_{i=1}^{k}\prod_{r=1}^{n}(a_{ri})_{y_r}\right)\cdot\left(\prod_{i=1}^{j}\prod_{r=1}^{n}(b_{ri})_{y_r}\right)^{-1}\cdot\left(\prod_{i=1}^{n}x_i^{y_i}\right) \tag{3.24b}$$

to be well-poised in $SU(n)$ if m is a nonnegative integer, $|q|<1$, $(A)_r$ is given by (2.3a), $(b_{ri})_{y_r}\neq 0$, $A_{ir}\neq 1$ $n\geq 2$, and

$$j\geq n, \tag{3.25a}$$

$$A_{\ r}/A_{is}=A_{sr},\ \text{for } s<r, \tag{3.25b}$$

$$a_{ir}/a_{sr}=A_{is},\ \text{for } i<s, \tag{3.25c}$$

$$b_{ir}/b_{sr}=A_{is},\ \text{for } i<s, \tag{3.25d}$$

$$b_{ii}=q,\ 1\leq i\leq n. \tag{3.25e}$$

We will call the a's numerator parameters and the b's denominator parameters. We denote the series in (3.24) by $[W]_m^{(n)}((A)|(a)|(b)|(x))$, or just $[W]_m^{(n)}$.

The related series $[F]^{(n)}((A)|(a)|(b)|(x))$ are determined by

Definition 3.26. (basic hypergeometric series in $U(n)$.

$$[F]^{(n)}\left(\begin{array}{c|c|c|c} (A_{rs}) & (a_{rs}) & (b_{rs}) & (x_i) \\ 1\leq r<s\leq n & 1\leq r\leq n & 1\leq r\leq n & 1\leq i\leq n \\ & 1\leq s\leq k & 1\leq s\leq j & \end{array}\right) \tag{3.27a}$$

(3.27b)

$$\equiv \sum_{m=0}^{\infty}\frac{(1-q)^m}{(q)_m}\cdot[W]_m^{(n)}\left(\begin{array}{c|c|c|c} (A_{rs}) & (a_{rs}) & (b_{rs}) & (x_i) \\ 1\leq r<s\leq n & 1\leq r\leq n & 1\leq r\leq n & 1\leq i\leq n \\ & 1\leq s\leq k & 1\leq s\leq j & \end{array}\right)$$

$$\equiv \sum_{y_1, \cdots, y_n \geq 0} (1-q)^{(j-k)(y_1+\cdots+y_n)} \cdot \left[\prod_{1 \leq i < r \leq n} (1-A_{ir} \cdot q^{y_i - y_r})/(1-A_{ir})\right]$$

$$\cdot \left[\prod_{i=1}^{k} \prod_{r=1}^{n} (a_{ri})_{y_r}\right] \cdot \left[\prod_{i=1}^{j} \prod_{r=1}^{n} (b_{ri})_{y_r}\right]^{-1} \cdot \left[\prod_{i=1}^{n} x_i^{y_i}\right], \tag{3.27c}$$

where the arrays (A), (a), and (b) satisfy the conditions in (3.25). We continue to call the a's numerator parameters and the b's denominator parameters. The series in (3.27) is balanced provided that $k \geq n$ and

$$\left[\prod_{s=n+1}^{j} (b_{is})\right] = [(a_{11}a_{22} \cdots a_{nn})q] \cdot \left[\prod_{s=n+1}^{k} (a_{is})\right], \text{ for } 1 \leq i \leq n. \tag{3.28}$$

Remark 3.29. The conditions in (3.25) reduce the number of free parameters in (3.27). Just set

$$A_{rs} = (z_r/z_s), \text{ for } 1 \leq r < s \leq n, \tag{3.30a}$$

and then note that the relations in (3.25) transform the arrays (a_{rs}) and (b_{rs}) into

$$b_{rs} = q(z_r/z_s), \text{ if } 1 \leq r, s \leq n, \tag{3.30b}$$

$$b_{r,n+s} = (b_{n,n+s})(z_r/z_n), \text{ if } 1 \leq r \leq n \text{ and } 1 \leq s \leq j-n, \tag{3.30c}$$

$$a_{rs} = (a_{ss})(z_r/z_s), \text{ if } 1 \leq r, s \leq n, \tag{3.30d}$$

$$a_{r,n+s} = (a_{n,n+s})(z_r/z_n), \text{ if } 1 \leq r \leq n \text{ and } 1 \leq s \leq k-n. \tag{3.30e}$$

We have the free parameters

$\{z_1, \cdots, z_n\}$, $\{b_{n,n+s} | 1 \leq s \leq j-n\}$, $\{a_{ss} | 1 \leq s \leq n\}$, and

$\{a_{n,n+s} | 1 \leq s \leq k-n\}$ subject to the condition that each term in (3.27) is always defined.

Theorem 3.1 is an immediate consequence of (3.27b-c), Remark 3.29, the

$$a = a_{11}a_{22} \cdots a_{nn} \equiv a_1 a_2 \cdots a_n \tag{3.31}$$

case of Theorem 2.1, and the summation theorem given by

Theorem 3.32. Let $[W]_m^{(n)}((A)|(a)|(b)|(x))$ be defined by Definition 3.23. We then have

$$[W]_m^{(n)}\left(\begin{array}{c|c|c|c} (A_{rs}) & (a_{rs}) & (b_{rs}) & q^{(i-1)} \\ 1\le r<s\le n & 1\le r,s\le n & 1\le r,s\le n & 1\le i\le n \end{array}\right) \tag{3.33a}$$

$$=\frac{(a_{11}a_{22}\cdots a_{nn})_m}{(1-q)^m}, \tag{3.33b}$$

where $(A)_r$ is defined by (2.3a).

We derived Theorem 3.32 in [71] by induction on m, the general q-difference equation for $[W]_m^{(n)}$ given by Theorem 1.31 of [69], and the fundamental

Lemma 3.34. Let $\{x_1, \cdots, x_n\}$ and $\{y_1, \cdots, y_n\}$ be indeterminants with the y_i distinct. We then have

$$1-x_1x_2\cdots x_n=\sum_{p=1}^{n}(1-x_p)\cdot\prod_{\substack{i=1\\ i\neq p}}^{n}\left(\frac{y_p-x_iy_i}{y_p-y_i}\right). \tag{3.35}$$

Lemma 3.34 was first proven in section 2 of [69]. This proof relied upon elementary properties of symmetric function and an important summation theorem (see Theorem 1.20 of [69]) due to Louck and Biedenharn [61,62] which appears frequently in dealing with the explicit matrix elements which arise in the unitary groups. Louck and Biedenharn [61,62] gave a rather complicated analytic proof of their result. In [43] we utilized the determinantal definition of Schur functions [64] and the Laplace expansion formula for the determinant of an $n\times n$ matrix to give a simple direct proof of an elegant identity, involving Schur functions, which contains the result of Louck and Biedenharn as a special case.

In sections 7 and 8 of [74] we presented additional elementary proofs of Lemma 3.34 which were based on a partial fraction expansion, the Lagrange interpolation formula, or an induction argument using symmetry and recursion, respectively.

Several recent applications of Lemma 3.34 are of independent interest. Lemma 3.34 is responsible for the q-difference equations in [69] which support the analytical results in [70-76]. Lemma 3.34 is also central to the work in [44]. Furthermore, as described in this section (and explained in detail in [71]) the Macdonald identities for $A_l^{(1)}$ are a consequence of Lemma 3.34, Theorem 2.1, and the product formula for a Vandermonde determinant (classical denominator formula for $sl(l+1,\mathbb{C})$).

4. A $U(n)$ Generalization of the ${}_6\Psi_6$ Summation Theorem.

R.A. Gustafson's higher-dimensional generalization of Theorem 2.24 is given by

Theorem 4.1. ($U(n)$ generalization of the ${}_6\Psi_6$ summation theorem). let $0 < |q| < 1$, $n \geq 2$, and

$$|q^{(1-n)}(b_1 \cdots b_n)/(a_1 \cdots a_n)| < 1. \tag{4.2}$$

We then have

$$\sum_{\substack{y_1+\cdots+y_n=0 \\ y_i \in \mathbf{Z}}} \left(\prod_{1 \leq i < r \leq n} (1-(z_i/z_r)q^{y_i-y_r})/(1-(z_i/z_r)) \right) \tag{4.3a}$$

$$\cdot \left(\prod_{1 \leq i,r \leq n} ((a_i(z_r/z_i))_{y_r} \cdot (b_i(z_r/z_i))_{y_r}^{-1}) \right) \tag{4.3b}$$

$$\cdot q^{(y_2+2y_3+\cdots+(n-1)y_n)} \tag{4.3c}$$

$$= \left\{ \frac{(q/(a_1a_2\cdots a_n))_\infty (q^{(1-n)}(b_1 \cdots b_n))_\infty}{(q^{(1-n)}(b_1 \cdots b_n)/(a_1 \cdots a_n))_\infty (q)_\infty} \right\} \tag{4.3d}$$

$$\cdot \left\{ \prod_{1\le i,r\le n} \left[\frac{((b_r/a_i)(z_i/z_r))_\infty (q(z_r/z_i))_\infty}{((q/a_i)(z_i/z_r))_\infty (b_i(z_r/z_i))_\infty} \right] \right\}, \tag{4.3e}$$

where

$$z_i \neq z_r, \text{ if } 1 \le i < r \le n; \tag{4.4a}$$

$$(a_iz_r/z_i) \neq q^p, \text{ if } 1 \le i,r \le n, \ p \in \mathbf{Z}, \text{ and } p \ge 1; \tag{4.4b}$$

$$(b_iz_r/z_i) \neq q^p, \text{ if } 1 \le i,r \le n, \ p \in \mathbf{Z}, \text{ and } p \le 0. \tag{4.4c}$$

It is not difficult to see that the $n=2$ case of Theorem 4.1 is equivalent to Theorem 2.24.

In [42] Gustafson proved Theorem 4.1 by an induction argument involving certain multiple contour integrals. The starting point for the induction was the $U(n)$ nonterminating ${}_6\Phi_5$ summation theorem from [73] that appears as Theorem 4.13 below. This induction was on the number of summation indices which assume negative as well as positive integer values. The most difficult part of Gustafson's proof was finding the correct integrand which allowed this type of induction to work.

By an argument similar to that in [72] which led from Theorem 3.4 to Theorem 3.10 and 3.13, Gustafson [42] utilized Theorems 2.12 and 4.1 to derive

Theorem 4.5. (distinct b_i case of $U(n)$ generalization of Ramanujan's ${}_1\Psi_1$ summation). Let $n \ge 1$,

$$0 < |q| < 1 \tag{4.6a}$$

and

$$|q^{(1-n)}(b_1 \cdots b_n)/(a_1 \cdots a_n)| < |t| < 1. \tag{4.6b}$$

Then

$$\sum_{y_1=-\infty}^{+\infty} \cdots \sum_{y_n=-\infty}^{+\infty} \left\{ \prod_{1 \le i < r \le n} (1-(z_i/z_r) \cdot q^{y_i - y_r})/(1-(z_i/z_r)) \right\} \tag{4.7a}$$

$$\cdot \left\{ \prod_{1 \le i, r \le n} ((a_i(z_r/z_i))_{y_r} (b_i(z_r/z_i))_{y_r}^{-1}) \right\} \tag{4.7b}$$

$$\cdot q^{(y_2+2y_3+ \cdots +(n-1)y_n)} \cdot t^{(y_1+ \cdots +y_n)} \tag{4.7c}$$

$$= \left\{ \frac{(a_1 a_2 \cdots a_n t)_\infty (q(a_1 a_2 \cdots a_n t)^{-1})_\infty}{(t)_\infty (q^{(1-n)}(b_1 \cdots b_n)/(a_1 a_2 \cdots a_n t))_\infty} \right\} \tag{4.7d}$$

$$\cdot \left\{ \prod_{1 \le i, r \le n} \left[\frac{((b_r/a_i)(z_i/z_r))_\infty (q(z_r/z_i))_\infty}{((q/a_i)(z_i/z_r))_\infty (b_i(z_r/z_i))_\infty} \right] \right\}, \tag{4.7e}$$

where the condition in (4.4) hold.

Clearly, the $n=1$ case of Theorem 4.5 is the classical Ramanujan ${}_1\Psi_1$ summation in Theorem 2.12. It is also immediate that (4.7) is identical to (3.6) when the b_i's are all equal to b. Furthermore, this $b_i = b$ case of Theorem 4.1 is exactly the $M=0$ case of Theorem 3.10, and is also equivalent to Theorem 3.13. In fact, the same argument that leads from Theorem 3.4 to Theorem 3.10 also gives Theorem 4.1 directly from Theorem 4.5. Consequently, Theorem 4.5 is a common generalization of Ramanujan's ${}_1\Psi_1$ summation, the ${}_6\Psi_6$ summation theorem, and the Macdonald identities for $A_l^{(1)}$.

In particular, the $n=2$ case of Theorem 4.5 implies the $n=2$ case of Theorem 4.1, which is equivalent to the classical ${}_6\Psi_6$ summation theorem in (2.25). That is, the classical ${}_6\Psi_6$ summation is much more natural when viewed as a 2-dimensional result-a simple consequence of the 2-dimensional ${}_1\Psi_1$ summation theorem. Note that the infinite products in (2.25b) are much more symmetrical when written as in the $n=2$ case of (4.3d-e).

A very useful special limiting case of (2.14) is obtained by replacing t by (t/a), simplifying, and then letting $a \to \infty$. In chapter 4 of [4] Andrews applied this identity, together with constant term arguments, to the original pair of Rogers-Ramanujan-Schur identities to derive Rogers' additional identities of the same type. Here, for future reference, we write down the higher-dimensional generalization of Andrews' identity. We have

Corollary 4.8. Let $0 < |q| < 1$, $n \geq 1$, and

$$|b_1 \cdots b_n| < |q^{(n-1)}t|. \tag{4.9}$$

If in (4.7) we make the substitution

$$t \to (t/(a_1 \cdots a_n)), \tag{4.10}$$

and then let each $a_i \to \infty$, we obtain the identity

$$\sum_{y_1=-\infty}^{+\infty} \cdots \sum_{y_n=-\infty}^{+\infty} \left(\prod_{1 \leq i < r \leq n} (1-(z_i/z_r)q^{y_i-y_r})/(1-(z_i/z_r)) \right) \tag{4.11a}$$

$$\cdot \left(\prod_{1 \leq i,r \leq n} (b_i(z_r/z_i))_{y_r}^{-1} \right) \left(\prod_{i=1}^{n} z_i^{(ny_i-(y_1+\ldots+y_n))} \right) \tag{4.11b}$$

$$\cdot q^{n[\binom{y_1}{2}+\ldots+\binom{y_n}{2}]} \cdot q^{(y_2+2y_3+\ldots+(n-1)y_n)} \tag{4.11c}$$

$$\cdot (-1)^{n(y_1+\ldots+y_n)} \cdot t^{(y_1+\ldots+y_n)} \tag{4.11d}$$

$$= \left\{ \frac{(t)_\infty (q/t)_\infty}{(q^{1-n} \cdot t^{-1} \cdot (b_1 \cdots b_n))_\infty} \right\} \tag{4.11e}$$

$$\cdot \left\{ \prod_{1 \leq i,r \leq n} \frac{(q(z_r/z_i))_\infty}{(b_i((z_r/z_i))_\infty} \right\}. \tag{4.11f}$$

Remark 4.12. Setting each $b_i = 0$ in (4.11) gives a version of (3.20). If we then set $t = -qx$, we get exactly (3.20).

Since it was the starting point for deriving Theorem 4.1, we now state the multdimensional ${}_6\Phi_5$ summation theorem from [73].

Theorem 4.13. ($U(n)$ generalization of the nonterminating ${}_6\Phi_5$ summation theorem.) Let

$$0 < |q| < 1 \tag{4.14a}$$

and

$$|q/(a_1 a_2 \cdots a_n c)| < 1. \tag{4.14b}$$

Then

$$\left\{ \left(\frac{(q(a_1 \cdots a_n)^{-1})_\infty (q(a_n c)^{-1})_\infty}{(q(a_n)^{-1})_\infty (q(a_1 \cdots a_n c)^{-1})_\infty} \right) \cdot \tag{4.15a}\right.$$

$$\left.\left.\left(\prod_{i=1}^{n-1} \frac{((qz_i)/(z_n))_\infty((qz_i)/(cz_n a_i))_\infty}{((qz_i)/(z_n a_i))_\infty((qz_i)/(cz_n))_\infty}\right)\right]\right\} \tag{4.15b}$$

$$= \sum_{y_1,\ldots,y_{n-1}\geq 0} \left\{\left[\left(\prod_{i=1}^{n-1} (z_i/z_n)_{(y_1+\ldots+y_{n-1})}\right)\cdot\left(\prod_{i=1}^{n-1}(q)_{y_i}\right)\right]^{-1}\right. \tag{4.16a}$$

$$\cdot\left[\left(\prod_{i=1}^{n-1} (1-z_i/z_n)\cdot q^{[y_i+(y_1+\ldots+y_{n-1})]})/(1-z_i/z_n)\right)\right] \tag{4.16b}$$

$$\cdot\left[(c)_{(y_1+\ldots+y_{n-1})}\cdot\left(\prod_{i=1}^{n-1}((qz_i)/(cz_n))_{y_i}\right)\right]^{-1} \tag{4.16c}$$

$$\cdot\left[\left(\prod_{1\leq r<s\leq n-1} (1-(z_r/z_s)\cdot q^{y_r-y_s})/(1-(z_r/z_s))\right)\right] \tag{4.16d}$$

$$\cdot\left[\left(\prod_{1\leq r<s\leq n-1} ((qz_r)/(z_s))_{y_r}((qz_s)/(z_r))_{y_s}\right)^{-1}\right] \tag{4.16e}$$

$$\cdot\left[\left(\prod_{1\leq r<s\leq n-1} (((a_s z_r)/(z_s))_{y_r}\cdot((a_r z_s)/(z_r))_{y_s})\right)\right] \tag{4.16f}$$

$$\cdot\left[\left(\prod_{i=1}^{n-1}(a_i)_{y_i}\right)\cdot\left(\prod_{i=1}^{n-1}((qz_i)/(z_n a_i))_{(y_1+\ldots+y_{n-1})}\right)\right]^{-1} \tag{4.16g}$$

$$\cdot\left[\left(\prod_{i=1}^{n-1}((a_n z_i)/(z_n))_{y_i}\right]\cdot\left((q/a_n)_{(y_1+\ldots+y_{n-1})}\right)^{-1}\right]\Bigg\} \tag{4.16h}$$

$$\cdot\left\{(a_1a_2\ \cdots\ a_n c)^{-(y_1+\ldots+y_{n-1})}\cdot q^{(y_1+2y_2+\ldots+(n-1)y_{n-1})}\right\} \tag{4.16i}$$

where $\{z_1, \ldots, z_n\}$ are indeterminants such that (3.29) holds, the corresponding arrays (A), (a), and (b) satisfy the conditions in (3.25), and we have

$$(z_r/z_s)\neq q^p,\ \text{if } 1\leq r<s\leq n-1, \tag{4.17a}$$

$$(z_i/z_n)\neq 1,\ \text{if } 1\leq i\leq n-1, \tag{4.17b}$$

$$(qz_i)/(cz_n)\neq q^{-p},\ p\geq 0 \text{ and } 1\leq i\leq n-1, \tag{4.17c}$$

$$(qz_i)/(z_n a_i)\neq q^{-p},\ p\geq 0 \text{ and } 1\leq i\leq n-1, \tag{4.17d}$$

$$(a_1\ \cdots\ a_n c)\neq q^p,\ p\geq 1, \tag{4.17e}$$

$$(a_1\ \cdots\ a_n c)\neq 0, \tag{4.17f}$$

$$a_n\neq q^p,\ p\geq 1, \tag{4.17g}$$

with $p\in\mathbf{Z}$ restricted as shown.

There are two natural ways to terminate the multiple sum in (4.16). The first is to set

$$c=q^{-N}, \tag{4.18}$$

for N a nonnegative integer. The second is to make the substitution

$$a_i=q^{-N_i},\ \text{for } 1\leq i\leq n, \tag{4.19}$$

and each N_i a nonnegative integer.

Our original proof of Theorem 4.13 in [73] involved (4.18). In particular,
we first showed that Theorem 3.32 is equivalent to the (4.18) case of the identity (4.15)-(4.16). Next, we observed that both (4.15) and (4.16) are analytic
functions of $z = (1/c)$ in a disk of positive radius about the origin. But, by the
(4.18) case of (4.15)-(4.16), these two analytic functions agree when
$z = q^m$, $m = 0,1,2, \cdots$. Thus, the general identity (4.15)-(4.16) follows.

From the above outline of the proof of Theorem 4.13 it is immediate that
the (4.19) case of (4.15)-(4.16) is a consequence of the (4.18) case. Nonetheless,
the (4.19) case of (4.15)-(4.16) is very interesting and we are studying it further
elsewhere.

Our proof of Theorem 4.13 helped motivate the multiple very well poised
$[H]^{(n)}$ series determined by

Definition 4.20. (basic hypergeometric series very well-poised in $U(n)$). We
define

$$
[H]^{(n)} \begin{bmatrix} (A_{rs}) \\ (A_{in}/c) \end{bmatrix} \begin{array}{|c|} (a_{rs};k) \\ (ca_{ni};k) \end{array} \begin{array}{|c|} (b_{rs};n-1),(b_{in}/c),(b_{rs};j) \\ (cb_{ni};n-1),(b_{nn}),(cb_{ni};j) \end{array} \begin{array}{|c} x_1 \\ \vdots \\ x_n \end{array} \Bigg] \tag{4.21}
$$

$$
\equiv \sum_{y_1, \ldots, y_{n-1} \geq 0} \left\{ \left[\left(\prod_{i=1}^{n-1} (A_{in})_{(y_1+\ldots+y_{n-1})} \right) \left(\prod_{i=1}^{n-1} (q)_{y_i} \right)^{-1} \right] \right.
$$

$$
\cdot \left[\left(\prod_{i=1}^{n-1} (1-A_{in} \cdot q^{[y_i+(y_1+\ldots+y_{n-1})]}) / (1-A_{in}) \right) \right]
$$

$$
\left. \cdot \left[(c)_{(y_1+\ldots+y_{n-1})} \cdot \left(\prod_{i=1}^{n-1} ((qA_{in})/c)_{y_i} \right)^{-1} \right] \right\} \tag{4.22a}
$$

(4.22b)

$$\left\{\cdot\left[\prod_{1\le i<l\le n-1}(1-A_{il}q^{y_i-y_l})/(1-A_{il})\right]\cdot\left[\prod_{1\le r<s\le n-1}(qA_{rs})_{y_r}(q/A_{rs})_{y_s}\right]^{-1}\right\}$$

$$\cdot\left[\frac{\left[\prod_{i=1}^{k}\prod_{l=1}^{n-1}(a_{li})_{y_l}\right]\cdot\left[\prod_{i=n+1}^{j}(q/b_{ni})_{(y_1+\ldots+y_{n-1})}\right]}{\left[\prod_{i=1}^{k}(q/a_{ni})_{(y_1+\ldots+y_{n-1})}\right]\cdot\left[\prod_{i=n+1}^{j}\prod_{l=1}^{n-1}(b_{li})_{y_l}\right]}\right] \tag{4.22c}$$

$$\cdot\left\{(-1)^{(j+k)(y_1+\ldots+y_{n-1})}\cdot q^{\left[n(y_1+\ldots+y_{n-1})-(j-k)\binom{1+(y_1+\ldots+y_{n-1})}{2}\right]}\right\} \tag{4.22d}$$

$$\cdot\left[\frac{(b_{n,n+1}b_{n,n+2}\cdots b_{n,j})}{(c)(a_{n1}a_{n2}\cdots a_{nk})(A_{1n}A_{2n}\cdots A_{n-1,n})}\right]^{(y_1+\ldots+y_{n-1})} \tag{4.22e}$$

$$\cdot\left[\prod_{i=1}^{n-1}(x_i/x_n)^{y_i}\right], \tag{4.22f}$$

to be very well-poised in $U(n)$ if $|q|<1$, $(A)_l$ is given by (2.3a), $(b_{li})_{y_l}\neq 0$, $A_{il}\neq 1$, $n\geq 2$, and the relations in (3.25) hold. We will call c and the a's numerator parameters and the b's denominator parameters. We sometimes denote the multiple series in (4.21) by the notation

$$[H]^{(n)}[(A)|(a),c|(b)|(x)]. \tag{4.23}$$

The very well-poised ${}_m\Phi_n$ series corresponds to a well-poised ${}_{m-2}\Phi_{n-2}$ series in the same way that

$$[H]^{(n)}[(A)|(a),c|(b)|(x)] \tag{4.24}$$

is related to the $n \longrightarrow (n-1)$ case of the multiple series

$$[F]^{(n)}((A)|(a)|(b)|(x)). \tag{4.25}$$

When comparing (4.24) to (4.25) it is useful to view (4.25) as simply a multivariable generalization of the classical (general) basic hypergeometric series in (2.16).

Remark 4.26. The multiple series (4.16) is obtained from (4.22) by first setting

$$k = j = n, \tag{4.27}$$

$$x_i = q^{i-1}, \; 1 \leq i \leq n, \tag{4.28}$$

and then replacing A_{rs} by

$$A_{rs} = (z_r/z_s), \text{ for } 1 \leq r < s \leq n. \tag{4.29}$$

That is, (4.22a-c) becomes (4.16a-h), and (4.22d-f) is written in (4.16i).

The $[H]^{(n)}$ series appear again in section 6.

5. A q-Analog of the Gauss Summation Theorem for $[F]^{(n)}$ Series.

In this section we present our q-analogs of W.J. Holman III's [50] $U(n)$ generalization of the summation theorems of Gauss and Pfaff-Saalschutz.

We first state

Theorem 5.1. ($q-U(n)$ Gauss summation theorem for $[F]^{(n)}$).

$$[F]^{(n)}\left(\begin{matrix} (z_r/z_s) \\ 1 \leq r < s \leq n \end{matrix} \;\middle|\; \begin{matrix} (a_s)(z_r/z_s), & b(z_i/z_n) \\ 1 \leq r,s \leq n & 1 \leq i \leq n \end{matrix} \;\middle|\; \begin{matrix} q(z_r/z_s), & c(z_i/z_n) \\ 1 \leq r,s \leq n & 1 \leq i \leq n \end{matrix} \;\middle|\; \begin{matrix} x_i \\ 1 \leq i \leq n \end{matrix}\right) \tag{5.2a}$$

$$= \sum_{y_1, \ldots, y_n \geq 0} \left(\prod_{1 \leq r < s \leq n} (1-(z_r/z_s) \cdot q^{y_r - y_s})/(1-(z_r/z_s)) \right) \tag{5.2b}$$

$$\cdot \left[\left(\prod_{1 \leq r, s \leq n} \frac{(a_s z_r/z_s)_{y_r}}{(q z_r/z_s)_{y_r}} \right) \cdot \left(\prod_{i=1}^{n} \frac{(b z_i/z_n)_{y_i}}{(c z_i/z_n)_{y_i}} \right) \right] \tag{5.2c}$$

$$\cdot \left(\prod_{i=1}^{n} [q^{(i-1)} \cdot c/(a_1 a_2 \cdots a_n b)]^{y_i} \right) \tag{5.2d}$$

$$= \frac{(c/b)_\infty}{(c/(a_1 a_2 \cdots a_n b))_\infty} \cdot \left(\prod_{i=1}^{n} \frac{((c z_i)/(z_n a_i))_\infty}{((c z_i)/z_n)_\infty} \right), \tag{5.2e}$$

where $n \geq 1$, $0 \leq |q| < 1$, and

$$x_i = q^{(i-1)} \cdot c/(a_1 a_2 \cdots a_n b), \text{ if } 1 \leq i \leq n; \tag{5.3a}$$

$$|c| < |a_1 a_2 \cdots a_n b|, \tag{5.3b}$$

$$(c z_i)/z_n \neq q^{-p}, \text{ if } p \geq 0 \text{ and } 1 \leq i \leq n, \tag{5.3c}$$

$$(z_r/z_s) \neq q^p, \text{ if } 1 \leq r < s \leq n, \tag{5.3d}$$

with p any integer.

We prove Theorem 5.1 in [74] by iterating a multivariable q-analog of the Gauss reduction formula (for a classical ${}_2F_1$) that is a direct consequence of the general contiguous relation for $[F]^{(n)}$ series in

Theorem 5.4. Let $[F]^{(n)}((A)|(a)|(b)|(x))$ be defined by Definition 3.26, and ${}_j\Phi_{j-1}$ by Definition 2.15. Also assume that $k = j \geq n$, $1 \leq \nu \leq n$, and $\{b_{v,n+1}, \ldots, b_{v,j}\}$ are distinct. We then have

$$\left[1-(b_{v,n+1} \cdots b_{v,j})(a_{11} \cdots a_{nn})^{-1}(a_{v,n+1} \cdots a_{v,j})^{-1}\right] \tag{5.5a}$$

$$\cdot [F]^{(n)} \left(\begin{array}{c|c|c|c} (A_{rs}) & (a_{rs}) & (b_{rs}) & (x_i) \\ 1 \leq r < s \leq n & \begin{array}{c} 1 \leq r \leq n \\ 1 \leq s \leq j \end{array} & \begin{array}{c} 1 \leq r \leq n \\ 1 \leq s \leq j \end{array} & 1 \leq i \leq n \end{array} \right) \tag{5.5b}$$

$$=\sum_{p=1}^{n}\left\{\left[(q^{(1-p)}\cdot x_p)-(b_{v,n+1}\cdots b_{v,j})(a_{11}\cdots a_{nn})^{-1}(a_{v,n+1}\cdots a_{v,j})^{-1}\right]\right. \tag{5.5c}$$

$$\left.\cdot\left[(-1)^{(p-1)}\cdot\left(\prod_{i=1}^{p-1}\frac{(A_{ip})}{(1-A_{ip})}\right)\left(\prod_{i=p+1}^{n}(1-A_{pi})\right)^{-1}\cdot\left(\prod_{i=1}^{j}(1-a_{pi})\right)\cdot\left(\prod_{i=n+1}^{j}(1-b_{pi})\right)^{-1}\right]\right\} \tag{5.5d}$$

$$\cdot\,{}_j\Phi_{j-1}\left[\begin{matrix}qa_{p1},\ \ldots,\ qa_{pj}\\ b_{p1},\ \ldots,\ b_{p,p-1},b_{p,p+1},\ \ldots,\ b_{p,n},\ qb_{p,n+1},\ \ldots,\ qb_{p,j}\end{matrix}\;\middle|\;x_p\cdot q^{(1-p)}\right] \tag{5.5e}$$

$$\cdot\,[F]^{(n-1)}\left(\begin{matrix}(\bar{A}_{rs})\\ 1\le r<s\le n-1\end{matrix}\;\middle|\;\begin{matrix}(\bar{a}_{rs})\\ 1\le r\le n-1\\ 1\le s\le j\end{matrix}\;\middle|\;\begin{matrix}(\bar{b}_{rs})\\ 1\le r\le n-1\\ 1\le s\le j\end{matrix}\;\middle|\;\begin{matrix}(\bar{x}_i)\\ 1\le i\le n-1\end{matrix}\right) \tag{5.5f}$$

$$+\sum_{p=n+1}^{j}\left\{\left(\prod_{i=1}^{n}(1-(b_{ip}/a_{ii}))/(1-b_{ip})\right)\cdot\left(\prod_{i=n+1}^{j}(1-(b_{vp}/a_{vi}))\right)\left(\prod_{\substack{i=n+1\\ i\neq p}}^{j}(1-(b_{vp}/b_{vi}))\right)^{-1}\right\} \tag{5.5g}$$

$$\cdot\,[F]^{(n)}\left(\begin{matrix}(A_{rs})\\ 1\le r<s\le n\end{matrix}\;\middle|\;\begin{matrix}(a_{rs})\\ 1\le r\le n\\ 1\le s\le j\end{matrix}\;\middle|\;\begin{matrix}(b_{rs}),\\ 1\le r\le n\\ 1\le s\le p-1\end{matrix}\ \ \begin{matrix}(qb_{i,p}),\\ 1\le i\le n\\ \ \end{matrix}\ \ \begin{matrix}(b_{rs})\\ 1\le r\le n\\ p<s\le j\end{matrix}\;\middle|\;\begin{matrix}(qx_i)\\ 1\le i\le n\end{matrix}\right),$$

where $(\bar{A}_{rs})$, $(\bar{a}_{rs})$, $(\bar{b}_{rs})$, $(\bar{x}_i)$ are given by

$$\bar{A}_{rs}=A_{rs},\ \text{if } 1\le r<s<p, \tag{5.6a}$$

$$=A_{r,s+1},\ \text{if } 1\le r<p\le s<n, \tag{5.6b}$$

$$=A_{r+1,s+1},\ \text{if } p\le r<s<n; \tag{5.6c}$$

$$\overline{a}_{rs} = a_{rs}, \text{ if } 1 \le r < p \text{ and, } 1 \le s \le j, \tag{5.7a}$$
$$= a_{r+1,s}, \text{ if } p \le r < n, \text{ and } 1 \le s \le j; \tag{5.7b}$$
$$\overline{b}_{rs} = b_{rs}, \text{ if } 1 \le r, s < p, \tag{5.8a}$$
$$= b_{r,s+1}, \text{ if } 1 \le r < p \text{ and } p \le s < j, \tag{5.8b}$$
$$= b_{r+1,s}, \text{ if } p \le r < n \text{ and } 1 \le s < p, \tag{5.8c}$$
$$= b_{r+1,s+1}, \text{ if } p \le r < n \text{ and } p \le s < j, \tag{5.8d}$$
$$= b_{rp}, \text{ if } 1 \le r < p \text{ and } s = j, \tag{5.8e}$$
$$= b_{r+1,p}, \text{ if } p \le r < n \text{ and } s = j; \tag{5.8f}$$

and the $\overline{x}_1, \ldots, \overline{x}_{n-1}$ are given by

$$\overline{x}_i = qx_i, \text{ if } 1 \le i < p, \tag{5.9a}$$
$$= x_{i+1}, \text{ if } p \le i < n. \tag{5.9b}$$

Furthermore, $\overline{A}_{rs}$, $\overline{a}_{rs}$, and $\overline{b}_{rs}$ satisfy the well-poised conditions in (3.25).

Motivated by sections 33 and 48 of [77] and section I.7 of [79] we derive Theorem 5.4 in [74] from certain q-differential operators in [70] and two special cases of Lemma 3.34.

The special value of x_i in (5.3a) was discovered by setting each coefficient in the $j = (n+1)$ case of (5.5c) equal to 0. It turns out that (5.5d) and (5.5e) are absolutely convergent for this choice of the x_i. Thus, each of the n terms in (5.5c-e) become 0, and (5.5a-b) and (5.5f-g) yield a two-term q-difference equation which is our multivariable q-analog of the Gauss reduction formula. Iterating this relation an infinite number of times gives Theorem 5.1.

Two equivalent forms of the Vandermonde summation theorem for $[F]^{(n)}$ are consequences of Theorem 5.1. We write these results in terms of the original arrays (A), (a), and (b) in (3.25).

We first have

Theorem 5.10. (terminating Gauss summation theorem for $[F]^{(n)}$ series).

$$[F]^{(n)}\left(\begin{array}{c|c|c|c} (A_{rs}) & (a_{rs}) & (b_{rs}) & x_i \\ 1\le r<s\le n & 1\le r\le n & 1\le r\le n & 1\le i\le n \\ & 1\le s\le n+1 & 1\le s\le n+1 & \end{array}\right) \tag{5.11a}$$

$$=(b_{n,n+1}/a_{n,n+1})_{(N_1+\ldots+N_n)}\cdot\left[\prod_{i=1}^{n}(b_{i,n+1})_{N_i}\right]^{-1}, \tag{5.11b}$$

where $n\ge 1$, q is arbitrary, and

$$a_{ii}=q^{-N_i},\ \text{for } 1\le i\le n \ \text{with } N_i \text{ nonnegative integers}, \tag{5.12a}$$

$$x_i=q^{(i-1)}\cdot q^{(N_1+\ldots+N_n)}\cdot(b_{n,n+1}/a_{n,n+1}),\ \text{for } 1\le i\le n, \tag{5.12b}$$

$$b_{li}\ne q^{-p},\ \text{if } p\ge -1,\ 1\le l\ne i\le n, \tag{5.12c}$$

$$b_{l,n+1}\ne q^{-p},\ \text{if } p\ge 0,\ 1\le l\le n, \tag{5.12d}$$

$$A_{il}\ne q^{p},\ \text{if } 1\le i<l\le n, \tag{5.12e}$$

$$\text{with } p \text{ any integer}. \tag{5.12f}$$

It is clear from (2.4) that if a_{ii} is given by (5.12a) then (5.2e) becomes (5.11b). Furthermore, since (5.11a) is a finite sum (terminates) and (5.11b) are finite products, (5.11) is equivalent to a polynomial identity in q. Thus, (5.11) is valid whenever each term is defined and the restrictions $0<|q|<1$ and (5.3b) can be eliminated.

The $n=1$ case of Theorem 5.10 is the same identity as equation (3.3.2.6) on page 97 of [79], and is known as one of the two q-analogs of Vandermonde's summation theorem [33,77,79].

Motivated by the classical ($n=1$) case [30] we next invert the base q, or reverse the order of summation, in Theorem 5.10 to obtain

Theorem 5.13. (second q-analog of the Vandermonde summation theorem for $[F]^{(n)}$ series).

Let $n \geq 1$, and q be arbitrary. Also assume that a_{ii} is given by (5.12a), and that (5.12c-f) holds. We then have

$$[F]^{(n)}\left(\begin{array}{c|c|c|c} (A_{rs}) & (a_{rs}) & (b_{rs}) & q^i \\ 1 \leq r < s \leq n & 1 \leq r \leq n & 1 \leq r \leq n & 1 \leq i \leq n \\ & 1 \leq s \leq n+1 & 1 \leq s \leq n+1 & \end{array}\right) \tag{5.14a}$$

$$= \left\{ (b_{n,n+1}/a_{n,n+1})_{(N_1+\cdots+N_n)} \cdot \left[\prod_{i=1}^{n} (b_{i,n+1})_{N_i}\right]^{-1} \right\} \tag{5.14b}$$

$$\cdot \left\{ \left[\prod_{i=1}^{n} (a_{i,n+1})^{N_i}\right] \cdot q^{-\sigma_2(N_1, \ldots, N_n)} \right\}, \tag{5.14c}$$

where $\sigma_2(N_1, \ldots, N_n)$ is the second elementary symmetric function of $\{N_1, \ldots, N_n\}$.

The $n=1$ case of Theorem 5.13 is equivalent to equation (3.3.2.7) on page 97 of [79]. Slater views (3.3.2.7) as the "usual" q-analog of the Vandermonde summation and, despite the discussion on page 88 of [79], regards (3.3.2.6) and (3.3.2.7) as distinct identities. However, as pointed out in [30], and generalized in [74,75], (3.3.2.6) and (3.3.2.7) are in fact equivalent.

Inverting the base q in terminating $[F]^{(n)}$ series in which

$$a_{ii} = q^{-N_i}, \text{ for } 1 \leq i \leq n \text{ and } N_i \text{ nonnegative integers,} \tag{5.15}$$

transforms $[F]^{(n)}((A)|(a)|(b)|(x))$ into a multiple series of the same type, but with the base q replaced by q^{-1}. This transformation depends upon various special cases of

$$(A;q)_l = (A^{-1};q^{-1})_l \cdot ((-1)^l A^l q^{l(l-1)/2}), \tag{5.16}$$

noting that

$$(a_{ii})^{-1} = q^{N_i} = (q^{-1})^{-N_i}, \text{ for } 1 \le i \le n, \tag{5.17}$$

and observing that

$$\begin{aligned}&(1 - A_{il} \cdot q^{(y_i - y_l)})/(1 - A_{il})\\ &= q^{(y_i - y_l)} \cdot ((1 - (A_{il})^{-1} \cdot (q^{-1})^{(y_i - y_l)})/(1 - (A_{il})^{-1})),\end{aligned} \tag{5.18}$$

and

$$\left(\prod_{1 \le i < l \le n} q^{(y_i - y_l)} \right) = \prod_{i=1}^{n} q^{(n-2i+1)y_i}. \tag{5.19}$$

In section 4 of [74] we deduce Theorem 5.13 from 5.10 by inverting the base q in (5.14a), applying Theorem 5.10, and then simplifying the resulting products. In fact, these two theorems are equivalent under this transformation.

Theorems 5.13 and 5.10 are also equivalent under multivariable reversal of terminating $[F]^{(n)}$ series where

$$k \ge n \tag{5.20a}$$

and

$$a_{ii} = q^{-N_i}, \text{ for } 1 \le i \le n \text{ and } N_i \text{ nonnegative integers.} \tag{5.20b}$$

Reversal of $[F]^{(n)}$ series, subject to (5.20), consists of making the substitution

$$y_l \longrightarrow (N_l - y_l), \text{ for } 1 \le l \le n, \tag{5.21}$$

in $[F]^{(n)}((A)|(a)|(b)|(x))$ and then applying certain special cases of

$$(a;q)_{N-m} = \frac{(a;q)_N \cdot q^{m(m+1)/2}}{(a^{-1}q^{1-N};q)_m \cdot (-a)^m \cdot q^{Nm}}, \tag{5.22}$$

and some algebra, to obtain a new $[F]^{(n)}$ series that is equal to the original. Writing everything out explicitly gives the identity between $[F]^{(n)}$ series contained in Theorem 6.6 of [75]. The special case in which $j = k$ is Corollary 6.29

of [75] and is given by

Lemma 5.23. ($k=j\geq n$ case of reversal of $[F]^{(n)}$ series). Let (5.20) hold, $j=k$, and suppose that x_i are independent of $\{y_1,\ldots,y_n\}$ for $1\leq i\leq n$. We then have

$$[F]^{(n)}\left(\begin{array}{c|c|c|c} (A_{rs}) & (a_{rs}) & (b_{rs}) & (x_i) \\ 1\leq r<s\leq n & 1\leq r\leq n & 1\leq r\leq n & 1\leq i\leq n \\ & 1\leq s\leq j & 1\leq s\leq j & \end{array}\right) \tag{5.24a}$$

$$=\left\{\left(\prod_{i=1}^{n}((-1)^{N_i}\cdot q^{-iN_i}\cdot q^{-\binom{N_i}{2}}\cdot x_i^{N_i})\right)\cdot q^{-\sigma_2(N_1,\ldots,N_n)}\right\} \tag{5.24b}$$

$$\cdot\left\{\left(\prod_{i=n+1}^{j}\prod_{l=1}^{n}((a_{li})_{N_l}\cdot\left(b_{li}\right)_{N_1}^{-1}\right)\right\} \tag{5.24c}$$

$$\cdot[F]^{(n)}\left(\begin{array}{c|c|c|c} (\overline{A}_{rs}) & (\overline{a}_{rs}) & (\overline{b}_{rs}) & (\overline{x}_i) \\ 1\leq r<s\leq n & 1\leq r\leq n & 1\leq r\leq n & 1\leq i\leq n \\ & 1\leq s\leq j & 1\leq s\leq j & \end{array}\right), \tag{5.24d}$$

where $(\overline{A}_{rs}),(\overline{a}_{rs}),(\overline{b}_{rs}),(\overline{x}_i)$ are given by

$$\overline{A}_{rs}=(A_{rs})^{-1}\cdot q^{(N_s-N_r)},\text{ if }1\leq r<s\leq n, \tag{5.25a}$$

$$\overline{a}_{rs}=((b_{rs})^{-1}\cdot q^{1-N_r}),\text{ if }1\leq r\leq n\text{ and }1\leq s\leq j, \tag{5.25b}$$

$$\overline{b}_{rs}=((a_{rs})^{-1}\cdot q^{1-N_r}),\text{ if }1\leq r\leq n\text{ and }1\leq s\leq j, \tag{5.25c}$$

$$\overline{x}_i=\left\{\left(\prod_{l=1}^{j}(b_{il}/a_{il})\right)\cdot q^{(2i-n-1)}\cdot(x_i)^{-1}\right\},\text{ if }1\leq i\leq n. \tag{5.25d}$$

The identity (5.24) preserves the conditions in both (3.25) and (3.28).

As an application of Lemma 5.23 we obtain Theorem 5.13 from 5.10 in section 6 of [75]. Similarly, Theorem 5.10 follows from Theorem 5.13.

One of our primary applications of Theorems 5.10 and 5.13 has been to derive a q-analog of Holman's [50] $U(n)$ generalization of the Pfaff-Saalschutz or balanced ${}_3F_2$ summation theorem [33,77,79] contained in

Theorem 5.26. (q-analog of the $U(n)$ balanced ${}_3F_2$ summation theorem). Assume $n \geq 1$ and that N_i is a nonnegative integer for $1 \leq i \leq n$. We then have

$$[F]^{(n)}\left(\begin{array}{c} (z_r/z_s) \\ 1 \leq r < s \leq n \end{array} \middle| \begin{array}{ccc} (q^{-N_s}(z_r/z_s)), & (a(z_i/z_n)), & (b(z_i/z_n)) \\ 1 \leq r,s \leq n & 1 \leq i \leq n & 1 \leq i \leq n \end{array} \middle| \right. \tag{5.27a}$$
$$\left. \middle| \begin{array}{ccc} (q(z_r/z_s)), & (c(z_i/z_n)), & (d(z_i/z_n)) \\ 1 \leq r,s \leq n & 1 \leq i \leq n & 1 \leq i \leq n \end{array} \middle| \begin{array}{c} (q^i) \\ 1 \leq i \leq n \end{array} \right)$$

$$= \left\{(c/a)_{(N_1+\ldots+N_n)} \cdot (c/b)_{(N_1+\ldots+N_n)}\right\} \tag{5.27b}$$

$$\cdot \left\{\prod_{i=1}^{n} \left((c(z_i/z_n))_{N_i}^{-1} \cdot ((c/(ab))(z_n/z_i)q^{[(N_1+\ldots+N_n)-N_i]})_{N_i}^{-1}\right)\right\}, \tag{5.27c}$$

where

$$cd = (ab)q^{1-(N_1+\ldots+N_n)}. \tag{5.28}$$

Theorem 5.26 provides a multivariable generalization of Jackson's [53] classical q-analog of the balanced ${}_3F_2$ summation theorem.

We prove Theorem 5.26 in [75] by an induction argument based upon a new general q-difference equation for balanced $[F]^{(n)}$ series and both Theorems 5.10 and 5.13. Our proof of Theorem 5.26 amounts to inductively factoring (5.27a) into lower order $[F]^{(n)}$ series, each of which can be summed by either Theorem 5.10 or 5.13.

R.A. Gustafson's [41] elegant generalization of F.J.W. Whipple's [81,82] classical transformation of a very-well poised ${}_7F_6(1)$ into a balanced ${}_4F_3(1)$ was partly responsible for our discovery of the new q-difference equations for $[F]^{(n)}$. Gustafson found a transformation between the ordinary $(q=1)$ multiple hypergeometric series $W_m^{(n)}$ and $F^{(n-1)}$. This transformation allowed us to deduce difference equations for special $F^{(n-1)}$ series from the corresponding general difference equations for $W_m^{(n)}$ which appeared in [67,69]. These crucial examples led us to general difference equations for $F^{(n)}$, which in turn made it much easier to discover our q-difference equations for $[F]^{(n)}$ in Theorems 1.46 and 1.49 of [75]. We made use of elementary series manipulations and standard partial fraction expansions to give a direct proof of these q-difference equations for $[F]^{(n)}$.

In section 6 of [75] we showed that Theorem 5.26 is invariant under both inversion of the base q in (5.15-19) and multivariable reversal of terminating $[F]^{(n)}$ series in (5.20-25). These symmetry results show that Theorems 5.10, 5.13, and 5.26 are particularly natural generalizations of the classical one-variable theory.

6. A q-Analog of a Whipple's Transformation for $[F]^{(n)}$ Series.

The q-difference equations in Theorems 1.46 and 1.49 of [75] not only lead to Theorem 5.26. They also enable us to prove

Theorem 6.1. (special case of first form of $q-U(n)$ Whipple). Let $[W]_m^{(n)}((A)|(a)|(b)|(x))$ and $[F]^{(n)}((A)|(a)|(b)|(x))$ be defined by Definitions 3.23 and 3.26, respectively. Also assume that $n \geq 2$, m is a nonnegative integer, and

$$a_{ii} = q^{-N_i}, \text{ for } 1 \le i \le n-1 \text{ and } N_i \text{ nonnegative integers.} \tag{6.2}$$

We the have

$$[W]_m^{(n)} \left(\begin{array}{c} (A_{rs}) \\ 1 \le r < s \le n \end{array} \middle| \begin{array}{c} (a_{rs}) \\ 1 \le r \le n \\ 1 \le s \le n+1 \end{array} \middle| \begin{array}{c} (b_{rs}) \\ 1 \le r \le n \\ 1 \le s \le n+1 \end{array} \middle| \begin{array}{c} q^{i-1} \\ 1 \le i \le n \end{array} \right) \tag{6.3a}$$

$$= \left\{ \left[\prod_{i=1}^{n-1} ((b_{in})_{N_i} ((a_{nn} a_{i,n+1})^{-1} \cdot q^{[1-m+(N_1+\ldots+N_{n-1})-N_i]})_{N_i}) \right] \right. \tag{6.3b}$$

$$\cdot \left[\left(q^{1-m} / a_{nn} \right)^{-1}_{(N_1+\ldots+N_{n-1})} \cdot \left(q^{1-m} / a_{n,n+1} \right)^{-1}_{(N_1+\ldots+N_{n-1})} \right] \tag{6.3c}$$

$$\left. \cdot \left[(a_{nn})_m (a_{n,n+1})_m \left(b_{n,n+1} \right)_m^{-1} (a_{11} \cdots a_{n-1,n-1})^m \cdot (1-q)^{-m} \right] \right\} \tag{6.3d}$$

$$\cdot [F]^{(n-1)} \left(\begin{array}{c} (A_{rs}) \\ 1 \le r < s \le n-1 \end{array} \middle| \begin{array}{c} (a_{rs}) \\ 1 \le r \le n-1 \\ 1 \le s \le n+1 \end{array} , \begin{array}{c} (b_{i,n+1} q^m) \\ 1 \le i \le n-1 \end{array} \right|$$

$$\left| \begin{array}{c} (b_{rs}) \\ 1 \le r \le n-1 \\ 1 \le s \le n+1 \end{array} , \begin{array}{c} ((a_{11} a_{22} \cdots a_{nn})(a_{i,n+1} q^m)) \\ 1 \le i \le n-1 \end{array} \middle| \begin{array}{c} q^i \\ 1 \le i \le n-1 \end{array} \right). \tag{6.3e}$$

In [76] we utilized q-difference equations and induction on m to prove Theorem 6.1. The general q-difference equations for $[F]^{(n)}$ in Theorem 1.46 of [75] imply that both sides of (6.3) satisfy the same special case of the general q-difference equation for $[W]_m^{(n)}$ in [69]. Our proof of Theorem 6.1 is completed by uniqueness and the fact that the $m=0$ case of (6.3) is equivalent to Theorem

5.26.

R.A. Gustafson's [41] transformation of $[W]_m^{(n)}$ into $F^{(n-1)}$ can be written as the $q=1$ case of Theorem 6.1.

It turns out that Theorem 6.1 is a key step in deriving the higher-dimensional generalization of Theorem 2.22 given by

Theorem 6.4. (general case of second form of $q-U(n)$ Whipple). Let $[F]^{(n)}((A)|(a)|(b)|(x))$ and $[H]^{(n)}[(A)|(a),c|(b)|(x)]$ be defined by Definitions 3.26 and 4.20, respectively. Also assume that $n \geq 2$ and that (6.2) holds. We then have

$$[H]^{(n)}\left[\begin{matrix}(A_{rs}) \\ (A_{in}/c)\end{matrix} \;\middle|\; \begin{matrix}(a_{rs};n+1) \\ (ca_{ni};n+1)\end{matrix} \;\middle|\; \begin{matrix}(b_{rs};n-1),\,(b_{in}/c),\,(b_{i,n+1}) \\ (cb_{ni};n-1),\,(b_{nn}),\,(cb_{n,n+1})\end{matrix} \;\middle|\; \begin{matrix}q^{i-1} \\ 1\leq i\leq n\end{matrix}\right] \tag{6.5a}$$

$$= \left\{ \left[\prod_{i=1}^{n-1} ((b_{in})_{N_i} \cdot ((a_{nn}\, a_{i,n+1})^{-1} \cdot q^{[1+(N_1+\ldots+N_{n-1})-N_i]})_{N_i}) \right] \right. \tag{6.5b}$$

$$\left. \cdot \left[\left(q/a_{nn}\right)^{-1}_{(N_1+\ldots+N_{n-1})} \cdot \left(q/a_{n,n+1}\right)^{-1}_{(N_1+\ldots+N_{n-1})} \right] \right\} \tag{6.5c}$$

$$\cdot [F]^{(n-1)} \left(\begin{matrix}(A_{rs}) \\ 1\leq r<s\leq n-1\end{matrix} \;\middle|\; \begin{matrix}(a_{rs}) \\ 1\leq r\leq n-1 \\ 1\leq s\leq n+1\end{matrix} \quad \begin{matrix},\,(b_{i,n+1}/c) \\ 1\leq i\leq n-1 \\ \end{matrix} \;\middle|\; \right.$$

$$\left|\begin{array}{cccc} (b_{rs}) & ,(b_{in}/c) & ,(b_{i,n+1}) & ,((a_{11}\cdots a_{nn})a_{i,n+1}) \\ 1\le r\le n-1 & 1\le i\le n-1 & 1\le i\le n-1 & 1\le i\le n-1 \\ 1\le s\le n-1 & & & \end{array}\right| \left.\begin{array}{c} q^{i} \\ 1\le i\le n-1 \end{array}\right). \tag{6.5d}$$

The connection between Theorem 6.1 and 6.4 is provided by

Lemma 6.6. Let m be a nonnegative integer and

$$c = q^{-m}. \tag{6.7}$$

We then have the identity

$$[H]^{(n)}\left[\begin{array}{c|c|c|c} (A_{rs}) & (a_{rs};k) & (b_{rs};n-1),\ (q^{m}b_{in}),\ (b_{rs};j) & x_i \\ (q^{m}A_{in}) & (q^{-m}a_{ni};k) & (q^{-m}\cdot b_{ni};n-1),\ (b_{nn}),\ (q^{-m}b_{ni};j) & 1\le i\le n \end{array}\right] \tag{6.8a}$$

$$= \left\{ \left(\prod_{i=1}^{k}(q^{-m}\cdot a_{ni})_m\right)^{-1} \cdot \left(\prod_{i=n+1}^{j}(q^{-m}\cdot b_{ni})_m\right) \cdot \left(\prod_{i=1}^{n-1}(qA_{in})_m\right) \right.$$

$$\left. \cdot\left((-1)^{(n-1)}\cdot x_n\right)^{-m}\cdot(1-q)^{(k+1-j)m}\cdot(A_{1n}A_{2n}\cdots A_{n-1,n})^{-m}\cdot q^{-(n-1)\binom{m}{2}} \right\} \tag{6.8b}$$

$$\cdot\,[W]_m^{(n)}\left(\begin{array}{c|c|c|c} (A_{rs}) & (a_{rs};k) & (b_{rs};n-1),\ (q^{m}b_{in}),\ (b_{rs};j) & x_1 \\ & & & \vdots \\ (q^{m}A_{in}) & (q^{-m}a_{ni};k) & (q^{-m}\cdot b_{ni};n-1),\ (b_{nn}),\ (q^{-m}b_{ni};j) & x_n \end{array}\right), \tag{6.8c}$$

where $[H]^{(n)}$ and $[W]_m^{(n)}$ are defined by Definitions (4.20) and 3.23), respectively.

Lemma 6.6 is proved in [73] by elementary series manipulations.

Now, it is not hard to see that both sides of (6.5) are analytic functions of

$$z = (1/c) \tag{6.9}$$

in a disk of positive radius about the origin. From Theorem 6.1 and Lemma 6.6 it follows that these two analytic functions agree when

$$z = (1/c) = q^m, \text{ for } m = 0,1,2,\cdots. \tag{6.10}$$

Thus, both sides of (6.5) are equal for general c if $0 < |q| < 1$. However, the condition $0 < |q| < 1$ can then be removed by analytic continuation, and we finally obtain Theorem 6.4.

This proof of Theorem 6.4 from Theorem 6.1 is the same argument that led from Theorem 3.32 to 4.13, from Theorem 3.1 to 3.4, and from Theorem 2.1 to 2.12.

It follows by relabeling parameters that Theorem 2.22 is the $n = 2$ case of Theorem 6.4.

We conclude this section with some applications of Theorem 6.4.

The terminating case of Theorem 4.13 in which (4.19) holds is a direct consequence of Theorem 6.4. By setting

$$a_{i,n+1} = b_{i,n+1}, \text{ for } 1 \leq i \leq n, \tag{6.11}$$

in Theorem 6.4, using Theorem 5.26 to sum the resulting $[F]^{(n-1)}$ series in (6.5d), and simplifying, we obtain (4.15-16), subject to (4.19).

Theorem 6.4 is also responsible for a higher-dimensional generalization of Jackson's q-analog of Dougall's [54] ${}_7F_6$ summation theorem. If we assume that

$$(b_{i,n+1}/c) = (a_{11}a_{22}\cdots a_{nn})a_{i,n+1}, \text{ for } 1 \leq i \leq n-1, \tag{6.12}$$

in (6.5), then it is not hard to see that Theorem 5.26 allows us to sum the series in (6.5d). Recalling the relations

$$a_{nn} = (a_{in}\, q / b_{in}),\ \text{for } 1 \le i \le n, \tag{6.13a}$$

$$(q / a_{nn}) = (b_{n-1,n} / a_{n-1,n}), \tag{6.13b}$$

and

$$(q / a_{n,n+1}) = (b_{n-1,n} / a_{n-1,n+1}), \tag{6.13c}$$

and simplifying the products resulting from (6.5b-d), we are immediately led to

Theorem 6.14. ($U(n)$ generalization of Jackson's q-analog of Dougall's theorem). Let $n \ge 2$ and assume that (6.2) holds. Furthermore, suppose that

$$(b_{in}\, b_{i,n+1}) = c\,(a_{in}\, a_{i,n+1})(a_{11} \cdots a_{n-1,n-1})q,\ \text{for } 1 \le i \le n. \tag{6.15}$$

We then have

$$[H]^{(n)} \left[\begin{matrix} (A_{rs}) \\ (A_{in}/c) \end{matrix} \;\middle|\; \begin{matrix} (a_{rs}; n+1) \\ (ca_{ni}; n+1) \end{matrix} \;\middle|\; \begin{matrix} (b_{rs}; n-1), (b_{in}/c), (b_{i,n+1}) \\ (cb_{ni}; n-1), (b_{nn}), (cb_{n,n+1}) \end{matrix} \;\middle|\; \begin{matrix} q^{i-1} \\ 1 \le i \le n \end{matrix} \right] \tag{6.16a}$$

$$= \left\{ \prod_{i=1}^{n-1} \left((b_{in})_{N_i} (b_{in}/c)_{N_i}^{-1} \right) \right\} \tag{6.16b}$$

$$\left\{ \left[\prod_{i=1}^{n-1} \left((b_{in}\, a_{ii}) \cdot [(a_{in}\, a_{i,n+1})(a_{11} \cdots a_{n-1,n-1})]^{-1} \right)_{N_i} \right] \right.$$

$$\left. \cdot \left[\prod_{i=1}^{n-1} \left((b_{in}\, a_{ii}) \cdot [(ca_{in}\, a_{i,n+1})(a_{11} \cdots a_{n-1,n-1})]^{-1} \right)_{N_i}^{-1} \right] \right\} \tag{6.16c}$$

$$\left\{ \left[(b_{n-1,n} / (ca_{n-1,n}))_{(N_1 + \ldots + N_{n-1})} \cdot \left(b_{n-1,n} / a_{n-1,n} \right)_{(N_1 + \ldots + N_{n-1})}^{-1} \right] \right.$$

$$\cdot \left[(b_{n-1,n}/(ca_{n-1,n+1}))_{(N_1+\ldots+N_{n-1})} \cdot \left(b_{n-1,n}/a_{n-1,n+1} \right)^{-1}_{(N_1+\ldots+N_{n-1})} \right] \Bigg\} . \tag{6.16d}$$

The $n=2$ case of (6.16) is Jackson's q-analog of Dougall's theorem.

When $c=q^{-m}$, Lemma 6.6 and a fair amount of algebraic simplification transforms this case of Theorem 6.14 into

Theorem 6.17. ($U(n)$ generalization of Jackson's q-analog of Dougall's theorem for $[W]_m^{(n)}$ series). Let $n \geq 2$, m a nonnegative integer, and suppose that (6.2) holds. Also, assume that

$$(b_{in}\, b_{i,n+1}) = (a_{in}\, a_{i,n+1})(a_{11} \cdots a_{n-1,n-1})q, \text{ for } 1 \leq i \leq n-1. \tag{6.18}$$

We then have

$$[W]_m^{(n)} \left(\begin{array}{c|c|c|c} (A_{rs}) & (a_{rs}) & (b_{rs}) & q^{i-1} \\ 1 \leq r < s \leq n & 1 \leq r \leq n & 1 \leq r \leq n & 1 \leq i \leq n \\ & 1 \leq s \leq n+1 & 1 \leq s \leq n+1 & \end{array} \right) \tag{6.19a}$$

$$= \left\{ (1-q)^{-m} \cdot \left[(b_{n-1,n+1}/a_{n-1,n+1})_m \cdot (b_{n-1,n+1}/a_{n-1,n})_m \cdot \left(b_{n,n+1} \right)_m^{-1} \right] \right\} \tag{6.19b}$$

$$\cdot \left\{ \prod_{i=1}^{n-1} \left((b_{i,n+1}/a_{ii})_m \cdot (b_{i,n+1})_m^{-1} \right) \right\} . \tag{6.19c}$$

It is also possible to obtain Theorem 6.17 directly from Theorem 6.1 and Theorem 5.26.

R.A. Gustafson's [41] generalization of Dougall's summation theorem for $W_m^{(n)}$ can be simplified to the $q=1$ case of Theorem 6.17.

Letting $q \rightarrow 1$ in Theorem 6.14 involves the ordinary series $H^{(n)}$ very-well poised in $U(n)$, that were introduced in [73].

Further applications of Theorem 6.4 appear in [76]. These include a $U(n)$ generalization of the Rogers-Selberg identity [5], which is a major ingredient in several proofs of the Rogers-Ramanujan-Schur identities [2,3,4].

References

1. C. Adiga, B.C. Berndt, S. Bhargava, and G.N.Watson, *Chapter 16 of Ramanujan's second notebook: theta-functions and q-series,* Mem. Amer. Math. Soc. **53** (1985), No. 315, v + 85 pp.

2. G.E. Andrews, "*The Theory of Partitions*", Vol. 2, "*Encyclopedia of Mathematics and Its Applications*", (G.-C. Rota, Ed.), Addison-Wesley, Reading, Mass., 1976.

3. G.E. Andrews, "*Partitions: yesterday and today*", New Zealand Math. Soc., Wellington, 1979.

4. G.E. Andrews, "*q-Series: Their development and application in analysis, number theory, combinatorics, physics and computer algebra*", NSF-CBMS Regional Conference Series, Number **66** (1986), 110 pages.

5. G.E. Andrews, *An analytic proof of the Rogers-Ramanujan-Gordon identities, Amer. J. Math.* **88** (1966), 844-846.

6. G.E. Andrews, *On Ramanujan's summation of* ${}_1\Psi_1(a,b,z)$, Proc. Amer. Math. Soc. **22** (1969), 552-553.

7. G.E. Andrews, *On a transformation of bilateral series with applicatins,* Proc. Amer. Math. Soc., **25** (1970), 554-558.

8. G.E. Andrews, *Applications of basic hypergeometric functions,* SIAM Rev. **16** (1974), 441-484.

9. G.E. Andrews, *Problems and prospects for basic hypergeometric functions, in "Theory and Applications of Special Functions"* (R. Askey, Ed.), pp. 191-

224. Academic Press, New York, 1975.

10. G.E. Andrews, *Partitions, q-series and the Lusztig-Macdonald-Wall conjectures,* Invent. Math. **41** (1977), 91-102.

11. G.E. Andrews, *An introduction to Ramanujan's "lost" notebook,* Amer. Math. Monthly **86** (1979), 89-108.

12. G.E. Andrews, *Ramanujan's "lost" notebook: I. partial theta functions,* Adv. in Math. **41** (1981), 137-172.

13. G.E. Andrews, *Ramanujan's "lost" notebook: II. θ-function expansions,* Adv. in Math. **41** (1981), 173-185.

14. G.E. Andrews, *Ramanujan's "lost" notebook: III. the Rogers-Ramanujan continued fraction,* Adv. in Math. **41** (1981), 186-208.

15. G.E. Andrews, *The Mordell integrals and Ramanujan's "lost" notebook, "Analytic Number Theory",* (M.I. Knopp, Editor), Lectures Notes in Math., No. **899,** Springer-Verlag, Berlin and New York, 1981, pp. 10-48.

16. G.E. Andrews, *Generalized Frobenius partitions,* Mem. Amer. Math. Soc. **49** (1984), No. 301, iv + 44 pp.

17. G.E. Andrews, Ramanujan and SCRATCHPAD, *Proc. of the 1984 MACSYMA Users' Conference, General Electric,* Schenectady, New York, 1984, pp. 384-408.

18. G.E. Andrews, *Multiple series Rogers-Ramanujan type identities,* Pacific J. Math. **114** (1984), 267-283.

19. G.E. Andrews, *Hecke modular forms and the Kac-Peterson identities,* Trans. Amer. Math. Soc. **283** (1984), 451-458.

20. G.E. Andrews, *Ramanujan's "lost" notebook: IV. stacks and alternating parity in partitions,* Adv. in Math. **53** (1984), 55-74.

21. G.E. Andrews, *Combinatorics and Ramanujan's "lost" notebook,* London Math. Soc. Lecture Note Series, No. **103,** Cambridge Univ. Press, London, 1985, pp. 1-23.

22. G.E. Andrews, *The fifth and seventh order mock theta functions,* Trans. Amer. Math. Soc. **293** (1986), 113-134.

23. G.E. Andrews, *Ramanujan's "lost notebook: V. Euler's partition identity,* Adv. in Math. **61** (1986), 156-164.

24. G.E. Andrews, *The Rogers-Ramanujan's identities without Jacobi's triple product,* The Rocky Mtn. Journal, to appear.

25. G.E. Andrews and R. Askey, *Enumeration of partitions: the role of Eulerian series and q-orthogonal polynomials,* "Higher Combinatorics" (M. Aigner, Editor), Reidel, Dordrecht, 1977, pp. 3-26.

26. G.E. Andrews, and R.A. Askey, *A simple proof of Ramanujan's summation of the* ${}_1\Psi_1$, Aequationes Math. **18** (1978), 333-337.

27. G.E. Andrews, R.J. Baxter, and P.J. Forrester, *Eight-vertex SOS model and generalized Rogers-Ramanujan-type identities,* J. Statist. Phys. **35** (1984), 193-266.

28. P.Appéll and J. Kampé de Fériet, "*Fonctions Hypergéometriques et Hypersphériques; Polynomes d'Hermites*", Gauthier-Villars, Paris, 1926.

29. R. Askey, *Ramanujan's extension of the gamma and beta functions,* Amer. Math. Monthly **87** (1980), 346-359.

30. R. Askey, *Book review in "Zentralblatt für Mathematik (Mathematics Abstracts)"*, Vol. **514** (1984), pp. 161-163. Review #33001.

31. R. Askey and M. Ismail, *The Rogers q-ultraspherical polynomials, "Approximation Theory. III"*, (E.W. Cheney, Editor), Academic Press, 1980, pp. 175-182.

32. R. Askey and J.A. Wilson, *Some basic hypergeometric orthogonal polynomials that generalize Jacobi polynomials,* Mem. Amer. Math. Soc. **54** (1985), No. 319, *iv* + 55 pp.

33. W.N. Bailey, "*Generalized Hypergeometric Series*", Cambridge Mathematical Tract No. **32,** Cambridge Univ. Press, Cambridge, 1935.

34. R.J. Baxter, *Hard hexagons: exact solution,* J. Phys. A **13** (1980), L61-L70.

35. R.J. Baxter, *Rogers-Ramanujan identities in the hard hexagon model,* J. Statist. Phys. **26** (1981), 427-452.

36. R.J. Baxter, "*Exactly Solved Models in Statistical Mechanics*", Academic Press, London and New York, 1982.

37. L.C. Biedenharn and J.D. Louck, "*Angular Momentum in Quantum Physics: Theory and Applications*", *Vol.* **8**, "*Encyclopedia of Mathematics and Its Applications*" (G.-C. Rota, Ed.), Addison-Wesley, Reading, Mass., 1981.

38. L.C. Biedenharn and J.D. Louck, "*The Racah-Wigner Algebra in Quantum Theory*", *Vol.* **9**, "*Encyclopedia of Mathematics and Its Applications*" (G.-C. Rota, Ed.), Addison-Wesley, Reading, Mass., 1981.

39. A. Cauchy, "*Oeuvres*", 1re Série Vol. **8**, p. 45, Gauthier-Villars, Paris, 1893.

40. F.J. Dyson, *Missed opportunities,* Bull. Amer. Math. Soc. **78** (1972), 635-653.

41. R.A. Gustafson, *A Whipple's transformation for hypergeometric series in* $U(n)$ *and multivariable hypergeometric orthogonal polynomials,* SIAM J. Math. Anal. **18** (1987), 495-530.

42. R.A. Gustafson, *Multilateral summation theorems for ordinary and basic hypergeometric series in* $U(n)$, SIAM J. Math. Anal., (to appear).

43. R.A. Gustafson and S.C. Milne, *Schur functions, Good's identity, and hypergeometric series well poised in* $SU(n)$, Adv. in Math. **48** (1983), 177-188.

44. R.A. Gustafson and S.C. Milne, *A q-analog of transposition symmetry for invariant G-functions,* J. of Math. Anal. and Appl. **114** (1986), 210-240.

45. W. Hahn, *Über orthogonal polynome, die q-differenzengleichungen genügen,* Math. Nachr. Berlin **2** (1949), 4-34.

46. W. Hahn, *Beitrage zur theorie der Heinesehen reihen, die 24 integrale der hypergeometrischen q-differenzengleichung das q-analogen der Laplace transformation,* Math. Nachr. **2** (1949), 263-278.

47. W. Hahn, *Beitrage zur Theorie der Heineschen Reihen,* Math. Nachr. **2** (1949), 340-379.

48. W. Hahn, *Über die hoheren Heineschen Rechen und eine einheitliche Theorie der Sogen-nanten speziellen Funktionen,* Math. Nachr. **3** (1950), 257-294.

49. G.H. Hardy and E.M. Wright, "*An Introduction to the Theory of Numbers*", 5th ed., Oxford Univ. Press, London/New York, 1979.

50. W.J. Holman III, *Summation theorems for hypergeometric series in $U(n)$*, SIAM J. Math. Anal. **11** (1980), 523-532.

51 W.J. Holman III, L.C. Biedenharn, and J.D. Louck, *On hypergeometric series well-poised in $SU(n)$*, SIAM J. Math. Anal. **7** (1976), 529-541.

52. M.E.H. Ismail, *A simple proof of Ramanujan's ${}_1\Psi_1$ sum,* Proc. Amer. Math. Soc. **63** (1977), 185-186.

53. F.H. Jackson, *Transformations of q-series,* Messenger of Math. **39** (1910), 145-153.

54. F.H. Jacson, *Summation of q-hypergeometric series,* Messenger of Math. **47** (1917), 101-112.

55. M. Jackson, *On Lerch's transcendent and the basic bilateral hypergeometric series ${}_2\Psi_2$,* J. London Math. Soc. **25** (1950), 189-196.

56. C.G.J. Jacobi, . "*Fundamenta nova theoriese functionum ellipticarum*", (1829), Regiomnoti, fratrum Bornträger (reprinted in "Gesammelte Werke", Vol. **1,** pp. 49-239, Reimer, Berlin, 1881).

57. V.G. Kac and D.H. Peterson, *Affine Lie algebras and Hecke modular forms,* Bull. Amer. Math. Soc. **3** (1980), 1057-1061.

58. V.G. Kac, "*Infinite Dimensional Lie Algebras*", Progress in Mathematics, Vol. **44,** Birkhäuser, Boston 1983.

59. J. Lepowsky, *Affine Lie algebras and combinatorial identities,* in "*Lie Algebras and Related Topics*", pp. 130-156, Rutgers Univ. Press, New Brunswick, N.J., 1981, Lecture Notes in Mathematics, Vol. **933,** Springer-Verlag, Berlin, 1982.

60. J. Lepowsky and S. Milne, *Lie algebraic approaches to classical partition identities,* Adv. in Math. **29** (1978), 15-59.

61. J.D. Louck, "*Theory of Angular Momentum in N-Dimensional Space*", Los Alamos Scientific Laboratory Report LA-2451, 1960; and the cited contribution of E.D. Cashwell.

62. J.D. Louck and L.C. Biedenharn, *Canonical unit adjoint tensor operators in $U(n)$,* J. Math. Phys. **11** (1970), 2368-2414.

63. I.G. Macdonald, *Affine root systems and Dedekind's η-function,* Invent. Math. **15** (1972), 91-143.

64. I.G. Macdonald, "*Symmetric Functions and Hall Polynomials*", Oxford Univ. Press, London/New York, 1979.

65. I.G. Macdonald, *Some conjectures for root systems,* SIAM J. Math. Anal. **13** (1982), 988-1007.

66. A.M. Mathai and R.K. Saxena, "*Generalized Hypergeometric Functions with Applications in Statistics and Physical Sciences*", Lecture Notes in Mathematics, Vol. **348,** Springer-Verlag, New York/Berlin, 1973.

67. S.C. Milne, *Hypergeometric series well-poised in $SU(n)$ and a generalization of Biedenharn's G-functions*", Adv. in Math. **36** (1980), 169-211.

68. S.C. Milne, *A new symmetry related to $SU(n)$ for classical basic hypergeometric series,* Adv. in Math. **57** (1985), 71-90.

69. S.C. Milne, *A q-analog of hypergeometric series well-poised in $SU(n)$ and invariant G-functions,* Adv. in Math. **58** (1985), 1-60.

70. S.C. Milne, *A q-analog of the ${}_5F_4(1)$ summation theorem for hypergeometric series well-poised in $SU(n)$,* Adv. in Math. **57** (1985), 14-33.

71. S.C. Milne, *An elementary proof of the Macdonald identities for $A_l^{(1)}$,* Adv. in Math. **57** (1985), 34-70.

72. S.C. Milne, *A $U(n)$ generalization of Ramanujan's ${}_1\Psi_1$ summation,* J. of Math. Anal. and Appl. **118** (1986), 263-277.

73. S.C. Milne, *Basic hypergeometric series very well-poised in $U(n)$,* J. of Math. Anal. and Appl. **122** (1987) 223-256.

74. S.C. Milne *A q-analog of the Gauss summation theorem for hypergeometric series in $U(n)$,* Adv. in Math., accepted.

75. S.C. Milne, *A q-analog of the balanced ${}_3F_2$ summation theorem for hypergeometric series in $U(n)$,* submitted for publication.

76. S.C. Milne, *A q-analog of a Whipple's transformation for hypergeometric series in $U(n)$,* submitted for publication.

77. E.D. Rainville, "*Special Functions*", Macmillan Co., New York, 1960.

78. L.J. Slater, *A new proof of Roger's transformation of infinite series,* Proc. London Math. Soc. (2) **53** (1951), 460-475.

79. L.J. Slater, "*Generalized hypergeometric functions*", Cambridge Univ. Press, London and New York, 1966.

80. G.N. Watson, *A new proof of the Rogers-Ramanujan identities,* J. London Math. Soc. **4** (1929), 4-9.

81. F.J.W. Whipple, *On well-poised series, generalized hypergeometric series having parameters in pairs, each pair with the same sum,* Proc. London Math. Soc. (2) **24** (1924), 247-263.

82. F.J.W. Whipple, *Well-poised series and other generalized hypergeometric series,* Proc. London Math. Soc. (2) **25** (1926), 525-544.

83. L. Winquist, *An elementary proof of* $p(11m+6)\equiv 0(mod\,11)$, J. Comb. Th. 6 (1969), 56-59.

84. D. Zeilberger and D.M. Bressoud, *A proof of Andrews' q-Dyson conjecture,* Discrete Math. **54** (1985), 201-224.

Recent results for the q-Lagrange inversion formula

Dennis Stanton†

Abstract. A survey of the q-Lagrange inversion formula is given, including recent work of Garsia, Gessel, Hofbauer, Krattenthaler, Remmel, and Stanton. Some applications to identities of Rogers-Ramanujan type are stated.

1. Introduction.

One of Ramanujan's favorite topics was the expansion of a given function in a series of other functions. For example, given a formal power series $f(x)$ such that $f(0) = 0$ and $f'(0) \neq 0$, one may ask for the coefficients a_k in the expansion

$$x = \sum_{k=1}^{\infty} a_k f(x)^k. \tag{1.1}$$

This question is answered by the *Lagrange inversion formula* [24, §7.32].

Ramanujan's notebooks [23] contain several examples of expansions which can be found from the Lagrange inversion formula, particularly in Chapters 3 and 9. Even though Ramanujan was aware of the Lagrange inversion formula, he had his own form of it, which Berndt [6] has called Ramanujan's Master Theorem. It is clear from Cauchy's integral theorem that a contour integral can be given for a_k. Ramanujan gave a real integral instead.

In this paper we shall survey recent work on q-analogues of Lagrange's Theorem. We also show how these analogues are related to q-series and the Rogers-Ramanujan identities.

The following notation will be used for formal power series. The coefficient of x^k in $g(x), f(x), F(x)$, etc., will be denoted g_k, f_k, F_k. If these coefficients are functions of q they will be denoted $f_k(q)$. In §2 all formal power series have complex coefficients; in later sections the coefficients are rational functions of q. Let $\langle x^n | F(x) \rangle$ denote the coefficient of x^n in $F(x)$. A formal Laurent series is a formal power series plus a finite number of negative integral powers. Let $\underset{x}{Res} F(x)$ denote the coefficient of x^{-1} in a formal Laurent series $F(x)$. Thus for any formal power series $F(x)$

$$\langle x^n | F(x) \rangle = \underset{x}{Res} \frac{F(x)}{x^{n+1}}.$$

---

†School of Mathematics, University of Minnesota, Minneapolis, MN 55455. This work was partially supported by a fellowship from the Sloan Foundation, and by NSF grant DMS:8700995.

ISBN 0-12-058560-X

We also adopt the usual notation from q-series,

$$\begin{aligned}(a;q)_k = (a)_k &= \prod_{m=1}^{k}(1-aq^{m-1}),\\(a,b,c,\cdots)_k &= (a)_k(b)_k(c)_k\cdots,\\k!_q &= (q)_k/(1-q)^k,\\[k] &= (1-q^k)/(1-q)\end{aligned}$$

and the q-binomial coefficient

$$\binom{n}{k}_q = \frac{(q)_n}{(q)_k(q)_{n-k}}.$$

2. Lagrange's Theorem.

Not only can the coefficients a_k of the inverse function to $f(x)$ in (1.1) be found, but also the coefficients for any formal power series $F(x)$ in x. This is Lagrange's Theorem.

THEOREM 1 (LAGRANGE INVERSION FORMULA). *Let $f(x)$ be a formal power series with $f(0)=0$ and $f'(0)\neq 0$. For any formal power series $F(x)$, if*

$$F(x) = \sum_{k=0}^{\infty} a_k f(x)^k \tag{2.1}$$

then

$$a_k = \operatorname*{Res}_x \frac{F(x)f'(x)}{f(x)^{k+1}} \tag{2.2}$$

$$= \operatorname*{Res}_x \frac{F'(x)}{kf(x)^k}. \tag{2.3}$$

Proof. Equation (2.2) follows from

$$\operatorname*{Res}_x(f(x)^{k-j}f'(x)) = \operatorname*{Res}_x(f(x)^{k-j+1})'/(k-j+1)$$

$$= \begin{cases}0 \text{ for } j\neq k+1,\\ 1 \text{ for } j=k+1.\end{cases} \tag{2.4}$$

Equation (2.2) follows from (2.3) and

$$\operatorname*{Res}_x\left(\frac{F(x)}{f(x)^k}\right)' = 0. \quad \square$$

It is clear that if $F(x)$ is replaced by $F(x)/f'(x)$, then (2.2) simplifies. This is sometimes called the second form of the Lagrange inversion formula.

THEOREM 2 (SECOND FORM OF THE LAGRANGE INVERSION FORMULA). *Let $f(x)$ be a formal power series with $f(0) = 0$ and $f'(0) \neq 0$. Then for any formal power series $F(x)$, if*

$$F(x)/f'(x) = \sum_{k=0}^{\infty} a_k f(x)^k$$

then

$$a_k = \operatorname*{Res}_x \frac{F(x)}{f(x)^{k+1}}. \tag{2.5}$$

A classical example of these two theorems is Abel's theorem

$$e^{ax} = \sum_{k=0}^{\infty} \frac{a(a-bk)^{k-1}}{k!} x^k e^{kbx} \tag{2.6}$$

and

$$e^{(a-b)x}/(1+bx) = \sum_{k=0}^{\infty} \frac{(a-b(k+1))^k}{k!} x^k e^{kbx}. \tag{2.7}$$

Frequently Theorems 1 and 2 are stated in another way. First replace x by the functional inverse $f^{\langle -1 \rangle}(x)$, to obtain

$$F(f^{\langle -1 \rangle}(x)) = \sum_{k=0}^{\infty} a_k x^k \tag{2.8}$$

where a_k is given by (2.2). For $F(x) = x^n$, (2.8) is

$$f^{\langle -1 \rangle}(x)^n = \sum_{k=0}^{\infty} a_k x^k. \tag{2.9}$$

Next let $x/R(x) = g(x)$, and put $g(x) = f^{\langle -1 \rangle}(x)$ so that $g(x)$ satisfies

$$g(x) = xR(g(x)).$$

Then (2.2) becomes

$$\langle x^k | g(x)^n \rangle = \frac{k}{n} \langle x^{n-k} | R(x)^k \rangle. \tag{2.10}$$

A calculation shows that (2.4) becomes, if $g(x) = xR(g(x))$,

$$\langle x^k | \frac{g(x)^n}{1 - xR'(g(x))} \rangle = \langle x^{k-n} | R(x)^k \rangle. \tag{2.11}$$

3. q-Lagrange inversion.

There have been two different approaches, each with its own goal, to the q-Lagrange inversion problem. The first approach is the most natural: write down a q-analogue of (2.1) and then give some formula for the coefficients a_k which is a q-analogue of (2.2) or (2.3). Of course to be a satisfactory solution, the q-analogue to (2.1) must be reasonable, and the resulting formula for a_k must be simple enough to be useful. In particular any such general theorem should easily reproduce the known examples of q-Lagrange inversion. Unfortunately these two goals have not simultaneously been met, and the second approach, in lieu of the first, is necessary. Find non-trivial and important families of q-Lagrange inversion.

Let $f(x,q)$ be a formal power series in x, with coefficients that are rational functions of q. Sometimes we shall suppress q and write $f(x)$ instead of $f(x,q)$. As usual, we can assume that $f_0(q) = 0$ and $f_1(q) = 1$. A good candidate for the q-analogue of the inverse to $f(x)$ is a formal power series $\phi(x)$ such that

$$\sum_{k=1}^{\infty} f_k(q)\phi(x)\phi(xq)\cdots\phi(xq^{k-1}) = x. \tag{3.1}$$

Clearly (3.1) is a q-analogue of $f(\phi(x)) = x$, and the relation $\phi(f(x)) = x$ could become

$$\sum_{k=1}^{\infty} \phi_k(q)f(x)f(xq^{-1})\cdots f(xq^{1-k}) = x. \tag{3.2}$$

Garsia [10] has shown that these two formulations of a q-analogue of a functional inverse are equivalent.

THEOREM 3 (GARSIA). *Equation (3.1) holds if, and only if, (3.2) holds.*

Andrews [2], Gessel [13], and Garsia [10] have each given versions of a general form of q-Lagrange inversion. Good expositions of these papers are given in [10], [17], or [19]. They were motivated by an example of Carlitz [8], who gave a q-analogue of Theorem 1 for the function $f(x) = x/(1-x)$. He replaced (2.1) by

$$F(x) = \sum_{k=0}^{\infty} a_k \frac{x^k}{(1-x)(1-xq)\cdots(1-xq^{k-1})}. \tag{3.3}$$

It is clear that a general form of (3.3) for $f(x) = x/r(x)$ is

$$F(x) = \sum_{k=0}^{\infty} a_k \frac{x^k}{r(x)r(xq)\cdots r(xq^{k-1})}. \tag{3.4}$$

Andrews [2] gave a general formula for the coefficients a_k as a determinant in the coefficients F_k of $F(x)$, but his result is very difficult to apply.

Garsia [10] has a very elegant form of q-analogue of Theorem 1 for the expansion of $F(f^{\langle -1\rangle}(x))$ in (2.7). Suppose that $f(x)$ and $\phi(x)$ satisfy (3.1) and (3.2). Then we are expanding

$$\sum_{k=0}^{\infty} F_k(q)\phi(x)\phi(xq)\cdots\phi(xq^{k-1}) = \sum_{k=0}^{\infty} a_k x^k. \tag{3.5}$$

Garsia's analogue of (2.2) for a_k involves a miraculous q-analogue of the derivative $f'(x)$, which he called $^{\circ}f(x)$. Again let $f(x) = x/r(x)$ and define the "roofing" and "starring" operators by

$$^{*}r(x) = \prod_{m=0}^{\infty} r(xq^{-m}), \tag{3.6}$$

$$\check{r}(x) = \sum_{k=0}^{\infty} r_k(q) q^{\binom{k}{2}} x^k. \tag{3.7}$$

Then $^{\circ}f(x)$ is defined by

$$^{\circ}f(x) = {}^{*}r(xq^{-1}) \left(\frac{1}{^{*}(\check{r}(xq))}\right)^{\check{}}. \tag{3.8}$$

It is not at all obvious that (3.8) is a q-analogue of $f'(x)$.

THEOREM 4 (GARSIA'S Q-LAGRANGE INVERSION FORMULA). *Let $f(x)$ and $\phi(x)$ satisfy (3.1), and $F(x)$ satisfy (3.5). Then*

$$a_k = \operatorname*{Res}_x \frac{^{\circ}f(xq^{-k})F(x)}{f(x)\cdots f(xq^{-k})},$$

where $^{\circ}f(x)$ is defined by (3.8).

Moreover Garsia shows that

$$\sum_{k=0}^{\infty} F_k(q)\phi(x)\phi(xq)\cdots\phi(xq^{k-1}) = \frac{(F(x)^{*}r(x))^{\check{}}}{(^{*}r(x))^{\check{}}} \tag{3.9}$$

which corresponds to no known result for $q = 1$.

Gessel [13, Th. 6.9] gave a q-analogue of the alternative (2.11) to Theorem 2. He replaced the functional equation $f(x) = xR(f(x))$ by

$$f(x,q) = qx \sum_{k=0}^{\infty} R_k(q) f(x,q) f(xq,q)\cdots f(xq^{k-1},q), \tag{3.11}$$

and found the next theorem. We shall use the notation

$$f^{[k]}(x,q) = f(x,q)f(xq,q)\cdots f(xq^{k-1},q). \tag{3.12}$$

THEOREM 5 (GESSEL'S Q-LAGRANGE INVERSION FORMULA). *Let R(x) and f(x) satisfy (3.11). Then*

$$\langle x^k | f^{[k]}(x,q)/(1-xd(x))\rangle = q^{n(n+1)/2}\langle x^{k-n}|R^{[k]}(x,q^{-1})\rangle.$$

where

$$d(x) = \sum_{i,j=0}^{\infty} R_{i+j+1}(q) f^{[i]}(x,q) f^{[j]}(x,q^{-1}).$$

Note that the denominator of (2.10) has been replaced by a double sum in Theorem 3. Garsia [10, Theorem 2.5] gave another form of the denominator using his q-analogue of the derivative (3.9).

4. More q-Lagrange inversion.

Cigler [9], Hofbauer [16], Krattenthaler [19], and Paule [20] have another approach to q-Lagrange inversion for special families of functions. They replaced $f^k(x)$ by a function $x^k/r_k(x,q)$ instead of $x^k/r(x)r(xq)\cdots r(xq^{k-1})$. Naturally unless the function $r_k(x,q)$ has some properties mimicking $r^k(x)$, there is no hope for an explicit formula for a_k in the expansion

$$F(x) = \sum_{k=0}^{\infty} a_k \frac{x^k}{r_k(xq,q)}. \tag{4.1}$$

We may assume that $r_k(0,q) = 1$.

The key property is a q-analogue of (2.4), which for $f(x) = x/r(x)$ is

$$\operatorname*{Res}_x \frac{r(x)^{n-k}}{x^{n+1-k}}\left(1 - \frac{xr'(x)}{r(x)}\right) = \begin{cases} 0 \text{ for } & k \neq n, \\ 1 \text{ for } & k = n. \end{cases}$$

A q-analogue could be

$$\operatorname*{Res}_x \frac{r_n(x,q)}{r_k(xq,q)x^{n+1-k}}(1 - x\rho(x)) = \begin{cases} 0 \text{ for } & k \neq n, \\ 1 \text{ for } & k = n, \end{cases} \tag{4.2}$$

where $\rho(x)$ is some q-analogue of $r'(x)/r(x)$. In fact, (4.2) holds if $r_k(x)$ has the following property:

$$D_q r_k(x) = [k]\rho(x) r_k(x) \text{ for all } k \geq 0, \tag{4.3}$$

where D_q is the q-derivative

$$D_q f(x) = \frac{f(xq) - f(x)}{(q-1)x}.$$

To prove (4.2), just compute

$$\operatorname*{Res}_x D_q\left(\frac{r_n(x)}{r_k(x)x^{n-k}}\right) = 0.$$

THEOREM 6 (HOFBAUER'S Q-LAGRANGE INVERSION). *Let $F(x)$ satisfy (4.1), where $r_k(x)$ satisfies (4.3). Then*

$$a_k = \operatorname*{Res}_x \frac{F(x)r_k(x)(1 - x\rho(x))}{x^{k+1}}.$$

Proof. Equation (4.2) immediately gives the theorem. □

Krattenthaler [19] generalized Theorem 6 by allowing simultaneously two different analogues of the denominator $r^k(x)$. Suppose that $r_k(x,q)$ and $s_k(x,q)$ satisfy $r_k(0,q) = 1$, $s_k(0,q) = 1$, and

$$\begin{aligned} D_q r_a(x) &= [k]\rho(x)r_a(x) \text{ for all real } a, \\ D_q s_b(x) &= [k]\sigma(x)s_b(x) \text{ for all real } b. \end{aligned} \tag{4.4}$$

THEOREM 7 (KRATTENTHALER'S Q-LAGRANGE INVERSION). *Let $F(x)$ satisfy*

$$F(x) = \sum_{k=0}^{\infty} a_k \frac{x^k s_{-k-b}(x,q)}{r_{k+a}(xq,q)}.$$

where $r_a(x)$ and $s_b(x)$ satisfy (4.4). Then

$$a_k = \operatorname*{Res}_x F(x)\frac{r_{k+a}(x)}{x^{k+1}s_{-k-b}(qx)}(1 - x\rho(x) - x\sigma(x) + x^2\rho(x)\sigma(x)(1 - q^{a-b})).$$

Proof. The proof is similar to the proof of Theorem 6, by establishing the appropriate version of (4.2) (see [19, Lemma 1]). □

Krattenthaler also gave a nice version of (2.3) for the $a = b = 0$ special case of Theorem 7

$$a_k = \frac{1}{[k]}\operatorname*{Res}_x \frac{D_q(F(x))r_k(x)}{s_{-k}(x)x^k}. \tag{4.5}$$

Note that the (4.5) also gives a version of (2.3) for Theorem 6.

Paule has given a generalization of Theorem 6 [20, Theorem 4].

5. Even more q-Lagrange inversion.

Gessel and Stanton [14], [15] took the point of view that the Lagrange inversion theorem is a matrix inversion result. Specifically, if

$$f^k(x) = \sum_{n=k}^{\infty} B_{nk}x^n \tag{5.1}$$

then (2.1) holds if, and only if, the matrix equation $Ba = f$. holds. The Lagrange inversion theorem gives a formula for the coefficients a_k, $a = B^{-1}f$, thus gives the inverse matrix B^{-1}.

They took a special family of functions replacing $f^k(x)$, namely $x^k/(1-x)^{a+(b+1)k}$, so that

$$B_{nk} = \prod_{j=1}^{n-k}(a+(b+1)k+j-1)/(n-k)!. \tag{5.2}$$

Theorem 1 implies

$$B_{km}^{-1} = \prod_{j=1}^{k-m-1}(1-a-(b+1)k+j)(-a-(b+1)m)/(k-m)!. \tag{5.3}$$

The q-analogue of Lagrange inversion for $x/(1-x)^{b+1}$ is given by q-analogues of the matrices in (5.2) and (5.3).

THEOREM 8 (Q-LAGRANGE INVERSION FOR $x/(1-x)^{b+1}$). *Let*

$$G_k(x) = \sum_{n=k}^{\infty} B_{nk}x^n,$$

where

$$B_{nk} = q^{-nk}(Aq^kp^k;p)_{n-k}/(q)_{n-k}.$$

Then

$$F(x) = \sum_{k=0}^{\infty} a_kG_k(x)$$

if, and only if,

$$a_k = \sum_{m=0}^{k}(Aq^kp^{k-1};p^{-1})_{k-m-1}(1-Ap^mq^m)q^{(k^2+m^2+k-m)/2}F_m(q)/(q)_{k-m}.$$

Garsia and Remmel [11] have yet another q-Lagrange inversion formula. They replaced $f_k(x)$ by a q-analogue of $(g(x)-1)^k$,

$$\sum_{s=0}^{k}\binom{k}{s}_q q^{\binom{s}{2}}(-1)^s g(x)g(xq)\cdots g(xq^{k-s-1}). \tag{5.4}$$

Let B_{nk} be the coefficient of x^n in (5.4). They give an explicit formula for the inverse matrix B^{-1}.

THEOREM 9 (GARSIA AND REMMEL'S Q-LAGRANGE INVERSION). *Let $G_k(x)$ be defined by (5.4), where $g(0) = 1$. Then*

$$F(x) = \sum_{k=0}^{\infty} a_k G_k(x)$$

if, and only if,

$$a_k = \sum_{m=0}^{k} A_{km} F_m(q),$$

where

$$A_{km} = q^{-\binom{k}{2}} \sum_{s=m}^{k} \frac{(-1)^s q^{\binom{k-s}{2}} \theta_{s-m}}{(q)_s (q)_{k-s} \theta_s}$$

and

$$\theta(x) = 1/\prod_{n=0}^{\infty} g(xq^n).$$

6. Two classical examples.

The first example of q-Lagrange inversion formula was given by Jackson [18, Eq.(5)], who gave a q-analogue of Abel's theorem (2.6). It is

$$E_q(ax) = \sum_{k=0}^{\infty} \frac{a(a-[2]b)\cdots(a-[k]b)}{k!_q} x^k E_q([k]bxq^{1-k}), \tag{6.1}$$

where $E_q(x)$ is a q-analogue of the exponential function

$$E_q(x) = (x(1-q))_\infty. \tag{6.2}$$

Carlitz's example [8] is a q-Lagrange inversion formula for $f(x) = x/(1-x)$. If $F(x)$ satisfies (3.3), then he gave

$$a_k = \frac{1}{[k]} \operatorname*{Res}_x \frac{D_q(F(x))(1-x)\cdots(1-xq^{k-1})}{x^k}. \tag{6.3}$$

7. Comparisons.

In this section the strengths and weaknesses of the various approaches will be given.

First we consider to which functions $f_k(x)$ the q-Lagrange inversion theorems apply. The Garsia-Gessel Theorems and the Garsia-Remmel Theorem apply to all of the corresponding analogues of $f^k(x)$. The Hofbauer-Krattenthaler Theorems apply to a quotient of functions satisfying (4.4). One may ask which functions $r_k(x) = r(x)r(xq)\cdots r(xq^{k-1})$ satisfy (4.3). An easy calculation shows

$$D_q r_k(x) = [k] r_k(x) \frac{D_{q^k} r(x)}{r(x)},$$

so that (4.3) holds, if, and only if,

$$\frac{D_{q^k} r(x)}{r(x)} = \rho(x), \text{ for all } k \geq 0. \tag{7.1}$$

Clearly a linear function is the only solution to (7.1), and we then obtain Carlitz's example.

Next we consider for which classical functions the inversion formulas given can be explicitly computed. The Garsia-Gessel Theorems give only Carlitz's example. There are applications to continued fractions, however, because the functional equations are appropriate. Garsia has used his roofing and starring operators to give new proofs of Rogers-Ramanujan type identities. He did not find any new such identities. His roofing and starring operators certainly deserve more attention. The Garsia-Remmel Theorem applies to $e^x - 1$, and $(1-x)^a - 1$. Hofbauer's Theorem includes Jackson's and Carlitz's examples, while Krattenthaler's Theorem also gives the $b = 1$ and $b = -1/2$ examples of Gessel-Stanton. The $b = 1$ case is particularly important. The entire theory of basic hypergeometric series can be based upon this case. As Andrews has shown [3], the Rogers-Ramanujan identities follow from this case, and it has led to the idea of the Bailey lattice [1]. Recent work of Gasper [12] and Rahman [21] indicates that many applications of bibasic identities (as in Theorem 8) to basic hypergeometric series remain.

8. Rogers-Ramanujan identities.

Consider the Rogers-Ramanujan continued fraction

$$\phi(x) = \cfrac{x}{1 - \cfrac{xq}{1 - \cfrac{xq^2}{\ddots}}}. \tag{8.1}$$

Garsia [10] has shown that the evaluation of (8.1) as a quotient of Rogers-Ramanujan series follows from (3.9). It is easy to see that the defining relation for the continued fraction is

$$\phi(x) - \phi(x)\phi(xq) = x, \tag{8.2}$$

so that we may take $f(x) = x - x^2$ in (3.1). Then (3.9), with $r(x) = 1/(1-x)$ and $F(x) = x$ easily gives the evaluation. In fact Garsia proves the key identity for the Rogers-Ramanujan identities that Rogers and Ramanujan [22] had. Several other examples of continued fractions are given by Gessel [13].

We now give some examples of new identities of Rogers-Ramanujan type that were found by q-Lagrange inversion in [14, Eq.(7.13) and (7.15)]. The first two examples are closely related,

$$1 + \sum_{n=1}^{\infty} \frac{(-q)_{n-1}}{(q)_n} q^{\binom{n+1}{2}} = \frac{1}{(q;q^2)_\infty (q^4, q^6, q^8, q^{10}, q^{22}, q^{24}, q^{26}, q^{28}; q^{32})_\infty} \tag{8.3}$$

and

$$\sum_{n=1}^{\infty} \frac{(-q)_{n-1}}{(q)_n} q^{\binom{n+1}{2}} = \frac{q}{(q;q^2)_\infty (q^2, q^8, q^{12}, q^{14}, q^{18}, q^{20}, q^{24}, q^{30}; q^{32})_\infty}. \tag{8.4}$$

Since the left sides of (8.3) and (8.4) differ by one, Andrews [4, 5] noted that (8.3) and (8.4) imply the next theorem.

THEOREM 10. *The number of partitions of n into parts which are odd or congruent to ± 4, ± 6, ± 8, or ± 10 modulo 32 is equal to the number of partitions of $n-1$ into parts which are odd or congruent to ± 2, ± 8, ± 12, or ± 14 modulo 32.*

Andrews also gave a combinatorial interpretation for (8.3) and (8.4) individually as a "colored" Rogers-Ramanujan identity. We state here only the version for (8.3). A *two-color partition* is an ordered pair of partitions (λ, μ), which are called *red* and *green* respectively. Such a two-color partition is called a partition of n if the sum of the parts of λ and μ is n.

THEOREM 11. *The number of two-color partitions of n such that*

(1) *the parts are distinct,*

(2) *the largest part is red, and*

(3) *each green part is at least two smaller than the next largest part*

is equal to the number of partitions of n into parts which are odd or congruent to ± 4, ± 6, ± 8, or ± 10 modulo 32.

Finally we give Bressoud's [7] combinatorial interpretation of [14, Eq. 7.24]

$$\sum_{k=0}^{\infty} \frac{(-q;q^2)_{2k} q^{2k^2}}{(q^2;q^4)_k (q^8;q^8)_k} = (-q^2, -q^3, -q^5; q^8)_\infty.$$

THEOREM 12. *The number of partitions of n into distinct parts whose odd parts are congruent to ± 3 modulo 8 is equal to the number of partitions of n with the following properties:*

(1) *the parts which are congruent to 2 modulo 4 are 2, 6, ..., $4k-2$, with multiplicity at least one,*

(2) *the parts which are congruent to 0 modulo 4 are $\leq 4k$ and have even multiplicities,*

(3) *all of the odd parts are distinct and less than $4k$.*

REFERENCES

[1] A. Agarwal, G. Andrews, and D. Bressoud, *The Bailey lattice*, 1987, (to appear).

[2] G. Andrews, *Identities in combinatorics. II: A q-analog of the Lagrange inversion theorem*, Proc. Amer. Math. Soc., 53 (1975), pp. 240-245.

[3] ———, *Connection coefficient problems and partitions*, D. Ray-Chaudhuri, ed., Proc. Sympos. Pure Math., 34 (1979), pp. 1–34.

[4] ———, *Further problems on partitions*, Amer. Math. Monthly, 94 (1987), pp. 437–439.

[5] ———, *Rogers-Ramanujan identities for two-color partitions*, Indian J. Math. (to appear).

[6] B. Berndt, *Ramanujan's Notebooks, Part I*, Springer, New York, 1985.

[7] D. Bressoud, *personal communication*, (1985).

[8] L. Carlitz, *Some q-expansion formulas*, Glas. Mat. Ser. III, 8 (1973), pp. 205–214.

[9] J. Cigler, *Operatormethoden für q-Identitäten III: Umbrale Inversion und die Lagrangesche Formel*, Arch. Math., 35 (1980), pp. 533–543.

[10] A. Garsia, *A q-analogue of the Lagrange inversion formula*, Hous. J. Math., 7 (1981), pp. 205–237.

[11] A. Garsia and J. Remmel, *A novel form of q-Lagrange inversion*, Hous. J. Math., 12 (1986), pp. 503–523.

[12] G. Gasper, *Summation, transformation, and expansion formulas for bibasic series*, (1987) (to appear).

[13] I. Gessel, *A noncommutative generalization and q-analog of the Lagrange inversion formula*, Trans. Amer. Math. Soc., 257 (1980), pp. 455–482.

[14] I. Gessel and D. Stanton, *Applications of q-Lagrange inversion to basic hypergeometric series*, Trans. Amer. Math. Soc., 277 (1983), pp. 173–201.

[15] ———, *Another family of q-Lagrange inversion formulas*, Rocky Mtn. J. Math., 16 (1986), pp. 373–384.

[16] J. Hofbauer, *A q-analogue of the Lagrange expansion*, Arch. Math., 42 (1984), pp. 536–544.

[17] ———, *Lagrange-Inversion*, Seminaire Lotharingien de Combinatoire, V. Strehl, ed., (1982), pp. 1–38.

[18] F. Jackson, *A q-generalization of Abel's series*, Rend. Palermo, 29 (1910), pp. 340–346.

[19] C. Krattenthaler, *A new q-Lagrange formula and some applications*, Proc. Amer. Math. Soc., 90 (1984), pp. 338–344.

[20] P. Paule, *Ein neuer Weg zur q-Lagrange inversion*, Bayreuther Math. Schr., 18 (1985), pp. 1–37.

[21] M. Rahman, *Some quadratic and cubic summation formulas for basic hypergeometric series*, (1987) (to appear).

[22] S. Ramanujan, *Proof of certain identities in combinatory analysis*, Proc. Camb. Phil. Soc., 19 (1919), pp. 214–216.

[23] ———, *Notebooks of Srinivasa Ramanujan, Volume II*, Tata Institute of Fundamental Research, Bombay, 1957.

[24] E. Whittaker and G. Watson, *A Course of Modern Analysis*, Cambridge Univ. Press, Cambridge, 1927.

RAMANUJAN'S SECOND NOTEBOOK:
ASYMPTOTIC EXPANSIONS FOR HYPERGEOMETRIC SERIES AND RELATED FUNCTIONS

Ronald J. Evans
Department of Mathematics
University of California, San Diego
La Jolla, CA 92093

We discuss and enlarge upon some of Ramanujan's most beautiful asymptotic expansions for functions related to hypergeometric series. We present generalizations, applications, and problems for further research. The expansions we've chosen appear in Chapters 3 and 10-13 of Ramanujan's second notebook [24], and were likely discovered sometime in the period 1904-1912, when Ramanujan was in his late teens and early twenties.

Asymptotic expansions for confluent hypergeometric functions are discussed in §1. Hypergeometric series with more parameters are considered in §2. For a discussion of further aspects of Ramanujan's work on hypergeometric series in the notebooks, consult [3], [7], and [8].

1. Confluent hypergeometric functions.

For any complex x, define

$$(x)_0 = 1, \quad (x)_k = x(x+1)\cdots(x+k-1), \text{ for } k = 1, 2, 3, \ldots.$$

ISBN 0-12-058560-X

As in [18, (9.9.1)], define the confluent hypergeometric function

$$\Phi(a,c;z) = \sum_{k=0}^{\infty} \frac{(a)_k z^k}{(c)_k k!}, \tag{1.1}$$

where a, c, z can take arbitrary complex values except that $c \neq 0, -1, -2, \ldots$. Define the confluent hypergeometric function of the second kind [18, (9.11.6)] by

$$\Psi(a,c;z) = \frac{1}{\Gamma(a)} \int_0^{\infty} e^{-zt} t^{a-1} (1+t)^{c-a-1} dt, \tag{1.2}$$

where $\mathrm{Re}(a) > 0, \mathrm{Re}(z) > 0$. The asymptotic behavior of $\Phi(a,c;z)$ and $\Psi(a,c;z)$ is well-known when $z \to \infty$ with a, c fixed [18, (9.12.3), (9.12.7)]. It is useful, in addition, to have estimates for the growth of these functions as several of the variables a, c, z tend to ∞. For some results in this direction, see [19, §4.8], [14, Vol. 1, §6.13], [13], [29], [30], [26, Ch. 4], and especially Olver's papers [21], [22]. For application of such estimates in number theory, see, e.g., [17, §§5-8]. The focus of our discussion in this section will be asymptotic expansions for $\Phi(1,c;z)$ and $\Psi(1,c;z)$ as both c, z tend to ∞ in such a way that $c - z$ is bounded (see Theorems 1 and 6 below). Ramanujan obtained such expansions in Chapters 12 and 13 of his second notebook. We will concentrate on real c, z, although the results can be extended to complex values.

Theorem 1 [9, Entry 6]. *Let b, z be real with b fixed, $z \to \infty$. Then*

$$\begin{aligned}\Psi(1, z+2+b; z) = {} & \frac{e^z \Gamma(z+b+1)}{2z^{z+b+1}} + (2/3+b)z^{-1} + (-4/135 + b^2(1+b)/3)z^{-2} \\ & + (8/2835 - 2b(1+b)/135 + b(1-b^2)(2-3b^2)/45)z^{-3} \\ & + 0(z^{-4}).\end{aligned}$$

Expanding the main term $e^z\Gamma(z+b+1)/(2z^{z+b+1})$ in Theorem 1 by a version of

Stirling's formula [1, (6.1.37)], namely,

$$\Gamma(z) = z^{z-1/2} e^{-z}\sqrt{2\pi}\left(1 + \frac{1}{12z} + \frac{1}{288z^2} - \frac{139}{51840z^3} - \frac{571}{2488320z^4} + O(z^{-5})\right), \tag{1.3}$$

we can obtain an asymptotic expansion of $\Psi(1, z+2+b; z)$ in descending powers of $\sqrt{z}$; for example:

Corollary 2. Let b, z be real with b fixed, $z \to \infty$. Then

$$\Psi(1, z+2+b; z) = \sqrt{\frac{\pi}{2z}} + (2/3+b)z^{-1} + O(z^{-3/2}).$$

In the case $b = 0$ of Theorem 1, Ramanujan gave more terms of the expansion, as follows.

Theorem 3 [11, Entry 48]. *For real* $z \to \infty$,

$$\Psi(1, z+2; z) = \frac{e^z\Gamma(z+1)}{2z^{z+1}} + \frac{2}{3z} - \frac{4}{135z^2} + \frac{8}{2835z^3} + \frac{16}{8505z^4} - \frac{8992}{12629925z^5} + O(z^{-6}).$$

Watson [31] and Szegö [28] established this asymptotic expansion up through the term $16/(8505z^4)$. For those interested in the coefficient of z^{-6} in the expansion, it is $-334144/492567075$; see (2.16) below.

As an application of Theorem 1, we prove:

Theorem 4. *Let n be a positive integer and let b be real with $b \neq -1, -2, -3, \ldots$. If b is fixed and $n \to \infty$, then*

$$\sum_{k=0}^{n} \frac{n^k}{(b+1)_k} = \frac{e^n \Gamma(b+1)}{2n^b} \left\{ 1 + (2/3 + b)\sqrt{\frac{2}{\pi n}} - \frac{1}{n}\sqrt{\frac{2}{\pi n}}\,(b^3/6 + b^2/2 + 5b/12 + 23/270) + 0(n^{-5/2}) \right\}.$$

Proof. By (1.2),

$$\Psi(1, n+2; n) = \int_0^\infty e^{-nx}(1+x)^n dx. \tag{1.4}$$

Integrating by parts $\Lambda n + 1$ times in (1.4), we obtain

$$\frac{(b+1)_n}{n^{n+1}} \sum_{k=0}^{n} \frac{n^k}{(b+1)_k} = \Psi(1, n+2+b; n) - \frac{(b)_{n+1}}{n^{n+1}} \Psi(1, b+1; n).$$

Thus,

$$\sum_{k=0}^{n} \frac{n^k}{(b+1)_k} = \frac{n^{n+1}}{(b+1)_n} \Psi(1, n+2+b; n) - b\Psi(1, b+1; n). \tag{1.5}$$

The last term in (1.5) is $0(1/n)$ by (1.2), so by Theorem 1,

$$\begin{aligned}\sum_{k=0}^{n} \frac{n^k}{(b+1)_k} &= \frac{n^{n+1}}{(b+1)_n} \left\{ \frac{e^n (b+1)_n \Gamma(b+1)}{2n^{n+b+1}} + \frac{(2/3+b)}{n} + \frac{(-4/135 + b^2(1+b)/3)}{n^2} + 0(n^{-3}) \right\} \\ &= \frac{e^n \Gamma(b+1)}{2n^b} + \frac{n^n \Gamma(b+1)}{\Gamma(b+1+n)} \left(\frac{2}{3} + b + \frac{(-4/135 + b^2(1+b)/3)}{n} + 0(n^{-2}) \right).\end{aligned}$$

The result now follows from (1.3).

The special case $b = 0$ of Theorem 4 yields the following estimate for the nth partial sum of the Taylor series for e^n (cf. [11, §48]).

Theorem 5. *For integer* $n \to \infty$,

$$\sum_{k=0}^{n} \frac{n^k}{k!} = \frac{e^n}{2}\left\{1 + \frac{2}{3}\sqrt{\frac{2}{\pi n}} - \frac{23}{270n}\sqrt{\frac{2}{\pi n}} + 0(n^{-5/2})\right\}.$$

For estimates of nth partial sums of related functions of n, such as e^{-n}, and for further generalizations, see the references in [8] and [11, p. 305], especially the paper of Paris [23].

We now turn from $\Psi(1, c; z)$ to

$$\Phi(1, c; z) = \sum_{k=0}^{\infty} \frac{z^k}{(c)_k}. \tag{1.6}$$

An asymptotic expansion for $\Phi(1, c; z)$ as real $c, z \to \infty$ with $c - z$ fixed can be obtained from Theorem 6 below. Such an expansion is equivalent to one for the incomplete gamma function

$$\gamma(c, z) = \int_0^z e^{-t} t^{c-1} dt. \tag{1.7}$$

This is because by the integral representation [18, (9.11.1)]

$$\Phi(a, c; z) = \frac{\Gamma(c)}{\Gamma(a)\Gamma(c - a)} \int_0^1 e^{zt} t^{a-1}(1 - t)^{c-a-1} dt,$$

we have

$$\begin{aligned} \Phi(1, c + 1; z) &= c\int_0^1 e^{zt}(1 - t)^{c-1} dt \\ &= ce^z \int_0^1 e^{-zt} t^{c-1} dt = ce^z z^{-c} \gamma(c, z). \end{aligned} \tag{1.8}$$

Theorem 6. *Let n, b, z be real with n, b fixed, $n > 0$. As $z \to \infty$,*

$$\sum_{k=0}^{\infty} \left(\frac{z^k}{(z+1+b)_k}\right)^n = \sqrt{\frac{\pi z}{2n}} + \frac{1}{3n} - b + 0\left(\frac{1}{\sqrt{z}}\right).$$

In the case $b = 0$, $n = 1$ of Theorem 6, more terms of the expansion have been given, as follows.

Theorem 7 [9, p. 317]. *As real $z \to \infty$,*

$$\Phi(1, z+1; z) = \sum_{k=0}^{\infty} \frac{z^k}{(z+1)_k} = \sum_{k=1}^{\infty} \frac{z^k}{(z)_k}$$
$$= \sqrt{\frac{\pi z}{2}} + \frac{1}{3} + \frac{1}{24}\sqrt{\frac{2\pi}{z}} + \frac{4}{135z} + 0\left(\frac{1}{z^{3/2}}\right).$$

The following corollary should be compared with the results in [21, p. 119], [1, (6.5.35)], [14, Vol. 2, §9.5], and [29].

Corollary 8. *As real $z \to \infty$,*

$$\gamma(z, z) = z^{z-1}e^{-z} \sum_{k=0}^{\infty} \frac{z^k}{(z+1)_k}$$
$$= z^{z-1}e^{-z}\left(\sqrt{\frac{\pi z}{2}} + \frac{1}{3} + \frac{1}{24}\sqrt{\frac{2\pi}{z}} + \frac{4}{135z} + 0\left(\frac{1}{z^{3/2}}\right)\right).$$

Proof. Apply (1.8) and Theorem 7.

Theorem 6 is in fact the special case $\phi(x) = (1+x)^n$, $\alpha = \delta = 0$, $\gamma = 1$, $\beta = 1 + b$, $h = 1/z$ of the following very general result.

Theorem 9 [9, Entry 10]. *Fix real $\alpha, \beta, \gamma, \delta$ with $\alpha > \delta \geq 0$. Assume that for some* *fixed $d > 0$, we have: $\phi(x)$ is analytic and nonzero in the disk $|x| \leq d$; $\phi(x)$ and $\phi'(x)$ are positive for $x \geq -d$; and there exists a constant $M > 0$ such that $x\phi'(x) \geq M\phi(x)$ for all $x \geq d$. Let $h > 0$. Then as $h \to 0$,*

$$\sum_{k=0}^{\infty} \prod_{j=1}^{k} \frac{\phi(h(\alpha + j\delta))}{\phi(h(\beta + j\gamma))} = \sqrt{\frac{\pi\phi(0)}{2h(\gamma-\delta)\phi'(0)}} + \frac{\alpha-\beta}{\gamma-\delta} + \frac{(\gamma+\delta)}{3(\gamma-\delta)}\left(1 - \frac{\phi(0)\phi''(0)}{\phi'(0)^2}\right) + o(\sqrt{h}).$$

Let C denote the class of functions $\phi(x)$ satisfying the hypotheses of Theorem 9. Then $e^x \in C$ and $(1+x)^n \in C$ for all real $n > 0$. Indeed, the class C is quite large. For if $\phi, \psi \in C$, then C also contains e^ϕ, $n\phi$, $n + \phi$, ϕ^n, and $\phi\psi$ for all real $n > 0$.

Problem. Enlarge the class C of functions $\phi(x)$ for which Theorem 9 holds, and find more terms in the asymptotic expansion. What happens if $\alpha, \beta, \gamma, \delta$ are allowed to vary?

2. Hypergeometric functions.

We begin this section with Ramanujan's remarkable asymptotic expansion for the series $\sum_{k=0}^{\infty} \phi(k)z^k/k!$, as $z \to \infty$, where $\phi(z)$ belongs to a certain class of functions of polynomial growth. This class will be seen to include all rational functions and indeed all functions

$$\phi(z) = \frac{(a_1)_z \cdots (a_r)_z}{(c_1)_z \cdots (c_r)_z}, \quad r = 0, 1, 2, \cdots, \quad c_i \neq 0, -1, -2 \ldots.$$

For each such $\phi(z)$, the series $\sum_{k=0}^{\infty} \phi(k)z^k/k!$ reduces to the generalized hypergeometric series

$$\sum_{k=0}^{\infty} \frac{(a_1)_k \cdots (a_r)_k z^k}{(c_1)_k \cdots (c_r)_k k!}. \tag{2.1}$$

The special case $r = 0$ of (2.1) yields e^z. The case $r = 1$ yields the general confluent hypergeometric function $\Phi(a_1, c_1; z)$ defined in (1.1). The case $r = 2$ produces associated Bessel functions [19, (6.2.9), Eq. (25)] and integrals of Bessel functions [19, (6.2.10), Eq. (3)].

Theorem 10 [10, Entry 10]. *Suppose that there exist constants $A \geq 1$, $c > 0$ and functions $\phi(x)$, $G(x)$ of a real variable x such that*

$$G(x) >> e^{-c\sqrt{x}} \quad as \quad x \to \infty, \tag{2.2}$$

and both $\phi(x)$, $G(x)$ have at most polynomial growth as $x \to \infty$. Suppose moreover that for all sufficiently large x and all nonnegative integers m, the derivatives $\phi^{(m)}(x)$ exist and satisfy

$$|\phi^{(m)}(x)/m!| \leq G(x)(A/x)^m. \tag{2.3}$$

Define

$$\phi_\infty(x) = e^{-x} \sum_{k=0}^{\infty}{}^{*} \phi(k)x^k/k!, \tag{2.4}$$

where the asterisk on the summation sign indicates that the (finitely many) terms for which $\phi(k)$ may be undefined are not included in the sum. Then for any fixed positive integer M, as $x \to \infty$,

$$\phi_\infty(x) = \phi(x) + \sum_{k=2}^{M} \sum_{n=k}^{2k-2} S_2(n, n+1-k)x^{n+1-k}\phi^{(n)}(x)/n! \tag{2.5}$$
$$+0(G(x)x^{-M}),$$

where $S_2(n,m)$ is the 2-associated Stirling number of the second kind [12, pp. 221-222], [25, pp. 74-78] defined by $S_2(n,m) = 0$ for $m \leq 0$ or $2m > n$, $S_2(n,1) = 1$ for all $n \geq 2$, and, for $2 \leq m \leq (n+1)/2$, $S_2(n+1,m) = nS_2(n-1,m-1) + mS_2(n,m)$.

Theorem 10 shows that as $x \to \infty$, $\phi_\infty(x)$ is asymptotic to $\phi(x)$ for a large class of functions $\phi(x)$. As is noted below, this class includes all rational functions of x; for other examples, see Corollaries 11-14. However, the choice $\phi(x) = e^{-x}$ shows that $\phi_\infty(x)$ is not asymptotic to $\phi(x)$ in general.

We take this opportunity now to correct some errors appearing in [7, Ch. 3, §10] and [10, §10]. The condition (2.2) above should be included in Entry 10 in both [7, p. 57], [10, p. 139]. The second paragraph below Entry 10 is incorrect and should be deleted. In the definition of S_2 below (10.18) in [7], [10], a factor of e^{-x} is missing. In the last inequality of the proof of Entry 10, replace " $\leq$ " by " $<<$ ". In the string of inequalities just above this, replace all occurrences of " $\leq$ " by " $<<$ ", and replace the very last exponent "$2k$" by "k". In [7, p. 63], this string of inequalities has a symbol "m" which should be replaced by "M". Finally, to make the proof of Entry 10 go through for all $G(x)$ satisfying (2.2) above, observe that the terms $0(2^{-N})$ in the proof can be replaced by $0(T^{-N})$ for any constant $T > 0$, by an argument virtually identical to the one given.

If $\phi(z)$ is a function of a complex variable z of at most polynomial growth as $|z| \to \infty$ which is analytic in some right half-plane (for example, any rational function), then there exist constants A, c and a function $G(x)$ satisfying the conditions of Theorem 10. This follows from the Cauchy integral formula for derivatives. Consequently, Theorem 10 yields an asymptotic expansion for the hypergeometric series (2.1).

If U denotes a Poisson random variable with mean x and ϕ is, say, a rational function with no poles at the nonnegative integers, then $\phi_\infty(x)$ is the expected value of $\phi(U)$. Write E for expected value. Thus (2.5) yields an asymptotic formula for the difference $\phi_\infty(x) - \phi(x) = E(\phi(U)) - \phi(E(U))$, as the mean $E(U)$ tends to ∞. (Of course in the case $\phi(x) = x^2$, this difference is the variance of U, which has the exact value x.) It may be of interest to obtain asymptotic expansions for $E(\phi(U)) - \phi(E(U))$ for other random variables U.

Corollary 11 [9, (11.2)]. *As real $x \to \infty$,*

$$e^{-x} \textstyle\sum_{k=0}^{\infty} (\frac{xe}{k})^k = \sqrt{2\pi x}\left(1 - \frac{1}{24x} - \frac{23}{1152x^2} - \frac{11237}{414720x^3} + 0\left(\frac{1}{x^4}\right)\right).$$

Proof. By Theorem 10, as $x \to \infty$,

$$e^{-x} \textstyle\sum_{k=0}^{\infty} \phi(k)x^k/k! = \phi(x) + \frac{x}{2}\phi^{(2)}(x) + \frac{x}{6}\phi^{(3)}(x)$$

$$+\frac{x^2}{8}\phi^{(4)}(x) + \frac{x}{24}\phi^{(4)}(x) + \frac{x^2}{12}\phi^{(5)}(x) + \frac{x^3}{48}\phi^{(6)}(x), \tag{2.6}$$

with $\phi(x) = e^x\Gamma(x+1)/x^x$. By (1.3),

$$\phi(x) = \sqrt{2\pi x}\left(1 + \frac{1}{12x} + \frac{1}{288x^2} - \frac{139}{51840x^3} + \cdots\right). \tag{2.7}$$

One can obtain asymptotic expansions of $\phi^{(m)}(x)$ by differentiating m times in (2.7), term by term (see [15, p. 21] or [20, p. 21]). Substituting these expansions in (2.6), we complete the proof.

Corollary 12 [9, p. 324]. *As real $x \to \infty$,*

$$e^{-x} \sum_{k=0}^{\infty} \log(k+1)x^k/k!$$
$$= \log x + \frac{1}{2x} + \frac{1}{12x^2} + \frac{1}{12x^3} + \frac{19}{120x^4} + \frac{9}{20x^5} + 0\left(\frac{1}{x^6}\right).$$

Corollary 13 [7, Ch. 3, p. 64]. *Fix real a, s. As real $x \to \infty$,*

$$e^{-x} \sum_{k=0}^{\infty}{}^{*}(k+a)^{-s}x^k/k!$$

$$= (x+a)^{-s} + \frac{s(s+1)}{2}x(x+a)^{-s-2} - \frac{s(s+1)(s+2)}{6}x(x+a)^{-s-3}$$

$$+\frac{s(s+1)(s+2)(s+3)}{8}x^2(x+a)^{-s-4} + 0(x^{-s-3})$$

$$= x^{-s}(1 + x^{-1}(s^2+s-2as)/2$$

$$+x^{-2}(3s^4 - 12as^3 + 14s^3 + 12a^2s^2 - 36as^2$$

$$+21s^2 + 12a^2s - 24as + 10s)/24$$

$$+0(x^{-3})).$$

The following corollary has applications to data compression schemes for digitally encoded radiographic images, and it proves a conjecture of Appledorn [2].

Corollary 14. *As real $x \to \infty$,*

$$H := e^{-x} \sum_{k=0}^{\infty} \frac{x^k}{k!} \log\left(\frac{k!}{x^k e^{-x}}\right) = \frac{1}{2}\log(2\pi e x) - \frac{1}{12x} + 0(x^{-2}).$$

Proof. In the notation of (2.4), with $\phi(x) = \log\Gamma(x+1)$, we have $H = x(1-\log x) + \phi_\infty(x)$. By (2.5), as $x \to \infty$,

$$\phi_\infty(x) = \phi(x) + \frac{x}{2}\phi^{(2)}(x) + \frac{x\phi^{(3)}(x)}{6} + \frac{x^2\phi^{(4)}(x)}{8} + 0(x^{-2}).$$

The result now follows after substitution of the well-known asymptotic expansions for the $\phi^{(n)}(x)$ [1, (6.1.41), (6.3.18), (6.4.11)].

We next turn to a special case of the hypergeometric series

$${}_2F_1\left(\begin{matrix}a\ b\\ c\end{matrix}\Big|z\right) = \sum_{k=0}^{\infty} \frac{(a)_k(b)_k z^k}{(c)_k k!},$$

specifically, the series

$$ {}_2F_1\left(\begin{matrix} a\ 1 \\ c \end{matrix}\,\middle|\,\frac{c}{a}\right) = \sum_{k=0}^{\infty} \frac{(a)_k c^k}{a^k (c)_k}, \tag{2.8} $$

where $a = c + d \to \infty$ with $c, d > 0$. As might be expected, (2.8) is considerably more difficult to estimate than the analogous one-parameter series

$$ \sum_{k=1}^{\infty} \frac{c^k}{(c)_k} = \Phi(1, c+1; c) $$

discussed in Theorem 7. Theorem 15 below deals with the case where c is bounded (so $d \to \infty$). Theorem 16 deals with the case where d is bounded (so $c \to \infty$). Finally, Theorem 17 deals with the very difficult case where both $c, d \to \infty$, or equivalently, $a/(cd) \to 0$. This is the case handled by Ramanujan in a remarkable tour de force [9, Entry 7].

Theorem 15. *Let c vary in a fixed interval $(0, M)$. Then as $a \to \infty$,*

$$ {}_2F_1\left(\begin{matrix} a\ 1 \\ c \end{matrix}\,\middle|\,\frac{c}{a}\right) = \sum_{k=0}^{\infty} \frac{c^k}{(c)_k} + a^{-1} \sum_{k=0}^{\infty} \binom{k}{2} \frac{c^k}{(c)_k} + 0(a^{-2}). $$

Proof. The left member above equals $S + T$, where

$$ S = \sum_{0 \le k \le a} \frac{c^k}{(c)_k} \frac{(a)_k}{a^k}, \qquad T = \sum_{k > a} \frac{c^k}{(c)_k} \frac{(a)_k}{a^k} $$

Let a be large. For $c \in (0, M)$ and $k > a$,

$$ \frac{c^k}{(c)_k} \frac{(a)_k}{a^k} = \prod_{r=1}^{k-1} \frac{1 + r/a}{1 + r/c} << \prod_{r=1}^{k-1} \frac{1}{2} < \left(\frac{1}{2}\right)^k, $$

so

$$ T << \sum_{k > a} \left(\frac{1}{2}\right)^k = 0(2^{-a}) = 0(a^{-2}). $$

For $k \le a$,

$$\frac{(a)_k}{a^k} = \prod_{r=1}^{k-1}\left(1+\frac{r}{a}\right) = 1 + a^{-1}\binom{k}{2} + 0\left(\sum_{m=2}^{k}\binom{k}{m}\left(\frac{k}{a}\right)^m\right)$$
$$= 1 + a^{-1}\binom{k}{2} + 0(a^{-2}k^2 2^k).$$

Thus, summing on k, $0 \le k \le a$, we deduce that

$$S = \sum_{k=0}^{\infty}\frac{c^k}{(c)_k} + a^{-1}\sum_{k=2}^{\infty}\binom{k}{2}\frac{c^k}{(c)_k} + 0(U) + 0(V) + 0(Wa^{-2}),$$

where

$$U = \sum\nolimits_{k>a}\frac{c^k}{(c)_k}, \quad V = \sum_{k>a}\binom{k}{2}\frac{c^k}{(c)_k}, \quad W = \sum_{0\le k\le a} k^2\frac{(2c)^k}{(c)_k}.$$

For all $c \in (0, M)$,

$$U < V = \sum_{k>a-1}\binom{k+1}{2}\frac{c^k}{(c+1)_k} < \sum_{k>a-1}\binom{k+1}{2}\frac{M^k}{k!}$$
$$< \sum_{k>a} 2^{-k} << 2^{-a} = 0(a^{-2}),$$

and

$$W < \sum_{k=1}^{\infty}\frac{k^2(2c)^k}{(c)_k} = 2\sum_{k=0}^{\infty}\frac{(k+1)^2(2c)^k}{(c+1)_k} < 2\sum_{k=0}^{\infty}\frac{(k+1)^2(2M)^k}{k!} = 0(1).$$

The result now follows.

Theorem 16. *Let d vary in a fixed interval $(0, M)$. Then as $a = c + d \to \infty$,*

$${}_2F_1\left(\begin{matrix} a\ 1 \\ c \end{matrix}\Big|\frac{c}{a}\right) = a\Psi(1, d+2; d) + 0(1),$$

where Ψ is defined by (1.2).

Proof. Let a be large. By [18, (9.5.7)],

$$\frac{1}{(c-1)}\,{}_2F_1\left(\begin{matrix} a\ 1 \\ c \end{matrix}\Big|\frac{c}{a}\right) + \frac{1}{(d+1)}\,{}_2F_1\left(\begin{matrix} a\ 1 \\ d+2 \end{matrix}\Big|\frac{d}{a}\right) = \frac{a^a\Gamma(c-1)\Gamma(d+1)}{\Gamma(a)c^{c-1}d^{d+1}}.$$

Thus,

$$ {}_2F_1\left(\begin{matrix} a\ 1 \\ c \end{matrix}\Big|\frac{c}{a}\right) = \frac{a^a\Gamma(c)\Gamma(d)}{\Gamma(a)c^{c-1}d^d} - \frac{(c-1)}{(d+1)}\ {}_2F_1\left(\begin{matrix} a\ 1 \\ d+2 \end{matrix}\Big|\frac{d}{a}\right). $$

By Theorem 15,

$$ {}_2F_1\left(\begin{matrix} a\ 1 \\ d+2 \end{matrix}\Big|\frac{d}{a}\right) = \sum_{k=0}^{\infty} \frac{d^k}{(d+2)_k} + 0(a^{-1}), $$

so

$$ {}_2F_1\left(\begin{matrix} a\ 1 \\ c \end{matrix}\Big|\frac{c}{a}\right) = \frac{a^a\Gamma(c)\Gamma(d)}{\Gamma(a)c^{c-1}d^d} - \frac{a}{(d+1)} \sum_{k=0}^{\infty} \frac{d^k}{(d+2)_k} + 0(1). $$

The first term on the right is, by (1.3), $a\Gamma(d)e^d d^{-d} + 0(1)$. Thus

$$ \begin{aligned} {}_2F_1\left(\begin{matrix} a\ 1 \\ c \end{matrix}\Big|\frac{c}{a}\right) &= a\left\{\frac{\Gamma(d)e^d}{d^d} - \frac{1}{(d+1)} \sum_{k=0}^{\infty} \frac{d^k}{(d+2)_k}\right\} + 0(1) \\ &= a\Psi(1, d+2; d) + 0(1) \end{aligned} $$

by [18, (9.11.5)].

Theorem 17 [9, Entry 7]. *Let $a = c + d$ with $c, d > 0$. Then as $a, c, d \to \infty$ (equivalently, as $a/(cd) \to 0$), we have the asymptotic expansion*

$$ {}_2F_1\left(\begin{matrix} a\ 1 \\ c \end{matrix}\Big|\frac{c}{a}\right) = c\left\{\frac{a^a\Gamma(c)\Gamma(d)}{2\Gamma(a)c^c d^d} + B_1\left(\frac{a}{cd}\right) + B_2\left(\frac{a}{cd}\right)^2 + B_3\left(\frac{a}{cd}\right)^3 + \cdots\right\}, $$

where the B_k are effectively computable polynomials of degree $2k-1$ over $\mathbf{Q}$ in the variable $x = d/a$ such that $B_k = 0(1)$ for each $k \geq 1$, and where

$$ B_1 = \frac{2}{3}(x+1) \tag{2.9} $$

$$ B_2 = -\frac{4}{135}(x+1)(x-2)(x-1/2) \tag{2.10} $$

$$ B_3 = \frac{8}{2835}(x+1)(x-2)(x-1/2)(x^2-x+1) \tag{2.11} $$

and

$$B_4 = \frac{16}{8505}(x+1)(x-2)(x-1/2)(x^2-x+1)^2. \tag{2.12}$$

In fact,

$$B_k = \frac{(k-1)!}{2}\,\mathrm{Res}_{z=0}(h^k(z)) - \frac{x(k-2)!}{2}\,\mathrm{Res}_{z=0}(h^{k-1}(z)), \tag{2.13}$$

where $x = d/a$ *and*

$$h(z) = z^{-2}\Big(\sum_{r=0}^{\infty} \frac{(-z)^r}{r+2}(1+x+x^2+\cdots+x^r)\Big)^{-1}. \tag{2.14}$$

We make the following observations regarding Theorem 17.

(1) For each k, the coefficients of the polynomial $B_k = B_k(x)$ are symmetric about the middle one, i.e., $x^{2k-1}B_k(x^{-1}) = B_k(x)$. This follows easily from (2.13) and (2.14).

(2) Formulas (2.9) - (2.12) seem to suggest that $B_k(x)$ divides $B_{k+1}(x)$ over $\mathbb{Q}[x]$. However, from (2.13), one can compute

$$B_5 = -\frac{8992}{12629925}(x+1)(x-2)\left(x-\frac{1}{2}\right) \times \left(x^6 - 3x^5 + \frac{1308}{281}x^4 - \frac{1211}{281}x^3 + \frac{1308}{281}x^2 - 3x + 1\right) \tag{2.15}$$

which is not divisible by B_4.

(3) The coefficients $2/3$, $-4/135$, ... of z^{-k} appearing in Theorem 3 are the respective constant terms of the polynomials B_k in Theorem 17. This follows because, by (2.13) - (2.14), the constant term of B_k is

$$\frac{(k-1)!}{2}\mathrm{Res}_{z=0}(z-\log(z+1))^{-k}, \tag{2.16}$$

and the proof in, say [9, §6] shows that (2.16) gives the coefficient of z^{-k} in Theorem 3.

Corollary 18. *Let $a = c + d$ with $c, d > 0$. Then as $a/(cd) \to 0$,*

$$ {}_2F_1\left({a\ 1 \atop c} \Big| \frac{c}{a} \right) = c\sqrt{\frac{\pi}{2}}\left(\sqrt{\frac{a}{cd}} + 0\left(\frac{a}{cd}\right)\right). $$

Proof. Use (1.3) in Theorem 17.

Problem. Estimate, for $n > 0$,

$$ \sum_{k=0}^{\infty}\left(\frac{(a)_k}{(c)_k}\frac{c^k}{a^k}\right)^n, $$

where $a = c + d \to \infty$ with $c, d > 0$. Cf. Theorem 6. (This problem is solved for $n = 1$ in Theorems 15-17.)

We now turn to a special case of the hypergeometric series

$$ {}_3F_2\left({a\ b\ c \atop d\ e} \Big| z \right) = \sum_{k=0}^{\infty} \frac{(a)_k(b)_k(c)_k z^k}{(d)_k(e)_k k!}, \tag{2.17} $$

where, for simplicity, z is real. Suppose for the moment that $d, e \notin \{0, -1, -2, \ldots\}$. By the ratio test, the series in (2.17) converges if $|z| < 1$. If $\mathrm{Re}(d + e - a - b - c) > 0$, the series even converges when $z = 1$, by Stirling's formula (1.3). Thus, if the series is 0-balanced, i.e., $a + b + c = d + e$, then as $z \uparrow 1$, the series tends to ∞. Ramanujan estimated its rate of growth as follows.

Theorem 19 [6, §24, Cor. 2]. *If* $a+b+c = d+e$ *and* $\mathrm{Re}(c) > 0$, *then as* $z \uparrow 1$,

$$\frac{\Gamma(a)\Gamma(b)\Gamma(c)}{\Gamma(d)\Gamma(e)}\, {}_3F_2\left(\begin{matrix} a\ b\ c \\ d\ e \end{matrix}\Big| z\right) = -\log(1-z) + L + O((1-z)\log(1-z)),$$

where

$$L = -2\gamma - \frac{\Gamma'(a)}{\Gamma(a)} - \frac{\Gamma'(b)}{\Gamma(b)} + \sum_{k=1}^{\infty} \frac{(d-c)_k(e-c)_k}{k(a)_k(b)_k}. \tag{2.18}$$

The difficulty in the proof is in verifying Ramanujan's explicit formula for the constant L in (2.18); see [16, §6]. A proof of Theorem 19 and a q-analogue are given in [16]. It is also shown there that for $z = 1$, the mth partial sum of the ${}_3F_2$ series in (2.17) equals

$$\frac{\Gamma(d)\Gamma(e)}{\Gamma(a)\Gamma(b)\Gamma(c)} (\log m + L + \gamma) + O(1/m),$$

as $m \to \infty$.

In the special case $e = c$, Theorem 19 reduces to the following well-known result (see [14, Vol. 1, p. 110, Eq. (12)], [6, Entry 26]).

Corollary 20. *Let* $d = a+b$. *As* $z \uparrow 1$,

$$\frac{\Gamma(a)\Gamma(b)}{\Gamma(a+b)}\, {}_2F_1\left(\begin{matrix} a\ b \\ d \end{matrix}\Big| z\right) = -\log(1-z) - 2\gamma - \frac{\Gamma'(a)}{\Gamma(a)} - \frac{\Gamma'(b)}{\Gamma(b)} + O((1-z)\log(1-z)).$$

Problem. Find analogues of Theorem 19 for ${}_4F_3$ and higher order hypergeometric series.

In the sequel, all hypergeometric series ${}_pF_q(\ )$ under consideration will have argument 1, and, as is customary, the argument 1 will be omitted in the notation ${}_pF_q(\ )$.

Furthermore, given a hypergeometric series ${}_pF_q(\ ) = \sum_{k=0}^{\infty}(\ )$, we write ${}_pF_q(\ )_m$ to denote its partial sum $\sum_{k=0}^{m}(\ )$. Write $\psi = \Gamma'/\Gamma$.

The following estimate generalizes Ramanujan's result in [5, §29, Cor. 2]. Cf. [5, Entry 35(i)].

Theorem 21. *For real c tending to* ∞,

$$\frac{\Gamma(a)\Gamma(b)}{\Gamma(a+b)}\ {}_3F_2\left(\begin{matrix} a & b & c \\ a+b & c+1 & \end{matrix}\right) = \log c - \gamma - \psi(a) - \psi(b) + 0\left(\frac{\log c}{c}\right). \tag{2.19}$$

Proof. Without loss of generality, assume $a, b \notin \{0, -1, -2, \ldots\}$. Let $N = [c]$. The left member of (2.19) equals

$$\sum_{k=0}^{\infty} \frac{\Gamma(a+k)\Gamma(b+k)\ c}{\Gamma(a+b+k)\Gamma(1+k)(c+k)} = S_N + T_N, \tag{2.20}$$

where

$$S_N = \sum_{k=0}^{N} \frac{\Gamma(a+k)\Gamma(b+k)\ c}{\Gamma(a+b+k)\Gamma(1+k)(c+k)},$$

$$T_N = \sum_{k=N+1}^{\infty} \frac{\Gamma(a+k)\Gamma(b+k)\ c}{\Gamma(a+b+k)\Gamma(1+k)(c+k)}.$$

Now, $S_N = U_N - V_N$, where

$$U_N = \sum_{k=0}^{N} \frac{\Gamma(a+k)\Gamma(b+k)}{\Gamma(a+b+k)\Gamma(1+k)}, \quad V_N = \sum_{k=1}^{N} \frac{\Gamma(a+k)\Gamma(b+k)}{\Gamma(a+b+k)\Gamma(k)(c+k)}.$$

By [19, p. 110, Eq. (35)], [5, Entry 15], as $N \to \infty$,

$$U_N = \log N - \gamma - \psi(a) - \psi(b) + 0(1/N). \tag{2.21}$$

For fixed A, B, as $z \uparrow \infty$,

$$\frac{\Gamma(z+A)}{\Gamma(z+B)} = z^{A-B}(1+O(1/z)), \tag{2.22}$$

by [19, p. 33, Eq. (12)]; thus

$$V_N = \sum_{k=1}^{N} \frac{1}{c+k}(1+O(1/k)).$$

Since by [19, p. 13, Eq. (5)],

$$\sum_{k=1}^{n} \frac{1}{z+k} = \psi(z+1+n) - \psi(z+1) \tag{2.23}$$

for all positive integers n, and since

$$\sum_{k=1}^{N} \frac{1}{(c+k)k} < \sum_{k=1}^{N} \frac{1}{ck} = O\left(\frac{\log c}{c}\right),$$

we have

$$V_N = \psi(c+1+N) - \psi(c+1) + O\left(\frac{\log c}{c}\right). \tag{2.24}$$

Next, by (2.22),

$$T_N = \sum_{k=N+1}^{\infty} \frac{c}{c+k}\left(\frac{1}{k}+O\left(\frac{1}{k^2}\right)\right) = \sum_{k=N+1}^{\infty} \frac{c}{k(c+k)} + O\left(\sum_{k=N+1}^{\infty} \frac{1}{k^2}\right).$$

The last term is $O(1/N)$, while

$$\begin{aligned}\sum_{k=N+1}^{\infty} \frac{c}{k(c+k)} &= \sum_{k=0}^{\infty} \left(\frac{1}{k+N+1} - \frac{1}{c+k+N+1}\right) \\ &= \psi(c+N+1) - \psi(N+1),\end{aligned}$$

since by [19, p. 12, Eq.(2)],

$$\sum_{k=0}^{\infty} \left(\frac{1}{k+z} - \frac{1}{k+x}\right) = \psi(x) - \psi(z). \tag{2.25}$$

Thus,

$$T_N = \psi(c+N+1) - \psi(N+1) + 0(1/N). \tag{2.26}$$

Combining (2.26), (2.24), and (2.21), we see that the members of (2.20) equal

$$\log N - \gamma - \psi(a) - \psi(b) + \psi(c+1) - \psi(N+1) + 0\left(\frac{\log c}{c}\right). \tag{2.27}$$

By [19, p. 33, Eq.(8)], as $z \uparrow \infty$,

$$\psi(z) = \log z + 0(1/z). \tag{2.28}$$

As $N = [c]$, the expression in (2.27) thus equals

$$\log c - \gamma - \psi(a) - \psi(b) + 0\left(\frac{\log c}{c}\right),$$

as desired.

Finally, we present a new proof of a magnificent estimate of Ramanujan for partial sums of a ${}_5F_4$.

Theorem 22 [5, Entry 6]. *If $a+b+c \notin \{0,-1,-2,\ldots\}$, then, as the integer m tends to ∞,*

$$\frac{\Gamma(a+b+c)\Gamma(a)\Gamma(b)\Gamma(c)}{\Gamma(b+c)\Gamma(a+c)\Gamma(a+b)}\,{}_5F_4\left(\begin{matrix}(a+b+c+1)/2,\ a+b+c-1,\ a,b,c\\ (a+b+c-1)/2,\ b+c,a+c,a+b\end{matrix}\right)_m$$
$$= 2\log m - \gamma - \psi(a) - \psi(b) - \psi(c) + 0\left(\frac{\log m}{m}\right). \tag{2.29}$$

Proof. Without loss of generality, assume that $a,b,c \notin \{0,-1,-2,\ldots\}$. By [5, (6.2)], the left member of (2.29) equals

$$\frac{\Gamma(a+b+c)\Gamma(a)\Gamma(b)\Gamma(c)}{\Gamma(b+c)\Gamma(a+c)\Gamma(a+b)}\,\frac{(a+b+c)_m(a+1)_m}{(b+c)_m(1)_m}\,{}_4F_3\left(\begin{matrix}a,\ a,\ a+b+c+m,\ -m\\ a+c,\ a+b,\ a+1\end{matrix}\right). \tag{2.30}$$

We now apply a transformation for 1- balanced terminating ${}_4F_3$ series [27, (4.3.5.1)], [4], namely

$$
{}_4F_3\left(\begin{matrix} w & v & u & -m \\ & y & x & z \end{matrix}\right)_m = \frac{(y-w)_m(z-w)_m}{(y)_m(z)_m} \times {}_4F_3\left(\begin{matrix} x-u, & x-v, & w, & -m \\ x, & 1+w-y-m, & 1+w-z-m \end{matrix}\right)_m ,
$$

where $x+y+z = 1-m+u+v+w$. (In [27, (4.3.5.1)], the rightmost w should be u.) Choosing $w=a,\ v=a,\ u = a+b+c+m,\ y=a+c,\ x=a+b$, and $z=a+1$, we see that the ${}_4F_3$ in (2.30) equals

$$
\frac{(c)_m(1)_m}{(a+c)_m(a+1)_m}\ {}_3F_2\left(\begin{matrix} a, & b, & -c-m \\ a+b, & 1-c-m \end{matrix}\right)_m .
$$

Thus the expression in (2.30) equals

$$
\frac{\Gamma(a+b+c+m)\Gamma(c+m)}{\Gamma(b+c+m)\Gamma(a+c+m)} R_m, \tag{2.31}
$$

where

$$
\begin{aligned}
R_m &= \frac{\Gamma(a)\Gamma(b)}{\Gamma(a+b)}\ {}_3F_2\left(\begin{matrix} a, & b, & -c-m \\ a+b, & 1-c-m \end{matrix}\right)_m \\
&= \sum_{k=0}^{m} \frac{\Gamma(a+k)\Gamma(b+k)(m+c)}{\Gamma(a+b+k)\Gamma(1+k)(m+c-k)}.
\end{aligned}
$$

The coefficient of R_m in (2.31) equals $1+0(1/m)$ by (2.22), so it remains to prove that

$$
R_m = 2\log m - \gamma - \psi(a) - \psi(b) - \psi(c) + 0\left(\frac{\log m}{m}\right).
$$

We have $R_m = U_m + W_m$, where

$$
\begin{aligned}
U_m &= \sum_{k=0}^{m} \frac{\Gamma(a+k)\Gamma(b+k)}{\Gamma(a+b+k)\Gamma(1+k)}, \\
W_m &= \sum_{k=1}^{m} \frac{\Gamma(a+k)\Gamma(b+k)}{\Gamma(a+b+k)\Gamma(k)(m+c-k)}.
\end{aligned}
$$

In view of (2.21), it remains to show that

$$
W_m = \log m - \psi(c) + 0\left(\frac{\log m}{m}\right). \tag{2.32}
$$

By (2.22),

$$W_m = \sum_{k=1}^{m} \frac{1}{m+c-k}(1+0(1/k))$$
$$= \sum_{k=1}^{m} \frac{1}{m+c-k} + 0\left(\frac{1}{m+c}\sum_{k=1}^{m}\left(\frac{1}{m+c-k}+\frac{1}{k}\right)\right).$$

By (2.23) and then (2.28),

$$\sum_{k=1}^{m} \frac{1}{m+c-k} = \psi(m+c)-\psi(c) = \log m - \psi(c) + 0(1/m),$$

and (2.32) now follows.

W. Bühring (The behavior at unit argument of the hypergeometric function ${}_3F_2$, SIAM J. Math. Anal. 18 (1987), 1227-1234) has established a generalization of Theorem 19 for s-balanced ${}_3F_2$ series.)

References

1. M. Abramowitz and I. Stegun, eds., **Handbook of Mathematical Functions**, Dover, N.Y., 1965.
2. C. Appledorn, *Problem 87-6**, **SIAM Review 29** (1987), p. 297.
3. R. Askey, *Ramanujan and hypergeometric functions,* to appear.
4. W. Bailey, **Generalized Hypergeometric Series,** Stechert-Hafner, N.Y., 1964.
5. B. Berndt, *Chapter 10 of Ramanujan's second notebook,* **J. Indian Math. Soc. 46** (1982), 31-76.
6. B. Berndt, *Chapter 11 of Ramanujan's second notebook*, **Bull. London Math. Soc. 15** (1983), 273-320.
7. B. Berndt, **Ramanujan's Notebooks, Part I**, Springer-Verlag, N.Y., 1985.
8. B. Berndt, **Ramanujan's Notebooks, Part II,** Springer-Verlag, N.Y., to appear.

9. B. Berndt and R. Evans, *Chapter 13 of Ramanujan's second notebook: Integrals and asymptotic expansions*, **Expo. Math. 2** (1984), 289-347.

10. B. Berndt, R. Evans, and B. Wilson, *Chapter 3 of Ramanujan's second notebook*, **Advances Math. 49** (1983), 123-169.

11. B. Berndt, R. Lamphere, and B. Wilson, *Chapter 12 of Ramanujan's second notebook: Continued fractions*, **Rocky Mountain J. Math. 15** (1985), 235-310.

12. L. Comtet, **Advanced Combinatorics**, Reidel, Dordrecht, 1974.

13. R. Dingle, **Asymptotic Expansions: Their Derivation and Interpretation**, Academic Press, N.Y., 1973.

14. A. Erdélyi, ed., **Higher Transcendental Functions**, Vols. 1-3, McGraw-Hill, N.Y., 1953.

15. A. Erdélyi, **Asymptotic Expansions**, Dover, N.Y., 1956.

16. R. Evans and D. Stanton, *Asymptotic formulas for zero-balanced hypergeometric series*, **SIAM J. Math. Anal. 15** (1984), 1010-1020.

17. J. Hafner, *Zeros on the critical line for Maass wave form L-functions,* **J. reine angew. Math. 377** (1987), 127-158.

18. N. Lebedev, **Special Functions and Their Applications**, Dover, N.Y., 1972.

19. Y. Luke, **The Special Functions and Their Approximations, Vol. 1**, Academic Press, N.Y., 1969.

20. F. Olver, **Introduction to Asymptotics and Special Functions**, Academic Press, N.Y., 1974.

21. F. Olver, *Unsolved problems in the asymptotic estimation of special functions,* in: **Theory and Application of Special Functions**, R. Askey, ed., Academic Press, N.Y., 1975.

22 F. Olver, *Whittaker functions with both parameters large: uniform approximations in terms of parabolic cylinder functions*, **Proc. Royal Soc. Edinburgh 86A** (1980), 213-234.

23. R. Paris, *On a generalisation of a result of Ramanujan connected with the exponential series,* **Proc. Edinburgh Math. Soc. 24** (1981), 179-195.

24. S. Ramanujan, **Notebooks**, 2 vols., Tata Institute of Fundamental Research, Bombay, 1957.

25. J. Riordan, **An Introduction to Combinatorial Analysis**, Wiley, N.Y., 1958.

26. L. Slater, **Confluent Hypergeometric Functions**, Cambridge University Press, 1960.

27. L. Slater, **Generalized Hypergeometric Functions**, Cambridge University Press, 1966.

28. G. Szegö, *Über einige von S. Ramanujan gestellte Aufgaben*, **J. London Math. Soc. 3** (1928), 225-232; Collected Papers, R. Askey, ed., Birkhauser, Boston, 1982.

29. N. Temme, *Uniform asymptotic expansions of the incomplete gamma functions and the incomplete beta function*, **Math. Comp. 29** (1975), 1109-1114.

30. N. Temme, *Uniform asymptotic expansions of confluent hypergeometric functions*, **J. Inst. Math. Appl. 22** (1978), 215-223.

31. G. Watson, *Theorems stated by Ramanujan (V): approximations connected with* e^x, **Proc. London Math. Soc. (2) 29** (1929), 293-308.

Beta integrals in Ramanujan's papers, his unpublished work and further examples

Richard Askey

Abstract. Ramanujan evaluated a number of integrals that extend the classical beta integral of Wallis and Euler. Further extensions have been found, and these integrals or special cases of them have associated orthogonal polynomials that are very attractive and have played a role in the development of some important mathematics, including the first derivation of the Rogers-Ramanujan identities. Some of these integrals will be explained, and a new proof of the value of one of the most general will be given.

1. Introduction. In the first chapter of his book Ramanujan, Hardy [20, pp. 7-8] listed fifteen statements from Ramanujan's first letter to him. These included five integrals. Two of these integrals were evaluated as continued fractions. One was transformed into a second integral. The other two were evaluated, one as a quotient of gamma functions, the other as the reciprocal of an infinite series, which could have been written as an infinite product if Ramanujan had cared to. The last two integrals are

ISBN 0-12-058560-X

(1.1) $$\int_0^\infty \frac{1+\left(\frac{x}{b+1}\right)^2}{1+\left(\frac{x}{a}\right)^2} \cdot \frac{1+\left(\frac{x}{b+2}\right)^2}{1+\left(\frac{x}{a+1}\right)^2} \cdots dx$$

$$= \frac{1}{2}\pi^{1/2} \frac{\Gamma(a+\frac{1}{2})\Gamma(b+1)\Gamma(b-a+\frac{1}{2})}{\Gamma(a)\Gamma(b+\frac{1}{2})\Gamma(b-a+1)}$$

(1.2) $$\int_0^\infty \frac{dx}{(1+x^2)(1+x^2r^2)(1+x^2r^4)\ldots} = \frac{\pi}{2(1+r+r^3+r^6+r^{10}+\ldots)} .$$

The numbers above are not those Hardy used, but will be used here for the sake of easy reference. Hardy wrote that as an expert on definite integrals he thought he could prove these two and "did so, though with a great deal more trouble than I had expected." He then said "On the whole the integral formulae seemed the least impressive."

Next, in commenting on four infinite series Ramanujan had sent, Hardy wrote: "The series formula (1.1)-(1.4) (his numbers, not those used in this paper) I found much more intriguing, and it soon became obvious that Ramanujan must possess much more general theorems and was keeping a great deal up his sleeve." Hardy could have written that about the integral (1.2). In his first notebook, Ramanujan had the following integral.

(1.3) $$\int_0^\infty \frac{(1+arx)(1+ar^2x)\ldots}{(1+x)(1+rx)\ldots} x^{n-1}dx$$

$$= \frac{\pi}{\sin \pi n} \prod_{m=1}^\infty \frac{(1-r^{m-n})(1-ar^m)}{(1-r^m)(1-ar^{m-n})}$$

when $0 < r < 1$, $n > 0$ and $0 < a < r^{n-1}$, unless n is an integer or a is of the form r^p, p a positive integer.

This statement is taken from a later paper [29], but it is in both the first and second notebooks of Ramanujan [30, p. 182], [31, p. 195]. In the first notebook this integral is on a left hand page, and these pages were almost surely used after most of the more systematic right hand pages, but even so, it is very likely this integral had been evaluated before Ramanujan wrote to Hardy.

The section in [29] that contains (1.3) starts with the sentence: "Another curious formula is the following." Then it continues with the statement of (1.3). This sentence sounds like it was written by Hardy rather than Ramanujan. I do not think that Ramanujan thought of any beautiful integral as "curious". Ramanujan did not have a proof of (1.3) according to a statement in [29]. Here is the relevant sentence. "My own proofs of the above results make use of a general formula, the truth of which depends on conditions that I have not investigated completely." While this statement does not say Ramanujan did not have a proof of his general formula under some conditions, Hardy has given the general formula in [20, Chapter XI], and it is clear that Ramanujan did not know enough function theory to have proven this general fact. However he could have proven (1.3) by the argument given in [2]. He used this type of argument to prove the q-binomial theorem in [29].

I have nothing to add to the very nice treatment of Ramanujan's general formula that Hardy gave in [20, Chapter XI], so will say nothing about it here. However the word "curious" is inappropriate, as will be seen.

Further evidence that Hardy is responsible for "curious" comes from a paper of his that follows Ramanujan's paper. In [19], Hardy wrote: "I have succeeded in evaluating another curious integral involving the function $F(z)$, viz.,"

$$(1.4) \qquad \int_0^\infty \exp\{\frac{-(\log x)^2}{2\log 1/b}\}F(ab^2x)x^{\frac{1}{2}-\nu}dx$$

$$= \frac{[2\pi \log 1/b]^{1/2}b^{-1/2(3/2-\nu)^2}}{(1-ab^\nu)(1-ab^{\nu+1})(1-ab^{\nu+2})\dots}$$

where $0 < b < 1$, $\nu + [\log(1/a)/\log(1/b)] > 0$ and

$$F(x) = \prod_{n=0}^{\infty}(1+xb^n) .$$

While (1.4) seemed curious to Hardy in 1915, I claim it is a reasonably natural integral, and in fact Ramanujan extended it and probably knew that it fits in with other extensions of the gamma and beta integrals.

2. Gamma and beta functions and integrals and some q-extensions.

Euler's definition of the gamma function is equivalent to

$$(2.1) \qquad \frac{1}{\Gamma(a)} = \lim_{n\to\infty} \frac{(a)_n}{n!}n^{1-a}$$

where the shifted factorial $(a)_n$ is defined by

(2.2) $$(a)_n = a(a+1)\cdots(a+n-1), \quad n = 1,2,\ldots,$$
$$= 1 \qquad\qquad , \quad n = 0 .$$

A q-extension of n! is given by

(2.3) $$n!_q = 1(1+q) \cdots (1+q+\cdots+q^{n-1}), \quad n = 1,2,\ldots .$$

This can be rewritten as

(2.4) $$n!_q = \frac{(1-q)\cdots(1-q^n)}{(1-q)^n} = \frac{(q;q)_\infty (1-q)^{1-(n+1)}}{(q^{n+1};q)_\infty}$$

when $0 < q < 1$ and

(2.5) $$(a;q)_\infty = \prod_{n=0}^{\infty} (1-aq^n)$$

is used. The right hand side of (2.4) makes sense for $n + 1$ a complex number, so define

(2.6) $$\Gamma_q(a) = \frac{(q;q)_\infty}{(q^a;q)_\infty}(1-q)^{1-a}$$

when the denominator does not have any zeros. It is immediate that

$$\Gamma_q(n+1) = n!_q ,$$

that

$$\Gamma_q(a+1) = \frac{(1-q^a)}{(1-q)}\Gamma_q(a) \ , \tag{2.7}$$

and Gosper has given a simple proof that

$$\lim_{q\to 1} \Gamma_q(a) = \Gamma(a) \ . \tag{2.8}$$

See [1, Appendix 1].

The q-extension of the shifted factorial (2.2) is

$$(a;q)_n = (a;q)_\infty/(aq^n;q)_\infty \ . \tag{2.9}$$

The q-binomial theorem that was mentioned in section 1 is

$$\frac{(ax;q)_\infty}{(x;q)_\infty} = \sum_{n=0}^{\infty} \frac{(a;q)_n}{(q;q)_n} x^n \ . \tag{2.10}$$

With this notation we can rewrite (1.3) as

$$\int_0^\infty x^{c-1} \frac{(-ax;q)_\infty}{(-x;q)_\infty} dx = \frac{\pi}{\sin \pi c} \frac{(q^{1-c};q)_\infty (a;q)_\infty}{(q;q)_\infty (aq^{-c};q)_\infty} \ . \tag{2.11}$$

When $a = q^{b+c}$ and Euler's reflection formula

$$\Gamma(c)\Gamma(1-c) = \frac{\pi}{\sin \pi c}$$

is used, (2.11) can be written as

$$(2.12) \qquad \int_0^\infty x^{c-1} \frac{(-xq^{b+c};q)_\infty}{(-x;q)_\infty} dx = \frac{\Gamma(c)\Gamma(1-c)\Gamma_q(b)}{\Gamma_q(1-c)\Gamma_q(b+c)} .$$

A limit needs to be taken when c is an integer. I will not mention this or other obvious restrictions below.

Euler's evaluation of the beta integral

$$(2.13) \qquad \int_0^1 x^{a-1}(1-x)^{b-1} dx = \frac{\Gamma(a)\Gamma(b)}{\Gamma(a+b)}$$

is well known. The change of variables $x \to x/(x+1)$ gives

$$(2.14) \qquad \int_0^\infty \frac{x^{a-1}}{(1+x)^{a+b}} dx = \frac{\Gamma(a)\Gamma(b)}{\Gamma(a+b)}$$

which looks similar to (2.12). In fact

$$(2.15) \qquad \lim_{q\to 1} \int_0^\infty x^{a-1} \frac{(-xq^{a+b};q)_\infty}{(-x;q)_\infty} dx = \int_0^\infty \frac{x^{a-1}}{(1+x)^{a+b}} dx$$

so not only do the values of (2.12) and (2.14) agree when $q \to 1$ (by (2.8)), the integrals agree. To see that (2.15) holds, first observe that for $|x| < 1$,

$$(2.16) \qquad \lim_{q\to 1} \frac{(q^a x;q)_\infty}{(x;q)_\infty} = \lim_{q\to 1} \sum_{n=0}^\infty \frac{(q^a;q)_n}{(q;q)_n} x^n$$

$$= \sum_{n=0}^\infty \frac{(a)_n}{n!} x^n = (1-x)^{-a} .$$

When $|x| \geq 1$, x not positive, then

$$\lim_{q\to 1} \frac{(q^a x;q)_\infty}{(x;q)_\infty} = \lim_{q\to 1} \frac{(q^a x;q)_\infty}{(x;q)_k (xq^k;q)_\infty}$$

$$= (1-x)^{-k}(1-x)^{-a+k} = (1-x)^{-a}$$

when k is chosen large enough so that $|xq^k| < 1$.

Euler's integral (2.14) has one attractive feature missing in Ramanujan's integral (2.12). The right hand side of (2.14) is symmetric in a and b, while the right hand side of (2.12) is not symmetric in b and c. There is an extension of (2.12) that restores the symmetry.

$$(2.17) \qquad \int_0^\infty \frac{x^{c-1}(-q^{b+c}x;q)_\infty(-q^{a+1-c}/x;q)_\infty}{(-x;q)_\infty(-q/x;q)_\infty}\, dx$$

$$= \frac{\Gamma(c)\Gamma(1-c)\Gamma_q(a)\Gamma_q(b)}{\Gamma_q(c)\Gamma_q(1-c)\Gamma_q(a+b)} .$$

This was proven in [5], but it would be a rash mathematician who would claim this was not known to Ramanujan. It is not included in the sheets from Trinity College that Andrews calls the lost notebook, but a very closely related integral is there, so if we ever find more sheets of work of Ramanujan, I would not be surprised to see that (2.17) was found by him. As was shown in [5], formula (2.17) is an easy consequence of (2.12).

The gamma integral

(2.18) $$\int_0^\infty x^{a-1}e^{-x}dx = \Gamma(a)$$

is an easy consequence of either (2.13) or (2.14) and the limit result

(2.19) $$\lim_{b\to\infty} \frac{b^a\Gamma(b)}{\Gamma(a+b)} = 1 .$$

In the q-case one can just take $a = 0$ in (2.11) or $q^b = 0$ in (2.12). The result is

(2.20) $$\int_0^\infty \frac{x^{c-1}dx}{(-x;q)_\infty} = \frac{\Gamma(c)\Gamma(1-c)(1-q)^c}{\Gamma_q(1-c)}$$

or

(2.21) $$\int_0^\infty \frac{x^{c-1}}{(-(1-q)x;q)_\infty}\, dx = \frac{\Gamma(c)\Gamma(1-c)}{\Gamma_q(1-c)} .$$

This is an extension of (2.18), since

$$\lim_{q\to 1^-}(-(1-q)x;q)_\infty = e^x .$$

When $c = 1/2$ in (2.20) and x is replaced by x^2 the result is equivalent to (1.2) after the series in (1.2) is written as a product. The product will be given below after a sum of Ramanujan is given. It is now clear that (1.2) is an extension of the normal integral

$$\int_{-\infty}^{\infty} e^{-x^2} dx = \sqrt{\pi} , \tag{2.22}$$

and so is probably a fundamental integral.

3. <u>Sums and integrals</u>. A strong analogy between sums and integrals is something we try to stress in elementary calculus, but we often are unaware of exactly how close they can be.

Consider the q-binomial theorem (2.10). Take $x = q^a$, $a = q^b$ and rewrite it as

$$\sum_{n=0}^{\infty} \frac{(q^{n+1};q)_\infty}{(q^{n+b};q)_\infty} q^{an} = \frac{(q^{a+b};q)_\infty (q;q)_\infty}{(q^a;q)_\infty (q^b;q)_\infty} .$$

Multiply by $(1-q)$ and rewrite the right hand side in terms of the q-gamma function. The result is

$$(1-q) \sum_{n=0}^{\infty} \frac{(q^{n+1};q)_\infty}{(q^{n+b};q)_\infty} q^{(a-1)n} q^n = \frac{\Gamma_q(a)\Gamma_q(b)}{\Gamma_q(a+b)} . \tag{3.1}$$

The right hand side suggests Euler's integral (2.13). To see that the left hand side can be interpreted as an integral consider the measure $d_q x$ which puts mass $(1-q)q^n$ at $x = q^n$, $n = 0,1,\dots,$ and zero elsewhere. Then (3.1) can be written as

$$\int_0^1 x^{a-1} \frac{(xq;q)_\infty}{(xq^b;q)_\infty} d_q x = \frac{\Gamma_q(a)\Gamma_q(b)}{\Gamma_q(a+b)} . \tag{3.2}$$

But

$$\lim_{q\to 1^-} \frac{(xq;q)_\infty}{(xq^b;q)_\infty} = (1-x)^{b-1}, \quad 0 \le x < 1 ,$$

and

$$\lim_{q\to 1^-} \int_0^1 f(x)d_qx = \int_0^1 f(x)dx$$

when $f(x)$ is continuous on $0 \le x \le 1$, so (3.2) is an extension of (2.13) when $b \ge 1$ (and when $b > 0$ after a little work). This was first observed by Thomae [39], and later by Jackson [21].

Ramanujan found a sum that extends Euler's integral on $(0,\infty)$. He evaluated

$$(3.3) \qquad \sum_{-\infty}^{\infty} \frac{(a;q)_n}{(b;q)_n} x^n = \frac{(ax;q)_\infty(q/ax;q)_\infty(q;q)_\infty(b/q;q)_\infty}{(x;q)_\infty(b/ax;q)_\infty(b;q)_\infty(q/a;q)_\infty} .$$

If the measure d_qx is extended to the positive reals to taking mass $(1-q)q^n$ at $x = q^n$, $n = 0, \pm 1, \pm 2, \ldots,$ then (3.3) can be rewritten as

$$(3.4) \qquad \int_0^\infty \frac{x^{a-1}(q^{a+b}\gamma x;q)_\infty}{(\gamma x;q)_\infty} d_qx = \frac{\Gamma_q(a)\Gamma_q(b)(q^a\gamma;q)_\infty(q^{1-a}/\gamma;q)_\infty}{\Gamma_q(a+b)(\gamma;q)_\infty(q/\gamma;q)_\infty}$$

which clearly extends (2.14).

One can try to extend (3.4) in the same way (2.17) extends (2.12) but the extension is really without content. For

$$\int_0^\infty x^{c-1} \frac{(q^{b+c}\gamma x;q)_\infty (q^{a+1-c}/\gamma x;q)_\infty}{(\gamma x;q)_\infty (q/\gamma x;q)_\infty} d_q x$$

$$= (1-q) \sum_{-\infty}^{\infty} q^{nc} \frac{(q^{n+b+c}\gamma;q)_\infty (q^{a+1-c-n}/\gamma;q)_\infty}{(q^n\gamma;q)_\infty (q^{1-n}/\gamma;q)_\infty}$$

$$= \frac{(1-q)(q^{b+c}\gamma;q)_\infty (q^{a+1-c}\gamma^{-1};q)_\infty}{(\gamma;q)_\infty (q\gamma^{-1};q)_\infty} \sum_{-\infty}^{\infty} q^{nc} \frac{(\gamma;q)_n (q^{a+1-c-n}\gamma^{-1};q)_n}{(q^{b+c}\gamma;q)_n (q^{1-n}\gamma^{-1};q)_n}$$

$$= \frac{(1-q)(q^{b+c}\gamma;q)_\infty (q^{a+1-c}\gamma^{-1};q)_\infty}{(\gamma;q)_\infty (q\gamma^{-1};q)_\infty} \sum_{-\infty}^{\infty} \frac{(q^{c-a}\gamma;q)_n}{(q^{b+c}\gamma;q)_n} q^{an} .$$

Thus this integral is just Ramanujan's sum in disguise. Since the disguise might be useful, the sum is given now.

$$(3.5) \qquad \int_0^\infty x^{c-1} \frac{(q^{b+c}\gamma x;q)_\infty (q^{a+1-c}/\gamma x;q)_\infty}{(\gamma x;q)_\infty (q/\gamma x;q)_\infty} d_q x$$

$$= \frac{\Gamma_q(a)\Gamma_q(b)}{\Gamma_q(a+b)} \frac{(\gamma q^c;q)_\infty (q^{1-c}\gamma^{-1};q)_\infty}{(\gamma;q)_\infty (q\gamma^{-1};q)_\infty}$$

and the symmetry in a and b that is missing in (3.4) has been restored.

In (3.3) replace x by x/a and let $a \to \infty$. The result is

$$(3.6) \qquad \sum_{-\infty}^{\infty} \frac{(-1)^n q^{n(n-1)/2} x^n}{(b;q)_n} = \frac{(x;q)_\infty (q/x;q)_\infty (q;q)_\infty}{(b/x;q)_\infty (b;q)_\infty}$$

or

$$(3.7)\qquad \sum_{-\infty}^{\infty} (bq^n;q)_\infty q^{n(n-1)/2} x^n = \frac{(-x;q)_\infty(-q/x;q)_\infty(q;q)_\infty}{(-b/x;q)_\infty} .$$

When $b = 0$ this is

$$(3.8)\qquad \sum_{-\infty}^{\infty} q^{n(n-1)/2} x^n = (-x;q)_\infty(-q/x;q)_\infty(q;q)_\infty .$$

This is the triple product formula for the theta function. When q is replaced by q^2 and x by qx the result is

$$(3.9)\qquad \sum_{-\infty}^{\infty} q^{n^2} x^n = (-qx;q^2)_\infty(-q/x;q^2)_\infty(q^2;q^2)_\infty .$$

This is another q-extension of the normal integral (2.22). When $x = 1$ in (3.8) the sum is

$$2\sum_{n=0}^{\infty} q^{n(n+1)/2} = (-1;q)_\infty(-q;q)_\infty(q;q)_\infty$$

so

$$\sum_{n=0}^{\infty} q^{n(n+1)/2} = (-q;q)_\infty^2(q;q)_\infty = \frac{(-q;q)_\infty^2(q;q)_\infty^2}{(q;q)_\infty}$$

$$= \frac{(q^2;q^2)_\infty^2}{(q;q^2)_\infty(q^2;q^2)_\infty} = \frac{(q^2;q^2)_\infty}{(q;q^2)_\infty} .$$

Thus (1.2) can be rewritten as

$$\int_{-\infty}^{\infty} \frac{dx}{(-x^2;q^2)_\infty} = \frac{\pi(q;q^2)_\infty}{(q^2;q^2)_\infty} \tag{3.10}$$

or

$$\int_{-\infty}^{\infty} \frac{dx}{(-(1-q)x^2;q)_\infty} = \frac{\pi}{\Gamma_q(1/2)} . \tag{3.11}$$

It is now easy to see how this generalizes the normal integral (2.22).

In the pages of results of Ramanujan that Andrews found in the Wren Library in Trinity College there are a few integrals. Two of them fit into the general picture described above. These are

$$\int_{-\infty}^{\infty} e^{-x^2+2mx}(-ae^{2kx};q)_\infty(-be^{-2kx};q)_\infty dx \tag{3.12}$$

$$= \sqrt{\pi} \frac{(abq;q)_\infty e^{m^2}}{(aq^{1/2}e^{2mk};q)_\infty(bq^{1/2}e^{-2mk};q)_\infty} , \quad q = e^{-2k^2}$$

$$\int_{-\infty}^{\infty} \frac{e^{-x^2+2mx}dx}{(aq^{1/2}e^{2ikx};q)_\infty(bq^{1/2}e^{-2ikx};q)_\infty} \tag{3.13}$$

$$= \sqrt{\pi}\, e^{m^2} \frac{(-aq^{1/2}e^{2imk};q)_\infty(-bq^{1/2}e^{-2imk};q)_\infty}{(abq;q)_\infty} , \quad q = e^{-2k^2}.$$

See [3].

The first of these two contains Hardy's integral (1.4) when $b = 0$ in (3.12) and a change of variables is made. It is a beta integral, and is analogous to (2.17), with e^{-x^2} taking the role of $[(-x;q)_\infty(-q/x;q)_\infty]^{-1}$ with x in the second being replaced by e^{2kx}, $q = \exp(-2k^2)$. These two functions have the same moments when exponential moments are considered and a trivial change of variables is made. Thus Hardy's integral (1.4) is analogous to a limiting case of Ramanujan's integral (1.3), and so is not as curious as Hardy thought. It is an extension of the gamma integral. Pastro [27] has worked out the corresponding orthogonal polynomials. The moment problem is indeterminate, for (1.4), the case $q^a = 0$ of (2.17) and (3.5) have essentially the same moments (exponential or polynomial as appropriate), so the same polynomials are orthogonal with respect to each of these distributions. These polynomials were introduced by Hahn [18] and studied in some detail by Moak [24]. The special case where the lognormal distribution is used was introduced in one case by Stieltjes [36] and by Wigert [41] in the general case.

Ramanujan's other q beta integral (3.13) can be transformed to be an extension of Cauchy's beta integral

$$\frac{1}{2\pi}\int_{-\infty}^{\infty} \frac{dx}{(a+ix)^\alpha(b-ix)^\beta} = \frac{\Gamma(\alpha+\beta-1)}{\Gamma(\alpha)\Gamma(\beta)}(a+b)^{1-\alpha-\beta} \tag{3.14}$$

when $\operatorname{Re} a > 0$, $\operatorname{Re} b > 0$, $\alpha + \beta > 1$. See Pastro [27] for this and how to use a transformation of this integral to find polynomials biorthogonal on the unit circle with weight function a q-version of a beta integral.

4. Further q-beta integrals. The ultraspherical polynomials $C_n^\lambda(x)$ can be given by the generating function

$$(4.1)\qquad (1 - 2xr + r^2)^{-\lambda} = \sum_{n=0}^{\infty} C_n^\lambda(x) r^n .$$

They satisfy

$$(4.2)\qquad \int_{-1}^{1} C_n^\lambda(x) C_m^\lambda(x)(1-x^2)^{\lambda-1/2} dx = 0, \quad m \neq n, \quad \lambda > -1/2 .$$

L. J. Rogers [33], [34] introduced an important extension of these polynomials. His polynomials are now called continuous q-ultraspherical polynomials and are denoted by $C_n(x;\beta|q)$. They are generated by

$$(4.3)\qquad \prod_{n=0}^{\infty} \frac{(1-2x\beta rq^n+\beta^2r^2q^{2n})}{(1-2xrq^n+r^2q^{2n})} = \sum_{n=0}^{\infty} C_n(x;\beta|q) r^n , \quad |r| < 1 .$$

They satisfy the three term recurrence relation

$$(4.4)\qquad 2x(1-\beta q^n)C_n(x;\beta|q) = (1-q^{n+1})C_{n+1}(x;\beta|q) + (1-\beta^2q^{n-1})C_{n-1}(x;\beta|q),$$

$$C_0(x;\beta|q) = 1, \; C_1(x;\beta|q) = 2x(1-\beta)/(1-q) .$$

When $\beta = q^\lambda$ and (4.4) is divided by $(1-q)$, the result of letting $q \to 1$ is

$$(4.5) \quad 2x(n+\lambda)C_n^{\lambda}(x) = (n+1)C_{n+1}^{\lambda}(x) + (n+2\lambda-1)C_{n-1}^{\lambda}(x) .$$

From the three term recurrence it is possible to prove that $C_n(x;\beta|q)$ are orthogonal with respect to a positive measure when $-1 < \beta < 1$, $-1 < q < 1$ (and even for other values of β, q but these will not be considered here). The appropriate theorem is called Favard's theorem, but it is older than the 1935 date of Favard's paper. See the comments to [38] for references. Rogers did not know this theorem in 1895, since the necessary mathematics had only been introduced by Stieltjes [36] shortly before, and the first complete statement of the theorem I have found is by Perron in 1912. Stieltjes essentially knew the theorem, but he died in 1894 without knowlege of Rogers's work. The first connection with orthogonal polynomials came in 1926 when Szegö discovered closely related orthogonal polynomials on the unit circle whose weight function is a theta function. The general polynomials were rediscovered by Feldheim [11] and Lanzewizky [23]. They knew Favard's theorem and so knew the polynomials were orthogonal, but were unable to find or guess the weight function. The weight function was first found as a special case of a more general orthogonality relation for polynomials with four free parameters in addition to the q. See [7]. The orthogonality is

$$(4.6) \quad \int_{-1}^{1} C_n(x;\beta|q)C_m(x;\beta|q)\prod_{k=0}^{\infty}\left[\frac{1-2(2x^2-1)q^k+q^{2k}}{1-2(2x^2-1)\beta q^k+\beta^2 q^{2k}}\right]\frac{dx}{(1-x^2)^{1/2}} = 0,$$

$m \neq n, \quad -1 < \beta, \quad q < 1.$

This is not the most obvious extension of (4.2), but it is an extension as can be seen from (2.16). For

$$\prod_{k=0}^{\infty} (1-2(2x^2-1)\beta q^k+\beta^2 q^{2k}) = (\beta e^{2i\theta};q)_\infty(\beta e^{-2i\theta};q)_\infty$$

when $x = \cos\theta$, and $\beta = q^\lambda$ and (2.10) gives the required limit for the weight function.

In [7] there is an extension of (4.6) to include three more free parameters. This paper has two parts. One is the evaluation of an integral. The rest of the paper deals with some of what can be done with this integral. A special case of the general integral is

$$(4.7) \quad \frac{1}{2\pi}\int_{-1}^{1} \frac{h(x,1)h(x,-1)h(x,q^{1/2})h(x,-q^{1/2})dx}{h(x,a)h(x,b)h(x,c)h(x,d)(1-x^2)^{1/2}}$$

$$= \frac{(abcd;q)_\infty}{(q;q)_\infty(ab;q)_\infty(ac;q)_\infty(ad;q)_\infty(bc;q)_\infty(bd;q)_\infty(cd;q)_\infty}$$

when $-1 < a,b,c,d,q < 1$ and

$$h(x,a) = \prod_{n=0}^{\infty} (1-2axq^n + a^2q^{2n}) .$$

Recently Nassrallah and Rahman [25] found an extension of Euler's integral representation of the ${}_2F_1$ hypergeometric function that uses a q-beta integral of the type of (4.7) to replace the ordinary beta integral. Included in their integral is the following integral that was first isolated by Rahman [28].

$$(4.8)\quad \frac{1}{2\pi}\int_{-1}^{1} \frac{h(x,1)h(x,-1)h(x,q^{1/2})h(x,-q^{1/2})h(x,\prod_{i=1}^{5} a_i)dx}{\prod_{j=1}^{5} h(x,a_j) \qquad (1-x^2)^{1/2}}$$

$$= \frac{\prod_{i=1}^{5} (a_1a_2a_3a_4a_5a_i^{-1};q)_\infty}{(q;q)_\infty \prod_{1\le i<j\le 5} (a_ia_j;q)_\infty} .$$

This is a beautiful integral, and once one knows the value (or suspects what it is), it is easy to prove (4.8). Since no proofs have been given in this paper, the following proof will serve for the one that Halmos said should be included in every talk on mathematics. A similar proof was given for (4.7) in [4], but the present proof is even easier since the starting values for the induction are easier to obtain.

Let $L(a_1,a_2,\cdots,a_5)$ denote the left hand side of (4.7), $R(a_1,a_2,\cdots,a_5)$ denote the right hand side, and call $a_1 = a$, $a_2 = b$. Let $L = L(a,b)$ and $R = R(a,b)$ denote these functions as functions of a and b with the other parameters fixed. Finally, let

$$K(a,b) = \frac{h(x,abcde)}{h(x,a)h(x,b)} .$$

Then

$$(4.9)\qquad bK(aq,b) - aK(a,bq) = \frac{(b-a)(1-ab)h(x,abcdeq)}{h(x,a)h(x,b)}$$

and

$$(1+b^2)K(aq,b) - (1+a^2)K(a,bq) = \frac{2x(b-a)(1-ab)h(x,abcdeq)}{h(x,a)h(x,b)} . \tag{4.10}$$

These combine to give

$$\{[1+(abcde)^2]b - abcde(1+b^2)\}K(aq,b) - \{[1+(abcde)^2]a-abcde(1+a^2)\}K(a,bq) = (b-a)(1-ab)K(a,b). \tag{4.11}$$

Then $L(a,b)$ satisfies the same functional equation. To complete the proof of (4.7) it is sufficient to show that $R(a,b)$ satisfies the functional equation (4.11) and that $L(a,b)$ and $R(a,b)$ agree sufficiently often. A calculation shows that

$$\{[1+(abcde)^2]b - abcde(1+b^2)\}R(aq,b) - \{[1+(abcde)^2]a - abcde(1+a^2)\}R(a,bq) = (1-ab)R(a,b)V(a,b)$$

where

$$V(a,b) = \frac{\{[1+(abcde)^2]b-abcde(1+b^2)\}(1-ac)(1-ad)(1-ae)}{(1-abcd)(1-abce)(1-abde)(1-acde)} - \frac{\{[1+(abcde)^2]a-abcde(1+a^2)\}(1-bc)(1-bd)(1-be)}{(1-abcd)(1-abce)(1-abde)(1-bcde)}$$

$$= \frac{U(a,b)}{(1-abcd)(1-abce)(1-abde)(1-acde)(1-bcde)} .$$

To show that $V(a,b) = (b-a)$ it is sufficient to show that $U(a,b) = (1-abcd)(1-abce)(1-abde)(1-acde)(1-bcde)(b-a)$. $U(a,b)$ is a polynomial of degree 5 in a and $U(b,b) = 0$. A simple calculation shows that $U((bcd)^{-1},b) = 0$. Symmetry then gives $U((bce)^{-1},b) = U((bde)^{-1},b) = 0$. Finally $U((cde)^{-1},b) = 0$ since both terms in $U(a,b)$ vanish when $acde = 1$. To complete the proof that $V(a,b) = b-a$ observe that the constant term in $U(a,b)$ as a function of a is $b(1-bcde)$. Thus $U(a,b)$ has the same roots and same constant term as $(1-abcd)(1-abce)(1-abde)(1-acde)(1-bcde)(b-a)$ and both are polynomials of degree 5. Therefore they are identical. Then $R(a,b)$ satisfies (4.11). To show that $L(a,b) = R(a,b)$ it is now sufficient to show they agree sufficiently often. When $b = 1$, $c = q^{1/2}$, $d = -1$, $e = -q^{1/2}$,

$$L(a,1,q^{1/2},-1,-q^{1/2}) = \frac{1}{2\pi}\int_{-1}^{1} \frac{h(x,aq)dx}{h(x,a)\sqrt{1-x^2}}$$

$$= \frac{1}{2\pi}\int_{-1}^{1} \frac{dx}{(1-2ax+a^2)\sqrt{1-x^2}} = \frac{1}{2\pi}\int_{0}^{\pi} \frac{d\theta}{1-2a\cos\theta+a^2}$$

$$= \frac{1}{4\pi(1-a^2)}\int_{-\pi}^{\pi} \frac{1-a^2}{1-2a\cos\theta+a^2}\, d\theta$$

$$= \frac{1}{4\pi(1-a^2)}\int_{-\pi}^{\pi} [1+2\sum_{n=1}^{\infty} a^n\cos n\theta]d\theta = \frac{1}{2(1-a^2)} .$$

But

$$R(a,1,q^{1/2},-1,-q^{1/2}) = \frac{1}{2(1-a)(1+a)(q;q^2)_\infty^2(-q;q)_\infty^2}$$

$$= \frac{1}{2(1-a^2)} \frac{(q;q)_\infty^2}{(q;q^2)_\infty^2(q^2;q^2)_\infty^2} = \frac{1}{2(1-a^2)} .$$

Thus $L(a,1,q^{1/2},-1,-q^{1/2}) = R(a,1,q^{1/2},-1,-q^{1/2})$. The functional equation then gives equality for $(a,q^k,q^{1/2},-1,-q^{1/2})$, $k = 0,1,\ldots$. But both $R(a,b)$ and $L(a,b)$ are analytic functions of b, so $R(a,b) = L(a,b)$. The same argument shows that $L(a,b,c,d,e) = R(a,b,c,d,e)$ for $|a| < 1$, $|b| < 1$, $|c| < 1$, $|d| < 1$, $|e| < 1$.

I call the integrals (4.7) and (4.8) very well poised and call (4.8) balanced. To explain these names it will be necessary to recall some facts about hypergeometric and basic hypergeometric series. A series Σc_n is a hypergeometric series if c_{n+1}/c_n is a rational function of n. If

$$\frac{c_{n+1}}{c_n} = \frac{(n+a_1)\cdots(n+a_p)x}{(n+b_1)\cdots(n+b_q)(n+1)}$$

it is traditional to write

$$(4.12) \qquad {}_pF_q\left[\begin{matrix} a_1,\cdots,a_p \\ b_1,\cdots,b_q \end{matrix}; x\right] = \sum_{n=0}^{\infty} \frac{(a_1)_n\cdots(a_p)_n}{(b_1)_n\cdots(b_q)_n} \frac{x^n}{n!} .$$

The series (4.12) is said to be well poised if $p = q+1$, and $a_1+1 = a_2+b_1 = \cdots = a_{q+1}+b_q$. It is very well poised if it is well poised and $a_2 = b_1+1$. This series is said to be k-balanced if $p = q+1$, one of the numerator parameters is a negative integer, $x = 1$, and $\Sigma a_i + k = \Sigma b_i$ for some positive integer k. It is called balanced if $k = 1$. Dougall [10] summed the 2-balanced very well poised ${}_7F_6$.

$$(4.13)\quad {}_7F_6\left[\begin{matrix}a,\ (a/2)+1,\ b,\ c,\ d,\ e,\ -n\\ a/2,\ a+1-b,\ a+1-c,\ a+1-d,\ a+1-e,\ a+1+n\end{matrix};1\right]$$

$$= \frac{(a+1)_n(a+1-b-c)_n(a+1-b-d)_n(a+1-c-d)_n}{(a+1-b)_n(a+1-c)_n(a+1-d)_n(a+1-b-c-d)_n}$$

when $2a+1 = b+c+d+e-n$.

When $d \to \infty$, $e \to -\infty$ the sum (4.13) becomes

$$(4.14)\quad {}_5F_4\left[\begin{matrix}a,\ (a/2)+1,\ b,\ c,\ -n\\ a/2,\ a+1-b,\ a+1-c,\ a+1+n\end{matrix};a\right] = \frac{(a+1)_n(a+1-b-c)_n}{(a+1-b)_n(a+1-c)_n}.$$

This is the weight function for a set of orthogonal polynomials called the Racah polynomials. These polynomials have an absolutely continuous version, called the Wilson polynomials. The integral that is used in the orthogonality is

$$(4.15)\quad \int_{-\infty}^{\infty} \left| \frac{\Gamma(a+ix)\Gamma(b+ix)\Gamma(c+ix)\Gamma(d+ix)}{\Gamma(ix)\Gamma(\frac{1}{2}+ix)} \right|^2 dx$$

$$= \frac{\Gamma(a+b)\Gamma(a+c)\Gamma(a+d)\Gamma(b+c)\Gamma(b+d)\Gamma(c+d)}{\Gamma(a+b+c+d)}$$

when $a,b,c,d > 0$. See [42]. The series in (4.14) is very well poised so it is natural to call the integral very well poised. The characteristic property of a Mellin-Barnes integral that makes it well poised is the ability to pair the gamma functions so that the contour is a line that cuts the plane so the poles and the zeros of the appropriate gamma functions are symmetric with respect to this line. That is, if the line is taken to be the real axis, for each factor $\Gamma(a+ix)$ there is $\Gamma(a-ix)$ multiplying it. From Euler's reflection formula

$$\Gamma(a+ix)\Gamma(a-ix) = \frac{\Gamma(a+ix)}{\Gamma(1-a+ix)} f(x)$$

and the arguments of the gamma function add to give a number that is the same for each pair. That is the connection with the classical definition of well poised for hypergeometric series. The very well poised integral has the factors $\Gamma(ix)\Gamma(\frac{1}{2}+ix) = 2^{2ix}A\Gamma(2ix)$, and $[\Gamma(2ix)\Gamma(-2ix)]^{-1} = 2\pi x/\sinh 2\pi x$. The x plays the role of $(\frac{a}{2}+1)_n/(\frac{a}{2})_n = (2n+a)/a$ in the very well poised series. See Wilson [42] for the orthogonality with respect to the integrand in (4.15) and a more general contour integral that contains both (4.15) and (4.14) as a limiting case.

The basic hypergeometric extension of (4.13) was given by Jackson [22], and earlier Rogers [34, p. 29] not only had the basic extension of (4.14) but also the corresponding nonterminating series. Basic hypergeometric series are Σc_n with c_{n+1}/c_n a rational function of q^n. The q-polynomials that correspond to the Racah polynomials were treated in [6], and the absolutely continuous case was given in [7]. The appropriate contour for well poised basic Mellin-Barnes integrals is a circle with factors of the form $(ae^{i\theta};q)_\infty(ae^{-i\theta};q)_\infty$. The very part of very well poised comes from the four pairs of factors in the numerator of (4.7). These can be written as $(e^{2i\theta};q)_\infty(e^{-2i\theta};q)_\infty$ when $x = \cos\theta$.

The balanced condition on the integral comes from writing $h(x,a) = (ae^{i\theta};q)_\infty(ae^{-i\theta};q)_\infty$, $x = \cos\theta$, and observing that $1\cdot q^{1/2}\cdot(-1)\cdot(-q^{1/2}) = q$. At present I do not know enough to be able to define a balanced basic hypergeometric integral that is not well poised.

There are other q-extensions of Mellin-Barnes integrals. See Watson [40] for the first example, Askey and Roy [5] for a recent example, and Gasper and Rahman [12] for a detailed treatment of basic hypergeometric series and integrals. As far as we know Ramanujan did not consider basic hypergeometric extensions of Mellin-Barnes integrals, but he did consider some Mellin-Barnes integrals. For example, he showed [29] that

$$(4.16)\qquad \int_{-\infty}^{\infty} |\Gamma(a+ix)\Gamma(b+ix)|^2 dx = \frac{\Gamma(\frac{1}{2})\Gamma(a)\Gamma(a+\frac{1}{2})\Gamma(b)\Gamma(b+\frac{1}{2})\Gamma(a+b)}{\Gamma(a+b+\frac{1}{2})} .$$

Barnes [9] showed that

$$(4.17)\qquad \frac{1}{2\pi}\int_{-\infty}^{\infty} \Gamma(a+ix)\Gamma(b+ix)\Gamma(c-ix)\Gamma(d-ix)dx$$

$$= \frac{\Gamma(a+c)\Gamma(a+d)\Gamma(b+c)\Gamma(b+d)}{\Gamma(a+b+c+d)} , \quad a,b,c,d > 0 ,$$

so there were a few obvious integrals of the type that Ramanujan considered that he never wrote down. However it would be silly to claim that he had not considered them. Bailey [8] wrote the following about Ramanujan.

"Ramanujan remains in my memory as a strange squat figure making his way to lectures with slippers on his feet. He attended a course of lectures given by Professor Hardy, which I also attended, and I remember that when Hardy wanted the value of an infinite integral he turned to Ramanujan and asked him for the value, and Ramanujan immediately supplied him with the answer."

5. What next? We have finally found all the classical orthogonal polynomials in one variable. This is a strong statement, and I hope it is wrong, but it seems very likely to be true. However there is still a lot to do. We need to understand and use the polynomials we have. Much more work will be done here. See Stanton [35] and Nikiforov, Suslov and Uvarov [26] for two recent surveys of some of these polynomials. We need to find the corresponding multidimensional polynomials, hypergeometric functions, and use them. Here the work has just started. See papers by Aomoto, Kadell and Milne in this book, and the recent continuing series of papers by Gel'fand and coworkers [13], [14], [15], [16]. Also see Gustafson [17]. There will be many multivariate extensions, and each will probably only contain part of the one variable results.

In any case I hope I have convinced the reader of two things. First, these integrals are more than "curious". They are natural extensions of some very important integrals, and will in the long run be useful. Second, when Hardy wrote that it was a shame that Ramanujan had not lived one hundred years earlier, he was thinking about the mathematics that had been developed up to his time and tried to place Ramanujan where he would have had the largest impact. I would rather have had Ramanujan born seventy-five years later. Try to imagine what someone with Ramanujan's ability could do now with the computer algebra systems that exist and the problems we have in several variables, where we need more explicit results to try to understand what is really happening. I write seventy-five because I am selfish, and would like to have a twenty-five year old Ramanujan to help me now. However I suspect he would be even more useful in twenty-five years, so all that was wrong with Hardy's statement was a minus sign.

REFERENCES

[1] G. E. Andrews, q-Series: Their Development and Application in Analysis, Number Theory, Combinatorics, Physics, and Computer Algebra. Regional Conference Series in Mathematics, 66, Amer. Math. Soc., Providence, RI, 1986.

[2] R. Askey, Ramanujan's extensions of the gamma and beta functions, Amer. Math. Monthly 87 (1980), 346-359.

[3] R. Askey, Two integrals of Ramanujan, Proc. Amer. Math. Soc. 85 (1982), 192-194.

[4] R. Askey, An elementary evaluation of a beta type integral, Indian J. Pure Appl. Math. 14 (1983), 892-895.

[5] R. Askey and R. Roy, More q-beta integrals, Rocky Mountain J. Math. 16 (1986), 365-372.

[6] R. Askey and J. Wilson, A set of orthogonal polynomials that generalize the Racah coefficients or 6-j symbols, SIAM J. Math. Anal. 10 (1979), 1008-1016.

[7] R. Askey and J. Wilson, Some basic hypergeometric orthogonal polynomials that generalize Jacobi polynomials, Memoirs Amer. Math. Soc. (1985), #319, 55pp.

[8] W. N. Bailey, Extracts from Inaugural Lecture on Ramanujan, at Bedford College, unpublished.

[9] E. W. Barnes, A new development of the theory of hypergeometric functions, Proc. London Math. Soc. (2) 6 (1908), 141-177.

[10] J. Dougall, On Vandermonde's theorm and more general expansions, Proc. Edinburgh Math. Soc. 25 (1907), 114-132.

[11] E. Feldheim, Sur les polynomes généralisés de Legendre, Izv. Akad. Nauk. SSSR, Ser. Math. 5 (1941), 241-248, Russian translation, ibid. 248-254.

[12] G. Gasper and M. Rahman, Basic Hypergeometric Series, Cambridge Univ. Press, to appear.

[13] I. M. Gel'fand, General theory of hypergeometric functions, Dokl. Akad. Nauk SSSR, 288 (1986), no. 1, 14-18, translation in Soviet Math. Doklady 33 (1986), no. 3, 573-577.

[14] I. M. Gel'fand and S. I. Gel'fand, Generalized hypergeometric equations, Dokl. Akad. Nauk SSSR, 288 (1986), no. 2, 279-282, translation in Soviet Math. Doklady 33 (1986), no. 3, 643-646.

[15] I. M. Gel'fand and M. I. Graev, A duality theorem for general hypergeometric functions, Dokl. Akad. Nauk. SSSR 289 (1986), no. 1, translation in Soviet Math. Dokl. 34 (1987), no. 1, 9-13.

[16] I. M. Gel'fand and A. V. Zelevinskii, Algebraic and combinatorial aspects of the general theory of hypergeometric functions, Functional Analysis and Its Applications, 20, no. 3 (1986), 17-34, translation, 20, no. 3 (1986), 183-197.

[17] R. Gustafson, A Whipple's transformation for hypergeometric series in U(n) and multivariable hypergeometric orthogonal polynomials, SIAM J. Math. Anal. 18 (1987), 495-530.

[18] W. Hahn, Über Orthogonalpolynome, die q-Differenzengleichungen genügen, Math. Nach. 2 (1949), 263-278.

[19] G. H. Hardy, Proof of a formula of Mr. Ramanujan, Messenger Math. 44 (1915), 18-21, Reprinted in Collected Papers, vol. 5, 594-597.

[20] G. H. Hardy, Ramanujan, Cambridge Univ. Press, 1940, reprinted Chelsea, New York, 1959.

[21] F. H. Jackson, On q-definite integrals, Quart. J. Pure Appl. Math. 41 (1910), 193-203.

[22] F. H. Jackson, Summation of q-hypergeometric series, Messenger Math. 50 (1921), 101-112.

[23] I. L. Lanzewizky, Über die Orthogonalität der Fejér-Szegöschen Polynome, C. R. (Dokl.) Acad. Sci. URSS, 31 (1941), 199-200.

[24] D. S. Moak, The q-analogue of the Laguerre polynomials, J. Math. Anal. Appl. 81 (1981), 20-47.

[25] B. Nassrallah and M. Rahman, Projection formulas, a reproducing kernel and a generating function for q-Wilson polynomials, SIAM J. Math. Anal. 16 (1985), 186-196.

[26] A. F. Nikiforov, S. K. Suslov and V. B. Uvarov, Classical Orthogonal Polynomials of a Discrete Variable, Nauka, Moscow, 1985 (in Russian).

[27] P. I. Pastro, Orthogonal polynomials and some q-beta integrals of Ramanujan, J. Math. Anal. Appl. 112 (1985), 517-540.

[28] M. Rahman, An integral representation of a ${}_{10}\varphi_9$ and continuous biorthogonal ${}_{10}\varphi_9$ rational functions, Canadian J. Math. 38 (1986), 605-618.

[29] S. Ramanujan, Some definite integrals, Messenger Math. 44 (1915), 10-18.

[30] S. Ramanujan, Notebook, vol. I, Tata Inst. Fundamental Research, Bombay, 1957.

[31] S. Ramanujan, Notebook, vol. II, Tata Inst. Fundamental Research, Bombay, 1957.

[32] S. Ramanujan, unpublished material in library, Trinity College, Cambridge.

[33] L. J. Rogers, Second memoir on the expansion of certain infinite products, Proc. London Math. Soc. 25 (1894), 318-343.

[34] L. J. Rogers, Third memoir on the expansion of certain infinite products, Proc. London Math. Soc. 26 (1895), 15-32.

[35] D. Stanton, Orthogonal polynomials and Chevalley groups, in Special Functions: Group Theoretical Aspects and Applications, ed. R. Askey, T. H. Koornwinder and W. Schempp, Reidel, Dordrecht, 1984, 87-128.

[36] T. J. Stieltjes, Recherches sur les fractions continues, Annales de la Faculté des Sciences de Toulouse, 8 (1894) 122 pp., 9 (1895), 47 pp. Reprinted in Oeuvres Complètes, vol. 2, 402-566.

[37] G. Szegö, Ein Beitrag zur Theorie der Thetafunktionen, Sitz. Preuss. Akad. Wiss. Phys. Math. Kl. XIX (1926), 242-252, reprinted in Collected Papers, Vol. 1, Birkhäuser-Boston, 1982, 795-803.

[38] G. Szegö, An outline of the history of orthogonal polynomials, Proc. Conf. Orthogonal Expansions and Their Continuous Analogues, ed. D. Haimo, Southern Illinois Univ. Press, Carbondale, 1968, 3-11. Reprinted in Collected Papers, vol. 3, Birkhäuser-Boston, 1982, 857-865. Comments follow the reprinted version, 866-869.

[39] J. Thomae, Beiträge zur Theorie der durch die Heinesche Reihe; $1 + ((1-q^{\alpha})(1-q^{\beta})/(1-q)(1-q^{\gamma}))x + \ldots$ darstellbaren Functionen, J. reine angew. Math. 70 (1869), 258-281.

[40] G. N. Watson, The continuations of functions defined by generalized hypergeometric series, Trans. Cambridge Phil. Soc. 21 (1910), 281-299.

[41] S. Wigert, Contributions à la théorie des polynomes d'Abel-Laguerre, Ark. Mat. Astronom. Fsy. 15 (24) (1921).

[42] J. A. Wilson, Some hypergeometric orthogonal polynomials, SIAM J. Math. Anal. 11 (1980), 690-701.

University of Wisconsin
Madison, WI 53706

Supported in part by NSF grant DMS-8701439

CORRELATION FUNCTIONS OF THE SELBERG INTEGRAL

K. Aomoto

ABSTRACT. Structures of correlation functions of the Selberg density are investigated. Some results about difference structure and asymptotic behaviour of them with respect to the dimension n are obtained by using a new integral representation.

1. Recurrence formula for moments.

Let $D = D_{\lambda_1,\lambda_2,\lambda}$ be the Selberg density

$$\Pi_{j=1}^{n} x_j^{\lambda_1}(1-x_j)^{\lambda_2} \prod_{1\le j<k\le n} |x_j-x_k|^{\lambda} \qquad \text{for } \lambda_1,\lambda_2,\lambda>0.$$

Given an arbitrary polynomial $\varphi(x_1,\ldots,x_n)$, we denote by $<\varphi(x_1,\ldots,x_n)>$ the correlation function

$$(1.1) \qquad \int_{(0,1)^n} \varphi(x_1,\ldots,x_n)\, D_{\lambda_1,\lambda_2,\lambda}(x_1,\ldots,x_n)\, dx_1\wedge\ldots\wedge dx_n.$$

In particular for each μ $(n\ge\mu\ge0)$ and each sequence of non-negative integers $k_1,\ldots,k_\mu$ such that $k_1\ge\cdots\ge k_\mu\ge0$ we consider the monomial $<k_1,\ldots,k_\mu> = (x_1\cdots x_{k_\mu})^{\mu}$ $(x_{k_\mu+1}\cdots x_{k_{\mu-1}})^{\mu-1}\cdots(x_{k_2+1}\cdots x_{k_1})$ and denote by $<<k_1,\ldots,k_\mu>>$ the correlation function (moment) $<\varphi>$ for $\varphi=<k_1,\ldots,k_\mu>$. When $\mu=0$, $<<k_1,\ldots,k_\mu>>$ reduces to the original

ISBN 0-12-058560-X

Selberg integral denoted by $\langle\langle\phi\rangle\rangle$. It is convenient to let k_0 be n.

<u>Definition</u> 1. We denote by $\Delta_\nu^\pm$ the two operations of displacement defined by : $\langle\langle k_1,\dots,k_\nu,\dots,k_n\rangle\rangle \to \langle\langle k_1,\dots,k_\nu\pm 1, k_{\nu+1},\dots,k_n\rangle\rangle$ respectively. They are well defined if $k_{\nu-1}>k_\nu$ and $k_\nu>k_{\nu+1}$ respectively.

Also we define $\langle\langle k_1,\dots,k_{\mu-1},0\rangle\rangle=\langle\langle k_1,\dots,k_{\mu-1}\rangle\rangle$.

We start from proving the following formula.

Proposition 1. <u>The multi sequence</u> $\{\langle\langle k_1,\dots,k_n\rangle\rangle\}$ <u>satisfies the following recurrence relation</u> :

(1.2) $$0 = A_0 + A_1 + \cdots + A_\mu$$

<u>where</u> A_ν <u>is given by</u>

(1.3) $$A_0 = \{\lambda_1+\lambda_2+\mu+1+\lambda(-\frac{k_\mu+1}{2}+n)\}\langle\langle k_1,\dots,k_\mu\rangle\rangle,$$

$$A_1 = -\{\lambda_1+\mu+\lambda(-\frac{k_{\mu-1}+k_\mu}{2}+n)\}\ \Delta_\mu^-\ \langle\langle k_1,\dots,k_\mu\rangle\rangle$$

and

(1.4) $$A_{2\rho}= \frac{\lambda}{2}(k_{\mu-2\rho}-k_{\mu-2\rho+1})\{\ \Sigma_{j=\mu-2\rho+1}^{\mu-1}\ \Delta_{\mu-2\rho+1}^+\cdots\Delta_j^+\cdot \Delta_{2\mu-2\rho-j+1}^-\cdots\Delta_\mu^- \ -\ \Sigma_{j=\mu-2\rho+1}^{\mu-2}\ \Delta_{\mu-2\rho+1}^+\cdots\Delta_j^+\cdot \Delta_{2\mu-2\rho-j}^-\cdots\Delta_\mu^-\ \}\ \langle\langle k_1,\dots,k_\mu\rangle\rangle,$$

$$A_{2\rho+1}= \frac{\lambda}{2}\ (k_{\mu-2\rho-1}-k_{\mu-2\rho})\{\ \Sigma_{j=\mu-2\rho}^{\mu-1}\ \Delta_{\mu-2\rho}^+\cdots\Delta_j^+\cdot$$

$$\Delta^-_{2\mu-2\rho-j}\cdots\Delta^-_\mu - \Sigma^{\mu-2}_{j=\mu-2\rho}\Delta^+_{\mu-2\rho}\cdots\Delta^+_j\cdot\Delta^-_{2\mu-2\rho-j-1}\cdots\Delta^-_\mu\}$$

$$<<k_1,\ldots,k_\mu>>.$$

We note that each A_ν is well-defined. A_2 and A_3 are equal to $\frac{\lambda}{2}(k_{\mu-2}-k_{\mu-1})\Delta^+_{\mu-1}\Delta^-_{\mu-2}<<k_1,\ldots,k_\mu>>$ and

$\frac{\lambda}{2}(k_{\mu-3}-k_{\mu-2})(\Delta^+_{\mu-2}\Delta^-_\mu - \frac{1}{2}\Delta^+_{\mu-2}\Delta^-_{\mu-1}\Delta^-_\mu)<<k_1,\ldots,k_\mu>>$

respectively . Thus $<<k_1,\ldots,k_\nu>>$ can be computed from $<<\phi>>$ in an inductive way as follows :

$$<<\phi>> \to <<k_1>> \to \cdots \to <<k_1,\ldots,k_{\mu-1}>> \to <<k_1,\ldots,k_\mu>>.$$

When $\mu=1,2,3$, then (1.2) becomes

$$(1.5)\qquad 0 = \{\lambda_1+\lambda_2+2+\lambda(n-\frac{k_1+1}{2})\}<<k_1>> - $$
$$- \{\lambda_1+1+\frac{\lambda}{2}(n-k_1)\}<<k_1-1>>.$$

$$(1.6)\qquad 0 = (\{\lambda_1+\lambda_2+3+\lambda(n-\frac{k_1+1}{2})\} +$$
$$\frac{\lambda}{2}(n-k_1)\Delta^+_1\Delta^-_2 - \{2+\lambda_1+\lambda(n-\frac{k_1+k_2}{2})\}\Delta^-_2)<<k_1,k_2>>$$

respectively. Before proving Prop 1 we need two lemmas. For an $(n-1)$-form ψ, we denote by $\nabla\psi$ the n-form defined by the covariant differentiation : $d(D\psi)=D\nabla\psi$, i.e. $\nabla\psi = d\psi + d\log D\wedge\psi$. Then by Stokes formula we have obviously

Lemma 1.1. $<\nabla\psi> = 0$.

Lemma 1.2. <u>For an arbitrary polynomial</u> u <u>in</u> $x_1,\ldots,x_n$ <u>which is symmetric in</u> x_i, x_j

$$(1.7)\qquad \left\langle \frac{x_i^{2\rho}\cdot u}{(i,j)} \right\rangle = \sum_{\sigma=0}^{\rho-1} \langle x_i^{2\rho-\sigma-1} x_j^{\sigma} \cdot u\rangle ,$$

$$\left\langle \frac{x_i^{2\rho+1}\cdot u}{(i,j)} \right\rangle = \sum_{\sigma=0}^{\rho-1} \langle x_i^{2\rho-\sigma} x_j^{\sigma} \cdot u\rangle + \frac{1}{2} \langle x_i^{\rho} x_j^{\rho} \cdot u\rangle.$$

<u>where</u> (i,j) <u>denotes</u> $x_i - x_j$.

<u>Proof</u>. These two equalities follow from nullity of the integral $\left\langle \frac{v}{(i,j)} \right\rangle$ for an arbitrary polynomial v which is symmetric in x_i and x_j.

<u>Proof of Proposition</u> 1. We put

$$(1.8)\qquad \psi = (x_1 - 1) \langle k_1, \ldots, k_\mu\rangle\, dx_2 \wedge \cdots \wedge dx_n$$

and apply Lemma 1.1. By the Leibniz formula

$$(1.9)\qquad 0 = \langle \nabla\psi\rangle = (\mu+\lambda_1)\left\langle \frac{x_1-1}{x_1} \langle k_1, \ldots, k_\mu\rangle\right\rangle +$$

$$+ (\lambda_2+1)\langle\langle k_1, \ldots, k_\mu\rangle\rangle +$$

$$\sum_{j=2}^{n} \lambda \left\langle \frac{(x_1-1)}{(1,j)} \cdot \langle k_1, \ldots, k_\mu\rangle\right\rangle.$$

The first term in the right hand side equals $\langle\langle k_1, \ldots, k_\mu\rangle\rangle - \langle\langle k_1, \ldots, k_\mu - 1\rangle\rangle$. Suppose $1+k_\sigma \le j \le k_\sigma$. Then

$$(1.10)\qquad \left\langle \frac{(x_1-1)}{(1,j)} \cdot \langle k_1, \ldots, k_\mu\rangle\right\rangle = \left\langle \frac{(x_1-1)}{(1,j)}\, x_1^{\mu}\, x_j^{\sigma} \cdot f\right\rangle$$

$$= \left\langle \frac{(x_1-1)}{(1,j)} \cdot x_i^{\mu-\sigma} (x_1 x_j)^{\sigma} \cdot f\right\rangle$$

where f is independent of x_1 and x_j. The last one equals

$$(1.11)\qquad \left\langle \frac{x_1^{\mu-\sigma+1}}{(1,j)} (x_1 x_j)^{\sigma} \cdot f\right\rangle - \left\langle \frac{x_1^{\mu-\sigma}}{(1,j)} (x_1 x_j)^{\sigma} \cdot f\right\rangle$$

which is, from Lemma 1.2, equal to

$$(1.12)\qquad \Sigma_{\sigma'=0}^{\rho} <x_1^{2\rho+\sigma+1-\sigma'} x_j^{\sigma+\sigma'}\cdot f> - \Sigma_{\sigma'=0}^{\rho-1} <x_1^{2\rho+\sigma-\sigma'} x_j^{\sigma+\sigma'}\cdot f> - \frac{1}{2} <x_1^{\rho+\sigma} x_j^{\sigma+\rho}\cdot f>$$

or

$$(1.13)\qquad \Sigma_{\sigma'=0}^{\rho-1} <x_1^{2\rho+\sigma-\sigma'} x_j^{\sigma+\sigma'}\cdot f> + \frac{1}{2} <x_1^{\rho+\sigma} x_j^{\rho+\sigma}\cdot f> - - \Sigma_{\sigma'=0}^{\rho-1} <x_1^{2p+\sigma-1-\sigma'} x_j^{\sigma+\sigma'}\cdot f>$$

according as $\sigma = \mu-2\rho-1$ or $\sigma=\mu-2\rho$. Hence one obtains

$$(1.14)\qquad \Sigma_{j=1+k_\mu}^{k_{\mu-1}} \lambda <\frac{x_1-1}{(1,j)} <k_1,\dots,k_\mu>> = (1 - \frac{1}{2}\Delta_\mu^-)<<k_1,\dots,k_\mu>>,$$

and

$$(1.15)\qquad \Sigma_{\sigma=k_{\sigma-1}+1}^{k_\sigma} <\frac{x_1-1}{(1,j)} <k_1,\dots,k_\mu>> = = (1 - \Delta_\mu^-)<<k_1,\dots,k_\mu>> + A_{\mu-\sigma}$$

for $0\le\sigma\le\mu-2$. Proposition 1 thus follows.

The moment functions $<<k_1,\dots,k_\mu>>$ can be extended for all $(k_1,\dots,k_\mu)$, $k_\mu\ge 0$ such that (1,2) and the relation $<<k_1,\dots,k_{\mu-1},0>> = <<k_1,\dots,k_{\mu-1}>>$ hold. These are no more represented by (1.1) unless $k_1\ge \cdots \ge k_\mu$.

2. Integral representation for generating functions.

Defintion 2. We fix $\mu\ge 0$. The generating function for the multi sequence $\{<<k_1,\dots,k_\mu>>\}$ is defined as follows :

(2.1) $$G_\mu(\xi_1,\dots,\xi_\mu) = = \Sigma_{k_1\geq \dots \geq k_\mu \geq 0} \langle\langle k_1,\dots,k_\mu\rangle\rangle\ \xi_1^{k_1}\cdots\ \xi_\mu^{k_\mu}.$$

Then G_μ is holomorphic at $\xi_\mu = 0$ and

(2.2) $$G_\mu(\xi_1,\dots,\xi_{\mu-1},0) = G_{\mu-1}(\xi_1,\dots,\xi_{\mu-1}).$$

G_0 is equal to a constant which reduces to $\langle\langle\phi\rangle\rangle$. (See (S) and (A2)). The following is a rephrase of Prop 1.

Proposition 2. <u>The sequence</u> $\{G_\mu\}$ <u>satisfies a recurrent system of linear partial differential equations</u> :

(2.3) $$B_0 G_\mu + \Sigma_{j=1}^{\mu} B_j \frac{\partial G_\mu}{\partial \xi_\mu} = G_{\mu-1}\ (B_0)_{\xi_\mu=0}\quad ,\ \mu\geq 1,$$

<u>where</u> $B_0, B_1, \dots, B_\mu$ <u>are defined as</u>

(2.4) $$B_0 = \lambda_1+\lambda_2+\mu+1+\lambda(n-\tfrac{1}{2}) - \{\lambda_1+\mu+\lambda(n-\tfrac{1}{2})\}\,\xi_\mu + $$
$$+ \lambda\ \Sigma_{\sigma=1}^{\mu-2}\ \xi_{\mu-\sigma}\xi_\mu\ H_{\mu-\sigma} + (n+1)\lambda\xi_1^{-1}\xi_\mu H_1,$$
$$B_{\mu-2\rho} = \lambda(-H_{\mu-2\rho} + \xi_{\mu-2\rho}\xi_{\mu-2\rho+1}^{-1}H_{\mu-2\rho+1})\,\xi_\mu,$$
$$B_{\mu-2\rho-1} = \lambda(-H_{\mu-2\rho-1} + \xi_{\mu-2\rho-1}\xi_{\mu-2\rho}^{-1}H_{\mu-2\rho})\,\xi_\mu,$$

<u>and</u> $$(B_0)_{\xi_\mu=0} = \lambda_1 + \lambda_2 + \mu + 1 + (n - \tfrac{1}{2})\lambda.$$

$H_{\mu-2\rho}$ <u>and</u> $H_{\mu-2\rho-1}$ <u>denote the following</u> :

(2.5) $$z_{\mu-2\rho+1}H_{\mu-2\rho} = \tfrac{1}{2}\ \Sigma_{j=\mu-2\rho+1}^{\mu}\ z_j\ z_{2\mu-2\rho-j+1} - $$
$$- \tfrac{1}{2}\ \Sigma_{j=\mu-2\rho+1}^{\mu-1}\ z_j\ z_{2\mu-2\rho-j},$$
$$z_{\mu-2\rho}H_{\mu-2\rho-1} = \tfrac{1}{2}\ \Sigma_{j=\mu-2\rho}^{\mu}\ z_j\ z_{2\mu-2\rho-j}$$

$$- \frac{1}{2} \Sigma_{j=\mu-2\rho}^{\mu-1} z_j \, z_{2\mu-2\rho-j-1}$$

<u>for</u> $z_{\mu-\sigma} = \xi_{\mu-\sigma} \cdots \xi_{\mu-1}$ <u>and</u> $z_\mu = 1$. <u>For example</u>,

(2.6) $$B_\mu = \frac{\lambda}{2} \xi_\mu (\xi_\mu - 1), \quad B_{\mu-1} = \frac{\lambda}{2} \xi_\mu (\xi_{\mu-1} - 1),$$

$$B_{\mu-2} = \lambda \xi_\mu \left(\frac{1}{2} \xi_{\mu-2} \xi_{\mu-1}^{-1} - 1 + \frac{1}{2} \xi_{\mu-1} \right),$$

$$B_{\mu-3} = \lambda \xi_\mu \left(\xi_{\mu-3} \xi_{\mu-2}^{-1} - \frac{1}{2} \xi_{\mu-3} \xi_{\mu-2}^{-1} \xi_{\mu-1} - \right.$$

$$\left. - \frac{1}{2} \xi_{\mu-2}^{-1} \xi_{\mu-1} + \xi_{\mu-1} \right).$$

<u>Definition</u> 3. The characteristic vector field $\mathfrak{X}_\mu$ of (2.3) is defined by the following vector field :

(2.7) $$d\xi_1 : \cdots : d\xi_\mu = B_1 : \cdots : B_\mu.$$

It is important to remark that $\mathfrak{X}_\mu$ does not depend on any of $\lambda_1, \lambda_2, \lambda$.

Lemma 2.1. $\mathfrak{X}_\mu$ <u>is equivalent to the following ordinary differential equations</u> :

(2.8) $$\frac{d\xi_\mu}{ds} = \frac{\xi_\mu - 1}{s},$$

$$\frac{dz_{\mu-\sigma}}{ds} = - 2 \frac{z_{\mu-\sigma+1}}{s} H_{\mu-\sigma} + \frac{z_{\mu-\sigma}}{s}$$

for $\sigma = 2, 3, 4, \ldots$. where s denotes $z_{\mu-1} - 1$.

These equations can be solved inductively and in an elementary way. But a complete expression seems hard to write down. The general expressions for $\xi_\mu, z_{\mu-1}, z_{\mu-2}, z_{\mu-3}$ are as follows :

(2.9) $$\xi_\mu = 1 + C_1 s, \quad z_{\mu-1} = 1 + s,$$

$$z_{\mu-2} = 1 + s + s^2 + C_2 s,$$

$$z_{\mu-3} = 1 + s + s^2 + s^3 + 2C_2 s^2 + C_3 s,$$

where C_1, C_2, C_3 are arbitrary constants.

In general one can prove

Lemma 2.2. $z_{\mu-\sigma}$, $\sigma = 1, 2, 3, \ldots$ <u>is a polynomial in</u> s <u>of degree</u> σ.

We denote by

(2.10) $$\xi_j = \xi_j(\xi_{\mu-1}, C_2, \ldots, C_{\mu-1}), \quad 0 \le j \le \mu-2, \text{ and}$$

$$\xi_\mu = 1 + C_1(\xi_{\mu-1} - 1)$$

a general trajectory of $\mathfrak{X}_\mu$ depending on arbitrary constants $C_1, C_2, \ldots, C_{\mu-1}$. Then

(2.11) $$\xi'_j = \xi_j(\xi'_{\mu-1}, C_2, \ldots, C_{\mu-j}), \quad 1 \le j \le \mu-2 \quad \text{and}$$

$$\xi'_\mu = 1 + C_1(\xi'_{\mu-1} - 1)$$

is the trajectory of (2.7) passing through $(\xi_1, \ldots, \xi_\mu)$ at $\xi'_{\mu-1} = \xi_{\mu-1}$.

By the standard Jacobi method, one can solve (2.3). The result is represented by the integral along trajectories of the vector field $\mathfrak{X}_\mu$:

(2.12) $$G_\mu(\xi_1, \ldots, \xi_\mu) = \xi_1^{n+1} \xi_2^{n+2} \cdots \xi_{\mu-1}^{n+\mu-1} \; \xi_\mu^{\kappa_{\mu,0}}$$

$$(\xi_{\mu-1} - 1)^{\kappa_{\mu,1}} \cdot \kappa_{\mu,0} \int_0^{\xi_\mu} d\xi'_\mu$$

$$\xi_1'^{\,-n-1} \xi_2'^{\,-n-2} \cdots \xi_{\mu-1}'^{\,-n-\mu+1} \; \xi_\mu'^{\,-\kappa_{\mu,0}} \; (\xi'_\mu - 1)^{-\kappa_{\mu,1}}$$

$$\frac{G_{\mu-1}(\xi'_1,\ldots,\xi'_{\mu-1})}{\xi'_\mu(\xi'_\mu-1)} .$$

where $\kappa_{\mu,0}$ and $\kappa_{\mu,1}$ denote $\frac{2}{\lambda}(\lambda_1+\lambda_2+\mu+1)+2n-1$ and $-\frac{2}{\lambda}(\lambda_2+1)-\mu-n+1$ respectively. The path of integration is fixed as $|\xi'_\mu|\le|\xi_\mu|$ and $\xi'_\mu/\xi_\mu \ge 0$.

The integral has a well defined meaning if $\kappa_{\mu,0}< 1$ and $|\xi_\mu|$ is small. If $\kappa_{\mu,0} \ge 1$, it must be taken "finite part" i.e. a regularization at the origin (See [A2] for a construction).

The successive application of (2.12) to G_μ , $G_{\mu-1}, G_{\mu-2},\ldots$ shows the following

Proposition 3. <u>The quotient</u>

(2.13) $$\tau^*_\mu(n) = G_\mu(\xi_1,\ldots,\xi_\mu)/\langle\langle\phi\rangle\rangle$$

<u>has an integral representation</u> :

(2.14) $$\int_{\mathbb{C}_0} L_0(\xi^*_1,\ldots,\xi^*_\mu)^n\, M_0(\xi^*_1,\ldots,\xi^*_\mu)\; d\xi^*_1\wedge\cdots\wedge d\xi^*_\mu$$

with $\xi^*_j = \xi_j^{(\mu+1-j)}$ $(\xi^*_\mu = \xi'_\mu)$ <u>where</u> $\mathbb{C}_0$ <u>denotes the cycle defined by</u>

(2.15) $$|\xi_\mu|\ge|\xi_\mu^{(1)}|,\ |\xi_{\mu-1}^{(1)}|\ge|\xi_{\mu-1}^{(2)}|,\ \ldots,\ |\xi_1^{(\mu-1)}|\ge|\xi_1^{(\mu)}|$$

and $$\xi_\mu^{(1)}/\xi_\mu \ge 0,\ \xi_{\mu-1}^{(2)}/\xi_{\mu-1}^{(1)} \ge 0,\ldots,\ \xi_1^{(\mu)}/\xi_1^{(\mu-1)}\ge 0 ,$$

<u>or its regularization</u>. L_0 <u>and</u> M_0 <u>are determined inductively through the formula</u> (2.12). L_0 <u>does not depend on</u> $\lambda_1,\lambda_2,\lambda$.

$(\xi_1^{(\sigma+1)},\dots,\xi_{\mu-\sigma}^{(\sigma+1)})$ _are related to_ $(\xi_1^{(\sigma)},\dots,\xi_{\mu-\sigma}^{(\sigma)})$ _as in_ (2.11) , _replaced by_ $\xi_j^{(\sigma)}$, $\xi_j^{(\sigma+1)}$ _in place of_ ξ_j _and_ ξ'_j _respectively_.

Corollary. _For_ $\mu = 1,2$, (2.12) _may be simplified as follows_ :

(2.16) $$G_1(\xi_1)/\langle\langle\phi\rangle\rangle = \xi^{\kappa_{1,0}}(\xi_1-1)^{\kappa_{1,1}}\kappa_{1,0}$$

$$\int_0^{\xi_1}\xi_1'^{-\kappa_{1,0}-1}\cdot(\xi_1'-1)^{-\kappa_{1,1}-1}d\xi_1',$$

(2.17) $$G_2(\xi_1,\xi_2)=\xi_1^{n+1}\ \xi_2^{\kappa_{2,0}}(\xi_2-1)^{\kappa_{2,1}}$$

$$\kappa_{2,0}\int_0^{\xi_2}\xi_1'^{-n-1}\xi_2'^{-\kappa_{2,0}-1}(\xi_2'-1)^{-\kappa_{2,1}-1}G_1(\xi_1')\,d\xi_2'.$$

3. Asymptotic behaviour of correlation functions.

Definition 4. The μ-point correlation function $F_{n,\mu}(t_1,\dots,t_\mu)$ is ,by definition, equal to the polynomial of $t_1,\dots,t_\mu$, $\langle\Pi_{k=1}^{\mu}\Pi_{j=1}^{n}(x_j-t_k)\rangle$.

The following is an immediate consequence of Cauchy formula.

Lemma 3.1. $F_{n,\mu}$ _has a_ μ-_dimensional integral representation using_ G_μ :

(3.1) $$F_{n,\mu}=\left(\frac{1}{2\pi i}\right)^{\mu}\int_{\Delta_\epsilon}\left(\Sigma_{j=0}^{\mu}x_{\mu-j}\ \xi_1^{-1}\cdots\xi_j^{-1}\right)^n\cdot$$

$$\frac{G_\mu(\xi_1,\dots,\xi_\mu)}{\xi_1\cdots\xi_\mu}d\xi_1\wedge\cdots\wedge d\xi_\mu,$$

where Δ_ε _denotes the cycle_ $|\xi_1| = \cdots = |\xi_\mu| = \varepsilon$ _in_ $\mathbf{C}^n$ _for_ a small positive number ε.

We denote by $\tau_\mu(n)$ the quotient $F_{n,\mu}/\langle\langle\phi\rangle\rangle$. Then

Proposition 4.

$$\tau_\mu(n) = \left(\frac{1}{2\pi i}\right)^\mu \int_{\Delta_\varepsilon\times\mathbb{C}_0} L(\xi_1,\dots,\xi_\mu;\xi_1^*,\dots,\xi_\mu^*)^n \cdot M(\xi_1,\dots,\xi_\mu;\xi_1^*,\dots,\xi_\mu^*)\, d\xi_1\wedge\cdots\wedge d\xi_\mu\wedge d\xi_1^*\wedge\cdots\wedge d\xi_\mu^*, \tag{3.2}$$

where $L = (\sum_{j=0}^{\mu} x_{\mu-j}\, \xi_1^{-1}\cdots\xi_j^{-1})\, L_0$, and $M = (\xi_1\cdots\xi_\mu)^{-1} M_0$. L is independent of $\lambda_1, \lambda_2, \lambda$.

From a result about linear difference equations in (A1), one can conclude that

Corollary. $\tau_\mu(n)$ satisfies a certain linear difference equation in n over coefficients of polynomials. In other words there exists ℓ polynomials $a_j(n)$ in n, $1\le j\le\ell$, such that

$$\sum_{n=0}^{\ell} a_j(n)\,\tau_\mu(n+j) = 0. \tag{3.3}$$

From (2.14) and (3.2) one can make conjectures about asymptotic behaviours for $n\to\infty$ of $\tau_\mu^*(n)$ and $\tau_\mu(n)$ which we want to state below :

Conjecture I.

$$\tau_\mu^*(n) = n^{\frac{\mu}{2}}\, V_0\, U_0^n\, \{1 + O(\tfrac{1}{n})\}, \tag{3.4}$$

provided $(\xi_1,\dots,\xi_\mu)$ lies in a neighbourhood of the real set

$1\le\xi_\mu\le\cdots\le\xi_1$ _and_ $\xi_i\ne\xi_j$ _for_ $i\ne j$, _where_ U_0 _denotes a function of the type_ $\Pi_j^\mu\ \xi_j^{\alpha_j}(\xi_j-1)^{\beta_j}\cdot\Pi_{1\le j<k\le\mu}(\xi_j-\xi_k)^{\gamma_{j,k}}$ _for constants_ $\alpha_j, \beta_j, \gamma_{j,k}$ _independent of_ $\lambda_1, \lambda_2, \lambda$.

In the same manner

Conjecture II. _For_ $(t_1,\ldots,t_\mu)\in R^\mu$,

$$\tau_\mu(n)= \Sigma_{i=1}^{\ell}\ V_i\ U_i^n\ \{1+0(\tfrac{1}{n})\} \tag{3.5}$$

where U_i _are all independent of_ $\lambda_1, \lambda_2, \lambda$.

We note that (3.4) does not hold in a neighbourhood of the origin. The saddle point method cannot be applicable for the cycle $\Delta_\epsilon\times\mathbb{C}_0$. Δ_ϵ must be deformed homotopically to a stable cycle with respect to the vector field Re log L_0 in the vicinity of the set $1\le\xi_\mu\le\ldots\le\xi_1$ so that a saddle point becomes the summit of this cycle. This seems to be a somewhat difficult task.

When $\lambda = 2$, the classical theory of orthogonal polynomials can be used and $F_{n,\mu}$ has been computed in terms of determinants by M.L. Mehta (See [M]). In this sense, if the conjectures are true, our correlation functions do not give any essential new features for $n\to\infty$ other than the ones involved in classical Jacobi polynomials where $\lambda = 2$.

When $\mu = 1,\ 2$ (2,14) becomes simpler as follows :

$$\tau_1(n) = \frac{1}{2\pi i}\int_{\Delta_\epsilon\times\mathbb{C}_0} L(\xi_1,\xi_1')^n\ M(\xi_1,\xi_1')\ d\xi_1\wedge d\xi_1' \tag{3.6}$$

where $L=(-t_1+\xi_1^{-1})\xi_1^2\ (\xi_1-1)^{-1}\xi_1'^{-2}(\xi_1'-1)$, and $M = \kappa_{1,0}$.

$$\xi_1^{\frac{2}{\lambda}(\lambda_1+\lambda_2+2)-2} (\xi_1-1)^{-\frac{2}{\lambda}(\lambda_2+1)} \xi_1'^{-\frac{2}{\lambda}(\lambda_1+\lambda_2+2)} (\xi_1'-1)^{\frac{2}{\lambda}(\lambda_2+1)-1},$$

which was proved to be $P_n^{(\alpha,\beta)}(1-2t_1) \dfrac{n!}{\pi_{j=1}^n (\alpha+\beta+n+j-2)}$ in (A2).

The symptotic behaviour is well known owing to the classical Szegö's limit formula(See (S)); so we omit it.

On the other hand , as for $\tau_2(n)$, one need further delicate estimates for the integral (2. 14), where (2. 17) shows

(3. 7) $$L = (x_2 + x_1\xi_1^{-1} + \xi_1^{-1}\xi_2^{-1})\ \xi_1\xi_2^2\ (\xi_2-1)^{-1} \cdot \xi_1'(\xi_1'-1)^{-1}\xi_2'^{-2}(\xi_2'-1)\ \xi_1''^{-2}(\xi_1''-1).$$

$$M = \kappa_{1,0}\ \kappa_{2,0}\ \xi_2^{\frac{2}{\lambda}(\lambda_1+\lambda_2+3)-2} (\xi_2-1)^{-\frac{2}{\lambda}(\lambda_2+1)} \cdot$$

$$\xi_1'^{\frac{2}{\lambda}(\lambda_1+\lambda_2+2)-2} (\xi_1'-1)^{-\frac{2}{\lambda}(\lambda_2+1)} \xi_2'^{-\frac{2}{\lambda}(\lambda_1+\lambda_2+3)}$$

$$(\xi_2'-1)^{\frac{2}{\lambda}(\lambda_2+1)} \xi_1''^{-\frac{2}{\lambda}(\lambda_1+\lambda_2+2)} (\xi_1''-1)^{\frac{2}{\lambda}(\lambda_2+1)-1},$$

with the relation $\xi_2' -1 = \dfrac{\xi_2-1}{\xi_1-1}(\xi_1-1)$.

We state only a result. We denote by A and B , t_1t_2 and $(1-t_1)(1-t_2)$ respectively. Then the following Theorem can be deduced from saddle point methods :

Theorem. (i) <u>If both</u> $t_1, t_2 > 1$ <u>or both</u> $t_1, t_2 < 0$, <u>then</u>

(3. 8) $$\tau_2(n) \sim V(t_1, t_2)\ U(t_1, t_2)^n\ \{1 + 0(\tfrac{1}{n})\},$$

<u>where</u> U <u>is equal to</u> $\{\sqrt{A} + \sqrt{B} + \sqrt{-1 + (\sqrt{A} + \sqrt{B})^2}\}^2$ <u>which is</u>

real and greater then 1. V *denotes a function independent of* n.

(ii) *Otherwise*.

$$(3.9) \qquad \tau_2(n) \sim \sum_{j=1}^{4} V_j\, U_j^{\,n}\, \{1 + 0(\tfrac{1}{n})\}$$

where U_i *denotes one of* $\{\pm\sqrt{A} + \sqrt{B} \pm \sqrt{-1 + (\pm\sqrt{A} + \sqrt{B})^2}\}^2$, and V_i *is independent of* n. *Remark that each two of the pairs* (U_i, V_i) *are complex conjugate. If further* $0<t_1, t_2<1$, *then all* U_i *are of absolute value* 1. *So in this case* τ_2 *has a purely oscillatory nature for* $n \to \infty$.

Details of this result will appear elsewhere.

Remark. The asymptotic formulae for general $F_{n,\mu}$, $\mu\geq 3$, cannnot yet be explicitely given. Perhaps one need a entirely new method. Kadell's formula for Selberg-Jack polynomials seems to me interesting in this sense (See [K] in this Volume).

References

[A1] K. Aomoto, Les équations aux différences linéares et les intégrales des fonctions multiformes, J. Fac. Sci. Univ. Tokyo, 22(1975), 271-297.

[A2] ——, Jacobi polynomials associated with Selberg integrals, SIAM J. Math. Anal., 18(1987), 545-549.

[A3] ——, Scaling limit formula for 2-point correlation function of random matrices, to appear in Ad. Studies in Pure Math, Kinokuniya, Tokyo.

[A4] R. Askey, Some basic hypergeometric extensions of integrals of Selberg and Andrews, SIAM J. Math. Anal., 11 (1980), 938-951.

[D] F. Dyson, A class of matrix ensembles, J. Math. Phys.,

13(1972), 90-97.
[K] K. Kadell, The Selberg-Jack polynomials, preprint, 1987, to appear in this Volume.
[M] M. Mehta, Random matrices and the statistical theory of energy levels, Acad. Press, 1967.
[S] G. Szegö, Orthogonal polynomials, A.M.S, Colloq. Publ., 1975.

Some Identities, for Your Amusement

R. Wm. Gosper*

Haste and hedonism leave me time for only a token contribution to these proceedings, in the form of some miscellaneous results I had lying around. Those marked with a $(*)$ are merely conjectures. I wonder how many seconds Ramanujan would have stared at each of these, before muttering "Of course," and moving on to the next.

$$(1)\qquad \prod_{n\geq 1} \frac{n!}{\sqrt{2\pi(n+\frac{1}{6})}\left(\frac{n}{e}\right)^n} = \sqrt{\tfrac{1}{6}!}\left(\sqrt{2\pi e}\,\exp\left(\frac{\zeta'(2)}{\zeta(2)}-\gamma\right)\right)^{1/6}$$

$$\approx 1+\cfrac{1}{128+\cfrac{1}{40+\cfrac{1}{18-\ddots}}}$$

$$(2)\qquad \lim_{n\to\infty} \frac{\pi/2}{\arctan n}\,\frac{\pi/2}{\arctan(n+1)}\cdots\frac{\pi/2}{\arctan(2n)} = \sqrt[\pi]{4} = 1.55468\ldots.$$

$$(3)\qquad \sum_{n\geq 0} \frac{c^n}{z^{(-1/2)^n}}\left(1-c\sqrt{z^3}\right)\left(1-\frac{c}{\sqrt{\sqrt{z^3}}}\right)\cdots\left(1-cz^{-3(-1/2)^{n+1}}\right) = \frac{z^{-1}-c^2z^2}{1+c^3},$$

$$|(1-c)c|<1.$$

$$(4)\qquad \frac{0\cdot 1}{2\cdot 3\cdot 4}\ln 1+\frac{1\cdot 2}{3\cdot 4\cdot 5}(\ln 1-\ln 2)+\frac{2\cdot 3}{4\cdot 5\cdot 6}(\ln 1-2\ln 2+\ln 3)+\cdots = -\frac{3\zeta(3)}{4\pi^2}.$$

$$(5)\qquad \prod_{n\geq 1} 1-\sqrt{3}\tan\frac{z}{(-2)^n} = z\left(\frac{1}{\sqrt{3}}+\cot z\right).$$

$$(6)\qquad \sum_{n>-69} q^n \prod_{k\geq n}(1-q^{k+1})\frac{1+aq^k}{1+aq^{2k}} = \sum_{n\geq 0} a^n q^{n^2}, \qquad |q|<1.$$

$$\lim_{\substack{n=\lfloor n\rfloor\\ n\to\infty}} (-ab)^n q^{(n-1)(n+4)/2} \sum_{j\geq\lfloor j_0\rfloor}(1-cq^{dj-fn})\frac{(a^3b^3, b^3q^3/a^3;q^6)_j}{(abq^{1-2n}, bq^{4-2n}/a^5;q^2)_j}\frac{(b^2q^{3-4n}/a^4;q^2)_{2j}}{(b^3q^{6-3n}/a^3;q^3)_{2j}}\,q^{2j}$$

$$(7*)\qquad = \frac{a^3b^3}{(a^3q^3/b^3;q^3)_\infty}\frac{(a^3b^3;q^6)_\infty}{(b^3/a^3;q^6)_\infty}\frac{(b^2/qa^4, a^4q^3/b^2;q^2)_\infty}{(a^5/b, ab/q, bq^2/a^5, q^3/ab;q^2)_\infty}\sum_{j\geq 0}(-a^6)^j q^{3j^2}$$

$$+\frac{b^4}{a^2}\frac{(ab;q^2)_\infty(a^3b^3,q^6;q^6)_\infty}{(ab/q;q)_\infty(q^3/ab;q^2)_\infty(a^3q^3/b^3;q^6)_\infty}, \qquad |q|<1,\ d>f>0.$$

---

* Symbolics, Inc., 700 El Camino Real, Mountain View, Cal., 94040

ISBN 0-12-058560-X

This one is instructively slippery. Note that the left hand sum not only vanishes termwise with large n, even its term ratio vanishes, indicating nonlinearly rapid convergence. Yet this sum is $O(q^{-n^2/2})$! In fact, as n increases, an endlessly growing "hump" forms in the term sequence, but tries to evade detection by sliding endlessly to the right, leaving each individual term to vanish. Thus the limit is independent of the sum's starting point $\lfloor j_0 \rfloor$. Note also that in the factor $1 - cq^{dj-fn}$, the q term seems to dominate the 1, yet the answer has no c, d, or f. Evidently, an ever shrinking percentage of the hump lies to the left of $j/n < 1$, and when $j/n > 1$, the 1 dominates the cq^{dj-fn}. Cursory numerical experiments indicate that the limit is finite for $f = d$, but the righthand side becomes dependent on c and d. For $f > d$ the limit appears to blow up.

Formula (7*) can also be generalized by the insertion of factors of the form $(gp^n; p)_j$ (with $|p| < 1$) into the left summand, which does not affect the righthand side for $d > f > 0$.

$$A := -\frac{1 - is}{2}$$

$$f(t) = \begin{cases} Af(2-2t) + P, & \text{if } 1 \ge t \ge \frac{1}{2}; \\ \overline{A}f(1-2t) + \overline{P}, & \text{if } \frac{1}{2} \ge t \ge 0; \\ e^{2in\pi/3} f(t-n), & \text{integer } n. \end{cases} \qquad P := \left(1 - \frac{s}{\sqrt{3}}\right) e^{i\pi/6}$$

$$|s| < \sqrt{3}$$

(8)

$$= \frac{\sqrt{3}}{2\pi^2} \sum_{k>-\infty} (-)^k \frac{e^{i\pi(k-1/3)(1-2t)}}{(k-\frac{1}{3})^2} \prod_{n\ge 1} 1 - s \tan \frac{k-1/3}{(-2)^n}\pi, \qquad |s| \le \sqrt{3}.$$

Then the Fourier series can be given in closed form for many t, such as explicit rationals, with easily described radix 2 expansions.

(9)

$$\begin{aligned}
f(\tfrac{1}{2}) &= \frac{\sqrt{3}}{2\pi^2} \sum_{k>-\infty} (-)^k \frac{\prod_{n\ge 1} 1 - s \tan \frac{k-1/3}{(-2)^n}\pi}{(k-\frac{1}{3})^2} = \frac{1}{\sqrt{3}} - s \\
f(\tfrac{1}{3}) &= \frac{1}{\sqrt{3}} + i + \frac{4}{3i - s} \\
f(\tfrac{1}{4}) &= \frac{1}{\sqrt{3}} + i\frac{s^2-1}{2} \\
f(\tfrac{1}{5}) &= \frac{1}{\sqrt{3}} + i\frac{s^2-3}{s^2+5} \\
f(\tfrac{2}{5}) &= \frac{1}{\sqrt{3}} - \frac{4s + i(s^2+1)}{s^2+5} \\
f(\tfrac{1}{7}) &= \frac{1}{\sqrt{3}} - \frac{4(s^2+1)s - i(s^2-3)(s^2+5)}{s^4+6s^2+21} \\
f(\theta) &= \frac{1}{\sqrt{3}} - \frac{4s}{s^2+5} - i\frac{s^2+1}{4} \prod_{n\ge 0} 1 - \left(\frac{s^2+1}{4}\right)^{2^n},
\end{aligned}$$

where

$$\begin{aligned}\theta :&= (.0110100110010110\ldots)_2 \\ &= (.6996966996696996\ldots)_{16} \\ &= \left(\prod_{n\geq 0} 1-2^{-2^n}\right)\sum_{n\geq 0}\frac{2^{-2^n}}{(1-2^{-1})\ldots(1-2^{-2^{n-1}})} \\ &= \frac{1}{2}-\frac{1}{4}\prod_{n\geq 0} 1-2^{-2^n}.\end{aligned}$$

Also, since $f(0) = 1/\sqrt(3) - i$,

$$\sum_{k>-\infty}\frac{\prod_{n\geq 1} 1 - s\tan\frac{k-1/3}{(-2)^n}\pi}{(k-\frac{1}{3})^2} = \tfrac{4}{3}\pi^2, \quad |s|<\sqrt{3}. \tag{10}$$

Finally, elaborating on identity (5),

$$\prod_{n\geq 1} 1 - s\tan\frac{k-\frac{1}{3}}{(-2)^n}\pi = -\frac{\pi}{3}\left(k-\frac{1}{3}\right)(-2)^{1+p_2(3k-1)}(s-\sqrt{3}) + O((s-\sqrt{3})^2), \quad \text{(integer k)} \tag{11}$$

$$\frac{\prod_{n\geq 1} 1 - s\tan\frac{z}{(-2)^n}}{z\left(\frac{1}{\sqrt{3}}+\cot z\right)} = 1 - \left(\frac{z}{\pi^2}\sum_{k>-\infty}\frac{1}{k-\frac{1}{3}-\frac{z}{\pi}}\frac{(-2)^{p_2(3k-1)-1}}{k-\frac{1}{3}}\right)(s-\sqrt{3}) + O((s-\sqrt{3})^2), \tag{12}$$

where $p_2(m) :=$ the largest power of 2 dividing m:

$$m = \pm 2^{p_2(m)}3^{p_3(m)}5^{p_5(m)}\cdots.$$

Consider this an IOU for the justifications of whichever identities you find interesting, but with no promise as to when. Although we lament that Ramanujan was not granted the longevity to honor his own (much greater) IOUs, we can hardly condemn a strategy to spend one's youth exploring, and one's senescence explaining. (Thus is life reduced to the single but nontrivial problem of denying senescence.)